T0138662

ARTIFICIAL INTELLIGENCE

CRITICAL CONCEPTS

ARTIFICIAL INTELLIGENCE

Critical Concepts

Edited by Ronald Chrisley
Editorial Assistant: Sander Begeer

Volume IV

London and New York

First published 2000
by Routledge
11 New Fetter Lane, London EC4P 4EE

Simultaneously published in the USA and Canada
by Routledge
29 West 35th Street, New York, NY 10001

Routledge is an imprint of the Taylor & Francis Group

Typeset in Times by RefineCatch Limited, Bungay, Suffolk
Printed and bound in Great Britain by
TJ International Ltd, Padstow, Cornwall

British Library Cataloguing in Publication Data
A catalogue record for this book is available from the British Library

Library of Congress Cataloging in Publication Data
Artificial intelligence: critical concepts/edited by Ronald Chrisley with Sander Begeer.
p. cm
Includes bibliographical references
ISBN 0–415–19331–1 (set)—ISBN 0–415–19332–X (v. 1)—ISBN 0–415–19333–8 (v. 2)
—ISBN 0–415–19334–6 (v. 3)—ISBN 0–415–19335–4 (v. 4)
1. Artificial intelligence. I. Chrisley, Ronald. II. Begeer, Sander.

Q335.5.A7825 2000
006.3—dc21   00–062568

ISBN 0–415–19331–1 (set)
ISBN 0–415–19335–4 (volume 4)

References within each chapter are as they appeared in the original complete work.

CONTENTS

VOLUME IV

PART I
Conceptual issues   **1**

    Introduction: What is AI? What is A? What is I?   **3**

SECTION 1.1: CHARACTERISATIONS OF ARTIFICIAL INTELLIGENCE

66   **Introduction to *Artificial Intelligence: The Very Idea***   **13**
    JOHN HAUGELAND

67   **What is AI, anyway?**   **22**
    ROGER C. SCHANK

68   **Artificial intelligence as craftwork**   **34**
    LUCY A. SUCHMAN AND RANDALL H. TRIGG

69   **The soul gained and lost: Artificial intelligence as a philosophical project**   **64**
    PHILIP E. AGRE

SECTION 1.2: THE NATURE OF THE ARTIFICIAL

70   **Understanding the natural and the artificial world**   **87**
    H. SIMON

SECTION 1.3: INTELLIGENCE AND THE TURING TEST

71 **Intelligence: Knowns and unknowns**   109
    U. NEISSER, G. BOODOO, T. J. BOUCHARD Jr., A. W. BOYKIN,
    N. BRODY, S. J. CECI, D. F. HALPERN, J. C. LOEHLIN, R. PERLOFF,
    R. J. STERNBERG AND S. URBINA

72 **Psychologism and behaviorism**   165
    NED BLOCK

73 **The Turing Test: AI's biggest blind alley?**   195
    BLAY WHITBY

PART II
Broader context   205

    Introduction: The concept of artificial intelligence in a
    wider perspective   207

SECTION 2.1: ARTIFICIAL MENTALITY

74 **Consciousness: Perspectives from symbolic and connectionist AI** 215
    WILLIAM BECHTEL

75 **Towards a design-based analysis of emotional episodes**   232
    IAN P. WRIGHT, AARON SLOMAN AND LUC BEAUDOIN

76 **Creativity and artificial intelligence**   271
    MARGARET A. BODEN

SECTION 2.2: ETHICS

77 **Ethics, mind and artifice**   285
    STEVE TORRANCE

78 **Artificial intelligence and ethics: An exercise in the**
    moral imagination   303
    MICHAEL R. LACHAT

SECTION 2.3: SOCIAL ISSUES

79 **Attitudes towards intelligent machines**   325
    PAUL ARMER

CONTENTS

80 **The social acceptability of AI systems: Legitimacy,
epistemology and marketing**   343
ROMAIN LAUFER

81 **Why not a sociology of machines? The case of sociology and
artificial intelligence**   371
STEVE WOOLGAR

82 **The knowing subject in AI**   390
A. ADAM

83 **Artificial intelligence**   419
J. D. BOLTER

Part I

CONCEPTUAL ISSUES

Section 1: Characterisations of artificial intelligence
Section 2: The nature of the artificial
Section 3: Intelligence and the Turing Test

INTRODUCTION

What is AI? What is A? What is I?

Ronald Chrisley

Although the preceding articles have represented changes in the concept of artificial intelligence, the papers in these three sections explicitly address the question: what is artificial intelligence? – either directly, in section 1, or by way of trying to clarify one of the constituent concepts (artificiality or intelligence), in sections 2 and 3 that follow.

1 Characterisations of artificial intelligence

Haugeland's paper brings up the key issues, starting with a rather orthodox support of the Turing Test – for objections to this view, see section 3. On the question of whether artificial intelligence must be like natural intelligence, Haugeland, like Dreyfus, answers yes on grounds of intelligibility. He dismisses IQ metrics as irrelevant to the question 'what is intelligence?', as it is really assuming that we know what is intelligent, and only tells us how much intelligence someone has. But it seems that the same consideration that leads one to reject IQ tests – parochiality – should also lead one to reject the Turing Test, which is in a way a kind of IQ *Viva Voce* Examination. Haugeland rebuts the Lovelace objection (article 12 in Volume I) on the grounds that it would imply an unacceptable scepticism concerning our own intelligence – following Descartes, it seems that intelligence must be the kind of thing that it is impossible for us not to have. He bravely attempts to justify the lack of interest in learning on the part of symbolic artificial intelligence. On a more historical note, Haugeland notes that the computer is responsible for the modern-day ambitions and interest in artificial intelligence, explaining it as a consequence of the idea that both the mind and the computer are essentially symbol-processing devices. Although this view did indeed become orthodoxy in symbolic artificial intelligence, it ignores another important factor in the rise of computational artificial intelligence: universality. At least one reason why it was thought that the computer could allow artificial intelligence to begin in earnest was Turing's result that a universal Turing machine can compute any function. Since human behaviour can be characterised in terms of a function (it was thought), it follows that a universal computer which could behave like a human is possible. This is true quite independently of whether or not both humans and computers process symbols.

Schank criticises mathematical, software engineering and simplistic linguistic approaches to characterising artificial intelligence. Although he is more sympathetic to a psychological understanding of the concept, he reveals his notion to be just as unprincipled when he states that we won't know for sure what artificial intelligence is until a machine 'begins to really be the way writers of science fiction have imagined it'!

The standard distinction between the two goals of artificial intelligence is made: to build an intelligent machine, and to find out about the nature of intelligence. Pointing out that there is little agreement about what intelligence is, Schank lists some of his criteria (communication, internal knowledge, world knowledge (including learning), goals and plans, creativity) – but there is no attempt to make these anything other than armchair reflections. Furthermore, it is unclear in what sense the capabilities he mentions are criteria, given that they are neither necessary nor sufficient for intelligence. Schank is better seen as implicitly making a distinction between what we might call criterial vs. ordinal features. The latter are not necessary nor sufficient for intelligence, but their presence or absence leads us to say that there is more or less intelligence present (cf. Haugeland's discussion of IQ). Unfortunately, Schank forgets this insight when discussing the idea that the number of plans one has might serve as a measure of intelligence. Next, he quickly evaluates how far the field of artificial intelligence has come in achieving these features, criticising expert systems *en route*: their hype has led to disruption, prompting only two responses: applications or science. He considers a common definition of artificial intelligence – getting computers to do that which only humans can do. But he also notes a familiar problem with this definition: as soon as one gets a program to do something thought to be distinctively human, one thereby changes one's opinion of the activity, taking the computer realisation of it as evidence that it was not a distinctively human activity after all. Thus, artificial intelligence becomes conceptually impossible. 'Much of the good work in AI has just been answering the question of what the issues are'. Schank proposes that artificial intelligence is not defined by the methodologies it employs, but by the problems attacked: 'it is an AI program if it addresses an AI issue' (although talk of programs assumes a particular methodology). But the issues change, yet (for an unspecified reason) Schank wants a static ('under all circumstances') definition of artificial intelligence. He observes that some issues are perennial, and so tend to define AI: representation (*pace* Brooks, et al.; see Volume III, Part I), decoding (the world is to be "decoded" into representations, making the world the code and the representations the reality!), inference, control of combinatorial explosion, indexing (perhaps too technology-relative), prediction and recovery, dynamic modification (learning), generalisation, curiosity, creativity. But again, no attempt is made, no theory given, to explain *why* these issues are crucial. Schank's claim that learning is the most important of these issues goes entirely against Haugeland's comments, but Schank concedes that there has been a conceptual shift on this issue between early work in artificial intelligence and "now". The conclusion confusingly contradicts the foregoing, talking of artificial intelligence as a methodology, and saying 'All subjects are really AI. All fields discuss the nature of man.' And then immediately after, Schank contradicts himself again, by identifying a supposed *difference* between artificial intelligence and other fields: 'AI tries to do something about it.' What about politics? Clinical psychology? Clearly, the contributions of this paper are not to be found in this final section.

Science studies and ethnomethodology unite in the paper by Suchman and Trigg to give a different approach to characterising artificial intelligence. They look at the actual activities of a pair of researchers (almost certainly in Brian Cantwell Smith's group, probably including Smith himself): talking, interrupting, gesturing, drawing, erasing, etc. Of particular interest is the role of representations: how do the whiteboard technology, the duo-dynamics, etc. permit the construction of representations that mediate between the 'common conceptions of rational cognition' and processes which can be realised in a computer? In this sense, ethnomethodological studies of artificial intelligence are unlike those of other scientific endeavours. The reflexive nature of this kind of research (forming representations about representations, reasoning about reasoning, as opposed to constructing formulae about quarks or thinking about proteins) creates a further constraint on work in artificial intelligence that can be respected or ignored: what one's research *says* intelligence is should be consistent with what one *does* when doing that research. Suchman and Trigg, following Agre, note that the researchers they studied were accountable to the *scenario* of scheduling as it exists in the 'pseudo narratives' constructed by the fields and communities in which they participate, more than to the *phenomenon* of scheduling in itself, as activity. Along with Lave, they wonder what would happen 'if the bases for AI's theorizing about everyday activity were not scenarios but actual scenes, captured in some rich medium and inspected in detail for their sense, their local structures, and their relations to other systems of activity?' A defensive response would be: in a way, expert system work, with its interaction between actual doctors, patients, researchers and machines, is based on 'scenes', although without the precision and care Suchman and Trigg would no doubt like. But to ask for that is to berate artificial intelligence for not being something else: ethnomethodological anthropology.

Agre argues that a study of the place of artificial intelligence in the history of ideas, the kind of work which this set is meant to assist, is necessary for the prevention of sterility in artificial intelligence research. To illustrate this, he conducts a mini-study of his own, tracing the tensions in the symbolic approach to planning as exemplified in the STRIPS formalism of Fikes and Nilsson back through Lashley and eventually Descartes. Although, or rather because, artificial intelligence rejects Descartes' ontological dualism while adopting the rest of his project, an impasse arises when researchers attempt to accept the soul as functionally defined yet replace its esoteric metaphysics with computationally tractable processes. Although most practitioners would see the appearance of this impasse as a failure, Agre takes it to be a contribution of artificial intelligence to our understanding of the mind and its intellectual history: Descartes' soul is not problematic because of its ontology, but because of its 'causal distance from the realm of practical action'. In this sense, Agre takes seriously his contention that artificial intelligence is philosophy (to the extent that engineering 'failures' are valuable if they illuminate philosophical issues). Thus, the interaction between artificial intelligence and the humanities is (or can be) truly two-way. Agre closes with a discussion of the role of formalism in artificial intelligence research. Like Suchman and Trigg, he sees artificial intelligence as struggling on the interface between actual rational activity and representations of that activity which are formal enough to realise it in machines. He concludes that a reformed artificial intelligence would begin with an awareness of this struggle, and an openness to alternative ways of characterising that which is to be formalised when impasses arise, so that the map does not become the territory. That is, he proposes a shift of allegiance away from theory and back to the phenomena of cognitive activity itself, or rather to the cyclic interplay between theory and phenomena.

2 The nature of the artificial

It would seem that the concept of artificial intelligence depends heavily on the concept of artificiality, but there is almost no discussion, on the part of artificial intelligence practitioners, of the artificial/natural distinction. An important exception is Simon's analysis. He initially gives the impression of making a simple, strict divide between the two ('a forest may be a phenomenon of nature; a farm certainly is not') based on the criterion of being 'man-made'. However, he (rightly) complicates this by pointing out that 'artifacts are not apart from nature' in the sense that they do not violate natural law. Their artificiality lies in the fact that they are adapted to our goals and purposes. Given that his interest is in determining whether we can have a science of artefacts, it is unfortunate that Simon falls short of asking the following questions: Are *we* natural? If not, what makes us artificial? Adaptation to a creator's goals? If, on the other hand, we are natural, what singles us out so that adaptation to *our* goals constitutes artificiality? Or is it adaptation to anything's goals that makes something artificial? Are we then the only things with natural goals? Or does artificiality extend beyond the human sphere?

Simon thinks we can have sciences of the artificial, but that since the artificial is defined in terms of human purpose, it will be a science that, unlike the natural sciences (and like psychology?), does not exclude the intentional and the normative from its discussion (he cites Rosenblueth, Wiener and Bigelow (Volume I, article 19) on this point). He summarises his discussion by giving 'indicia' of the artificial (synthesised by man, imitate appearances while lacking the reality, characterised in terms of functions, discussed in terms of imperatives as well as descriptive), but leaves it open as to whether these are necessary or sufficient conditions.

The artefact, according to Simon, can be thought of as an interface between two environments: the outer and the inner ('the substance and organization of the artifact itself'). The advantage of this view is that it allows us to understand the artefact without having to know details of the inner environment, outer environment, or both. (Strikingly, Simon says that the interface view can be applied to many things that are not man-made, suggesting either that many organisms are artefacts, or that being adapted is not a hallmark of the artificial, as suggested by his third indicium, above.)

The discussion now turns to simulation, because computers are artefacts which are good at being artificial, i.e. simulating (although Simon never seems to acknowledge that he is employing this equivocation between two senses of 'artificial'): 'Because of its abstract character and its symbol-manipulating generality, the digital computer has greatly extended the range of systems whose behaviour can be imitated'. A crucial question is: '*how could a simulation ever tell us anything that we do not already know?*' Simon offers two answers: the obvious one is that a simulation can help us calculate the consequences of our theory; the more subtle answer is that we can simulate systems that we do not fully understand, and acquire knowledge thereby. Artificial systems themselves are particularly susceptible to this latter approach. It is this ability to abstract away from inner and outer detail that makes computers susceptible to mathematical analysis. But Simon stresses that there can be an empirical science of computation as well. By this, he does not mean a physical science of the components of computers, but an empirical science of their performance as systems. To support this, he cites cases in the past in which the properties of computational systems could only be determined by building those systems and observing them. But it is unclear that this shows computers to be empirical objects in any interesting sense; a quick response would be that mathematicians often cannot determine the truth of a proposition without getting out pencil and paper and writing down formulae and proofs, yet presumably Simon would not want to conclude thereby that mathematics is empirical (if he does, then he trivialises his claim concerning computers).

Moving on to concerns more central to artificial intelligence, Simon notes

that 'if it is the organisation of components, and not their physical properties, which largely determine behaviour', then computer-assisted psychology
can proceed in advance of neurophysiology. But in the preceding paragraph, he invokes his view that complexity of behaviour derives mainly
from complexity of the outer rather than complexity of the inner (a view
made famous by his image, later in the same book, of an ant's complex
path being the product of the interaction of the ant's simple structure with
the complexity of the landscape though which it travels). So which is it:
behaviour is primarily the upshot of internal, abstract organisation, so
symbolic artificial intelligence may proceed; or primarily the consequence
of external complexity, and thus a less internalist, more activity-based
approach is required? Simon does not explicitly consider the question, but
it seems he is assuming that artificial intelligence must be concerned with
the internal components, despite their secondary role in generating complex
behaviour.

Simon again complicates his natural artificial distinction when he claims
that the human mind and brain are members 'of an important family of
artifacts called symbols systems'. It is ironic that he thinks of symbol systems as 'almost the quintessential artifacts, for adaptivity to an environment
is their *raison d'être*', given that connectionist networks, usually thought of
in opposition to symbol systems, showed the architectures Simon concerned
himself with to be particularly inflexible and static. Simon concludes with a
statement of the physical symbol system hypothesis (see Volume II, article
31): a physical symbol system has the necessary and sufficient means for
general intelligent action.

3 Intelligence and the Turing test

Although artificial intelligence practitioners have paid more attention to the
concept of intelligence than to the concept of artificiality, it usually takes the
form of introspective musings about what motivates them to do their
research, what they are striving for; the scientific psychological literature on
intelligence has been largely ignored, often consciously so (see the discussion
of IQ in Haugeland, above). This is in some ways justified, as much of what
is studied in psychology has to do with the contingencies of the human case,
rather than intelligence in its most abstract form. Nevertheless, a proper
assessment of artificial intelligence should include an examination of the
ways in which its concept of intelligence aligns with or grates against the
concept of intelligence in a closely related area of investigation. Neisser et
al.'s review is included for this reasons. Although it is true that little outside
of the first section of the paper has direct relevance to artificial intelligence, it
was thought that the paper should be included in its entirety to make clear
the differences in interest, and to provide context for what is said that is
relevant. The report distinguishes five approaches to studying, or concepts
of, intelligence: psychometric, multidimensional, cultural, developmental

and biological. The first approach, which is caricatured by the slogan 'intelligence is whatever intelligence tests measure', remains the most dominant notion of intelligence, but it is increasingly giving way to the view that there are many independent aspects to intelligence, or several varieties of intelligence (Sternberg proposes three aspects: analytic, creative and practical).

An interesting finding of the cultural approach is that at least in some cases, to be considered as intelligent, 'one must excel in the skills valued by one's own group'. The thinkers whose ideas have had the most impact on our conceptions, including our conceptions of intelligence, are those who have been able to communicate them effectively and in a lasting form (writing). Furthermore, given the linguistic nature of this set, the points of view contained herein have been those of people with exceptional linguistic skills, who are members of communities which value highly such skills. Small wonder, then, that our notion of intelligence has been lingui-centric, going back to Descartes, Turing and continuing through much of the symbolic approach. But then what of the recent approaches to artificial intelligence, with their non-linguistic notions of intelligence as adaptive situated activity or pattern recognition? Are we to conclude that they are repounded by members of communities in which language is less valued than previously? To some extent, perhaps; ironically, it would be the rise of the computer and its supposed diminution of the importance of verbal skills – or indeed, the relatively non-communicative activity of the isolated artificial intelligence hacker – which would promote a non-linguistic (and therefore not traditionally computational) conception of intelligence.

The developmental approach, unlike the others, does not emphasise individual differences in intelligence, but seeks to understand how intelligence arises through interaction with the world. Piaget, for example, sees the development of intelligence as a way of preserving the balance between incorporating new experiences into existing cognitive structures on the one hand, and modifying those structures in the light of new experiences on the other. In this regard, the development of intelligence recapitulates scientific progress. Vygotsky emphasises the role of society, and especially the parent, in scaffolding the development of intelligence. Thus, an agent's intelligence might be best measured in terms of what they can achieve given scaffolding of some kind, rather than in terms of its static cognitive abilities at any one moment.

When, in artificial intelligence, attention does turn to the concept of intelligence, it more often than not focuses on the Turing Test (see Volume II, article 25). As counterpoint to this preoccupation, two papers have been included that cast doubt on the relevance of the Turing Test to intelligence, be it natural or artificial. Block, in effect, maintains that the Turing Test is too easy: it could be passed by a lookup table – a machine that searches through a set of canned responses to what has just been said. (Although the Turing Test is behaviouristic, and artificial intelligence is supposedly a cognitivist enterprise, Block does not find the test's popularity in artificial intelligence circles surprising.) He shows that the Turing Test conception of intelligence can be beefed up so that it is not refutable using three standard objections to behaviourism, but still falls afoul of his lookup table objection. The second half of the paper is spent, in true philosophical style, responding to various possible objections to the main argument. Along the way, a couple of points of interest arise. First, it is striking how much some of Block's examples resemble Searle's Chinese Room thought experiment, although I am making no scholarly claims here as to which one came first. Second, Block makes clever use of Putnam's theory of reference to argue that he is not changing the meaning of the word 'intelligence' by denying that term's application to a lookup table: 'it is part of the logic of natural kind terms that what seems to be a stereotypical X can turn out not to be an X at all if it fails to belong to the same scientific natural kind as the main body of things we have referred to as Xs'. It is curious, then, that in the next response two paragraphs later he says: 'if someone offered a definition of "life" that had the unnoticed consequence that small stationery items such as paper clips are alive, one could refute him by pointing out the absurdity of the consequence, even if one had no very detailed account of what life is with which to replace his.' One wonders why Putnam cannot be invoked here to say: it is part of the logic of natural kind terms that what seems not to be a living thing can turn out to be a living thing if it turns out to belong to the same scientific natural kind as the main body of things we have referred to as living things. This issue of how we can make sense of a concept's reference or meaning changing over time is very relevant to this set as a whole, concerned as it is with the development of the concept of artificial intelligence (cf. the General Introduction).

By contrast, Whitby's paper can be read as arguing that the Turing test is too hard: there are forms of intelligence which may be easily distinguishable from human intelligence, and thus fail the test. Whitby ironically uses the analogy with flight, which has been used by artificial intelligence practitioners to justify their disregard of biological details (see the Armer paper in Part II, section 3 of this Volume), to argue against the Turing Test: as the development of artificial flight was not assisted by trying to imitate the performance of birds (indeed, as Whitby points out, we could not even now build a machine which could pass a 'bird flight' version of the imitation game), so also is the development of artificial intelligence not assisted by trying to imitate human performance. In fact, Whitby contends, such work has been hindered by this faulty operational definition of intelligence. He contends that Turing never intended it to be such, and offers an alternative, historically situated account of the function the game was playing in Turing's paper, and how it became misconstrued as an objective for research into intelligent machines.

Section 1.1: Characterisations of Artificial Intelligence

INTRODUCTION TO *ARTIFICIAL INTELLIGENCE: THE VERY IDEA*

John Haugeland

Source: J. Haugeland, *Artificial Intelligence: The Very Idea*, MIT Press, 1985, pp. 2–12.

Minds: artificial and natural

What are minds? What is thinking? What sets people apart, in all the known universe? Such questions have tantalized philosophers for millennia, but (by scientific standards anyway) scant progress could be claimed ... until recently. For the current generation has seen a sudden and brilliant flowering in the philosophy/science of the mind; by now not only psychology but also a host of related disciplines are in the throes of a great intellectual revolution. And the epitome of the entire drama is *Artificial Intelligence*, the exciting new effort to make computers think. The fundamental goal of this research is not merely to mimic intelligence or produce some clever fake. Not at all. 'AI' wants only the genuine article: *machines with minds*, in the full and literal sense.[1] This is not science fiction, but real science, based on a theoretical conception as deep as it is daring: namely, we are, at root, *computers ourselves*. That idea—the idea that thinking and computing are radically the same—is the topic of this book.

We've all chuckled nervously over the cartoon computer typing out 'I think, therefore I am' or some comparable profundity. But when it comes to taking Artificial Intelligence seriously, people tend to split into 'scoffers' and 'boosters.' Scoffers find the whole idea quite preposterous—not just false, but ridiculous—like imagining that your car (really) hates you or insisting that a murderous bullet should go to jail. Boosters, on the other hand, are equally certain that it's only a matter of time; computers with minds, they say, are as inevitable as interplanetary travel and two-way pocket TV. The remarkable thing is how utterly confident each side is: 'It's so obvious,' they both say (while thumping the table), 'only a *fanatic* could disagree.' Well, here we shall not be fanatics in either direction, no matter who disagrees. Artificial Intelligence is neither preposterous nor inevitable. Rather, it is based on a powerful idea, which very well might be right (or right in some respects) and just as well might not.

More specifically, we have three ambitions: first and foremost, to explain, clearly and with an open mind, what AI is really all about; second, to exhibit the philosophical and scientific credentials behind its enormous appeal; and finally, to take a look at what actually has and has not been accomplished. Along the way we shall have to develop an abstract account of what computers are; confront some knotty metaphysical puzzles about 'meaning' in a material universe; disentangle various common-sense confusions about language, knowledge, personality, and even common sense itself; and, in general, delve into quite a stack of tricky and controversial issues. Since this is an unusual juxtaposition of problems, some part of what follows will be new, even to professional scientists and philosophers. But the discussion as a whole is designed deliberately for nonspecialists; technical assumptions in any area have been carefully avoided.

Fiction, technology, and theory

The concept of Artificial Intelligence did not, of course, spring up from nowhere, nor did it originate with computers. Its proper intellectual heritage is the subject of chapter 1; but in the meantime, we can distinguish two familiar and well-developed themes on intelligent artifacts in science fiction. One is the 'creature feature' genre, starring monsters or androids—basically like natural animals except for being man-made (and thus somehow peculiar, superior, or horribly flawed). Included are the mythical creations of Hephaestus and Dr. Frankenstein as well as miscellaneous anthropoid slaves, indistinguishable from ordinary people save for serial numbers, emotional oddities, and the like. The other genre is populated by various mechanical 'robots': typically blinking, clanking contraptions, with springs and pulleys in lieu of flesh, wires for nerves, and maybe wheels instead of legs—plus emotional limitations even more serious than the androids'.

While the monster theme often invokes mystery and black magic, robots tend to be extrapolations of industry's latest hightech marvel. Early designs were based on the intricate gear and ratchet mechanisms that so enchanted Europe when clockworks were new; and, through the years, steam engines, automatic looms, hydraulic controls, and telephone switchboards have all fueled fantastic projections. Contemporary Artificial Intelligence, needless to say, is rooted in fancy programmable electronics; in particular, no current work is based on chemical wizardry or bioengineering (it belongs at IBM, not at du Pont or Genentech). AI, therefore, is direct heir to the contraption line. But there's one crucial difference: whereas few respectable scientists ever tried to build intelligent clockworks or switchboards (let alone androids), research on intelligent computers is big time. Why?

The real issue has nothing to do with advanced technologies (or corporate specialties), but with deep theoretical assumptions. According to a central tradition in Western philosophy, thinking (intellection) essentially *is* rational manipulation of mental symbols (viz., ideas). Clocks and switchboards, however, don't do anything at all like rational symbol manipulation. Computers, on the other hand, can manipulate arbitrary 'tokens' in any specifiable manner whatever, so apparently we need only arrange for those tokens to be symbols, and the manipulations to be specified as rational, to get a machine that *thinks*. In other words, AI is new and different because computers actually do something very like what minds are supposed to do. Indeed, if that traditional theory is correct, then our imagined computer ought to have 'a mind of its own': a (genuine) *artificial mind*.

To call something a symbol or a manipulation is to characterize it quite abstractly. That doesn't mean the characterization is vague, formless, or even hard to understand, but rather that inessential details are omitted. Consider, for instance, two ways of specifying the motor for an appliance. One engineer might describe it in great detail, giving the precise shape of each little part, what it's made of, how it's attached, and so on. (That would be a 'concrete' characterization, the opposite of abstract.) Another engineer, however, might stipulate only the minimum horsepower required, the space into which it has to fit, and how quietly it must run—leaving the details up to the motor designer. The resulting motor could be made of metal or plastic, be round or square, be based on one physical principle or another, and still satisfy the abstract specifications exactly.

According to the symbol manipulation theory, intelligence depends only on a system's organization and functioning as a symbol manipulator—which is even more abstracted from concrete details than are horsepower and noise level. Hence low-level specifics, such as what the symbols are made of or their precise shapes, are irrelevant to whether the system might be intelligent; the symbols need only satisfy some higher-level, abstract specifications. In other words, various 'details,' like whether the underlying structure is electronic or physiological (or hydraulic or fiber optical or whatever), are entirely beside the point. By the same token, contemporary computer technology is relevant only for economic reasons: electronic circuits just happen to be (at the moment) the cheapest way to build flexible symbol manipulating systems.

But the lesson goes deeper: if Artificial Intelligence really has little to do with computer technology and much more to do with abstract principles of mental organization, then the distinctions among AI, psychology, and even philosophy of mind seem to melt away. One can study those basic principles using tools and techniques from computer science, or with the methods of experimental psychology, or in traditional philosophical terms—but it's the same subject in each case. Thus a grand interdisciplinary marriage seems imminent; indeed, a number of enthusiasts have already taken the vows. For their new 'unified' field, they have coined the name *cognitive science*. If you believe the advertisements, Artificial Intelligence and psychology, as well as parts of philosophy, linguistics, and anthropology, are now just 'subspecialties' within one coherent study of cognition, intelligence, and mind—that is, of symbol manipulation.

Artificial Intelligence in this sense (as a branch of cognitive science) is the only kind we will discuss. For instance, we will pay no attention to commercial ventures (so-called 'expert systems,' etc.) that make no pretense of developing or applying psychological principles. We also won't consider whether computers might have some alien or inhuman kind of intellect (like Martians or squids?). My own hunch, in fact, is that anthropomorphic prejudice, 'human chauvinism,' is built into our very concept of intelligence. This concept, of course, could still apply to all manner of creatures; the point is merely that it's the only concept we have—if we escaped our 'prejudice,' we wouldn't know what we were talking about.

Be that as it may, the only *theoretical* reason to take contemporary Artificial Intelligence more seriously than clockwork fiction is the powerful suggestion that our own minds work on computational principles. In other words, we're really interested in AI as part of the theory that *people* are computers—and we're all interested in people.

What is intelligence?

How shall we define intelligence? Doesn't everything turn on this? Surprisingly, perhaps, very little seems to turn on it. For practical purposes, a criterion proposed by Alan Turing (1950) satisfies nearly everyone. Turing was annoyed by fruitless disputes over word meanings; he thought you could never find out anything interesting about what machines could do by armchair philosophizing about what we mean by 'think' and 'intelligent'. So he suggested that we ignore the verbal issue and adopt a simple test which he devised; then we could concentrate on building and observing the machines themselves. He predicted that by the year 2000 computer systems would be passing a modest version of his test and that contrary 'definitions' would eventually just look silly (and quietly fade away).

Turing's test is based on a game, called the 'imitation game,' played by three mutual strangers. Two of them are 'witnesses,' and they are of opposite sex; the third player, the 'interrogator,' tries to guess which witness is which, purely on the basis of how they answer questions. The trick is that one witness (say the man) is trying to fool the interrogator (by systematically pretending to be the woman), while the other (the woman) is doing all she can to help the interrogator. If the interrogator guesses correctly, the woman wins, otherwise the man does. In order to avoid any extraneous clues, like tone of voice, all questions and answers are transmitted via teletype. So far no computers are involved. Turing's idea, however, was to substitute a computer for the male witness and see whether, against average women

---

Box 1
Why IQ Is Irrelevant

It might seem that we already have a perfectly reasonable standard of intelligence: namely, performance on an IQ test. There are, however, two things wrong with that supposition. First, IQ tests are intended to measure *degree* of intelligence, on the assumption that the subject has some intelligence to measure. But for computers that assumption is the issue; we must know whether it makes sense to attribute intelligence to them at all before we can ask how much of it they have. Second, IQ tests are designed specifically for people, and thus they may depend on indicators that are actually valid only in this special case.

To take a simplified example, it might be found that some peculiar skill, like solving logic problems or comparing line diagrams, is reliably correlated with how smart a person is; so a test could take advantage of this correlation, for purposes of convenient measurement. But that doesn't mean that such a task actually requires intelligence; it could happen that a manifestly unintelligent device could perform spendidly, by virtue of some coincidence or gimmick. (The fact that many people can't remember how to extract square roots doesn't mean that pocket calculators are more intelligent than they.) What we need is a general test for whether an entity is intelligent at all (in the human sense, of course) and not a special purpose measuring device convenient for use in schools or the army.

---

opponents, it can fool the average (human) interrogator as often as the average man can. If it can, it 'passes' the test.[2]

But why would such a peculiar game be a test for general (human-like) intelligence? Actually, the bit about teletypes, fooling the interrogator, and so on, is just window dressing, to make it all properly 'experimental.' The crux of the test is *talk*: does the machine talk like a person? Of course this doesn't mean sounding like a person, but rather saying the sorts of things that people say in similar situations. But again, why should that be a sign of general intelligence? What's so special about talking? Turing says: 'The question and answer method seems to be suitable for introducing almost any one of the fields of human endeavor that we wish to include.' That is, we can talk about pretty much anything.

Further, and more important, to converse beyond the most superficial level, you have to know what you're talking about. That is, understanding the words alone is not enough; you have to understand the topic as well. Turing points out (1950, p. 446) how similar his imitation game is to an oral quiz and gives us a sample:

Interrogator:	In the first line of your sonnet which reads 'Shall I compare thee to a summer's day,' would not 'a spring day' do as well or better?
Witness:	It wouldn't scan.
Interrogator:	How about 'a winter's day'? That would scan all right.
Witness:	Yes, but nobody wants to be compared to a winter's day.
Interrogator:	Would you say Mr. Pickwick reminded you of Christmas?
Witness:	In a way.
Interrogator:	Yet Christmas is a winter's day, and I do not think Mr. Pickwick would mind the comparison.
Witness:	I don't think you're serious. By a winter's day one means a typical winter's day, rather than a special one like Christmas.

This student has displayed not only competence with the English language, but also a passable understanding of poetry, the seasons, people's feelings, and so on—all just by talking. The same could be done for politics, fine wines, electrical engineering, philosophy . . . you name it. What if a machine could pass all those examinations? That's why the Turing test is so powerful and compelling.

It's also quite convenient in practice; typing and reading at a terminal, after all, are the standard means of interacting with a computer. Since there's no physical barrier to having a friendly conversation with a machine, AI research is free to attack the underlying theoretical issues. By accepting the Turing test (in spirit, if not the letter), scientists can concentrate almost entirely on the 'cognitive' aspects of the problem: what internal structure and operations would enable a system to say the right thing at the right time? In other words, they can dispense with messy incidentals and get on with computational psychology.

'They can only . . . '

Many people are especially doubtful about 'automating' creativity, freedom, and the like. No computer, they suppose, could ever be truly inventive, artistic, or responsible, because 'it can only do what it's programmed to do.' Everything depends, however, on just what this alleged limitation means. In one technical and boring sense, of course, it's perfectly true that computers always follow their programs, since a program is nothing but a careful specification of all the relevant processes inside the machine. That, however, doesn't prove anything because a similar point might be made about us. Thus, assuming there were a 'careful specification' of all the relevant processes in our brains (laws of neuropsychology, or something like that), it would be equally easy to say: 'We—or rather our brain parts—always act only as specified.'[3] But, obviously, no such fact could show that we are never creative or free— and the corresponding claim about computers is no more telling.

The underlying problem with the argument is that it ignores distinctions of *organizational level*. A stereo, for instance, can be described as a device for reproducing recorded music, as a complicated tangle of electronic components, or as a giant cloud of subatomic particles. What you can say about it depends on the level of description you adopt. Thus, none of the components (let alone the particles) could properly be termed 'high fidelity'; that characteristic makes sense only at the level of music reproduction. Likewise, none of our individual brain functions, and none of the individual operations in a computer, could properly be termed 'creative' or 'free'; such descriptions belong at a completely different level—a level at which one speaks of the system or person as a whole.[4]

Unfortunately, confusions remain because the notion 'is-programmed-to' is ambiguous. Instead of the above sense, in which programming refers to a detailed specification of internal processes, one can use the term more broadly, to describe a system's overall design or intended capacities. For example, I might say 'this computer is programmed to keep the payroll accounts' or 'that computer is programmed to find the best flight path in bad weather.' These descriptions apply to the system as a whole; yet even at this level it seems that the systems 'can only do what they're programmed to do'—as long, anyway, as they don't malfunction. Here the underlying problem is quite different: namely, it's simply not clear that being 'programmed' (in this sense) is incompatible with being creative or free. After all, why not just program the system to be creative, free, or whatever? Then it would have those characteristics by design.

You might think that being 'programmed for creativity' is a contradiction in terms. But it can't be, as we can see by again considering ourselves. In some sense, surely, we are elaborate integrated systems with an overall design—the result of evolution, perhaps. Thus when we're healthy (not malfunctioning), we 'only do what we're designed to do.' But then, assuming that creativity and freedom are not (always) unhealthy, we must be 'designed for creativity,' etc. This is no contradiction because the relevant sense of 'design' relates only to overall capacities and characteristics; but that's also the very sense of 'programming' in question.

Still, there's one last argument: it's only a metaphor to say that we were 'designed' by evolution; evolution is not an actual designer, but only a mindless natural process. Computers, on the other hand, are quite literally *programmed* by actual (human) programmers. So when we're creative, it's all our own; but when a computer printout contains something artistic, that's really the programmer's artistry, not the machine's. But wait: how does that follow? Why should an entity's potential for inventiveness be determined by its ancestry (like some hereditary title) and not by its own manifest competence? What if, for instance, the very same computer system had resulted from an incredible laboratory accident; could *that* make any difference to whether the resulting system was creative? Or, turning the tables, what if you or I had

---

Box 2
Why Not Start with Learning?

Sometimes it seems that learning is to psychology what energy is to physics or reproduction to biology: not merely a central research topic, but a virtual definition of the domain. Just as physics is the study of energy transformations and biology is the study of self-reproducing organisms, so psychology is the study of systems that learn. If that were so then the essential goal of AI should be to build systems that learn. In the meantime, such systems might offer a shortcut to artificial adults: systems with the "raw aptitude" of a child, for instance, could learn for themselves—from experience, books, and so on—and save AI the trouble of codifying mature common sense. But, in fact, AI more or less ignores learning. Why?

In other words, Artificial Intelligence must start by trying to understand knowledge (and skills and whatever else is acquired) and them, on that basis, tackle learning. It may even happen that, once the fundamental structures are worked out, acquisition and adaptation will be comparatively easy to include. Certainly the ability to learn is essential to full intelligence; AI cannot succeed without it. But it does not appear that learning is the most basic problem, let alone a shortcut or a natural starting point.

Learning is *acquisition* of knowledge, skills, etc. The issue is typically conceived as: given a system capable of knowing, how can we make it capable of acquiring? Or: starting from a static knower, how can we make an adaptable or educable knower? This tacitly assumes that knowing as such is straightforward and that acquiring or adapting it is the hard part; but that turns out to be false. AI has discovered that knowledge itself is extraordinarily complex and difficult to implement—so much as that even the general structure of a system with common sense is not yet clear. Accordingly, it's far from apparent *what* a learning system needs to acquire; hence the project of acquiring some can't get off the ground.[5]

---

been concocted out of petroleum by-products at Exxon; would that mean that all our later inventions and artworks automatically belonged to a team of chemists? I certainly hope not.

Of course, if those inventions had actually been dreamt up in advance by the relevant programmers or chemists and merely stored in the machine or us for later 'playback,' then the credit would be theirs. But that's not at all the way AI works, even today. What gets programmed directly is just a bunch of general information and principles, not unlike what teachers instill in their pupils. What happens after that, what the system does with all this input, is not predictable by the designer (or teacher or anybody else). The most striking current examples are chess machines that outplay their programmers, coming up with brilliant moves that the latter would never have found. Many people are amazed by this fact; but if you reflect that invention is often just a rearrangement (more or less dramatic) of previously available materials, then it shouldn't seem so surprising.

None of this proves that computer systems *can* be truly creative, free, or artistic. All it shows is that our initial intuitions to the contrary are not trustworthy, no matter how compelling they seem at first. If you're sitting there muttering: 'Yes, yes, but I *know* they can't; they just couldn't,' then you've missed the point. Nobody knows. Like all fundamental questions in cognitive science, this one awaits the outcome of a great deal more hard research. Remember, the real issue is whether, in the appropriate abstract sense, we are computers ourselves.

Notes

1 Perhaps Artificial Intelligence should be called "Synthetic Intelligence" to accord better with commercial parlance. Thus artificial diamonds are fake imitations, whereas synthetic diamonds are genuine diamonds, only manufactured instead of dug up (compare also artificial maple flavoring versus, say, synthetic insulin). Despite the name, AI clearly aims at genuine intelligence, not a fake imitation.

2 Turing doesn't mention whether the interrogator is told that a computer has been substituted for the man; and that would surely make a difference to the questioning. But, as the next paragraph shows, the essence of the test is much simpler, and the ambiguity doesn't really matter.

3 One might reject this comparison on the grounds that *our* thoughts take place in *immaterial* (perhaps immortal) souls and have at most incidental relations to our brains. Such a position, however, would rule out Artificial Intelligence from the start. Hence, for purposes of discussion, this book must and will assume that human intelligence is (or at least could be) realized in matter—such as brains.

4 Philosopher Dan Dennett has been particularly assiduous in making this point in a variety of contexts (see, for instance, his 1978 and 1984).

5 Essentially, this point was made a quarter of a century ago by McCarthy (1959): "We base ourselves on the idea that in order for a program to be capable of learning something it must first be capable of being told it" (Minsky 1968, p. 405). Time has borne McCarthy out; but see Schank (1983) for a plea that learning should now be reactivated as a central research topic.

67

WHAT IS AI, ANYWAY?

Roger C. Schank

Source: D. Partridge and Y. Wilks (eds), *The Foundations of Artificial Intelligence: A Sourcebook*, Cambridge University Press, 1990, pp. 3–13.

Artificial intelligence is a subject that, due to the massive, often quite unintelligible, publicity that it gets, is nearly completely misunderstood by people outside the field. Even AI's practitioners are somewhat confused with respect to what AI is really about.

Is AI mathematics? A great many AI researchers believe strongly that knowledge representations used in AI programs must conform to previously established formalisms and logics or else the field will be unprincipled and *ad hoc*. Many AI researchers believe that they *know* how the answer will turn out before they have figured out what exactly the questions are. They *know* that some mathematical formalism or other must be the best way to express the contents of the knowledge that people have. Thus, to them, AI is an exercise in the search for the proper formalisms to use in representing knowledge.

Is AI software engineering? A great many AI practitioners seem to think so. If you can put knowledge into a program, then that program must be an AI program. This conception of AI, derived as it is from much of the work going on in industry in expert systems, has served to confuse AI people tremendously about what the correct focus of AI ought to be, and about what the fundamental issues in AI are. If AI is just so much software engineering, if building an AI program means primarily the addition of domain knowledge such that a program "knows about" insurance or geology, for example, then what is to differentiate an AI program in insurance from any other computer program that works within the field of insurance? Under this conception, it is very difficult to determine where software engineering leaves off and where AI begins.

Is AI linguistics? A great many AI researchers seem to think that building grammars of English and putting those grammars on a machine is AI. Of course, linguists have never thought of their field as having very much to do with AI at all. But, as money for linguistics has begun to disappear, while money for AI has increased, it has become increasingly convenient to claim that work on language that had nothing to do with computers at all, has some computational relevance. Suddenly theories of language that were never considered by their creators to be process models at all, are now proposed as AI models.

Is AI psychology? Would building a complete model of human thought processes and putting it on a computer be considered a contribution to AI? Many AI researchers couldn't care less about the human mind. Yet, the human mind is the only kind of intelligence that we can reasonably hope to study. We have an existence proof. We know the human mind works. But, in adopting this view, one still has to worry about computer models that display intelligence but yet are clearly in no way related to how humans function. Are such models intelligent? Such issues inevitably force one to focus on the issue of the nature of intelligence apart from its particular physical embodiment.

In the end, the question of what AI is all about probably does not have only one answer. What AI is depends heavily upon the goals of the researchers involved. And any definition of AI is very dependent upon the methods that are being employed in building AI models. Last, of course, it is a question of results. These issues about what AI is exist precisely because AI has not yet been completed. They will disappear entirely when a machine begins to really be the way writers of science fiction have imagined it.

There are two main goals in AI that most practitioners would agree upon. First and foremost, the goal is to build an intelligent machine. And, second, the goal is to find out about the nature of intelligence. Both of these goals have at their heart a need to define intelligence. AI people are fond of talking about intelligent machines, but when it comes down to it, there is very little agreement on exactly what constitutes intelligence. And, it thus follows, there is very little agreement in AI about exactly what AI is and what it should be. We all agree that we would like to endow machines with an attribute that we really can't define. Needless to say, AI suffers from this lack of definition of its scope.

One way to attack this problem is to attempt to list some features that we would expect an intelligent entity to have. None of these features would define intelligence – indeed a being could lack any one of them and still be considered to be intelligent. Nevertheless each is an integral part of intelligence in its way.

Let me list the features I consider to be critical and then I shall briefly discuss them. They are: communication, internal knowledge, world knowledge, goal and plans, and creativity.

Communication

An intelligent entity can be communicated with. We can't talk to rocks or tell trees what we want, no matter how hard we try. With dogs and cats we cannot express many of our feelings, but we can let them know when we are angry. Communication is possible with them. If it is very difficult to communicate with someone, we might consider him to be unintelligent. If the communication lines are very narrow with a person, if he can only understand a few things, we might consider him to be unintelligent. No matter how smart your dog is, he can't understand when you discuss physics with him. This does not mean that he doesn't understand something about physics. You can't discuss physics with your pet rock either, but it doesn't understand physics at all. Your small child may know some physics, but discussions of that subject with him will have to be put in terms he can understand. In other words, the easier it is to communicate with an entity, the more intelligent the entity seems. Obviously there are many exceptions to this general feature of intelligence. There are people who are considered to be very intelligent who are impossible to talk to, for example. Nevertheless, this feature of intelligence is still significant, even if it is not absolutely essential.

Internal knowledge

We expect intelligent entities to have some knowledge about themselves. They should know when they need something; they should know what they think about something; and, they should know that they know it. Presently, probably only humans can do all this – we cannot really know what dogs know about what they know. We could program computers to seem as if they know what they know, but it would be hard to tell if they really did. To put this another way, we really cannot examine the insides of an intelligent entity in such a way as to establish what it actually knows. Our only choice is to ask and observe. If we get an answer that seems satisfying then we tend to believe that the entity we are examining has some degree of intelligence. Of course, this is another subjective criterion, a feature that when it is absent may signify nothing.

World knowledge

Intelligence also involves being aware of the outside world and being able to find and utilize the information that one has about the outside world. It also implies having a memory in which past experience is encoded and which can be used as a guide for processing new experiences. You cannot understand and operate in the outside world if you treat every experience as if it were brand new. Thus, intelligent entities must have an ability to see new experiences in terms of old ones. This implies an ability to retrieve old experiences which would have had to have been codified in such a way as make them available in a variety of different circumstances. Entities that do not have this ability can be momentarily intelligent but not globally intelligent. There are cases of people who are brain-damaged who perform adequately in a given moment, but forget what they have done soon after. The same is true of simple machines that can do a given job but do not know that they have done it, and have no ability to draw on that or other experiences to guide them in future jobs.

Goals and plans

Goal-driven behavior means knowing when one wants something and knowing a plan to get what one wants. There is usually a presumed correspondence between the complexity of the goals that an entity has and the sheer number of plans that an entity has available for accomplishing those goals. So, a tree has none or next to none of these, a dog has somewhat more, and a person has quite a few; very intelligent people probably have more. Of course, sheer number of recorded plans would probably not be a terrific measure of intelligence. If it were, machines could easily be constructed that met that criterion. The real criterion with respect to plans has to do with interrelatedness of plans and their storage in an abstract enough way as to allow a plan constructed for situation A to be adapted and used in situation B.

Creativity

Finally, every intelligent entity is assumed to have some degree of creativity. Creativity can be defined very weakly, including for example, the ability to find a new route to one's food source when the old one is blocked. But, of course, creativity can also mean finding a new way to look at something that changes one's world in some significant way. And, it certainly means being able to adapt to changes in one's environment and being able to learn from experience. Thus, an entity that doesn't learn is probably not intelligent, except momentarily.

Now, as I said, one needn't have all of these things to be intelligent, but each is an important part of intelligence. That having been said, where do current AI programs fit in? It seems clear that no AI model is very creative as of yet, although various ideas have been proposed in this regard lately. It also seems clear that no AI models have a great deal of internal knowledge. In general, AI programs don't know what they know, nor are they aware of what they can do. They may be able to summarize a news wire, but they don't know that they are summarizing it.

On the other hand, programs that have goals and plans to accomplish those goals have been around since the inception of AI. Work on such programs has spawned a variety of ideas on how planning can be accomplished, particularly within the domain of problem solving. Programs that have external knowledge usually have not been considered to be part of AI at all. Database retrieval is not in any way connected with AI, although it has seemed clear to AI researchers that they must eventually concern themselves with how knowledge is best organized in order to have really intelligent machines. Nevertheless, many programs for organizing and retrieving knowledge do, of course, exist.

Programs that communicate with computers have been around as long as there have been computers, of course. But this communication has been less than satisfactory. Most non-computer professionals complain bitterly about the difficulty in getting a computer to do what is wanted, and of course, the computer industry has been responsive to this, producing better and better interfaces. But, in the end, computers will not really be easy to use until they can see, hear, read, and generally understand what we say to them and what we want them to do.

In AI, these subjects have always been considered to be important parts of the field and much research has been done on them.

As AI has become more commercialized, the parts of AI research that have been the most advanced in terms of engineering would, one might have imagined, become those areas where the commercial action would begin. But, as often happens, salesmanship and market readiness often determine what gets sold. So AI entered the world through the creation of so-called expert systems, which were engineering attempts to take some of the problem solving and planning models that had been proposed in AI and give them real world relevance. The problem was that these experts lacked what I have termed internal knowledge and creativity. And, it is very difficult to have an expert who doesn't know what he knows, how he came to know it, or how to adapt if circumstances are somewhat different than they were supposed to be. Most of all, experts with no memories are no experts at all.

Partly as a result of the commercialization of expert systems, equating AI with expert systems in the public eye, and partly as a result of the usual battles AI has always faced with older fields of inquiry that relate to it, AI is in a serious state of disruption.

Most AI people seem to have chosen one of two routes, to get them out of their state of confusion. The first of these routes I will call the *applications route*. In this view of AI, the job is to build real working systems. Whether these systems are AI or not loses its import as one begins to work on them. The problem is making them work at all, not to be a purist about what is or is not AI. As anyone who has ever worked on a large software engineering program knows, this task is so complex as to make all other problems pale by comparison. Making big programs work is hard. And when they are finished are they AI? Does it matter?

The second route is what I will call the *scientific route*. This route sounds good in principle and it has as its premise a desire to avoid the commercial-ization of AI and work only on impossible problems like the brain, or neat problems like logic. Let the applications route people do as they will, the scientific route people have chosen simply to ignore them and bolt the door.

Thus, without actually deciding to do so, AI has made a decision. Either one defines AI as a modern methodological tool now being used in the ancient enterprise of the study of mind, the *scientific answer*, or, one's defin-ition of AI is, in essence, the *applications answer*, namely an attempt to create certain new computer technology that relates to some behaviors previously done only by humans.

This seems fine in principle – many fields have a scientific, theoretical group and an applications group that derives its work from the scientific work. And, this would be nice in AI too, if it were the case. What actually is the case is that the scientific workers are, for the most part, concerned with issues that are very far away from potential applications, and the applications folk have been busy applying results from earlier days which are known to be seriously inadequate. This does not mean that they are not building useful applications, sometimes they are. But, it does mean that, for all intents and purposes, the two routes have nothing to do with each other.

One problem with the applications answer is that it is very imprecise. Is all new computer technology to be labeled AI? Certainly, if one reads the advertisements in the computer magazines, it is easy to believe that AI is anything anyone says it is, that there is no definition. But, to an AI researcher (as opposed to an AI businessman), only a small fraction of advances in computer software and hardware would seem to qualify as advances in AI. The technology that AI people want to create usually involves solving some fundamental problem, and the solution itself involves decisions on the nature of what kinds of things are part of a computer program. Further, AI usually means getting a machine to do what previously only humans have done before (rather than simply improving existing techniques). The problem with this definition has been obvious to AI people for some time. As soon as something radically new has been accomplished, then, since computers have at that point done it, it is thus no longer uniquely human, and thus no longer AI. So, one question that needs to be answered on the technological side is, "Can some definition as to the nature of AI software be made such that, under all circumstances, it will be seen as uniquely part of or derivative from AI?"

What is really the case is that it is not possible to define very clearly which pieces of new software are AI and which are not. In actuality, AI must have an issues-related definition. In other words, people do arithmetic and so do computers. The fact is, however, that no one considers a program that calcu-lates to be an AI program, nor would they, even if that program calculated in exactly the way that people do. The reason that this is so is that calculation is not seen as a fundamental problem of intelligent behavior and also that computers are already better at calculation than people are. This two-sided definition, based upon the perception of the fundamental centrality of an issue with respect to its role in human intelligence, and the practical viewpoint of how good current computers are at accomplishing such a task already, constitutes how one defines whether a given problem is legitimately an AI problem. For this reason, much of the good work in AI has been just answering the question of what the issues are.

Or, to put this another way, what is AI is defined not by the methodologies used in AI, but by the problems attacked by those methodologies. A program is not an AI program because it uses LISP or PROLOG certainly. By the same token, a program is not an AI program because it uses some form of logic or if-then rules. Expert systems are only AI programs if they attack some AI issue. A rule-based system is not an AI program just because it uses rules or was written with an expert system shell. It is an AI program if it addresses an AI issue.

One thing about AI issues though, is that they change. What was an issue yesterday may not be one today. Similarly, the issues that I believe to be critical today may disappear ten years from now. Given that that is the case, defining AI by issues can make AI a rather odd field, with a constantly changing definition. But, there are some problems that will endure, that tend to define AI. I will discuss some of these below:

1 Representation
2 Decoding
3 Inference
4 Control of combinatorial explosion
5 Indexing
6 Prediction and recovery
7 Dynamic modification
8 Generalization
9 Curiosity
10 Creativity

1 Representation

Probably the most significant issue in AI is the old problem of the representation of knowledge. *What do we know?*, and *how do we get a machine to know it?* is the central issue in AI. An AI program or theory that makes a statement about how knowledge that is of a generality greater than the range of knowledge covered by the program itself ought to be represented is a contribution to AI.

2 Decoding

It is of no use to have a very nice knowledge representation if there is no way to translate from the real world into that representation. In natural language, or vision systems, for example, decoding is often the central problem in constructing an AI program. Sometimes, of course, the decoding work is so difficult that the programmers forget to concern themselves with what they are decoding into, that is, what the ideal representation ought to be, so that they make the work harder for themselves. Deciding that the representation is a given fact, that it is predicate calculus, or syntactic phrase markers, for example, can complicate the problem, relegating the decoding work to some other, often non-existent, program.

3 Inference

Information is usually more than the sum of its parts. Once we have decoded a message (visual, verbal, symbolic, or whatever) we must begin to attempt to extract the content of that message. Usually the content is much more than has been expressed directly. We don't say every nuance of what we mean. We expect our hearer to be smart enough to figure some of it out for himself. Similarly, we must attempt to figure out the significance of what we have seen, making assumptions about what it all means. This is the problem of inference.

Human memory is highly inferential, even about prior experiences, and retrieval of information. People are capable of answering questions from very incomplete data. They can figure out if they should know something and whether they might be able to figure it out. Such self-awareness depends strongly upon an ability to know how the world works in general, or, the representation problem again. Building a program that knows if it would know a thing is a very important task.

4 Control of combinatorial explosion

Once you allow a program to make assumptions about what may be true beyond what it has been told, the possibility that it could go on forever doing this, becomes quite real. At what point do you turn off your mind and decide that you have thought enough about a problem? Arbitrary limits are just that, arbitrary. It seems a safe assumption that it is the structure of our knowledge that guides the inference process. Knowing what particular knowledge structure we are in while processing can help us to determine how much we want to know about a given event. Or, to put this another way, contexts help narrow the inference process. There are many possible ways to control the combinatorics of the inference process – deciding among them and implementing them is a serious AI problem if the combinatorial explosion was started by an AI process in the first place.

5 *Indexing*

It is all well and good to know a great deal, but the more you know, the harder it should get to find what you know. The most knowledgeable man on earth should also be the slowest to say anything, by that reasoning. This is called the paradox of the expert in psychology. It is a paradox precisely because it is untrue. Obviously, people must have ways of organizing their knowledge so that they can find what they need when they need it. Originally this problem was called the search problem in AI. But, viewed as a search problem, the implication was that faster search methods were what was needed. This would imply that experts were people who searched their data bases quickly and that seems quite absurd. It is the organization and labeling of memory and episodes in memory that is the key issue here. For any massive system, that is for any real AI system, indexing is a central, and possibly the central problem. AI programs are not usually large enough to make their answers to the indexing question meaningful, but the construction of programs of the appropriate size should become more important in the years ahead.

6 *Prediction and recovery*

Any serious AI program should be able to make predictions about how events in its domain will turn out. This is what understanding really means, that is, knowing to some extent what is coming. When these predictions fail, which they certainly must in any realistic system, an intelligent program should not only recover from the failure, but it must also explain the failure. That is, programs must understand their own workings well enough to know what an error looks like, and be able to correct the rule that caused that error in addition to being able to recognize that situation when it occurs again. As an example of the kind of thing I am talking about, a computer should be able, by use of the same basic scientific theory, to do an adequate job of forecasting stocks or weather, or playing a game of chess, or coaching a football team. What I mean by *the same basic theory* is that the theory of prediction, recovery from error, error explanation, and new theory creation should be identical in principle, regardless of domain.

7 *Dynamic modification*

AI went through a long period of trying to find out how to represent knowledge. We needed to find out what was learned before we could even consider working on learning itself. But, most of us have always wanted to work on learning. Learning is, after all, the quintessential AI issue. What makes people interesting, what makes them intelligent, is that they learn. People change with experience. The trouble with almost all the programs that we have written is that they are not modified by their experiences. No matter how sophisticated a story understander may seem, it loses all credibility as an intelligent system when it reads the same story three times in a row and it fails to get mad, bored, or even to notice. Programs must change as a result of their experiences or else they will not do anything very interesting.

Similarly, any knowledge structures, or representations of knowledge that AI researchers create, no matter how adequately formulated initially, must change over time. Understanding how they are changed by actual use during the course of processing information is one of the major problems in representation itself. Deciding when to create a new structure or abandon an old one is a formidable problem. Thus, new AI programs should be called upon to assimilate information and change the nature of the program in the course of that assimilation. Clearly such programs are necessary before the knowledge acquisition problem can be adequately attacked. It should also be clear that an AI program that cannot build itself up gradually, without requiring all its knowledge stuffed in at the beginning, is not really intelligent.

I will now give a definition of AI that most of our programs will fail. AI is the science of endowing programs with the ability to change themselves for the better as a result of their own experiences. The technology of AI is derived from the science of AI and is, at least for now, unlikely to be very intelligent. But, it should be the aim of every current AI *researcher* to endow his programs with that kind of *dynamic* intelligence.

8 Generalization

A program that can form a generalization from experience that can be tested would be of great significance. This program would have to be able to draw conclusions from disparate data. The key aspect of a good generalization maker is his ability to connect together experiences that are not obviously connectable. This is the essence of creativity. A key AI problem, therefore is to understand new events and make predictions about future events by generalizing from prior events. These generalizations would likely be inadequate at first, but eventually new theories that fit the data should emerge. Ultimately human expertise is embodied not in rules but in cases. People can abstract rules about what they do of course, but the essence of their expertise, that part which is used in the most complex cases, is derived from particular and rather singular cases that stand out in their minds. The job of the expert is to find the most relevant case to reason from in any given instance. Phenomena such as reminding enhance this ability to generalize by providing more data to consider. The very consideration of seemingly irrelevant data makes for a good generalizer. In other words, AI programs should be able to come up with ideas on their own, so to speak.

9 Curiosity

Cats, small children, and some adults, are curious. They ask questions about what they see, wonder about what they hear, and object to what they are told. This curiosity is not so wondrous when we realize that once a system makes predictions, those predictions may fail, and the system should wonder why. The ability to wonder why, to generate a good question about what is going on, and the ability to invent an answer, to explain what has gone on to oneself, is at the heart of intelligence. We would accept no human who failed to wonder or failed to explain, as being very intelligent. In the end, we shall have to judge AI programs by the same criteria.

10 Creativity

Scientists and technologists would both agree that what is most fascinating of all is the possibility that computers will someday surpass human beings. They are most likely to do this by being creative in some way. Principles of creativity, combined with the other powers of the computer, are likely to create this ultimate fantasy. To this end, I believe it to be necessary for AI people to become familiar with work in other fields that bears upon this issue. Other issues such as consciousness and development relate here also. Thus, another issue is relating ideas in AI to those in allied fields with the purpose of coming to some new scientific conclusions.

Which problems are most important?

All of them are important, of course. But there is one thing above all: an AI program that does not learn is no AI program. Now, I understand that this maxim would not have made much sense in the past. But, one of the problems of defining AI is, as I have said, that AI could, by past definitions, be nearly anything. We have reached a new stage. We have a much better idea of what is learned, therefore it is time to demand learning of our programs. AI programs have always been a promise for the future, a claim about what we could build someday. Each thesis has been the prototype of what we might build if only we would. Well, from the technological perspective, the time to build is now. From the scientific perspective, after the issue of what is learned is taken care of, the issue for AI is learning, although we probably do not have to wait for the former to be finished in order to start.

AI should, in principle, be a contribution to a great many fields of study. AI has already made contributions to psychology, linguistics, and philosophy as well as other fields. In reality, AI is, potentially, the algorithmic study of processes in every field of inquiry. As such, the future should produce AI/anthropologists, AI/doctors, AI/political scientists and so on. There might also be some AI/computer scientists, but on the whole, I believe, AI has less to say, in principle, to computer science than to any other discipline. The reason that this has not been so heretofore is an accident of birth. AI people have been computer scientists, therefore they have tended to contribute to computer science. Computer science has needed tools, as has AI, and, on occasion, these tools have coincided. AI is actually a methodology applicable to many fields. It is just a matter of time until AI becomes part of other fields, and the issue of what constitutes a contribution to AI will be reduced to the question of what constitutes a contribution in the allied field. At that time what will remain of AI will be precisely the issues that transcend these allied fields, whatever they may turn out to be. In fact, that may be the best available working definition of what constitutes a successful contribution in AI today, namely a program whose inner workings apply to similar problems in areas completely different from the one that was tackled originally.

In some sense, all subjects are really AI. All fields discuss the nature of man. AI tries to do something about it. From a technological point of view AI matters to the extent that its technology matters, and the significance of a specific technology is always hard to justify. But from a scientific point of view, we are trying to answer the only questions that really do matter.

68

ARTIFICIAL INTELLIGENCE AS CRAFTWORK

Lucy A. Suchman and Randall H. Trigg

Source: S. Chaiklin and J. Lave (eds), *Understanding Practice: Perspectives on Activity and Context*, Cambridge University Press 1993, pp. 144–78.

> There are two ways in which the visualization processes we are all interested in may be ignored; one is to grant to the scientific mind what should be granted to the hands, to the eyes and to the signs; the other is to focus exclusively on the signs qua signs, without considering the mobilization of which they are but the fine edge.
>
> (Latour, 1986, p. 26)

The goal of research in artificial intelligence (AI) is to design runnable computer programs that replicate some aspect of human behavior. A common first step in the design process is to represent in some form the behavior to be replicated. In this chapter we consider representational practice in AI as the practical activity of two researchers working together at a whiteboard (i.e., a white 'blackboard' used with colored markers).[1] In locating the science there, we aim to bring into focus its character as socially organized craftsmanship – the crafting together of a complex machinery made of heterogeneous materials, mobilized in the service of developing a theory of mind. In this effort we align ourselves with recent developments in the investigation and respecification of science as practice, beginning with Garfinkel's recommendations (1967) that we take sociology's subject matter to be the identifying details of particular forms of practical action, and Lave's analyses (1988) of the social and material structuring of specifically situated activity systems. Prior ethnomethodological studies of science orient us as well to the centrality of representational devices in the structuring of science practice (see, e.g., Garfinkel, Lynch, & Livingston, 1981; Lynch, 1985; Lynch, Livingston, &

Garfinkel, 1983; Livingston, 1986; Lynch & Woolgar, 1990), as does Latour's notion of inscription devices (1986). Finally, we take inspiration from Latour's discussion (1986) of science as craftwork and Law's view (1987) of technological development as heterogeneous engineering.

Our objective here is to view the work of designing intelligent machines as a specific form of social practice – a form made the more interesting by AI's own concern with the delegation of social practice to machines (see also Dreyfus, 1979; Woolgar, 1987; and Collins 1987). We begin with an ethnomethodological interest in the 'worldly observability of reasoning' as socially organized, embodied activity (Lynch et al., 1983, p. 206). With respect to science, this leads to a concern with the practical accomplishment of specific instances of scientific inquiry, 'motivated by the attempt to rediscover the problem of social order in and as the real-world detail of scientific praxis' (ibid., p. 205). The interest in science, in other words, is not only an interest in a particular arena of human activity but in that arena as a window onto the general problem of the situated structuring of ordinary practice.

Of particular interest in science studies is the relation of scientific practice to various devices for seeing. Devices for seeing include re-representations of the world as texts, diagrams, formulas, models, and a host of other artifacts taken to stand for the structure of an investigated phenomenon. As proxies for the phenomena of interest, such artifacts underwrite the accountability both of the phenomena and of the claims to be made about them. Ethnomethodological studies of work, Lynch (1985) points out, 'are distinguished by the way in which they topicalize embodied practices with "paper," "pages," "blackboards," and "typewriter symbols" as of fundamental importance in studies of "intellectual" activities' (p. 294). A major insight of such studies is that the practice of science and other 'nonmanual' forms of labor crucially involves a material basis. Moreover, the use of representational devices organizes the conduct of such activities in a way that is methodical but also contingent and therefore necessarily ad hoc. The meaning of signs and the actions of scientists are mutually constituted, the intelligibility of each presupposing the other. And insofar as the work of scientific inquiry comprises an emergent interaction between scientists and their materials, the structuring of scientific practice is a skilled improvisation, organized in orderly ways that are designed to maintain a lively openness to the possibilities that the materials at hand present.

Latour (1986) offers another insight into the role of representation in science and elsewhere. He calls for a view of science practice that 'deflates grandiose schemes and conceptual dichotomies [e.g., of prescientific versus scientific culture] and replaces them by simple modifications in the way in which groups of people argue with one another using paper, signs, prints and diagrams' (p. 3). In particular, he points to the centrality of such inscription devices in the mobilization of credibility and other associated resources. What makes such devices efficacious, he argues, are their properties of 'immutable mobility'; that is, their capacity to embody processes occurring at one time and place in a form that can be reproduced at another. At the same time, ethnomethodology's observations regarding the reflexive relation of activities to artifacts underscore the extent to which the persuasive power of such devices relies not on the devices themselves, but on the specific achievements of their design and use.

According to Law (1987) 'the stability and form of artifacts should be seen as a function of the interaction of heterogeneous elements as these are shaped and assimilated into a network . . . I call such activity *heterogeneous engineering* and suggest that the product can be seen as a *network* of juxtaposed components' (p. 113, original emphasis). Technology, on this view, is 'a family of methods for associating and channeling other entities and forces, both human and nonhuman. It is a method, one method, for the conduct of heterogeneous engineering, for the construction of a relatively stable system of related bits and pieces with emergent properties' (p. 115). In this respect things engineered are not constituted as such once and for all, but rely upon the continuing cooperation of the world in which they are embedded.

In the case of artificial intelligence, the technology relies upon this cooperation at the same time that it is intended to participate successfully in the social order. The work of AI comprises a process by which researchers, drawing upon lived experience and their culturally constituted common sense of the social world, inscribe scenarios of activity as text, graphical formalisms, and computer programs intended to delegate human competence to machines. The process is not a simple encoding of behavior, but rather a series of transformations involving the simplification of action for purposes of its inscription, followed by implementation of the resulting inscriptions in the machine. The inscriptions produced must be interpretable with reference to common conceptions of rational action on the one hand, while meeting requirements of computability on the other.

We view the enterprise of designing intelligent machines as both 'a cultural practice and an operationalization of beliefs about rationality' (Lave, 1988, p. 172). Lave warns that 'constructing research in terms of mythological views of scientific thought insures blindness to questions of the structuring of everyday activities themselves' (p. 174). This study is a first attempt to replace mythological views of reasoning with the details of AI researchers' practice, as a contribution to the larger project of replacing mentalist myths about reasoning with an understanding of the structuring of embodied action. More specifically, our interest here is in understanding how AI researchers produce and reproduce the sense and sociality of scenarios, formalisms, and intelligent machines on the specific occasions of their creation and use.

The work's setting

The focus of this analysis is a particular episode of technical work in AI. The episode is located in a stream of activities whose concerns are both historically given and projected forward in time. The work makes use of certain resources, is accountable to persistent technical problems and concerns, and is judged in relation to common, albeit controvertible, conceptions of adequacy. In the course of their work, researchers selectively reproduce, make relevant, extend, and transform problems and solutions given by their membership in progressively more specialized technical communities, each with their own assumptions, commitments, and identifying technologies.

The field of artificial intelligence

Artificial intelligence is, most generally, a project to delegate human competence to computing machines. The possibility for such delegation depends on a starting premise of AI; namely, that the phenomenon of intelligent agency can be understood independent of its particular embodiment in human beings. For the case at hand, our practitioners follow what Searle (1980) calls the 'weak AI programme,' that is, they explicitly do not make claims for the psychological reality of their computer-based artifacts. The goal for them is rather to achieve effective delegation of competence; that is, to use the structure and functionality of computation to craft machines that are capable of participating successfully in interactions with the human world.

At this stage in the project, however, the goal is less to build a usable artifact than to develop a new formalism within a subfield of AI known as *knowledge representation*, and to demonstrate the formalism's efficacy to other practitioners. The enterprise of knowledge representation lies at the heart of AI:

> The notion of the *representation of knowledge* ... has to do with writing down, in some language or communicative medium, descriptions or pictures that correspond in some salient way to the world or a state of the world. In Artificial Intelligence (AI), we are concerned with writing down descriptions of the world in such a way that an intelligent machine can come to new conclusions about its environment by formally manipulating these descriptions ... just about every current AI program has what is called a 'knowledge base' containing symbolic descriptions represented in some 'representation scheme.'
>
> (Brachman & Levesque, 1985, p. xiii)

But knowledge representations are more than inert data: 'In AI, a *representation of knowledge* is a combination of data structures and interpretive procedures that, if used in the right way in a program, will lead to 'knowledgeable' behavior' (Barr & Feigenbaum, 1981, p. 143). It is the problem of combining structures and procedures to produce behavior that constitutes the work at hand. In this particular session, researchers focus on the means of interpreting and manipulating symbolic representations already given, rather than on designing the representations themselves. In the process, however, the representations are transformed.

The laboratory

The technological implications of artificial intelligence have led to industrial as well as academic interest in the progress of its work. The institution in which this work takes place is a corporate laboratory comprising activities that, though not directly related to a product line, can be argued to have potential relevance to the design of more powerful or more useful machines. This rationale supports the financing by the corporation of projects identified as 'basic research': that is, research whose relevance to corporate profits is justified in the long-term and admittedly speculative future.

Work in the laboratory includes a range of projects involving the design of computer systems and the development of 'system sciences' broadly defined. Although the prevalent field is computer science, there is value placed on multidisciplinary research; the laboratory includes cognitive psychologists, linguists, typographers and graphic designers, physicists, mathematicians, logicians, philosophers, and anthropologists. Self-organizing collaborations emerge through mutual interests discovered in everyday interaction as well as in more explicitly organized projects.

In addition, multiple ties to universities nationally and internationally are maintained through a steady stream of graduate students and members of the laboratory who hold joint industry—university appointments. Perhaps most salient to members of the laboratory is their identification with the academic community, as both resource and audience for their work.

The project

The AI project on which our analysis is based took place under the combined auspices of the laboratory and an affiliated institute at a nearby university. As described in the center's fourth-year report, 'The Center for the Study of Language and Information is a research institute that aims to develop theories about the nature of information and how it is conveyed, processed, stored, and transformed through language and in computation' (CSLI, 1987, p. 1). Many of the center's projects are conducted jointly with the laboratory. One of these is the Embedded Computation (EC) project, described in the same report as having two goals: '(1) to develop a theory of computation that views computers as situated information processors, and (2) to design and implement specific computational architectures consonant with that theory' (p. 45). Researchers on the project see their efforts as leading to a significantly different view of computation than is standard in computer science. This view includes the notion that computers are physically 'embodied' and contextually 'embedded,' such that their abilities and limitations depend upon a physical substrate and a surrounding situation.

The project involves two related enterprises: (1) constructing scenarios of activity that raise certain thorny representational issues in AI, and (2) designing and implementing a computer program that runs the scenarios, providing evidence that the behaviors (and problems) identified there are realizable (and solvable) in a machine that could participate in the original activity. As with most work in AI, the project is expected to produce a running computer program that realizes and serves as a sufficiency test for the theories that stand behind it. The artifact created, accordingly, is designed to serve researchers' purposes of theorizing more than the purposes attributed to the projected user. At the same time, the program must ultimately succeed in the interactions it is designed for if it is to gain credibility for the theories on which it is based.

The EC project is distinguished by its stated commitment to modeling 'situated inference' about time, place, persons, and the like. The model is to be tested through the design of a computer artifact called the Situated Inference Engine (SIE), intended to embody ideas about 'nonformal inference, situated language, parallel architecture, and representation' (p. 46). The report motivates the SIE subproject as follows:

> Most models of computational inference – particularly those for which rigorous semantical analyses have been given – depend in large measure on theoretical notions from mathematical logic. These theories, however, typically sidestep considerations of various kinds of context. For example, mathematical proofs do not deal with such expressions as TO-THE-RIGHT-OF(TIGER,HIM,NOW), whose semantical interpretation depends on surrounding circumstantial facts. Human conversation, however, systematically exploits exactly this kind of physical, temporal, and discourse relativity.
>
> (p. 50)

Researchers working on the SIE see as their goal the design of an 'inference engine' capable of taking advantage of the implicit context and embedding circumstances of its interactions with a human user. The test case is to design a meeting scheduler capable of interacting with a hypothetical user to maintain a weekly calendar. The first version of the SIE is intended to carry out simple 'dialogues' with a human user about times, places, persons, and the like.

The scenario

The SIE's interactions with its user are modeled by a scenario which, standing as a proxy on behalf of the social world, conceives the activity of scheduling in terms of puzzles of logic and representation interesting from the point of view of AI. Scenarios are a particularly powerful form of what Latour (1986) calls 'immutable mobiles'; that is, representations produced in one place and time, able to be transported more or less intact in order to be deployed again somewhere else:

> One example will illustrate what I mean. La Perouse travels through the Pacific for Louis XVI with the explicit mission of bringing *back* a better map. One day, landing on what he calls Sakhalin he meets with Chinese and tries to learn from them whether Sakhalin is an island or a peninsula. To his great surprise the Chinese understand geography quite well. An older man stands up and draws a map of his island on the sand with the scale and the details needed by La Perouse. Another, who is younger, sees that the rising tide will soon erase the map and picks up one of La Perouse's notebooks to draw the map again with a pencil.
>
> (p. 5)

Following Latour, we take a primary advantage of the inscription of an imagined activity into a scenario to be the latter's *simplicity, mobility,* and *immutability*. The scenario is crafted to pose just and only those problems that the scientist is, a priori, committed to solve. And rather than being contingent on the times and places in which others choose to act, the scientist using the scenario can have access to the problem whenever and wherever he or she chooses. Finally, an inscription has immutability insofar as it, or at least the basis for reproducing it, remains unchanged as it is displaced from one situation of use to a next. It is through these properties that the scenario serves as a coordinating device for project activities distributed over time and space.

At the same time, the mobility and immutability of the scenario are ongoing achievements of project participants, as they selectively reproduce the scenario's significance on successive occasions of its use. Through the scenario, received problems in the field are exemplified as simple invented interactions, which in turn establish requirements for the work at hand. In the meeting analyzed here, participants are concerned with the sequence from the scheduling scenario depicted in Figure 1. Their task is to extend the machinery of AI to handle the puzzles that the sequence poses.

The researchers in this meeting make extensive use of the scenario. Yet they do so constructively, transforming the scenario's opening statement, for example, to 'Wednesday mornings are for graduate students' from the ori-

("us" = user, "ss" = system)

us > On Wednesday mornings I only meet with graduate students.
ss > OK

      . . . later . . .

us > Schedule a meeting with Tore for Wednesday morning!
ss >> Is Tore a graduate student?
us >> Yes.
ss >> How is 9:30?
us >> Fine
ss > Done.

Figure 1. Part of a scheduling scenario.

ginal 'On Wednesday mornings I only meet with graduate students.' The shorter form is equivalent for their purposes at hand, while it maintains the theoretical concerns that motivated the original scenario's design.[2] More specifically, for the researchers the first line of this sequence indexes the canonical AI problem of representing constraints on behavior, and it is that problem with which they are currently engaged.

Figure 1 shows a sequence of the scenario wherein the user informs the system of a scheduling rule, which it successfully makes use of at a later time. This piece of the scenario is made of a rule and directive and embedded question-answer sequence. The problem at hand is to encode the rule in such a way that the machine asks the embedded question regarding Tore's status if and only if the question has not previously been answered. The machine should not, in other words, act stupidly.

Work at the board

Where the physical sciences traditionally rely upon experimentation to produce the objectively accountable evidence of their phenomena and to test their theories, artificial intelligence relies upon the design of computational artifacts. Along with the computer, however, the representational technology of choice among AI researchers is the whiteboard. Whether the concern of the moment is theorizing or system design, much of laboratory activity on a day-to-day basis consists in talk that takes place in front of a whiteboard. Visitors to the laboratory often remark on the ubiquity of the whiteboard as a feature of the general decor. Whiteboards, some covering an entire wall from floor to ceiling, are to be found in 'common' areas as well as in offices, conference rooms, and laboratories. Alongside the computer, the whiteboard constitutes the 'bench' for the laboratory's work practices.

In the case at hand our focus is on a specific occasion of whiteboard work; namely, the production and use of the inscriptions depicted in Figure 2a and

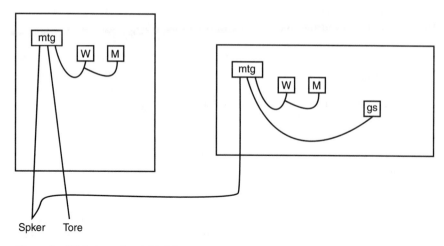

Figure 2a Whiteboard at 1:01:06.

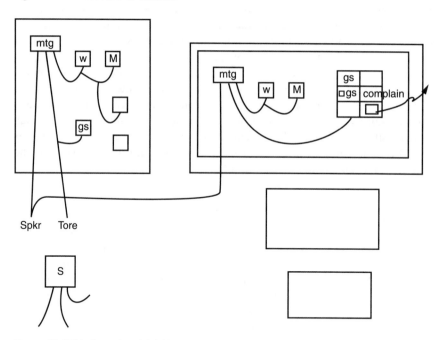

Figure 2b Whiteboard at 1:21:48.

their development into Figure 2b. Ethnomethodological studies of lecturing and of mathematicians' work (Garfinkel & Burns, 1979; Livingston, 1986) have identified the essential, mutually constitutive relationship between marks and the activity of their production and use. Rather than analyze whiteboard inscriptions as such, therefore, we are interested in viewing them in relation to activity, through the use of video records. Viewed as free-standing signs left behind by the work, we assume that the sense of these marks is largely undecipherable. Viewed in relation to the activity of their production and use, in contrast, they come alive as the material production of 'thinking with eyes and hands' that constitutes science as craftwork. Our task here is to provide for the reader, through text, a sense for the sense of these marks as the embodied practice of work at the board.

The analysis is based on video records of a 1.5-hour working session of two researchers, C and M, on the SIE project. Our focus in this analysis is on the design activity occurring after the construction of scenarios and before the creation of computer software. Given the world inscribed as a textual scenario, C and M employ a further device to re-represent the text in a form closer to the program they are eventually after. Previous work on the project, both their own and others', provides them with a graphical formalism and a set of representational conventions. With these, they construct the local setting for their work.

In the analysis we focus on a sequence near the end of the meeting, during which C and M deal specifically with the issues raised by the scenario of Figure 1. Though they continually hold their designs accountable to the scenario, and though they often look ahead to the requirements for implementation in a physical computer, the inscriptions with which they work are neither scenario texts nor computer programs, but hand-drawn diagrammatic representations written on the shared drawing space of the whiteboard.

The creation of the marks in Figure 2a occurs about an hour into the meeting.[3] In the course of their subsequent use, running for roughly 20 minutes until shortly before C and M conclude their work for the day, and resulting in the inscription depicted in Figure 2b, a design dilemma is posed, debated, and resolved. The problem is to design the mechanisms of SIE responsible for combining input from the user with prior knowledge and constraints inscribed in the system, in order to yield requirements on the system's response. In particular, C and M's immediate task is to design the behavior of the SIE system when a schedule command is received for which one or more scheduling rules or 'constraints' are applicable.

The scenario posits that the part of the SIE that takes input from the user has just received the command, 'Schedule a meeting with Tore on Wednesday morning.' Among other 'knowledge' captured in the SIE is a representation of the earlier directive, 'Wednesday mornings are for graduate students.' Combining this directive with the user's schedule command should yield a requirement that Tore be a graduate student:

58:14
001 C: So. Right so we, run the constraint about Wednesday mornings

002   being for graduate students, to get the requirement that Tore is a
           graduate student.

In this case, the slot in the user's weekly calendar corresponding to Wednesday mornings is constrained to be filled (if at all) with meetings with graduate students. As it turns out, the problem for C and M is not how to represent this constraint. Rather, their struggle is over how and when it is to be
applied.

At the outset of the sequence, in the space of 1 minute, C constructs all of
the objects depicted in Figure 2a:[4]

59:54

031 C: (turns back to board) But so, we've got this, this isolated
032   impression structure (looks to M, who looks up at sketch)
033 M: //Right.
034 C: //That's come from the parser essentially. Now the lisp code that
035   runs scheduling could certainly make up (turns to upper left of the
036   wb) a piece (draws large box on left) of what it's going to melt into
037   the larger memory later (turns to M, waving hands in circular
038   motion around box.) (.) (back to box) which says you know meeting,
039   (draws smaller 'mtg' box in upper left corner of large box)
040 M: Right.
041 C: Uh (line down from 'mtg' box to 'spkr' written outside large box)
042   Speaker. (another down from 'mtg' box to 'Tore') Tore. (draws
043   'w' and 'm' boxes and connecting lines to the right of 'mtg' box)
044   Wednesday morning.
045 M: //(inaudible)
046 C: (puts cap on marker, takes step back)//And then (.) (moves again
047   to board and draws second large box to right of the first) So, what's
048   going to be in the biplane, someplace else, outside, is you know
049   (filling in smaller boxes 'mtg,' 'w,' 'm') meeting, Wednesday
050   morning (adds connecting line from 'mtg' in large right-hand box
051   to 'spkr' below large left-hand box, writes 'gs' in box in right half
052   of large right-hand box, cap back onto marker, steps back).
053 M: Are for graduate students, ah right.

As with any occasion of work, C and M's work here is constructed in relation to, and makes use of the products of, previous activities. Most immediately, they have on hand a collection of graphical objects that they themselves have produced on the board earlier in this meeting – for example, the
'impression structure' mentioned by C in lines 031–032 (not pictured). But
those objects, in turn, are selectively reproduced from previous work of
theirs, of others in their project, and of still others in the larger field of which
they are members. Some of these objects are recreated by them here but

treated, at least for present purposes, as closed. Others are the subject matter of their work now, open for invention or transformation. In either case, the objects produced and reproduced constitute the setting for C and M's subsequent activity.

The inscription of objects and the alignment of fields

Lynch and Woolgar (1990) propose that occasions of scientific practice distributed in time and space can be aligned, through the juxtaposition of inscriptions from one occasion with those produced on another. Relations between activities are thereby constituted through the relationship of their inscriptions:

> Representations can represent other representations in complex socio-technical networks: the sense conveyed by a picture may derive as much from a spatiotemporal order of other representations as from its resemblance or symbolization of some external object. Relationships between representational objects and expressions are of particular interest for any effort to reveal the 'social' organization of technical work in science.
>
> (pp. 5–6)

Similarly, Latour (1986) proposes that the progress of science relies upon scientists' successful deployment of a set of 'well aligned and faithful allies,' including techniques, technologies, arguments, and inscriptions. The alignment of these allies does not come without effort however, insofar as they comprise a heterogeneous mix of objects and processes drawn from a diverse collection of fields. For AI in general and for the SIE project in particular, the fields from which such allies are drawn include philosophy, psychology, linguistics, mathematics, electronics, computer science, and engineering. Figure 3 shows the fields brought to bear on constructing the SIE formalism and on the work at hand.

The scientists' problem is to transform this diverse collection of allies, through their superimposition and alignment, into a consistent theory or working artifact. That such alignment succeeds at all is largely due to the metaphorical quality of scientific language. That is, through their ways of talking and inscribing, researchers establish a metaphorical relationship between the various fields without having to say what exactly that relationship is (see Agre, 1990).

A requirement for C and M is to bring a particular set of heterogeneous devices – the scenario, the graphical formalism, the program – into meaningful relationship. Each device is accountable to its adjacent fields. Figure 4 depicts their alignment as a series of transformations from activity to machine.

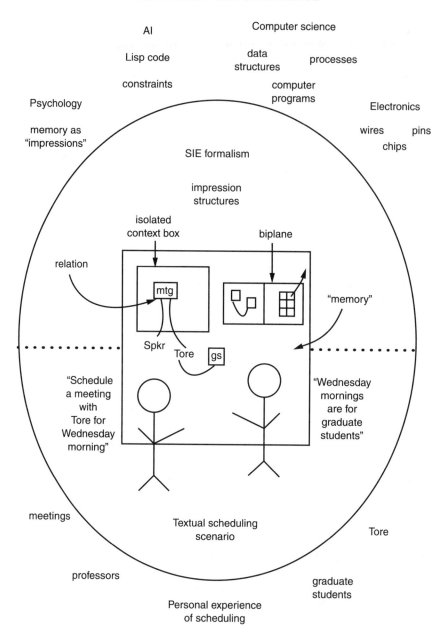

Figure 3 Objects and fields of origin

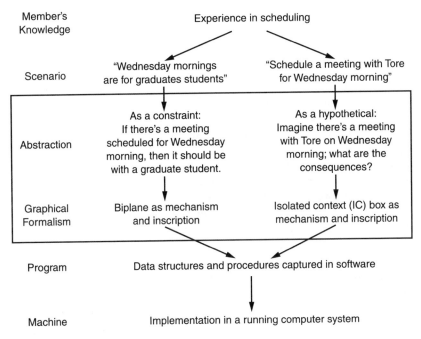

Figure 4 A series of transformations.

Experience is recast as scenarios, which are transformed into abstractions and graphical formalisms, transformed in turn into programs. To succeed, the scenario must be plausible as a representation of scheduling practices, at the same time that it sets up the conditions for their transformation to graphical formalisms. Graphical formalisms, in their turn, must inscribe the scenario, at the same time that they set up the conditions for its inscription as a program runnable on a machine.

The graphical formalism under development in this session at the board lies in some sense midway in the transformation from scheduling activity to program. Notions of scheduling are inscribed as passages in a scenario, reconceptualized in turn as abstractions (e.g., 'constraints' and 'hypotheticals'). These abstractions are recast as a formal notation inscribed as two-dimensional graphical objects (e.g., 'biplanes' and 'IC boxes') on the whiteboard, designed to be encoded as a computer program, to be implemented finally on a machine. The two-dimensionality of the whiteboard facilitates this appropriation of the social world to the world of machines. The crossing of boundaries between heterogeneous phenomena is made easier by the flatness and consequent homogeneity of their inscriptions, such that 'realms of reality that seem far apart ... are inches apart, once flattened out onto the same surface' (Latour, 1986, p. 27). Through this process of flattening and layering, the order of heterogeneous fields and their attendant phenomena are aligned.

Impression structures

The whiteboard is a medium for the construction of what we might call *concrete conceptual objects*. Constructs depicted on the board are conceptual in that they inscribe ideas, but they are also concrete objects – visible, tangible marks that can be produced, used, and transformed. The computer also is an inscribable medium at several levels. At the lowest level, computer software can be characterized as zeros and ones inscribed in the registers of the machine. For most programmers, however, the activity of creating software involves inscribing information in the computer by writing and storing instructions. The computer then 'contains' the information so inscribed, in the same sense that the whiteboard contains the marks inscribed on it.

Impression structure is a generic term used in the SIE project to refer to any data inscribed in the computer's memory. Taking off from an early notion in psychology of memories as analogous to 'impressions' made in soft wax, impression structure in the SIE formalism projects computational and psychological fields onto a single graphical object. Whereas the notion of computer 'memory' itself superimposes computation over psychology, the terms used to denote the contents of memory in computer science traditionally do not draw on psychology. Rather than 'memories,' inscriptions in the computer are called 'data structures,' 'records,' 'bytes.' The notion that a computer's memory could be 'impressed' upon, in contrast, not only allies computation with psychology and computers with minds, but implies a relation of the computer to the social world as the source of its inscriptions.

Isolated contexts

Assuming the inscription of the user's command to the SIE as an impression or data structure inside the machine, C creates the large box to the left in Figure 2a (lines 034–039). The box inscribes the text 'Schedule a meeting on Wednesday morning with Tore' as a graphical formalism that represents the meeting itself, but in a way meant to assign it a provisional status. C describes the box he draws as, 'a piece of what [the system's] going to melt into the larger memory later,' that is once the meeting has been verified (lines 035–038). For now, the box and its contents must be 'isolated' from the rest of the system's memory in case this meeting needs to be retracted from the schedule because it is found to violate some constraint.

To get at their provisional nature, such objects are referred to by project members as *isolated contexts* (ICs). An IC box contains a data or impression structure that is 'isolated' from the rest of memory. One can think of the 'walls' of such a box as a kind of one-way glass. From inside the box, the rest of memory is accessible for purposes of verifying the box's contents against the given constraints. From elsewhere in memory outside the box, however, the contents of the box are unavailable.

Boxes and wires

In lines 041–044, C draws several small labeled rectangles and connecting lines. Each small rectangle represents an association between objects. For example a (two-person) meeting ('mtg') is taken to be a relation between two people ('Spkr' meaning speaker, or the user of SIE and 'Tore,' the name of a graduate student), a time ('W' for Wednesday, 'M' for morning), and a place.[5] *Relation instance boxes* capture this grouping through connecting *wires*. Thus the rectangle labeled 'mtg' appearing inside the IC box (on the left in Figure 2a) has three wires connected to its bottom edge, one each for the two people meeting and one for the time of the meeting. The inscription 'Tore' appearing below the IC box is not itself an entity in memory (thus the absence of a box) but rather indexes for purposes of talk at the board the totality of relations in which Tore participates – that is, a possibly complex but here left unspecified set of wires and connected boxes in the system's memory.

The device of boxes and wires aligns social, psychological, and computational relations through electrical engineering. Digital circuit design is a familiar activity to many computer scientists. Manipulating and constructing digital circuits are largely matters of linking (or wiring) together a number of chips (essentially 'black boxes' with well-documented behavior) containing simple logical or processing elements. The goal is a network whose behavior can be 'read off' of the resulting diagram.

Memory

In lines 046–052, C moves to the right of the IC box and draws a divided rectangle called a *biplane* (i.e., a flat plane divided in two) to represent the constraint 'Wednesday mornings are for graduate students.' As C begins to draw the biplane he says, 'So, what's going to be in the biplane, someplace else, outside . . . ' (lines 047–048). Both 'someplace else' and 'outside' convey his intention that the biplane exists outside of the hypothetical context represented by the IC box. In this case, the biplane is presumed to exist as an impression structure in the computer's 'memory' before this particular schedule command is received. (The placement of 'Tore' and 'Spkr' outside the IC box suggests that they too have been inscribed in memory prior to receiving this command.) As boxes are drawn on the whiteboard, the memory – that which the IC box isolates the context from – becomes the space on the board surrounding the box. As a consequence, a decision about whether something is part of the hypothetical meeting or part of the memory is trivially reversible; one erases the object's inscription from outside the box and redraws it inside (or vice versa).

Constraints

The standard definition of *constraint* that comes closest to C and M's technical usage is 'something that restricts, limits, or regulates' (*American Heritage*, 1976, p. 286). In this representation scheme the constraint takes the form of a logical if-then rule: If there is a meeting scheduled for Wednesday morning, then it must be with a graduate student. M's reading of C's inscription as 'Are for graduate students, ah right' (line 053), however, reflects a preference among researchers in AI to represent constraints in a 'declarative' rather than a 'procedural' fashion; that is, independently of the mechanism by which they are enforced. The goal of representing constraints in a declarative fashion, in turn, reflects a more basic assumption in AI; namely, that there is a distinction between the knowledge one has and how one uses it. Knowledge of the kind 'Wednesday mornings are for graduate students' should be represented in a form that is independent of the procedures comprising its use or application, so as to make the knowledge representation formalism independent of its implementation in a particular system. One should be able to read off from the representation the meaning of the constraint – that is, which objects are restricted to be in what relationships one to another – *without* having to know how the system will maintain such relationships, or what action will be taken if it finds them to be violated.

Designing the behavior of objects

We have noted that all of the objects of Figure 6.2a are reconstituted by C and M from prior work on the project. Rather than invent new objects, C and M's task on this occasion is to design the behavior of those already in hand. More specifically, they take as their task to specify the response of the system when a schedule command is received to which some previously specified rules of scheduling apply.

The scenario with which C and M are concerned prescribes an order of scheduling based on an allocation of times to social categories, for example, 'Wednesday mornings are for graduate students.' Social identity is at once a major organizing device for interaction and a practical problem for everyday interactants (Schegloff, 1972). Institutional interactions, or interactions between strangers, frequently involve demonstrating one's own membership in a particular social category and inferring the membership of others. Various means are available for such demonstrations and inferences, including evidence provided by time, place, appearances, and talk. Troubles of uncertainty or misidentification are detected and resolved (more and less successfully) as they arise.

50

A basic requirement for successful interaction, remarkable only when trouble arises, is to know what constitutes adequate grounds for inference. For example, if I infer something about you based on appearance and turn out to be wrong, or if I question your status when the answer should be obvious, my own competence as a member of the local group is called into question. For C and M, the immediate question is how the system should combine the command 'Schedule a meeting with Tore for Wednesday morning' with the requirement that anyone scheduled for such a meeting must be a graduate student. In this sense, their problem is first and foremost a members' one. That is, given the command to schedule a meeting with Tore, what inference regarding Tore's social status is warranted?

1:00:58
053 M: . . . And the problem here is that (.) we don't want to infer (3.0)
054   It's not supposed to be an inference.
055 (2.0)
056 C: What.
057 M: We're not supposed to infer that Tore is a graduate student, (C
058   sits down on table still holding marker) we're supposed to ask it.
059   That's one-
060 (7.0)
061 M: So::
062 (2.5)

In designing the SIE formalism C and M have a dual accountability, to the social world on the one hand, and to the world of computing on the other. Their problem becomes a technical one insofar as their commitment is to the capabilities of the computer – in particular, how to inscribe knowledge of the social world into the computer in such a way that it will appropriately combine the directive with the constraint. A standard approach to solving the problem is actually to inscribe in the machine some rules of conduct in the form of procedures that, when run, will reproduce the prescribed behavior. In what follows M proposes such procedures as a way of dealing with the constraints on meeting scheduling. More specifically, in lines 068–104 he describes what the computer would do under his plan:

1:01:31
062 C: Right. (.5) Well, first of all, y'just more basically,
063 M: Yeah.
064 C: (stands up, moves to wb.) we have to, take this (points to IC box)
065   piece of structure and, ask whether it matches any constraint
066   (points to biplane box), the left hand side of any constraint in
067   the memory.
068 (2.0)

069 M: The left hand side of that. (C waves at biplane.) No, what I was
070   going to do (stands, moves toward wb) was just imagine that we
071   have a whole bun – (two-handed wave at biplane box) I mean.
072   (Looks for marker on tray.) Turn this into a procedure (draws
073   box around the biplane box, figure 2b) and we have a whole wad
074   of these things (draws two smaller boxes below biplane box),
075   basically each constraint (1.0)//(inaudible)
076 C: // corresponds to a constr-, to a procedure.
077 M: corresponds to a procedure, and just have a set of them. And we
078   just (holds finger of left hand on IC box), start with this context
079   thing and we just go, constraint (taps, with marker, on wb at
080   biplane box), constraint (taps again on new lower box), constraint
081   (points to but doesn't tap the lower of the three boxes).
082   Fire up- fire them all off. Some of them could just, produce
083   contradictions in which case (2.0) uhhm some of them could
084   produce some contradictions, some of them could, in- the
085   Wednesday mornings are for graduate students one, would actually
086   (picks up eraser) if we have it this way (pointing at right
087   side of biplane box) it says, if you have a meeting on a Wednesday
088   morning (turns to look at C) with a grad- then assume it's
089   with a graduate student. That's not what we want, we want: then
090   (erases 'gs' in right side of biplane fig 2a)
091 C: //Uh
092 M: //Actually what we'd is, what we probably want (.) is to have
093   (starts drawing new 3-part box in right side of biplane fig 2b) I
094   mean there's a couple of ways to do this, but we might, um do,
095   if it's a graduate student then do nothing, (filling in parts of
096   3-part box) if it's not a graduate student, then complain (1.0) and
097   if it's unknown, then (.) a- then ask the user (.) I mean then go
098   off to a lisp, (draw arrow pointing out of 3-part box) function
099   which is going to ask user is this, a graduate student. (puts cap
100   on marker) Or something like that//(inaudible)
101 C: //Yeah, but can't we-
102 M: (puts marker on tray) Can we make that =
103 C: = This is going to be very stylized.
104 M: (sits down on table) Yes//so that we want to-
105 C: //Can't we
106 (1.0)
107 C: embed it in the lisp procedure? (.) Rather than in the memory?

C and M are designing the mechanisms by which biplanes and IC boxes, or rules of action and hypothetical situations, will interact. M's proposal assumes the medium of the computer, where processes can be inscribed in a form manipulable by the machine. The whiteboard, however, has no access to, and therefore cannot 'run,' the text and graphical objects inscribed there. The graphical formalism C and M use at the whiteboard is designed for them, in other words, rather than for the machine. To use the formalism to design the machine, M must simulate its intended activity. In lines 077–081 he 'animates' the whiteboard objects so as to simulate the behavior of constraints. Holding a finger of one hand on the IC box, he taps his marker on three newly inscribed 'constraint procedure' boxes to indicate the manner in which they behave. In this respect, the behavior of the constraints is not inscribed so much as it is performed (see also Star & Gerson, 1988; Bly, 1988; Tang, 1989). The constitution of the formalism relies upon a reflexive relation between whiteboard inscriptions and practices, the inscriptions on the board being produced and used through activities that are not themselves reconstructible from these 'docile records,' but whose presence the records presuppose (Garfinkel & Burns, 1979).

On this occasion, however, the performance is intended not for the machine but for C. M needs to prescribe a procedure that the machine would run, but only to the extent that is required to convey the idea to C. He does this by extending the biplane representation to capture the three-part conditional, pointing off to an unspecified mechanism for the interaction with the user. Precisely because the whiteboard is indifferent to these inscriptions, is not 'running' over them, it imposes no requirements for completeness beyond their usefulness for the communicative task at hand.

M's proposal arises from the concern that there are different types of constraints, some of which may warrant automatic inference and others of which do not. To be a competent scheduling assistant, the SIE must maintain the social order of 'Wednesday mornings are for graduate students.' The competence that this rule implies is identified in ethnomethodological studies of social order as the 'ad hoc elaboration of rules in use' (Zimmerman & Wieder, 1970). The central observation of those studies is that maintaining any rule of action requires the local elaboration by participants of just what the rule could mean in relation to specific circumstances of its application. The ad hoc constitution of special purpose procedures to handle those contingencies, however, violates C's sense of adequate design. In struggling with this problem of how rules for scheduling should be applied, C and M return to the importance of the tentativeness of the desired meeting with Tore on Wednesday morning.

1:11:12

247 C: Uhhm. See, I'm pinning my hopes (chuckle)
248 M: //(chuckle)
249 C: //here on the notion that, this box that we've made up,
250 M: right =
251 C: = isn't yet, a fact that we claim about the world.
252 (1.0)

253 C: When I say//schedule
254 M: //Right,
255 C: with//Tore
256 M: //right
257 C: on Wednesday morning I don't mean, there's a meeting on, I'm
258   having a meeting with T – it's not the same as claiming that
259   there is such a meeting.
260 M: Right. That's true.
261 C: Therefore, even if, the SIE didn't make the distinction between,
262   natural law and, nominal constraints and conventional ones,
263 M: Right =
264 C: = uhhm, it could, nevertheless, not assume that Tore's a graduate
265   student, in good faith. (1.0) Because of the fact that, we
266   haven't yet claimed that there's a meeting with Tore on
267   Wednesday morning, but rather that, we would like there to be
268   one.

In superimposing their formalism onto the world of scheduling, C is able to argue that for the SIE to take a meeting inscribed inside the IC box as actual (and therefore as evidence for Tore's status) rather than hypothetical (leaving Tore's status still in question) would violate a normative order. The notion of 'good faith' (line 265) invokes the moral premise that participants in an interaction will neither deliberately mislead each other nor deliberately mis-read each others' intent. Inscriptions inside the IC box are to be taken as proposals rather than claims, leaving open the question of their adherence to the rules of orderly scheduling. In specifying a procedure whereby the SIE would answer the question of Tore's status, a mapping between hypothetical situations and specific circumstances emerges as the new problem:

1:18:36

364 C: Except that what what's actually been tr- true is that you've been
365   asked, the SIE has been asked to schedule a meeting. There's
366   still isn't a meeting. (.) There's still no claim that there's a
367   meeting on Wednesday morning.
368 (.)
369 M: Right. (.) Right that would be (2.0) Ah. See, I still think that the
370   right way to get the inference here is to imagine there being, a
371   meeting on Wednesday morning and see what the consequences
372   of that would be.
373 C: uh-hmm. So, one of the consequences would be, because of
374   this constraint, (indicates biplane) that Tore is a graduate student.
375   (.) Right?
376 (1.5)
377 M: Right.

378 C: But so then, the question is how you match up, this: inductively
379   filled out world, that uh, that you have imagined,
380 M: Right
381 C: with what you know of the real world.
382 M: But the problem is that with, the semantics of the memory
383   structure, (.) you already believe that Tore is a graduate student
384   so, stating that Tore is a graduate student inside it, is not, I
385   mean is a//null operation.
386 C: //Why do you already believe this?
387 M: Cause the semantics o:f, nested contexts is that they inherit
388   beliefs. (1.0) That's just (.) a basic property of the memory.
389 (1.0)
390 C: Wait wait wait wait wait.
391 (5.5)
392 C: hhh.
393 (1.5)
394 C: Well, (stands, moves to wb) I mean no no. I mean (picks up
395   marker, points at IC box), if this is the imaginary world now
396   (erases gs box with hand), then it's gonna have to be the case
397   that, you know (writes gs box and wire inside IC box) the, the
398   graduate student gets added in here =
399 M: = Oh ah. Uh right. (.) Right, if graduate student isn't already
400   outside then, okay. So the idea is you would build more structure
401   in (C points to IC box) there.
402   C:Yeah.

M's initial objection to C's proposal in lines 382–388 arises from a misalign-
ment between M and C, corresponding to loss of alignment between the
whiteboard inscriptions and their talk. M at line 382 is looking at the whiteboard, on which is inscribed the representation of 'gs' outside the IC box, in
memory (signifying that Tore's status as a graduate student is already
known), while C is looking away from the whiteboard, worrying about the
unknown case. C points to the whiteboard while stating, 'one of the consequences would be, because of this constraint . . . ' But then, while presumably making reference to the IC box ('the question is how you match up this
inductively filled out world . . . ') he uses his hands to form a closed spherical
container in the air in front of him, without referring to or looking toward
the whiteboard. M protests that since SIE already 'believes' that Tore is a
graduate student (presumably, because that is inscribed in memory), restat-
ing that fact *inside* the IC box gains nothing. C asks why M 'believes this,'
meaning why does M believe that the SIE already knows that Tore is a
graduate student. M hears that as, why would it be a 'null operation' to
represent Tore's status inside the box, and answers by appealing to the nature
of 'nested contexts,' that is, isolated, insulated boxes and their relations to

memory outside. C at that point looks from M over to the whiteboard and sees that indeed, it depicts the very situation that M has described, namely that Tore's status is represented in memory, outside the box. (This inscription occurred over 15 minutes earlier.)

The trouble reveals the extent to which C and M's shared understandings are tied to shared inscriptions on the board. In this case a 'garden path' misunderstanding arises from the fact that C and M are not at one moment referring to the same objects. M takes the inscriptions on the board, the residue of their previous work, as the current context, whereas C is referring to a revised representation he has constructed 'in the air.'

Seeing the source of the confusion, C goes to the whiteboard, erases the gs inscription 'outside,' and redraws it inside the IC box. This simple action captures the crux of their solution; namely, to assume a consistency between rules of scheduling and requests for meetings, but place any resulting new inferences (e.g., that Tore must be a graduate student) in the same isolated context that contains the meeting. Thus, if processing the constraint 'Wednesday mornings are for graduate students' results in the inference that Tore is a graduate student, that piece of structure will have the same *hypothetical* status as the meeting itself.

1:20:34

398 M: You'd still inherit (inaudible), okay. See, in the case where there
399   was already a graduate student outside (C replaces marker on
400   tray) it wouldn't even build the interior one but that's not a
401   problem.
402 C: (Steps back from wb.) That's cool, yeah.
403 M: n'kay. So the- so it's just this case where it builds an outer one.
404   A:nd (C moves in to wb, grabs marker),//so what you're saying
405   is,
406 C: //Right, there are sort of three cases. One is this (points to gs
407   box outside IC box, not pictured) is empty.
408   One is, this (overwrites 'gs' in same box) has graduate student,
409   in which case this (points to new gs box just added to IC box)
410   doesn't happen. And the other this has (starts writing 'not' box
411   above gs box) gradua- not graduate student (.) in which case
412   (2.0)
413 M: It's//gonna contrad-
414 C: //Well, I don't know.
415 M: it's gonna generate//a contradiction. (Stands and moves toward
416   wb.)
417 C: //This (points to new gs box inside IC box) isn't gonna get built,
418   the contradiction's gonna,//gonna happen in one sort of (in-
419   audible).
420 M: //It's gonna, it's gonna [inaudible] this (points to IC box), it's

421   gonna say, right, it's gonna say this context is contradictory,
422 C: Right =
423 M: = which is okay. So (C replaces marker on tray while M grabs
424   marker), on on this other picture (grabs eraser) then, so we
425   would go along (erases gs box outside IC box) we would, fire off
426   all these constraints and it would build structuring here (points
427   to IC box).
428 C: uh hm.
429 M: And then at the end it would go along and go (turns around to
430   face C, back to wb) how about this (.) structure. And actually
431   that sort of fits with the, how about, I mean it's sort of along the
432   same lines of, how about nine-thirty. Cause that's other structure
433   that's being built in here, it runs all the structure. It has all
434   this, I mean it runs all this (.) things it now builds this structure
435   in here.
436 C: Yeah.
437 M: And now it queries you to, agree to essentially all the things it's
438   about to deduce, it seems like.

Although M's concern about the contingency of the scheduling rules still holds, M and C's accomplishment is to design the behavior of the machine so that its internal architecture ignores the distinction, handing judgments of warranted inference off to the user. The solution requires inscribing a consistent set of relations inside the machine and then enlisting the user in reconciling that inscription with the social world. By finessing the problem for social interaction, they satisfy the adequacy requirements of computer science, in that the objects in memory behave in a uniform, consistent manner. The user, moreover, is consulted only once to pass judgment on the adequacy of the resulting structure. Aligning the scenario with the formalism at the time of design, they rely upon the alignment of formalism with circumstances of the social world at the time of use.

Conclusion

This analysis has been concerned with the in situ work of representing human behavior as the skilled, socially and materially organized practice of AI. The sense of 'representation' we have developed here is an anthropological one, viewing representation as socially organized activity producing certain publicly available artifacts, used in subsequent interactions with others and with the material world. We have proposed that the work of AI involves a series of transformations or re-representations, originating in researchers' connected experience of the social world, moving from a simplified textual scenario that transforms and stands on behalf of that experience, to a formalism that inscribes the scenario, to the inscription of the formalism as code implemented on a machine, and finally to a reconnection of the machine into the social world through its interaction with a human user. Although certain logical relations hold, this process is not a unilinear progression. Scenarios, abstractions, formalisms, and programs comprise the objects of the work under discussion by AI researchers, objects that mediate between experience on the one hand and machines on the other.

Through the devices of scenarios and formalisms, AI researchers attempt to bring practical activity under the jurisdiction of runnable programs. At the same time, a scenario as written provides only a sketch of what the research problems and their solutions could be.[6] The production of relevant problems and appropriate solutions is itself a practical problem for researchers, solved on specific occasions of technical work. That problem is characterized by a tension between researchers' intuitions about the logic of everyday practice on the one hand, and their allegiance to the logic of AI and computation on the other. In the case at hand, the graphical formalisms inscribed on the board mediate between the two.

Through their skilled work at the board, researchers make scenarios and formalisms relevant to their practical purposes at hand. This work constitutes the 'performance' that, according to Star and Gerson (1988), is the necessary companion to inscriptions in use: 'Where inscriptions attempt to freeze natural phenomena to make them more manageable, performances 'fiddle' and adjust representations to make them fit local circumstances' (p. 2).

These performances, the 'unformulated practices' (Lynch, 1985) of AI design, mediate between the requirements of persons and machines. As a medium for inscribing formalisms, the whiteboard mediates between persons and machines as well. The two-dimensional objects on the board are designed to be manipulated and talked about as representations of persons and schedules that anticipate the requirements of the machine. Their success, however, depends upon the artful practice of researchers as they exploit certain properties of the objects while treating others as irrelevant. As Livingston (1986) has discovered for the practice of mathematics:

> If we consider the primordial setting of mathematics to be those occasions when mathematicians, in the presence of one another, work in such a way so as to exhibit to each other the recognizable adequacy of their work, then one of the things that we have seen is that mathematicians work in such a way so as to disengage the mathematical object from the situated work that makes it available and, therein, to disengage that object from the situated work that makes it its naturally accountable properties. Thus, the first major point is that the naturally accountable mathematical object is the local achievement of mathematical provers.
>
> (p. 10)

Like any product of skilled practice, the formalism inscribed on the board leaves behind the logic of its own production and use, seen here as collaborative craftwork of hands, eyes, and signs. But analyses of situated practice such as this one point to the contingencies of practical action on which logic-in-use, including the production and use of scenarios and formalisms, inevitably and in every instance relies. In this way such analyses provide an alternative to idealized formulations of reasoning as disembodied mental operations.

In taking AI as a subject of inquiry we are faced with an outstanding issue regarding the representation of human practice. The issue can be formulated, at least initially, as follows: Ethnomethodological studies of the physical and biological sciences eschew any interest in the adequacy of scientific representations as other than a member's concern. The point of such studies is specifically not to find ironies in the relation between analysts' constructions of the phenomenon and those of practitioners (Garfinkel, 1967, p. viii; Woolgar, 1983). Rather, the analyst's task is to take the ways by which practitioners come to an understanding of their phenomenon as the identifying accomplishment of their scientific practice. In turning to AI and cognitive science, however, one is confronted with fields whose phenomenon of interest itself is practice. For cognitive science theorizing, the object is mind and its manifestation in rational action. And in designing so-called intelligent computer systems, representations of practice provide the grounds for achieving rationality in the behavior of the machine.

To the extent that AI is an enterprise dedicated to explicating the social world, it shares with the other social sciences a central question; that is, to what rendering of the phenomenon of interest is the enterprise accountable? In our own case, working from video records presupposes that 'it is the embodiment of speech and gesture which provides work with its visibility for practitioners' (Lynch, 1985, p. 7). Moreover, we assume that the identifying problems and solutions of the practice in which we are interested are to be found in the analysis of actual, specific instances of practitioners working together. At the same time, we recognize the produced-and-analyzed character of these video records, as materials with which we are actively engaged rather than as 'data' whose sense can be read off directly from the record that the videotape provides.

Without setting up a simple irony, then, in the comparison of AI's enterprise with our own, we wish to open the question of accountability in relation to the project of engineering intelligent machines. AI is interested in reproducing practical reasoning computationally as a means of modeling and thereby understanding it. However, rather than beginning with documented instances of situated inference (e.g., inferring whether someone is a graduate student), researchers begin with what Agre (1990) calls 'pseudo-narratives': in this case, postulates and problems handed down by the ancestral communities of computer science, systems engineering, philosophical logic, and the like.[7] Scheduling operates here not as a category of activity in the world but as a pretext for the resolution of problems in constraint-based reasoning. The scenario disciplines and constrains C and M's intuitions in the service of an intellectual enterprise defined not by scheduling activities but by the communities of practice from which the scenario comes and to which it is accountable. C and M's primary concern must be with the accountability of their representations to the scenario and its ancestral communities, rather than with the scenario's relation to the activity it purports to model and for which on this occasion it stands.

The communities of practice of which AI is a part, and from which its resources are drawn, have traditionally taken the production of definitive, decontextualized renderings of a phenomenon of interest as the measure of understanding. In accord with this standard, AI has as a goal to escape from the indeterminacies of argumentation about intelligence through the design of machines that could successfully and definitively reproduce it. The successful design of intelligent machines is to be the proverbial 'pudding' that proves the validity of researchers' theories and the efficacy of their methods. However, to the extent that practical reasoning is comprised of the juxtaposition, *bricoleur*-fashion, of disparate elements available in specific, historically and culturally constituted settings, the situated inference of AI research must come to terms with its own irreducibly contingent and ad hoc character.

Lave (1988) has argued that 'theoretically charged, unexamined, normative models of thinking lose their descriptive and predictive power when research is moved to everyday settings and relaxes its grip on the structuring of activity' (p. 172) and asks:

> What would happen to theorizing about cognition if investigation were moved to the sites of the activity whose interpretation was under debate? What changes in theoretical orientation would be required in order to make such travels seem sensible and of value in the first place? What further theoretical reformulations would follow from a multi-faceted approach to observation and analysis of everyday activity? The argument has been formulated as a journey from the laboratory into the everyday world.
>
> (p. 170)

The laboratory Lave has in mind here is the psychology laboratory, but we find her questions equally relevant to the laboratory of AI research. What would happen, we wonder, if the bases for AI's theorizing about everyday activity were not scenarios but actual scenes, captured in some rich medium and inspected in detail for their sense, their local structures, and their relations to other systems of activity? What changes in theoretical orientation would be required for this shift in methods to happen? The design of machines as situated reasoning engines would seem to implicate them in specific sociocultural, historical, temporal, and spatial locations. Yet AI scenarios routinely hold such circumstances in abeyance, implicitly relying upon designer and user to fill in the machine's social location as needed, while systematically neglecting to consider that process itself as an object of research. If, however, as Lave suggests, 'thought (embodied and enacted) is situated in socially and culturally structured time and space' (p. 171) the locus of AI theorizing must be opened up to the larger constitutive order of which persons, machines, and activities are invariably and essentially a part.

Acknowledgement

We are grateful to Phil Agre, Urs Fuhrer, Charles Goodwin, Brigitte Jordan, Bruno Latour, Jean Lave, and Susan Newman for their comments on earlier drafts. Seth Chaiklin and Jean Lave provided extremely valuable substantive as well as editorial suggestions. Most crucially we are indebted to researchers on the SIE project for allowing us to look in on their work.

Notes

1 The work reported here is the result of a collaboration between the authors, an anthropologist, and a computer scientist. The study draws on our combined knowledge and experience of ethnography, ethnomethodology, interaction analysis, computer system design, and AI. The project described here was part of the research program of another division of the laboratory in which we were both members. This provided us with ready access to the researchers we studied and a familiarity with aspects of their work's larger context, both of which contributed to our analysis of the video records.

2 The shortened version used in the meeting may also be a reference to the version, 'Wednesday mornings are reserved for graduate students,' appearing later in the scenario. Presumably the researchers are familiar with the entire scenario though they only demonstrate their concern here with the first few lines.

3 Figures 2a and 2b represent the upper left corner of a whiteboard on which various other textual and graphic inscriptions are also lying about as the result of the meeting's first hour. We select this piece of the board and the corresponding episode because they are relatively self-contained, but also because they are perspicuous with respect to the issues of AI in which we have an interest.

4 For the sake of readability in dealing with these technically complex materials, we provide only a standard, nonconversation analytic transcription, though we are sure that these materials would repay careful analysis. In the transcript segments numbers in parentheses indicate elapsed time in seconds. Thus '(3.0)' indicates a pause of three seconds. A dot in parentheses '(.)' indicates an untimed pause, an equals sign ' = ' indicates 'latching,' i.e., the beginning of one utterance following directly on the end of the prior with no gap. Double slashes '//' indicate the onset of overlapped talk. Colons ':' indicate prolongation of the immediately preceding sound. Line numbers refer to the place of a segment in the full transcript.

5 The meeting place is left unrepresented during this discussion, as the larger issue of place is a piece of the problem they are holding aside. For the moment, at least, focusing on time and time-related constraints is sufficient for their purposes.

6 The problems posed in the scenario include representing unanticipated information (say, Tore's status), building objects in a machine that track the changing real world (again, Tore's status, which might change from year to year), and

representing indexicals, objects like Wednesday, Speaker, and 'I,' which depend for their meaning on a situation of use.

7 Agre's point is that these are fictional narratives constructed to resemble 'ordinary' narratives read forward from recounted events, whereas in fact they are actually (and covertly) read backward from technical categories and from the need to illustrate, motivate, or exemplify technical proposals cast within those categories. Such 'pseudo-narratives' are constructed for the specific purpose of reconstructing commonsense knowledge as something that can be transparently read off of the particular technical representations at hand. For a practitioner's critique of current AI practice and recommendations for an alternative, see Agre (in press).

References

Agre, P. (1990, July). *Portents of planning: A critical reading of the first paragraph of Miller, Galanter and Pribram's* Plans and the Structure of Behavior. Paper presented at the Conference on Narrative in the Human Sciences, Iowa City.

Agre, P. (in press). *Computation and human experience.* Cambridge: Cambridge University Press.

American Heritage Dictionary (1976). Boston: Houghton Mifflin.

Barr, A., & Feigenbaum, E. (1981). Representation of knowledge. In A. Barr & E. Feigenbaum (Eds.), *The handbook of artificial intelligence* (Vol. 1, pp. 141–222). Los Altos, CA: Morgan Kaufmann.

Bly, S. (1988). A use of drawing surfaces in different collaborative settings. *Proceedings of the Second Conference on Computer-Supported Cooperative Work* (pp. 250–256). New York: Association of Computing Machinery.

Brachman, R., & Levesque, H. (1985). Introduction. In R. Brachman & H. Levesque (Eds.), *Readings in knowledge representation* (pp. xiii–xix). Los Altos, CA: Morgan Kaufmann.

Collins, H. M. (1987). Expert systems and the science of knowledge. In W. Bijker, T. Hughes, & T. Pinch (Eds.), *The social construction of technological systems* (pp. 329–348). Cambridge, MA: MIT Press.

CSLI (1987). *Fourth year report of the situated language research program* (CSLI-87–111). Stanford, CA: Center for the Study of Language and Information.

Dreyfus, H. (1979). *What computers can't do.* New York: Harper and Row.

Garfinkel, H. (1967). *Studies in ethnomethodology.* Englewood Cliffs, NJ: Prentice-Hall.

Garfinkel, H., & Burns, S. (1979). *Lecturing's work of talking introductory sociology.* Unpublished manuscript, Department of Sociology, University of California, Los Angeles.

Garfinkel, H., Lynch, M., & Livingston, E. (1981). The work of a discovering science construed with materials from the optically discovered pulsar. *Philosophy of the Social Sciences, 11,* 131–158.

Latour, B. (1986). Visualization and cognition: Thinking with eyes and hands. *Knowledge and Society, 6,* 1–40.

Lave, J. (1988). *Cognition in practice.* Cambridge: Cambridge University Press.

Law, J. (1987). Technology and heterogeneous engineering: The case of Portuguese expansion. In W. Bijker, T. Hughes, & T. Pinch (Eds.), *The social construction of technological systems* (pp. 111–134). Cambridge, MA: MIT Press.

Livingston, E. (1986). *The ethnomethodological foundations of mathematics*. London: Routledge and Kegan Paul.

Lynch, M. (1985). *Art and artifact in laboratory science: A study of shop work and shop talk in a research laboratory*. London: Routledge and Kegan Paul.

Lynch, M., Livingston, E., & Garfinkel, H. (1983). Temporal order in laboratory work. In K. Knorr-Cetina & M. Mulkay (Eds.), *Science observed: Perspectives on the social study of science* (pp. 205–238). Beverly Hills, CA: Sage.

Lynch, M., & Woolgar, S. (1990). Introduction: Sociological orientations to representational practice in science. In M. Lynch & S. Woolgar (Eds.), *Representation in scientific practice* (pp. 1–18). Cambridge, MA: MIT Press.

Schegloff, E. (1972). Notes on a conversational practice: Formulating place. In D. Sudnow (Ed.), *Studies in social interaction* (pp. 75–115). New York: Free Press.

Searle, J. (1980). Minds, brains, and programs. *Behavioral and Brain Sciences, 3*, 417–457.

Star, S. L., & Gerson, E. (1988). *Representation and re-representation in scientific work*. Unpublished manuscript, Tremont Research Institute, San Francisco.

Tang, J. (1989). *Listing, drawing and gesturing in design: A study of the use of shared workspaces by design teams* (Research Center Technical Report SSL-89-3). Palo Alto, CA: Xerox Palo Alto.

Woolgar, S. (1983). Irony in the social study of science. In K. Knorr-Cetina and M. Mulkay (Eds.), *Science observed: Perspectives on the social study of science* (pp. 239–265). Beverly Hills, CA: Sage.

Woolgar, S. (1987). Reconstructing man and machines: A note on sociological critiques of cognitivism. In W. Bijker, T. Hughes, & T. Pinch (Eds.), *The social construction of technological systems* (pp. 311–328). Cambridge, MA: MIT Press.

Zimmerman, D. H., & Wieder, D. L. (1970). Ethnomethodology and the problem of order: Comment on Denzin. In J. D. Douglas (Ed.), *Understanding everyday life: Toward the reconstruction of sociological knowledge* (pp. 285–298). Chicago: Aldine.

THE SOUL GAINED AND LOST

Artificial intelligence as a philosophical project

Philip E. Agre

Source: *Stanford Humanities Review* 4(2), 1995: 1–19.

Introduction

When I was a graduate student in Artificial Intelligence (AI), the humanities were not held in high regard. They were vague and woolly, they employed impenetrable jargons, and they engaged in 'meta-level bickering that never decides anything.' Although my teachers and fellow students were almost unanimous in their contempt for the social sciences, several of them (not all, but many) were moved to apoplexy by philosophy. Periodically they would convene impromptu two-minute hate sessions to compare notes on the arrogance and futility of philosophy and its claims on the territory of AI research. 'They've had two thousand years and look what they've accomplished. Now it's our turn.' 'Anything that you can't explain in five minutes probably isn't worth knowing.' They distinguished between 'just talking' and 'doing,' where 'doing' meant proving mathematical theorems and writing computer programs. A new graduate student in our laboratory, hearing of my interest in philosophy, once sat me down and asked in all seriousness, 'Is it true that you don't actually do anything, that you just say how things are?' It was not, in fact, true, but I felt with great force the threat of ostracism implicit in the notion that I was 'not doing any real work.'

These anecdotes may provide some sense of the obstacles facing any attempt at collaboration between AI and the humanities. In particular, they illustrate certain aspects of AI's conception of itself as a discipline. According to this self-conception, AI is a self-contained technical field. In particular, it is a practical field; to do AI is to prove theorems, write software, and build hardware whose purpose is to 'solve' previously defined technical 'problems.' The whole test of these activities lies in 'what works.' The criterion of 'what works' is straightforward, clear, and objective in the manner of engineering design; arguments and criticisms from outside the field can make no claim at all against it. The substance of the field consists in the 'state of the art' and its history is a history of computer programs. The technical methods underlying these programs might have originated in other fields, but the real work consisted in formalizing, elaborating, implementing, and testing those ideas. Fields which do not engage in these painstaking activities, it is said, are sterile debating societies which do not possess the intellectual tools—most particularly mathematics—to do more than gesture in the general direction of an idea, as opposed to really working it out.

I will be thought to exaggerate. Technicians will protest their respect for great literature, and the attitudes I have reported will be put down to a minority of fundamentalists. Yet the historical record makes plain that interactions between AI and the humanities have been profoundly shaped by the disciplinary barriers that such attitudes both reflect and reproduce. Serious research in history and literature, for example, has had almost no influence on AI. This is not wholly due to ignorance on the part of technical people, many of whom have had genuine liberal educations. Rather AI, as a technical field, is constituted in such a way that its practitioners honestly cannot imagine what influence those fields *could* have.

Philosophy has had a little more influence. Research on AI's constitutive questions in the philosophy of mind is widely read and discussed among AI research people, and is sometimes included in the curriculum; but these discussions are rarely considered part of the work of AI—judging, for example, by journal citations—and any influence they might have had on the day-to-day work of AI has been subtle at best. Contemporary ideas from the philosophies of language and logic have been used as raw material for AI model-making, though, and philosophers and technical people have collaborated to some degree in specialized research on logic.

Perhaps the principal humanistic influence on AI has derived from a small number of philosophical critics of the field, most particularly Hubert Dreyfus. For Dreyfus, the project of writing 'intelligent' computer programs ran afoul of the critique of rules in Wittgenstein, and of Heidegger's analysis of the present-at-hand way of relating to beings (in this case, symbolic rules).[1] The use of a rule in any practical activity, Dreyfus argues, requires a prior participation in the culturally specific form of life within which such activities take place. The attempt to fill in the missing 'background knowledge' through additional rules would suffer the same problem and thus introduce a fatal regress.[2] Although most senior AI researchers of my acquaintance stoutly deny having been affected by Dreyfus's arguments, a reasonable amount of research has addressed the recurring difficulties with AI research that Dreyfus predicted. One of these is the 'brittleness' of symbolic, rule-based AI systems, which derives from their tendency to fail catastrophically in situations that depart even slightly from the whole background of operating assumptions that went into the system's design. For the most part, the response of AI researchers to these difficulties, and to Dreyfus's analyses generally, is to interpret them as additions to AI's agenda that require no fundamental rethinking of its premises.[3]

Within the field itself, critical reflection is largely a prerogative of the field's most senior members, and even these papers are published separately from the narrowly technical reports, either in non-archival publications like the *AI Magazine* or in special issues of archival publications devoted to the founders' historical reflections. In 1990 I received a referee's report on an AAAI (American Association for Artificial Intelligence) conference paper that read in part,

> In general, avoid writing these 'grand old man' style papers until you've built a number of specific systems & have become a grand old man.

The boundaries of 'real AI research,' in short, have been policed with great determination.

Yet this is now changing. In part the current changes reflect sociological shifts in the field: in particular, its decentralization away from a few heavily funded laboratories and the resulting, albeit modest, trend toward interdisciplinary pluralism. But the change in atmosphere has also been influenced by genuine dissatisfactions with the field's original technical ideas. AI's practices of formalizing and 'working out' an idea constitute a powerful method of inquiry, but precisely for this reason they are also a powerful way to force an idea's internal tensions to the surface through prolonged technical frustrations: excessive complexity, intractable inefficiency, difficulties in 'scaling up' to realistic problems, and so forth. These patterns of frustration have helped clear the ground for a new conception of technical work, one that recognizes the numerous, deep continuities between AI and the humanities. Although these continuities reach into the full range of humanistic inquiry, I will restrict myself here to the following five assertions about AI and its relationship to philosophy:

1. AI ideas have their genealogical roots in philosophical ideas.
2. AI research programs attempt to work out and develop the philosophical systems they inherit.
3. AI research regularly encounters difficulties and impasses that derive from internal tensions in the underlying philosophical systems.
4. These difficulties and impasses should be embraced as particularly informative clues about the nature and consequences of the philosophical tensions that generate them.
5. Analysis of these clues must proceed outside the bounds of strictly

technical research, but they can result in both new technical agendas and in revised understandings of technical research itself.

In short, AI is philosophy underneath. These propositions are not entirely original, of course, and some version of them underlies Dreyfus's early critique of the field. My own purpose here is to illustrate how they might be fashioned into a positive method of inquiry that maintains a dialogue between the philosophical and technical dimensions of AI research. To this end, I will present a brief case study of one idea's historical travels from philosophy through neurophysiology and into AI, up to 1972. Although much of this particular story has been told many times, some significant conclusions from it appear to have escaped analysis. It is an inherently difficult story to tell, since it requires a level of technical detail that may intimidate the uninitiated without nearly satisfying the demands of initiates. It is a story worth telling, though, and I will try to maintain a firm sense of the overall point throughout. I will conclude by briefly discussing recent developments that have been motivated in part by critical reevaluations of this tradition, and by sketching the shape of the new, more self-critical AI that is emerging in the wake of this experience.

René Descartes: criteria of intelligence

In a famous passage in his Discourse on Method Descartes summarizes a portion of his suppressed treatise on *The World* as follows:

> . . . the body is regarded as a machine which, having been made by the hands of God, is incomparably better arranged, and possesses in itself movements which are much more admirable, than any of those which can be invented by man . . . if there had been such machines, possessing the organs and outward form of a monkey or some other animal without reason, we should not have had any means of ascertaining that they were not of the same nature as those animals. On the other hand, if there were machines which bore a resemblance to our body and imitated our actions as far as it was morally possible to do so, we should always have two very certain tests by which to recognize that, for all that, they were not real men. The first is, that they could never use speech or other signs as we do when placing our thoughts on record for the benefit of others. For we can easily understand a machine's being constituted so that it can utter words, and even emit some responses to action on it of a corporeal kind, which brings about a change in its organs; for instance, if it is touched in a particular part it may ask what we wish to say to it; if in another part it may exclaim that it is being hurt, and so on. But it never happens that it arranges its speech in various ways, in order to reply

appropriately to everything that may be said in its presence, as even the lowest type of man can do. And the second difference is, that although machines can perform certain things as well as or perhaps better than any of us can do, they infallibly fail short in others, by the which means we may discover that they did not act from knowledge, but only from the disposition of their organs. For while reason is a universal instrument which can serve for all contingencies, these organs have need of some special adaptation for every particular action. From this it follows that it is morally impossible that there should be sufficient diversity in any machine to allow it to act in all the events of life in the same way as our reason causes us to act.[4]

It is worth quoting Descartes's words at such length because they contained the seeds of a great deal of subsequent intellectual history. Distinctions between the body and the soul were, of course, of great antiquity, as was the idea that people could be distinguished from animals by their reasoned use of language. Descartes, though, extended these ideas with an extremely detailed physiology. His clearly drawn dualism held that automata, animals, and the human body could all be explained by the same mechanistic laws of physics, and he set about partitioning functions between body and mind.[5] In establishing this partition, one of the tests was the conventional distinction between animal capabilities, which reside in the body, and specifically human capabilities, which required the exercise of the soul's faculties of reason and will. Thus, for example, automata or animals might utter isolated words or phrases in response to specific stimuli, but lacking the faculty of reason they could not combine these discrete units of language in an unbounded variety of situationally appropriate patterns. The soul itself has ideas, but it has no physical extent or structure. Thus, as Descartes explains in *The Passions of the Soul* (Articles 42 and 43), memory is a function of the brain; when the soul wishes to remember something, it causes animal spirits to propagate to the spot in the brain where the memory is stored, whereupon the original image is presented once again to the soul in the same manner as a visual perception.

The attraction of Descartes's proposals lay not in their particulars, many of which were dubious even to his contemporaries. Rather, Descartes provided a model for a kind of theory-making that contrasted with late scholastic philosophy in every way: it was specific and detailed, it was grounded in empirical physiology, and it was written in plain language.

Karl Lashley: language as a model for action

The American cognitivists of the 1950s often modeled themselves after Descartes, and they intended their research to have much of the same appeal. Despite the intervening three centuries, the lines of descent are indeed clear.

This is evident in the case of Chomsky, for example, who argued in explicitly Cartesian terms for a clear distinction between the physiology of speech, including the biological basis of linguistic competence, and the capacity for actually choosing what to say. While not a dualist, Chomsky nonetheless epitomized his conception of human nature in terms of 'free creation within a system of rule.' Miller used Descartes's *Rules for the Direction of the Mind* to motivate his search for ways that people might more efficiently use their limited memories.[6]

The first and most influential revival of research into mental mechanisms, Karl Lashley's 1951 paper 'The Problem of Serial Order in Behavior,' did not acknowledge any sources beyond the linguistics, psychology, and neurophysiology of the 1940s.[7] Nonetheless, the underlying continuities are important for the computational ideas that followed. Despite his own complex relationship to behaviourism, Lashley's paper argued clearly that behaviorist psychology could not adequately explain the complexity of human behavior. Lashley focused on a particular category of behavior, namely speech. He pointed out that linguists could demonstrate patterns to the grammar and morphology of human languages that are hard to account for by using the theory of 'associative chains,' whereby each action's effects in the world give rise to stimuli that then trigger the next action in turn. The formal structures exhibited by human language, then, were sufficient reason to restore some notion of mental processing to psychology.

Moreover, Lashley suggested that *all* action be understood on the model of language. He regarded both speech and physical movement as having a 'syntax,' and he sought the physiological basis of both the syntax of movement and the choice of specific movements from among the syntactically possible combinations. This suggestion was enormously consequential for the subsequent development of cognitivist psychology, and particularly for AI. Lashley summarized the idea in this way:

> It is possible to designate, that is, to point to specific examples of, the phenomena of the syntax of movement that require explanation, although those phenomena cannot be clearly defined. A real definition would be a long step toward solution of the problem. There are at least three sets of events to be accounted for. First, the activation of the expressive elements (the individual words or adaptive acts) which do not contain the temporal relations. Second, the determining tendency, the set, or idea. This masquerades under many names in contemporary psychology, but is, in every case, an inference from the restriction of behavior within definite limits. Third, the syntax of the act, which can be described as an habitual order or mode of relating the expressive elements; a generalized pattern or schema of integration which may be imposed upon a wide range and a wide variety of specific acts. This is the essential problem of serial order;

the existence of generalized schemata of action which determine the sequence of specific acts, acts which in themselves or in their associations seem to have no temporal valence.[8]

Two things are new to cognitive theorizing here: grammar as a principle of mental structure and the generalization of grammatical form to all action. But a great deal in Lashley's account is continuous with that of Descartes. To start with, it is an attempt at an architecture of cognition. Indeed, it is considerably less detailed than Descartes's architecture, although Descartes provided no account of the mechanics of speech. Both Lashley and Descartes assign the ability to speak individual words—or in Lashley's case, to make individual discrete physical movements—to individual bits of machinery, without being very specific about what these bits of machinery are like; and they both view the human capacity for putting these elements together as the signature of the mind. To be sure, Lashley's argument rests on the formal complexity of speech whereas Descartes's points at the appropriateness of each utterance to the specific situation. In each case, though, what counts is the capacity of the mind to order the elements of language in an unbounded variety of ways.

The continuities go deeper. Lashley, as a neurophysiologist, shows no signs of believing in an ontological dualism such as Descartes's. Yet the conceptual *relations* among the various components of his theory are analogous to those of Descartes. In each case, the brain subserves a repertoire of bodily capacities, and on every occasion the mind orders these in accord with its choices, which themselves are not explained. For Descartes, the mind's choices simply *cannot* be explained in causal terms, though its operations can be described in the normative terms of reason, as for example in his *Rules for the Direction of the Mind*. Lashley does not express any overt skepticism about his 'determining tendency,' but neither does he have anything very definite to say about it; the concept stays nebulous throughout. This is not simply an incompleteness of Lashley's paper but is inherent in its design: the purpose of the determining tendency is not to *have* structure in itself but to *impose* structure upon moment-to-moment activities from the repertoire of action schemata made available to it by the brain.

In retrospect, then, Lashley's paper makes clear the shape of the challenge that the cognitivists had set themselves. They wished to rout their sterile behaviorist foes in the same way that Descartes had routed the schoolmen, by providing a scientific account of cognitive processes. The problem, of course, is that Descartes was not a thoroughgoing mechanist. So long as the cognitivists retained the relational system of ideas that they had inherited from Descartes, and from the much larger tradition of which Descartes is a part, each of their models would include a component corresponding to the soul. No matter how it might be squeezed or divided or ignored, there would always remain one black box that seemed fully as intelligent as the person as a whole, capable of making intelligent choices from a given range of options on a regular basis. As the field of AI developed, this recalcitrant box acquired several names. Dennett, for example, spoke of the need for 'discharging the homunculus,' something he imagined to be possible by dividing the intelligent homunculus into successively less intelligent pieces, homunculi within homunculi like the layers of an onion, until one reached a homunculus sufficiently dumb to be implemented in a bit of computer code.[9] AI researchers' jargon spoke of subproblems as being 'AI-complete' (an analogy: so-called NP-complete computational problems are thought to be unsolvable except through an enumeration of possible solutions—an efficient algorithm for any one such problem would yield efficient algorithms for all of them). Furthermore, several exceedingly skilled programmers devised computer systems that were capable of reasoning about their own operation, including reasoning about their reasoning about their own operation, and so on *ad infinitum*.[10] In each case, the strategy was to reduce the soul's infinite choices to finite mechanical means.

But beyond sketching the shape of a future problem, Lashley also sketched the principal strategy of a whole generation for solving it. The operation of the determining tendency might be a mystery, but the general form of its accomplishment was not. While the linguistic metaphor for action envisions an infinite variety of possible actions, it also imposes a great deal of structure on them. In mathematical terms the possible actions form a 'space.' The generative principle of this space lies in the 'schemata of action,' which are modeled on grammatical rules. A simple schema for English sentences might be:

Sentence → NounPhrase IntransitiveVerb.

That is, roughly speaking 'one way to make a sentence is to utter a noun phrase followed by an intransitive verb.' Other rules might spell out these various 'categories' further, for example:

NounPhrase → ArticleNoun
Article → *a*
Article → *the*
Noun → *cat*
Noun → *dog*
IntransitiveVerb → *slept*
IntransitiveVerb → *died*

These mean, roughly, 'one way to make a noun phrase is to utter an article followed by a noun,' 'some possible articles are *a* and *the*,' 'some possible nouns are *cat* and *dog*,' and 'some possible intransitive verbs are *slept* and *died*.' There might be other ways to make sentences, for example:

Sentence → NounPhrase TransitiveVerb NounPhrase
TransitiveVerb → *saw*
TransitiveVerb → *ate*

This particular set of grammatical rules generates a finite space of English sentences, for example:

the cat saw a dog
a dog ate a dog

The process of 'deriving' a sentence with these rules is simple and orderly. One begins with the category Sentence, and then at each step one makes two choices: (1) which category to 'expand,' and (2) which rule to apply in doing so, until no categories are left. For example, one might proceed as follows:

1.Sentence
2. NounPhrase TransitiveVerb NounPhrase
3. NounPhrase TransitiveVerb Article Noun
4. NounPhrase *saw* Article Noun
5. Article Noun *saw* Article Noun
6. *the* Noun *saw* Article Noun
7. *the* Noun *saw* Article *dog*
8. *the cat saw* Article *dog*
9. *the cat saw a dog*

The space of possible sentences, then, resembles a branching road with a definite set of choices at each point. The process of choosing a sentence is reduced to a series of much smaller choices among a small array of alternatives. The virtue of this reduction becomes clearer once the grammar generates an infinite array of sentences, as becomes the case when the following grammatical rules are added to the ones above:

Sentence → NounPhrase CognitiveVerb   *that* Sentence
CognitiveVerb → *thought*
CognitiveVerb → *forgot*

It now becomes possible to generate sentences such as

the cat thought that the dog forgot that a cat slept

Chomsky in particular made a great deal of this point; following Humboldt, he spoke of language as making 'infinite use of finite means.'[11] Further, although he believes that the mind ultimately has a biological (and thus mechanical) explanation, he has focused his research on the level of

72

grammatical competence rather than trying to uncover this explanation himself.[12]

Allen Newell and Herbert Simon: the mechanization of the soul

Instead the first steps in mechanizing this idea of generative space were due to Newell and Simon.[13] Whereas Chomsky was concerned simply with the precise extent of the generative space of English grammar, Newell and Simon's computer program had to make actual choices within a generative space. Whereas Lashley posited the existence of a 'determining tendency' whose genealogical origins lay in a non-mechanical soul, Newell and Simon had to provide some mechanical specification of it. Here the generative structure of the space was crucial. Newell and Simon did not employ linguistic vocabulary. Nonetheless, just as grammatical rules and derivations provide a simple, clear means of generating any grammatical sentence, the application of 'operators' provided Newell and Simon with a simple, easily mechanized means of generating any possible sequence of basic actions. Choosing *which* sequence of actions to adopt was a matter of 'search.' The mechanism that conducted the search did not have to make correct choices all the time; it simply had to make good enough choices eventually as it explored the space of possibilities.

Newell and Simon placed enormous significance on this idea, and justifiably so.[14] While maintaining the system of conceptual relations already found in Descartes, Lashley, and Chomsky, their program nonetheless embodied a serious proposal for the mechanization of the soul.[15] Their strategy was ingenious: rather than endow the soul with an internal architecture—something incomprehensible within the system of ideas they inherited—they effectively proposed interpreting the soul as an epiphenomenon. Ironically, given Descartes's polemics against scholastic philosophy, the idea is approximately Aristotelian: the soul as the form of the person, not a discrete component. More specifically, rather than being identified with any particular device, the soul was *contained* by the generative structure of the search space and *manifested* through the operation of search mechanisms. These search mechanisms were 'heuristic' in the sense that no single choice was ever guaranteed to be correct, yet the overall effect of sustained searching was the eventual discovery of a correct outcome. Despite the simplicity and limitations of their early programs, Newell and Simon were willing to refer to these programs' behavior as 'intelligent' because they met this criterion. In addition, they regarded their proposal as promising because so many human activities could readily be cast as search problems.

Up to this point, the story of the mechanization of the soul is a conventional chapter in the history of ideas: to tell this story, we trace the unfolding of an intellectual project within an invariant framework of continuities or analogies among idea-systems. With Newell and Simon's program, though, the story clearly changes its character. But how exactly? So far as the disciplinary culture of AI is concerned, the formalization and implementation of an idea bring a wholly new day—a discontinuity between the prehistory of (mere) questions and ideas and the history, properly speaking, of problems and techniques. Once this 'proper' history has begun, technical people can put their proposals to the test of implementation: either it works or it does not work.

Yet despite this conception, and indeed partly because of it, the development of technical methods can be seen to continue a long trajectory largely determined by the defining projects and internal tensions of the ancestral systems of ideas. In particular, these projects and tensions continue to manifest themselves in the goals and tribulations of AI's technical work. In the case of Newell and Simon's proposal, the central goals and tribulations clustered around the 'problem' of *search control*: that is, making heuristic search choices well enough—not perfectly, just well enough—to allow the search process to 'terminate' with an acceptable answer within an acceptable amount of time. An enormous AI subliterature addresses this problem in a wide variety of ways. Within this literature, searches are said to 'explode' because of the vastness of search spaces. It should be emphasized that mediocre search control ideas do not kill a mechanism; they only slow it down. Yet this research has long faced a troubling aporia: the more complicated the world is, the more choices become possible at each point in the search, and the more ingenuity is required to keep the search process under control. The metaphors speak of a struggle of containment between explosion and control. Such a struggle, indeed, seems inherent in any theory for which action is said to result from formal reason conducted by a finite being.[16]

Newell and Simon's achievement thus proved tenuous. So long as AI's self-conception as a self-sufficient technical discipline has remained intact, however, these difficulties are readily parsed as technical problems seeking technical solutions. An endless variety of solutions to the search control problem has indeed been proposed, and each of them more or less 'works' within the bounds of one or another set of 'assumptions' about the world of practical activity.

Richard Fikes and Nils Nilsson: mechanizing embodied action

To watch the dynamics of this process unfold, it will help to consider one final chapter; the STRIPS program.[17] The purpose of STRIPS is to automatically derive 'plans' for a robot to follow in transporting objects around in a maze of rooms. The program constructs these plans through a search process modeled on those of Newell and Simon.[18] The search space consists of partially specified plans, with each 'operator' adding another step to the plan. Returning to the linguistic metaphor, the authors of STRIPS understand the robot's action within a grammar of possible plans. They refer to the units of action that Lashley called 'expressive elements' as 'primitive actions,' and the 'syntax of the act' strings these actions into sequences that can be 'executed' in the same manner as a computer program. In Descartes's terms, the soul's faculty of reason specifies an appropriate sequence of bodily actions, each of which may well be complicated, its faculty of will decides to undertake them, and the body then physically performs them.

To those who have had experience getting complex symbolic programs to work, the STRIPS papers make intense reading. Because the authors were drawing together so many software techniques for the first time, the technically empathetic reader gets a vivid sense of struggle: the unfolding logic of what the authors unexpectedly felt compelled to do, given what seemed to be required to get the program to work. A detailed consideration of the issues would take us much too far afield, but the bottom line is easy enough to explain. As might be expected, this bottom line concerns the technical practicalities of search control. A great deal is at stake: if the search can be controlled without making absurdly unrealistic assumptions about the robot's world, then the program can truly be labeled 'intelligent' in some non-trivial sense.

Consider, though, what this search entails. The STRIPS program is searching for a correct plan: that is, a plan which, if executed in the world as it currently stands, would achieve a given goal. This condition—achieving a given goal—is not simply a property of the plan; it is a property of the robot's interactions with its world. In order to determine whether a given plan is correct, then, the program must effectively conduct a simulation of the likely outcome of each action. For example, if a candidate plan contains the primitive action 'step forward,' it matters whether the robot is facing a wall, a door, a pile of rubbish, or an open stretch of floor. If 'step forward' is the *first* step in the plan, then the robot can predict its outcome simply by activating its video camera and looking ahead of itself. But if 'step forward' is the seventh step in the plan, subsequent to several other movements, then complex reasoning will be required to determine its likely outcome.

This is a severely challenging problem, and Fikes and Nilsson approached it, reasonably enough given the state of computer technology in 1971, through brute force: they encoded the robot's world in the form of a set of formulate in the predicate calculus, and they incorporated into STRIPS a general-purpose program for proving predicate-calculus theorems by means of a search through the space of possible formal proofs. This approach 'works' in the same sense that any search method works: if the search ever terminates, then the answer is correct, but how long this takes depends heavily on the perspicacity of the program's search control policies. And adequately perspicuous search control policies are notoriously elusive. As programmers like Fikes and Nilsson quickly learned, the trick is to design the world, and the robot's representations of the world, in such a way that long, involved chains of reasoning are not required to predict the outcomes of actions.

Yet predicting the outcomes of actions was, as programmers say, only the 'inner loop' of the plan-construction process. Recall that the overall process of choosing possible actions is also structured as a search problem; extending Lashley's linguistic metaphor, it is as if the grammaticality of a spoken sentence depended on the listener's reaction to each successive word. Moreover, the space of possible plans is enormous: at any given time, the robot can take any of about a dozen primitive actions, depending on its immediate circumstances, and even a simple plan will have several steps. Once again, search control policies are crucial. At each point in the search process, the program must make two relatively constrained choices among a manageable list of options: it must choose a partially specified plan to further refine, and it must choose a means of further refining it—roughly speaking, it must add another primitive action to the plan.

As with any search, making these choices correctly every time would require 'intelligence' that no mechanism could probably possess. The point, instead, is to make the choices correctly *often enough* for the search to settle on a correct answer in a reasonable amount of time. This, once again, is the appeal of heuristic search: intelligent action emerges from a mass of readily mechanizable decisions. In other words, the problem for Fikes and Nilsson was that they had to write bits of code whose outcomes approximated two hopelessly uncomputable notions: 'partially specified plan most likely to lead to a correct plan' and 'best primitive action to add to this subplan.' Their solution to these problems was unsurprising in technical retrospect, and the details do not matter here. Briefly, they chose whatever partially specified plan seemed to have gotten the furthest toward the goal with the smallest number of primitive actions, and they chose a new primitive action that allowed the theorem-proving program to make further progress toward proving that the goal had been achieved. Both of these criteria are virtually guaranteed to lead the plan-construction process down blind alleys (such as telling the robot to head for the door before getting the key). The important point is that these blind alleys did not hurt the robot; they only kept the robot waiting longer to be given a plan to execute.

How big a step was the STRIPS program toward mechanized intelligence? Reasonable people could disagree. It is certainly an impressive thing to watch such a program in operation—provided you have long enough to wait. But the question of search control was daunting. To the AI research people of that era, search control in STRIPS-like plan-construction programs was a 'problem' to be addressed through a wide variety of technical means. Yet this approach accepts as given the underlying structure of the situation: a steep trade-off between the complexity of the world and the practicality of the search control problem. If the robot can perform many possible actions, or if the results of these actions depend in complex ways on the circumstances, then the search space grows rapidly—in mathematical terms, exponentially—in size. If it is impossible to predict the outcomes of actions—say, because the robot is not the only source of change in the world—then the search space will have to include all of the *possible* outcomes as well. In a prescient aside in the sequel to the original STRIPS paper, Fikes, Hart, and Nilsson pointed this out:

> One of the novel elements introduced into artificial intelligence research by work on robots is the study of execution strategies and how they interact with planning activities. Since robot plans must ultimately be executed in the real world by a mechanical device, as opposed to being carried out in a mathematical space or by a simulator, consideration must be given by the executor to the possibility that operations in the plan may not accomplish what they were intended to, that data obtained from sensory devices may be inaccurate, and that mechanical tolerances may introduces errors as the plan is executed.
>
> Many of these problems of plan execution would disappear if our system generated a whole new plan after each execution step. Obviously, such a strategy would be too costly, so we instead seek a plan execution scheme with the following properties:
>
> 1. When new information obtained during plan execution implies that some remaining portion of the plan need not be executed, the executor should recognize such information and omit the unneeded plan steps.
> 2. When execution of some portion of the plan fails to achieve the intended results, the executor should recognize the failure and either direct reexecution of some portion of the plan or, as a default, call for a replanning activity.[19]

Thus, although they recognized the tension that was inherent in the system of concepts they had inherited, the technical imagination of that time provided Fikes, Hart, and Nilsson with no other way of structuring the basic question of intelligent action. It was fifteen years before the inherent dilemma of plan-construction was given definite mathematical form, first by Chapman and then more compactly by McAllester and Rosenblitt.[20] This kind of research does not decisively discredit the conceptual framework of planning-as-search; rather, it clarifies the precise nature of the trade-offs generated by that framework. Indeed, productive research continues to this day into the formal structure of plan-construction search problems.

Beyond the Cartesian soul

The previous sections offer a critical reconstruction of a single strand of intellectual history, a single intellectual proposition worked out in increasingly greater technical detail such that its internal tensions become manifest. To diagnose the resulting impasse and move beyond it, it will be necessary to transcend AI's conception of itself as a technical, formalizing discipline, and instead to reconsider the larger intellectual path of which AI research has been a part. No matter how esoteric AI literature has become, and no matter how thoroughly the intellectual origins of AI's technical methods have been forgotten, the technical work of AI has nonetheless been engaged in an effort to domesticate the Cartesian soul into a technical order in which it does not belong. The problem is not that the individual operations of Cartesian reason cannot be mechanized—they can be—but that the role assigned to the soul in the larger architecture of cognition is untenable. This incompatibility has shown itself in a pervasive and ever more clear pattern of technical frustrations. The difficulty can be shoved into one area or another through programmers' choices about architectures and representation schemes, but it cannot be made to go away.

This impasse, however, is not a failure. To the contrary, tracing the precise shape of the impasse allows us to delineate with particular confidence the internal tensions in the relational system of ideas around the Cartesian soul. According to this hypothesis, the fundamental embarrassment of Descartes's theory does not lie in the untenability of ontological dualism. Rather, it lies in the soul's causal distance from the world of practical action. As this world grows more complex (or, more precisely, as one's representational schemes reflect this world's complexity more fully), and as one becomes more fully immersed in that world, the soul's job becomes astronomically difficult. Yet Descartes performed his analysis of the soul in sedentary conditions: introspecting, visualizing, and isolating particular episodes of perception. When he did discuss complex activities, he focused not on the practicalities of their organization but on the struggles they engendered between the body and the soul.[21]

In order to impose intelligent order on its body's actions, the Cartesian soul faces a stern task. For example, to visualize a future course of events, the soul must stimulate the brain to assemble the necessary elements of memory. The reasoning which guides this visualization process must be based in turn upon certain knowledge of the world, obtained through the senses: enough information to visualize fully the outcomes of the individual's planned sequence of actions. Our judgment that such a scheme places an excessive burden on the soul—or, as technical people would say, makes the soul into a 'bottleneck'—is not a logical refutation; it is only an engineer's embodied judgment of the implausibility of a design. But within the logic of Descartes's project that is a lot.

The underlying difficulty takes perhaps its clearest form in Lashley. At the beginning of his lecture, he opposes his own view to the behaviorist and reflexological tale of stimuli and responses as follows:

> My principal thesis today will be that the input is never into a quiescent or static system, but always into a system which is already actively excited and organized. In the intact organism, behavior is the result of interaction of this background of excitation with input from any designated stimulus. Only when we can state the general characteristics of this background of excitation, can we understand the effects of a given input.[22]

In contradistinction to a scheme that focuses upon the effects of an isolated stimulus, Lashley proposes giving due weight both to a stimulus and to the ongoing flux of brain activity into which the stimulus intervenes. People, in other words, are always thinking as well as interacting with the world. Having said this, though, he immediately gives priority to the internal 'background' of neural activity; and his paper never returns to any consideration of external stimuli and their effects. As with his silence about the nature of the determining tendency, this is not a simple omission but rather is intrinsic to his relational system of concepts. His analysis of action on the model of speech portrays speakers as laying out a complex series of sounds through internal processing and then producing them in a serially ordered sequence, without in any way interacting with the outside world.[23] As we have already seen in the case of STRIPS, this obscurity about the relationship between 'planning' (of action sequences) and 'interaction' (with the world while those actions are going on) structured cognitive theorizing about action, and AI research in particular, for many years afterward.[24]

It is precisely this pattern of difficulty that has impelled an emerging interdisciplinary movement of computational modelers to seek a conception of intelligent behavior whose focal point is the fullness of embodied activity, not the reticence of thought. An organizing theme of this movement is the principled characterization of interactions between agents and their environments, and the use of such characterizations to guide design and explanation. When the 'agents' in question are robots, this theme opens out onto a systems view of robotic activity within the larger dynamics of the robot's world. When the 'agents' are animals, it opens out onto biology, and specifically onto a conception of ethology in which creatures and their behavior appear thoroughly adapted to the dynamics of a larger ecosystem. When the 'agents' in question are people, it opens out onto philosophical and anthropological conceptions of human beings as profoundly embedded in their social environments. In lieu of detailed references to these directions of research, allow me to direct the reader to an issue of *Artificial Intelligence* on computational theories of interaction and agency that will appear in 1995.

AI and the humanities

I have argued that AI can become sterile unless it maintains a sense of its place in the history of ideas, and in particular unless it maintains a respect for the power of inherited systems of ideas to shape our thinking and our research in the present day. At the same time, AI also provides a powerful means of forcing into the open the internal structure of a system of ideas and the internal tensions inherent in the project of getting those ideas to 'work.' Thus, AI properly understood ought to be able to participate in a constructive symbiosis with humanistic analyses of ideas.

Putting this mode of cooperative work into practice will not be easy. The obstacles are many and varied, but I believe that the most fundamental ones pertain to the use in AI of mathematics and mathematical formalization. This is not the place for a general treatment of these topics, but it is possible at least to outline some of the issues. The most obvious issue, perhaps, is the symbolic meaning attached to mathematics in the discursive construction of technical disciplines. Technical people frequently speak of mathematics as 'clean' and 'precise,' as opposed to the 'messy' and 'vague' nature of the social world and humanistic disciplines. These metaphors clearly provide rich points of entry for critical research, but the important point here is that their practical uses go beyond the simple construction of hierarchies among disciplines. Most particularly, the notion of mathematics as the telos of reason structures AI researchers' awareness in profound ways.

To see this, let us briefly consider the role that mathematics plays in AI research. The business of AI is to build computer programs whose operation can be narrated in language that is normally used to describe human activities.[25] Since the function of computers is specified in terms of discrete mathematics, the daily work of AI includes the complex and subtle discursive practice of talking about human activities in ways that assimilate them to mathematical structures.[26] In the case of the computational models of action described above, this assimilation is achieved by means of a linguistic metaphor for action. This metaphor is not specific to AI; in fact, it structures a great deal of the practice of applied computing.[27] This fact in turn points to an inherent source of intellectual conservatism in AI: the field is not restricted *a priori* to speaking of human beings in particular terms, but it is restricted to speaking in terms that someone knows how to assimilate to mathematical structures that can be programmed on computers. In this way, the existing intellectual infrastructure of computing—its stock of discursive forms and technical methods—drags like an anchor behind any project that would reinvent AI using language drawn from alternative conceptions of human beings and their lives.

This observation goes far toward explaining the strange appearance that AI presents to fields such as literature and anthropology that routinely employ much more sophisticated and critically reflective conceptions of human life. The first priority for AI research is to get something working on a computer, and the field does not reward gnawing doubts about whether the conceptions of human life being formalized along the way are sufficiently subtle, accurate, or socially responsible—thus the emphasis, mentioned at the outset, on 'doing' as opposed to 'just talking.' Critical methods from the humanities are likely to appear pointless, inasmuch as they do not immediately deliver formalizations or otherwise explain what programs one might write. AI people see formalization as a trajectory with an endpoint, in which the vagueness and ambiguity of ordinary language are repaired through mathematical definition, and they are not greatly concerned with the semantic violence that might be done to that language in the process of formal definition. A word like 'action' might present real challenges to a philosophical project that aims to respect ordinary usage,[28] but the assimilation of action to formal language theory reduces the word to a much simpler form: a repertoire of possible 'actions' assembled from a discrete, finite vocabulary of 'expressive elements' or 'primitives.' Having thus taken its place in the technical vocabulary of AI, the word's original semantic ramifications are lost as potential resources for AI work. The ideology surrounding formalization accords no intrinsic value to these leftover materials. As a result, formalization becomes a highly organized form of social forgetting—and not only of the semantics of words, but of their historicity as well. This is why the historical provenance and intellectual development of AI's underlying ideas claim so little interest among the field's practitioners.

What would a reformed AI look like? It would certainly not reject or replace mathematics. Rather, it would draw upon critical research to cultivate a reflexive awareness of how mathematical formalization is used as part of the engineer's embodied work of building things and seeing what they do. In particular, it would cultivate an awareness of the cycle of formalization, the technical working-out, the emergence of technical impasses, the critical work of diagnosing an impasse as reflecting either a superficial or a profound difficulty with the underlying conception of action, and the initiation of new and more informed rounds of formal modeling. The privilege in this cycle does not lie with the formalization process, nor does it lie with the critical diagnosis of technical impasses. Rather, it lies with the cycle itself, in the researcher's 'reflective conversation with the materials' of technical and critical work.[29]

Humanistic critical practice can take up numerous relationships, cooperative or not, to this cycle of research. My own analysis in this paper has employed a relatively old-fashioned set of humanistic methods from the history of ideas, tracing the continuity of certain themes across a series of authors and their intellectual projects. Since formalization is a fundamentally metaphorical process, discursively interrelating one set of things with another, mathematical set, it can be particularly fruitful to trace the historical travels of a given metaphor among various institutional sites in society, technical and otherwise.[30] The purpose in doing so is not simply to debunk any claims that technical institutions might make to an ahistorical authority, but to prevent the passage to formalism from forgetting the underlying commitments that a given way of speaking about human activities draws from its broader cultural embedding.[31] This contextual awareness will be crucial when the technical research reaches an impasse and needs to be diagnosed as a manifestation of internal tensions within the underlying system of ideas. Any given set of ideas will be more easily given up when they are seen as simply one path among many others not taken. Indeed, this awareness of context will be crucial for recognizing that an impasse may have occurred in the first place. Viewed in this way, technical impasses are a form of social remembering, moments when a particular discursive form deconstructs itself and makes its internal tensions intelligible to anyone who is critically equipped to hear them.

The cycle of reaching and interpreting technical impasses, moving back and forth between technical design and critical inquiry, can be practiced on a variety of scales, depending upon the acuity of one's critical methods. The example I traced in the body of this paper was extremely coarse: whole decades of research could be seen in hindsight to have been working through a single, clear-cut intellectual problem. The difficulty was not that AI practitioners were insulated from the philosophical critiques of Cartesian reason that might have provided a diagnosis of their difficulties and defined the contours of alternative territories of research. To the contrary, Hubert Dreyfus was articulating some of these critiques all along. The real difficulty was that the critical apparatus of the field did not provide its practitioners with a living, day-to-day appreciation for the contingent nature of their formalisms. Although they viewed formalization as conferring upon language a cleanliness and precision that it did not otherwise possess, the effect was precisely the reverse. Lacking a conscious awareness of the immense historicity of their language, they could not understand it as it called out to them the very things they had discovered. A reformed technical practice would employ the tools of critical inquiry to engage in a richer and more animated conversation with the world.

Notes

This paper has been improved by comments from Harry Collins, Güven Güzeldere, Scott Mainwaring, Beth Preston, and Jozsef Toth.
1 See Hubert L. Dreyfus, *What Computers Can't Do: A Critique of Artificial Reason* (New York: Harper, 1972); Martin Heidegger, *Being and Time*, trans. John Macquarrie and Edward Robinson (1927; New York: Harper, 1961); Ludwig Wittgen-

stein, *Philosophical Investigations*, 3rd edition, trans. G.E.M. Anscombe (1953; New York: Macmillan, 1968).

2 For a detailed analysis of this argument see Elizabeth F. Preston, 'Heidegger and Artificial Intelligence,' *Philosophy and Phenomenological Research*, 53.1 (1993) 43–69.

3 Dreyfus, in joint work with Stuart Dreyfus, has been cautiously supportive of one alternative AI research program, the 'connectionist' attempt to build simulations of neural circuitry without necessarily formulating 'knowledge' in terms of symbolic 'rules.' See Hubert L. Dreyfus and Stuart Dreyfus, 'Making a Mind vs. Modeling the Brain: AI Back at a Branchpoint,' *Daedalus*, 117.1 (1988) 15–43. But as the Dreyfuses point out, this research program still faces a long, difficult learning curve and will not be discussed here.

4 René Descartes, *The Philosophical Works of René Descartes*, trans. Elizabeth S. Haldane and George R. T. Ross, vol. 1 (Cambridge, UK: Cambridge UP, 1972) 116.

5 The terms 'mechanism' and 'mechanistic' require more analysis than space permits here. Suffice it to say that a mechanism is a physical object whose workings are wholly explicable in causal terms. To speak of something as a mechanism, furthermore, is to insert it into a rhetoric of engineering design, whether divine or human, and whether on the model of the clockmaker or the computer programmer. For the modern mathematical intepretations of the term, which are obviously relevant to the foundations of computing if not immediately to the genealogy being traced here, see Judson Chambers Webb, *Mechanism, Mentalism, and Mathematics: An Essay on Finitism* (Dordrecht: Reidel, 1980). Note also that the intellectual culture of Descartes's day did not distinguish between 'mind' and 'soul,' and the two terms continue to be used interchangeably in Catholic philosophy; see, for example, Ludger Holscher, *The Reality of the Mind: Augustine's Philosophical Arguments for the the Human Soul as a Spiritual Substance* (London: Routledge, 1986). Even in the present day, these terms are usually not so much opposed as simply employed in different discourses with overlapping genealogies.

6 Noam Chomsky, *Problems of Knowledge and Freedom: The Russell Lectures* (New York: Pantheon, 1971) 50; George A. Miller, 'Information and Memory,' *Scientific American*, 195.2 (1956) 42–46.

7 Karl S. Lashley, 'The Problem of Serial Order in Behavior,' *Cerebral Mechanisms in Behavior: The Hixon Symposium*, ed. Lloyd A. Jeffress (New York: Wiley, 1951).

8 Lashley, 122.

9 Daniel Dennett, 'Why the Law of Effect Will Not Go Away,' *Brainstorms: Philosophical Essays on Mind and Psychology*, ed. Daniel Dennett. (Montgomery, VT: Bradford Books, 1978) 80–81.

10 Cf. Brain C. Smith, 'Prologue to *Reflection and Semantics in a Procedural Language*,' *Readings in Knowledge Representation*, ed. Ronald J. Brachman and Hector J. Levesque (Los Altos, CA: Morgan Kaufmann, 1985).

11 Noam Chomsky, *Aspects of the Theory of Syntax* (Cambridge, MA: MIT Press, 1965) 8.

12 Noam Chomsky, *Language and Responsibility*, trans. (from the French) John Viertel (New York: Pantheon, 1979) 66, 97.

13 Allen Newell and Herbert A. Simon, 'GPS: A Program That Simulates Human Thought,' *Computers and Thought*, ed. Edward A. Feigenbaum and Julian Feldman (New York: McGraw, 1963).

14 See, for example, Newell's comments in Philip E. Agre, 'Interview with Allen Newell,' *Artificial Intelligence*, 59.1–2 (1993) 415–449, 418.

15 C. R. Gallistel, *The Organization of Action: A New Synthesis* (Hillsdale, NJ: Erlbaum, 1980) 6–7.

16 Christopher Cherniak, *Minimal Rationality* (Cambridge, MA: MIT Press, 1986).
17 Richard E. Fikes and Nils J. Nilsson, 'STRIPS: A New Approach to the Application of Theorem Proving to Problem Solving,' *Artificial Intelligence*, 23 (1971) 189–208.
18 David Chapman, 'Planning for Conjunctive Goals,' *Artificial Intelligence*, 32.3 (1987), presents a genealogy of the AI 'planning' systems in this lineage.
19 Richard E. Fikes, Peter E. Hart, and Nils J. Nilsson, 'Learning and Executing Generalized Robot Plans,' *Artificial Intelligence*, 3.4 (1972) 251–288, 268.
20 Chapman; David McAllester and David Rosenblitt, 'Systematic Non-linear Planning,' *Proceedings of the National Conference on Artificial Intelligence* (Los Altos, CA: Kaufmann, 1991) 634–639.
21 See, for example, Descartes, *Passions of the Soul*, Article 47.
22 Lashley, 112.
23 Actual human speakers frequently do interact with their addresses and others during the real-time production of their utterances, but this fact is rarely taken into account in cognitive theories of grammar and speech. See Charles Goodwin, *Conversational Organization: Interaction Between Speakers and Hearers* (New York: Academic, 1981).
24 It is particularly clear in the opening chapter of Miller, Galanter, and Pribram's influential book *Plans and the Structure of Behavior* (New York: Holt, 1960).
25 Harry M. Collins, *Artificial Experts: Social Knowledge and Intelligent Machines* (Cambridge, MA: MIT Press, 1990).
26 See Philip E. Agre, 'Surveillance and Capture: Two Models of Privacy,' *The Information Society*, 10.2 (1994) 101–127. This is obviously an attribute that AI shares with a wide variety of other fields, for example mathematical economics, and much of the analysis here applies to these other fields as well. It should be noted that AI people themselves place great emphasis on a distinction between 'neat' forms of AI, which openly avow their commitment to mathematical formalization and employ large amounts of mathematical notation in their papers, and 'scruffy' forms, which do not (Cf. Diane E. Forsythe, 'Engineering Knowledge: The Construction of Knowledge in Artificial Intelligence,' *Social Studies of Science*, 23.3 (1993) 445–477). My argument, though, applies equally to both forms of AI research. Regardless of whether its author was consciously thinking in terms of mathematics, a computer program is a notation whose operational semantics can be specified in mathematical terms. While the formalizations in 'neat' research are frequently more consistent, systematic, and explicit than those of 'scruffy' research, the design of any computer program necessarily entails a significant level of formalization.
27 Different linguistic metaphors for human action are obviously possible, if perhaps equally problematic, see, for example, Paul Ricoeur, 'The Model of the Text: Meaningful Action Considered as a Text,' *Social Research*, 38 (1971) 529–562.
28 e.g., Alan R. White, ed., *The Philosophy of Action* (London: Oxford UP, 1968).
29 Donald A. Schön, *The Reflective Practitioner: How Professionals Think in Action* (New York: Basic, 1983).
30 See Emily Martin, *The Woman in the Body: A Cultural Analysis of Reproduction* (Boston: Beacon, 1987); Paul McReynolds, 'The Clock Metaphor in the History of Psychology,' *Scientific Discovery: Case Studies*, ed. Thomas Nickles (Dordrecht: Reidel, 1980); and Philip Mirowski, *More Heat Than Light: Economics as Social Physics, Physics as Nature's Economics* (Cambridge, UK: Cambridge UP, 1989).
31 For an impressive cultural analysis of the origins of AI, see Paul Edwards, *The Closed World: Computers and the Politics of Discourse in Cold War America* (Cambridge, MA: MIT Press, in press).

1.2: The Nature of Artificial

UNDERSTANDING THE NATURAL AND THE ARTIFICIAL WORLD

H. Simon

Source: H. Simon, *Sciences of the Artificial*, MIT Press, 1969, pp. 1–24.

About three centuries after Newton we are thoroughly familiar with the concept of natural science—most unequivocally with physical and biological science. A natural science is a body of knowledge about some class of things—objects or phenomena—in the world: about the characteristics and properties that they have; about how they behave and interact with each other.

The central task of a natural science is to make the wonderful commonplace: to show that complexity, correctly viewed, is only a mask for simplicity; to find pattern hidden in apparent chaos. The early Dutch physicist Simon Stevin, showed by an elegant drawing (figure 1) that the law of the inclined plane follows in 'self-evident fashion' from the impossibility of perpetual motion, for experience and reason tell us that the chain of balls in the figure would rotate neither to right nor to left but would remain at rest. (Since rotation changes nothing in the figure, if the chain moved at all, it would move perpetually.) Since the pendant part of the chain hangs symmetrically, we can snip it off without disturbing the equilibrium. But now the balls on the long side of the plane balance those on the shorter, steeper side, and their relative numbers are in inverse ratio to the sines of the angles at which the planes are inclined.

Stevin was so pleased with his construction that he incorporated it into a vignette, inscribing above it

Wonder, en is gheen wonder

that is to say: 'Wonderful, but not incomprehensible.'

This is the task of natural science: to show that the wonderful is not incomprehensible, to show how it can be comprehended—but not to destroy

Figure 1 The vignette devised by Simon Stevin to illustrate his derivation of the law of the inclined plane

wonder. For when we have explained the wonderful, unmasked the hidden pattern, a new wonder arises at how complexity was woven out of simplicity. The aesthetics of natural science and mathematics is at one with the aesthetics of music and painting—both inhere in the discovery of a partially concealed pattern.

The world we live in today is much more a man-made,[1] or artificial, world than it is a natural world. Almost every element in our environment shows evidence of human artifice. The temperature in which we spend most of our hours is kept artificially at 20 degrees Celsius; the humidity is added to or taken from the air we breathe; and the impurities we inhale are largely produced (and filtered) by man.

Moreover for most of us—the white-collared ones—the significant part of the environment consists mostly of strings of artifacts called 'symbols' that we receive through eyes and ears in the form of written and spoken language and that we pour out into the environment—as I am now doing—by mouth or hand. The laws that govern these strings of symbols, the laws that govern the occasions on which we emit and receive them, the determinants of their content are all consequences of our collective artifice.

One may object that I exaggerate the artificiality of our world. Man must obey the law of gravity as surely as does a stone, and as a living organism man must depend for food, and in many other ways, on the world of biological phenomena. I shall plead guilty to overstatement, while protesting that the exaggeration is slight. To say that an astronaut, or even an airplane pilot, is obeying the law of gravity, hence is a perfectly natural phenomenon, is true, but its truth calls for some sophistication in what we mean by 'obeying' a natural law. Aristotle did not think it natural for heavy things to rise or light ones to fall (*Physics*, Book IV); but presumably we have a deeper understanding of 'natural' than he did.

So too we must be careful about equating 'biological' with 'natural.' A forest may be a phenomenon of nature; a farm certainly is not. The very species upon which we depend for our food—our corn and our cattle—are artifacts of our ingenuity. A plowed field is no more part of nature than an asphalted street—and no less.

These examples set the terms of our problem, for those things we call artifacts are not apart from nature. They have no dispensation to ignore or violate natural law. At the same time they are adapted to human goals and purposes. They are what they are in order to satisfy our desire to fly or to eat well. As our aims change, so too do our artifacts—and vice versa.

If science is to encompass these objects and phenomena in which human purpose as well as natural law are embodied, it must have means for relating these two disparate components. The character of these means and their implications for certain areas of knowledge—economics, psychology, and design in particular—are the central concern of this book.

The artificial

Natural science is knowledge about natural objects and phenomena. We ask whether there cannot also be 'artificial' science—knowledge about artificial objects and phenomena. Unfortunately the term 'artificial' has a pejorative air about it that we must dispel before we can proceed.

My dictionary defines 'artificial' as, 'Produced by art rather than by nature; not genuine or natural; affected; not pertaining to the essence of the matter.' It proposes, as synonyms: affected, factitious, manufactured, pretended, sham, simulated, spurious, trumped up, unnatural. As antonyms, it lists: actual, genuine, honest, natural, real, truthful, unaffected. Our language seems to reflect man's deep distrust of his own products. I shall not try to assess the validity of that evaluation or explore its possible psychological roots. But you will have to understand me as using 'artificial' in as neutral a sense as possible, as meaning man-made as opposed to natural.[2]

In some contexts we make a distinction between 'artificial' and 'synthetic.' For example, a gem made of glass colored to resemble sapphire would be called artificial, while a man-made gem chemically indistinguishable from sapphire would be called synthetic. A similar distinction is often made between 'artificial' and 'synthetic' rubber. Thus some artificial things are imitations of things in nature, and the imitation may use either the same basic materials as those in the natural object or quite different materials.

As soon as we introduce 'synthesis' as well as 'artifice,' we enter the realm of engineering. For 'synthetic' is often used in the broader sense of 'designed' or 'composed.' We speak of engineering as concerned with 'synthesis,' while science is concerned with 'analysis.' Synthetic or artificial objects—and more specifically prospective artificial objects having desired properties—are the central objective of engineering activity and skill. The engineer, and more generally the designer, is concerned with how things *ought* to be—how they ought to be in order to *attain goals*, and to *function*. Hence a science of the artificial will be closely akin to a science of engineering—but very different, as we shall see in my fifth chapter, from what goes currently by the name of 'engineering science.'

With goals and 'oughts' we also introduce into the picture the dichotomy between normative and descriptive. Natural science has found a way to exclude the normative and to concern itself solely with how things are. Can or should we maintain this exclusion when we move from natural to artificial phenomena, from analysis to synthesis?[3]

We have now identified four indicia that distinguish the artificial from the natural; hence we can set the boundaries for sciences of the artificial:

1. Artificial things are synthesized (thought not always or usually with full forethought) by human beings.
2. Artificial things may imitate appearances in natural things while lacking, in one or many respects, the reality of the latter.
3. Artificial things can be characterized in terms of functions, goals, adaptation.
4. Artificial things are often discussed, particularly when they are being designed, in terms of imperatives as well as descriptive.

The environment as mold

Let us look a little more closely at the functional or purposeful aspect of artificial things. Fulfillment of purpose or adaptation to a goal involves a relation among three terms: the purpose or goal, the character of the artifact, and the environment in which the artifact performs. When we think of a clock, for example, in terms of purpose we may use the child's definition: 'a clock is to tell time.' When we focus our attention on the clock itself, we may describe it in terms of arrangements of gears and the application of the forces of springs or gravity operating on a weight or pendulum.

But we may also consider clocks in relation to the environment in which they are to be used. Sundials perform as clocks *in sunny climates*—they are more useful in Phoenix than in Boston and of no use at all during the Arctic winter. Devising a clock that would tell time on a rolling and pitching ship, with sufficient accuracy to determine longitude, was one of the great adventures of eighteenth-century science and technology. To perform in this difficult environment, the clock had to be endowed with many delicate properties, some of them largely or totally irrelevant to the performance of a landlubber's clock.

Natural science impinges on an artifact through two of the three terms of the relation that characterizes it: the structure of the artifact itself and the environment in which it performs. Whether a clock will in fact tell time depends on its internal construction and where it is placed. Whether a knife will cut depends on the material of its blade and the hardness of the substance to which it is applied.

The artifact as 'interface'

We can view the matter quite symmetrically. An artifact can be thought of as a meeting point—an 'interface' in today's terms—between an 'inner' environment, the substance and organization of the artifact itself, and an 'outer' environment, the surroundings in which it operates. If the inner environment is appropriate to the outer environment, or vice versa, the artifact will serve its intended purpose. Thus, if the clock is immune to buffeting, it will serve as a ship's chronometer. (And conversely, if it isn't, we may salvage it by mounting it on the mantel at home.)

Notice that this way of viewing artifacts applies equally well to many things that are not man-made—to all things in fact that can be regarded as adapted to some situation; and in particular it applies to the living systems that have evolved through the forces of organic evolution. A theory of the airplane draws on natural science for an explanation of its inner environment (the power plant, for example), its outer environment (the character of the atmosphere at different altitudes), and the relation between its inner and outer environments (the movement of an airfoil through a gas). But a theory of the bird can be divided up in exactly the same way.[4]

Given an airplane, or *given* a bird, we can analyze them by the methods of natural science without any particular attention to purpose or adaptation, without reference to the interface between what I have called the inner and outer environments. After all, their behavior is governed by natural law just as fully as the behavior of anything else (or at least we all believe this about the airplane, and most of us believe it about the bird).

Functional explanation

On the other hand, if the division between inner and outer environment is not necessary to the analysis of an airplane or a bird, it turns out at least to be highly convenient. There are several reasons for this, which will become evident from examples.

Many animals in the Arctic have white fur. We usually explain this by saying that white is the best color for the Arctic environment, for white creatures escape detection more easily than do others. This is not of course a natural science explanation; it is an explanation by reference to purpose or function. It simply says that these are the kinds of creatures that will 'work,' that is, survive, in this kind of environment. To turn the statement into an explanation, we must add to it a notion of natural selection, or some equivalent mechanism.

An important fact about this kind of explanation is that it demands an understanding mainly of the outer environment. Looking at our snowy surroundings, we can predict the predominant color of the creatures we are likely to encounter; we need know little about the biology of the creatures themselves, beyond the facts that they are often mutually hostile, use visual clues to guide their behavior, and are adaptive (through selection or some other mechanism).

Analogous to the role played by natural selection in evolutionary biology is the role played by rationality in the sciences of human behavior. If we know of a business organization only that it is a profit-maximizing system, we can often predict how its behavior will change if we change its environment—how it will alter its prices if a sales tax is levied on its products. We can sometimes make this prediction—and economists do make it repeatedly—without detailed assumptions about the adaptive mechanism, the decision-making apparatus that constitutes the inner environment of the business firm.

Thus the first advantage of dividing outer from inner environment in studying an adaptive or artificial system is that we can often predict behavior from knowledge of the system's goals and its outer environment, with only minimal assumptions about the inner environment. An instant corollary is that we often find quite different inner environments accomplishing identical or similar goals in identical or similar outer environments—airplanes and birds, dolphins and tunafish, weight-driven clocks and battery-driven clocks, electrical relays and transistors.

There is often a corresponding advantage in the division from the standpoint of the inner environment. In very many cases whether a particular system will achieve a particular goal or adaptation depends on only a few characteristics of the outer environment and not at all on the detail of that environment. Biologists are familiar with this property of adaptive systems under the label of homeostasis. It is an important property of most good designs, whether biological or artifactual. In one way or another the designer insulates the inner system from the environment, so that an invariant relation is maintained between inner system and goal, independent of variations over a wide range in most parameters that characterize the outer environment.

The ship's chronometer reacts to the pitching of the ship only in the negative sense of maintaining an invariant relation of the hands on its dial to the real time, independently of the ship's motions.

Quasi independence from the outer environment may be maintained by various forms of passive insulation, by reactive negative feedback (the most frequently discussed form of insulation), by predictive adaptation, or by various combinations of these.

Functional description and synthesis

In the best of all possible worlds—at least for a designer—we might even hope to combine the two sets of advantages we have described that derive from factoring an adaptive system into goals, outer environment, and inner environment. We might hope to be able to characterize the main properties of the system and its behavior without elaborating the detail of *either* the outer or inner environment. We might look toward a science of the artificial that would depend on the relative simplicity of the interface as its primary source of abstraction and generality.

Consider the design of a physical device to serve as a counter. If we want the device to be able to count up to one thousand, say, it must be capable of assuming any one of at least a thousand states, of maintaining itself in any given state, and of shifting from any state to the 'next' state. There are dozens of different inner environments that might be used (and have been used) for such a device. A wheel notched at each twenty minutes of arc, and with a ratchet device to turn and hold it, would do the trick. So would a string of ten electrical switches properly connected to represent binary numbers. Today instead of switches we are likely to use transistors or other solid-state devices.[5]

Our counter would be activated by some kind of pulse, mechanical or electrical, as appropriate, from the outer environment. But by building an appropriate transducer between the two environments, the physical character of the interior pulse could again be made independent of the physical character of the exterior pulse—the counter could be made to count anything.

Description of an artifice in terms of its organization and functioning—its interface between inner and outer environments—is a major objective of invention and design activity. Engineers will find familiar the language of the following claim quoted from a 1919 patent on an improved motor controller:

What I claim as new and desire to secure by Letters Patent is:
1 In a motor controller, in combination, reversing means, normally effective field-weakening means and means associated with said reversing means for rendering said field-weakening means ineffective during motor starting and thereafter effective to different degrees determinable by the setting of said reversing means . . . '

Apart from the fact that we know the invention relates to control of an electric motor, there is almost no reference here to specific, concrete objects or phenomena. There is reference rather to 'reversing means' and 'field-weakening means,' whose further purpose is made clear in a paragraph preceding the patent claims:

> The advantages of the special type of motor illustrated and the control thereof will be readily understood by those skilled in the art. Among such advantages may be mentioned the provision of a high starting torque and the provision for quick reversals of the motor.[7]

Now let us suppose that the motor in question is incorporated in a planing machine (see figure 2). The inventor describes its behavior thus:

> Referring now to [figure 2], the controller is illustrated in outline connection with a planer (100) operated by a motor M, the controller being adapted to govern the motor M and to be automatically operated by the reciprocating bed (101) of the planer. The master shaft of the controller is provided with a lever (102) connected by a link (103) to a lever (104) mounted upon the planer frame and projecting into the path of lugs (105) and (106) on the planer bed. As will be understood, the arrangement is such that reverse movements of the planer bed will, through the connections described, throw the master shaft of the controller back and forth between its extreme positions and in consequence effect selective operation of the reversing switches (1) and (2) and automatic operation of the other switches in the manner above set forth.[8]

In this manner the properties with which the inner environment has been endowed are placed at the service of the goals in the context of the outer environment. The motor will reverse periodically under the control of the position of the planer bed. The 'shape' of its behavior—the time path, say, of a variable associated with the motor—will be a function of the 'shape' of the external environment—the distance, in this case, between the lugs on the planer bed.

The device we have just described illustrates in microcosm the nature of artifacts. Central to their description are the goals that link the inner to the outer system. The inner system is an organization of natural phenomena capable of attaining the goals in some range of environments, but ordinarily there will be many functionally equivalent natural systems capable of doing this.

The outer environment determines the conditions for goal attainment. If the inner system is properly designed, it will be adapted to the outer environment, so that its behavior will be determined in large part by the

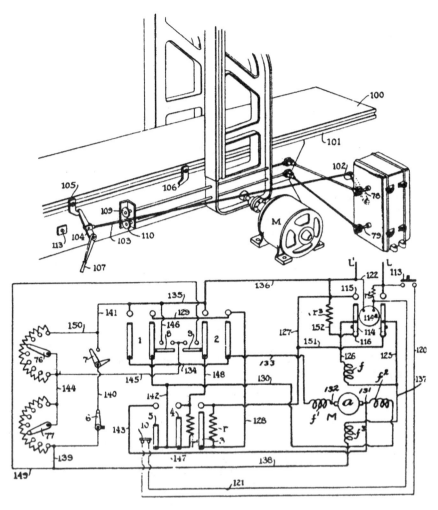

Figure 2 Illustrations from a patent for a motor controller

behavior of the latter, exactly as in the case of 'economic man.' To predict how it will behave, we need only ask, 'How would a rationally designed system behave under these circumstances?' The behavior takes on the shape of the task environment.[9]

Limits of adaptation

But matters must be just a little more complicated than this account suggests. 'If wishes were horses, all beggars would ride.' And if we could always specify a protean inner system that would take on exactly the shape of the task environment, designing would be synonymous with wishing. 'Means for scratching diamonds' defines a design objective, an objective that *might* be attained with the use of many different substances. But the design has not been achieved until we have discovered at least one realizable inner system obeying the ordinary natural laws—one material, in this case, hard enough to scratch diamonds.

Often we shall have to be satisfied with meeting the design objectives only approximately. Then the properties of the inner system will 'show through.' That is, the behavior of the system will only partly respond to the task environment; partly, it will respond to the limiting properties of the inner system.

Thus the motor controls described earlier are aimed at providing for 'quick' reversal of the motor. But the motor must obey electromagnetic and mechanical laws, and we could easily confront the system with a task where the environment called for quicker reversal than the motor was capable of. In a benign environment we would learn from the motor only what it had been called upon to do; in a taxing environment we would learn something about its internal structure—specifically about those aspects of the internal structure that were chiefly instrumental in limiting performance.[10]

A bridge, under its usual conditions of service, behaves simply as a relatively smooth level surface on which vehicles can move. Only when it has been overloaded do we learn the physical properties of the materials from which it is built.

Understanding by simulating

Artificiality connotes perceptual similarity but essential difference, resemblance from without rather than within. In the terms of the previous section we may say that the artificial object imitates the real by turning the same face to the outer system, by adapting, relative to the same goals, to comparable ranges of external tasks. Imitation is possible because distinct physical systems can be organized to exhibit nearly identical behavior. The damped spring and the damped circuit obey the same second-order linear differential equation; hence we may use either one to imitate the other.

Techniques of simulation

Because of its abstract character and its symbol manipulating generality, the digital computer has greatly extended the range of systems whose behavior can be imitated. Generally we now call the imitation 'simulation,' and we try to understand the imitated system by testing the simulation in a variety of simulated, or imitated, environments.

Simulation, as a technique for achieving understanding and predicting the behavior of system, predates of course the digital computer. The model basin and the wind tunnel are valued means for studying the behavior of large systems by modeling them in the small, and it is quite certain that Ohm's law was suggested to its discoverer by its analogy with simply hydraulic phenomena.

Simulation may even take the form of a thought experiment, never actually implemented dynamically. One of my vivid memories of the Great Depression is of a large multicolored chart in my father's study that represented a hydraulic model of an economic system (with different fluids for money and goods). The chart was devised by a technocratically inclined engineer named Dahlberg. The model never got beyond the pen-and-paint stage at that time, but it could be used to trace through the imputed consequences of particular economic measures or events—provided the theory was right![11]

As my formal education in economics progressed, I acquired a disdain for that naive simulation, only to discover after World War II that a distinguished economist, Professor A. W. Phillips had actually built the Moniac, a hydraulic model that simulated a Keynesian economy.[12] Of course Professor Phillips's simulation incorporated a more nearly correct theory than the earlier one and was actually constructed and operated—two points in its favor. However, the Moniac, while useful as a teaching tool, told us nothing that could not be extracted readily from simple mathematical versions of Keynesian theory and was soon priced out of the market by the growing number of computer simulations of the economy.

Simulation as a source of new knowledge

This brings me to the crucial question about simulation. *How can a simulation ever tell us anything that we do not already know?* The usual implication of the question is that it can't. As a matter of fact, there is an interesting parallelism, which I shall exploit presently, between two assertions about computers and simulation that one hears frequently:

1. A simulation is no better than the assumptions built into it.
2. A computer can do only what it is programmed to do.

I shall not deny either assertion, for both seem to me to be true. But despite both assertions simulation can tell us things we do not already know.

There are two related ways in which simulation can provide new knowledge—one of them obvious, the other perhaps a bit subtle. The obvious point is that, even when we have correct premises, it may be very difficult to discover what they imply. All correct reasoning is a grand system of tautologies, but only God can make direct use of that fact. The rest of us must painstakingly and fallibly tease out the consequences of our assumptions.

97

Thus we might expect simulation to be a powerful technique for deriving, from our knowledge of the mechanisms governing the behavior of gases, a theory of the weather and a means of weather prediction. Indeed, as many people are aware, attempts have been under way for some years to apply this technique. Greatly oversimplified, the idea is that we already know the correct basic assumptions, the local atmospheric equations, but we need the computer to work out the implications of the interactions of vast numbers of variables starting from complicated initial conditions. This is simply an extrapolation to the scale of modern computers of the idea we use when we solve two simultaneous equations by algebra.

This approach to simulation has numerous applications to engineering design. For it is typical of many kinds of design problems that the inner system consists of components whose fundamental laws of behavior—mechanical, electrical, or chemical—are well known. The difficulty of the design problem often resides in predicting how an assemblage of such components will behave.

Simulation of poorly understood systems

The more interesting and subtle question is whether simulation can be of any help to us when we do not know very much initially about the natural laws that govern the behavior of the inner system. Let me show why this question must also be answered in the affirmative.

First, I shall make a preliminary comment that simplifies matters: we are seldom interested in explaining or predicting phenomena in all their particularity; we are usually interested only in a few properties abstracted from the complex reality. Thus, a NASA-launched satellite is surely an artificial object, but we usually do not think of it as 'simulating' the moon or a planet. It simply obeys the same laws of physics, which relate only to its inertial and gravitational mass, abstracted from most of its other properties. It *is* a moon. Similarly electric energy that entered my house from the early atomic generating station at Shippingport did not 'simulate' energy generated by means of a coal plant or a windmill. Maxwell's equations hold for both.

The more we are willing to abstract from the detail of a set of phenomena, the easier it becomes to simulate the phenomena. Moreover we do not have to know, or guess at, all the internal structure of the system but only that part of its that is crucial to the abstraction.

It is fortunate that this is so, for if it were not, the topdown strategy that built the natural sciences over the past three centuries would have been infeasible. We knew a great deal about the gross physical and chemical behavior of matter before we had a knowledge of molecules, a great deal about molecular chemistry before we had an atomic theory, and a great deal about atoms before we had any theory of elementary particles—if indeed we have such a theory today.

This skybook-skyscraper construction of science from the roof down to the yet unconstructed foundations, was possible because the behavior of the system at each level depended on only a very approximate, simplified, abstracted characterization of the system at the level next beneath.[13] This is lucky, else the safety of bridges and airplanes might depend on the correctness of the 'Eightfold Way,' of looking at elementary particles.

Artificial systems and adaptive systems have properties that make them particularly susceptible to simulation via simplified models. The characterization of such systems in the previous section of this chapter explains why. Resemblance in behavior of systems without identity of the inner systems is particularly feasible if the aspects in which we are interested arise out of the *organization* of the parts, independently of all but a few properties of the individual components. Thus for many purposes we may be interested in only such characteristics of a material as its tensile and compressive strength. We may be profoundly unconcerned about its chemical properties, or even whether it is wood or iron.

The motor control patent cited earlier illustrates this abstraction to organizational properties. The invention consisted of a 'combination' of 'reversing means,' of 'field weakening means,' that is to say, of components specified in terms of their functioning in the organized whole. How many ways are there of reversing a motor, or of weakening its field strength? We can simulate the system described in the patent claims in many ways without reproducing even approximately the actual physical device that is depicted. With a small additional step of abstraction, the patent claims could be restated to encompass mechanical as well as electrical devices. I suppose that any undergraduate engineer at Berkeley, Carnegie Mellon University, or MIT could design a mechanical system embodying reversibility and variable starting torque so as to simulate the system of the patent.

The computer as artifact

No artifact devised by man is so convenient for this kind of functional description as a digital computer. It is truly protean, for almost the only ones of its properties that are detectable in its behavior (when it is operating properly!) are the organizational properties. The speed with which it performs it basic operations may allow us to infer a little about its physical components and their natural laws; speed data, for example, would allow us to rule out certain kinds of 'slow' components. For the rest, almost no interesting statement that one can make about an operating computer bears any particular relation to the specific nature of the hardware. A computer is an organization of elementary functional components in which, to a high approximation, only the function performed by those components is relevant to the behavior of the whole system.[14]

Computers as abstract objects

This highly abstractive quality of computers makes it easy to introduce mathematics into the study of their theory—and has led some to the erroneous conclusion that, as a computer science emerges, it will necessarily be a mathematical rather than an empirical science. Let me take up these two points in turn: the relevance of mathematics to computers and the possibility of studying computers empirically.

Some important theorizing, initiated by John von Neumann, has been done on the topic of computer reliability. The question is how to build a reliable system from unreliable parts. Notice that this is not posed as a question of physics or physical engineering. The components engineer is assumed to have done his best, but the parts are still unreliable! We can cope with the unreliability only by our manner of organizing them.

To turn this into a meaningful problem, we have to say a little more about the nature of the unreliable parts. Here we are aided by the knowledge that *any* computer can be assembled out of a small array of simple, basic elements. For instance, we may take as our primitives the so-called Pitts-McCulloch neurons. As their name implies, these components were devised in analogy to the supposed anatomical and functional characteristics of neurons in the brain, but they are highly abstracted. They are formally isomorphic with the simplest kinds of switching circuits—'and,' 'or,' and 'not' circuits. We postulate, now, that we are to build a system from such elements and that each elementary part has a specified probability of functioning correctly. The problem is to arrange the elements and their interconnections in such a way that the complete system will perform reliably.

The important point for our present discussion is that the parts could as well be neurons as relays, as well relays as transistors. The natural laws governing relays are very well known, while the natural laws governing neurons are known most imperfectly. But that does not matter, for all that is relevant for the theory is that the components have the specified level of unreliability and be interconnected in the specified way.

This example shows that the possibility of building a mathematical theory of a system or of simulating that system does not depend on having an adequate microtheory of the natural laws that govern the system components. Such a microtheory might indeed be simply irrelevant.

Computers as empirical objects

We turn next to the feasibility of an *empirical* science of computers—as distinct from the solid-state physics or physiology of their componentry.[15] As a matter of empirical fact almost all of the computers that have been designed have certain common organizational features. They almost all can be decomposed into an active processor (Babbage's 'Mill') and a memory

(Babbage's 'Store') in combination with input and output devices. (Some of the larger systems, somewhat in the manner of colonial algae, are assemblages of smaller systems having some or all of these components. But perhaps I may oversimplify for the moment.) They are all capable of storing symbols (program) that can be interpreted by a program-control component and executed. Almost all have exceedingly limited capacity for simultaneous, parallel activity—they are basically one-thing-at-a-time systems. Symbols generally have to be moved from the larger memory components into the central processor before they can be acted upon. The systems are capable of only simple basic actions: recoding symbols, storing symbols, copying symbols, moving symbols, erasing symbols, and comparing symbols.

Since there are now many such devices in the world, and since the properties that describe them also appear to be shared by the human central nervous system, nothing prevents us from developing a natural history of them. We can study them as we would rabbits or chipmunks and discover how they behave under different patterns of environmental stimulation. Insofar as their behavior reflects largely the broad functional characteristics we have described, and is independent of details of their hardware, we can build a general—but empirical—theory of them.

The research that was done to design computer time-sharing systems is a good example of the study of computer behavior as an empirical phenomenon. Only fragments of theory were available to guide the design of a time-sharing system or to predict how a system of a specified design would actually behave in an environment of users who placed their several demands upon it. Most actual designs turned out initially to exhibit serious deficiencies, and most predictions of performance were startlingly inaccurate.

Under these circumstances the main route open to the development and improvement of time-sharing systems was to build them and see how they behaved. And this is what was done. They were built, modified, and improved in successive stages. Perhaps theory could have anticipated these experiments and made them unnecessary. In fact it didn't, and I don't know anyone intimately acquainted with these exceedingly complex systems who has very specific ideas as to how it might have done so. To understand them, the systems had to be constructed, and their behavior observed.[16]

In a similar vein computer programs designed to play games or to discover proofs for mathematical theorems spend their lives in exceedingly large and complex task environments. Even when the programs themselves are only moderately large and intricate (compared, say, with the monitor and operating systems of large computers), too little is known about their task environments to permit accurate prediction of how well they will perform, how selectively they will be able to search for problem solutions.

Here again theoretical analysis must be accompanied by large amounts of experimental work. A growing literature reporting these experiments is beginning to give us precise knowledge about the degree of heuristic power of particular heuristic devices in reducing the size of the problem spaces that must be searched. In theorem proving, for example, there has been a whole series of advances in heuristic power based on and guided by empirical exploration: the use of the Herbrand theorem, the resolution principle, the set-of-support principle, and so on.[17]

Computers and thought

As we succeed in broadening and deepening our knowledge—theoretical and empirical—about computers, we discover that in large part their behavior is governed by simple general laws, that what appeared as complexity in the computer program was to a considerable extent complexity of the environment to which the program was seeking to adapt its behavior.

This relation of program to environment opened up an exceedingly important role for computer simulation as a tool for achieving a deeper understanding of human behavior. For if it is the organization of components, and not their physical properties, that largely determines behavior, and if computers are organized somewhat in the image of man, then the computer becomes an obvious device for exploring the consequences of alternative organizational assumptions for human behavior. Psychology could move forward without awaiting the solutions by neurology of the problems of component design—however interesting and significant these components turn out to be.

Symbol systems: rational artifacts

The computer is a member of an important family of artifacts called symbol systems, or more explicitly, physical symbol systems.[18] Another important member of the family (some of us think, anthropomorphically, it is the *most* important) is the human mind and brain. It is with this family of artifacts, and particularly the human version of it, that we will be primarily concerned in this book. Symbol systems are almost the quintessential artifacts, for adaptivity to an environment is their whole *raison d'être*. They are goal-seeking, information-processing systems, usually enlisted in the service of the larger systems in which they are incorporated.

Basic capabilities of symbol systems

A physical symbol system holds a set of entities, called symbols. These are physical patterns (e.g., chalk marks on a blackboard) that can occur as components of symbol structures (sometimes called 'expressions'). As I have already pointed out in the case of computers, a symbol system also possesses a number of simple processes that operate upon symbol structures—processes that create, modify, copy, and destroy symbols. A physical symbol system is a machine that, as it moves through time, produces an evolving collection of symbol structures.[19] Symbol structures can, and commonly do, serve as internal representations (e.g., 'mental images') of the environments to which the symbol system is seeking to adapt. They allow it to model that environment with greater or less veridicality and in greater or less detail, and consequently to reason about it. Of course, for this capability to be of any use to the symbol system, it must have windows on the world and hands, too. It must have means for acquiring information from the external environment that can be encoded into internal symbols, as well as means for producing symbols that initiate action upon the environment. Thus it must use symbols to *designate* objects and relations and actions in the world external to the system.

Symbols may also designate processes that the symbol system can interpret and execute. Hence the programs that govern the behavior of a symbol system can be stored, along with other symbol structures, in the system's own memory, and executed when activated.

Symbol systems are called 'physical' to remind the reader that they exist as real-world devices, fabricated of glass and metal (computers) or flesh and blood (brains). In the past we have been more accustomed to thinking of the symbol systems of mathematics and logic as abstract and disembodied, leaving out of account the paper and pencil and human minds that were required actually to bring them to life. Computers have transported symbol systems from the platonic heaven of ideas to the empirical world of actual processes carried out by machines or brains, or by the two of them working together.

Intelligence as computation

The three chapters that follow rest squarely on the hypothesis that intelligence is the work of symbol systems. Stated a little more formally, the hypothesis is that a physical symbol system of the sort I have just described has the necessary and sufficient means for general intelligent action.

The hypothesis is clearly an empirical one, to be judged true or false on the basis of evidence. One task of chapters 3 and 4 will be to review some of the evidence, which is of two basic kinds. On the one hand, by constructing computer programs that are demonstrably capable of intelligent action, we provide evidence on the sufficiency side of the hypothesis. On the other hand, by collecting experimental data on human thinking that tend to show that the human brain operates as a symbol system, we add plausibility to the claims for necessity, for such data imply that all known intelligent systems (brains and computers) are symbol systems.

Economics: abstract rationality

As prelude to our consideration of human intelligence as the work of a physical symbol system, chapter 2 introduces a heroic abstraction and idealization—the idealization of human rationality which is enshrined in modern economic theories, particularly those called neoclassical. These theories are an idealization because they direct their attention primarily to the external environment of human thought, to decisions that are optimal for realizing the adaptive system's goals (maximization of utility or profit). They seek to define the decisions that would be substantively rational in the circumstances defined by the outer environment.

Economic theory's treatment of the limits of rationality imposed by the inner environment—by the characteristics of the physical symbol system—tends to be pragmatic, and sometimes even opportunistic. In the more formal treatments of general equilibrium and in the so-called 'rational expectations' approach to adaptation, the possibilities that an information-processing system may have a very limited capability for adaptation are almost ignored. On the other hand, in discussions of the rationale for market mechanisms and in many theories of decision making under uncertainty, the procedural aspects of rationality receive more serious treatment.

In chapter 2 we will see examples both of neglect for and concern with the limits of rationality. From the idealizations of economics (and some criticisms of these idealizations) we will move, in chapters 3 and 4, to a more systematic study of the inner environment of thought—of thought processes as they actually occur within the constraints imposed by the parameters of a physical symbol system like the brain.

Notes

1 I will occasionally use 'man' as an androgynous noun, encompassing both sexes, and 'he,' 'his,' and 'him' as androgynous pronouns including women and men equally in their scope.

2 I shall disclaim responsibility for this particular choice of terms. The phrase 'artificial intelligence,' which led me to it, was coined, I think, right on the Charles River, at MIT. Our own research group at Rand and Carnegie Mellon University have preferred phrases like 'complex information processing' and 'simulation of cognitive processes.' But then we run into new terminological difficulties, for the dictionary also says that 'to simulate' means 'to assume or have the mere appearance or form of, without the reality; imitate; counterfeit; pretend.' At any rate, 'artificial intelligence' seems to be here to stay, and it may prove easier to cleanse the phrase than to dispense with it. In time it will become sufficiently idiomatic that it will no longer be the target of cheap rhetoric.

3 This issue will also be discussed at length in my fifth chapter. In order not to keep readers in suspense, I may say that I hold to the pristine empiricist's position of the irreducibility of 'ought' to 'is,' as in chapter 3 of my *Administrative Behavior* (New York: Macmillan, 1976). This position is entirely consistent with treating natural or artificial goal-seeking systems as phenomena, without commitment to their

goals. *Ibid.*, appendix. See also the well-known paper by A. Rosenbluth, N. Wiener, and J. Bigelow, 'Behavior, Purpose, and Teleology,' *Philosophy of Science*, 10 (1943):18–24.

4 A generalization of the argument made here for the separability of 'outer' from 'inner' environment shows that we should expect to find this separability, to a greater or lesser degree, in *all* large and complex systems, whether they are artificial or natural. In its generalized form it is an argument that all nature will be organized in 'levels.' My essay 'The Architecture of Complexity,' included in this volume as chapter 8, develops the more general argument in some detail.

5 The theory of functional equivalence of computing machines has had considerable development in recent years. See Marvin L. Minsky, *Computation: Finite and Infinite Machines* (Englewood Cliffs, N.J.: Prentice-Hall, 1967), chapters 1–4.

6 U.S. Patent 1,307,836, granted to Arthur Simon, June 24, 1919.

7 Ibid.

8 Ibid.

9 On the crucial role of adaptation or rationality—and their limits—for economics and organization theory, see the introduction to part IV, 'Rationality and Administrative Decision Making,' of my *Models of Man* (New York: Wiley, 1957); pp. 38–41, 80–81, and 240–244 of *Administrative Behavior*; and chapter 2 of this book.

10 Compare the corresponding proposition on the design of administrative organizations: 'Rationality, then, does not determine behavior. Within the area of rationality behavior is perfectly flexible and adaptable to abilities, goals, and knowledge. Instead, behavior is determined by the irrational and nonrational elements that bound the area of rationality ... administrative theory must be concerned with the limits of rationality, and the manner in which organization affects these limits for the person making a decision.' *Administrative Behavior*, p. 241. For a discussion of the same issue as it arises in psychology, see my 'Cognitive Architectures and Rational Analysis: Comment,' in Kurt VanLehn (ed.), *Architectures for Intelligence* (Hillsdale, NJ: Erlbaum, 1991).

11 For some published versions of this model, see A. O. Dahlberg, *National Income Visualized* (N.Y.: Columbia University Press, 1956).

12 A. W. Phillips, 'Mechanical Models in Economic Dynamics,' *Economica*, New Series, *17* (1950):283–305.

13 This point is developed more fully in 'The Architecture of Complexity,' chapter 8 in this volume. More than fifty years ago, Bertrand Russell made the same point about the architecture of mathematics. See the 'Preface' to *Principia Mathematica*: ' ... the chief reason in favour of any theory on the principles of mathematics must always be inductive, i.e., it must lie in the fact that the theory in question enables us to deduce ordinary mathematics. In mathematics, the greatest degree of self-evidence is usually not to be found quite at the beginning, but at some later point; hence the early deductions, until they reach this point, give reasons rather for believing the premises because true consequences follow from them, than for believing the consequences because they follow from the premises.' Contemporary preferences for deductive formalisms frequently blind us to this important fact, which is no less true today than it was in 1910.

14 On the subject of this and the following paragraphs, see M. L. Minsky, *op. cit.*; then John von Neumann, 'Probabilistic Logics and the Synthesis of Reliable Organisms from Unreliable Components,' in C. E. Shannon and J. McCarthy (eds.), *Automata Studies* (Princeton: Princeton University Press, 1956).

15 A. Newell and H. A. Simon, 'Computer Science as Empirical Inquiry,' *Communications of the ACM, 19*(March 1976):113–126. See also H. A. Simon, 'Artificial Intelligence: An Empirical Science,' *Artificial Intelligence, 77*(1995): 95–127.

16 The empirical, exploratory flavor of computer research is nicely captured by the account of Maurice V. Wilkes in his 1967 Turing Lecture, 'Computers Then and Now,' *Journal of the Association for Computing Machinery, 15* (January 1968):1–7.

17 Note, for example, the empirical data in Lawrence Wos, George A. Robinson, Daniel F. Carson, and Leon Shalla, 'The Concept of Demodulation in Theorem Proving,' *Journal of the Association for Computing Machinery*, 14 (October 1967):698–709, and in several of the earlier papers referenced there. See also the collection of programs in Edward Feigenbaum and Julian Feldman (eds.), *Computers and Thought* (New York: McGraw-Hill, 1963). It is common practice in the field to title papers about heuristic programs, 'Experiments with an *XYZ* Program.'

18 In the literature the phrase *information-processing system* is used more frequently than symbol system. I will use the two terms as synonyms.

19 Newell and Simon, 'Computer Science as Empirical Inquiry,' p. 116.

1.3: Intelligence and the Turing Test

71

INTELLIGENCE: KNOWNS AND UNKNOWNS

U. Neisser, G. Boodoo, T. J. Bouchard Jr., A. W. Boykin, N. Brody,
S. J. Ceci, D. F. Halpern, J. C. Loehlin, R. Perloff, R. J. Sternberg
and S. Urbina

Source: *American Psychologist* 51, 1996: 77–101.

In the fall of 1994, the publication of Herrnstein and Murray's book The Bell
Curve *sparked a new round of debate about the meaning of intelligence test
scores and the nature of intelligence. The debate was characterized by strong
assertions as well as by strong feelings. Unfortunately, those assertions often
revealed serious misunderstandings of what has (and has not) been demonstrated by scientific research in this field. Although a great deal is now known,
the issues remain complex and in many cases still unresolved. Another
unfortunate aspect of the debate was that many participants made little effort
to distinguish scientific issues from political ones. Research findings were often
assessed not so much on their merits or their scientific standing as on their
supposed political implications. In such a climate, individuals who wish to make
their own judgments find it hard to know what to believe.*

*Reviewing the intelligence debate at its meeting of November 1994, the
Board of Scientific Affairs (BSA) of the American Psychological Association
(APA) concluded that there was urgent need for an authoritative report on
these issues—one that all sides could use as a basis for discussion. Acting by
unanimous vote, BSA established a Task Force charged with preparing such a
report. Ulric Neisser, Professor of Psychology at Emory University and a
member of BSA, was appointed Chair. The APA Board on the Advancement of
Psychology in the Public Interest, which was consulted extensively during this
process, nominated one member of the Task Force; the Committee on Psychological Tests and Assessment nominated another; a third was nominated by the
Council of Representatives. Other members were chosen by an extended con-
sultative process, with the aim of representing a broad range of expertise and
opinion.*

The Task Force met twice, in January and March of 1995. Between and after these meetings, drafts of the various sections were circulated, revised, and revised yet again. Disputes were resolved by discussion. As a result, the report presented here has the unanimous support of the entire Task Force.

1 Concepts of intelligence

Individuals differ from one another in their ability to understand complex ideas, to adapt effectively to the environment, to learn from experience, to engage in various forms of reasoning, to overcome obstacles by taking thought. Although these individual differences can be substantial, they are never entirely consistent: A given person's intellectual performance will vary on different occasions, in different domains, as judged by different criteria. Concepts of "intelligence" are attempts to clarify and organize this complex set of phenomena. Although considerable clarity has been achieved in some areas, no such conceptualization has yet answered all the important questions and none commands universal assent. Indeed, when two dozen prominent theorists were recently asked to define intelligence, they gave two dozen somewhat different definitions (Sternberg & Detterman, 1986). Such disagreements are not cause for dismay. Scientific research rarely begins with fully agreed definitions, though it may eventually lead to them.

This first section of our report reviews the approaches to intelligence that are currently influential, or that seem to be becoming so. Here (as in later sections) much of our discussion is devoted to the dominant *psychometric* approach, which has not only inspired the most research and attracted the most attention (up to this time) but is by far the most widely used in practical settings. Nevertheless, other points of view deserve serious consideration. Several current theorists argue that there are many different 'intelligences' (systems of abilities), only a few of which can be captured by standard psychometric tests. Others emphasize the role of culture, both in establishing different conceptions of intelligence and in influencing the acquisition of intellectual skills. Developmental psychologists, taking yet another direction, often focus more on the processes by which all children come to think intelligently than on measuring individual differences among them. There is also a new interest in the neural and biological bases of intelligence, a field of research that seems certain to expand in the next few years.

In this brief report, we cannot do full justice to even one such approach. Rather than trying to do so, we focus here on a limited and rather specific set of questions:

- What are the significant conceptualizations of intelligence at this time? (Section 1)
- What do intelligence test scores mean, what do they predict, and how well do they predict it? (Section 2)

- Why do individuals differ in intelligence, and especially in their scores on intelligence tests? Our discussion of these questions implicates both genetic factors (Section 3) and environmental factors (Section 4).
- Do various ethnic groups display different patterns of performance on intelligence tests, and if so what might explain those differences? (Section 5)
- What significant scientific issues are presently unresolved? (Section 6)

Public discussion of these issues has been especially vigorous since the 1994 publication of Herrnstein and Murray's *The Bell Curve*, a controversial volume which stimulated many equally controversial reviews and replies. Nevertheless, we do not directly enter that debate. Herrnstein and Murray (and many of their critics) have gone well beyond the scientific findings, making explicit recommendations on various aspects of public policy. Our concern here, however, is with science rather than policy. The charge to our Task Force was to prepare a dispassionate survey of the state of the art: to make clear what has been scientifically established, what is presently in dispute, and what is still unknown. In fulfilling that charge, the only recommendations we shall make are for further research and calmer debate.

The psychometric approach

Ever since Alfred Binet's great success in devising tests to distinguish mentally retarded children from those with behavior problems, psychometric instruments have played an important part in European and American life. Tests are used for many purposes, such as selection, diagnosis, and evaluation. Many of the most widely used tests are not intended to measure intelligence itself but some closely related construct: scholastic aptitude, school achievement, specific abilities, etc. Such tests are especially important for selection purposes. For preparatory school, it's the SSAT; for college, the SAT or ACT; for graduate school, the GRE; for medical school, the MCAT; for law school, the LSAT; for business school, the GMAT. Scores on intelligence-related tests matter, and the stakes can be high.

Intelligence tests

Tests of intelligence itself (in the psychometric sense) come in many forms. Some use only a single type of item or question; examples include the Peabody Picture Vocabulary Test (a measure of children's verbal intelligence) and Raven's Progressive Matrices (a nonverbal, untimed test that requires inductive reasoning about perceptual patterns). Although such instruments are useful for specific purposes, the more familiar measures of general intelligence—such as the Wechsler tests and the Stanford-Binet—include many different types of items, both verbal and nonverbal. Test-takers may be asked to give the meanings of words, to complete a series of pictures, to indicate which of several words does not belong with the others, and the like. Their performance can then be scored to yield several subscores as well as an overall score.

By convention, overall intelligence test scores are usually converted to a scale in which the mean is 100 and the standard deviation is 15. (The standard deviation is a measure of the variability of the distribution of scores.) Approximately 95% of the population has scores within two standard deviations of the mean, i.e., between 70 and 130. For historical reasons, the term 'IQ' is often used to describe scores on tests of intelligence. It originally referred to an 'Intelligence Quotient' that was formed by dividing a so-called mental age by a chronological age, but this procedure is no longer used.

Intercorrelations among tests

Individuals rarely perform equally well on all the different kinds of items included in a test of intelligence. One person may do relatively better on verbal than on spatial items, for example, while another may show the opposite pattern. Nevertheless, subtests measuring different abilities tend to be positively correlated: people who score high on one such subtest are likely to be above average on others as well. These complex patterns of correlation can be clarified by factor analysis, but the results of such analyses are often controversial themselves. Some theorists (e.g., Spearman, 1927) have emphasized the importance of a general factor, g, which represents what all the tests have in common; others (e.g., Thurstone, 1938) focus on more specific group factors such as memory, verbal comprehension, or number facility. As we shall see in Section 2, one common view today envisages something like a hierarchy of factors with g at the apex. But there is no full agreement on what g actually means: it has been described as a mere statistical regularity (Thomson, 1939), a kind of mental energy (Spearman, 1927), a generalized abstract reasoning ability (Gustafsson, 1984), or an index measure of neural processing speed (Reed & Jensen, 1992).

There have been many disputes over the utility of IQ and g. Some theorists are critical of the entire psychometric approach (e.g., Ceci, 1990; Gardner, 1983; Gould, 1978), while others regard it as firmly established (e.g., Carroll, 1993; Eysenck, 1973; Herrnstein & Murray, 1994; Jensen, 1972). The critics do not dispute the stability of test scores, nor the fact that they predict certain forms of achievement—especially school achievement—rather effectively (see Section 2). They do argue, however, that to base a concept of intelligence on test scores alone is to ignore many important aspects of mental ability. Some of those aspects are emphasized in other approaches reviewed below.

Multiple forms of intelligence

Gardner's theory

A relatively new approach is the theory of 'multiple intelligences' proposed by Howard Gardner in his book *Frames of Mind* (1983). Gardner argues that our conceptions of intelligence should be informed not only by work with 'normal' children and adults but also by studies of gifted persons (including so-called 'savants'), of virtuosos and experts in various domains, of valued abilities in diverse cultures, and of individuals who have suffered selective forms of brain damage. These considerations have led him to include musical, bodily-kinesthetic, and various forms of personal intelligence in the scope of his theory along with more familiar linguistic, logical-mathematical, and spatial abilities. (Critics of the theory argue, however, that some of these are more appropriately described as special talents than as forms of 'intelligence.')

In Gardner's view, the scope of psychometric tests includes only linguistic, logical, and some aspects of spatial intelligence; other forms have been almost entirely ignored. Even in the domains on which they are ostensibly focused, the paper-and-pencil format of most tests rules out many kinds of intelligent performance that matter a great deal in everyday life, such as giving an extemporaneous talk (linguistic) or being able to find one's way in a new town (spatial). While the stability and validity of performance tests in these new domains are not yet clear, Gardner's argument has attracted considerable interest among educators as well as psychologists.

Sternberg's theory

Robert Sternberg's (1985) triarchic theory proposes three fundamental aspects of intelligence—analytic, creative, and practical—of which only the first is measured to any significant extent by mainstream tests. His investigations suggest the need for a balance between analytic intelligence, on the one hand, and creative and especially practical intelligence on the other. The distinction between analytic (or 'academic') and practical intelligence has also been made by others (e.g., Neisser, 1976). Analytic problems, of the type suitable for test construction, tend to (a) have been formulated by other people, (b) be clearly defined, (c) come with all the information needed to solve them, (d) have only a single right answer, which can be reached by only a single method, (e) be disembedded from ordinary experience, and (f) have little or no intrinsic interest. Practical problems, in contrast, tend to (a) require problem recognition and formulation, (b) be poorly defined, (c) require information seeking, (d) have various acceptable solutions, (e) be embedded in and require prior everyday experience, and (f) require motivation and personal involvement.

One important form of practical intelligence is *tacit knowledge*, defined by Sternberg and his collaborators as 'action-oriented knowledge, acquired without direct help from others, that allows individuals to achieve goals they personally value' (Sternberg, Wagner, Williams, & Horvath, 1995, p. 916). Questionnaires designed to measure tacit knowledge have been developed for various domains, especially business management. In these questionnaires, the individual is presented with written descriptions of various work-related situations and asked to rank a number of options for dealing with each of them. Measured in this way, tacit knowledge is relatively independent of scores on intelligence tests; nevertheless it correlates significantly with various indices of job performance (Sternberg & Wagner, 1993; Sternberg et al., 1995). Although this work is not without its critics (Jensen, 1993; Schmidt & Hunter, 1993), the results to this point tend to support the distinction between analytic and practical intelligence.

Related findings

Other investigators have also demonstrated that practical intelligence can be relatively independent of school performance or scores on psychometric tests. Brazilian street children, for example, are quite capable of doing the math required for survival in their street business even though they have failed mathematics in school (Carraher, Carraher, & Schliemann, 1985). Similarly, women shoppers in California who had no difficulty in comparing product values at the supermarket were unable to carry out the same mathematical operations in paper-and-pencil tests (Lave, 1988). In a study of expertise in wagering on harness races, Ceci and Liker (1986) found that the reasoning of the most skilled handicappers was implicitly based on a complex interactive model with as many as seven variables. Nevertheless, individual handicappers' levels of performance were not correlated with their IQ scores. This means, as Ceci as put it, that 'the assessment of the experts' intelligence on a standard IQ test was irrelevant in predicting the complexity of their thinking at the racetrack' (1990, p. 43).

Cultural variation

It is very difficult to compare concepts of intelligence across cultures. English is not alone in having many words for different aspects of intellectual power and cognitive skill (*wise, sensible, smart, bright, clever, cunning* . . .); if another language has just as many, which of them shall we say corresponds to its speakers' 'concept of intelligence'? The few attempts to examine this issue directly have typically found that, even within a given society, different cognitive characteristics are emphasized from one situation to another and from one subculture to another (Serpell, 1974; Super, 1983; Wober, 1974). These differences extend not just to conceptions of

114

intelligence but also to what is considered adaptive or appropriate in a broader sense.

These issues have occasionally been addressed across subcultures and ethnic groups in America. In a study conducted in San Jose, California, Okagaki and Sternberg (1993) asked immigrant parents from Cambodia, Mexico, the Philippines, and Vietnam—as well as native-born Anglo-Americans and Mexican Americans—about their conceptions of child-rearing, appropriate teaching, and children's intelligence. Parents from all groups except Anglo-Americans indicated that such characteristics as motivation, social skills, and practical school skills were as or more important than cognitive characteristics for their conceptions of an intelligent first-grade child.

Heath (1983) found that different ethnic groups in North Carolina have different conceptions of intelligence. To be considered as intelligent or adaptive, one must excel in the skills valued by one's own group. One particularly interesting contrast was in the importance ascribed to verbal versus nonverbal communication skills—to saying things explicitly as opposed to using and understanding gestures and facial expressions. Note that while both these forms of communicative skill have their uses, they are not equally well represented in psychometric tests.

How testing is done can have different effects in different cultural groups. This can happen for many reasons. In one study, Serpell (1979) asked Zambian and English children to reproduce patterns in three different media: wire models, pencil and paper, or clay. The Zambian children excelled in the wire medium to which they were most accustomed, while the English children were best with pencil and paper. Both groups performed equally well with clay. As this example shows, differences in familiarity with test materials can produce marked differences in test results.

Developmental progressions

Piaget's theory

The best-known developmentally-based conception of intelligence is certainly that of the Swiss psychologist Jean Piaget (1972). Unlike most of the theorists considered here, Piaget had relatively little interest in individual differences. Intelligence develops—in all children—through the continually shifting balance between the assimilation of new information into existing cognitive structures and the accommodation of those structures themselves to the new information. To index the development of intelligence in this sense, Piaget devised methods that are rather different from conventional tests. To assess the understanding of 'conservation,' for example (roughly, the principle that material quantity is not affected by mere changes of shape), children who have watched water being poured from a shallow to a tall beaker may be asked if there is now more water than before. (A positive answer would suggest that the child has not yet mastered the principle of conservation.) Piaget's tasks can be modified to serve as measures of individual differences; when this is done, they correlate fairly well with standard psychometric tests (for a review see Jensen, 1980).

Vygotsky's theory

The Russian psychologist Lev Vygotsky (1978) argued that all intellectual abilities are social in origin. Language and thought first appear in early interactions with parents, and continue to develop through contact with teachers and others. Traditional intelligence tests ignore what Vygotsky called the 'zone of proximal development,' i.e., the level of performance that a child might reach with appropriate help from a supportive adult. Such tests are 'static,' measuring only the intelligence that is already fully developed. 'Dynamic' testing, in which the examiner provides guided and graded feedback, can go further to give some indication of the child's latent potential. These ideas are being developed and extended by a number of contemporary psychologists (Brown & French, 1979; Feuerstein, 1980; Pascual-Leone & Ijaz, 1989).

Biological approaches

Some investigators have recently turned to the study of the brain as a basis for new ideas about what intelligence is and how to measure it. many aspects of brain anatomy and physiology have been suggested as potentially relevant to intelligence; the arborization of cortical neurons (Ceci, 1990), cerebral glucose metabolism (Haier, 1993), evoked potentials (Caryl, 1994), nerve conduction velocity (Reed & Jensen, 1992), sex hormones (see Section 4), and still others (cf. Vernon, 1993). Advances in research methods, including new forms of brain imaging such as PET and MRI scans, will surely add to this list. In the not-too-distant future it may be possible to relate some aspects of test performance to specific characteristics of brain function.

This brief survey has revealed a wide range of contemporary conceptions of intelligence and of how it should be measured. The psychometric approach is the oldest and best established, but others also have much to contribute. We should be open to the possibility that our understanding of intelligence in the future will be rather different from what it is today.

2 Intelligence tests and their correlates

The correlation coefficient, r, can be computed whenever the scores in a sample are paired in some way. Typically this is because each individual is measured twice: he or she takes the same test on two occasions, or takes two different tests, or has both a test score and some criterion measure such as grade point average or job performance. (In Section 3 we consider cases where the paired scores are those of two different individuals, such as twins or parent and child.) The value of r measures the degree of relationship between the two sets of scores in a convenient way, by assessing how well one of them (computationally it doesn't matter which one) could be used to predict the value of the other. Its sign indicates the direction of relationship: when r is negative, high scores on one measure predict low scores on the other. Its magnitude indicates the strength of the relationship. If $r = 0$, there is no relation at all; if r is 1 (or -1), one score can be used to predict the other score perfectly. Moreover, the square of r has a particular meaning in cases where we are concerned with predicting one variable from another. When $r = .50$, for example, r^2 is .25: this means (given certain linear assumptions) that 25% of the variance in one set of scores is predictable from the correlated values of the other set, while the remaining 75% is not.

Basic characteristics of test scores

Stability

Intelligence test scores are fairly stable during development. When Jones and Bayley (1941) tested a sample of children annually throughout childhood and adolescence, for example, scores obtained at age 18 were correlated $r = .77$ with scores that had been obtained at age 6 and $r = .89$ with scores from age 12. When scores were averaged across several successive tests to remove short-term fluctuations, the correlations were even higher. The mean for ages 17 and 18 was correlated $r = .86$ with the mean for ages 5, 6, and 7, and $r = .96$ with the mean for ages 11, 12, and 13. (For comparable findings in a more recent study, see Moffitt, Caspi, Harkness, & Silva, 1993.) Nevertheless, IQ scores do change over time. In the same study (Jones & Bayley, 1941), the average change between age 12 and age 17 was 7.1 IQ points; some individuals changed as much as 18 points.

Is it possible to measure the intelligence of young infants in a similar way? Conventional tests of 'infant intelligence' do not predict later test scores very well, but certain experimental measures of infant attention and memory—originally developed for other purposes—have turned out to be more successful. In the most common procedure, a particular visual pattern is shown to a baby over and over again. The experimenter records how long the infant subject looks at the pattern on each trial; these looks get shorter and shorter as the baby becomes 'habituated' to it. The time required to reach a certain level of habituation, or the extent to which the baby now 'prefers' (looks longer at) a new pattern, is regarded as a measure of some aspect of his or her information-processing capability.

These habituation-based measures, obtained from babies at ages ranging from three months to a year, are significantly correlated with the intelligence test scores of the same children when they get to be 2 or 4 or 6 years old (for reviews see Bornstein, 1989; Columbo, 1993; McCall & Garriger, 1993). A few studies have found such correlations even at ages 8 or 11 (Rose & Feldman, 1995). A recent meta-analysis, based on 31 different samples, estimates the average magnitude of the correlations at about $r = .36$ (McCall & Garriger, 1993). (The largest rs often appear in samples that include 'at risk' infants.) It is possible that these habituation scores (and other similar measures of infant cognition) do indeed reflect real cognitive differences, perhaps in 'speed of information processing' (Columbo, 1993). It is also possible, however, that—to a presently unknown extent—they reflect early differences in temperament or inhibition.

It is important to understand what remains stable and what changes in the development of intelligence. A child whose IQ score remains the same from age 6 to age 18 does not exhibit the same performance throughout that period. On the contrary, steady gains in general knowledge, vocabulary, reasoning ability, etc. will be apparent. What does *not* change is his or her score in comparison to that of other individuals of the same age. A six-year-old with an IQ of 100 is at the mean of six-year-olds; an 18-year-old with that score is at the mean of 18-year-olds.

Factors and g

As noted in Section 1, the patterns of intercorrelation among tests (i.e., among different kinds of items) are complex. Some pairs of tests are much more closely related than others, but all such correlations are typically positive and form what is called a 'positive manifold.' Spearman (1927) showed that in any such manifold, some portion of the variance of scores on each test can be mathematically attributed to a 'general factor,' or g. Given this analysis, the overall pattern of correlations can be roughly described as produced by individual differences in g plus differences in the specific abilities sampled by particular tests. In addition, however, there are usually patterns of intercorrelation among groups of tests. These commonalities, which played only a small role in Spearman's analysis, were emphasized by other theorists. Thurstone (1938), for example, proposed an analysis based primarily on the concept of group factors.

While some psychologists today still regard g as the most fundamental measure of intelligence (e.g., Jensen, 1980), others prefer to emphasize the distinctive profile of strengths and weaknesses present in each person's performance. A recently published review identifies over 70 different abilities that can be distinguished by currently available tests (Carroll, 1993). One way to represent this structure is in terms of a hierarchical arrangement with a general intelligence factor at the apex and various more specialized abilities arrayed below it. Such a summary merely acknowledges that performance levels on different tests are correlated; it is consistent with, but does not prove, the hypothesis that a common factor such as g underlies those correlations. Different specialized abilities might also be correlated for other reasons, such as the effects of education. Thus while the g-based factor hierarchy is the most widely accepted current view of the structure of abilities, some theorists regard it as misleading (Ceci, 1990). Moreover, as noted in Section 1, a wide range of human abilities—including many that seem to have intellectual components—are outside the domain of standard psychometric tests.

Tests as predictors

School performance

Intelligence tests were originally devised by Alfred Binet to measure children's ability to succeed in school. They do in fact predict school performance fairly well: the correlation between IQ scores and grades is about .50. They also predict scores on school achievement tests, designed to measure knowledge of the curriculum. Note, however, that correlations of this magnitude account for only about 25% of the overall variance. Successful school learning depends on many personal characteristics other than intelligence, such as persistence, interest in school, and willingness to study. The encouragement for academic achievement that is received from peers, family, and teachers may also be important, together with more general cultural factors (see Section 5).

The relationship between test scores and school performance seems to be ubiquitous. Wherever it has been studied, children with high scores on tests of intelligence tend to learn more of what is taught in school than their lower-scoring peers. There may be styles of teaching and methods of instruction that will decrease or increase this correlation, but none that consistently eliminates it has yet been found (Cronbach & Snow, 1977).

What children learn in school depends not only on their individual abilities but also on teaching practices and on what is actually taught. Recent comparisons among pupils attending school in different countries have made this especially obvious. Children in Japan and China, for example, know a great deal more math than American children even though their intelligence test scores are quite similar (see Section 5). This difference may result from many factors, including cultural attitudes toward schooling as well as the sheer amount of time devoted to the study of mathematics and how that study is organized (Stevenson & Stigler, 1992). In principle it is quite possible to improve the school learning of American children—even very substantially—without changing their intelligence test scores at all.

Years of education

Some children stay in school longer than others; many go on to college and perhaps beyond. Two variables that can be measured as early as elementary school correlate with the total amount of education individuals will obtain: test scores and social class background. Correlations between IQ scores and total years of education are about .55, implying that differences in psychometric intelligence account for about 30% of the outcome variance. The correlations of years of education with social class background (as indexed by the occupation/education of a child's parents) are also positive, but somewhat lower.

There are a number of reasons why children with higher test scores tend to get more education. They are likely to get good grades, and to be encouraged by teachers and counselors; often they are placed in 'college preparatory' classes, where they make friends who may also encourage them. In general, they are likely to find the process of education rewarding in a way that many low-scoring children do not (Rehberg & Rosenthal, 1978). These influences are not omnipotent: some high scoring children do drop out of school. Many personal and social characteristics other than psychometric intelligence determine academic success and interest, and social privilege may also play a role. Nevertheless, test scores are the best single predictor of an individual's years of education.

In contemporary American society, the amount of schooling that adults complete is also somewhat predictive of their social status. Occupations considered high in prestige (e.g., law, medicine, even corporate business) usually require at least a college degree—16 or more years of education—as a condition of entry. It is partly because intelligence test scores predict years of education so well that they also predict occupational status—and, to a smaller extent, even income (Herrnstein & Murray, 1994; Jencks, 1979). Moreover, many occupations can only be entered through professional schools which base their admissions at least partly on test scores: the MCAT, the GMAT, the LSAT, etc. Individual scores on admission-related tests such as these are certainly correlated with scores on tests of intelligence.

Social status and income

How well do IQ scores (which can be obtained before individuals enter the labor force) predict such outcome measures as the social status or income of adults? This question is complex, in part because another variable also predicts such outcomes: namely, the socioeconomic status (SES) of one's parents. Unsurprisingly, children of privileged families are more likely to attain high social status than those whose parents are poor and less educated. These two predictors (IQ and parental SES) are by no means independent of one another; the correlation between them is around .33 (White, 1982).

One way to look at these relationships is to begin with SES. According to Jencks (1979), measures of parental SES predict about one-third of the variance in young adults' social status and about one-fifth of the variance in their income. About half of this predictive effectiveness depends on the fact that the SES of parents also predicts children's intelligence test scores, which have their own predictive value for social outcomes; the other half comes about in other ways.

We can also begin with IQ scores, which by themselves account for about one-fourth of the social status variance and one-sixth of the income variance. Statistical controls for parental SES eliminate only about a quarter of this predictive power. One way to conceptualize this effect is by comparing the occupational status (or income) of adult brothers who grew up in the same family and hence have the same parental SES. In such cases, the brother with the higher adolescent IQ score is likely to have the higher adult social status and income (Jencks, 1979). This effect, in turn, is substantially mediated by education: the brother with the higher test scores is likely to get more schooling, and hence to be better credentialled as he enters the workplace.

Do these data imply that psychometric intelligence is a major determinant of social status or income? That depends on what one means by 'major.' In fact, individuals who have the same test scores may differ widely in occupational status and even more widely in income. Consider for a moment the distribution of occupational status scores for all individuals in a population, and then consider the conditional distribution of such scores for just those individuals who test at some given IQ. Jencks (1979) notes that the standard deviation of the latter distribution may still be quite larger; in some cases it amounts to about 88% of the standard deviation for the entire population. Viewed from this perspective, psychometric intelligence appears as only one of a great many factors that influence social outcomes.

Job performance

Scores on intelligence tests predict various measures of job performance: supervisor ratings, work samples, etc. Such correlations, which typically lie between $r = .30$ and $r = .50$, are partly restricted by the limited reliability of those measures themselves. They become higher when r is statistically corrected for this unreliability: in one survey of relevant studies (Hunter, 1983), the mean of the corrected correlations was .54. This implies that, across a wide range of occupations, intelligence test performance accounts for some 29% of the variance in job performance.

Although these correlations can sometimes be modified by changing methods of training or aspects of the job itself, intelligence test scores are at least weakly related to job performance in most settings. Sometimes IQ scores are described as the 'best available predictor' of that performance. It is worth noting, however, that such tests predict considerably less than half the variance of job-related measures. Other individual characteristics— interpersonal skills, aspects of personality, etc.—are probably of equal or greater importance, but at this point we do not have equally reliable instruments to measure them.

Social outcomes

Psychometric intelligence is negatively correlated with certain socially undesirable outcomes. For example, children with high test scores are less likely than lower-scoring children to engage in juvenile crime. In one study, Moffitt, Gabrielli, Mednick, and Schulsinger (1981) found a correlation of— .19 between IQ scores and number of juvenile offenses in a large Danish sample; with social class controlled, the correlation dropped to −.17. The correlations for most 'negative outcome' variables are typically smaller than .20, which means that test scores are associated with less than 4% of their total variance. It is important to realize that the causal links between psychometric ability and social outcomes may be indirect. Children who are unsuccessful in—and hence alienated from—school may be more likely to engage in delinquent behaviors for that very reason, compared to other children who enjoy school and are doing well.

In summary, intelligence test scores predict a wide range of social outcomes with varying degrees of success. Correlations are highest for school achievement, where they account for about a quarter of the variance. They are somewhat lower for job performance, and very low for negatively valued outcomes such as criminality. In general, intelligence tests measure only some of the many personal characteristics that are relevant to life in contemporary America. Those characteristics are never the only influence on outcomes, though in the case of school performance they may well be the strongest.

Test scores and measures of processing speed

Many recent studies show that the speeds with which people perform very simple perceptual and cognitive tasks are correlated with psychometric intelligence (for reviews see Ceci, 1990; Deary, 1995; Vernon, 1987). In general, people with higher intelligence test scores tend to apprehend, scan, retrieve, and respond to stimuli more quickly than those who score lower.

Cognitive correlates

The modern study of these relations began in the 1970s, as part of the general growth of interest in response time and other chronometric measures of cognition. Many of the new cognitive paradigms required subjects to make same/different judgments or other speeded responses to visual displays. Although those paradigms had not been devised with individual differences in mind, they could be interpreted as providing measures of the speed of certain information processes. Those speeds turned out to correlate with psychometrically-measured verbal ability (Hunt, 1978; Jackson & McClelland, 1979). In some problem solving tasks, it was possible to analyze the subjects' overall response times into theoretically motivated 'cognitive components' (Sternberg, 1977); component times could then be correlated with test scores in their own right.

Although the size of these correlations is modest (seldom accounting for more than 10% of the variance), they do increase as the basic tasks were made more complex by requiring increased memory or attentional capacity. For instance, the correlation between paired associate learning and intelligence increases as the pairs are presented at faster rates (Christal, Tirre, & Kyllonen, 1984).

Choice reaction time

In another popular cognitive paradigm, the subject simply moves his or her finger from a 'home' button to one of eight other buttons arranged in a semicircle around it; these are marked by small lights that indicate which one is the target on a given trial (Jensen, 1987). Various aspects of the choice reaction times obtained in this paradigm are correlated with scores on intelligence tests, sometimes with values of r as high as $-.30$ or $-.40$ (r is negative because higher test scores go with shorter times). Nevertheless, it has proved difficult to make theoretical sense of the overall pattern of correlations, and the results are still hard to interpret (cf. Brody, 1992; Longstreth, 1984).

Somewhat stronger results have been obtained in a variant of Jensen's paradigm devised by Frearson and Eysenck (1986). In this 'odd-man-out' procedure, three of the eight lights are illuminated on each trial. Two of these are relatively close to each other while the third is more distant; the subject must press the button corresponding to the more isolated stimulus. Response times in this task show higher correlations with IQ scores than those in Jensen's original procedure, perhaps because it requires more complex forms of spatial judgment.

Inspection time

Another paradigm for measuring processing speed, devised to be relatively independent of response factors, is the method of 'inspection time' (IT). In the standard version of this paradigm (Nettelbeck, 1987; Vickers, Nettelbeck & Wilson, 1972), two vertical lines are shown very briefly on each trial, followed by a pattern mask; the subject must judge which line was shorter. For a given subject, IT is defined as the minimum exposure duration (up to the onset of the mask) for which the lines must be displayed if he or she is to meet a pre-established criterion of accuracy—e.g., nine correct trials out of ten.

Inspection times defined in this way are consistently correlated with measures of psychometric intelligence. In a recent meta-analysis, Kranzler and Jensen (1989) reported an overall correlation of −.30 between IQ scores and IT; this rose to −.55 when corrected for measurement error and attenuation. More recent findings confirm this general result (e.g., Bates & Eysenck, 1993; Deary, 1993). IT usually correlates best with performance subtests of intelligence; its correlation with verbal intelligence is usually weaker and sometimes zero.

One apparent advantage of IT over other chronometric methods is that the task itself seems particularly simple. At first glance, it is hard to imagine that any differences in response strategies or stimulus familiarity could affect the outcome. Nevertheless, it seems that they do. Brian Mackenzie and his colleagues (e.g., Mackenzie, Molloy, Martin, Lovegrove, & McNicol, 1991) discovered that some subjects use apparent-movement cues in the basic IT task while others do not; only in the latter group is IT correlated with intelligence test scores. Moreover, standard IT paradigms require an essentially spatial judgment; it is not surprising, then, that they correlate with intelligence tests which emphasize spatial ability. With this in mind, Mackenzie et al. (1991) devised a *verbal* inspection time task based on Posner's classical same-letter/different-letter paradigm (Posner, Boies, Eichelman, & Taylor, 1969). As predicted, the resulting ITs correlated with verbal but not with spatial intelligence. It is clear that the apparently simple IT task actually involves complex modes of information processing (cf. Chaiken, 1993) that are as yet poorly understood.

Neurological measures

Recent research has begun to explore what seem to be still more direct indices of neural processing. Reed and Jensen (1992) have used measures based on visual evoked potentials (VEP) to assess what they call 'nerve conduction velocity' (NCV). To estimate that velocity, distance is divided by time: each subject's head length (a rough measure of the distance from the eye to the primary visual cortex) is divided by the latency of an early component (N70 or P100) of his or her evoked potential pattern. In a study with 147 college-student subjects, these NCVs correlated $r = .26$ with scores on an unspeeded test of intelligence. (A statistical correction for the restricted range of subjects raised the correlation to .37.) Other researchers have also reported correlations between VEP parameters and intelligence test scores (Caryl, 1994). Interestingly, however, Reed and Jensen (1993) reported that their estimates of 'nerve conduction velocity' were *not* correlated with the same subjects' choice reaction times. Thus while we do not yet understand the basis of the correlation between NCV and psychometric intelligence, it is apparently not just a matter of overall speed.

Problems of interpretation

Some researchers believe that psychometric intelligence, especially g, depends directly on what may be called the 'neural efficiency' of the brain (Eysenck, 1986; Vernon, 1987). They regard the observed correlations between test scores and measures of processing speed as evidence for their view. If choice reaction times, inspection times, and VEP latencies actually do reflect the speed of basic neural processes, such correlations are only to be expected. In fact, however, the observed patterns of correlation are rarely as simple as this hypothesis would predict. Moreover, it is quite possible that high- and low-IQ individuals differ in other ways that affect speeded performance (cf. Ceci, 1990). Those variables include motivation, response criteria (emphasis on speed vs. accuracy), perceptual strategies (cf. Mackenzie et al., 1991), attentional strategies, and—in some cases—differential familiarity with the material itself. Finally, we do not yet know the direction of causation that underlies such correlations. Do high levels of 'neural efficiency' promote the development of intelligence, or do more intelligent people simply find faster ways to carry out perceptual tasks? Or both? These questions are still open.

3 The genes and intelligence

In this section of the report we first discuss individual differences generally, without reference to any particular trait. We then focus on intelligence, as measured by conventional IQ tests or other tests intended to measure general cognitive ability. The different and more controversial topic of group differences will be considered in Section 5.

We focus here on the relative contributions of genes and environments to individual differences in particular traits. To avoid misunderstanding, it must be emphasized from the outset that gene action always involves an environment—at least a biochemical environment, and often an ecological one. (For humans, that ecology is usually interpersonal or cultural.) Thus all genetic effects on the development of observable traits are potentially modifiable by environmental input, though the practicability of making such modifications may be another matter. Conversely, all environmental effects on trait development involve the genes or structures to which the genes have contributed. Thus there is always a genetic aspect to the effects of the environment (cf. Plomin & Bergeman, 1991).

Sources of individual differences

Partitioning the variation

Individuals differ from one another on a wide variety of traits: familiar examples include height, intelligence, and aspects of personality. Those differences are often of considerable social importance. Many interesting questions can be asked about their nature and origins. One such question is the extent to which they reflect differences among the genes of the individuals involved, as distinguished from differences among the environments to which those individuals have been exposed. The issue here is not whether genes and environments are both essential for the development of a given trait (this is always the case), and it is not about the genes or environment of any particular person. We are concerned only with the observed variation of the trait across individuals in a given population. A figure called the 'heritability' (h^2) of the trait represents the proportion of that variation that is associated with genetic differences among the individuals. The remaining variation ($1 - h^2$) is associated with environmental differences and with errors of measurement. These proportions can be estimated by various methods described below.

Sometimes special interest attaches to those aspects of environments that family members have in common (for example, characteristics of the home). The part of the variation that derives from this source, called 'shared' variation or c^2, can also be estimated. Still more refined estimates can be made: c^2 is sometimes subdivided into several kinds of shared variation; h^2 is sometimes subdivided into so-called 'additive' and 'nonadditive' portions (the part that is transmissible from parent to child vs. the part expressed anew in each generation by a unique patterning of genes.) Variation associated with correlations and statistical interactions between genes and environments may also be identifiable. In theory, any of the above estimates may vary with the age of the individuals involved.

A high heritability does not mean that the environment has no impact on the development of a trait, or that learning is not involved. Vocabulary size, for example, is very substantially heritable (and highly correlated with general psychometric intelligence) although every word in an individual's vocabulary is learned. In a society in which plenty of words are available in everyone's environment—especially for individuals who are motivated to seek them out—the number of words that individuals actually learn depends to a considerable extent on their genetic predispositions.

Behavior geneticists have often emphasized the fact that individuals can be active in creating or selecting their own environments. Some describe this process as active or reactive genotype—environment correlation (Plomin, DeFries, & Loehlin, 1977). (The distinction is between the action of the organism in selecting its own environment and the reaction of others to its gene-based traits.) Others suggest that these forms of gene-environment relationship are typical of the way that genes are normally expressed, and simply include them as part of the genetic effect (Roberts, 1967). This is a matter of terminological preference, not a dispute about facts.

How genetic estimates are made

Estimates of the magnitudes of these sources of individual differences are made by exploiting natural and social 'experiments' that combine genotypes and environments in informative ways. Monozygotic (MZ) and dizygotic (DZ) twins, for example, can be regarded as experiments of nature. MZ twins are paired individuals of the same age growing up in the same family who have all their genes in common; DZ twins are otherwise similar pairs who have only half their genes in common. Adoptions, in contrast, are experiments of society. They allow one to compare genetically unrelated persons who are growing up in the same family as well as genetically related persons who are growing up in different families. They can also provide information about genotype-environment correlations: in ordinary families genes and environments are correlated because the same parents provide both, whereas in adoptive families one set of parents provides the genes and another the environment. An experiment involving both nature and society is the study of monozygotic twins who have been reared apart (Bouchard, Lykken, McGue, Segal, & Tellegen, 1990; Pedersen, Plomin, Nesselroade, & McClearn, 1992). Relationships in the families of monozygotic twins also offer unique possibilities for analysis (e.g., R. J. Rose, Harris, Christian, & Nance, 1979). Because these comparisons are subject to different sources of potential error, the results of studies involving several kinds of kinship are often analyzed together to arrive at robust overall conclusions. (For general discussions of behavior genetic methods, see Plomin, DeFries, & McClearn, 1990, or Hay, 1985.)

Results for IQ scores

Parameter estimates

Across the ordinary range of environments in modern Western societies, a sizable part of the variation in intelligence test scores is associated with genetic differences among individuals. Quantitative estimates vary from one study to another, because many are based on small or selective samples. If one simply combines all available correlations in a single analysis, the heritability (h^2) works out to about .50 and the between-family variance (c^2) to about .25 (e.g., Chipuer, Rovine, & Plomin, 1990; Loehlin, 1989). These overall figures are misleading, however, because most of the relevant studies have been done with children. We now know that the heritability of IQ changes with age: h^2 goes up and c^2 goes down from infancy to adulthood

(McCartney, Harris, & Bernieri, 1990; McGue, Bouchard, Iacono, & Lykken, 1993). In childhood h^2 and c^2 for IQ are of the order of .45 and .35; by late adolescence h^2 is around .75 and c^2 is quite low (zero in some studies). Substantial environmental variance remains, but it primarily reflects within-family rather than between-family differences.

These adult parameter estimates are based on a number of independent studies. The correlation between MZ twins reared apart, which directly estimates h2, ranged from .68 to .78 in five studies involving adult samples from Europe and the United States (McGue et al., 1993). The correlation between unrelated children reared together in adoptive families, which directly estimates c^2, was approximately zero for adolescents in two adoption studies (Loehlin, Horn, & Willerman, 1989; Scarr & Weinberg, 1978) and .19 in a third (the Minnesota transracial adoption study: Scarr, Weinberg, & Waldman, 1993).

These particular estimates derive from samples in which the lowest socio-economic levels were under-represented (i.e., there were few very poor families), so the range of between-family differences was smaller than in the population as a whole. This means that we should be cautious in generalizing the findings for between-family effects across the entire social spectrum. The samples were also mostly White, but available data suggest that twin and sibling correlations in African American and similarly selected White samples are more often comparable than not (Loehlin, Lindzey, & Spuhler, 1975).

Why should individual difference in intelligence (as measured by test scores) reflect genetic differences more strongly in adults than they do in children? One possibility is that as individuals grow older their transactions with their environments are increasingly influenced by the characteristics that they bring to those environments themselves, decreasingly by the conditions imposed by family life and social origins. Older persons are in a better position to select their own effective environments, a form of genotype-environment correlation. In any case the popular view that genetic influences on the development of a trait are essentially frozen at conception while the effects of the early environment cumulate inexorably is quite misleading, at least for the trait of psychometric intelligence.

Implications

Estimates of h^2 and c^2 for IQ (or any other trait) are descriptive statistics for the populations studied. (In this respect they are like means and standard deviations.) They are outcome measures, summarizing the results of a great many diverse, intricate, individually variable events and processes, but they can nevertheless be quite useful. They can tell us how much of the variation in a given trait the genes and family environments explain, and changes in them place some constraints on theories of how this occurs. On the other hand they have little to say about specific mechanisms, i.e., about how genetic and environmental differences get translated into individual physiological and psychological differences. Many psychologists and neuroscientists are actively studying such processes; data on heritabilities may give them ideas about what to look for and where or when to look for it.

A common error is to assume that because something is heritable it is necessarily unchangeable. This is wrong. Heritability does not imply immutability. As previously noted, heritable traits can depend on learning, and they may be subject to other environmental effects as well. The value of h^2 can change if the distribution of environments (or genes) in the population is substantially altered. On the other hand, there can be effective environmental changes that do not change heritability at all. If the environment relevant to a given trait improves in a way that affects all members of the population equally, the mean value of the trait will rise without any change in its heritability (because the differences among individuals in the population will stay the same). This has evidently happened for height: the heritability of stature is high, but average heights continue to increase (Olivier, 1980). Something of the sort may also be taking place for IQ scores—the so-called 'Flynn effect' discussed in Section 4.

In theory, different subgroups of a population might have different distributions of environments or genes and hence different values of h^2. This seems not to be the case for high and low IQ levels, for which adult heritabilities appear to be much the same (Saudino, Plomin, Pedersen, & McClearn, 1994). It is also possible that an impoverished or suppressive environment could fail to support the development of a trait, and hence restrict individual variation. This could affect estimates of h^2, c^2, or both, depending on the details of the process. Again (as in the case of whole populations), an environmental factor that affected every member of a subgroup equally might alter the group's mean without affecting heritabilities at all.

Where the heritability of IQ is concerned, it has sometimes seemed as if the findings based on differences between group means were in contradiction with those based on correlations. For example, children adopted in infancy into advantaged families tend to have higher IQs in childhood than would have been expected if they had been reared by their birth mothers; this is a mean difference implicating the environment. Yet at the same time their individual resemblance to their birth mothers persists, and this correlation is most plausibly interpreted in genetic terms. There is no real contradiction: the two findings simply call attention to different aspects of the same phenomenon. A sensible account must include both aspects: there is only a single developmental process, and it occurs in individuals. By looking at means or correlations one learns somewhat different but compatible things about the genetic and environmental contributions to that process (Turkheimer, 1991).

As far as behavior genetic methods are concerned, there is nothing unique

129

about psychometric intelligence relative to other traits or abilities. Any reliably measured trait can be analyzed by these methods, and many traits including personality and attitudes have been. The methods are neutral with regard to genetic and environmental sources of variance: if individual differences on a trait are entirely due to environmental factors, the analysis will reveal this. These methods have shown that genes contribute substantially to individual differences in intelligence test performance, and that their role seems to increase from infancy to adulthood. They have also shown that variations in the unique environments of individuals are important, and that between-family variation contributes significantly to observed differences in IQ scores in childhood although this effect diminishes later on. All these conclusions are wholly consistent with the notion that both genes and environment, in complex interplay, are essential to the development of intellectual competence.

4 Environmental effects on intelligence

The 'environment' includes a wide range of influences on intelligence. Some of those variables affect whole populations, while others contribute to individual differences within a given group. Some of them are social, some are biological; at this point some are still mysterious. It may also happen that the proper interpretation of an environmental variable requires the simultaneous consideration of genetic effects. Nevertheless, a good deal of solid information is available.

Social variables

It is obvious that the cultural environment—how people live, what they value, what they do—has a significant effect on the intellectual skills developed by individuals. Rice farmers in Liberia are good at estimating quantities of rice (Gay & Cole, 1967); children in Botswana, accustomed to story-telling, have excellent memories for stories (Dube, 1982). Both these groups were far ahead of American controls on the tasks in question. On the other hand Americans and other Westernized groups typically out-perform members of traditional societies on psychometric tests, even those designed to be 'culture-fair.'

Cultures typically differ from one another in so many ways that particular differences can rarely be ascribed to single causes. Even comparisons between subpopulations can be difficult to interpret. If we find that middle-class and poor Americans differ in their scores on intelligence tests, it is easy to suppose that the environmental difference has caused the IQ difference (i.e., that growing up in the middle class produces higher psychometric intelligence than growing up poor). But there may also be an opposite direction of causation: individuals can come to be in one environment or another because of differences in their own abilities. Waller (1971) has shown, for example, that adult sons whose IQ scores are above those of their fathers tend to have higher social-class status than those fathers; conversely, sons with IQ scores below their fathers' tend to have lower social-class status. Since all the subjects grew up with their fathers, the IQ differences in this study cannot have resulted from class-related differences in childhood experience. Rather, those differences (or other factors correlated with them) seem to have had an influence on the status that they achieved. Such a result is not surprising, given the relation between test scores and years of education reviewed in Section 2.

Occupation

In Section 2 we noted that intelligence test scores predict occupational level, not only because some occupations require more intelligence than others but also because admission to many professions depends on test scores in the first place. There can also be an effect in the opposite direction, i.e., work-places may affect the intelligence of those who work in them. Kohn and Schooler (1973), who interviewed some 3,000 men in various occupations (farmers, managers, machinists, porters, etc.), argued that more 'complex' jobs produce more 'intellectual flexibility' in the individuals who hold (them. Although the issue of direction of effects was not fully resolved in their study—and perhaps not even in its longitudinal follow-up (Kohn & Schooler, 1983)—this remains a plausible suggestion.

Among other things, Kohn and Schooler's hypothesis may help us understand urban/rural differences. A generation ago these were substantial in the United States, averaging about 6 IQ points or 0.4 standard deviations (Terman & Merrill, 1937; Seashore, Wesman, & Doppelt, 1950). In recent years the difference has declined to about 2 points (Kaufman & Doppelt, 1976; Reynolds, Chastain, Kaufman, & McLean, 1987). In all likelihood this urban/rural convergence primarily reflects environmental changes: a decrease in rural isolation (due to increased travel and mass communications), an improvement in rural schools, the greater use of technology on farms. All these changes can be regarded as increasing the 'complexity' of the rural environment in general or of farm work in particular. (However, processes with a genetic component—e.g., changes in the selectivity of migration from farm to city—cannot be completely excluded as contributing factors.)

Schooling

Attendance at school is both a dependent and an independent variable in relation to intelligence. On the one hand, children with higher test scores are less likely to drop out and more likely to be promoted from grade to grade and then to attend college. Thus the number of years of education that adults complete is roughly predictable from their childhood scores on intelligence tests. On the other hand, schooling itself changes mental abilities, including those abilities measured on psychometric tests. This is obvious for tests like the SAT that are explicitly designed to assess school learning, but it is almost equally true of intelligence tests themselves.

The evidence for the effect of schooling on intelligence test scores takes many forms (Ceci, 1991). When children of nearly the same age go through school a year apart (because of birthday-related admission criteria), those who have been in school longer have higher mean scores. Children who attend school intermittently score below those who go regularly, and test performance tends to drop over the summer vacation. A striking demonstration of this effect appeared when the schools in one Virginia county closed for several years in the 1960s to avoid integration, leaving most Black children with no formal education at all. Compared to controls, the intelligence-test scores of these children dropped by about 0.4 standard deviations (6 points) per missed year of school (Green, Hoffman, Morse, Hayes, & Morgan, 1964).

Schools affect intelligence in several ways, most obviously by transmitting information. The answers to questions like 'Who wrote Hamlet?' and 'What is the boiling point of water?' are typically learned in school, where some pupils learn them more easily and thoroughly than others. Perhaps at least as important are certain general skills and attitudes: systematic problem-solving, abstract thinking, categorization, sustained attention to material of little intrinsic interest, and repeated manipulation of basic symbols and operations. There is no doubt that schools promote and permit the development of significant intellectual skills, which develop to different extents in different children. It is because tests of intelligence draw on many of those same skills that they predict school achievement as well as they do.

To achieve these results, the school experience must meet at least some minimum standard of quality. In very poor schools, children may learn so little that they fall farther behind the national IQ norms for every year of attendance. When this happens, older siblings have systematically lower scores than their younger counterparts. This pattern of scores appeared in at least one rural Georgia school system in the 1970s (Jensen, 1977). Before desegregation, it must have been characteristic of many of the schools attended by Black pupils in the South. In a study based on Black children who had moved to Philadelphia at various ages during this period, Lee (1951) found that their IQ scores went up more than half a point for each year that they were enrolled in the Philadelphia system.

Interventions

Intelligence test scores reflect a child's standing relative to others in his or her age cohort. Very poor or interrupted schooling can lower that standing substantially; are there also ways to raise it? In fact many interventions have been shown to raise test scores and mental ability 'in the short run' (i.e., while the program itself was in progress), but long-run gains have proved more elusive. One noteworthy example of (at least short-run) success was the Venezuelan Intelligence Project (Herrnstein, Nickerson, de Sanchez, & Swets, 1986), in which hundreds of seventh-grade children from under-privileged backgrounds in that country were exposed to an extensive, theoretically-based curriculum focused on thinking skills. The intervention produced substantial gains on a wide range of tests, but there has been no follow-up.

Children who participate in 'Head Start' and similar programs are exposed to various school-related materials and experiences for one or two years. Their test scores often go up during the course of the program, but these gains fade with time. By the end of elementary school, there are usually no significant IQ or achievement-test differences between children who have been in such programs and controls who have not. There may, however, be other differences. Follow-up studies suggest that children who participated in such programs as preschoolers are less likely to be assigned to special education, less likely to be held back in grade, and more likely to finish high school than matched controls (Consortium for Longitudinal Studies, 1983; Darlington, 1986; but see Locurto, 1991).

More extensive interventions might be expected to produce larger and more lasting effects, but few such programs have been evaluated systematically. One of the more successful is the Carolina Abecedarian Project (Campbell & Ramey, 1994), which provided a group of children with enriched environments from early infancy through preschool and also maintained appropriate controls. The test scores of the enrichment-group children were already higher than those of controls at age two; they were still some 5 points higher at age 12, seven years after the end of the intervention. Importantly, the enrichment group also outperformed the controls in academic achievement.

Family environment

No one doubts that normal child development requires a certain minimum level of responsible care. Severely deprived, neglectful, or abusive environments must have negative effects on a great many aspects—including intellectual aspects—of development. Beyond that minimum, however, the role of family experience is now in serious dispute (Baumrind, 1993; Jackson, 1993; Scarr, 1992, 1993). Psychometric intelligence is a case in point. Do differences between children's family environments (within the normal range) produce differences in their intelligence test performance? The problem here is to disentangle causation from correlation. There is no doubt that such variables as resources of the home (Gottfried, 1984) and parents' use of language (Hart & Risley, 1992, in press) are correlated with children's IQ scores, but such correlations may be mediated by genetic as well as (or instead of) environmental factors.

Behavior geneticists frame such issues in quantitative terms. As noted in Section 3, environmental factors certainly contribute to the overall variance of psychometric intelligence. But how much of that variance results from differences between families, as contrasted with the varying experiences of different children in the same family? Between-family differences create what is called 'shared variance' or c^2 (all children in a family share the same home and the same parents). Recent twin and adoption studies suggest that while the value of c^2 (for IQ scores) is substantial in early childhood, it becomes quite small by late adolescence.

These findings suggest that differences in the life styles of families— whatever their importance may be for many aspects of children's lives— make little long-term difference for the skills measured by intelligence tests. We should note, however, that low-income and non-White families are poorly represented in existing adoption studies as well as in most twin samples. Thus it is not yet clear whether these surprisingly small values of (adolescent) c^2 apply to the population as a whole. It remains possible that, across the full range of income and ethnicity, between-family differences have more lasting consequences for psychometric intelligence.

Biological variables

Every individual has a biological as well as a social environment, one that begins in the womb and extends throughout life. Many aspects of that environment can affect intellectual development. We now know that a number of biological factors—malnutrition, exposure to toxic substances, various prenatal and perinatal stressors—result in lowered psychometric intelligence under at least some conditions.

Nutrition

There has been only one major study of the effects of prenatal malnutrition (i.e., malnutrition of the mother during pregnancy) on long-term intellectual development. Stein, Susser, Saenger, and Marolla (1975) analyzed the test scores of Dutch 19-year-old males in relation to a wartime famine that had occurred in the winter of 1944–45, just before their birth. In this very large sample (made possible by a universal military induction requirement), exposure to the famine had no effect on adult intelligence. Note, however, that the famine itself lasted only a few months; the subjects were exposed to it prenatally but not after birth.

In contrast, prolonged malnutrition during childhood does have long-term intellectual effects. These have not been easy to establish, in part because many other unfavorable socioeconomic conditions are often associated with chronic malnutrition (Ricciuti, 1993; but cf. Sigman, 1995). In one intervention study, however, preschoolers in two Guatemalan villages (where undernourishment is common) were given ad lib access to a protein dietary supplement for several years. A decade later, many of these children (namely, those from the poorest socioeconomic levels) scored significantly higher on school-related achievement tests than comparable controls (Pollitt, Gorman, Engle, Martorell, & Rivera, 1993). It is worth noting that the effects of poor nutrition on intelligence may well be indirect. Malnourished children are typically less responsive to adults, less motivated to learn, and less active in exploration than their more adequately nourished counterparts.

Although the degree of malnutrition prevalent in these villages rarely occurs in the United States, there may still be nutritional influences on intelligence. In studies of so-called 'micro-nutrients,' experimental groups of children have been given vitamin/mineral supplements while controls got placebos. In many of these studies (e.g., Schoenthaler, Amos, Eysenck, Peritz, & Yudkin, 1991), the experimental children showed test-score gains that significantly exceeded the controls. In a somewhat different design, Rush, Stein, Susser, and Brody (1980) gave dietary supplements of liquid protein to pregnant women who were thought to be at risk for delivering low birth-weight babies. At one year of age, the babies born to these mothers showed faster habituation to visual patterns than did control infants. (Other research has shown that infant habituation rates are positively correlated with later psychometric test scores: Columbo, 1993.) Although these results are encouraging, there has been no long-term follow-up of such gains.

Lead

Certain toxins have well-established negative effects on intelligence. Exposure to lead is one such factor. In one long-term study (Baghurst et al., 1992; McMichael et al., 1988), the blood lead levels of children growing up near a lead smelting plant were substantially and negatively correlated with intelligence test scores throughout childhood. No 'threshold dose' for the effect of lead appears in such studies. Although ambient lead levels in the United States have been reduced in recent years, there is reason to believe that some American children—especially those in inner cities—may still be at risk from this source (cf. Needleman, Geiger, & Frank, 1985).

Alcohol

Extensive prenatal exposure to alcohol (which occurs if the mother drinks heavily during pregnancy) can give rise to fetal alcohol syndrome, which includes mental retardation as well as a range of physical symptoms. Smaller 'doses' of prenatal alcohol may have negative effects on intelligence even when the full syndrome does not appear. Streissguth, Barr, Sampson, Darby, and Martin (1989) found that mothers who reported consuming more than 1.5 oz. of alcohol daily during pregnancy had children who scored some 5 points below controls at age four. Prenatal exposure to aspirin and antibiotics had similar negative effects in this study.

Perinatal factors

Complications at delivery and other negative perinatal factors may have serious consequences for development. Nevertheless, because they occur only rarely, they contribute relatively little to the population variance of intelligence (Broman, Nichols, & Kennedy, 1975). Down's syndrome, a chromosomal abnormality that produces serious mental retardation, is also rare enough to have little impact on the overall distribution of test scores.

The correlation between birth weight and later intelligence deserves particular discussion. In some cases low birth weight simply reflects premature delivery; in others, the infant's size is below normal for its gestational age. Both factors apparently contribute to the tendency of low-birth-weight infants to have lower test scores in later childhood (Lubchenko, 1976). These correlations are small, ranging from .05 to .13 in different groups (Broman et al., 1975). The effects of low birth weight are substantial only when it is very low indeed (less than 1,500 gm). Premature babies born at these very low birth weights are behind controls on most developmental measures; they often have severe or permanent intellectual deficits (Rosetti, 1986).

Continuously rising test scores

Perhaps the most striking of all environmental effects is the steady worldwide rise in intelligence test performance. Although many psychometricians had noted these gains, it was James Flynn (1984, 1987) who first described them systematically. His analysis shows that performance has been going up ever since testing began. The 'Flynn effect' is now very well documented, not only in the United States but in many other technologically advanced countries. The average gain is about 3 IQ points per decade—more than a full standard deviation since, say, 1940.

Although it is simplest to describe the gains as increases in population IQ, this is not exactly what happens. Most intelligence tests are 'restandardized' from time to time, in part to keep up with these very gains. As part of this process the mean score of the new standardization sample is typically set to 100 again, so the increase more or less disappears from view. In this context, the Flynn effect means that if 20 years have passed since the last time the test was standardized, people who now score 100 on the new version would probably average about 106 on the old one.

The sheer extent of these increases is remarkable, and the rate of gain may even be increasing. The scores of 19-year-olds in the Netherlands, for example, went up more than 8 points—over half a standard deviation—between 1972 and 1982. What's more, the largest gains appear on the types of tests that were specifically designed to be free of cultural influence (Flynn, 1987). One of these is Raven's Progressive Matrices, an untimed nonverbal test that many psychometricians regard as a good measure of *g*.

These steady gains in intelligence test performance have not always been accompanied by corresponding gains in school achievement. Indeed, the relation between intelligence and achievement test scores can be complex. This is especially true for the Scholastic Aptitude Test (SAT), in part because the ability range of the students who take the SAT has broadened over time. That change explains some portion—not all—of the prolonged decline in SAT scores that took place from the mid-1960s to the early 1980s, even as IQ scores were continuing to rise (Flynn, 1984). Meanwhile, however, other more representative measures show that school achievement levels have held steady or in some cases actually increased (Herrnstein & Murray, 1994). The National Assessment of Educational Progress (NAEP), for example, shows that the average reading and math achievement of American 13- and 17-year-olds improved somewhat from the early 1970s to 1990 (Grissmer, Kirby, Berends, & Williamson, 1994). An analysis of these data by ethnic group, reported in Section 5, shows that this small overall increase actually reflects very substantial gains by Blacks and Latinos combined with little or no gain by Whites.

The consistent IQ gains documented by Flynn seem much too large to result from simple increases in test sophistication. Their cause is presently unknown, but three interpretations deserve our consideration. Perhaps the most plausible of these is based on the striking cultural differences between successive generations. Daily life and occupational experience both seem more 'complex' (Kohn & Schooler, 1973) today than in the time of our parents and grandparents. The population is increasingly urbanized; television exposes us to more information and more perspectives on more topics than ever before; children stay in school longer; and almost everyone seems to be encountering new forms of experience. These changes in the complexity of life may have produced corresponding changes in complexity of mind, and hence in certain psychometric abilities.

A different hypothesis attributes the gains to modern improvements in nutrition. Lynn (1990) points out that large nutritionally-based increases in height have occurred during the same period as the IQ gains: perhaps there have been increases in brain size as well. As we have seen, however, the effects of nutrition on intelligence are themselves not firmly established.

The third interpretation addresses the very definition of intelligence. Flynn himself believes that real intelligence—whatever it may be—cannot have increased as much as these data would suggest. Consider, for example, the number of individuals who have IQ scores of 140 or more. (This is slightly above the cutoff used by L. M. Terman [1925] in his famous longitudinal study of 'genius.') In 1952 only 0.38% of Dutch test takers had IQs over 140; in 1982, scored by the same norms, 9.12% exceeded this figure! Judging by these criteria, the Netherlands should now be experiencing 'a cultural renaissance too great to be overlooked' (Flynn, 1987, p. 187). So too should France, Norway, the United States, and many other countries. Because Flynn (1987) finds this conclusion implausible or absurd, he argues that what has risen cannot be intelligence itself but only a minor sort of 'abstract problem solving ability.' The issue remains unresolved.

Individual life experiences

Although the environmental variables that produce large differences in intelligence are not yet well understood, genetic studies assure us that they exist. With a heritability well below 1.00, IQ must be subject to substantial environmental influences. Moreover, available heritability estimates apply only within the range of environments that are well-represented in the present population. We already know that some relatively rare conditions, like those reviewed earlier, have large negative effects on intelligence. Whether there are (now equally rare) conditions that have large positive effects is not known.

As we have seen, there is both a biological and a social environment. For any given child, the social factors include not only an overall cultural/social/ school setting and a particular family but also a unique 'micro-environment' of experiences that are shared with no one else. The adoption studies reviewed in Section 3 show that family variables—differences in parenting style, in the resources of the home etc.—have smaller long-term effects than we once supposed. At least among people who share a given SES level and a given culture, it seems to be unique individual experience that makes the largest environmental contribution to adult IQ differences.

We do not yet know what the key features of those micro-environments may be. Are they biological? Social? Chronic? Acute? Is there something especially important in the earliest relations between the infant and its caretakers? Whatever the critical variables may be, do they interact with other aspects of family life? Of culture? At this point we cannot say, but these questions offer a fertile area for further research.

5 Group differences

Group means have no direct implications for individuals. What matters for the next person you meet (to the extent that test scores matter at all) is that person's own particular score, not the mean of some reference group to which he or she happens to belong. The commitment to evaluate people on their own individual merit is central to a democratic society. It also makes quantitative sense. The distributions of different groups inevitably overlap, with the range of scores within any one group always wider than the mean differences between any two groups. In the case of intelligence test scores, the variance attributable to individual differences far exceeds the variance related to group membership (Jensen, 1980).

Because claims about ethnic differences have often been used to rationalize racial discrimination in the past, all such claims must be subjected to very careful scrutiny. Nevertheless, group differences continue to be the subject of intense interest and debate. There are many reasons for this interest: some are legal and political, some social and psychological. Among other things, facts about group differences may be relevant to the need for (and the effectiveness of) affirmative action programs. But while some recent discussions of intelligence and ethnic differences (e.g., Herrnstein & Murray, 1994) have made specific policy recommendations in this area, we will not do so here. Such recommendations are necessarily based on political as well as scientific considerations, and so fall outside the scope of this report.

Besides European Americans ('Whites'), the ethnic groups to be considered are Chinese and Japanese Americans, Hispanic Americans ('Latinos'), Native Americans ('Indians'), and African Americans ('Blacks'). These groups (we avoid the term 'race') are defined and selfdefined by social conventions based on ethnic origin as well as on observable physical characteristics such as skin color. None of them are internally homogeneous. Asian Americans, for example, may have roots in many different cultures: not only China and Japan but also Korea, Laos, Vietnam, the Philippines, India, and Pakistan. Hispanic Americans, who share a common linguistic tradition, actually differ along many cultural dimensions. In their own minds they may be less 'Latinos' than Puerto Ricans, Mexican Americans, Cuban Americans, or representatives of other Latin cultures. 'Native American' is an even more diverse category, including a great many culturally distinct tribes living in a wide range of environments.

Although males and females are not ethnic or cultural groups, possible sex differences in cognitive ability have also been the subject of widespread interest and discussion. For this reason, the evidence relevant to such differences is briefly reviewed in the next section.

Sex differences

Most standard tests of intelligence have been constructed so that there are no overall score differences between females and males. Some recent studies do report sex differences in IQ, but the direction is variable and the effects are small (Held, Alderton, Foley, & Segall, 1993; Lynn, 1994). This overall equivalence does not imply equal performance on every individual ability. While some tasks show no sex differences, there are others where small differences appear and a few where they are large and consistent.

Spatial and quantitative abilities

Large differences favoring males appear on visual-spatial tasks like mental rotation and spatiotemporal tasks like tracking a moving object through space (Law, Pellegrino, & Hunt, 1993; Linn & Petersen, 1985). The sex difference on mental rotation tasks is substantial: a recent meta-analysis (Masters & Sanders, 1993) puts the effect size at $d = 0.9$. (Effect sizes are measured in standard deviation units. Here, the mean of the male distribution is nearly one standard deviation above that for females.) Males' achievement levels on movement-related and visual-spatial tests are relevant to their generally better performance in tasks that involve aiming and throwing (Jardine & Martin, 1983).

Some quantitative abilities also show consistent differences. Females have a clear advantage on quantitative tasks in the early years of school (Hyde, Fennema, & Lamon, 1990), but this reverses sometime before puberty; males then maintain their superior performance into old age. The math portion of the Scholastic Aptitude Test shows a substantial advantage for males ($d = 0.33$ to 0.50), with many more males scoring in the highest ranges (Benbow, 1988; Halpern, 1992). Males also score consistently higher on tests of proportional and mechanical reasoning (Meehan, 1984; Stanley, Benbow, Brody, Dauber, & Lupkowski, 1992).

Verbal abilities

Some verbal tasks show substantial mean differences favoring females. These include synonym generation and verbal fluency (e.g., naming words that start with a given letter), with effect sizes ranging from $d = 0.5$ to 1.2 (Gordon & Lee, 1986; Hines, 1990). On average females score higher on college achievement tests in literature, English composition, and Spanish (Stanley, 1993); they also excel at reading and spelling, Many more males than females are diagnosed with dyslexia and other reading disabilities (Sutaria, 1985), and there are many more male stutterers (Yairi & Ambrose, 1992). Some memory tasks also show better performance by females, but the size (and perhaps even the direction) of the effect varies with the type of memory being assessed.

Causal factors

There are both social and biological reasons for these differences. At the social level there are both subtle and overt differences between the experiences, expectations, and gender roles of females and males. Relevant environmental differences appear soon after birth. They range from the gender-differentiated toys that children regularly receive to the expectations of adult life with which they are presented, from gender-differentiated household and leisure activities to assumptions about differences in basic ability. Models that include many of these psychosocial variables have been successful in predicting academic achievement (Eccles, 1987).

Many biological variables are also relevant. One focus of current research is on differences in the sizes or shapes of particular neural structures. Numerous sexually dimorphic brain structures have now been identified, and they may well have implications for cognition. There are, for example, sex-related differences in the sizes of some portions of the corpus callosum; these differences are correlated with verbal fluency (Hines, Chiu, McAdams, Bentler, & Lipcamon, 1992). Recent brain imaging studies have found what may be differences in the lateralization of language (Shaywitz et al., 1995). Note that such differences in neural structure could result from differences in patterns of life experience as well as from genetically-driven mechanisms of brain development; moreover, brain development and experience may have bidirectional effects on each other. This research area is still in a largely exploratory phase.

Hormonal influences

The importance of prenatal exposure to sex hormones is well established. Hormones influence not only the developing genitalia but also the brain and certain immune system structures (Geschwind & Galaburda, 1987; Halpern & Cass, 1994). Several studies have tested individuals who were exposed to abnormally high androgen levels in utero, due to a condition known as congenital adrenal hyperplasia (CAH). Adult CAH females score significantly higher than controls on tests of spatial ability (Resnick, Berenbaum, Gottesman & Bouchard, 1986); CAH girls play more with 'boys' toys' and less with 'girls' toys' than controls (Berenbaum & Hines, 1992).

Other experimental paradigms confirm the relevance of sex hormones for performance levels in certain skills. Christiansen and Knussman (1987) found testosterone levels in normal males to be correlated positively (about .20) with some measures of spatial ability and negatively (about −.20) with some measures of verbal ability. Older males given testosterone show improved performance on visual-spatial tests (Janowsky, Oviatt, & Orwoll, 1994). Many similar findings have been reported, though the effects are often nonlinear and complex (Gouchie & Kimura, 1991; Nyborg, 1984). It is clear that any adequate model of sex differences in cognition will have to take both biological and psychological variables (and their interactions) into account.

Mean scores of different ethnic groups

Asian Americans

In the years since the Second World War, Asian Americans—especially those of Chinese and Japanese extraction—have compiled an outstanding record of academic and professional achievement. This record is reflected in school grades, in scores on content-oriented achievement tests like the SAT and GRE, and especially in the disproportionate representation of Asian Americans in many sciences and professions. Although it is often supposed that these achievements reflect correspondingly high intelligence test scores, this is not the case. In more than a dozen studies from the 1960s and 1970s analyzed by Flynn (1991), the mean IQs of Japanese and Chinese American children were always around 97 or 98; none was over 100. Even Lynn (1993), who argues for a slightly higher figure, concedes that the achievements of these Asian Americans far outstrip what might have been expected on the basis of their test scores.

It may be worth noting that the interpretation of test scores obtained by Asians in Asia has been controversial in its own right. Lynn (1982) reported a mean Japanese IQ of 111 while Flynn (1991) estimated it to be between 101 and 105. Stevenson et al. (1985), comparing the intelligence-test performance of children in Japan, Taiwan, and the United States, found no substantive differences at all. Given the general problems of cross-cultural comparison, there is no reason to expect precision or stability in such estimates. Nevertheless, some interest attaches to these particular comparisons: they show that the well-established differences in school achievement among the same three groups (Chinese and Japanese children are much better at math than American children) do not simply reflect differences in psychometric intelligence. Stevenson, Lee, and Stigler (1986) suggest that they result from structural differences in the schools of the three nations as well as from varying cultural attitudes toward learning itself. It is also possible that spatial ability—in which Japanese and Chinese obtain somewhat higher scores than Americans—plays a particular role in the learning of mathematics.

One interesting way to assess the achievements of Chinese and Japanese Americans is to reverse the usual direction of prediction. Data from the 1980 census show that the proportion of Chinese Americans employed in managerial, professional, or technical occupations was 55% and that of Japanese was 46%. (For Whites, the corresponding figure was 34%.) Using the well-established correlation between intelligence test scores and occupational level, Flynn (1991, p. 99) calculated the mean IQ that a hypothetical White group 'would have to have' to predict the same proportions of upper-level employment. He found that the occupational success of these Chinese Americans—whose mean IQ was in fact slightly below 100—was what would be expected of a White group with an IQ of almost 120! A similar calculation for Japanese Americans shows that their level of achievement matched that of Whites averaging 110. These 'overachievements' serve as sharp reminders of the limitations of IQ-based prediction. Various aspects of Chinese American and Japanese American culture surely contribute to them (Schneider, Hieshima, Lee, & Plank, 1994); gene-based temperamental factors could conceivably be playing a role as well (Freedman & Freedman, 1969).

Hispanic Americans

Hispanic immigrants have come to America from many countries. In 1993, the largest Latino groups in the continental United States were Mexican Americans (64%), Puerto Ricans (11%), Central and South Americans (13%), and Cubans (5%) (U.S. Bureau of the Census, 1994). There are very substantial cultural differences among these nationality groups, as well as differences in academic achievement (Duran, 1983; United States National Commission for Employment Policy, 1982). Taken together, Latinos make up the second largest and the fastest-growing minority group in America (Davis, Haub, & Willette, 1983; Eyde, 1992).

In the United States, the mean intelligence test scores of Hispanics typically lie between those of Blacks and Whites. There are also differences in the patterning of scores across different abilities and subtests (Hennessy & Merrifield, 1978; Lesser, Fifer, & Clark, 1965). Linguistic factors play a particularly important role for Hispanic Americans, who may know relatively little English. (By one estimate, 25% of Puerto Ricans and Mexican Americans and at least 40% of Cubans speak English 'not well' or 'not at all' [Rodriguez, 1992]). Even those who describe themselves as bilingual may be at a disadvantage if Spanish was their first and best-learned language. It is not surprising that Latino children typically score higher on the performance than on the verbal subtests of the English-based Wechsler Intelligence Scale for Children—Revised (WISC-R; Kaufman, 1994). Nevertheless, the predictive validity of Latino test scores is not negligible. In young children, the WISC-R has reasonably high correlations with school achievement measures (McShane & Cook, 1985). For high school students of moderate to high English proficiency, standard aptitude tests predict first-year college grades about as well as they do for non-Hispanic Whites (Pennock-Roman, 1992).

Native Americans

There are a great many culturally distinct North American Indian tribes (Driver, 1969), speaking some 200 different languages (Leap, 1981). Many Native Americans live on reservations, which themselves represent a great variety of ecological and cultural settings. Many others presently live in metropolitan areas (Brandt, 1984). Although few generalizations can be appropriate across so wide a range, two or three points seem fairly well established. The first is a specific relation between ecology and cognition: the Inuit (Eskimo) and other groups that live in the arctic tend to have particularly high visual-spatial skills. (For a review see McShane & Berry, 1988.) Moreover, there seem to be no substantial sex differences in those skills (Berry, 1974). It seems likely that this represents an adaptation—genetic or learned or both—to the difficult hunting, traveling, and living conditions that characterize the arctic environment.

On the average, Indian children obtain relatively low scores on tests of verbal intelligence, which are often administered in school settings. The result is a performance-test /verbal-test discrepancy similar to that exhibited by Hispanic Americans and other groups whose first language is generally not English. Moreover, many Indian children suffer from chronic middle-ear infection (otitis media), which is 'the leading identifiable disease among Indians since record-keeping began in 1962' (McShane & Plas, 1984a, p. 84). Hearing loss can have marked negative effects on verbal test performance (McShane & Plas, 1984b).

African Americans

The relatively low mean of the distribution of African American intelligence test scores has been discussed for many years. Although studies using different tests and samples yield a range of results, the Black mean is typically about one standard deviation (about 15 points) below that of Whites (Jensen, 1980; Loehlin et al., 1975; Reynolds et al., 1987). The difference is largest on those tests (verbal or nonverbal) that best represent the general intelligence factor g (Jensen, 1985). It is possible, however, that this differential is diminishing. In the most recent restandardization of the Stanford-Binet test, the Black/White differential was 13 points for younger children and 10 points for older children (Thorndike, Hagen, & Sattler, 1986). In several other studies of children since 1980, the Black mean has consistently been over 90 and the differential has been in single digits (Vincent, 1991). Larger and more definitive studies are needed before this trend can be regarded as established.

Another reason to think the IQ mean might be changing is that the Black/White differential in *achievement* scores has diminished substantially in the last few years. Consider, for example, the mathematics achievement of 17-year-olds as measured by the National Assessment of Educational Progress (NAEP). The differential between Black and White scores, about 1.1 standard deviations as recently as 1978, had shrunk to .65 SD by 1990 (Grissmer et al., 1994) because of Black gains. Hispanics showed similar but smaller gains; there was little change in the scores of Whites. Other assessments of school achievement also show substantial recent gains in the performance of minority children.

In their own analysis of these gains, Grissmer et al. (1994) cite both demographic factors and the effects of public policy. They found the level of parents' education to be a particularly good predictor of children's school achievement; that level increased for all groups between 1970 and 1990, but most sharply for Blacks. Family size was another good predictor (children from smaller families tend to achieve higher scores); here too, the largest change over time was among Blacks. Above and beyond these demographic effects, Grissmer et al. believe that some of the gains can be attributed to the many specific programs, geared to the education of minority children, that were implemented during that period.

Test bias

It is often argued that the lower mean scores of African Americans reflect a bias in the intelligence tests themselves. This argument is right in one sense of 'bias' but wrong in another. To see the first of these, consider how the term is used in probability theory. When a coin comes up heads consistently for any reason it is said to be 'biased,' regardless of any consequences that the outcome may or may not have. In this sense the Black/ White score differential is *ipso facto* evidence of what may be called 'outcome bias.' African Americans are subject to outcome bias not only with respect to tests but along many dimensions of American life. They have the short end of nearly every stick: average income, representation in high-level occupations, health and health care, death rate, confrontations with the legal system, and so on. With this situation in mind, some critics regard the test score differential as just another example of a pervasive outcome bias that characterizes our society as a whole (Jackson, 1975; Mercer, 1984). Although there is a sense in which they are right, this critique ignores the particular social purpose that tests are designed to serve.

From an educational point of view, the chief function of mental tests is as *predictors* (Section 2). Intelligence tests predict school performance fairly well, at least in American schools as they are now constituted. Similarly, achievement tests are fairly good predictors of performance in college and postgraduate settings. Considered in this light, the relevant question is whether the tests have a 'predictive bias' against Blacks. Such a bias would exist if African American performance on the criterion variables (school achievement, college GPA, etc.) were systematically higher than the same subjects' test scores would predict. This is not the case. The actual regression lines (which show the mean criterion performance for individuals who got various scores on the predictor) for Blacks do not lie above those for Whites; there is even a slight tendency in the other direction (Jensen, 1980; Reynolds & Brown, 1984). Considered as predictors of future performance, the tests do not seem to be biased against African Americans.

.

Characteristics of tests

It has been suggested that various aspects of the way tests are formulated and administered may put African Americans at a disadvantage. The language of testing is a standard form of English with which some Blacks may not be familiar; specific vocabulary items are often unfamiliar to Black children; the tests are often given by White examiners rather than by more familiar Black teachers; African Americans may not be motivated to work hard on tests that so clearly reflect White values; the time demands of some tests may be alien to Black culture. (Similar suggestions have been made in connection with the test performance of Hispanic Americans, e.g., Rodriguez, 1992.) Many of these suggestions are plausible, and such mechanisms may play a role in particular cases. Controlled studies have shown, however, that none of them contributes substantially to the Black/White differential under discussion here (Jensen, 1980; Reynolds & Brown, 1984; for a different view see Helms, 1992). Moreover, efforts to devise reliable and valid tests that would minimize disadvantages of this kind have been unsuccessful.

Interpreting group differences

If group differences in test performance do not result from the simple forms of bias reviewed above, what is responsible for them? The fact is that we do not know. Various explanations have been proposed, but none is generally accepted. It is clear, however, that these differences—whatever their origin—are well within the range of effect sizes that can be produced by environmental factors. The Black/White differential amounts to one standard deviation or less, and we know that environmental factors have recently raised mean test scores in many populations by at least that much (Flynn, 1987; see Section 4). To be sure, the 'Flynn effect' is itself poorly understood: it may reflect generational changes in culture, improved nutrition, or other factors as yet unknown. Whatever may be responsible for it, we cannot exclude the possibility that the same factors play a role in contemporary group differences.

Socioeconomic factors

Several specific environmental/cultural explanations of those differences have been proposed. All of them refer to the general life situation in which contemporary African Americans find themselves, but that situation can be described in several different ways. The simplest such hypothesis can be framed in economic terms. On the average, Blacks have lower incomes than Whites; a much higher proportion of them are poor. It is plausible to suppose that many inevitable aspects of poverty—poor nutrition, frequently inadequate prenatal care, lack of intellectual resources—have negative effects on children's developing intelligence. Indeed, the correlation between 'socio-economic status' (SES) and scores on intelligence tests is well-known (White, 1982).

Several considerations suggest that this cannot be the whole explanation. For one thing, the Black/White differential in test scores is not eliminated when groups or individuals are matched for SES (Loehlin et al., 1975). Moreover, the data reviewed in Section 4 suggest that—if we exclude extreme conditions—nutrition and other bioligical factors that may vary with SES account for relatively little of the variance in such scores. Finally, the (relatively weak) relationship between test scores an income is much more complex than a simple SES hypothesis would suggest. The living conditions of children result in part from the accomplishments of their parents: If the skills measured by psychometric tests actually matter for those accomplishments, intelligence is affecting SES rather than the other way around. We do not know the magnitude of these various effects in various populations, but it is clear that no model in which 'SES' directly determines 'IQ' will do.

A more fundamental difficulty with explanations based on economics alone appears from a different perspective. To imagine that any simple income- and education-based index can adequately describe the situation of African Americans is to ignore important categories of experience. The sense of belonging to a group with a distinctive culture—one that has long been the target of oppression—and the awareness or anticipation of racial discrimination are profound personal experiences, not just aspects of socio-economic status. Some of these more deeply rooted differences are addressed by other hypotheses, based on caste and culture.

Caste-like minorities

Most discussions of this issue treat Black/White differences as aspects of a uniquely 'American dilemma' (Myrdal, 1944). The fact is, however, that comparably disadvantaged groups exist in many countries: the Maori in New Zealand, scheduled castes ('untouchables') in India, non-European Jews in Israel, the Burakumin in Japan. All these are 'caste-like' (Ogbu, 1978) or 'involuntary' (Ogbu, 1994) minorities. John Ogbu distinguishes this status from that of 'autonomous' minorities who are not politically or economically subordinated (like Amish or Mormons in the United States), and from that of 'immigrant' or 'voluntary' minorities who initially came to their new homes with positive expectations. Immigrant minorities expect their situations to improve; they tend to compare themselves favorably with peers in the old country, not unfavorably with members of the dominant majority. In contrast, to be born into a caste-like minority is to grow up firmly convinced that one's life will eventually be restricted to a small and poorly-rewarded set of social roles.

Distinctions of caste are not always linked to perceptions of race. In some countries lower and upper caste groups differ by appearance and are assumed to be racially distinct; in others they are not. The social and educational consequences are the same in both cases. All over the world, the children of caste-like minorities do less well in school than upper-caste children and drop out sooner. Where there are data, they have usually been found to have lower test scores as well.

In explaining these findings, Ogbu (1978) argues that the children of caste-like minorities do not have 'effort optimism,' i.e., the conviction that hard work (especially hard schoolwork) and serious commitment on their part will actually be rewarded. As a result they ignore or reject the forms of learning that are offered in school. Indeed they may practice a sort of cultural inversion, deliberately rejecting certain behaviors (such as academic achievement or other forms of 'acting White') that are seen as characteristic of the dominant group. While the extent to which the attitudes described by Ogbu (1978, 1994) are responsible for African American test scores and school achievement has not been empirically established, it does seem that familiar problems can take on quite a different look when they are viewed from an international perspective.

African American culture

According to Boykin (1986, 1994), there is a fundamental conflict between certain aspects of African American culture on the one hand and the implicit cultural commitments of most American schools on the other. 'When children are ordered to do their own work, arrive at their own individual answers, work only with their own materials, they are being sent cultural messages. When children come to believe that getting up and moving about the classroom is inappropriate, they are being sent powerful cultural messages. When children come to confine their 'learning' to consistently bracketed time periods, when they are consistently prompted to tell what they know and not how they feel, when they are led to believe that they are completely responsible for their own success and failure, when they are required to consistently put forth considerable effort for effort's sake on tedious and personally irrelevant tasks . . . then they are pervasively having cultural lessons imposed on them' (1994, p. 125).

In Boykin's view, the combination of constriction and competition that most American schools demand of their pupils conflicts with certain themes in the 'deep structure' of African American culture. That culture includes an emphasis on such aspects of experience as spirituality, harmony, movement, verve, affect, expressive individualism, communalism, orality, and a socially defined time perspective (Boykin, 1986, 1994). While it is not shared by all African Americans to the same degree, its accessibility and familiarity give it a profound influence.

The result of this cultural conflict, in Boykin's view, is that many Black

148

children become alienated from both the process and the products of the education to which they are exposed. One aspect of that process, now an intrinsic aspect of the culture of most American schools, is the psychometric enterprise itself. He argues (Boykin, 1994) that the successful education of African American children will require an approach that is less concerned with talent sorting and assessment, more concerned with talent development.

One further factor should not be overlooked. Only a single generation has passed since the Civil Rights movement opened new doors for African Americans, and many forms of discrimination are still all too familiar in their experience today. Hard enough to bear in its own right, discrimination is also a sharp reminder of a still more intolerable past. It would be rash indeed to assume that those experiences, and that historical legacy, have no impact on intellectual development.

The genetic hypothesis

It is sometimes suggested that the Black/White differential in psychometric intelligence is partly due to genetic differences (Jensen, 1972). There is not much direct evidence on this point, but what little there is fails to support the genetic hypothesis. One piece of evidence comes from a study of the children of American soldiers stationed in Germany after the Second World War (Eyferth, 1961): there was no mean difference between the test scores of those children whose fathers were White and those whose fathers were Black. (For a discussion of possible confounds in this study, see Flynn, 1980.) Moreover, several studies have used blood-group methods to estimate the degree of African ancestry of American Blacks; there were no significant correlations between those estimates and IQ scores (Loehlin, Vandenberg, & Osborne, 1973; Scarr, Pakstis, Katz, & Barker, 1977).

It is clear (Section 3) that genes make a substantial contribution to individual differences in intelligence test scores, at least in the White population. The fact is, however, that the high heritability of a trait within a given group has no necessary implications for the source of a difference between groups (Loehlin et al., 1975). This is now generally understood (e.g., Herrnstein & Murray, 1994). But even though no such implication is *necessary*, some have argued that a high value of h^2 makes a genetic contribution to group differences more *plausible*. Does it?

That depends on one's assessment of the actual difference between the two environments. Consider Lewontin's (1970) well-known example of seeds from the same genetically variable stock that are planted in two different fields. If the plants in field X are fertilized appropriately while key nutrients are withheld from those in field Y, we have produced an entirely environmental group difference. This example works (i.e., h^2 is genuinely irrelevant to the differential between the fields) because the differences between the effective environments of X and Y are both large and consistent. Are the environmental and cultural situations of American Blacks and Whites also substantially and consistently different—different enough to make this a good analogy? If so, the within-group heritability of IQ scores is irrelevant to the issue. Or are those situations similar enough to suggest that the analogy is inappropriate, and that one can plausibly generalize from within-group heritabilities? Thus the issue ultimately comes down to a personal judgment: How different are the relevant life experiences of Whites and Blacks in the United States today? At present, this question has no scientific answer.

6 Summary and conclusions

Because there are many ways to be intelligent, there are also many conceptualizations of intelligence. The most influential approach, and the one that has generated the most systematic research, is based on psychometric testing. This tradition has produced a substantial body of knowledge, though many questions remain unanswered. We know much less about the forms of intelligence that tests do not easily assess: wisdom, creativity, practical knowledge, social skill, and the like.

Psychometricians have successfully measured a wide range of abilities, distinct from one another and yet intercorrelated. The complex relations among those abilities can be described in many ways. Some theorists focus on the variance that all such abilities have in common, which Spearman termed *g* ('general intelligence'); others prefer to describe the same manifold with a set of partially independent factors; still others opt for a multifactorial description with factors hierarchically arranged and something like *g* at the top. Standardized intelligence test scores ('IQs'), which reflect a person's standing in relation to his or her age cohort, are based on tests that tap a number of different abilities. Recent studies have found that these scores are also correlated with information processing speed in certain experimental paradigms (choice reaction time, inspection time, evoked brain potentials, etc.), but the meaning of those correlations is far from clear.

Intelligence test scores predict individual differences in school achievement moderately well, correlating about .50 with grade point average and .55 with the number of years of education that individuals complete. In this context the skills measured by tests are clearly important. Nevertheless, population levels of school achievement are not determined solely or even primarily by intelligence or any other individual-difference variable. The fact that children in Japan and Taiwan learn much more mathematics than their peers in America, for example, can be attributed primarily to differences in culture and schooling rather than in abilities measured by intelligence tests.

Test scores also correlate with measures of accomplishment outside of school, e.g., with adult occupational status. To some extent those correlations result directly from the tests' link with school achievement and from their roles as 'gatekeepers.' In the United States today, high test scores and grades are prerequisites for entry into many careers and professions. This is not quite the whole story, however: a significant correlation between psychometric intelligence and occupational status remains even when measures of education and family background have been statistically controlled. There are also modest (negative) correlations between intelligence test scores and certain undesirable behaviors such as juvenile crime. Those correlations are necessarily low: all social outcomes result from complex causal webs in which psychometric skills are only one factor.

Like every trait, intelligence is the joint product of genetic and environmental variables. Gene action always involves a (biochemical or social) environment; environments always act via structures to which genes have contributed. Given a trait on which individuals vary, however, one can ask what fraction of that variation is associated with differences in their genotypes (this is the *heritability* of the trait) as well as what fraction is associated with differences in environmental experience. So defined, heritability (h^2) can and does vary from one population to another. In the case of IQ, h^2 is markedly lower for children (about .45) than for adults (about .75). This means that as children grow up, differences in test scores tend increasingly to reflect differences in genotype and in individual life experience rather than differences among the families in which they were raised.

The factors underlying that shift—and more generally the pathways by which genes make their undoubted contributions to individual differences in intelligence—are largely unknown. Moreover, the environmental contributions to those differences are almost equally mysterious. We know that both biological and social aspects of the environment are important for intelligence, but we are a long way from understanding how they exert their effects.

One environmental variable with clear-cut importance is the presence of formal schooling. Schools affect intelligence in many ways, not only by transmitting specific information but by developing certain intellectual skills and attitudes. Failure to attend school (or attendance at very poor schools) has a clear negative effect on intelligence test scores. Preschool programs and similar interventions often have positive effects, but in most cases the gains fade when the program is over.

A number of conditions in the biological environment have clear negative consequences for intellectual development. Some of these—very important when they occur—nevertheless do not contribute much to the population variance of IQ scores because they are relatively rare. (Perinatal complications are one such factor.) Exposure to environmental lead has well-documented negative effects; so too does prenatal exposure to high blood levels of alcohol. Malnutrition in childhood is another negative factor for intelligence, but the level at which its effects become significant has not been clearly established. Some studies suggest that dietary supplements of certain micro-nutrients can produce gains even in otherwise well-nourished individuals, but the effects are still controversial and there has been no long-term follow-up.

One of the most striking phenomena in this field is the steady worldwide rise in test scores, now often called the 'Flynn effect.' Mean IQs have increased more than 15 points—a full standard deviation—in the last 50 years, and the rate of gain may be increasing. These gains may result from improved nutrition, cultural changes, experience with testing, shifts in schooling or child-rearing practices, or some other factor as yet unknown.

Although there are no important sex differences in overall intelligence test scores, substantial differences do appear for specific abilities. Males typically score higher on visual-spatial and (beginning in middle childhood) mathematical skills; females excel on a number of verbal measures. Sex hormone levels are clearly related to some of these differences, but social factors presumably play a role as well. As for all the group differences reviewed here, the range of performance within each group is much larger than the mean difference between groups.

Because ethnic differences in intelligence reflect complex patterns, no overall generalization about them is appropriate. The mean IQ scores of Chinese and Japanese Americans, for example, differ little from those of Whites though their spatial ability scores tend to be somewhat higher. The outstanding record of these groups in terms of school achievement and occupational status evidently reflects cultural factors. The mean intelligence test scores of Hispanic Americans are somewhat lower than those of Whites, in part because Hispanics are often less familiar with English. Nevertheless, their test scores, like those of African Americans, are reasonably good predictors of school and college achievement.

African American IQ scores have long averaged about 15 points below those of Whites, with correspondingly lower scores on academic achievement tests. In recent years the achievement-test gap has narrowed appreciably. It is possible that the IQ-score differential is narrowing as well, but this has not been clearly established. The cause of that differential is not known; it is apparently not due to any simple form of bias in the content or administration of the tests themselves. The Flynn effect shows that environmental factors can produce differences of at least this magnitude, but that effect is mysterious in its own right. Several culturally-based explanations of the Black/White IQ differential have been proposed; some are plausible, but so far none has been conclusively supported. There is even less empirical support for a genetic interpretation. In short, no adequate explanation of the differential between the IQ means of Blacks and Whites is presently available.

It is customary to conclude surveys like this one with a summary of what has been established. Indeed, much is now known about intelligence. A near-century of research, most of it based on psychometric methods, has produced an impressive body of findings. Although we have tried to do justice to those findings in this report, it seems appropriate to conclude on a different note. In this contentious arena, our most useful role may be to remind our readers that many of the critical questions about intelligence are still unanswered. Here are a few of those questions:

1. Differences in genetic endowment contribute substantially to individual differences in (psychometric) intelligence, but the pathway by which genes produce their effects is still unknown. The impact of genetic differences appears to increase with age, but we do not know why.

2. Environmental factors also contribute substantially to the development of intelligence, but we do not clearly understand what those factors are or how they work. Attendance at school is certainly important, for example, but we do not know what aspects of schooling are critical.

3. The role of nutrition in intelligence remains obscure. Severe childhood malnutrition has clear negative effects, but the hypothesis that particular 'micronutrients' may affect intelligence in otherwise adequately-fed populations has not yet been convincingly demonstrated.

4. There are significant correlations between measures of information-processing speed and psychometric intelligence, but the overall pattern of these findings yields no easy theoretical interpretation.

5. Mean scores on intelligence tests are rising steadily. They have gone up a full standard deviation in the last 50 years or so, and the rate of gain may be increasing. No one is sure why these gains are happening or what they mean.

6. The differential between the mean intelligence test scores of Blacks and Whites (about one standard deviation, although it may be diminishing) does not result from any obvious biases in test construction and administration, nor does it simply reflect differences in socioeconomic status. Explanations based on factors of caste and culture may be appropriate, but so far have little direct empirical support. There is certainly no such support for a genetic interpretation. At present, no one knows what causes this differential.

7. It is widely agreed that standardized tests do not sample all forms of intelligence. Obvious examples include creativity, wisdom, practical sense, and social sensitivity; there are surely others. Despite the importance of these abilities we know very little about them: how they develop, what factors influence that development, how they are related to more traditional measures.

In a field where so many issues are unresolved and so many questions unanswered, the confident tone that has characterized most of the debate on these topics is clearly out of place. The study of intelligence does not need politicized assertions and recriminations; it needs self-restraint, reflection, and a great deal more research. The questions that remain are socially as well as scientifically important. There is no reason to think them unanswerable, but finding the answers will require a shared and sustained effort as well as the commitment of substantial scientific resources. Just such a commitment is what we strongly recommend.

Note

This is a 'Report of a Task Force Established by the American Psychological Association.'

The Task Force appreciates the contributions of many members of the APA Board of Scientific Affairs (BSA) and the APA Board for the Advancement of Psychology in the Public Interest (BAPPI), who made helpful comments on a preliminary draft of this report. We also wish to acknowledge the indispensable logistical support of the APA Science Directorate during the preparation of the report itself.

Correspondence concerning the report should be addressed to Ulric Neisser, Department of Psychology, Emory University, Atlanta, GA 30322. Electronic mail may be sent via Internet to neisser@fs1.psy.emory.edu.

References

Baghurst, P. A., McMichael, A. J., Wigg, N. R., Vimpani, G. V., Robertson, E. F., Roberts, R. J., & Tong, S.-L. (1992). Environmental exposure to lead and children's intelligence at the age of seven years: The Port Pirie cohort study. *New England Journal of Medicine, 327,* 1279–1284.

Bates, T. C., & Eysenck, H. J. (1993). Intelligence, inspection time, and decision time. *Intelligence, 17,* 523–531.

Baumrind, D. (1993). The average expectable environment is not good enough: A response to Scarr. *Child Development, 64,* 1299–1317.

Benbow, C. P. (1988). Sex differences in mathematical reasoning ability in intellectually talented preadolescents: Their nature, effects, and possible causes. *Behavioral and Brain Sciences, 11,* 169–232.

Berenbaum, S. A., & Hines, M. (1992). Early androgens are related to childhood sex-typed toy preferences. *Psychological Science, 3,* 203–206.

Berry, J. W. (1974). Ecological and cultural factors in spatial perceptual development. In J. W. Berry & P. R. Dasen (Eds.), *Culture and cognition: Readings in cross-cultural psychology* (pp. 129–140). London: Methuen.

Bornstein, M. H. (1989). Stability in early mental development: From attention and information processing in infancy to language and cognition in childhood. In M. H. Bornstein & N. A. Krasnegor (Eds.), *Stability and continuity in mental development* (pp. 147–170). Hillsdale, NJ: Erlbaum.

Bouchard, T. J., Jr., Lykken, D. T., McGue, M., Segal, N. L., & Tellegen, A. (1990). Sources of human psychological differences. The Minnesota study of twins reared apart. *Science, 250,* 223–228.

Boykin, A. W. (1986). The triple quandary and the schooling of Afro-American children. In U. Neisser (Ed.), *The school achievement of minority children* (pp. 57–92). Hillsdale, NJ: Erlbaum.

Boykin, A. W. (1994). Harvesting talent and culture: African-American children and educational reform. In R. Rossi (Ed.), *Schools and students at risk* (pp. 116–138). New York: Teachers College Press.

Brandt, E. A. (1984). The cognitive functioning of American Indian children: A critique of McShane and Plas. *School Psychology Review*, *13*, 74–82.

Brody, N. (1992). *Intelligence* (2nd ed.), San Diego, CA: Academic Press.

Broman, S. H., Nichols, P. L., & Kennedy, W. A. (1975). *Preschool IQ: Prenatal and early developmental correlates*. Hillsdale, NJ: Erlbaum.

Brown, A. L., & French, A. L. (1979). The zone of potential development: Implications for intelligence testing in the year 2000. In R. J. Sternberg & D. K. Detterman (Eds.), *Human intelligence: Perspectives on its theory and measurement* (pp. 217–235). Norwood, NJ: Ablex.

Campbell, F. A., & Ramey, C. T. (1994). Effects of early intervention on intellectual and academic achievement: A follow-up study of children from low-income families. *Child Development*, *65*, 684–698.

Carraher, T. N., Carraher, D., & Schliemann, A. D. (1985). Mathematics in the streets and in schools. *British Journal of Developmental Psychology*, *3*, 21–29.

Carroll, J. B. (1993). *Human cognitive abilities: A survey of factor-analytic studies*. Cambridge, England: University of Cambridge Press.

Caryl, P. G. (1994). Early event-related potentials correlate with inspection time and intelligence. *Intelligence*, *18*, 15–46.

Ceci, S. J. (1990). *On intelligence . . . more or less: A bioecological treatise on intellectual development*. Englewood Cliffs, NJ: Prentice Hall.

Ceci, S. J. (1991). How much does schooling influence general intelligence and its cognitive components? A reassessment of the evidence. *Developmental Psychology*, *27*, 703–722.

Ceci, S. J., & Liker, J. (1986). A day at the races: A study of IQ, expertise, and cognitive complexity. *Journal of Experimental Psychology: General*, *115*, 255–266.

Chaiken, S. R. (1993). Two models for an inspection time paradigm: Processing distraction and processing speed versus processing speed and asymptotic strength. *Intelligence*, *17*, 257–283.

Chipuer, H. M., Rovine, M., & Plomin, R. (1990). LISREL modelling: Genetic and environmental influences on IQ revisited. *Intelligence*, *14*, 11–29.

Christal, R. E., Tirre, W., & Kyllonen, P. (1984). Two for the money: Speed and level scores from a computerized vocabulary test. In G. Lee & T. Ulrich (Eds.), *Proceedings, Psychology in the Department of Defense, Ninth Annual Symposium* (USAFA TR 8–2). Colorado Springs, CO: U.S. Air Force Academy.

Christiansen, K., & Knussmann, R. (1987). Sex hormones and cognitive functioning in men. *Neuropsychobiology*, *18*, 27–36.

Columbo, J. (1993). *Infant cognition: Predicting later intellectual functioning*. Newbury Park, CA: Sage.

Consortium for Longitudinal Studies. (1983). *As the twig is bent . . . lasting effects of preschool programs*. Hillsdale, NJ: Erlbaum.

Cronbach, L. J., & Snow, R. E. (1977). *Aptitudes and instructional methods*. New York: Irvington.

Darlington, R. B. (1986). Long-term effects of preschool programs. In U. Neisser (Ed.), *The school achievements of minority children* (pp. 159–167). Hillsdale, NJ: Erlbaum.

Davis, C., Haub, C., & Willette, J. (1983). U.S. Hispanics: Changing the face of America. *Population Bulletin*, *38*(No. 3).

Deary, I. J. (1993). Inspection time and WAIS-R IQ subtypes: A confirmatory factor analysis study. *Intelligence*, *17*, 223–236.

Deary, I. J. (1995). Auditory inspection time and intelligence: What is the causal direction? *Developmental Psychology*, *31*, 237–250.

Driver, H. E. (1969). *Indians of North America*. Chicago: University of Chicago Press.

Dube, E. F. (1982). Literacy, cultural familiarity, and 'intelligence' as determinants of story recall. In U. Neisser (Ed.), *Memory observed: Remembering in natural contexts* (pp. 274–292). New York: Freeman.

Duran, R. P. (1983). *Hispanics' education and background: Prediction of college achievement*. New York: College Entrance Examination Board.

Eccles, J. S. (1987). Gender roles and women's achievement-related decisions. *Psychology of Women Quarterly*, *11*, 135–172.

Eyde, L. D. (1992). Introduction to the testing of Hispanics in industry and research. In K. F. Geisinger (Ed.), *Psychological testing of Hispanics* (pp. 167–172). Washington, DC: American Psychological Association.

Eyferth, K. (1961). Leistangen verchiedener Gruppen von Besatzungskindern im Hamburg-Wechsler Intelligentztest fur Kinder (HAWIK) [The performance of different groups of occupation children in the Hamburg-Wechsler Intelligence Test for Children]. *Archive fur die gesamte Psychologie*, *113*, 222–241.

Eysenck, H. (1973). *The measurement of intelligence*. Baltimore: Williams & Wilkins.

Eysenck, H. J. (1986). Inspection time and intelligence: A historical introduction. *Personality and Individual Differences*, *7*, 603–607.

Feuerstein, R. (1980). *Instrumental enrichment: An intervention program for cognitive modifiability*: Baltimore: University Park Press.

Flynn, J. R. (1980). *Race, IQ, and Jensen*. London: Routledge & Kegan Paul.

Flynn, J. R. (1984). The mean IQ of Americans: Massive gains 1932 to 1978. *Psychological Bulletin*, *95*, 29–51.

Flynn, J. R. (1987). Massive IQ gains in 14 nations: What IQ tests really measure. *Psychological Bulletin*, *101*, 171–191.

Flynn, J. R. (1991). *Asian-Americans: Achievement beyond IQ*. Hillsdale, NJ: Erlbaum.

Frearson, W. M., & Eysenck, H. J. (1986). Intelligence, reaction time [RT], and a new 'odd-man-out' RT paradigm. *Personality and Individual Differences*, *7*, 807–817.

Freedman, D. G., & Freedman, N. C. (1969). Behavioral differences between Chinese-American and European-American newborns. *Nature*, *224*, 1227.

Gardner, H. (1983). *Frames of mind: The theory of multiple intelligences*. New York: Basic Books.

Gay, J., & Cole, M. (1967). *The new mathematics and an old culture. A study of learning among the Kpelle of Liberia*. New York: Holt, Rhinchart & Winston.

Geschwind, N., & Galaburda, A. M. (1987). *Cerebral lateralization Biological mechanisms, associations, and pathology*. Cambridge, MA: MIT Press.

Gordon, H. W., & Lee, P. (1986). A relationship between gonadotropins and visuospatial function. *Neuropsychologia*, *24*, 563–576.

Gottfried, A. W. (Ed.), (1984). *Home environment and early cognitive development: Longitudinal research*. New York: Academic Press.

Gouchie, C., & Kimura, D. (1991). The relationship between testosterone levels and cognitive ability patterns. *Psychoneuroendocrinology*, *16*, 323–334.

Gould, S. J. (1978). Morton's ranking of races by cranial capacity: Unconscious manipulation of data may be a scientific norm. *Science*, *200*, 503–509.

Green, R. L., Hoffiman, L. T., Morse, R., Hayes, M. E., & Morgan, R. F. (1964). *The educational status of children in a district without public schools* (Cooperative

Research Project No. 2321). Washington, DC: Office of Education, U.S. Department of Health, Education, and Welfare.

Grissmer, D. W., Kirby, S. N., Berends, M., & Williamson, S. (1994). *Student achievement and the changing American family*. Santa Monica, CA: RAND Corporation.

Gustafsson, J. E. (1984). A unifying model for the structure of intellectual abilities. *Intelligence, 8,* 179–203.

Haier, R. J. (1993). Cerebral glucose metabolism and intelligence. In P. A. Vernon (Ed.), *Biological approaches to the study of human intelligence* (pp. 317–332). Norwood, NJ: Ablex.

Halpern, D. (1992). *Sex differences in cognitive abilities* (2nd ed.), Hillsdale, NJ: Erlbaum.

Halpern, D. F., & Cass, M. (1994). Laterality, sexual orientation, and immune system functioning: Is there a relationship? *International Journal of Neuroscience, 77,* 167–180.

Hart, B., & Risley, T. R. (1992). American parenting of language-learning children: Persisting differences in family-child interactions observed in natural home environments. *Developmental Psychology, 28,* 1096–1105.

Hart, B., & Risley, T. R. (in press). *Meaningful differences in the everyday experience of young American children*. Baltimore: P. H. Brookes.

Hay, D. A. (1985). *Essentials of behavior genetics*. Melbourne, Australia: Blackwell.

Heath, S. B. (1983). *Ways with words*. New York: Cambridge University Press.

Held, J. D., Alderton, D. E., Foley, P. P., & Segall, D. O. (1993). Arithmetic reasoning gender differences: Explanations found in the Armed Services Vocational Aptitude Battery (ASVAB). *Learning and Individual Differences, 5,* 171–186.

Helms, J. E. (1992). Why is there no study of cultural equivalence in standardized cognitive ability testing? *American Psychologist, 47,* 1083–1101.

Hennessy, J. J., & Merrifield, P. R. (1978). Ethnicity and sex distinctions in patterns of aptitude factor scores in a sample of urban high school seniors. *American Educational Research Journal, 15,* 385–389.

Herrnstein, R. J., & Murray C. (1994). *The bell curve: Intelligence and class structure in American life*. New York: Free Press.

Hernstein, R. J., Nickerson R. S., de Sanchez, M., & Swets, J. A. (1986). Teaching thinking skills. *American Psychologist, 41,* 1279–1289.

Hines, M. (1990). Gonadal hormones and human cognitive development. In. J. Balthazart (Ed.), *Hormones, brains, and behaviors in vertebrates: 1. Sexual differentiation, neuroanatomical aspects, neurotransmitters, and neuropeptides,* (pp. 51–63). Basel, Switzerland: Karger.

Hines, M., Chiu, L., McAdams, L. A., Bentler, M. P., & Lipcamon, J. (1992). Cognition and the corpus callosum: Verbal fluency, visuospatial ability, language lateralization related to midsagittal surface areas of the corpus callosum. *Behavioral Neuroscience, 106,* 3–14.

Hunt, E. (1978). Mechanics of verbal ability. *Psychological Review, 85,* 109–130.

Hunter, J. E. (1983). A causal analysis of cognitive ability, job knowledge, job performance, and supervisor ratings. In F. Landy, S. Zedeck, & J. Cleveland (Eds.), *Performance measurement and theory* (pp. 257–266). Hillsdale, NJ: Erlbaum.

Hyde, J., Fennema, E., & Lamon, S. J. (1990). Gender differences in mathematics performance: A meta-analysis. *Psychological Bulletin, 107,* 139–155.

Jackson, G. D. (1975). On the report of the Ad Hoc Committee on Educational Uses of Tests with Disadvantaged Students: Another psychological view from the Association of Black Psychologists. *American Psychologist, 30*, 88–93.

Jackson, J. F. (1993). Human behavioral genetics, Scarr's theory, and her views on interventions: A critical review and commentary on their implications for African American children. *Child Development, 64*, 1318–1332.

Jackson, M., & McClelland, J. (1979). Processing determinants of reading speed. *Journal of Experimental Psychology: General, 108*, 151–181.

Janowsky, J. S., Oviatt, S. K., & Orwoll, E. S. (1994). Testosterone influences spatial cognition in older men. *Behavioral Neuroscience, 108*, 325–332.

Jardine, R., & Martin, N. G. (1983). Spatial ability and throwing accuracy. *Behavior Genetics, 13*, 331–340.

Jencks, C. (1979). *Who gets ahead? The determinants of economic success in America.* New York: Basic Books.

Jensen, A. R. (1972). *Genetics and education.* New York: Harper & Row.

Jensen, A. R. (1977). Cumulative deficit in IQ of Blacks in the rural South. *Developmental Psychology, 13*, 184–191.

Jensen, A. R. (1980). *Bias in mental testing.* New York: Free Press.

Jensen, A. R. (1985). The nature of the black-white difference on various psychometric tests: Spearman's hypothesis. *Behavioral and Brain Sciences, 8*, 193–263.

Jensen, A. R. (1987). Individual differences in the Hick paradigm. In P. A. Vernon (Ed.), *Speed of information processing and intelligence* (pp. 101–175). Norwood, NJ: Ablex.

Jensen, A. R. (1993). Test validity: g vs. 'tacit knowledge.' *Current Directions in Psychological Science, 2*, 9–10.

Jones, H. E., and Bayley, N. (1941). The Berkeley Growth Study. *Child Development, 12*, 167–173.

Kaufman, A. S. (1994). *Intelligent testing with the WISC-III.* New York: Wiley.

Kaufman, A. S., & Doppelt, J. E. (1976). Analysis of WISC-R standardization data in terms of the stratification variables. *Child Development, 47*, 165–171.

Kohn, M. L., & Schooler, C. (1973). Occupational experience and psychological functioning: An assessment of reciprocal effects. *American Sociological Review, 38*, 97–118.

Kohn, M. L., & Schooler, C. (1983). *Work and personality: An inquiry into the impact of social stratification.* Norwood, NJ: Ablex.

Kranzler, J., & Jensen, A. R. (1989). Inspection time and intelligence: A meta-analysis. *Intelligence, 13*, 329–347.

Lave, J. (1988). *Cognition in practice.* New York: Cambridge University Press.

Law, D. J., Pellegrino, J. W., & Hunt, E. B. (1993). Comparing the tortoise and the hare: Gender differences and experience in dynamic spatial reasoning tasks. *Psychological Science, 4*, 35–40.

Leap, W. L. (1981). American Indian languages. In C. Ferguson & S. B. Heath (Eds.), *Language in the USA.* Cambridge, England: Cambridge University Press.

Lee, E. S. (1951). Negro intelligence and selective migration: A Philadelphia test of the Klineberg hypothesis. *American Sociological Review, 16*, 227–232.

Lesser, G. S., Fifer, G., & Clark, D. H. (1965). Mental abilities of children from different social-class and cultural groups. *Monographs of the Society for Research in Child Development, 30*(Whole No. 102).

Lewontin, R. (1970). Race and intelligence. *Bulletin of the Atomic Scientists, 26*, 2–8.

Linn, M. C., & Petersen, A. C. (1985). Emergence and characterization of sex differences in spatial ability: A meta-analysis. *Child Development, 56*, 1479–1498.

Locurto, C. (1991). Beyond IQ in preschool programs? *Intelligence, 15*, 295–312.

Loehlin, J. C. (1989). Partitioning environmental and genetic contributions to behavioral development. *American Psychologist, 10*, 1285–1292.

Loehlin, J. C., Horn, J. M., & Willerman, L. (1989). Modeling IQ change: Evidence from the Texas Adoption Project. *Child Development, 60*, 993–1004.

Loehlin, J. C., Lindzey, G., & Spuhler, J. N. (1975). *Race differences in intelligence.* New York: Freeman.

Loehlin, J. C., Vandenberg, S. G., & Osborne, R. T. (1973). Blood group genes and Negro-White ability differences. *Behavior Genetics, 3*, 263–270.

Longstreth, L. E. (1984). Jensen's reaction-time investigations of intelligence: A critique. *Intelligence, 8*, 139–160.

Lubchenko, L. O. (1976). *The high-risk infant.* Philadelphia: Saunders.

Lynn, R. (1982). IQ in Japan and the United States shows a growing disparity. *Nature, 297*, 222–223.

Lynn, R. (1990). The role of nutrition in secular increases in intelligence. *Personality and Individual Differences, 11*, 273–285.

Lynn, R. (1993). Oriental Americans: Their IQ, educational attainment, and socioeconomic status. *Personality and Individual Differences, 15*, 237–242.

Lynn, R. (1994). Sex differences in intelligence and brain size: A paradox resolved. *Personality and Individual Differences, 17*, 257–271.

Mackenzie, B., Molloy, E., Martin, F., Lovegrove, W., & McNicol, D. (1991). Inspection time and the content of simple tasks: A framework for research on speed of information processing. *Australian Journal of Psychology, 43*, 37–43.

Masters, M. S., & Sanders, B. (1993). Is the gender difference in mental rotation disappearing? *Behavior Genetics, 23*, 337–341.

McCall, R. B., & Garriger, M. S. (1993). A meta-analysis of infant habituation and recognition memory performance as predictors of later IQ. *Child Development, 64*, 57–79.

McCartney, K., Harris, M. J., & Bernieri, F. (1990). Growing up and growing apart: A developmental meta-analysis of twin studies. *Psychological Bulletin, 107*, 226–237.

McGue, M., Bouchard, T. J., Jr., Iacono, W. G., & Lykken, D. T. (1993). Behavioral genetics of cognitive ability: A life-span perspective. In R. Plomin & G. E. McClearn (Eds.), *Nature, nurture, & psychology* (pp. 59–76). Washington, DC: American Psychological Association.

McMichael, A. J., Baghurst, P. A., Wigg, N. R., Vimpani, G. V., Robertson, E. F., & Roberts, R. J. (1988). Port Pirie cohort study: Environmental exposure to lead and children's abilities at the age of four years. *New England Journal of Medicine, 319*, 468–475.

McShane, D. A., & Berry, J. W. (1988). Native North Americans: Indian and Inuit abilities. In S. H. Irvine & J. W. Berry (Eds.), *Human abilities in cultural context* (pp. 385–426). New York: Cambridge University Press.

McShane, D. A., & Cook, V. J. (1985). Transcultural intellectual assessment: Performance by Hispanics on the Wechsler Scales. In B. B. Wolman (Ed.), *Handbook of intelligence: Theories, measurements, and applications.* New York: Wiley.

McShane, D. A., & Plas, J. M. (1984a). Response to a critique of the McShane & Plas review of American Indian performance on the Wechsler Intelligence Scales. *School Psychology Review, 13*, 83–88.

McShane, D. A., & Plas, J. M. (1984b). The cognitive functioning of American Indian children: Moving from the WISC to the WISC-R. *School Psychology Review, 13,* 61–73.

Meehan, A. M. (1984). A meta-analysis of sex differences in formal operational thought. *Child Development, 55,* 1110–1124.

Mercer, J. R. (1984). What is a racially and culturally nondiscriminatory test? A sociological and pluralistic perspective. In C. R. Reynolds & R. T. Brown (Eds.), *Perspectives on bias in mental testing.* New York: Plenum Press.

Moffitt, T. E., Caspi, A., Harkness, A. R., & Silva, P. A. (1993). The natural history of change in intellectual performance: Who changes? How much? Is it meaningful? *Journal of Child Psychology and Psychiatry, 34,* 455–506.

Moffitt, T. E., Gabrielli, W. F., Mednick, S. A., & Schulsinger, F. (1981). Socioeconomic status, IQ, and delinquency. *Journal of Abnormal Psychology, 90,* 152–156.

Myrdal, G. (1944). *An American dilemma: The Negro problem and modern democracy.* New York: Harper.

Needleman, H. L., Geiger, S. K., & Frank, R. (1985). Lead and IQ scores: A reanalysis. *Science, 227,* 701–704.

Neisser, U. (1976). General, academic, and artificial intelligence. In L. B. Resnick (Ed.), *The nature of intelligence* (pp. 135–144). Hillsdale, NJ: Erlbaum.

Nettelbeck, T. (1987). Inspection time and intelligence. In P. A. Vernon (Ed.), *Speed of information-processing and intelligence* (pp. 295–346). Norwood, NJ: Ablex.

Nyborg, H. (1984). Performance and intelligence in hormonally different groups. In G. J. De Vries, J. DeBruin, H. Uylings, & M. Cormer (Eds.), *Progress in brain research* (Vol. 61, pp. 491–508). Amsterdam: Elsevier Science.

Ogbu, J. U. (1978). *Minority education and caste: The American system in cross-cultural perspective.* New York: Academic Press.

Ogbu, J. U. (1994). From cultural differences to differences in cultural frames of reference. In P. M. Greenfield & R. R. Cocking (Eds.), *Cross-cultural roots of minority child development* (pp. 365–391). Hillsdale, NJ: Erlbaum.

Okagaki, L., & Sternberg, R. J. (1993). Parental beliefs and children's school performance. *Child Development, 64,* 36–56.

Olivier, G. (1980). The increase of stature in France. *Journal of Human Evolution, 9,* 645–649.

Pascual-Leone, J., & Ijaz, H. (1989). Mental capacity testing as form of intellectual-developmental assessment. In R. J. Samuda, S. L. Kong, et al. (Eds.), *Assessment and placement of minority students.* Toronto, Ontario, Canada: Hogrefe & Huber.

Pedersen, N. L., Plomin, R., Nesselroade, J. R., & McClearn, G. E. (1992). A quantitative genetic analysis of cognitive abilities during the second half of the life span. *Psychological Science, 3,* 346–353.

Pennock-Roman, M. (1992). Interpreting test performance in selective admissions for Hispanic students. In K. F. Geisinger (Ed.), *Psychological testing of Hispanics* (pp. 95–135). Washington, DC: American Psychological Association.

Piaget, J. (1972). *The psychology of intelligence,* Totowa, NJ: Littlefield Adams.

Plomin, R., & Bergeman, C. S. (1991). The nature of nurture: Genetic influence on 'environmental' measures. *Behavioral and Brain Sciences, 14,* 373–427.

Plomin, R., DeFries, J. C., & Loehlin, J. C. (1977). Genotype-environment interaction and correlation in the analysis of human behavior. *Psychological Bulletin, 84,* 309–322.

Plomin, R., DeFries, J. C., & McClearn (1990). *Behavioral genetics: A primer* (2nd ed.), New York: Freeman.

Pollitt, E., Gorman, K. S., Engle, P. L., Martorell, R., & Rivera, J. (1993). Early supplementary feeding and cognition. *Monographs of the Society for Research in Child Development, 58*(Serial No. 235).

Posner, M. I., Boies, S. J., Eichelman, W. H., & Taylor, R. L. (1969). Retention of visual and name codes of single letters. *Journal of Experimental Psychology, 79,* 1–16.

Reed, T. E., & Jensen, A. R. (1992). Conduction velocity in a brain nerve pathway of normal adults correlate with intelligence level. *Intelligence, 16,* 259–272.

Reed, T. E., & Jensen, A. R. (1993). Choice reaction time and visual pathway conduction velocity both correlates with intelligence but appear not to correlate with each other: Implications for information processing. *Intelligence, 17,* 191–203.

Rehberg, R. A., & Rosenthal, E. R. (1978). *Class and merit in the American high school.* New York: Longman.

Resnick, S. M., Berenbaum, S. A., Gottesman, I. I., & Bouchard, T. J., Jr. (1986). Early hormonal influences on cognitive functioning in congenital adrenal hyperplasia. *Developmental Psychology, 22,* 191–198.

Reynolds, C. R., & Brown, R. T. (1984). Bias in mental testing: An introduction to the issues. In C. R. Reynolds & R. T. Brown (Eds.), *Perspectives on bias in mental testing* (pp. 1–39). New York: Plenum Press.

Reynolds, C. R., Chastain, R. L., Kaufman, A. S., & McLean, J. E. (1987). Demographic characteristics and IQ among adults: Analysis of the WAIS-R standardization sample as a function of the stratification variables. *Journal of School Psychology, 25,* 323–342.

Ricciuti, H. N. (1993). Nutrition and mental development. *Current Directions in Psychological Science, 2,* 43–46.

Roberts, R. C. (1967). Some concepts and methods in quantitative genetics. In J. Hirsch (Ed.), *Behavior-genetic analysis* (pp. 214–257). New York: McGraw-Hill.

Rodriguez, O. (1992). Introduction to technical and societal issues in the psychological testing of Hispanics. In K. F. Geisinger (Ed.), *Psychological testing of Hispanics* (pp. 11–15). Washington, DC: American Psychological Association.

Rose, R. J., Harris, E. L., Christian, J. c., & Nance, W. E. (1979). Genetic variance in non-verbal intelligence: Data from the kinship of identical twins. *Science, 205,* 1153–1155.

Rose, S. A., & Feldman, J. (1995). The prediction of IQ and specific cognitive abilities at 11 years from infancy measures. *Developmental Psychology, 31,* 685–696.

Rosetti, L. (1986). *High risk infants: Identification, assessment, and intervention.* Boston: Little Brown.

Rush, D., Stein, Z, Susser, M., & Brody, N. (1980). Outcome at one year of age: Effects on somatic and psychological measures. In D. Rush, Z. Stein, & M. Susser (Eds.), *Diet in pregnancy: A randomized controlled trial of nutritional supplements.* New York: Liss.

Saudino, K. J., Plomin, R., Pedersen, N. L., & McClearn, G. E. (1994). The etiology of high and low cognitive ability during the second half of the life span. *Intelligence, 19*, 359–371.

Scarr, S. (1992). Developmental theories for the 1990s: Development and individual differences. *Child Development, 63*, 1–19.

Scarr, S. (1993). Biological and cultural diversity: The legacy of Darwin for development. *Child Development, 64*, 1333–1353.

Scarr, S., Pakstis, A. J., Katz, S. H., & Barker, W. B. (1977). Absence of a relationship between degree of White ancestry and intellectual skills within a Black population. *Human Genetics, 39*, 69–86.

Scarr, S., & Weinberg, R. A. (1978). The influence of 'family background' on intellectual attainment. *American Sociological Review, 43*, 674–692.

Scarr, S., Weinberg, R. A., & Waldman, I. D. (1993). IQ correlations in transracial adoptive families. *Intelligence, 17*, 541–555.

Schmidt, F. L., & Hunter, J. E. (1993). Tacit knowledge, practical intelligence, and job knowledge. *Current Directions in Psychological Science, 2*, 8–9.

Schneider, B., Hieshima, J. A., Lee, S., & Plank, S. (1994). East-Asian academic success in the United States: Family, school, and cultural explanations. In P. M. Greenfield & R. R. Cocking (Eds.), *Cross-cultural roots of minority child development* (pp. 332–350). Hillsdale, NJ: Erlbaum.

Schoenthaler, S. J., Amos, S. P., Eysenck, H. J., Peritz, E., & Yudkin, J. (1991). Controlled trial of vitamin-mineral supplementation: Effects on intelligence and performance. *Personality and Individual Differences, 12*, 351–362.

Seashore, H., Wesman, A., & Doppelt, J. (1950). The standardization of the Wechsler Intelligence Scale for Children. *Journal of Consulting Psychology, 14*, 99–110.

Serpell, R. (1974). *Estimates of intelligence in a rural community of Eastern Zambia: Human Development Research Unit Reports, 25*, Mimeo, Lusaka: University of Zambia.

Serpell, R. (1979). How specific are perceptual skills? A cross-cultural study of pattern reproduction. *British Journal of Psychology, 70*, 365–380.

Shaywitz, B. A., Shaywitz, S. E., Pugh, K. R., Constable, R. T., Skudlarski, P., Fulbright, R. K., Bronen, R. A., Fletcher, J. M., Shankweller, D. P., Katz, L., & Gore, J. C. (1995). Sex differences in the functional organization of the brain for language. *Nature, 373*, 607–609.

Sigman, M. (1995). Nutrition and child development: More food for thought. *Current Directions in Psychological Science, 4*, 52–55.

Spearman, C. (1927). *The abilities of man.* New York: Macmillan.

Stanley, J. (1993). Boys and girls who reason well mathematically. In G. R. Bock and K. Ackrill (Eds.), *The origins and development of high ability.* Chichester, England: Wiley.

Stanley, J. C., Benbow, C. P., Brody, L. E., Dauber, S., & Lupkowski, A. (1992). Gendre differences on eighty-six nationally standardized aptitude and achievement tests. In N. Colangelo, S. G. Assouline, & D. L. Ambroson (Eds.), *Talent development, Vol. 1: Proceedings from the 1991 Henry B. and Jocelyn Wallace National Research Symposium on Talent Development.* Unionville, NY: Trillium Press.

Stein, Z., Susser, M., Saenger, G., & Marolla, F. (1975). *Famine and human development: The Dutch hunger winter of 1944–45.* New York: Oxford University Press.

Sternberg, R. J. (1977). *Intelligence, information processing, and analogical reasoning: The componential analysis of human abilities.* Hillsdale, NJ: Eribaum.

Sternberg, R. J. (1985). *Beyond IQ: A triarchic theory of human intelligence*. New York: Cambridge University Press.

Sternberg, R. J. (Ed.). (1994). *Encyclopedia of human intelligence*. New York: MacMillan.

Sternberg, R. J., & Detterman, D. K. (Eds.). (1986). *What is intelligence? Contemporary viewpoints on its nature and definition*. Norwood, NJ: Ablex.

Sternberg, R. J., & Wagner, R. K. (1993). The geocentric view of intelligence and job performance is wrong. *Current Directions in Psychological Science, 2*, 1–4.

Sternberg, R. J., Wagner, R. K., Williams, W. M., & Horvath, J. A. (1995). Testing common sense. *American Psychologist, 50*, 912–927.

Stevenson, H. W., Lee, S. Y., & Stigler, J. W. (1986). Mathematics achievement of Chinese, Japanese, and American children. *Science, 231*, 693–699.

Stevenson, H. W., & Stigler, J. W. (1992). *The learning gap*. New York: Summit Books.

Stevenson, H. W., & Stigler, J. W., Lee, S. Y., Lucker, G. W., Kitamura, S., & Hsu, C. C. (1985). Cognitive performance and academic achievement of Japanese, Chinese, and American children. *Child Development, 56*, 718–734.

Streissguth, A. P., Barr, H. M., Sampson, P. D., Darby, B. L., & Martin, D. C. (1989). IQ at age 4 in relation to maternal alcohol use and smoking during pregnancy. *Developmental Psychology, 25*, 3–11.

Super, C. M. (1983). Cultural variation in the meaning and uses of children's 'intelligence.' In J. B. Deregowski, S. Dziurawiec, & R. C. Annis (Eds.), *Explorations in cross-cultural psychology*. Lisse, The Netherlands: Swets & Zeitlinger.

Sutaria, S. D. (1985). *Specific learning disabilities: Nature and needs*. Springfield, IL: Charles C Thomas.

Terman, L. M. (1925). *Genetic studies of genius: Mental and physical traits of a thousand gifted children*. Stanford, CA: Stanford University Press.

Terman, L. M., & Merrill, M. A. (1937). *Measuring intelligence: A guide to the administration of the new revised Stanford-Binet tests of intelligence*. Boston: Houghton Mifflin.

Thomson, G. H. (1939). *The factorial analysis of human ability*. Boston: Houghton Mifflin.

Thorndike, R. L., Hagen, E. P., & Sattler, J. M. (1986). *Stanford-Binet intelligence scale: Fourth edition (Technical Manual)*. Chicago: Riverside.

Thurstone, L. L. (1938). *Primary mental abilities*. Chicago: University of Chicago Press.

Turkheimer, E. (1991). Individual and group differences in adoption studies of IQ. *Psychological Bulletin, 110*, 392–405.

United States Bureau of the Census. (1994). *The Hispanic population of the United States: March 1993* (Current Population Reports, Series P20–475). Washington, DC: Author.

United States National Commission for Employment Policy. (1982). *Hispanics and jobs: Barriers to progress* (Report No. 14). Washington, DC: Author.

Vernon, P. A. (1987). *Speed of information processing and intelligence*. Norwood, NJ: Ablex.

Vernon, P. A. (1993). *Biological approaches to the study of human intelligence*. Norwood, NJ: Ablex.

Vickers, D., Nettelbeck, T., & Wilson, R. J. (1972). Perceptual indices of performance: The measurement of 'inspection time' and 'noise' in the visual system. *Perception, 1*, 263–295.

Vincent, K. R. (1991). Black/White IQ differences: Does age make the difference? *Journal of Clinical Psychology, 47*, 266–270.

Vygotsky, L. S. (1978). *Mind in society: The development of higher psychological processes*. Cambridge, MA: Harvard University Press.

Waller, J. H. (1971). Achievement and social mobility: Relationships among IQ score, education, and occupation in two generations. *Social Biology, 18*, 252–259.

White, K. R. (1982). The relation between socioeconomic status and academic achievement. *Psychological Bulletin, 91*, 461–481.

Wober, M. (1974). Towards an understanding of the Kiganda concept of intelligence. In J. W., Berry & P. R. Dasen (Eds.), *Culture and cognition: Readings in cross-cultural psychology* (pp. 261–280). London: Methuen.

Yairi, E., & Ambrose, N. (1992). Onset of stuttering in preschool children: Selected factors. *Journal of Speech and Hearing Research, 35*, 782–788.

72

PSYCHOLOGISM AND BEHAVIORISM

Ned Block

Source: *Philosophical Review* 90(1), 1981: 5–43.

Let psychologism be the doctrine that whether behavior is intelligent behavior depends on the character of the internal information processing that produces it. More specifically, I mean psychologism to involve the doctrine that two systems could have actual and potential behavior *typical* of familiar intelligent beings, that the two systems could be exactly alike in their actual and potential behavior, and in their behavioral dispositions and capacities and counterfactual behavioral properties (i.e., what behaviors, behavioral dispositions, and behavioral capacities they would have exhibited had their stimuli differed)—the two systems could be alike in all these ways, yet there could be a difference in the information processing that mediates their stimuli and responses that determines that one is not at all intelligent while the other is fully intelligent.

This paper makes two claims: first, psychologism is true, and thus a natural behaviorist analysis of intelligence that is incompatible with psychologism is false. Second, the standard arguments against behaviorism are inadequate to defeat this natural behaviorist analysis of intelligence or to establish psychologism.

While psychologism is of course anathema to behaviorists,[1] it also seems wrong-headed to many philosophers who would *not* classify themselves as behaviorists. For example, Michael Dummett says:

> If a Martian could learn to speak a human language, or a robot be devised to behave in just the ways that are essential to a language speaker, an implicit knowledge of the correct theory of meaning for the language could be attributed to the Martian or the robot with as much right as to a human speaker, even though their internal mechanisms were entirely different.[2]

Dummett's view seems to be that what is relevant to the possession of a certain mental state is a matter of actual and potential behavior, and that internal processing is *not* relevant except to the extent that internal processing affects actual and potential behavior. I think that this Dummettian claim contains an important grain of truth, a grain that many philosophers wrongly take to be incompatible with psychologism.

This grain of truth can be elucidated as follows. Suppose we meet Martians, and find them to be behaviorally indistinguishable from humans. We learn their languages and they learn ours, and we develop deep commercial and cultural relations with them. We contribute to their journals and enjoy their movies, and vice versa. Then Martian and human psychologists compare notes, only to find that in underlying psychological mechanisms the Martians are very different from us. The Martian and human psychologists soon agree that the difference could be described as follows. Think of humans and Martians as if they were the products of conscious design. In any artificial intelligence project, there will be a range of engineering options. For example, suppose one wants to design a machine that makes inferences from information fed into it in the form of English sentences. One strategy would be to represent the information in the machine in English, and to formulate a set of inference rules that operate on English sentences. Another strategy would be to formulate a procedure for translating English into an artificial language whose sentences wear their logical forms on their faces. This strategy would simplify the inference rules, though at the computational cost of implementing the translation procedure. Suppose that the Martian and human psychologists agree that Martians and humans differ as if they were the products of a whole series of engineering decisions that differ along the lines illustrated. Should we conclude that the Martians are *not* intelligent after all? Obviously not! That would be crude human chauvinism. I suggest that philosophers reject psychologism in part because they (wrongly) see psychologism as involving this sort of chauvinism.

One of my purposes in this paper will be to show that psychologism does not in fact involve this sort of chauvinism.

If I succeed in showing psychologism to be true, I will have provided aid and comfort to those of us who have doubts about functionalism (the view that mental states are functional states—states definable in terms of their causal roles). Doubts about functionalism stem in part from the possibility of entities that look and act like people (and possess a network of internal states whose causal roles mirror those of our mental states), but differ from people in being operated by a network of homunculi whose aim is to simulate the functional organization of a person.[3] The presence of the homunculi can be used to argue that the homunculi-heads lack mentality. Defenders of functionalism are often inclined to 'bite the bullet,' replying along the following lines: 'If I were to discover that my best friend and most valuable colleague was a homunculi-head, that should not lead me to regard him as lacking intelligence (or other aspects of mentality), since differences in internal goings-on that do not affect actual or potential behavior (or behavioral counterfactuals) are not relevant to intelligence.' If this paper shows psychologism to be true, it blocks this line of defense of functionalism.

Let us begin the main line of argument by focusing on the well-known Turing Test. The Turing Test involves a machine in one room, and a person in another, each responding by teletype to remarks made by a human judge in a third room for some fixed period of time, e.g., an hour. The machine passes the test just in case the judge cannot tell which are the machine's answers and which are those of the person. Early perspectives on the Turing Test reflected the contemporary view of what it was for something to be intelligent, namely that it act in a certain way, a way hard to define, but easy enough to recognize.

Note that the sense of 'intelligent' deployed here—and generally in discussion of the Turing Test[4]—is *not* the sense in which we speak of one person being more intelligent than another. 'Intelligence' in the sense deployed here means something like the possession of thought or reason.

One popular way of construing Turing's proposal is as a version of operationalism. 'Being intelligent' is defined as passing the Turing Test, if it is administered (or alternatively, à la Carnap: if a system is given the Turing Test, then it is intelligent if and only if it passes). Construed operationally, the Turing Test conception of intelligence shares with other forms of operationalism the flaw of stipulating that a certain measuring instrument (the Turing Test) is *infallible*. According to the operationalist interpretation of the Turing Test as a definition of intelligence, it is absurd to ask of a device that passes the Turing Test whether it is *really* intelligent, and it is equally absurd to ask of a device that fails it whether it failed for some extraneous reason, but is nonetheless intelligent.

This difficulty can be avoided by going from the crude operationalist formulation to a familiar behavioral disposition formulation. On such a formulation, intelligence is identified not with the property of passing the test (if it is given), but rather with a behavioral *disposition* to pass the test (if it is given). On this behaviorist formulation, failing the Turing Test is not taken so seriously, since we can ask of a system that fails the test whether the failure *really does* indicate that the system lacks the disposition to pass the test. Further, passing the test is not *conclusive* evidence of a disposition to pass it, since, for example, the pass may have been accidental.

But the new formulation is nonetheless subject to deep difficulties. One obvious difficulty is its reliance on the discriminations of a human judge. Human judges may be able to discriminate *too well*—that is, they may be able to discriminate some *genuinely* intelligent machines from humans. Perhaps the responses of some intelligent machines will have a machinish style that a good human judge will be able to detect.

This problem could be avoided by altering the Turing Test so that the judge is not asked to say which is the machine, but rather is asked to say whether one or both of the respondents are, say, as intelligent as the average human. However, this modification introduces circularity, since 'intelligence' is defined in terms of the judge's judgments of intelligence. Further, even ignoring the circularity problem, the modification is futile, since the difficulty just crops up in a different form: perhaps human judges will tend chauvinistically to regard some genuinely intelligent machines as unintelligent because of their machinish style of thought.

More importantly, human judges may be too easily fooled by mindless machines. This point is strikingly illustrated by a very simple program[5] (two hundred lines in BASIC), devised by Joseph Weizenbaum, which can imitate a psychiatrist by employing a small set of simple strategies. Its major technique is to look for key words such as 'I,' 'you,' 'alike,' 'father,' and 'everybody.' The words are ranked—for example, 'father' is ranked above 'everybody,' and so if you type in 'My father is afraid of everybody,' the machine will respond with one of its 'father' responses, such as 'What else comes to mind when you think of your father?' If you type in 'I know everybody laughed at me,' you will get one of its responses to 'everybody,' for example, 'Who in particular are you thinking of?' It also has techniques that simultaneously transform 'you' into 'I' and 'me' into 'you,' so that if you type in 'You don't agree with me,' it can reply: 'Why do you think that I don't agree with you?' It also *stores* sentences containing certain key words such as 'my.' If your *current* input contains no key words, but if you had earlier said 'My boyfriend made me come here,' it will 'ignore' your current remark, saying instead, 'Does that have anything to do with the fact that your boyfriend made you come here?' If all other tricks fail, it has a list of last ditch responses such as, 'Who is the psychiatrist here, you or me?' Though this system is *totally* without intelligence, it proves *remarkably* good at fooling people in short conversations. Of course, Weizenbaum's machine rarely fools anyone for very long if the person has it in mind to explore the machine's capacities. But the program's extraordinary success (Weizenbaum's secretary asked him to leave the room in order to talk to the machine privately) reminds us that human gullibility being what it is, some more complex (but nonetheless unintelligent) program may be able to fool most any human judge. Further, since our tendency to be fooled by such programs seems dependent on our degree of suspicion, sophistication about machines, and other contingent factors, it seems silly to adopt a view of the nature of intelligence or thought that so closely ties it to human judgment. Could the issue of whether a machine *in fact* thinks or is intelligent depend on how gullible human interrogators tend to be?

In sum, human judges may be unfairly chauvinist in rejecting genuinely intelligent machines, and they may be overly liberal in accepting cleverly-engineered, mindless machines.

The problems just described could be avoided if we could specify in a non-question-begging way what it is for a sequence of responses to verbal stimuli to be a typical product of one or another style of intelligence. For then we would be able to avoid the dependence on human powers of discrimination that lies at the root of the problems of the last paragraph. Let us suppose, for the sake of argument, that we *can* do this, that is, that we can formulate a non-question-begging definition—indeed, a behavioristically acceptable definition—of what it is for a sequence of verbal outputs to be, as we shall say, 'sensible,' relative to a sequence of inputs. Though of course it is very doubtful that 'sensible' can be defined in a non-question-begging way, it will pay us to *suppose* it can, for as we shall see, even such a definition would not save the Turing Test conception of intelligence.

The role of the judge in Turing's definition of intelligence is to avoid the problem of actually specifying the behavior or behavioral dispositions thought to constitute intelligence. Hence my supposition that 'sensible' can be defined in a non-question-begging way amounts to the suggestion that we ignore one of the usual criticisms of behaviorists—that they cannot specify their behavioral dispositions in a non-question-begging way. This is indeed an enormous concession to behaviorism, but it will not play an important role in what follows.

We can now propose a version of the Turing Test conception of intelligence that avoids the problems described:

> Intelligence (or more accurately, conversational intelligence) is the disposition to produce a sensible sequence of verbal responses to a sequence of verbal stimuli, whatever they may be.

The point of the 'whatever they may be' is to emphasize that this account avoids relying on anyone's ability to come up with clever questions; for in order to be intelligent according to the above-described conception, the system must be disposed to respond sensibly not only to what the interlocutor *actually* says, but to whatever he *might* have said as well.

While the definition just given is a vast improvement (assuming that 'sensible' can be adequately defined), it is still a clearly behaviorist formulation. Let us now review the standard arguments against behaviorism with an eye towards determining whether the Turing Test conception of intelligence is vanquished by them.

Probably the most influential argument against behaviorism is due to Chisholm and Geach.[6] Suppose a behaviorist analyzes someone's wanting an ice cream cone as his having a set of behavioral dispositions such as the disposition to grasp an ice cream cone if one is 'presented' to him. But someone who wants an ice cream cone will be disposed to grasp it only if he *knows* it is an ice cream cone (and not in general if he thinks it is a tube of axle grease being offered to him as a joke) and only if he does not *believe* that taking an ice cream cone would conflict with other *desires* of more import-ance to him (for example, the desire to avoid an obligation to return the favor). In short, which behavioral dispositions a desire issues in depends on the *other* mental states of the desirer. And similar points apply to behaviorist analyses of belief and of many other mental states. Conclusion: one cannot define the conditions under which a given mental state will issue in a given behavioral disposition without adverting to *other mental states.*

Another standard argument against behaviorism flows out of the Chisholm-Geach point. If a person's behavioral dispositions depend on a *group* of mental states, perhaps *different* mental groups can produce the *same* behavioral dispositions. This line of thought gave rise to the 'perfect actor' family of counter-example. As Putnam[7] argued in convincing detail, it is possible to imagine a community of perfect actors (Putnam's super-super-spartans) who, in virtue of lawlike regularities, lack the behavioral disposi-tions envisioned by the behaviorists to be associated with pain, even though they do in fact have pain. This shows that no behavioral disposition is neces-sary for pain, and an exactly analogous example of perfect pain-pretenders shows that no behavioral disposition is sufficient for pain either.

Another less important type of traditional counterexample to behaviorism is illustrated by paralytics and brains in vats. Like Putnam's super-super-spartans, they can have pain without the usual dispositions.

When I speak of the 'standard objections to behaviorism' in what follows, I shall have these three types of objection in mind: the Chisholm-Geach objection, the perfect actor objection, and the objection based on paralytics and the like.[8]

I Do the standard objections to behaviorism dispose of behaviorist conceptions of intelligence?

The three arguments just reviewed are generally and rightly regarded as decisive refutations of behaviorist analyses of many mental states, such as belief, desire, and pain. Further, they serve to refute one quite plausible behaviorist analysis of intelligence. Intelligence is plausibly regarded as a second order mental property, a property that consists in having first order mental states—beliefs, desires, etc.—that are caused to change in certain ways by changes in one another and in sensory inputs. If intelligence is indeed such a second order property, and given that the behaviorist analyses of the first order states are false, one can conclude that a plausible behavior-ist view of intelligence is false as well.[9]

But it would be unfair to behaviorism to leave the matter here. Behaviorists generally mean their dispositions to be 'pure dispositions.' Ryle, for example, emphasized that 'to possess a dispositional property is not to be in a particu-lar state or to undergo a particular change.'[10] Brittleness, according to Ryle, is not a *cause* of breaking, but merely *the fact* of breaking easily. Similarly, to attribute pain to a person is not to attribute a cause or effect of anything, but simply to say *what he would do* in certain circumstances. However, the notion just mentioned of intelligence as a second order property is at its most plausible when first order mental states are thought of as entities that *have causal roles*. Since pure dispositions do not have causal roles in any straightforward sense, the analysis of intelligence as a second order property should seem unsatisfactory to a behaviorist, even if it is the right analysis of intelligence. Perhaps this explains why behaviorists and behaviorist-sympathizers do not seem to have adopted a view of intelligence as a second order property.

Secondly, an analysis of intelligence along roughly the lines indicated in what I called the Turing Test conception of intelligence is natural for the behaviorist because it arises by patching a widely known operationalist formulation. It is not surprising that such a position is popular in artificial intelligence circles.[11] Further, it seems to be regarded sympathetically by many philosophers who accept the standard arguments against behaviorist analyses of beliefs, desires, etc.[12]

Another attraction of an analysis along the lines suggested by the Turing Test conception of intelligence is that such an analysis can *escape the standard objections to behaviorism*. If I am right about this, then it would certainly be foolish for the critic of behaviorism to regard behaviorism with respect to intelligence as obliterated by the standard objections, ignoring analyses along the lines of the Turing Test conception of intelligence. For these reasons, I will now return to an examination of how well the Turing Test conception of intelligence fares when faced with the standard objections.

The Turing Test conception of intelligence offers a necessary and sufficient condition of intelligence. The standard objections are effective against the necessary condition claim, but not against the sufficient condition claim. Consider, for example, Putnam's perfect actor argument. The super-super-spartans have pain, though they have no disposition to pain behavior. Similarly, a machine might *be* intelligent, but not be disposed to *act* intelligently because, for example, it might be programmed to believe that acting intelligently is not *in its interest*. But what about the converse sort of case? A perfect actor who pretends to *have* pain seems as plausible as the super-super-spartans who pretend to *lack* pain, but *this* sort of perfect actor case does *not* seem to transfer to intelligence. For how could an unintelligent system perfectly pretend to be intelligent? It would seem that any system that is *that* good at pretending to be intelligent would have to *be* intelligent. So no behavioral disposition is necessary for intelligence, but *as far as this standard objection is concerned*, a behavioral disposition may yet be sufficient for intelligence. A similar point applies with respect to the Chisholm-Geach objection. The Chisholm-Geach objection tells us that a disposition to pain behavior is not a sufficient condition of having pain, since the behavioral disposition could be produced by a number of different combinations of mental states, e.g., [pain + a normal preference function] or by [no pain + an overwhelming desire to appear to have pain]. Turning to intelligent behavior, we see that it normally is produced by [intelligence + a normal preference function]. But could intelligent behavior be produced by [no intelligence + an overwhelming desire to appear intelligent]? Indeed, could there be *any* combination of mental states and properties *not including intelligence* that produces a lawful and thoroughgoing disposition to act intelligently? It seems not. So it seems that the Chisholm-Geach objection does not refute the claim of the Turing Test conception that a certain disposition is sufficient for intelligence.

Finally, the standard paralytic and brain in the vat examples are only intended to apply to claims of necessary conditions—not sufficient conditions—of mental states.

The defect I have just pointed out in the case against the behaviorist view of intelligence is a moderately serious one, since behaviorists have tended to focus on giving sufficient conditions for the application of mental terms (perhaps in part because of their emphasis on the connection between the meaning of 'pain' and the circumstances in which we learned to apply it). Turing, for example, was willing to settle for a 'sufficient condition' formulation of his behaviorist definition of intelligence.[13] One of my purposes in this paper is to remedy this defect in the standard objections to behaviorism by showing that no behavioral disposition is sufficient for intelligence.

I have just argued that the standard objections to behaviorism are only partly effective against the Turing Test conception of intelligence. I shall now go one step further, arguing that there is a reformulation of the Turing Test conception of intelligence that avoids the standard objections *altogether*. The reformulation is this: substitute the term 'capacity' for the term 'disposition' in the earlier formulation. As mentioned earlier, there are all sorts of reasons why an intelligent system may fail to be disposed to act intelligently: believing that acting intelligently is not in its interest, paralysis, etc. But intelligent systems that do not want to act intelligently or are paralyzed still have *the capacity* to act intelligently, even if they do not or cannot exercise this capacity.

Let me say a bit more about the difference between a behavioral disposition and a behavioral capacity. A capacity to φ need not result in a disposition to φ unless certain *internal* conditions are satisfied—say, the appropriate views or motivation or not having curare in one's bloodstream. To a first approximation, a disposition can be specified by a set (perhaps infinite) of input-output conditionals.

If i_1 obtains, then o_1 is emitted
If i_2 obtains, then o_2 is emitted
and so on.[14]

A corresponding first stab at a specification of a capacity, on the other hand, would involve mentioning *internal states* in the antecedents of the conditionals.

If s_a and i_a obtain, then o_a is emitted
If s_b and i_b obtain, then o_b is emitted
and so on,

where s_a and s_b are internal states.[15] In humans, such states would include beliefs and desires and working input and output organs at a minimum, though a machine could have a capacity the exercise of which is contingent only on nonmental internal parameters, e.g., whether its fuses are intact.

What I have said about the difference between a disposition and a capacity is very sketchy, and clarification is needed, especially with regard to the question of what sorts of internal states are to be specified in the antecedents of the conditionals. If paralytics are to be regarded as possessing behavioral capacities, these internal states will have to include specifications of functioning input and output devices. And if the systems that believe that acting intelligently is not in their interest are to have the required capacity, internal states will have to be specified such that if they *were* to obtain, the system would believe that acting intelligently *is* in its interest. Notice, however, that the behaviorist need not be committed to these *mentalistic descriptions* of the internal states; physiological or functional descriptions will do.[16]

The reader may suspect that the reformulation of behaviorism in terms of capacities that I have suggested avoids the standard objections to behaviorism only because it concedes *too much*. The references to internal states— even under physiological or functional descriptions—may be seen as too great a concession to psychologism (or other nonbehavioristic doctrines) for any genuine behaviorist to make. I reply: so much the better for my purposes, for I intend to show that this concession is not *enough*, and that the move from behavioral dispositions to behavioral capacities *will not save behaviorism*.

I now propose the reformulation suggested by the preceding remarks; let us call it the *neo-Turing Test conception of intelligence.*

Intelligence (or, more accurately, conversational intelligence) is the capacity to produce a sensible sequence of verbal responses to a sequence of verbal stimuli, whatever they may be.

Let us briefly consider the standard objections to behaviorism in order to show that the neo-Turing Test conception avoids them. First, intelligent paralytics and brains in vats provide no counterexample, since they do have the capacity to respond sensibly, though they lack the means to exercise the capacity. Second, consider the 'perfect actor' objection. An intelligent being who perfectly feigns stupidity nonetheless has the capacity to respond sensibly. Further, as in the disposition case, it would seem that no one could have the capacity to pretend perfectly to be intelligent without actually being intelligent. Third, the new formulation entirely disarms the Chisholm-Geach objection. There are many combinations of beliefs and desires that could cause an intelligent being to fail to be *disposed* to respond sensibly, but these beliefs and desires would not destroy the being's *capacity* to respond sensibly. Further, as I have mentioned repeatedly, it is hard to see how any combination of mental states not including intelligence could result in the capacity to respond in an intelligent manner to arbitrary sequences of stimuli.

One final point. Notice that my concession that 'sensible' can be defined in a behavioristically adequate way is *not* what is responsible for the fact that the neo-Turing Test conception of intelligence evades the standard objections. What does the job is first the difficulty of conceiving of someone who can pretend perfectly to be intelligent without actually being intelligent, and second, the move from dispositions to capacities.

II The argument for psychologism and against behaviorism

My strategy will be to describe a machine that produces (and thus has the capacity to produce) a sensible sequence of verbal responses to verbal stimuli. The machine is thus intelligent according to the neo-Turing Test conception of intelligence (and also according to the cruder versions of this conception). However, according to me, a knowledge of the machine's internal information processing shows conclusively that it is totally lacking in intelligence.

I shall now describe my unintelligent machine. First, we require some terminology. Call a string of sentences whose members can be typed by a human typist one after another in an hour or less, a *typable* string of sentences. Consider the set of all typable strings of sentences. Since English has a finite number of words (indeed, a finite number of typable letter strings), this set has a very large, but nonetheless finite, number of members. Consider the subset of this set which contains all and only those strings which are naturally interpretable as conversations in which at least one party's contribution is sensible in the sense described above. Call a string which can be understood in this way a *sensible* string. For example, if we allot each party to a conversation one sentence per 'turn' (a simplification I will continue to use), and if each even-numbered sentence in the string is a reasonable conversational contribution, then the string is a sensible one. We need not be very restrictive as to what is to count as sensible. For example, if sentence 1 is 'Let's see you talk nonsense,' it would be sensible for sentence 2 to be nonsensical. The set of sensible strings so defined is a finite set that could in principle be listed by a very large and clever team working for a long time, with a very large grant and a lot of mechanical help, *exercising imagination and judgment* about what is to count as a sensible string.

Presumably the programmers will find that in order to produce really convincing sensible strings, they will have to think of themselves as simulating some definite personality with some definite history. They might choose to give the responses my Aunt Bertha might give if she were brought to a room with a teletype by her errant nephew and asked to answer 'silly' questions for a time.

Imagine the set of sensible strings recorded on tape and deployed by a very simple machine as follows. The interrogator types in sentence A. the machine searches its list of sensible strings, picking out those that begin with A. It then picks one of these A-initial strings at random, and types out its second sentence, call it 'B.' The interrogator types in sentence C. The machine searches its list, isolating the strings that start with A followed by B followed by C. It picks one of these ABC-initial strings and types out its fourth sentence, and so on.[17]

The reader may be helped by seeing a variant of this machine in which the notion of a sensible string is replaced by the notion of a sensible branch of a tree structure. Suppose the interrogator goes first, typing in one of $A_1 \ldots A_n$. The programmers produce *one* sensible response to each of these sentences, $B_1 \ldots B_n$. For each of $B_1 \ldots B_n$ the interrogator can make various replies, so many branches will sprout below each of $B_1 \ldots B_n$. Again, for each of these replies, the programmers produce one sensible response, and so on. In this version of the machine, all the X-initial strings can be replaced by a single tree with a single token of X as the head node; all the XYZ-initial strings can be replaced by a branch of that tree with Y and Z as the next nodes, and so forth. This machine is a tree-searcher instead of a string-searcher.

So long as the programmers have done their job properly, such a machine will have the capacity to emit a sensible sequence of verbal outputs, whatever the verbal inputs, and hence it is intelligent according to the neo-Turing Test conception of intelligence. But actually, the machine has the intelligence of a toaster. *All the intelligence it exhibits is that of its programmers.* Note also that its limitation to Turing Tests of an hour's length is not essential. For a Turing Test of *any* given length, the machine could in principle be programmed in just the same way to pass a Turing Test of that length.

I conclude that the capacity to emit sensible responses is *not* sufficient for intelligence, and so the neo-Turing Test conception of intelligence is refuted (along with the older and cruder Turing Test conceptions). I also conclude that whether behavior is intelligent behavior is in part a matter of how it is produced. Even if a system has the actual and potential behavior characteristic of an intelligent being, if its internal processes are like those of the machine described, it is not intelligent. So psychologism is true.

I haven't shown *quite* what I advertised initially, since I haven't shown that the machine could duplicate the response properties of a real person. But what I have shown is close enough for me, and besides, it doesn't change the essential point of the example if we imagine the programmers deciding *exactly* what Aunt Bertha would say on the basis of a psychological or physiological theory of Aunt Bertha.

We can now see why psychologism is not incompatible with the point made earlier in connection with the Martian example. The Martian example suggested that it was doubtful that there would be any single natural kind of information processing that must be involved in the production of all intelligent behavior. (I argued that it would be chauvinist to refuse to classify Martians as intelligent *merely* because their internal information processing is very different from ours.) Psychologism is not chauvinist because psychologism requires only that intelligent behavior *not* be the product of a (at least one) certain kind of internal processing. One can insist that behavior which has a certain etiology cannot be intelligent behavior without holding that all intelligent behavior must have the same 'kind' of etiology.

The point of the machine example may be illuminated by comparing it with a two-way radio. If one is speaking to an intelligent person over a two-way radio, the radio will normally emit sensible replies to whatever one says. But the radio does not do this in virtue of a capacity to make sensible replies that *it* possesses. The two-way radio is like my machine in being a *conduit* for intelligence, but the two devices differ in that my machine has a crucial capacity that the two-way radio lacks. In my machine, no causal signals from the interrogators reach those who think up the responses, but in the case of the two-way radio, the person who thinks up the responses has to hear the questions. In the case of my machine, the causal efficacy of the programmers is limited to what they have stored in the machine before the interrogator begins.

The reader should also note that my example is really an extension of the traditional perfect pretender counterexample, since the machine 'pretends' to be intelligent without actually being intelligent. Once one notes this, it is easy to see that a *person* could have a capacity to respond intelligently, even though the intelligence he exhibits is not *his*—for example, if he memorizes responses in Chinese though he understands only English.[18] An idiot with a photographic memory, such as Luria's famous mnemonist, could carry on a brilliant philosophical conversation if provided with strings by a team of brilliant philosophers.[19]

The machine, as I have described it thus far, is limited to typewritten inputs and outputs. *But this limitation is inessential, and that is what makes my argument relevant to a full-blooded behaviorist theory of intelligence*, not just to a theory of conversational intelligence. What I need to show to make my point is that the kind of finiteness assumption that holds with respect to typewritten inputs and outputs also holds with respect to the whole range of sensory stimulation and behavior. If I can show this, then I can generalize the idea of the machine I described to an unintelligent robot that nonetheless acts in every possible situation just as intelligently as a person.

The sort of finiteness claim that I need can be justified both empirically and conceptually. The empirical justifications are far too complex to present here, so I will only mention them briefly. First, I would claim that enough is now known about sensory physiology to back up the assertion that every stimulus parameter that is not already 'quantized' could be quantized without making any difference with respect to effects on the brain or on behavior, provided that the 'grain' of quantization is fine enough. Suppose that all of your sense organs were covered by a surface that effected an 'analog-to-digital conversion.' For example, if some stimulus parameter had a value of .111 ... units, the surface might change it to .11 units. Provided that the grain was fine enough (not too many decimal places are 'lopped off'), the analog-to-digital conversion would make no mental or behavioral difference. If this is right, then one could take the output of the analog-digital converter as the relevant stimulus, and so there would be a finite number of possible sequences of arrays of stimuli in a finite time.

I am told that a similar conclusion can actually be reached with respect to *any* physical system that can be regarded as having inputs and outputs. The crucial claim here is that no physical system could be an infinitely powerful amplifier, so given a 'power of amplification,' one could impose a corresponding quantization of the inputs that would not affect the outputs. I don't know enough physics to pursue this line further, so I won't.

The line of argument for my conclusion that I want to rely on is more conceptual than empirical. The point is that our *concept* of intelligence allows an intelligent being to have quantized sensory devices. Suppose, for example, that Martian eyes are like movie cameras in that the information that they pass on to the Martian brain amounts to a series of newspaper-like 'dot' pictures, i.e., matrices containing a large number of cells, each of which can be either black or white. (Martians are color-blind.) If Martians are strikingly like us in appearance, action, and even internal information processing, no one ought to regard their movie camera eyes (and other finitary sense organs) as showing they are not intelligent. However, note that since there are a finite number of such 'dot' pictures of a given grain, there are a finite number of *sequences* of such pictures of a given duration, and thus a finite number of *possible visual stimuli* of a given duration.

It is easy to see that both the empirical and the conceptual points support the claim that an intelligent being could have a finite number of possible sequences of types of stimuli in a finite time (and the same is also true of responses). But then the stimulus sequences could in principle be catalogued by programmers, just as can the interrogator's remarks in the machine described earlier. Thus, a robot programmed along the lines of the machine I described earlier could be given every behavioral capacity possessed by humans, via a method of the sort I have already described. In sum, while my remarks so far have dealt mainly with a behaviorist account of *conversational* intelligence, broadening the argument to cover a behaviorist theory of intelligence *simpliciter* would raise no new issues of principle. In what follows, I shall return for convenience to a discussion of conversational intelligence.

By this time, the reader may have a number of objections. Given the heavy use of the phrase 'in principle' above, you may feel that what this latest wrinkle shows is that the sense of 'in principle possible' in which *any* of the machines I described are in principle possible is a bit strange. Or you may object: 'Your machine's capacity to pass the Turing Test *does* depend on an arbitrary time limit to the test.' Or: 'You are just stipulating a new meaning for the word 'intelligent.'' Or you may want to know what I would say if *I* turned out to be one.

I will now attempt to answer these and other objections. If an objection has a subscripted numeral (e.g., 3a), then it depends on the immediately preceding objection or reply. However, the reader can skip any other objection or reply without loss of continuity.

Objection 1. Your argument is too strong in that it could be said of *any* intelligent machine that the intelligence it exhibits is that of its programmers.

Reply. I do *not* claim that the intelligence of *every* machine designed by intelligent beings is merely the intelligence of the designers, and no such principle is used in my argument. If we ever do make an intelligent machine, presumably we will do it by equipping it with mechanisms for learning, solving problems, etc. Perhaps we will find general principles of learning, general principles of problem solving, etc., which we can build into it. But though we *make* the machine intelligent, the intelligence it exhibits is *its* own, just as our intelligence is no less ours, even if it was produced mainly by the enormously skillful efforts of our parents.

By contrast, if my string-searching machine emits a clever pun *P*, in response to a conversation *C*, then the sequence *CP* is literally one that was thought of and included by the programmers. Perhaps the programmers will say of one of their colleagues, 'Oh, Jones thought of that pun—he is so clever.'

The trouble with the neo-Turing Test conception of intelligence (and its predecessors) is precisely that it does not allow us to distinguish between behavior that reflects a machine's *own* intelligence, and behavior that reflects *only the intelligence of the machine's programmers*. As I suggested, only a partly etiological notion of intelligent behavior will do the trick.

Objection 2. If the strings were recorded before this year, the machine would not respond the way a person would to a sentence like 'What do you think of the latest events in the Mid-East?'

Reply. A system can be intelligent, yet have no knowledge of current events. Likewise, a machine can *imitate* intelligence without *imitating* knowledge of current events. The programmers could, if they liked, choose to simulate an intelligent Robinson Crusoe who knows nothing of the last twenty-five years. Alternatively, they could undertake the much more difficult task of reprogramming periodically to simulate knowledge of current events.

Objection 3. You have argued that a machine with a certain internal mechanical structure is not intelligent, even though it seems intelligent in every *external* respect (that is, in every external respect examined in the Turing Test). But by introducing this internal condition, aren't you in effect merely suggesting a linguistic stipulation, a new meaning for the word 'intelligent'? We *normally* regard input-output capacities as criterial for intelligence. All you are doing is suggesting that we adopt a new practice, involving a *new* criterion which includes something about what goes on inside.

Reply. Jones plays brilliant chess against two of the world's foremost grandmasters at once. You think him a genius until you find out that his method is as follows. He goes second against grandmaster G_1 and first against G_2. He notes G_1's first move against him, and then makes the same move against G_2. He awaits G_2's response, and makes the same move against G_1, and so on. Since Jones's method itself was one he read about in a comic book, Jones's performance is no evidence of his intelligence. As this example[20] illustrates, it is a feature of our concept of intelligence, that to the degree that a system's performance merely echoes the intelligence of another system, the first system's performance is thereby misleading as an indication of its intelligence. Since my machine's performances are *all* echoes, these performances provide no reason to attribute intelligence to it.[21]

The point is that though we *normally* ascertain the intelligence of a system by trying to assess its input-output capacities, it is part of our ordinary concept of intelligence that input-output capacities can be misleading. As Putnam has suggested, it is part of the logic of natural kind terms that what seems to be a stereotypical X can turn out not to be an X at all if it fails to belong to the same scientific natural kind as the main body of things we have referred to as X's.[22] If Putnam is right about this, one can never accuse someone of 'changing the meaning' of a natural kind term *merely* on the ground that he says that something that satisfies the standard 'criteria' for X's is not an X.

Objection 3a. I am very suspicious of your reply to the last objection, especially your introduction of the Putnam point. Is it not rather chauvinist to suppose that a system has to be scientifically *like us* to be intelligent? Maybe a system with information processing very unlike ours does not belong in the extension of our term 'intelligence'; but it is equally true that we do not belong in the extension of *its* term 'shmintelligence.' And who is to say that intelligence is any better than shmintelligence?

Reply. I have not argued that the *mere fact* of an information processing *difference* between my machine and us cuts any ice. Rather, my point is based on the *sort* of information processing difference that exists. My machine lacks the kind of 'richness' of information processing requisite for intelligence. Perhaps this richness has something to do with the application of abstract principles of problem solving, learning, etc. I wish I could say more about just what this sort of richness comes to. But I have chosen a much less ambitious task: to give a clear case of something that *lacks* that richness, but nonetheless behaves as if it were intelligent. If someone offered a definition of 'life' that had the unnoticed consequence that small stationery items such as paper clips are alive, one could refute him by pointing out the absurdity of the consequence, even if one had no very detailed account of what life really is with which to replace his. In the same way, one can refute the neo-Turing Test conception by counterexample without having to say very much about what intelligence really is.

Objection 4. Suppose it turns out that human beings, including you, process information in just the way that your machine does. Would you insist that humans are not intelligent?

Reply. I'm not very sure of what I would say about human intelligence were someone to convince me that human information processing is the same as that of my machine. However, I do not see that there is any *clearly and obviously correct* response to this question against which the responses natural for someone with my position can be measured. Further, none of the more plausible responses that I can think of are incompatible with what I have said so far.

Assume, for example, a theory of reference that dictates that in virtue of the causal relation between the word 'intelligence' and human information processing, human information processing is intelligent *whatever* its nature.[23] Then, if I were convinced that humans process information in the manner of my machine, I should admit that my machine is intelligent. But how is this incompatible with my claim that my machine is not *in fact* intelligent? Tweaking me with 'What if *you* turned out to be one?' is a bit like tweaking an atheist with 'What if you turned out to be God?' The atheist would have to admit that if he were God, then God would exist. But the atheist could concede this counterfactual without giving up atheism. If the word 'intelligence' is firmly anchored to human information processing, as suggested above, then my position is committed to the *empirical claim* that human information processing is not like that of my machine. But this is a perfectly congenial claim, one that is supported both by common sense and by empirical research in cognitive psychology.

Objection 5. You keep insisting that we do not process information in the manner of your machine. What makes you so sure?

Reply. I don't see how someone could make such an objection without being somewhat facetious. You will have no difficulty coming up with responses to my arguments. Are we to take seriously the idea that someone long ago recorded both what I said and a response to it and inserted both in your brain? Common sense recoils from such patent nonsense. Further, pick any issue of any cognitive psychology journal, and you will see attempts at experimental investigation of our information processing mechanisms. Despite the crudity of the evidence, it tells overwhelmingly against the string-searching idea.

Our cognitive processes are undoubtedly much more mechanical than some people like to think. But there is a vast gap between our being more mechanical than some people like to think and our being a machine of the sort I described.

Objection 6. Combinatorial explosion makes your machine impossible. George Miller long ago estimated[24] that there are on the order of 10^{30} grammatical sentences 20 words in length. Suppose (utterly arbitrarily) that of these 10^{15} are semantically well formed as well. An hour-long Turing Test would require perhaps 100 such sentences. That makes 10^{1500} strings, a number which is greater than the number of particles in the universe.

Reply. My argument requires only that the machine be *logically* possible, not that it be feasible or even nomologically possible. Behaviorist analyses were generally presented as *conceptual analyses*, and it is difficult to see how conceptions such as the neo-Turing Test conception could be seen in a very different light. Could it be an *empirical hypothesis* that intelligence is the capacity to emit sensible sequences of outputs relative to input sequences? What sort of empirical evidence (other than evidence from *linguistics*) could there be in favor of such a claim? If the neo-Turing Test conception of intelligence is seen as something on the order of a claim about the concept of intelligence, then the mere *logical* possibility of an unintelligent system that has the capacity to pass the Turing Test is enough to refute the neo-Turing Test conception.

It may be replied that although the neo-Turing Test conception clearly is not a *straightforwardly* empirical hypothesis, still it may be *quasi-empirical.* For it may be held that the identification of intelligence with the capacity to emit sensible output sequences is a *background* principle or law of empirical psychology. Or it may be offered as a rational reconstruction (of our vague common sense conception of intelligence) which will be fruitful in future empirical psychological theories. In both cases, while no empirical evidence could *directly* support the neo-Turing Test conception, still it could be held to be part of a perspective that could be empirically supported as a whole.[25]

This reply would carry some weight if any proponent of the neo-Turing Test conception had offered the *slightest reason* for thinking that such a conception of intelligence is likely to contribute to the fruitfulness of empirical theories that contain it. In the absence of such a reason (and, moreover, in the presence of examples that suggest the contrary—behaviorist psychology and Turingish approaches to artificial intelligence—see footnote 11), why should we take the neo-Turing Test conception seriously as a quasi-empirical claim?

While this reply suffices, I shall add that my machine may indeed be nomologically possible. Nothing in contemporary physics prohibits the possibility of matter in some part of the universe that is infinitely divisible. Indeed, whenever the latest 'elementary' particle turns out not to be truly elementary, and when the number and variety of its constituents multiply (as has now happened with quarks), physicists typically entertain the hypothesis that *our* matter is not composed of any *really* elementary particles.

Suppose there is a part of the universe (possibly this one) in which matter *is* infinitely divisible. In that part of the universe there need be no upper bound on the amount of information storable in a given finite space. So my machine could perhaps exist, its tapes stored in a volume the size of, e.g., a human head. Indeed, one can imagine that where matter is infinitely divisible, there are creatures of all sizes, including creatures the size of electrons who agree to do the recording for us if we agree to wipe out their enemies by putting the lumps on which the enemies live in one of our particle accelerators.

Further, even if the story of the last paragraph is not nomologically possible, still it is not clear that the *kind* of nomological impossibility it possesses is relevant to my objection to the neo-Turing Test conception of intelligence. For if the neo-Turing Test conception of intelligence is an empirical 'background' principle or law, it is a background principle or law of human *cognitive psychology*, not of *physics*. But a situation can contravene laws of physics without contravening laws of human psychology. For example, in a logically possible world in which gravity obeyed an inverse cube law instead of an inverse square law, our laws of *physics* would be different, but our laws of *psychology* might not be.

Now if my machine contravenes laws of nature, these laws are presumably laws of physics, not laws of psychology. For the question of how much information can be stored in a given space and how fast information can be transferred from place to place depends on such physical factors as the divisibility of matter and the speed of light. Even if the electron-sized creatures just described contravene laws of physics, still they need not contravene laws of human psychology. That is, humans (with their psychological laws intact) could coexist with the little creatures.[26]

But if my machine does not contravene laws of human psychology—if it exists in a possible world in which the laws of human psychology are the same as they are here—then the neo-Turing Test conception of intelligence is false in a world where the laws of human psychology are the same as they are here. So the neo-Turing Test conception of intelligence cannot *be* one of the laws of human psychology.

In sum, the neo-Turing Test conception of intelligence can be construed either as some sort of conceptual truth or as a kind of psychological law. And it is false on both construals.

One final point: various sorts of modifications may make a variant of my machine nomologically possible in a much more straightforward sense. First, we could limit the vocabulary of the Turing Test to Basic English. Basic English has a vocabulary of only 850 words, as opposed to the hundreds of thousands of words in English, and it is claimed that Basic English is adequate for normal conversation, and for expression of a wide range of ideas. Second, the calculation made above was based on the string-searching version of the machine. The tree-searching version described earlier, however, avoids enormous amounts of duplication of parts of strings, and is no more intelligent.

More importantly, the machine as I have described it is designed to perform *perfectly* (barring breakdown); but perfect performance is far better than one could expect from any human, even ignoring strokes, heart attacks, and other forms of human 'breakdown.' Humans whose mental processes are functioning normally often misread sentences, or get confused; worse, any normal person engaged in a long Turing Test would soon get bored, and his attention would wander. Further, many loquacious souls would blather on from the very beginning, occasionally apologizing for not listening to the interlocutor. Many people would respond more by way of free association to the interlocutor's remarks than by grasping their sense and giving a considered reply. Some people might devote nearly every remark to complaints about the unpleasantness of these interminable Turing Tests. If one sets one's sights on making a machine that does only as well in the Turing Test as *most* people would do, one might try a hybrid machine, containing a relatively small number of trees plus a bag of tricks of the sort used in Weizenbaum's program.

Perhaps many tricks can be found to reduce the memory load without making the machine any smarter. Of course, no matter how sophisticated the memory-reduction tricks we find, they merely postpone, but do not avoid the inevitable combinatorial explosion. For the whole point of the machine is to substitute memory for intelligence. So for a Turing Test of *some* length, perhaps a machine of the general type that I have described will be so large that making it any larger will cause collapse into a black hole. My point is that technical ingenuity being what it is, the point at which nomological impossibility sets in may be beyond what is required to simulate human conversational abilities.

Objection 7. The fault of the Turing Test as you describe it is one of experimental design, not experimental concept. The trouble is that *your* Turing Test has a *fixed length*. The programmers must know the length in order to program the machine. In an *adequate* version of the Turing Test, the duration of any occasion of testing would be decided in some random manner. In short, the trouble with your criticism is that you've set up a straw man.

Reply. It is certainly true that my machine's capacity to pass Turing Tests depends on there being some upper bound to the length of the tests. But the same is true of *people*. Even if we allow, say, twelve hours between question and answer to give people time to eat and sleep, still, people eventually *die*. Few humans could pass a Turing Test that lasted ninety years, and no humans could pass a Turing Test that lasted five hundred years. You can (if you like) characterize intelligence as the capacity to pass a Turing Test of arbitrary length, but since *humans do not have this capacity*, your characterization will not be a necessary condition of intelligence, and even if it were a sufficient condition of intelligence (which I very much doubt—see below) a sufficient condition of intelligence that *humans do not satisfy* would be of little interest to proponents of views like the neo-Turing Test conception.

Even if medical advances remove any upper bound on the human life span, still people will die by accident. There is a nonzero probability that, in the course of normal thermal motion, the molecules in the two halves of one's body will move in opposite directions, tearing one in half. Indeed, the probability of escaping such accidental death literally *forever* is zero. Consider the 'half-life' of people in a world in which death is put off as long as is physically possible. (The half-life for people, as for radioactive atoms, is the median life span, the time it takes for half to pass away.) Machines of my sort could be programmed to last for that half-life and (assuming they are no more susceptible to accidental destruction than people) their median life span would be as long as that of the median person.

Objection 7a. Let me try another tack. Cognitive psychologists and linguists often claim that cognitive mechanisms of one sort or another have 'infinite capacities.' For example, Chomsky says that our mechanisms for understanding language have the capacity to understand sentences of any length. An upper bound on the length of sentences people can understand in practice is a matter of interferences due to distraction, boredom, going mad, memory limitations, and many other phenomena, including, of course, death. This point is often put by saying that under the appropriate idealization (i.e., ignoring 'interfering' phenomena of the sort mentioned) we have the capacity to understand sentences of any length. Now here is my point: under the same sort of idealization, we presumably have the capacity to pass a Turing Test of any length. But your string-searcher does *not* have this capacity, even under the appropriate idealization.

Reply. You seem to think you have objected to my claim, but really you have *capitulated* to it. I cheerfully concede that there is an idealization under which we probably have an 'infinite' capacity that my machine lacks. But in order to describe this idealization, you will have to indulge in a kind of theorizing about cognitive mechanisms that would be unacceptable to a behaviorist.

Consider the kind of reformulation of the neo-Turing Test conception of intelligence suggested by the idealization objection; it would be something like: 'intelligence = the possession of language-processing mechanisms such that, were they provided with unlimited memory, and were they directed by motivational mechanisms that assigned at least a moderately high preference value to responding sensibly, and were they 'insulated' from 'stop' signals from emotion centers, and so forth, then the language-processing mechanisms would have the capacity to respond sensibly indefinitely.' Notice that in order to state such a doctrine, one has to distinguish among various mental components and mechanisms. As an aside, it is worth nothing that these distinctions have substantive empirical presuppositions. For example, memory might be inextricably bound up with language-processing mechanisms so as to make nonsense of talk of supplying the processing mechanisms with unlimited memory. The main point, however, is that in order to state such an 'idealization' version of the neo-Turing Test conception one has to invoke mentalistic notions that no behaviorist could accept.

Objection 7b. I believe I can make my point without using mentalistic notions by idealizing away simply from nonaccidental causes of death. In replying to Objection 7, you said (correctly) that if medical advances removed an upper bound on human life, still the median string-searching machine could do as well as the median person. However, note that if non-accidental causes of death were removed, every *individual* human would have no upper bound on how long *he* could go on in a Turing Test. By contrast, any individual string-searching machine must by its very nature have some upper bound on its ability to go on.

Reply. What determines how long we can go on in a Turing Test is not just how long we live, but the nature of our cognitive mechanisms and their interactions with other mental mechanisms. Suppose, for example, that we have no mechanisms for 'erasing' information stored in long term memory. (Whether this is so is not known.) If we can't 'erase,' then when our finite memories are 'used up,' normal conversational capacity will cease.

If the behaviorist identifies intelligence with the capacity to go on indefinitely in a Turing Test, idealizing away only from nonaccidental death, then people may turn out not to be intelligent in his sense. Further, even if people do turn out to satisfy such a condition, it can't be regarded as *necessary* for intelligence. Beings that go senile within two hundred years because they lack 'erase' mechanisms can nonetheless be intelligent before they go senile.

Of course, the behaviorist could avoid this difficulty by further idealizing, explicitly mentioning erase mechanisms in his definition of intelligence. But that would land him back in the mentalistic swamp described in the last reply.

It is worth adding that even if we do have 'erase' mechanisms, and even if nonaccidental causes of death were eliminated, still we would have *finite* memories. A variant of my string-searcher could perhaps exploit the finiteness of our memories so as to do as well as a person in an indefinitely long Turing Test. Suppose, for example, that human memory cannot record more than two hundred years of conversation. Then one of my string-searchers could perhaps be turned into a *loop-searcher* that could go on indefinitely. Instead of 'linear' strings of conversation, it would contain circular strings whose ends rejoin the beginnings after, say, one thousand years of conversation. The construction of such loops would take much more inventiveness than the construction of ordinary strings. Even if it could be done, such a machine would seem intolerably repetitious to a being whose memory capacity far exceeded ours, but human conversation would seem equally repetitious to such a being.

Here is one final kind of rejoinder to the 'unbounded Turing Test' objection. Consider a variant of my machine in which the programmers simply continue on and on, adding to the strings. When they need new tape, they reuse tape that has already been passed by.[27] Note that it is *logically* possible for the everextending strings to come into existence by themselves—without the programmers (see note 21). Thus not even the capacity to go on indefinitely in a Turing Test is *logically* sufficient for intelligence.

Continuing on this theme, consider the infinitely divisible matter mentioned in the reply to Objection 6. It is logically and perhaps nomologically possible for a *man-sized* string-searching machine to contain creatures of everdecreasing size who work away making the tapes longer and longer without bound. Of course, neither of the two machines just mentioned has a *fixed* program, but since the programmers never see the stimuli, it is still the *machines* and not the programmers that are doing the responding. Contrast these machines with the infamous 'machine' of long ago that contained a midget hidden inside it who listened to the questions and produced the answers.

Objection 8. You remarked earlier that the neo-Turing Test conception of intelligence is widespread in artificial intelligence circles. Still, your machine cannot be taken as refuting any AI (artificial intelligence) point of view, because as Newell and Simon point out, in the AI view, 'the task of intelligence ... is to avert the ever-present threat of the exponential explosion of search.'[28] (In exponential explosion of search, adding one step to the task requires, e.g., 10 times the computational resources, adding two steps requires 10^2 (= 100) times the computational resources, adding three steps requires 10^3 (= 1000) times the computational resources, etc.) So it would be reasonable for AIers to amend their version of the neo-Turing conception of intelligence as follows:

> Intelligence is the capacity to emit sensible sequences of responses to stimuli, *so long as this is accomplished in a way that averts exponential explosion of search.*[29]

Reply. Let me begin by noting that for a proponent of the neo-Turing Test conception of intelligence to move to the *amended* neo-Turing Test conception is to capitulate to the psychologism that I have been defending. The *amended* neo-Turing Test conception attempts to avoid the problem I have posed by placing a *condition on the internal processing* (albeit a minimal one), viz., that it not be explosive. So the amended neo-Turing Test conception *does* characterize intelligence partly with respect to its internal etiology, and hence the amended neo-Turing Test conception is psychologistic.

While the amended neo-Turing Test conception is an improvement over the original neo-Turing Test conception in this one respect (it appeals to internal processing), it suffers from a variety of defects. One difficulty arises because there is an ambiguity in phrases such as 'averts the exponential explosion of search.' Such phrases can be understood as equivalent to '*avoids* exponential explosion altogether' (i.e., uses methods that do not require computational resources that go up exponentially with the 'length' of the task) or, alternatively, as '*postpones* exponential explosion long enough' (i.e., *does* use methods that require computational resources that go up exponentially with the 'length' of the task, but the 'length' of the task is short enough that the required resources are in fact available). If it is postponing that is meant, my counterexample may well be untouched by the new proposal, because as I pointed out earlier, my machine or a variant on it may postpone combinatorial explosion long enough to pass a reasonable Turing Test.

On the other hand, if it is *avoiding* combinatorial explosion altogether that is meant, then the amended neo-Turing Test conception may brand *us* as unintelligent. For it is certainly possible that *our* information processing mechanisms—like those of many AI systems—are ones that succeed not because they avoid combinatorial explosion altogether, but only because they *postpone* combinatorial explosion long enough for practical purposes.

In sum, the amended neo-Turing Test conception is faced with a dilemma. If it is postponing combinatorial explosion that is meant, my machine may count as intelligent. If it is avoiding combinatorial explosion altogether that is meant, *we* (or other intelligent organisms) may not count as intelligent.

Further, the proposed amendment to the neo-Turing Test conception is an entirely ad hoc addition. The trouble with such ad hoc exclusion of counter examples is that one can never be sure whether someone will come up with another type of counterexample which will require another ad hoc maneuver.

I shall now back up this point by sketching a set of devices that have sensible input-output relations, but arguably are not intelligent.

Imagine a computer which simulates your responses to stimuli by computing *the trajectories* of all the elementary particles in your body. This machine starts with a specification of the positions, velocities, and charges (I assume Newtonian mechanics for convenience) of all your particles at one moment, and computes the changes of state of your body as a function of these initial conditions and energy impinging on your sensory mechanisms. Of course, what is especially relevant for the Turing Test is the effect of light from your teletype monitor on your typing fingers. Now though this takes some discussion, I opine that a machine that computes your elementary particle trajectories in this way is not intelligent, though it could control a robot which has the capacity to behave exactly as you would in any situation. It behaves as you do when you are doing philosophy, but *it* is not doing philosophy; rather, what it is doing is computing elementary particle trajectories so as to mimic your doing philosophy.

Perhaps what I have described is not nomologically possible. Indeed, it may be that even if God told us the positions and velocities of all the particles in your body, no computer could compute the complex interactions, even assuming Newtonian mechanics. However, notice one respect in which this machine may be superior to the one this paper has been mainly concerned with: namely, if it can stimulate something for an hour, it may be able to simulate it for a year or a decade with the same apparatus. For continuing the simulation would be simply a matter of solving the same equations over and over again. For a wide variety of types of equations, solving the same equations over and over will involve no exponential explosion of search. If there is no exponential expansion of search here, the ad hoc condition added in the objection is eluded, and we are left with the issues about nomological possibility that we discussed in Objection 6.

The idea of the machine just sketched could be applied in another machine which is closer to nomological possibility, namely one that simulates your *neurophysiology* instead of your elementary particle physics. That is, this machine would contain a representation of some adequate neurological theory (say, of the distant future) and a specification of the current states of all your neurons. It would simulate you by computing the changes of state of your neurons. Still more likely to be nomologically possible would be a machine which, in an analogous manner, simulates your *psychology*. That is, it contains a representation of some adequate psychological theory (of the distant future) and a specification of the current states of your psychological mechanisms. It simulates you by computing the changes of state of those mechanisms given their initial states and sensory inputs. Again, if there is no exponential expansion of search, the modification introduced in the objection gains nothing.

I said that these three devices are *arguably* unintelligent, but since I have little space to give any such arguments, this part of my case will have to remain incomplete. I will briefly sketch part of one argument.

Consider a device that simulates you by using a theory of your psychological processes. It is a robot that looks and acts as you would in any stimulus situation. Instead of a brain it has a computer equipped with a description of your psychological mechanisms. You receive a certain input, cogitate about it, and emit a certain output. If your robot doppelganger receives that input, a transducer converts the input into a description of the input. The computer uses its description of your cognitive mechanisms to deduce the product of your cogitations; it then transmits a description of your output to a mechanism that causes the robot body to execute the output. It is hardly obvious that the robot's process of manipulation of descriptions of your cogitation is *itself* cogitation. It is still less obvious that the robot's manipulation of descriptions of your experiential and emotional processes are themselves experiential and emotional processes.

To massage your intuitions about this a bit, substitute for the description-manipulating computer in your doppelganger's head a very small *intelligent person* who speaks only Chinese, and who possesses a manual (in Chinese) describing your psychological mechanisms. You get the input 'Who is your favorite philosopher?' You cogitate a bit and reply 'Heraclitus.' Your robot doppelganger on the other hand contains a mechanism that transforms the question into a description of its sound; then the little man deduces that you would emit the noise 'Heraclitus,' and he causes the robot's voice box to emit that noise. The robot could simulate your input-output relations (and in a sense, simulate your internal processing, too) even though the person inside the robot understands nothing of the question or the answer. It seems that the robot simulates your thinking your thoughts without itself thinking those thoughts. Returning to the case where the robot has a description-manipulating computer instead of a description-manipulating person inside it, why should we suppose that the robot has or contains any thought processes at all?[30]

The string-searching machine with which this paper has been mainly concerned showed that behavior is intelligent only if it is *not* the product of a certain sort of information processing. Appealing to the Martian example described at the beginning of the paper, I cautioned against jumping to the conclusion that there is any positive characterization of the type of information processing underlying all intelligent behavior (except that it have at least a minimal degree of 'richness'). However, what was said in connection with the Martian and string-searching examples left it open that though there is no single natural kind of information processing underlying all intelligent behavior, still there might be a kind of processing common to all *un*intelligent entities that nonetheless pass the Turing Test (viz., very simple processes operating over enormous memories). What this last machine suggests, however, is that it is also doubtful that there will be any interesting type of information processing common to such unintelligent devices.[31]

Notes

1 Indeed, Ryle's *The Concept of Mind* (London: Hutchinson, 1949) is a direct attack on psychologism. Ryle considers what we are judging 'in judging that someone's performance is or is not intelligent,' and he concludes: 'Our inquiry is *not into causes* . . . but into capacities, skills, habits, liabilities and bents.' See Jerry Fodor's *Psychological Explanation* (New York: Random House, 1968) for a penetrating critique of Ryle from a psychologistic point of view.

2 'What Is a Theory of Meaning (II),' in *Truth and Meaning*, ed. G. Evans and J. McDowell (London: Oxford University Press, 1976).

3 See my 'Troubles with Functionalism,' in *Perception and Cognition: Issues in the Foundations of Psychology*, Minnesota Studies in the Philosophy of Science, 9, ed. C. W. Savage (Minneapolis: University of Minnesota Press, 1978). Direct criticisms appear in William Lycan's 'A New Lilliputian Argument against Machine Functionalism,' *Philosophical Studies*, 35 (1979) and in Lycan's 'Form, Function, and Feel,' forthcoming in the *Journal of Philosophy*. See also Sydney Shoemaker's 'Functionalism and Qualia,' *Philosophical Studies*, 27 (1975), my reply, 'Are Absent Qualia Impossible?' *Philosophical Review*, 89 (1980), and Shoemaker's rejoinder, 'The Missing Absent Qualia Argument—a Reply to Block,' forthcoming.

4 Turning himself said the question of whether the machine could *think* should 'be replaced by' the question of whether it could pass the Turing Test, but much of the discussion of the Turing Test has been concerned with *intelligence* rather than thought. (Turning's paper [in *Mind*, 1950] was called 'Computing Machinery and *Intelligence*' [emphasis added].)

5 'Eliza—A Computer Program for the Study of Natural Language Communication between Man and Machine,' *Communications of the Association for Computing Machinery*, 9 (1965). See also M. Boden, *Artificial Intelligence* (New York: Basic Books, 1977).

6 See Roderick Chisholm, *Perceiving* (Ithaca, N. Y.: Cornell University Press, 1957), ch. 11, and Peter-Geach, *Mental Acts* (London: Routledge, 1957), p. 8.

7 'Brains and Behavior,' in Putnam's collected papers (Volume II), *Mind, Language and Reality* (London: Cambridge University Press, 1975).

8 While the Chisholm-Geach objection and the perfect actor objection ought in my view to be considered the main objections to behaviorism in the literature, they are not on *everybody's* list. Rorty, for example (*Philosophy and the Mirror of Nature* [Princeton, N. J.: Princeton University Press, 1979]), has his own list (p. 98). Rorty and others make heavy weather of one common objection that I have ignored: that behaviorism's analyses of mental states are supposed to be analytic or true in virtue of the meanings of the mental terms. I have ignored analyticity objections in part because behaviorism's main competitors, physicalism and functionalism, are often held in versions that involve commitment to analytic truth (for example, by Lewis and Shoemaker). Further, many behaviorists have been willing to settle for conceptual connections 'weaker' than analyticity, and I see no point in exploring such weakened versions of the thesis when behaviorism can be refuted quite independently of the analyticity issue.

9 I am indebted here to Sydney Shoemaker.

10 Op. cit., p. 43.

11 See R. C. Schank and R. P. Abelson, *Scripts, Plans, Goals, and Understanding: An Inquiry into Human Knowledge Structures* (Hillsdale, N. J.: Lawrence Erlbaum Assoc., 1977). See also Weizenbaum's description of the reaction to his Eliza program in his *Computer Power and Human Reason* (San Francisco: Freeman, 1976).

12 There is, admittedly, something odd about accepting a behaviorist analysis of intelligence while rejecting (on the standard grounds) behaviorist theories of belief, desire, etc. Dennett's view, as I understand it, comes close to this (see note 29), though the matter is complicated by Dennett's skepticism about many first order mental states. (See *Brainstorms* [Montgomery: Bradford, 1978], especially the Introduction, and Dennett's support of Ryle against Fodor's psychologism— p. 96 of *Brainstorms*. See also Dennett's Mary-Ruth-Sally parable on p. 105 of *Brainstorms*.) In discussions among computer scientists who accept something like the Turing Test conception, the 'oddness' of the position doesn't come to the fore because these practitioners are simply not *interested* in making machines that believe, desire, feel, etc. Rather, they focus on machines that are intelligent in being able to reason, solve problems, etc.

13 Turing says:

> The game may perhaps be criticized on the ground that the odds are weighted too heavily against the machine. If the man were to try and pretend to be the machine he would clearly make a very poor showing. He would be given away at once by slowness and inaccuracy in arithmetic. May not machines carry out something which ought to be described as thinking but which is very different from what a man does? This objection is a very strong one, but at least we can say that if, nevertheless, a machine can be constructed to play the imitation game satisfactorily, we need not be troubled by this objection. [op. cit., p. 435]

14 A disposition to φ would be more revealingly described in terms of conditionals all of whose consequent are 'φ is emitted.' But in the cases of the 'pain behavior' or 'intelligent behavior' of interest to the behaviorist, what output is appropriate depends on the input.

15 Of the inadequacies of this sort of analysis of dispositions and capacities of which I am aware, the chief one is that it seems implausible that in attributing a disposition or a capacity, one commits oneself to an infinite (or even a very large) number of specific conditionals. Rather, it seems that in saying that x has the capacity to φ, one is saying something *quite vague* about the sort of internal and external conditions in which x would φ. Notice, however, that it won't do to be *completely* vague, to analyze 'x has the capacity to φ' as 'possibly, x φs,' using a notion of possibility that holds entirely unspecified features of the actual world constant. For such an analysis would commit its proponents to ascribing too many capacities. For example, since there is a possible world in which Jimmy Carter has had a womb and associated paraphernalia surgically inserted, Jimmy Carter (*the actual one*) would have the capacity to bear children. There is a difference between the capacities someone *has* and the capacities he *might have had*, and the analysis of 'x has the capacity to φ' as 'possibly, x φs' does not respect this distinction.

16 The departure from behaviorism involved in appealing to internal states, physiologically or functionally described, is mitigated somewhat when the point of the previous footnote is taken into account. The physiological/ functional descriptions in a *proper* analysis of capacities may be so vague as to retain the behavioristic flavor of the doctrine.

17 A version of this machine was sketched in my 'Troubles with Functionalism,' op. cit.

18 This sort of point is discussed in somewhat more detail at the end of the paper.

19 What I say here should not be taken as indicating that the standard objections *really do* vanquish the neo-Turing Test conception of intelligence after all. If the idiot can be said to have the mental state [no intelligence + an overwhelming desire to appear intelligent], the sense of 'intelligence' used is the 'comparative' sense, not the sense we have been concerned with here (the sense in which intelligence is the possession of thought or reason). If the idiot *wants* to appear intelligent (in the comparative sense) and *thinks* that be can do so by memorizing strings, then he *is* intelligent in the sense of possessing (at least minimally) thought or reason.

Whether one thinks my objection is really just a variant of the 'perfect actor' objection depends on how closely one associates the perfect actor objection with the Chisholm-Geach objection. If we associate the perfect actor objection quite closely with the Chisholm-Geach objection, as I think is historically accurate (see p. 324 of Putnam's *Mind, Language and Reality*), then we will take the point of the perfect actor objection to be that different *groups of mental states* can produce the same behavioral dispositions. [mental state x + a normal preference function] can produce the same behavioral disposition as [lack of mental state x + a preference function that gives infinite weight to seeming to have mental state x]. My machine is *not a perfect actor in this sense*, since it has no mental states, and hence no groups of mental states either.

20 Such examples were suggested by Dick Boyd and Georges Rey in their comments on an earlier rendition of this paper. Rey tells me the chess story is a true tale.

21 The reader should not conclude from the 'echo' examples that what *makes* my machine unintelligent is that its responses are echoes. Actually, what makes it unintelligent is that its responses are *mere* echoes, i.e., its information processing is of the most elementary sort (and the appearances to the contrary are merely the echoes of genuinely intelligent beings). Notice that such a machine would be just as unintelligent if it were produced by a cosmic accident rather than by the long creative labors of intelligent people. What makes this accidentally produced machine unintelligent is, as before, that its information processing is of the most elementary sort; the appearances to the contrary are produced in this case not via echoes, but by a cosmic accident.

22 Hilary Putnam, 'The Meaning of 'Meaning,'' in *Language, Mind and Knowledge*, Minnesota Studies in the Philosophy of Science, 7, ed. Keith Gunderson (Minneapolis: University of Minnesota Press, 1975). See also Saul Kripke, 'Naming and Necessity,' in *Semantics and Natural Language*, ed. G. Harman and D. Davidson (Dordrecht, Holland: Reidel, 1972).

23 The theory sketched in Putnam, op. cit., might be taken to have this consequence. Whether it does have this consequence depends on whether it dictates that there is *no* descriptive component at all to the determination of the reference of natural kind terms. It seems certain that there is *some* descriptive component to the determination of the reference of natural kind terms, just as there is some descriptive component to the determination of the reference of names. There is a possible world in which Moses was an Egyptian fig merchant who spread tall tales about himself, but is there a possible world in which Moses was a brick? Similarly, even if there is a possible world in which tigers are automata, is there a possible world in which tigers exist, but are ideas? I would argue, along these lines, that the word 'intelligence' attaches to whatever natural kind our information processing belongs to (assuming it belongs to a single natural kind) *unless* our information processing fails the minimal descriptive requirement for intelligence (as ideas fail

the minimal descriptive requirement for being tigers). String-searchers, I would argue, *do* fail to have the minimal requirement for intelligence.

24 G. Miller, E. Galanter, and K. Pribram, *Plans and the Structure of Behavior* (New York: Holt, 1960), p. 146.

25 What follows is one rejoinder for which I only have space for a brief sketch. If intelligence = sensible response capacity (and if the terms flanking the ' = ' are rigid), then the *metaphysical* possibility of my machine is enough to defeat the neo-Turing Test conception, even if it is not nomologically possible. (The claim that there are metaphysical possibilities that are not also nomological possibilities is one that I cannot argue for here.)

What if the neo-Turing Test conception of intelligence is formulated not as an identity claim, but as the claim that a certain capacity is nomologically necessary and sufficient for intelligence? I would argue that if F is nomologically necessary and sufficient for G, then one of the following holds:

(a) This nomological coextensivity is an ultimate law of nature.
(b) This nomological coextensivity can be explained in terms of an underlying mechanism.
(c) $F = G$.

In case (c), the claim is vulnerable to the point of the previous paragraph. Case (a) is obviously wrong. And in case (b), intelligence must be identifiable with something other than the capacity to give sensible responses. Suppose, for example, that we can give a mechanistic account of the correlation of intelligence with sensible response capacity by showing that intelligence requires a certain sort of cognitive structure, and creatures with such a cognitive structure have the required capacity. But then intelligence should be identified with *the cognitive structure* and not with the capacity. See my 'Reductionism,' in the *Encyclopedia of Bioethics* (New York: Macmillan, 1978), for a brief discussion of some of these ideas.

26 It may be objected that since brute force information processing methods are far more effective in the world in which matter is infinitely divisible than in ours, the laws of thought in that world *do* differ from the laws of thought in ours. But this objection begs the question, since if the string-searching machine I described cannot think in *any* world (as I would argue), the nomological difference which makes it possible is a difference in laws which affect the *simulation* of thought, not a difference in laws of thought.

27 This machine would get ever larger unless the programmers were allowed to abandon strings which had been rendered useless by the course of the conversation. (In the tree-searching version, this would amount to pruning by-passed branches.)

28 Alan Newell and Herbert Simon, 'Computer Science as Empirical Inquiry: Symbols and Search,' in *Communications of the Association for Computing Machinery*, 19 (1979), 123.

29 I am indebted to Dan Dennett for forcefully making this objection in his role as respondent to an earlier version of this paper in the University of Cincinnati Philosophy of Psychology Conference in 1978. Dennett tells me that he advocates the neo-Turing Test conception as amended above.

30 Much more needs to be said to turn this remark into a serious argument. Intuitions about homunculi-headed creatures are too easily manipulable to stand on their own. For example, I once argued against functionalism by describing a robot that is functionally equivalent to a person, but is controlled by an 'external brain' consisting of an army of people, each doing the job of a 'square' in a machine table that describes a person. William Lycan objected ('Form, Function, and Feel,' op. cit.) that the intuition that the aforementioned creature lacked mentality could

be made to go away by imagining yourself reduced to the size of a molecule, and standing inside a person's sensory cortex. Seeing the molecules bounce about, it might seem absurd to you that what you were watching was a series of events that constituted or was crucial to some being's experience. Similarly, Lycan suggests, the intuition that my homunculi-heads lack qualia is an illusion produced by missing the forest for the trees, that is, by focusing on 'the hectic activities of the little men, . . . seeing the homunculi-head as if through a microscope rather than as a whole macroscopic person.' (David Rosenthal made the same objection in correspondence with me.)

While I think that the Lycan-Rosenthal point does genuinely alter one's intuitions, it can be avoided by considering a variant of the original example in which a *single* homunculus does the whole job, his *attention to column* S_i of a machine table posted in his compartment playing precisely the causal role required for the robot he controls to *have* S_i. (See 'Are Absent Qualia Impossible?' op. cit., for a somewhat more detailed description of this case.) No 'forest for the trees' illusion can be at work here. Nonetheless, the Lycan-Rosenthal point does illustrate the manipulability of intuitions, and the danger of appealing to intuition without examining the source of the intuition. The role of most of the early objections and replies in this paper was to locate the source of our intuitions about the stupidity of the string-searching machine in its extremely simple information processing.

Another difficulty with the description-manipulator example is that it may seem that such an example could be used to show that *no symbol manipulation theory of thought processes* (such as those popular in cognitive psychology and artificial intelligence) *could be correct*, since one could always imagine a being in which the symbol-manipulating mechanisms are replaced by homunculi. (John Searle uses an example of the same sort as mine to make such a case in 'Minds, Brains and Programs,' forthcoming in *The Behavioral and Brain Sciences*. See my reply in the same issue.) While I cannot defend it here, I would claim that some symbol-manipulating homunculi-heads *are* intelligent, and that what justifies us in regarding some symbol-manipulating homunculus-heads (such as the one just described in the text) as unintelligent is that the causal relations among their states do not mirror the causal relations among our mental states.

31 Previous versions of this paper were read at a number of universities and meetings, beginning with the 1977 meeting of the Association for Symbolic Logic. I am indebted to the following persons for comments on previous drafts: Sylvain Bromberger, Noam Chomsky, Jerry Fodor, Paul Horwich, Jerry Katz, Israel Krakowski, Robert Kirk, Philip Kitcher, David Lewis, Hugh Lacey, William Lycan, Charles Marks, Dan Osherson, Georges Rey, Sydney Shoemaker, George Smith, Judy Thomson, Richard Warner, and Scott Weinstein.

73

THE TURING TEST

AI's biggest blind alley?

Blay Whitby

Source: P. Millican and A. Clark (eds), *Machines and Thought: The Legacy of Alan Turing*, Oxford University Press, 1996, pp. 53–62.

Introduction

Alan Turing's 1950 paper, 'Computing Machinery and Intelligence',[1] and the 'Turing Test' suggested in it are rightly seen as inspirational to the inception and development of artificial intelligence (AI). However, inspiration can soon become distraction in science, and it is not too early to begin to consider whether or not the Turing test is just such a distraction. What will be argued is that this is indeed the case with the Turing Test and AI.

AI has had an intimate relationship with the Turing Test throughout its brief history. The view of this relationship presented in this paper is that it has developed more or less as follows:

1950–66: A source of inspiration to all concerned with AI.
1966–73: A distraction from some more promising avenues of AI research.
1973–90: By now a source of distraction mainly to philosophers, rather than AI workers.
1990 onwards: Consigned to history.[2]

One conclusion that is implied by this view of the history of AI and Turing's 1950 paper is that for most of the period since its publication it has been a distraction. While not detracting from the brilliance of the paper and its central role in the philosophy of AI, it can be argued that Turning's 1950 paper, or perhaps some strong interpretations of it have, on occasion, hindered both the practical development of AI and the philosophical work necessary to facilitate that development. Thus one can make the claim that, in an important philosophical sense, 'Computing Machinery and Intelligence' has led AI into a blind alley from which it is only just beginning to extract itself.

One main source of this distraction has been the common, yet mistaken reading of 'Computing Machinery and Intelligence' as somehow 'showing' that one can attempt to build an intelligent machine without a prior understanding of the nature of intelligence. If we can, by whatever means, build a computer-based system which deceives a human interrogator for a while into suspecting that it might be human, then we have solved the many philosophical, scientific, and engineering problems of AI! This simplistic reading has, of course, proved both false and misleading in practice. The key to this misreading would seem to be the mistaken view that Turing's paper contains an adequate operational definition of intelligence. A later section of this paper suggests an interpretation of 'Computing Machinery and Intelligence' and of the 'imitation game' in their historical context. This interpretation does not imply the existence of an operational definition of intelligence.

That 'Computing Machinery and Intelligence' was almost immediately read as providing an operational definition of intelligence is witnessed by the change from the label 'imitation game' to 'Turning Test' by commentators. Turing himself was always careful to refer to 'the game'. The suggestion that it might be some sort of test involves an important extension of Turing's claims. This is not some small semantic quibble, but an important suggestion that Turning's paper was being interpreted as closer to an operational test than he himself intended.

It will be argued in the remainder of this paper that this general misreading of Turing's 1950 paper has led to the currency of three mistaken assertion, namely:

(1) Intelligence in computing machinery is (or is nearly or includes) being able to deceive a human interlocutor.
(2) The best approach to the problem of defining intelligence is through some sort of operational test, of which the imitation game is a paradigm example.
(3) Work specifically directed at producing a machine which could perform well in the imitation game is genuine (or perhaps even useful) AI research.

This paper will not pursue the falsity of assertions (1) and (2) in any great detail. On claim (1) it should be sufficient to remark that the comparative success of ELIZA[3] and programs like it at deceiving human interlocutors could not be held to indicate that they are closer to achieving intelligence than more sophisticated AI work. Other writers have convincingly attacked claim (2) on the grounds that the imitation game does not test for intelligence, but rather for other items such as cultural similarity.[4]

Instead this paper focuses on assertion (3) and the effect of this assertion on the history of AI. The claim is that work directed at success in the Turning Test is neither genuine nor useful AI research. In particular, the point will be stressed that, irrespective of whether or not Turing's 1950 paper provided one, the last thing that AI has needed since 1966 is an operational definition of intelligence.

Few, if any, philosophers and AI researchers would assent to claim (3) stated boldly. However, the influence of Alan Turing and his 1950 paper on the history of AI has been so profound that such mistaken claims can have a significant influence at a 'subconscious' (or more properly a subcultural) level.

In any case, the passing of more than forty years gives sufficient historical perspective to enable us to begin to debate the way in which 'Computing machinery and Intelligence' has influenced the development of AI. The basic theme of this paper is that the influence of Turning's 1950 paper has been largely unfortunate. This is not through any fault of the paper, but is rather a consequence of the historical circumstances which obtained at the time of its writing and some of the pressures which have affected the subsequent development of AI.

Some consequences of misinterpretation of 'computing machinery and intelligence'

The main consequence of perceiving intelligence in terms of some sort of imitation of human performance, such as success in the imitation game, is that AI research and experiment has paid far too much attention to the development of machinery and programs which seek directly or indirectly to imitate human performance. It might, at first, be thought that this was inevitable since human behaviour is the only practical clue to the nature of intelligence which is readily available. However, this is a mistaken view. We know so very little about the nature of human intelligence that we cannot produce a definition which is of use to an AI engineer. Such a definition would have to make no direct reference to either humans or machines.

This focus of AI research on imitation of human performance has at least three unfortunate consequences. First, it does not seem to have been very productive. Secondly, as I have argued at length elsewhere,[5] it is unlikely to lead to profitable or safe applications of AI. New technology is generally taken up quickly where there is a clear deficiency in existing technologies and very slowly, if at all, where it offers only a marginal improvement over existing technologies. Even an amateur salesman of AI should be able to see that researchers should be steered away from programs that imitate human beings. The old quip about there being no shortage of natural intelligence contains an important truth. There are many safe, profitable applications for AI, but programs inspired by the imitation game are unlikely to lead towards them. This sort of research is more likely to produce interesting curiosities such as ELIZA than working AI applications.

A third unfortunate consequence is the way in which the myth that intelligence can be operationally defined as some sort of imitation of human beings has apparently exempted both philosophers and AI researchers from the rather difficult task of providing the sort of definition of intelligence which would be of use to AI. To be useful in AI research any definition of intelligence needs to be independent of human capabilities. This is for a number of reasons. Among these are the lack of a clear understanding of human intellectual abilities and the lack of an uncontroversial framework within which such understanding might be achieved. Human psychology as a study is divided into factions which do not agree on basic methodological questions or on the definition of basic terms. It is not the purpose of this paper to be critical of human psychology, but simply to observe that human psychology is not, and is not for some time likely to be, in a position to provide AI with the theoretical basis which would turn it from a form of research into a form of engineering.

In various other places,[6] an analogy has been developed between AI and artificial flight. One feature of this analogy which is relevant here is the way in which direct imitation of natural flight proved a relatively fruitless avenue of research. It is true that many serious aviation pioneers did make a detailed study of bird flight, the most notable being Otto Lilienthal; but it must be stressed that working aircraft were developed by achieving greater understanding of the principles of aerodynamics. The Wright brothers were extremely thorough and precise scientists. They succeeded because they were thorough in their experimental methods, whereas others had failed because they were too hasty to build aircraft based upon incomplete theoretical work. There may be some important lessons for AI research in the methodology of the Wrights.[7]

It is also importantly true that our understanding of bird flight has stemmed from our knowledge of aerodynamics and not the reverse.[8] If there were an imitation game type of test for flight we would probably still not be able to build a machine which could pass it. Some aircraft can imitate some features of bird flight such as a glider when soaring in a thermal, but totally convincing imitation does not exist. We do not know how to build a practical ornithopter (an aircraft which employs a birdlike wing-flapping motion) but this is not of any real importance. Some of the purposes for which we use artificial flight, such as the speedy crossing of large distances, are similar to the purposes for which natural flight has evolved, but others, such as controlling the re-entry of spacecraft, are radically different. It is clear that AI, if it is to be a useful technology, should undergo a similar development. Many of the most useful applications for AI will be in areas which in no way replace or imitate natural intelligence. It is quite probable that we will never build a machine which could pass the Turing Test in its entirety, but this may well be because we can see little use for such a machine; indeed it could have danger-ous side-effects.

What is needed is a definition of intelligence which does not draw on our assumed intuitive knowledge of our own abilities. Such knowledge is at best vague and unreliable, and there may be Gödel-like[9] reasons for believing that we do not fully understand our own capabilities. Some writers have made tentative approaches to such a definition[10] and perhaps some common fea-tures are beginning to emerge, among which are that any intelligent entity must be able to form clearly discernible goals. This is a feature which is not suggested by the Turing Test nor possessed by programs which have reputedly done well in the imitation game, such as ELIZA, DOCTOR,[11] and PARRY.[12]

In considering AI as an engineering enterprise— concerned with the development of useful products— the effects of the imitation game are dif-ferent but equally misleading. If we focus future work in AI on the imitation of human abilities, such as might be required to succeed in the imitation game, we are in effect building 'intellectual statues' when what we need are 'intellectual tools'. This may prove to be an expensive piece of vanity. In other words, there is no reason why successful AI products should relate to us as if they were humans. They may instead resemble a workbench which enables a human operator to achieve much more than he could without it, or perhaps be largely invisible to humans in that they operate automatically and autonomously.

A more useful interpretation of 'computing machinery and intelligence'

If we are not to read Turing's 1950 paper as providing an operational defin-ition of intelligence, what are we to make of it? There has, of course, been a preponderance of interpretations which stress the use of the imitation game as a test for intelligence or the ability to think. In fact in the reported discus-sions about his work in the all too brief three years before his death in 1953, Turing seems to have allowed this sort of interpretation to have played a significant part.[13] It is possible to explain Turing's toleration of such inter-pretations of the paper as something more than the desire for a good argument.

There is little point in being sidetracked into a discussion of Turing's actual intention at the time of his writing. This is, probably correctly, known in literary criticism as 'the intentionalist fallacy'. What matters is the way in which the paper has been and is to be interpreted. However, in order to explain the first part of a better interpretation, it is necessary to set the paper in its historical context. The 1950 paper was in many ways based upon a report written for the National Physics Laboratory in August 1948.[14] This in turn, although ostensibly a technical report, drew together Turing's speculations on the possibility of building an intelligent machine which had been carried on in conversation at least as far back as 1940 at Bletchley Park.

During this period Turing (among others) was leading what Thomas Kuhn has christened a 'paradigm shift'.[15] This paradigm shift involved an understanding of what we would now call the logical and physical aspects of certain types of systems. The wartime work at Bletchley Park was crucial to the development of this paradigm shift, as Turing was one of the few men who could fully appreciate what the Polish cryptanalysts had done in the years immediately preceding 1939, in discovering how the *physical* nature of the Enigma coding machine could be deduced from the *logical* nature of its output. This work also involved the building of further *physical* machines such as the Colossi to assist in the deciphering of the intercepted traffic, that is, the *logical* output of another machine. The whole of computing is founded upon this understanding of the way in which physical and logical systems can be direct counterparts of each other. However, the fact that we all understand this now should not distract us from the fact that in 1940 only a few men of vision were capable of appreciating its importance. By 1950 this paradigm shift had spread more widely in computing and the sciences, but not to philosophy or the general public.

Thus a crucial part of 'Computing Machinery and Intelligence' is devoted to pursuing the philosophical implications of applying this paradigm shift to the question of whether or not machines can think. In the imitation game Turing picks a man and a woman because they would be obviously physically different. Turing assumes that the general public would have no difficult in appreciating that there are physical differences between participants in the imitation game. However, the observer is denied any access to the physical attributes of the participants in the imitation game and instead must try to deduce these from their logical output via a teletype. In a way it is Enigma revisited, but with human beings. Just as the wartime cryptanalysts had to deduce the physical nature of the Enigma coding device by observing logical patterns in its output, so the observer in the imitation game must attempt to distinguish the physical differences between the participants by discerning differing patterns of output.

When a machine is introduced into the game the observer is again forced to view it in terms of its logical output. Turing does not need to take a view on how successful the observer might be in distinguishing the man from the woman. He simply suggests that when a machine is introduced into the game and achieves comparable levels of success in producing indistinguishable output then we can no longer attach much importance to physical differences between women, men, and machines. What Turing managed creatively to show was that the paradigm shift in which he had a leading role could be applied to the familiar question: 'Can a machine think?' The imitation game contrived a method, understandable to a wide audience, of showing what

Turing and a few others had already clearly grasped: that observable physical features have a subordinate role in answering such questions.

The remaining portion of a useful interpretation of 'Computing Machinery and Intelligence' is more relevant today. It also explains the continuing appeal of the Turing Test to present-day writers. This is because 'Computing Machinery and Intelligence' clearly illustrates the importance of human attitudes in determining the answers to questions such as 'can machines think?'

Ascribing the label 'intelligent' is not a purely technical exercise; it involves a number of moral and social dimensions. Human beings consider themselves obligated to behave in certain ways toward intelligent items.

To claim that the ascription of intelligence has moral and social dimensions is not merely to claim that it has moral and social consequences. It may well be the case that certain moral and social criteria must be satisfied before such an ascription can be made. In a sense it is true that we feel more at ease in ascribing intelligence (and sometimes even the ability to think) to those entities with which we can have an interesting conversation than with radically different entities. It is this feature of the ascription of intelligence which makes the use of any sort of operational test of intelligence with human beings so unattractive.

These moral and social dimensions to the ascription of intelligence are also covered by 'Computing Machinery and Intelligence'. Turing wanted to ask (although he obviously could not answer) the question: 'What would be the human reaction to the sort of machine which could succeed in the imitation game?' If, as Turing clearly believed, digital computers could, by the end of the century, succeed in deceiving an interrogator 70 per cent of the time, how would we describe such a feat? This is not primarily a technical or philosophical question, but rather a question about human attitudes. As Turing himself observed, the meaning of words such as 'thinking' can change with changing patterns of usage. Although sampling human attitudes as a method of answering the question 'can a machine think?' is rejected in the first paragraph of 'Computing Machinery and Intelligence', we can read the entire paper as primarily concerned with human attitudes. The contrivance of the imitation game was intended to show the importance of human attitudes, not to be an operational definition of intelligence.

Given this interpretation of the paper, it is not surprising that Turing tolerated a certain amount of misinterpretation of the role of the imitation game. The paper itself was partly an exercise in testing and changing human attitudes. Turing fully expected it to provoke a certain amount of controversy. However, in the fourth decade of research in AI this sort of controversy is no longer productive.

Conclusions

After the passage of over forty years it is safe to assume that not only will Turing's prediction of machines succeeding in the imitation game by the end of the century not come about, but also that it probably never will be achieved. There would be little practical use for a machine aimed specifically at success in the imitation game. Furthermore, examination of AI products from a 1990s perspective prompts a high degree of cynicism about the possibility of success in the imitation game being simply an emergent property of computers with sufficient memory and performance.

It should be clear that at this stage in the development of AI there is nothing to be gained by clinging to the notion of the imitation game as an operational test for intelligence. It is now clear that we need AI for a number of practical purposes, including making computing machinery more useful. To imagine, for whatever reason, that this involves making computers more like human beings may well be a distracting vanity.

In conclusion it is worth repeating that the last thing needed by AI *qua* science is an operational definition of intelligence involving some sort of comparison with human beings. The need here is for an account of intelligence which makes no direct reference to either humans or machines. This is analogous to the account provided by the science of aerodynamics in the field of artificial flight. AI *qua* engineering should not be distracted into direct copying of human performance and methods. There is no reason to assume either that this is an easy task, or that it is likely to produce useful products.

Notes

I am grateful to Professor Aaron Sloman for his comments on an early draft of this paper.

1 A. M. Turing, 'Computing Machinery and Intelligence', *Mind*, 59/236: 433–60. I shall assume familiarity with the text of this paper throughout.
2 The (somewhat arbitrary) dates in this history are derived from the first publications describing ELIZA (1966) and PARRY (1973) and the Turing 1990 Colloquium.
3 J. Weizenbaum, 'ELIZA—A Computer Program for the Study of Natural Language Communication between Man and Machine', *Communications of the A.C.M.*, 9/1: 36–45.
4 See e.g. R. French (in this volume, pages 11–26) and D. Michie (in this volume, pages 27–51).
5 B. R. Whitby, *AI: A Handbook of Professionalism*, Ellis Horwood, Chichester (1988), ch. I.
6 e.g. in B. R. Whitby, ibid., ch. 2. and in M. Yazdani and B. R. Whitby 'Artificial Intelligence: Building Birds out of Beer Cans', *Robotica*, 5(1987): 89–92.
7 There are two features of the Wright's methodology which contrast sharply with other contemporary experimenters and which may have relevance to AI. First, they spent a good deal of time looking at the work, both successful and unsuccess-

ful, of previous aviation experimenters. They developed a coherent account of these successes and failures. Secondly and surprisingly, unlike most of their contemporaries they had a full appreciation of the need to control any aircraft in addition to simply getting it airborne. See e.g. D. Mondey (ed.), *The International Encyclopaedia of Aviation*, Octopus, London (1977), 38–49.

8 In 1928 the first successful soaring flight was made in a glider; the aircraft climbing in the rising air of a thermal. Birds had been observed doing so for centuries; but at this time many biologists maintained that they could do so by virtue of the air trapped within the hollow bones of their wings being expanded by the heat of the sun. In this case a young pilot was able to overturn biological theory by performing the same feat.

9 See e.g. J. R. Lucas, 'Minds Machines and Gödel', *Philosophy*, 36 (1961): 112–27 and in this volume, pp. 103–24.

10 e.g. R. C. Schank, *Explanation Patterns*, Lawrence Erlbaum, London (1986) and M. Yazdani (ed.), *Artificial Intelligence*, Chapman & Hall, London, 263.

11 For the claim that DOCTOR passed the 'Turing Test' see D. Michie, *On Machine Intelligence*, Ellis Horwood, Chichester (2nd edn., 1986), 241–2.

12 K. M. Colby, F. D. Hilf, Sylvia Weber, and H. C. Kraemer, 'Turing-Like Indistinguishability Tests for the Validation of a Computer Simulation of Paranoid Processes', in *Artificial Intelligence*, 3(1972): 199–222.

13 For the best account of this brief period see A. Hodges, *Alan Turing, The Enigma of Intelligence*, Unwin, London (1983), 413–46.

14 Eventually published (though perhaps incorrectly dated) in B. Meltzer and D. Michie (eds.), *Machine Intelligence 5*, Edinburgh University Press.

15 T. S. Kuhn, *The Structure of Scientific Revolutions*, University of Chicago Press (2nd edn., 1970).

Part II

BROADER CONTEXT

Section 2.1: Artificial Mentality
Section 2.2: Ethics
Section 2.3: Social Issues

INTRODUCTION

The concept of artificial intelligence in a
wider perspective

Sander Begeer

1 Artificial mentality

The final part of this volume broadens the consideration of the concept of artificial intelligence in three ways. The section on artificial mentality highlights features of an artificial mind that go beyond mere intelligence. The three chosen articles, though in no way representative of all the work in this field, provide the reader with illuminating and provocative discussions on consciousness, emotion and creativity. The cognitive revolution was in large part a repudiation of behaviourism's proscription against appealing to inner mental states, according to Bechtel. Artificial intelligence, as a central discipline of cognitive science, turned to information processing, rather than experience, as the kind of inner event on which it would focus. Some aspects of consciousness did seem critical to the information processing model though, and Bechtel asks here whether computational models can be thought to offer accounts of consciousness. Symbolic and connectionist perspectives are given that focus on the functional modelling of some aspects of consciousness. The need for physical explanations over functional ones is related to the intentionality, awareness and qualitative character of conscious mental states. In particular, Searle's Chinese Room argument against artificial intelligence (see the Introduction to Part II of Volume III) is evaluated.

Wright, Sloman and Beaudoin show how ideas in artificial intelligence can serve as ways of explaining emotional phenomena, deriving from suggestions made by Simon in 1967. A design-based approach is used, a methodology for investigating mechanisms capable of generating mental phenomena, whether they occur in humans, animals or machines. This approach is applied to the emotional phenomenon of grief, a topic chosen for its involvement of a loss of control of thought processes. Representing an early stage of a possible general architecture, the interpretative ground is provided for (some) emotional phenomena.

Boden, one of the most prominent scholars of artificial intelligence in its widest sense, discusses the challenge of modelling creativity. The novelty of creative ideas can be perceived with respect to an individual (psychological creativity), or the whole of previous history (historical creativity). Three types of creativity are distinguished here: producing novel combinations of familiar ideas, exploring potential and conceptual spaces, and making transformations that enable the generation of previously impossible ideas. Computer models of creativity are discussed that exhibit or model these kinds of creativity. Transformational creativity may be regarded as the ultimate creativity in humans, but many workers in artificial intelligence prefer to avoid this level, since transformation of the rules of an artificial intelligence program does not necessarily lead to a superior system. The evaluation of new ideas is a related problem, and the ultimate program that will persuade us of the value of its self-generated ideas remains fiction in the science of present day.

2 Ethics

Much has been written about the ethical implications of artificial intelligence, so the two included articles can only amount to scratching the surface, a starting point for further research.

Torrance's discussion of our moral duties towards intelligent artefacts pivots on the issue of consciousness. First, he makes a distinction between narrow and wide artificial intelligence, between merely reproducing some aspects of mentality (e.g. intelligence) in an artefact, and reproducing all of human mentality (including consciousness, emotion, etc.) in an artefact. Making an analogy with animals, he implies that our moral duties towards artefacts depend on the capacity of the artefact, e.g. to feel pain. So narrow artificial intelligence (which he thinks may be all that is on offer via the computational approach) would not produce the kinds of artefacts to which we would have moral obligations. However, Torrance does not consider the ethical tradition in which the wrong of doing harm to animals does not derive from the fact that it causes pain, but from the fact that it brutalises us, and desensitises us to human pain (see, e.g., Elton 2000). To put things simplistically, on the this line it would be wrong to do harm to (e.g., cheat) a chess-playing computer, even one which we believe to lack consciousness, emotion, etc., if doing so would make us more likely to cheat and distrust humans.

Torrance argues that it is not the artefactuality as such that makes people balk at (wide) artificial intelligence, but rather the clanking, clumsy, inflexible nature of the usual mechanical, computational visions of what such an artefact might be like (although he might not put it that way). He envisions a field ("psychotechnics") that attempts to create intelligent artefacts non-computationally, biologically (involving, e.g. "cells synthesised in a laboratory"). The products of this field would be artefacts in a sense (however, see the general introduction); yet one could not in any principled manner deny that we have moral duties to them.

The final part of the paper is a rejection of Sloman's idea that we do not first determine the *fact* of whether or not an agent is conscious, and then use that fact to conclude that we have moral obligations towards that agent; rather, Sloman says, first comes our behaviour towards that agent, and such behaviour will constitute (or not) our classification of it as a moral being. Torrance responds that taking ethical beliefs seriously calls Sloman's view into question. We can agree on all our ethical beliefs, and yet differ in our behaviour because we disagree on some factual beliefs, such as whether or not a machine is conscious.

In passing, Torrance worries about what he sees as the increasing domination of the field of artificial intelligence by military and corporate concerns. But if Edwards (Volume I, article 18) is correct, Torrance's perception is illusory: the field has been so dominated since its inception.

After a brief discussion of the possibilities of artificial intelligence and the Turing Test, LaChat looks at two ethical issues of artificial intelligence: the morality of making an intelligent artefact, and the question of whether such an artefact would itself be a moral agent. He likens "the AI experiment" to experimenting on persons, and argues that the latter is only justified if there are overwhelming benefits to society. He then argues (fallaciously, it seems) that since the production of artificial intelligence is not necessary to the survival of our species (we can reproduce without it), it is not of overwhelming benefit to us, and therefore the "experiment" cannot be justified. He also considers the suggestion that rather than an experiment, creating an artificial intelligence is analogous to giving birth, but rejects this because he sees birth, and not intelligent artefact creation, as something over which we have control (a bizarre converse of the view on these matters considered in the general introduction). As for whether intelligent artefacts can be moral agents, his discussion with respect to free will is best summarised as "confused". But what he says about morality and emotion is interesting: on the one hand, any supposed lack of emotion in an intelligent artefact (but see Wright, Sloman and Beaudoin, article 75) might count *in favour* of it being a moral agent, since its lack of emotional bias would make it, at least on one moral theory, an even better moral judge than we are. However, the same moral theory demands omnipercipience ("the ability to vividly imagine the feelings and circumstances of the parties involved, that is, something like empathy") of its ideal moral judge. So what the robot gains on the swings, it loses on the roundabouts: it has, by hypothesis, no emotions so empathising is out of the question. But perhaps LaChat is wrong to equate the imaginative ability of omnipercipience with empathy; perhaps the former does not require the ability to *have* emotions, only the ability to *know* what emotions would be possessed in any given situation. The artificial intelligence could then employ a *theory* of emotions to take the anticipated emotions into account during its moral deliberations. The discussion of casuistry, or the application of ethical rules, suffers from a focus on Asimov's "Three Laws of Robotics" (misquoted as "Rules for Robotics"). In his conclusion LaChat misquotes Hegel's "The owl of Minerva spreads its wings only with the coming of the dawn", but his point is clear: we cannot afford to wait before thinking about these issues.

3 Social issues

Any overview of social perspectives on the concept of an intelligent artefact will be inexhaustive. The dividing line between man and machine has been sought for in many fields besides artificial intelligence. The bridge between the artificial intelligence community and researchers in the humanities and sociology has been made apparent most significantly in issues of the *Stanford Electronic Humanities Review* (1995) and *Daedalus* (1988). One of the joint features of the papers included in this section is the emphasis on the subjectivity of artificial intelligence.

Armer, former head of the computer sciences department of the RAND Corporation, first published his paper as a Warr Technical report for the symposium on Bionics in 1960. It was included in one of the first collections of artificial intelligence papers, "Computers and Thought", edited by Feigenbaum and Feldman in 1962. Armer provides a review and analysis of various preconceived notions of machine intelligence, based on a survey of the literature and his own observations in the US and the USSR. A short overview of famous historical attitudes towards artificial intelligence precedes a recital of arguments against the possibility of an intelligent machine. An interesting, early account is given of an oft-used analogy between artificial intelligence and artificial flight (see for example Whitby and Yazdani 1987). Armer's subsequent description of the Soviet attitudes towards artificial intelligence is interesting both for its political and scientific point of view. The Soviet editors of the Russian-language version of "Computers and Thought" replaced, without requesting permission, Armer's paper with a Russian one.

Laufer discusses the social acceptability of artificial intelligence systems through the notions of legitimacy, epistemology and marketing. The emergence of the culture of the artificial is described from a French philosophical perspective here. In order to study the social acceptability of artificial intelligence systems, Laufer provides an analysis of the way people discuss artificial intelligence, rather than an analysis of artificial intelligence itself. He suggests that social acceptability can be defined as equivalent to the notion of legitimacy. Systems of legitimacy of Western societies are characterised by the central place reason and science occupy in them. Artificial intelligence is linked to the notion of epistemology, and will be defined as the "ultimate expression of the crisis affecting the very foundation of the system of legitimacy in our society, i.e. scientific reason".

Sociologist Steve Woolgar evaluates the prospects of an association between sociology and artificial intelligence, with particular reference to expert systems. Three key features are described: the distinction between the social and the scientific, that the fact that the interpretative flexibility of intelligence facilitates the constant redefinition of the operational correlate of these entities, and the appearance-essence distinction. Different styles of an internalist sociology of artificial intelligence are considered, referring to the genesis of artificial intelligence rather than its effects. Difficulties in "finding" science as a sociologist are compared to "finding" intelligence rather than mere signs of intelligence. According to Woolgar the distinction between the latter two has several consequences: the claim that the metaphysical entity is not reducible to epistemology preserves the object of inquiry and therefore the object's existence, and relieves it of the responsibility to reveal itself. Thus it can always be said that we have not yet got the object, which provides the artificial intelligence community with a seemingly endless research programme. It is important to examine how sociology presumes human behaviour to be unlike the performance of a machine. Woolgar asks: are machines the subject or object of sociology? The question whether human behaviour can be understood as distinctively social is reassessed by artificial intelligence.

The subjectivity of artificial intelligence devices is further challenged by Adam, who highlights the "gendered" vision of the world which is inscribed in artificial intelligence systems. The "knowing subject" in artificial intelligence is not an independent entity, but connected to others and grounded in its (male) culture. The impossibility of achieving a universal, perspectiveless viewpoint is revealed through the discussion of two well known artificial intelligence systems, CYC and SOAR, systems which have been described in detail in the papers in Volume II, Part I.

There was perhaps never a moment in the ancient or modern history of Europe when no one was pursuing the idea of making a human being by other than the ordinary reproductive means. Each age has found in the human mind precisely what it has brought to the search, Bolter writes. Metaphorical explanations, from the city-state of the ancient Greeks (see the discussion of Plato and Turing in the introduction to Volume II, Part I) through the clockworks of the middle ages to the digital computer of the present day, are discussed in this illuminating chapter, taken from "Turing's Man", a highly regarded history of Western culture in the computer age (and perhaps a perverse choice for an article to follow Adam's, given its title). Artificial intelligence is regarded as a special skill in engineering and logic rather than a science by the author, who describes artificial intelligence programs as decorations which should not be underestimated, much like the great Strasbourg clock in the time of Leibniz and Descartes. The modern computer man is fulfilling the same function as the ancient metaphors, an expression of both the possibilities and the limits of a new technology. All researchers in this area accept to some degree the idea that computers and humans are comparable things. Man the artificer and man the artefact merge, and a new freedom from nature is accomplished. Men tend to regard what they make as in some measure human. The artefact changes the artificer, and, as before, technology determines what part of the man will be illuminated.

References

The Stanford Electronic Humanities Review (1995) **4**:2.

Daedalus: Journal of the American Academy of Arts and Sciences (1988) **117**:1.

Elton, M. (2000) "Should Vegetarians Play Video Games?" Philosophical Papers (to appear).

Hegel, G. W. F. (1976) *The Philosophy of Right*, T. M. Knox, (trans.), Oxford: Oxford University Press.

Simon, H. A. (1967) "Motivational and Emotional Controls of Cognition", reprinted in H. A. Simon, (1979) *Models of Thought*, New Haven: Yale University Press.

Whitby, B. and Yazdani, M. (1987) "Artificial Intelligence: Building Birds out of Beer Cans", *Robotica* **5**:89–92.

Section 2.1: Artificial Mentality

74

CONSCIOUSNESS: PERSEPECTIVES FROM SYMBOLIC AND CONNECTIONIST AI

William Bechtel

Source: *Neuropsychologia* 33, 1994: 1075–86.

1 Computational models of consciousness

For many people, consciousness is one of the defining characteristics of mental states. Thus, it is quite surprising that consciousness has, until quite recently, had very little role to play in the cognitive sciences. Three very popular multi-authored overviews of cognitive science, Stillings et al. [33], Posner [26], and Osherson et al. [25], do not have a single reference to consciousness in their indexes. One reason this seems surprising is that the cognitive revolution was, in large part, a repudiation of behaviorism's proscription against appealing to inner mental events. When researchers turned to consider inner mental events, one might have expected them to turn to conscious states of mind. But in fact the appeals were to postulated inner events of information processing. The model for many researchers of such information processing is the kind of transformation of symbolic structures that occurs in a digital computer. By positing procedures for performing such transformation of incoming information, cognitive scientists could hope to account for the performance of cognitive agents. Artificial intelligence, as a central discipline of cognitive science, has seemed to impose some of the toughest tests on the ability to develop information processing accounts of cognition: it required its researchers to develop running programs whose performance one could compare with that of our usual standard for cognitive agents, human beings. As a result of this focus, for AI researchers to succeed, at least in their primary task, they did not need to attend to consciousness; they simply had to design programs that behaved appropriately (no small task in itself!)

This is not to say that conscious was totally ignored by artificial intelligence researchers. Some aspect of our conscious experience seemed critical to the success of any information processing model. For example, conscious agents exhibit selective attention. Some information received through their senses is attended to; much else is ignored. What is attended to varies with the task being performed: when one is busy with a conceptual problem, one may not hear the sounds of one's air conditioner going on and off, but if one is engaged in repairing the controls on the air conditioning system, one may be very attentive to these sounds. In order for AI systems to function in the real world (especially if they are embodied in robots) it is necessary to control attention, and a fair amount of AI research has been devoted to this topic.

Moreover, conscious thought seems to be linear: we are not aware of having multiple thoughts at once, but rather of one thought succeeding another. Typically other processing is occurring at the same time, but it is not brought into the linear sequence of consciousness. This is suggestive of the role of an executive in some AI systems, which is responsible for coordinating and directing the flow of information needed for action. Johnson-Laird [19], who argues for the need for much of the computation underlying behavior to proceed in parallel, proposes that consciousness arises with a high level processing system that coordinates lower level processes. Finally, conscious states are states people have access to, can report on to others, and can rely on in conducting their own actions. Capturing an aspect of this has turned out to be particularly important in a variety of computer programs, especially those we rely on to make or advise about decisions. We want to query them about their decisions or recommendations so as to evaluate whether they were reasonable. But Johnson-Laird points out that humans go much further: we can use information about our own states to guide our actions. He therefore proposes that what is needed for cognitive systems to be conscious is that they possess a recursive ability to model (albeit partially and incompletely) what is going on in themselves, and to use such models in controlling future activity (mental and physical).

The strategy employed by Johnson-Laird (himself a psychologist, albeit one with a strong computational perspective) and those AI researchers who have taken consciousness seriously has been to focus on the functions of conscious: how is it that our information processing is influenced by being conscious. They then try to capture these functional elements in either schematic designs or actual AI systems. Until recently most theorists who took up the question of how an AI system might exhibit consciousness operated within the framework of symbolic AI. A symbolic AI system is one in which explicit symbol structures within the computer represent pieces of information and the system employs rules to transform these rules. Symbolic AI has been quite successful in modeling a variety of cognitive activities but has also exhibited some clear limitations. Those frustrated with the problems of working in traditional AI have recently brought about a renaissance in another form of AI modeling, one that is not grounded on performing formal operations on complex representations. Drawing their inspiration from the basic conception of how a brain works, these theorists develop models using processing units which can take on activations and, as a result, excite or inhibit other units. Systems of such processing units are referred to as *connectionist* or *neural network* systems. (For introductions to connectionist modeling, see Rumelhart, McClelland, and the PDP Research Group [29] and Bechtel and Abrahamsen [2].) As we shall see below, connectionism provides quite different resources and challenges for someone seeking to explain consciousness. But for some connectionists, the enterprise is much like that for practitioners of more traditional AI: identify functional features of consciousness and show how they might be explicated using a connectionist model.

One connectionist who has approached consciousness in this way is Paul Churchland [5]. Churchland identifies the following features of consciousness:

1) Consciousness involves *short-term* memory.
2) Consciousness is *independent of sensory inputs*.
3) Consciousness displays *steerable attention*.
4) Consciousness has the capacity for *alternative interpretations* of complex or ambiguous data.
5) Consciousness *disappears in deep sleep*.
6) Consciousness *reappears in dreaming*, at least in muted or disjointed form.
7) Consciousness harbors the contents of the several basic sensory modalities within a *single unified experience*.

His strategy is then to show that connectionist models of a particular kind have the resources to explain these features of consciousness. The sort of model he appeals to is a recurrent networks, a network in which activation largely flows forward from input units to output units through one or more intermediate layers, but in which there is feedback from units later in the processing stream to those earlier [13]. One thing such feedback provides is a way to make processing of inputs supplied later sensitive to what happened in the processing of earlier inputs. That is, recurrent networks exhibit the first feature of consciousness, a kind of short-term memory. Second, these networks can continue to processes recurrent stimulation even when no new input is provided, and thus are independent of sensory inputs. Third, recurrent pathways provide a means of influencing the processing of a new input, in particular steering the network to attend and respond to certain features of the input rather than others. Fourth, recurrent pathways can cause the network to respond to the same input in multiple ways, thus exhibiting the capacity for generating multiple interpretations.

To explain other features of consciousness Churchland combines the appeal to artificial neural networks with information about the brain, in particular Llinas' discovery of 40 herz oscillations in the neural activity of the cortex, which seem to be due to recurrent neural pathways from the intralaminar nucleus, whose neurons have an intrinsic tendency to oscillate at 40 herz. Overlaying this oscillation are a variety of specific activation patterns which seem to constitute the brain's response to particular stimulations. This amplitude of this oscillatory pattern is greatly diminished in deep sleep when the neurons in the intralaminar nucleus are inactive. But it reappears in REM sleep, along with the overlaying activation patterns, which now, however, are not correlated with external inputs [20]. Churchland proposes that the recurrent pathways from the intralaminar nucleus can account for both the disappearance of consciousness in deep sleep and its muted or disjointed reappearance in REM sleep. Finally, Churchland proposes that the recurrent processing through the intralaminar nucleus explains the unified character of consciousness – all processing must go through the bottleneck of the intralaminar nucleus, and this imposes unification on the processing.

2 Perceived problems with computational approaches

As the previous section suggests, there is reason to be optimistic that computational models can capture many of the functional features of consciousness. To many critics, though, computational attempts to model consciousness, whether in more classical symbolic systems or in connectionist systems, miss the point. These critics contend that what is special about consciousness is not its functional aspects, but its qualitative character (see Chalmers [6]). The worry about the qualitative character of consciousness was presented crisply by Thomas Nagel [23] when he posed the question "What is it like to be a bat?" He contended that although we might come to understand the neurophysiology of bats and work out in detail the manner in which they process sonar information, we will never understand what it is like to experience the world as a bat does. This information simply is not there in the physical or functional information about bats. One must be a bat to appreciate how bats experience the world. And since it must be experienced to be appreciated, it cannot be explained in terms of the neurophysiology of the bat. What goes for bats also go for us: the qualitative character of our conscious states cannot be understood by knowing the physical processes occurring within us. If nothing about the neurophysiology of a bat or us could account for the way a bat or we experience the world, the consequences for AI, symbolic or connectionist, are rather dire: an important aspect of the cognition of humans and other animals may simply lie outside of the scope of AI (that is, outside of the scope of any computational model).

To undercut the potential of computational models to explain consciousness one need not adopt even such a strong position as Nagel's. It is common to differentiate the functional and physical aspects of events within physical systems. Functional features of a system have to do with the way operations components of the system perform and the way these are coordinated. The physical features concern the particular physical devices that perform those operations. This distinction corresponds to the distinction between hardware and software in the case of computers, but can be generalized to other complex systems. For example, one can differentiate the catalyzed reactions that are performed in different metabolic processes from the specific enzymes that catalyze the reactions. What Nagel and others who others who share his concern claim is that the qualitative character of mental events is not due to either the functional or physical character of cognitive systems but is in some way beyond the physical and functional dimension. However, to argue that AI is incapable of explaining consciousness, it is sufficient to argue that conscious is not a functional property but depends on the physical realization of our cognitive system. That is, one only needs to argue that consciousness can only be explained by details of brain physiology, and not the functional properties of the brain (its procedures for processing information). Consciousness would then be *program resistance* in contrast with the program receptive properties of sapience (Gunderson, [16]). Such a view has been advocated by John Searle [30] in what many have regarded as one of the most serious criticisms of AI.

Searle focuses his argument on intentionality, a feature which Brentano [4] identified as separating mental systems from physical ones. Intentionality is the characteristic that mental states enjoy of having content, or being *about* something. In contemplating a rose, one's thoughts are about the rose. In developing a theory of consciousness, one's thoughts are about consciousness. Mental states seem, in some way, to be linked to their objects. But this link is not, and cannot be, an ordinary physical relation. We can have thoughts about things that do not exist, such as Ponce de Leon's fountain of youth. And our thoughts of the fountain of youth are not the same as our thoughts of other nonexistent objects. This is not an idle worry, since many of our thoughts are directed at possible future states of affairs, many of which will never be realized. For Brentano, the fact that mental states seemed relation-like, but not actually relations, was an argument for dualism; for him, our mental states behaved differently than any phenomena in the physical universe. (One common response to Brentano's problem is to hold that in mental states we are not related to objects in the world, but to mental representations of those objects. There is nothing problematic, it seems, in having mental representations of nonexistent objects. But this fails to solve the problem. In order for mental states to account for our ability to function in the real world, for example, to allow us to make plans that lead to real actions, our mental states must be *about* the objects of the world, not just our representations. If one accepts the need for mental representations, the problem of intentional can be stated as the problem of how our mental representations relate to objects in the world. Now the problem that intentionality seems to be relation-like but not a relation arises again.)

Searle's contention is that real intentionality, which he calls *intrinsic intentionality* cannot be exhibited by computers because having intentionality is not a matter of having the right program. He argues for this claim by means of a thought experiment. Assume that we have a program that proposes to account for how a person engages in a conversation in Chinese and that a computer running this program is behaviorally indistinguishable from an actual Chinese speaker. The program takes in Chinese text, performs some formal operations on it (which might involve writing down other characters, storing them, retrieving them, etc.). Now, to show that the program does not account for intentionality, allow Searle to execute the program. He will be locked in a room with English directions that specify the steps in the program. Some Chinese text is slipped under the door, and Searle executes the operations specified in the program. After a time the operations specify that he should slide some new text back under the door, and he obliges. This process is repeated and Chinese speakers outside the room are satisfied that they are engaging in conversation with a fellow Chinese speaker. The only problem, Searle contends, is that he does not understand a word of Chinese (he did not even know he was working on Chinese text) and hence had no idea that he was carrying on a conversation or what it was about. Since he did not know the content of the conversation, he did not exhibit intentionality concerning the Chinese conversation. Nor, Searle contends, does a computer which is running the program.

Searle anticipated several obvious lines of response to this argument, one of the most compelling of which he labeled the *systems* reply. This response contends that when Searle is in the Chinese room he does not understand the Chinese text. But that is because the program and some of the intermediate states of processing are external to Searle, stored in the program which Searle consults and in the intermediate representations he stores on paper. Searle, however, revises the scenario so as to answer this. He proposes that he memorize the program and carry out all of the operations in his head. Now everything is inside Searle. Yet, he contends he still does not understand the Chinese conversation in which he is engaged. A real Chinese speaker, on the other hand, knows what he or she is talking about. Thus, Searle's simulation of the Chinese speaker fails to capture the intentionality of the Chinese speaker's mental states. It has failed to capture the Chinese speaker's conscious awareness of what he or she is talking about. Since any computer simulation would possess no more than Searle possesses, it too would fail to exhibit such conscious awareness of what its conversations were about. (The advantage of the thought experiment over any computer implementation, Searle contends, is that while we cannot get a reliable report from the computer as to what it is like to engage in the conversation, Searle, who already knows what it is like to engage in a real conversation in which he knows what he is talking about, can tell us that in the thought experiment he would have no such knowledge. Indeed, the computer might put out a response that it does know what it is talking about, but if the program Searle was executing directed him to produce such an output in English, he would be able to testify that it was an erroneous statement.)

Searle's diagnosis of the problem is that the computer simulation fails to capture the important causal element in conscious human performance. Intentional states have real causal roles to play in us, and they play this causal role in virtue of their intentionality. Computational models, being purely formal, fail to capture this causal role. The only way to capture this causal role is to turn to something that has true causal powers: the biological states in our brains. Just as plants generate oxygen from carbon dioxide as a result of possessing chlorophyll, our brains produce behavior because they have intentional states within them. This intentionality is, for Searle, an emergent property of the neural structures in our brains. Other natural phenomena might generate intentional states, but a purely formal analysis, such as is provided in an AI program, cannot realize the causal agency found in real brains. Thus, intrinsic intentionality is conceptually beyond the capacities of AI programmers. (It seems quite reasonable to object to Searle's appeal to biology by noting that functional explanations are not limited to psychology but appear in physiology, biochemistry, etc. Moreover, when we explain a feature of some system, we do so by finding a level of organization at which functional properties of the system's components can account for the features of the system. Thus, if Searle's rejection of functional or computational accounts of intentionality were correct, they would also rule out biological explanations of intentionality.)

More recently, Searle [31] has raised the stakes of his position with respect to consciousness. One might have responded to Searle's earlier position by agreeing that indeed AI simulations could not capture the intrinsic intentionality or conscious awareness of mental content exhibited in our conscious mental states, but that at least they could account for a great deal of mental life. A common assumption of many cognitive scientists is that most mental processes are non-conscious and these should be within the range of computational explanations. We can assign representational content to underlying mental states and explain behavior in terms of processes operating over these contentful states. But Searle contends that in order for a state to be representational it must possess what he refers to as its *aspectual* shape: a particular perspective on the object or event represented. For example, a representation of Clinton may represent him as a jogger, not as President. Since the referent of the representation remains the same for both the jogger and President representation, this aspectual shape is not captured by physical relations to Clinton but can only be identified and employed by us when we are conscious of it. (This claim seems problematic at best. Computational theorists would seek to capture the particular aspectual shape of a representation in terms of relations to other representations, not just to possible referents in the world.) Hence it makes no sense to attribute it to states that are inherently non-conscious and so it makes no sense to posit inherently non-conscious intentional states and to try to explain behavior in terms of them. When behavior arises without consciousness, the explanation for it must be purely neural, and make no reference to intentional mental representations. If Searle is right, therefore, not only do conscious mental states lie outside the scope of AI, but since only conscious or potentially conscious mental states can figure in real psychological explanations, so does any psychological phenomenon.

3 Strategies for capturing consciousness in computational systems

For the remainder of this paper I will take Searle's arguments to pose a serious challenge for anyone seeking to provide a computational account of consciousness and sketch ways in which computationalist might counter his arguments. The first step is to overcome the assumption that consciousness is a single, holistic phenomenon that is either present or not. This sense lies behind not only Searle's arguments but many attempts to argue that consciousness is a special property that we cannot hope to explain. It lies behind the claim that what differentiates AI systems, robots, or zombies from us is that in the first three cases there is no one home, while in our case there is a someone who is home. If conscious were such a phenomenon that it is either present or absent, then it is difficult to show how an underlying physical system could account for it. On the other hand, if the phenomenon of consciousness can be decomposed, and some aspects of it realized while others are not, then one has a basis for identifying underlying mechanisms whose presence or absence correlates with the features of consciousness that are present or absent (see Bechtel and Richardson [3] for an account of the development of scientific explanations via the strategies of decomposition and localization). Dennett [11] offers a sustained attack on the idea of consciousness as a unified or atomistic phenomenon, while the strategy of trying to show how different components of consciousness might be explained by different physical or functional processes and how we might use defects in consciousness to identify responsible mechanisms is well described in the work of Flanagan ([14] and this volume).

Inspired by Searle, I shall focus on three features that seem particularly prominent when we think of our conscious mental states. First is the intentionality of mental states. Intentionality is often viewed as principally a feature of cognitive states such those characterized in terms of propositional attitudes like belief and desire. But it is also characteristic of more purely phenomenal states such as perceiving colors or hearing tones: we see a red

222

circle or hear an offpitch tone. Second, we are aware of these states and their content; we have what appears to be reliable first person privileged access to their contents. Third, there is a distinctive qualitative character to each of these states. This is especially true of perceptual and imagistic states: seeing red feels qualitatively different from seeing blue. But it is also true of propositional attitude states: thinking today is a holiday feels qualitatively different than thinking that consciousness can be explained computationally. The question is whether any or all of these features of conscious states can be realized in an AI system.

In one respect, intentionality seems to be obviously present in symbolic AI systems. The symbols employed in these systems, over which the formal operations specified in the program are then performed, are understood to be representations. It is insofar as these symbols are interpreted as representing features of the world that the systems can be thought of as having knowledge of the world and figuring out solutions to the problems presented to the systems. But this intentionality is illusory. There is nothing about the representations in symbolic computer systems that makes them have specific content. This is easily seen by recognizing that a program designed to perform one task can be put to work to perform another task as long as the formal operations specified in the program are correct. A program to play tick-tack-toe, for instance, is not intrinsically a tick-tack-toe program. The program will do an equally good job of Simon's game of number scrabble, which consists of laying cards with values 1 through 9 on a table face up, and allowing two players to alternately choose one until one player has a set of three cards that add up to 15 ([32], p. 76). In the case of traditional symbolic AI programs, all of the work is done by the set of formal operations in the system, operations defined in terms of the formal composition of the symbols themselves (their syntax). If these operations are appropriate, then the program will provide the right responses when its symbols are interpreted as referring to entities in the real world. In Dennett's [9] characterization, a symbolic AI device is a syntactic engine which performs as a semantic engine. But all of the intentionality is supplied by the human being who interprets the AI system. This is what Searle refers to as *as if* intentionality: the system is behaving as if it were an intentional system, but it is not really such a system. (Searle holds much the same position with respect to the words of a natural language – in themselves they do not possess meaning or intentionality, but only insofar as they are interpreted as having particular meaning by human beings.)

One diagnosis of why traditional symbolic systems do not really possess intentionality is that there is not the right kind of connection between the representations within the system and what they represent. Some philosophers of language have attempted to explain the specific meanings of words in natural language in terms of historical links to occasions in which they were used to refer to particular objects. This approach encounters a number of problems, especially in terms of explaining how words could refer to nonexistent entities or to entities not directly encountered (e.g., words used to refer to theoretical posits). Another, related approach, focuses not on how words or mental representations were first connected with objects, but how they are adaptations which enable our cognitive system to better adapt to the environment we encounter. The model for this is the function of a biological trait. The function of a biological trait is usually construed as either the activity whose performance led to the selection of that trait by an organism or that which is now enabling it to meet selection forces [35, 36]. Dretske [12] and Millikan [22] are two philosophers who have advocated pursuing such a perspective with respect to mental states, arguing that it is the manner in which they have been selected within the system that determines their semantic content. Dretske, in particular, emphasizes the need for mental representations to be the product of a learning system (learning being, at least in part, a selective process). (The treatment of cognitive systems as adaptive provides a suggestion as to how we might explain our ability to refer to nonexistent entities. Our system, like any biological system, is only imperfectly adapted to its environment. At points of misfit our cognitive system may mischaracterize entities or represent nonexistent ones.)

Many traditional symbolic AI systems have not been learning systems, although recently there has been considerable interest in developing symbolic learning systems. But connectionist systems are generally learning systems. Learning occurs as a result of adjustment of weights within the system as the network performs the tasks assigned to it. One of the crucial advances leading to the reemergence of connectionist modeling in the 1980s was the development of a general learning algorithm, backpropagation, for networks consisting of multiple layers of units with feedforward processing [28]. It is common when analyzing connectionist networks to view various layers within the network as developing specific representations of the information provided at the input layer, representations that facilitate the network in performing the task it is being trained to do. This is clearly illustrated in a network Hinton [18] trained to respond to queries about relationships in two family trees. The two trees were isomorphic with each other, but one consisted of individuals with British names and the other with individuals with Italian names. Each tree consisted of three generations. The network was structured so as to receive as input a localist representation of one individual in the tree and of a relationship, and the network was trained to identify the other individual or individuals who stood in that relationship. (A localist representation is one in which a single unit, when activated, is designated to represent a particular entity or relation.) The network processed this information through three hidden layers. The first hidden layer consisted of two sets of six units, one of which received inputs from the units representing input individuals, the other from units representing input relationships. Hinton analyzed the connections leading from the input units to these hidden units, and was able to establish that these hidden units had learned to represent selected features of the input. For example, different hidden units receiving input from the units representing individuals learned to discriminate the generation of the individual, the nationality of the individual, and whether the individual was on the left side or right side of the tree. (Of course the network never saw the tree; it had to extract the relevant information from the problems it was given. Nonetheless, it determined that it needed to use its six hidden units to categorize the input information on different dimensions in order to solve the problem on which it was being trained.)

Analysis of the sort Hinton conducted is not generally possible, but connectionists have employed other techniques, such as cluster analysis [18] to determine how whole patterns of activation capture information supplied in the input. The success of these analyses makes it seem plausible to view these learned patterns as possessing real intentionality. The patterns of activation on hidden units result from the adjustment of weights between units as the network learns to respond correctly to inputs and these patterns of activation then supply all of the information about the input that is available to units later in the system. The assignment of a content to a particular pattern of activation is not simply an act of interpretation by the network designer. Rather, it is an interpretation that captures the causal relations within the network, particularly the causal relations that led to the pattern of activation occurring in the system in response to a particular input. The pattern of activation is as it is due to the causal history of the network, and it will affect the future behavior of the network as a result of possessing those causal powers. In this sense, the intentionality of network representations seems real.

When Searle argued that real cognitive systems possessed intrinsic intentionality, not mere *as if* intentionality, a major part of his case was that he, as a real cognitive system, knew the contents of his representations whereas the AI simulation did not. Only from an external perspective could one attribute content to the representations in the AI system. It is more difficult to run Searle's thought experiment in the case of a network since one of the feature of networks is that there is no central processing unit in which all operations are performed. Thus, there is no one set of tasks Searle might be imagined to perform in his head and evaluate whether, when he performs them, he achieves real intentionality with respect to that task. But even so, it seems plausible to argue that there is no awareness of what is being represented within the network. So, even if the above argument succeeds in showing that the attribution of intentionality in learning systems is capturing something real about the system, it still seems as if the AI system is fundamentally different from us in this respect. Hinton's network does not know what its representations represent. Part of this is due to the nature of the inputs and outputs of Hinton's network: it learns only to deal with symbolically encoded information, and its generates a symbolic representation. It never encounters members of the two families and never interacts with them. But that can be accommodated in a straight-forward manner: a network can be established inside a robot and receive its input from the sense organs of the robot and generate its output through the robot's motor system (see Nolfi, Elman, and Parisi [24] for a suggestive simulation of this sort). But even when the network is hooked up to the world in a more realistic manner, it does not seem likely that it will acquire the direct, first person awareness of the contents of its representations that humans seem to possess.

Accounting for the direct, first person awareness of content seems, at first, to be impossible in a computation system. The reason is that we have no plausible models of how such direct awareness might be accomplished in a physical system. A strategy one might pursue in this situation is to argue that such awareness is illusory (the strategy I am proposing here is similar to that Dennett [11] proposes for dealing with the qualitative character of mental events). But the feeling that we know the contents of our own conscious mental states is sufficiently powerful that if we are to hold that it is illusory, we are obliged to give a plausible account of how it arose. One suggestion is that it is due to the fact that we are language users. If one views language as a way of giving public expression to internal mental representations, and so dependent upon them, then appeal to language here cannot help us. But another possibility is that language is a relatively autonomous representational system, one which is learned in a public environment as a means of acquiring information from other and influencing their behavior (Bechtel [1]). Vygotsky [37] argues that only after language is learned in this public manner is its use internalized in private thinking. As we learn to use public language, one of the things we find useful is to characterize the mental states of ourselves and others. The activity of describing our mental lives in language is a separate activity from having the mental state. (Rosenthal [27] has argued for the claim that conscious awareness of a mental state is the result of having a second mental state directed at the first mental state.) We have information about our mental states that is not accessible to others as a result of them being states within us. We thereby account for the privileged access we have to our own mental states. But, just as importantly, this access is not direct in the way that would make it infallible. Having learned to use language to refer to events in the world, we must then learn to characterize the contents of our mental states in terms of features of the external world (see Gopnik [15] for supporting experimental evidence from developmental psychology for this suggestion).

So, perhaps we have a form of privileged access to our own mental states, and one that is more direct than other people are able to have, but not the less not direct and infallible access. We learn to use internal and perhaps behavioral cues to determine the content of our mental states and to express this content in language. If this account is correct, though, then it would seem possible for computational systems to achieve the same thing. We don't yet have computers fully capable of operating in a natural language, but progress is being made. What will be required, according to the analysis offered above, for computers to exhibit the same sort of access to mental states as we seem to have is for them not only to use language to characterize their environment, but also to characterize their own mental states in terms of how they represent the world. There do not seem to be any insuperable difficulties in developing computational systems of this kind, and one can even see a benefit of having such systems: by being able to represent their own mental states to themselves, such systems might be able to develop ways of revising their mental activity.

The final feature of consciousness that I set out above is the one that has been of most concern to philosophers. Mental states have distinctive qualitative characteristics. Seeing a blue object, for example, is a very different experience than seeing a red object. It is not just that we are able to differentiate the two experiences and so produce different verbal responses to them. They feel differently to us as we have them. Philosophers refer to the qualitative characteristics of mental states as *qualia*. Some philosophers (e.g., Dennett, 1988) deny the existence of qualia, arguing that nothing fits the definition of qualia as ineffable, intrinsic (atomic and unanalyzable), private, and directly accessible in consciousness. Dennett argues for this by a set of thought experiments or intuition pumps that attempt to break these properties apart and to show that to the degree any of the properties is satisfied it is not by means of mysterious entities known as qualia. Others have tried to show how qualia might be brought within the scope of physical explanation by showing how qualia are more complex than usually thought, and have features which co-vary with features of our underlying physical brain, such as features of our color or other sensory processing system (Hardin [17], Clark [7]). Both of these represent important advances towards developing a reductive explanation of our qualitative experience in terms of physical processes in the brain.

In this spirit, Lloyd [21] tries to show how a connectionist network might account for salient features of our phenomenal states. In addition to the four properties cited in Dennett's definition above, he claims that phenomenal states exhibit what he refers to as *phenomenal superposition* insofar as different features of objects presented to us are all integrated in our representation of the object. For example, our awareness of a red chair integrates our awareness of it as a chair and as red. The two features are not separately recorded as, for example, they are in a sentence describing the chair. The result is that subtle differences between two objects (e.g., subtle changes in shape or color) may result in similar but slightly different phenomenal states. The same characteristic is found in connectionist networks that distribute representational functions over sets of units so that a pattern of activation over a set of units serves to represent the relevant aspects of the input information and that same pattern represents a variety of pieces of information

227

about that input. Thus, information is *superimposed* rather than stored discretely. This allows the network, for example, to respond subtle differences between two very similar inputs by generating very similar outputs. This similarity in representational features suggests to Lloyd that connectionism has the potential to explain the phenomenal features of consciousness.

For some (e.g., Chalmers [6], Cottrell [8]), however, these steps are not sufficient. There remains the brute fact that seeing red has a certain qualitative character that we are aware of and which has not been explained. Why do the physical or functional processes yield phenomenal states of this character? There seems to be nothing about the physical or functional processes occurring in us that causes seeing red to have the qualitative character it in fact has. If, in fact, this explanatory gap cannot be closed, it seems difficult to figure out what one might do to make an AI system experience the right qualitative character. But it is worth attending to what makes it seem that mental states have a qualitative character that escapes physical or functional explanation. Historically scientists have found ways to bridge gaps between concepts that did not fit into the same explanatory scheme. For example, genetic factors and chromosomes were not part of the same conceptual domain, but earlier in this century researchers noted a few important correlations between the state of chromosomes and genetic effects, proposed that genetic factors were in fact located on chromosomes, and proceeded to develop a powerful explanatory framework that linked other features of genetic factors and chromosomes (see Wimsatt [35]). Cottrell allows that eventually a new framework integrating the processing states and qualitative characters might be developed. But to the critics of computational and physical accounts of consciousness, such as Chalmers, the case of qualia is inherently different. The reason is that we are aware of the qualitative character from a first person perspective, while the physical and functional properties of the brain are known from a third person perspective.

If this is right, then the challenge to the computationalist is great since there seems to be nothing about the subjective character of these states that the computationalist can model. If the computationalist is to succeed, he or she needs to question the nature of our first person perspective on our mental states. Perhaps, as I suggested above, it is not as direct as it seems. Perhaps we seem to have direct access to the qualitative character of our mental states only insofar as we use other mental states, ones that figure in linguistic production, to characterize them. Then the problematic character of qualitative experience may be dismissed as an obstacle. We only need to explain what leads us to make the sorts of reports about our mental states that we do and the path may be open to a computational account of the sort Lloyd proposes. We can develop systems whose information about its mental states is the same as ours and which can therefore describe their mental states in the same way. But denying that the subjective characteristics of our mental states are really there and experienced by us seems too radical for many. If it is too radical, however, the prospects are dim for a computational account of the subjective character of our conscious experiences.

4 Conclusions

Can computational models of thought offer accounts of consciousness? While there has been limited work in AI on consciousness, some features of consciousness seem to lend themselves relatively easily to computational modeling. This applies to some of the features of consciousness I extracted from Searle's criticism of AI, that conscious mental states are intentional and that we are aware of their contents. I offered a connectionist simulation that suggests how intentionality might be captured in computational systems. The latter feature seems problematic insofar as we tend to think of conscious agencies of having direct first person access to the contents of their states, but I suggested that this may be an illusion and that we have simply learned to describe some of our mental states through other mental activity involved in language use. The least tractable feature of consciousness from a computational perspective would seem to be the qualitative character that seems to attach to conscious states, e.g., the qualitative character associated with seeing red. While the functional features of such states might be analyzable, there seems always to be the additional question of why they have the qualitative character they do. What makes the qualitative character difficult to account for computationally is that we are only aware of it from the first-person perspective. For computational accounts to get a foothold in explaining this feature of consciousness, it seems that they need to deny that we really have experiences with these subjective characteristics and claim only that we so describe our conscious states. If such a move is rejected, then the subjective character of mental states my be program resistant.

References

1. Bechtel, W. Decomposing intentionality: Perspectives on intentionality drawn from language research with two species of chimpanzees. *Biology and Philosophy*, 8, 1–32, 1993.
2. Bechtel, W. and Abrahamsen, A. A. *Connectionism and the Mind*. Basil Blackwell, Oxford, 1991.
3. Bechtel, W. and Richardson, R. C. *Discovering complexity: Decomposition and localization as strategies in scientific research*. Princeton University Press, Princeton, 1993.
4. Brentano, F. *Psychology from an empirical standpoint* (A. C. Pancurello, D. B. Terrell, & L. L. McAlister, Translators). Humanities, New York, 1874/1973.
5. Churchland, P. M. *The engine of reason*. MIT Press, Cambridge, MA, in press
6. Chalmers, D. *Toward a theory of consciousness*. MIT Press, Cambridge, MA, in press.
7. Clark, A. *Sensory qualities*. Oxford, Oxford University Press, 1993.

8. Cottrell, A. Tertium datur? Reflections on Owen Flanagan's *Consciousness reconsidered. Philosophical Psychology*, in press.

9. Dennett, D. C. Three kinds of intentional psychology. In *Reduction, time, and reality*, R. Healey (Editor), pp. 37–61. Cambridge University Press, Cambridge, England, 1981

10. Dennett, D. C. Quining qualia. In *Consciousness in contemporary science*, A. J. Marcel and E. Bisiach (Editors). Oxford University Press, Oxford, 1988.

11. Dennett, D. C. *Consciousness explained*. Little, Brown, and Company, Boston, 1991.

12. Dretske, F. *Explaining behavior*. MIT Press, Cambridge, MA, 1988.

13. Elman, J. Finding structure in time. *Cognitive Science*, 14, 179–211, 1990.

14. Flanagan, O. *Consciousness reconsidered*. MIT Press, Cambridge, MA, 1992.

15. Gopnik, A. How we know our minds: The illusion of first-person knowledge of intentionality. *The Behavioral and Brain Sciences* 16, 1–14, 1993.

16. Gunderson, K. *Mentality and machines*. Anchor Book, Garden City, NY, 1971.

17. Hardin, C. L. *Color for philosophers: Unweaving the rainbow*. Hackett, Indianapolis, 1988.

18. Hinton, G. E. Learning distributed representations of concepts. *Proceedings of the Eighth Annual Conference of the Cognitive Science Society*, pp. 1–12. Erlbaum, Hillsdale, NJ, 1986.

19. Johnson-Laird, P. N. *Mental models*. Harvard University Press, Cambridge, MA, 1983.

20. Llinas, R. R. and Pare, D. On dreaming and wakefulness. *Neuroscience* 44, 521–535, 1991.

21. Lloyd, D. Consciousness: A connectionist manifesto, in preparation.

22. Millikan, R. G. *Language, thought, and other biological categories*. MIT Press, Cambridge, MA, 1984.

23. Nagel, T. What is it like to be a bat? *The Philosophical Review* 83, 435–450, 1974

24. Nolfi, S., Elman, J. L., and Parisi, D. Learning and evolution in neural networks. Technical Report 9019, Center for Research in Language, University of California, San Diego, 1990.

25. Osherson, D. N. and Lasnik, H. (Editors) *An invitation to cognitive science*. MIT Press, Cambridge, MA, 1990.

26. Posner, M. (Editor) *Foundations of cognitive science*. MIT Press, Cambridge, MA, 1989.

27. Rosenthal, D. M. Two concepts of consciousness. *Philosophical Studies* 49, 329–59, 1986.

28. Rumelhart, D. E., Hinton, G. E., and Williams, R. J. Learning representations by back-propagating errors. *Nature*, 323, 533–536, 1986.

29. Rumelhart, D. E., McClelland, J. L., and the PDP Research Group (Editors). *Parallel distributed processing: Explorations in the microstructure of cognition*, vol. 1: *Foundations*. MIT Press, Cambridge, MA, 1986.

30. Searle, J. R. Minds, brains, and programs. *The Behavioral and Brain Sciences* 3, 417–424, 1980.

31. Searle, J. R. Consciousness, explanatory inversion, and cognitive science. *The Behavioral and Brain Sciences* 13, 585–596, 1990.

32. Simon, H. A. *The sciences of the artificial*. MIT Press, Cambridge, MA, 1969

33. Stillings, N. A., Feinstein, M. H., Garfield, J. L., Rissland, E. L., Rosenbaum,

D. A., Weisler, S. E., Baker-Ward, L. (Editors) *Cognitive science: An introduction*. MIT Press, Cambridge, MA, 1987.

34. Wimsatt, W. C. Teleology and the logical structure of function statements. *Studies in the History and Philosophy of Science* 3, 1–80, 1972.

35. Wimsatt, W. C. Reductionism, levels of organization, and the mind-body problem. In *Consciousness and the brain: A scientific and philosophical inquiry*, pp. 205–267, G. Globus, G. Maxwell, and I. Savodnik (Editors). Plenum Press, New York, 1976

36. Wright, L. *Teleological explanations: An etiological analysis of goals and functions*, University of California Press, Berkeley, 1976.

37. Vygotsky, L. S. *Language and thought*. MIT, Cambridge, MA, 1962.

75

TOWARDS A DESIGN-BASED ANALYSIS OF EMOTIONAL EPISODES

Ian P. Wright, Aaron Sloman and Luc Beaudoin[1]

Source: *Philosophy Psychiatry and Psychology* 3(2), 1996: 101–26.

Abstract The design-based approach is a methodology for investigating mechanisms capable of generating mental phenomena, whether introspectively or externally observed, and whether they occur in humans, other animals or robots. The study of designs satisfying requirements for autonomous agency can provide new deep theoretical insights at the information processing level of description of mental mechanisms. Designs for working systems (whether on paper or implemented on computers) can systematically explicate old explanatory concepts and generate new concepts that allow new and richer interpretations of human phenomena. To illustrate this, some aspects of human grief are analysed in terms of a particular *information processing architecture* being explored in our research group.

We do not claim that *this* architecture is part of the causal structure of the human mind; rather, it represents an early stage in the iterative search for a deeper and more general architecture, capable of explaining more phenomena. However even the current early design provides an interpretative ground for some familiar phenomena, including characteristic features of certain emotional episodes, particularly the phenomenon of *perturbance* (a partial or total loss of control of attention).

The paper attempts to expound and illustrate the design-based approach to cognitive science and philosophy, to demonstrate the potential effectiveness of the approach in generating interpretative possibilities, and to provide first steps towards an information processing account of 'perturbant', emotional episodes.

1 Introduction

The human mind, and its underlying engine, the brain, are incredibly complex collections of mechanisms of many kinds, produced over millions of years of evolution. As a result of its origins there are several levels of control, of varying degrees of sophistication. Some, like reflex arcs, are shared with many other organisms. Some, like the mechanisms involved in arousal of various kinds, e.g. those involving the limbic system, seem to be shared with many other mammals. Some, like cortical mechanisms involved in the ability to long for recognition, the ability to enjoy the admiration and respect of others, the ability to be thrilled by a mathematical discovery, and the ability to grieve at the death of a friend, require sophisticated cognitive capabilities, which may be unique to humans. Because many researchers into emotions do not clearly distinguish the different types of phenomena, there is much confusion about what is being studied and what is explained by various theories. Our concern is primarily with mental processes that are typically to be found in human beings, which involve high level cognitive functions and which often have social consequences. They may also, in fact, involve older more primitive mechanisms, though those are not the concern of this paper. (A *complete* theory of the human mind would have to include them.)

This paper has two main goals: (a) to illustrate the design-based approach to the study of some "higher level" human mental processes; and (b) to make theoretical progress towards a design-based account of certain emotional episodes, namely those that involve a partial or total loss of control of thought processes. Our work derives ultimately from suggestions in (Simon 67), though we have extended and generalised Simon's ideas.

We try to show how a certain sort of information processing architecture, extending ideas in Artificial Intelligence, can serve as a new explanatory ground for some well-known emotional phenomena. Whether the proposed outline architecture is correct, how it might be implemented in neural mechanisms and what the implications of further refinements will be, remain questions for future investigation. The architecture certainly does not yet account for all aspects of grief, and it also leaves unexplained other important mental phenomena which points to the need for extensions to the architecture, which we shall continue to explore.

Section 2, which follows this introduction, is primarily theoretical: subsection 2.1 introduces key ideas of the design-based approach to the study of mind, including the idea of a 'broad but shallow' architecture. Subsections 2.2 and 2.3 sketch our high level design for autonomous agents, including the distinction between highly parallel 'automatic' attention-free processing and resource-bound 'management' and 'meta-management' processes (Beaudoin, 94). Allocation of 'management' resources is one aspect of attention (the management of thought).

Section 3 applies our theory to a concrete example: subsection 3.1 presents an example of a first-hand account of human grieving. We identify certain characteristic features of grieving to be explained (along with other phenomena which we ignore) by any complete theory of human emotions. Subsection 3.2 introduces the notion of self-control and limits to self-control. Subsection 3.3 introduces the type of personal attachment which plays a decisive role in states of grieving. Subsection 3.4 explains in outline how the theory provides architecturally grounded explanations for the phenomena of grief.

Section 4 provides concluding comments and reservations.

2 The design-based approach

This section outlines the design-based approach, sketches an architecture for autonomous resource-bounded agency, and introduces the notion of a 'hierarchy' of dispositional control states. Some known gaps in the theory are discussed later.

2.1 Ontology and the design-based approach

We assume (a) that information-processing architectures exist, are implemented on human brains, and mediate both internal and external behaviour; and (b) that our methodology allows a systematic approach towards high level functional congruity between artificial, explicitly designed architectures and certain important aspects of evolved, naturally occurring architectures, despite differences in low level implementation details.

Claim (a) underlies much contemporary Cognitive Science and has been argued for or presupposed by many theorists (e.g., see (Miller et al., 70), (Johnson-Laird, 88), (Simon, 67, 69, 95); and (Palmer & Kimchi, 84) for different sub-theses).

Claim (b) is more contentious and depends on finding appropriate levels of abstraction. There are other examples of congruity at high levels despite low level differences. Two physically quite different computing systems may both implement the same virtual machine architecture (e.g., both may be Prolog systems, or both may implement internet utilities, including mail, news, telnet and the World Wide Web). Similarly, it is often taken for granted that general principles of feedback control apply both to natural and artificial systems. What we need to add to this, following much work in Artificial Intelligence, and the ideas in Simon (67), is a level of explanation that involves richer and more profound forms of control of both external and internal behaviour using richer semantic structures and new sorts of control architectures to support various kinds of motivational processes (e.g., see Simon 67, Sloman & Croucher 81, Sloman 87, Beaudoin & Sloman 93, Sloman 93a, 93b, Beaudoin 94, Sloman 94, Sloman, Beaudoin & Wright 94.)

Brains appear to support several rich ontologies at different levels of abstraction. In computing systems, ontologies are often 'stacked' in layers of implementation. For instance, a word processor package that manipulates pages, paragraphs, sentences, words, letters, etc. may be implemented in a 'virtual machine' corresponding to a high level programming language, which, in turn, is implemented in a lower level machine language, and ultimately by quantum physical states of electronic components, with several machine levels in between. The abstract machines at all levels are compound objects, composed of many different kinds of entities, relations and processes.

Moreover, causal and functional relations may hold between the high level abstract machine structures. (Changes in an abstract data-structure, such as a database of information about employees, can cause changes in what gets printed on pay slips.) These data-structures may have *semantics* in that they refer to individuals and their salaries, etc. We have argued elsewhere that this can include semantics *for the machine* (e.g. Sloman 94).

In the case of human brains we do not know what the layers are. Yet causal relations between abstract structures clearly occur when a person's seeing something causes him to get angry, which in turn may cause him to strike out. The fact that ultimately people, like computers, are implemented in (ill-understood) physical mechanisms is not inconsistent with this. Even physical phenomena are normally explained well above the level of fundamental physics: most people who learn how a car engine works are not taught about quantum physics, but about carburettors, chokes, pistons, etc.

Though a designer often knows a great deal about how a complex system works, it may be impossible for others who merely observe the system, to infer the internal processing. (Sometimes even the designer does not understand all the internal interactions.) This means that any philosophy of science that assumes that theories must be directly or easily testable is ill-conceived: it will fail for complex information processing systems, most of whose behaviour is internal and unobservable. Moreover, even knowing how the system works may not provide a basis for predicting particular behaviours if the behaviour depends not only on the design and current circumstances but also on fine details of enduring changes produced by a long previous history.

When studying systems we have not designed we can, at best, hope for a succession of theories accounting for more and more phenomena, using increasingly powerful explanatory principles, tested in part by implementing the theories in working designs and in part by relating them to the ever growing body of knowledge in neuroscience. There may never be a total ordering of merit among such theories, and the ordering may change over time as new phenomena are discovered. Objections to our approach are often based on a naive philosophy of science, or misplaced 'physics envy'. (For a broader view see Lakatos 70, chapter 2 of Sloman 78, and Bhaskar 78, 94).

The design-based approach draws its inspiration from software engineering and conceptual analysis in philosophy (see chapter 4 of Sloman,

78). It construes AI as a methodology for exploring an abstract space of possible requirements for functioning agents (*niche space*) and the space of possible designs for such agents (*design space*) and the mappings between them (Sloman 94, Sloman 95). Research strategies vary: they may be top-down, bottom-up or middle-out. All are potentially useful. This paper is largely top-down, but we do not exclude other options, e.g. the use of genetic algorithms to create designs by simulating evolutionary processes.

Although it is often assumed that AI is concerned only with algorithms (e.g., Searle 80, Penrose 89), *architectures* are more important. We need to understand global designs for *complete* systems, including their functional decomposition into coexisting interacting subsystems. Early work, still exploring general principles, need not make any commitment to the implementation details of mechanisms; for example, we take a neutral stance towards symbolic or connectionist engines. We start with 'broad but shallow' (Bates et al. 91) architectures that combine many sorts of capabilities (such as perception, planning, goal management, and action). Each capability is initially implemented in a simplified fashion. Subsequent work gradually refines and deepens the implementations.

We claim that *architecture dominates mechanism* (Sloman, 93b), i.e. global design normally determines global capabilities to a greater extent than implementation details. Of course, we must ultimately link designs to neural details and will profit from the 'bottom up' studies of such details, which impose constraints on high level designs. Most of the constraints seem to be quite weak. Exceptions are the high level effects of drugs, which we have not taken into account.

We do not assume congruity between the design decisions 'taken' by evolution under environmental and competitive pressures and those taken by a designer when moving from initial requirements (what the system should do) to prototype design (how the system will do it). Rather we merely claim that the design-based methodology is a source of potential explanatory theories. Such theories will be improved under pressure of criticism, either because of things they fail to explain, or because they explain too much (e.g., capabilities people don't have), or because the designs could not have evolved naturally, or could not be implemented in brains.

Even an oversimplified or incorrect theory that yields a workable design can help our exploration of design space. Comparing it with other more 'realistic' theories aids our understanding of the latter, for we don't really understand any system if we don't know how changing it would produce different capabilities.

Designs satisfying the same information processing and control requirements may possess common design features, whether produced by natural selection or human engineering, just as birds and aeroplanes are both constrained by principles of aerodynamics. Over time the design-based approach may gradually approximate natural 'designs'. This could happen by increasingly taking account of empirical constraints and iterating the development cycle to deepen requirements and extend designs. Such designs can also be tested empirically and compared in more and more detail with their natural counterparts. The total research community is effectively engaged in a parallel cooperative search.[2]

To summarise: (a) An architecture has causal powers that determine the capabilities of an agent and explain its ability to 'fit' into a part of 'niche' space; and (b) the design-based approach generates candidate architectures that may correspond to naturally occurring high level causal structures implemented upon neural substrates. These candidates can guide empirical investigations to check such claims.

2.2 A motive-processing architecture

We now sketch an architecture[3] that is partly similar to Georgeff's Procedural Reasoning System (Georgeff & Ingrand, 89; Rao & Georgeff, 91; Rao & Georgeff, 92), but allows a richer mental ontology, including asynchronous goal generation, more coexisting concurrent sub-mechanisms, a richer set of representations relating to motivators, an attention filtering mechanism and meta-management processes. (Our ideas on all this are still evolving.)

A full account of the proposed architecture would be too long for this paper, so we focus mainly on the processing of motivators. 'Motivator' is used to refer to a subclass of information structures with dispositional powers to determine action (both internal and external). This subsumes desires, goals, intentions and wishes. The precise definitions of these structures and their powers can be given only in terms of the architecture, which is roughly sketched in Figure 1: an impressionistic diagram. For more details see (Beaudoin 94). Within this architecture, motivators can be generated or re-activated asynchronously as a result of internal or external events, and can generate processes of varying complexity, including evaluation, prioritisation, selection, planning, plan execution, plan suspension, and many more. Some of the processes that emerge from such interactions we call 'perturbances', and are described below.

The large shaded area represents 'automatic' processes (associative memory, low level sensory analysis, low level motor control processes, innate and trained reflexes) all implemented in highly parallel dedicated (but trainable) 'hardware'. We assume that such processes include mechanisms shared with many other animals. The larger unshaded area above that represent 'management' processes involved in (among other things) deciding whether new motivators should be adopted or not, assessing their relative importance and urgency, deciding how to achieve them, working out whether they are in conflict, deciding whether to abandon them, reasoning about new information, formulating questions about puzzling information, and so on. (All these processes can be implemented at least approximately using AI techniques.)

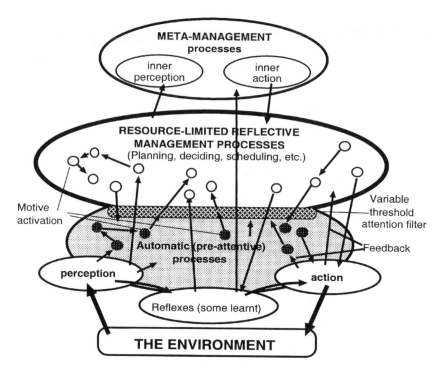

Figure 1 Towards an Intelligent Agent Architecture

The management processes, but not the low level processes, can create, consider and evaluate explicit (representations of) options before selecting between them, for deliberation, planning and problem-solving. This requires the ability to create temporary complex information structures, often with complex syntactic forms, often representing things that are not present to the senses (e.g. future possible actions) and to switch attention between the structures. We suspect that most other animals do not share this capability with humans: their architectures are not sufficiently rich. There are both empirical and design arguments supporting the claim that despite parallelism in the brain such high level cognitive processes are resource-limited: not all potentially useful management tasks can be performed concurrently. So not all new motives, thoughts, problems, can be considered simultaneously. This 'processing-limit' leads to a requirement for some type of filtering of 'attention-distractors', as explained below.

The architecture has the following components (among others), which coexist and operate concurrently. Many of these components require a depth and complexity that we cannot describe here.

Perceptual mechanisms

These are extremely complex systems, which detect potentially relevant sensory episodes and analyse and interpret them in terms of states and processes in the environment, creating or modifying internal representations. A perceptual control mechanism directs sensing operations. (Figure 1 over-simplifies drastically.)

Database of 'beliefs'

Information derived from perceptual representations, internal monitoring and reasoning processes is stored in a 'world model', which acts as a store of information. This will include both specific and general information, including a generic ontology for objects, processes, actions, etc. It need not look anything like current computer databases, for instance if implemented in a neural net. Planning may use temporary 'what-if' extensions to this store.

A changing collection of motivators

A motivator is a semantically rich information structure that tends to produce, modify or select between actions. It typically expresses a motivational attitude ('make false', 'keep true', etc.) towards a possible state of affairs ('short of food', 'warm', 'in danger', etc.), which may be expressed in propositional or non-propositional from. Motivators have various associated information items, including urgency, importance and an insistence value (Sloman, 87).[4]

A new motivator's *insistence level* determines its ability to penetrate a (variable threshold) filter in order to be considered by management processes. *Importance* helps to determine whether it is adopted as something to be achieved, if it is considered. In order not to divert scarce resources, mechanisms assigning insistence values must work using simple 'heuristic' measures of importance and urgency. Computing accurate measures of urgency and importance could be too slow and computationally expensive, possibly diverting management processes which the insistence mechanism is 'designed' to protect. However, insistence measures based on fallible heuristics can sometimes cause 'bad' decisions about what should and should not divert attention.

Pre-attentive and attentive motive generactivators (Beaudoin 94)

These express agent 'concerns' (Frijda 86; Moffat & Frijda, 95). They operate asynchronously in parallel, triggered by internal and external events. They generate and activate or reactivate motivators, and set or reset their insistence level. E.g. the concern to maintain fluid levels may activate a drink seeking motivator. A simple type of generactivator could scour the 'world model' for its 'firing' conditions, and when they are met a motivator is constructed and its insistence level set. Other generactivators may be built into the physiological control system or into perceptual mechanisms. Some may be very abstract and general, e.g. reacting to states where another agent is in difficulty and creating a desire to help. Some are innate, many are learnt and culturally determined.

Variable threshold attention filter

An attention filter protects management processes by allowing only items with insistence values 'higher' than the current filter threshold to divert management processes. When first learning to drive, many find it difficult to hold a conversation simultaneously, as all high level processes are required for driving and the filter threshold is set high. However, attention can still be diverted by, say, the passenger screaming (loud noises can trigger high insistence levels). Later, when the driver is an expert, lower level mechanisms derived from earlier management processes control most of the driving. This reduces the management load, allowing a lower filter threshold and easier diversion of attention. Filtering is content sensitive, with different thresholds for different contents (Beaudoin, 94): A baby's cry can divert attention even when other loud noises do not. Motivators that fail to surface may remain available, so as to take advantage later of a lower filter threshold, or they may die unless continually reactivated by the relevant generactivators. Motivators survive until they are satisfied or decay.

Motive management

Once a motivator has 'surfaced' it can cause many diverse and complex processes, including: assessing (evaluating its importance, urgency, costs and benefits etc.), deciding (whether to adopt the motive, i.e. form an intention), scheduling (when and under which conditions to act), expansion (how to do it, i.e. planning), prediction (projecting the effects of hypothetical decisions), detecting motive conflicts, detecting opportunities[5], abandoning a motive and changing filter thresholds. Information about current motivators (including intention structures discussed below) is stored in a 'motivator database'. Only a limited amount of parallelism is available for management processes.

Plans and other 'databases'

The system will have many short term and long term memories containing information about current, future, or possible activities. In particular, certain goals require plans, and some re-usable plans will be stored as well as information about how to create new plans. Other information stores will include collections of particular skills, e.g. linguistic skills, mathematical skills, skills relating to social activities, games, one's job, etc. Some of this will be stored in an opaque form among the pre-attentive mechanisms. Some will be accessible to management processes. Some will be innate, others learnt, some fixed and others modifiable.

- Meta-management

A meta-management process is any goal-directed process whose goal refers either to a management or to a meta-management process. Deciding whether to decide whether to adopt a goal, deciding which management process to run now, and deciding if too much motive-swapping is occurring, are all examples of meta-management processes, where motive management itself is the object of control. Meta-management requires some degree of ability to monitor and change the management processes. Conflicts can lead to 'loss of self control'. Again, resources are limited.

- Plan execution and effectors

Selected motivators are *intentions*. Executing them may occur with or without planning, with or without high level management, with or without monitoring. External actions are dispatched to an effector driver that controls agent actions within the environment. Internal actions may produce a succession of management states.

- Self-monitoring mechanisms

A variety of types of self-monitoring are required. Meta-management monitors include those that can detect global states of the management processes, such as noticing that new motivators are surfacing faster than they can be processed. This could lead to a raised filter threshold. Other states worth detecting include repeatedly considering the same goals or problems without making progress in solving them (described as 'maundering' in Beaudoin 94). A concept-learning mechanism would be required for discovering useful new ways of describing internal states. Humans can detect inconsistencies between internal management tendencies and personal ideals.

- Pleasure and pain mechanisms

Pleasure and pain have not been analysed adequately yet. They seem to involve phylogenetically old structures in the nervous system that are deeply implicated in mechanisms for both learning and online control: i.e. whether current activities should be maintained or terminated. Some people doubt that an information-processing architecture can fully account for such subjective states. For now we assume that there are mechanisms producing some motivational control states that are pleasurable in the sense of involving a disposition to preserve or extend some current state or activity, and some that are painful, involving dispositions to terminate or reduce some state or process. Some of the control states in the architecture may have a positive or negative valency that arises out of genetically programmed drives (e.g., seeking after novelty, urge to procreate and form attachments) and states of body arousal. Others involve learnt evaluations. For pain and pleasure to be *experienced* requires self-monitoring mechanisms that detect these 'preserve/terminate' control states. The mechanisms may be linked in that termination or reduction of pleasure inducing states functions as a pain inducing state and *vice versa*. In some cases these links will need to be built up through learnt associations. In others they may be 'hard-wired' in the architecture.

• Global control mechanisms

An agent sometimes needs to modulate global features of its processing, for instance speeding everything up in times of extreme danger, slowing things down when losing energy too fast, generally being cautious when the environment is unfriendly, not wasting time on caution when the environment is generally friendly. Other more subtle global changes may be required when the social context changes, for instance when an individual of higher status is present. These global changes of state seem to be related to the colloquial concept of 'mood'. In humans it seems that some of these global mood states are implemented in part at the chemical level (as shown by effects of drugs and hormones). Some control mechanisms may be 'global' only relative to a subset of a system: e.g. global changes in the ease with which unsuccessful attempts are abandoned.

We acknowledge that this design sketch is speculative, vague and subject to revision in the light of implementation problems or empirical evidence. Detailed designs may vary, e.g. some using rule-based systems, others neural nets. The components may exist within a virtual (abstract) machine whose components and processes do not correlate in any simple way with physical structures and processes.

A small subset of the architecture has been implemented (Wright, 94) and tested in a simulated domain, using very simple management processes. A more elaborate implementation is in progress, using a toolkit developed at Birmingham (Sloman & Poli 95).

The architecture is 'broad' in that it combines many different capabilities. It is 'shallow' in that the components are not themselves specified in any great depth. For testing purposes simple implementations are used at first. Much of the specification is still provisional and speculative, in that work on implementation may reveal serious problems. It is also speculative in that empirical checking has not yet been attempted (and may be very difficult.) Nevertheless we think the architecture already has explanatory power.

2.3 Varieties of control states

A mind can be viewed as a control system with a rich collection of control states (Sloman 93b), involving dispositions to respond to internal or external conditions with internal or external actions. Some control states are implemented in high level abstract machines, others in various sorts of neural states, or in states of chemicals in the blood or nervous system. The described architecture provides a framework within which many control states can coexist and interact.

Examples of control states referred to in folk psychology are beliefs, images, suppositions, desires, preferences, intentions, moods, learnt associations, innate or trained reflexes, personality traits, and emotional states. The dispositions may be of a high order (i.e. dispositions to invoke dispositions to invoke dispositions . . . (Ryle 49).)

Every architecture supports a family of concepts describing its states and processes. Exactly which control states are possible depends on the architecture. A leaf's movements may speed up or slow down, but it cannot be described as 'braking' because it lacks the architecture required for self-modification of speed, namely one sub-component which acts on others to slow them down.

The architectural presuppositions of ordinary mental terms are far more deep and difficult to analyse. By defining states in terms of an architecture that supports them we can offer a rational reconstruction of many ordinary mental concepts, just as theories of the architecture of matter rationalised concepts of physical and chemical stuff (e.g., 'iron', 'carbon', 'water', etc.). Folk psychology concepts may implicitly (pre-theoretically) refer to mechanisms of the general sort we describe, even though they contain contradictions and confusions. We use them only as first approximations. Later we hope to offer something more systematic and analogous to the periodic table defining chemical elements.

Every control state has structure, aetiology, powers, transformation capabilities, liabilities, and in some cases semantics. These ideas include analogues of the linguistic notions of syntax, semantics, pragmatics, and inference (Sloman, 94). For example, a motivator may have a complex internal structure (syntax), a content (based on that structure) referring to certain states of affairs (semantics), a functional role, i.e. dispositional powers to determine internal and external actions (pragmatics). It may also enter into processes that derive new motivators or plans (inference), it may be brought about or triggered in various ways (aetiology), and may be modified, suppressed or terminated by other processes (liabilities). Some control states are short-lived (e.g., a motivator which is immediately rejected, or whose goal is quickly achieved.) Others endure.

A control state may exist but not express its causal powers, or may express its causal powers but not determine action. Observed behaviour will generally fail to indicate the full richness of the underlying control states, especially the dormant states.

Certain high level, long-term (motivational) states (such as selfishness and other personality traits) are difficult to change, are modified only very slowly by learning and possess pervasive causal powers corresponding to their abstractness and general control applicability. Low-level, short-term states, such as a desire to scratch an itch or to repay a favour, are easier to change and have more direct causal powers corresponding to their specificity and narrower control applicability.

Some control states will gradually change their status over time, via a process we call *circulation* in which control states move around the system. Useful control states 'percolate' up the hierarchy, gaining in abstractness and resistance to change, and increasing their field of influence. Defunct long-term control states may gradually lose influence through lack of use, leaving only a few relatively specific active instances. An example may be standards and principles from a culture one has left.

Control states may be qualitatively transformed during circulation, for instance acquiring more general conditions of applicability. Higher level general attitudes such as generosity of spirit, may also spawn derivative specialised control states such as favouring a certain political party – another aspect of circulation. Internal connections between control states will set up suppressive or supportive relationships, dependencies, mutual dependencies and, occasionally, dead-locks.

The net effect of all this is a process of 'diffusion' in which the effects of a major motivator are gradually distributed in myriad enduring control substates, i.e. in motive generators, plan schemata, preferences, and predictive strategies. In some cases the effects will be *irreversibly* embedded in a host of reflexes and automatic responses. (This is loosely analogous to the process of compiling a high level language.)

The totality of control states is a dynamic structure with complex internal relations and many levels of control. High level control states amenable to some degree of self-monitoring are among the requirements for any architecture underlying human-like capabilities. Where there is appropriate self-monitoring (described below) the system may also acquire self-knowledge that triggers negative evaluations and new high-level motivators attempting to change some aspects of the system itself, whether previously learnt cognitive reflexes or high level attitudes.

A full specification of the architecture is work for the future. Nevertheless, we can begin to use it schematically to explain certain aspects of human mental functioning by mapping familiar experiences and processes into control states and processes that could occur in this sort of architecture; for instance, affectional bonds and 'perturbant' emotional states.

3 Architecture as explanatory ground

In this section we apply the architecture to a concrete emotional phenomenon: grief at the loss of a loved one. This is not a comprehensive 'theory of grief' but an application of a 'broad but shallow' architecture to the understanding of a complex cognitive phenomenon. It will be seen that a *complete* architecture can account better for the diversity of internal and external behaviour that can occur during grief than an explanation focusing only on some emotional mechanism.

3.1 Personal reports on grief

The following quotations (a) to (p) are based on extracts from a first-hand account of grief, edited to disguise the origin. After each item we make some preliminary comments in italics, relating it to the architecture. Later we expand on these comments.

(a) When the person finally passes on, the hurt is like no other . . . Now the memories of the good times seem to be like a film playing in my head.

> *This is one of many examples of partial loss of control of thought processes in emotional states: thoughts, motives and memories relating to the object of the emotion intrude and may even dominate thought processes, making it hard to attend to other matters, even those judged to be urgent and important.*

(b) XXX called us the day after his friend died suddenly. He was broke, alone, grieving and gravely ill, staying at the hospice where he'd spent the last month by his friend's bedside. I flew to YYY and brought him home, where he spent the next ten weeks in hospital. He was *so* ill that it was hard even for me – a medically sophisticated person – to comprehend and accept.

> *New facts may not easily fit into one's belief system. This is linked to the pain they cause: not physical pain but mental pain, a major phenomenon to be explained.*

(c) I started grieving the day I received the phone call, continued grieving the day I met him in the hospice in YYY, and all the time I sat by his bedside back in ZZZ. It tore me apart to see what this disease had done to him . . .

> *Grief can be both extended and highly disruptive. Notice that 'tore*

245

me apart' does not describe physical or physiological processes, but in a highly metaphorical way describes mental processes. Unpacking that sort of metaphor is part of the job of a deep theory of emotions.

(d) At least, that's all I wished for silently over and over again as I sat next to him in the hospital.

Powerful new motivators sometimes cause futile behaviour.

(e) When he died, I was initially in shock.

Shock can be physical or mental. We can't tell which was referred to here but it could easily have been both. One of the things to be explained is how mental events, e.g. learning about the death of a loved one, can produce profound physical effects. But we are primarily concerned with mental effects.

(f) And then there are details like writing obits, funeral arrangements, meeting his family, etc., which keep you busy. And then the grief resumes.

The ability of grief to control processing is a disposition in the sense of Ryle (49). (Dispositions and capabilities can exist for a long time without being manifested because their 'triggering' conditions do not occur, like the fragility of a wine glass, or countervailing processes prevent their expression, like a dam wall preventing a potential flood.) Grief involves dispositions that may be temporarily ineffective because urgent and important tasks manage to hold attention. But during that time the disposition remains and when there's a chance it regains control. From this point of view it is misleading to say 'the grief resumes'. It was there all along, though its manifestations were temporarily absent.

(g) It has been two-phased for me. This summer I kept confronting the *unreality* of it all. XXX, dead? I was wracked with insomnia. Every night as I'd try to go to bed, indeed, during much of the day too, I would replay the details of the previous three months over and over and over again.

(h) Each recollection was full of almost indescribable pain, but it was also fresh with his presence, something I cherished and which I'd missed daily for almost four years before. I wish I'd had some 'good times' to replay too, but they were from an earlier time, . . . and they were crowded out by the intensity of the recent months.

This helps to bring out some of the complexity of human emotional states: mixtures of different states are not uncommon. Several different dispositions can be 'fighting' for control and the balance may shift from time to time. Not long ago, in a BBC radio interview, the captain of a women's yacht in a round the world race described her emotional state on arriving at the final port. It was an enormously complex mixture of: pride in achievement, sadness that it was all over, joy at the prospect of seeing loved ones again, delight at the prospect of eating (rations had been exhausted two days earlier), regret that they had not won the race, happy memories of teamwork and obstacles overcome, sadness that the team would now be parting, and so on.

(i) I managed to keep up a bit of a social life during this summer.

In a state of grief, interactions that would normally be taken for granted and enjoyed may be difficult.

(j) My overall mood was somber, but I was at least willing to be distracted by friends . . .

Sometimes when self control of thoughts is hard, external help is effective. A mood is a type of global state, which need not have a semantic focus, unlike emotions. Moods also need to be explained by a theory of the architecture of a mind.

(k) I became more and more of a hermit. Things lost their savour for me, and I withdrew.

Some of the high level control states, which we may think of as forming the personality, can be profoundly changed by grief. This may affect a wide range of preferences, choices, strategies, plans, and behaviour.

(l) Grief isn't something you can show for too long. People are uncomfortable with it. They will indulge you only for so long, so you just hold it inside, slog along and try to get on with life.

Besides the control problems which relate to tasks and goals that form part of normal life, the observation that grief has undesirable social consequences can generate a new second order control problem – namely, not allowing the grief to be shown or to intrude in social interactions. Many emotions generate second-order motivations relating to the control of those emotional states themselves.

(m) The holidays and the new year are a natural marker, and they've kept me busy and distracted me.

Another example of external help with the control problem.

(n) I try to reintegrate myself with my social circle, and start seeing friends again more regularly. But I'm worried; I don't want to let go of the grief. Sometimes I think it's all I have left of XXX.

Motivation in relation to the control of the emotional state may be very mixed. The griever who manages to control the grief and get on with life may also suffer feelings of guilt or regret because another motivator involving one's duty to the deceased seems to be violated, or because of the feeling that overcoming the grief would itself be a sort of loss of contact with the deceased.

(o) I don't want to enter his bedroom one day with indifference, and wonder how we might use the space. I don't want to stop crying every day when reminded of another piece of our time together. Well, I *do*, eventually, and I know I will, but I am not comfortable with this yet.

Another example of mixed and conflicting second order motivation relating to the state of grief.

(p) This was a gruelling, soul-grinding and exhausting year. It has been the worst year of my life.

Emotional states normally involve evaluations. Powerful emotions often arise out of 'intense' evaluations. The emotional states themselves can be evaluated and contribute to the judgement that something bad, or something good, is happening.

Those who have grieved or had close contact with a griever may empathise with these extracts. Others will also understand, for these are pervasive phenomena and play a major role in many works of art. But we need to get beyond empathy and folk psychology to understand the architecture underlying grieving and other affective states. Our proposed architecture provides a provisional first draft explanation of certain characteristic cognitive features of mourning in terms of causal relations between underlying information processing mechanisms.

The following are among the surface phenomena of grieving, illustrated by the above extracts:

1. The continual and repeated interruption of attention by memories or thoughts relating to the friend's illness and death; i.e. loss of 'normal' control of thought processes (explained below). See [a, d, g, h].
2. The difficulty of accepting the fact of the friend's illness and death. See [b, e, g].
3. The disruptive effect on normal, day-to-day functioning. See [c, e, g, k, p].
4. Periods of relative normality when grief is 'backgrounded', sometimes because external factors help one regain 'normal' control. See [f, i, j, m].
5. Attempts to 'fight' the grief. [g: 'try to go to bed', l: 'hold it inside, slog along and try to get on with life'].
6. Second order motivators, some of them involving evaluation of the griev-

ing state as good or bad, including, in some cases, wishing the grief to continue. See [n, o].

7. The subjective 'pain' experienced by the mourner. There may be mental pain as well as bodily disturbances. See [a, h, p].

8. Crying. See [o].

These are not all the possible symptoms of long-term grief and neither are they unique to grief: excited anticipation of a long awaited event could also disrupt normal day-to-day functioning. Anger can also be 'background' when other demands control one's attention. Guilt feelings, or an undesirable infatuation may also be fought against.

Many theories of emotion concentrate either on the neural substrate, external behaviour or externally observable changes (facial expression, posture, muscular tension, sweating, etc.), i.e. evolutionarily old mechanisms shared with other animals. We are deliberately ignoring most of these, indeed regarding them as only marginally relevant, since, in principle, the mental phenomena that we are concerned with could occur without these other accompaniments, for instance, in beings from another planet whose mental functioning and social life were much like ours despite considerable bodily differences (see Sloman 92).

We do not wish to argue over whether these phenomena are or are not part of the definition of the word 'emotion'. Many words of folk psychology are notoriously ill-defined (Read & Sloman, 93; Kagan, 78), both in colloquial use, and in scientific contexts where different theorists offer different definitions. So instead of arguing over definitions we merely identify certain types of familiar phenomena and then ask what sorts of mechanisms might explain them. Since we are interested in information processing explanations of information processing phenomena we are not concerned that there are no behavioural or physiological definitions of the phenomena: for example, there are no behavioural or physical definitions of many of the states and processes in information systems that are of interest to software engineers. They are rightly not concerned that their work does not conform to narrow (and often misguided) criteria of what constitutes 'science'.

Our interest is in information processing theories of affective states because we expect they will be both theoretically and practically enormously fruitful in the long run, even though most of the people who should be most concerned, such as therapists, counsellors and educationalists, are usually unaware of them on account of current training regimes.

For those that remain uncomfortable with a functional analysis of affective states the following distinction may be helpful: many mental terms have, besides their physical basis, two non-physical aspects – phenomenological (subjective feelings states) and psychological (functional role) (Chalmers, 96). For example, 'pain' certainly denotes an unpleasant feeling state, but it also refers to a functional role of a pain control signal that leads to the withdrawal or avoidance of an aversive stimulus. In our discussion the 'phe-nomenological problem' is factored out and placed to one side. Our emphasis is on what causal mechanisms *do*, not *what it is to be like* these causal mechanisms.

3.2 Self-control and perturbance

A grieving person is partly 'out of control'. Explaining this requires an analysis of what it is to be in control. The ordinary notion of 'self-control' is not a unitary concept admitting of a unique analysis. Like many mental concepts it covers a variety of cases and further study is required to investigate how many of them can be accommodated within the design-based framework. In particular, not all agent architectures can support a distinction between being in control and not being in control of one's thought processes. For instance it is not clear that a rat ever has control of thought processes. In that case it cannot lose control. If that is so, the sorts of processes we are discussing cannot occur in a rat.

What kind of system can have control of its thought processes? A partial answer is that the system must be able to have goals relating to its own thought processes, and it has control when everything that occurs in it is consistent with all the currently adopted management and meta-management goals. This does not imply that everything that happens is *generated* by those goals, for that would rule out intrusions, such as feeling hungry, or a new desire to help someone in trouble. These can arise without contradicting one's view of what one should be like.

Our partial answer needs to be expanded in various ways. One is to allow that there need not be only *one* coherent global set of goals, preferences, etc. since some people seem to change personality from one context to another, like the kind father who is an aggressive car driver. The architecture might allow a number of *different* sets of mutually consistent high level dispositions that co-exist, though only one set is active at a time (as sketched in Ch. 10 of Sloman 78).

Detection of incongruent states requires some sort of self-monitoring of the global 'picture' and an explicit evaluation of it as fitting or not fitting the agent's ideals, long term objectives, or previous decisions regarding (for example) what to think about, or which desires are unacceptable. If a substantial amount of what is happening at any time is inconsistent with the agent's dominant evaluations and preferences, then the agent is, to that extent, partly out of control, even if all the disturbances and disruptions are generated entirely within the system, e.g. from lower level automatic, non-attentive, processes, or reflexes in the management system. Addictions are an extreme case.

We use the term *perturbant* for a state in which partial loss of control is due to the continual surfacing of postponed or rejected, or unwanted, motivators (Beaudoin, 94), or possibly disruptive thoughts, images, and the like (e.g., a catchy tune that won't 'go away'). Such disruption can interfere with the management of other, important goals. This is the type of information processing state that the 'attention filter penetration' theory posits as characteristic of many emotional states (Simon 67, Sloman & Croucher 81, Sloman 87, 92). It is what the filter normally prevents.

Perturbant *states* differ in several dimensions: duration; whether the source is internal or external; semantic content (what is referred to); type of disruption (it could be due to a goal, thought, or recollection); effect on management processes; frequency of disruption; positive or negative evaluation (compare grieving with being unable to stop thinking about the victory one has recently won – grieving and gloating have much in common); how the state develops; whether and how it decays; how easily it can be controlled, and so on.

Perturbances (like 'thrashing' in an overloaded computer operating system) are side-effects of mechanisms whose major role is to do something else (just as thrashing arises from the paging and swapping mechanisms in the operating system). Perturbances arise from the interactions between (a) resource-limited attentive processing, (b) a subsystem that generates new candidates for such processing and (c) a heuristic filter mechanism. These design elements arise from the requirements for coping with complex and rapidly changing environments. Perturbances do not arise because of some special perturbance generating (or emotion generating) mechanism. Thus it is misguided to ask what the *function* of perturbant states is or to postulate a perturbance mechanism.

Our architecture was described above as concerned with processing goals. However, other things should also be able to penetrate the filter mechanism and divert management processes, such as items of factual information about current or past events. Sometimes new information generates motivators as a result of high level reasoning which interacts with generactivators in the management system, for instance, discovering that one's bank balance is very low. Also new factual information may be required to interact with current plans and goals, for instance, showing that a goal has been satisfied and is now redundant, or that a short-cut is now available (Ch 6 of Sloman 78, Pryor & Collins 92). This means that perturbant states can be produced not only by new motivators but also episodic recollections, Simon's 'cognitive associations' (Simon, 67), or motivationally neutral thoughts.

Can perturbant states be controlled? Self-control requires self-knowledge. Control of motive management processes requires both knowledge of what they are and motivators expressing what they should be: a partly normative theory of the self, which can be used in detecting and categorising internal states, just as knowledge and desires are used in external perception and action. In humans there are wide differences in degree and kind of self-knowledge, though mourners usually know that they are mourning. People are aware of some aspects of their own mental state which they can describe with more or less precision and artistry.

Monitoring of management processes may be based on detection of such variables as the rate of surfacing of new motives, aspects of their semantic content, their effects on processing, the current filter threshold level, the rate of success of plans. Self-descriptions thus produced may vary in scope and content, as in 'My last goals were not achieved', 'I am usually calm', 'I am happy now', 'I am grieving over my lost brother', 'I feel depressed about life', 'I am worried about a job interview but looking forward to a hot bath'. Information sampled from the stream of management processing can be stored to provide data for the self-control mechanism.

Such 'internal perception', where the self-control mechanism is the per-ceiver and motive processing is the environment, requires non-intrusive or 'transparent' monitoring that does not change the processes observed, just as looking at a scene does not change the scene. This is also a requirement for 'software agent' architectures in computing systems, where agents need to be able to observe and react to actions of other agents in the system. Full trans-parency is difficult, or even impossible to achieve: architectures are always partly opaque. Attempts to 'trace' everything in a software system break down when the tracing processes are traced. Self-knowledge is always incomplete, for otherwise there would be an infinite regress, for instance, of beliefs about beliefs about beliefs . . .

The requirement for transparency of motive management processes may be satisfied to different degrees by different designs (e.g., a neural net moni-toring a lower level neural net by 'sampling' connections, or procedures that can be interrogated about their functionality without disrupting their oper-ation (Rozas, 93), or blackboard architectures with globally readable infor-mation spaces, or towers of self-referential processors (Bawden, 88), and so forth). Exactly which forms of transparency exist in which organisms is an empirical question. Which forms are useful for which purposes is a design question.

Access to information is not enough. The system must be able to produce adequate descriptions or categorisations. So self-reflective concepts are required for self-monitoring, including both concepts learnt from the utter-ances of others ('Don't be angry', 'Are you upset?') and concepts induced internally via generic concept-learning mechanisms. Thus both socially acquired descriptions and more or less idiosyncratic categories will be used to refer to internal states.

Besides self-monitoring, self-control requires selection of remedies and their application. Like medical treatment self-control uses a three-stage pro-cess of diagnosis (identifying the problem), selecting strategies (selection of medication and prognosis), and applying them within the system (treatment). There are numerous possible strategies, with details differing between archi-tectures. Some management strategies will be socially inculcated while others are induced by generic learning mechanisms from consequences of self-management decisions.

Such a meta-management system will have, or develop, ways of classifying internal states and associating appropriate strategies with them – often different strategies in different contexts. For example, raising the attention filter threshold to counter perturbance may be useful when it is difficult to keep up with new goals, but could be disastrous in situations where some highly urgent and important new information could turn up.

Some control strategies treat symptoms: for example, counting imaginary sheep to counteract insomnia. The sheep-counting strategy works by concentrating deliberative resources on a motivationally neutral task that requires full attention. The cause of insomnia remains but its ability to divert resources is diminished by a rival task. (This often fails.) Another case of treating symptoms is turning to drink in order to dull painful thoughts and emotional responses: a strategy which depends on close coupling between chemical processes and high level control states.

More powerful self-control strategies may be more difficult to apply: removing the cause of the problem (dismantling an attachment structure (defined below) or abandoning an unfulfilled desire – often difficult or impossible), suppressing external symptoms while internal turmoil continues (the stiff upper lip syndrome), diverting the system via tasks and external contexts that cause the attention filter threshold to be raised, undergoing explicit or implicit training (or therapy) that alters some of the links in the system (e.g. disabling some generactivators or changing them so that they assign lower insistence levels). Some of these are temporary palliatives, whilst others have long term effects. Some may lead to new re-integrated personalities, while others leave potentially harmful tensions within the control system.

Self-control is always limited. The difficulty in controlling perturbances may have different causes. (a) Self-control mechanisms have limited causal powers (hence the tension between the ease of representing what you want to become and the difficulty of becoming what you have represented (Smith, 86)); (b) self-monitoring is limited by architectural opacity; (c) the system may lack the concepts required to categories internal states and express appropriate remedial strategies; or (d) adequate control strategies may not yet be available.

Powers of self-control mechanisms can be extended by various kinds of training and practice. Opacity can sometimes be overcome by extra reasoning (after the event), like inferring the shape of an occluded object during visual perception. New meta-management strategies can be learnt through trial and error, social influences, or possibly therapy.

Psychological evidence exists for self-modelling, reflection and self-repair, e.g. (Kuhl & Kraska, 89). Selecting or creating control strategies requires a decision mechanism that can synthesise different kinds of information –

current state of motive management, environmental context, current goals, theory of the self and so on – and then decide on a strategy. This ability will vary between individuals.

3.3 Attachment structures

A raised surface can leave an impression on human skin; similarly, interaction with another person will leave an 'impression' on mentality. Before the advent of information processing architectures this metaphor could not be unpacked.

Bowlby's theory of attachment (Bowlby, 79 & 88) attempts to explain how affectional bonds are created and the effects that occur when such bonds are broken. Although criticised in recent times (particularly the emphasis on maternal deprivation in childhood to explain subsequent problems in adulthood; see (Smith & Cowie, 91), Ch. 3) attachment theory is still used to account for both childhood and adult mourning in clinical psychology. We shall explore this theory within our proposed architecture, showing how processes described above as percolation, circulation and diffusion allow a distributed multi-component 'structure of attachment' to an individual to develop and influence subsequent processing. Being deeply entrenched at many levels within the control hierarchy it manifests itself in multifarious ways when its object dies.

The perceptual system and belief systems of an agent will include information about other agents, including information about how to recognize them and what behaviour to expect from them in various situations. This may also include evaluations such as 'X is a good person' or 'X is dependable'. Interaction with X will lead to creation of motive generactivators expressing motivational attitudes towards X. Over time, enduring control states pertaining to X will be generated that interact with higher level attitudes and personality traits within the hierarchy of dispositional control states.

For example, various preferential mechanisms may be set up ('prefer to be in the company of X'), which could function as motive comparators; or unfocused and abstract wishes ('wish X is always happy and well'); also desires ('desire to holiday with X sometime soon' or 'desire to spend more time with X'), hopes ('hope X likes me', 'hope X enjoys my company', 'hope that X will remain close') and aims ('maintain friendship with X', 'avoid arguments with X'). High level preferences may generate lower level motive generators: for example, preferring to be in the company of X could generate the aim to maintain the friendship of X. In other words, a diverse collection of control states with complex interrelations and dispositional powers will be created alongside factual information collected through interactions with X.

The evaluations, generactivators and motivators will be positive towards some individuals, negative or neutral towards others, and with varying degrees of strength, possibly involving the pleasure and pain mechanisms.

Depending on the particular combinations of evaluations and other attitudes towards an individual, the death of that individual may cause grief or
some other kind of emotional state, or no emotional state. A pre-requisite
for grief is strong positive evaluation, though that is not sufficient, for the
death of a person whom one admires or respects greatly need not cause grief.
Something more is required, namely the sort of entanglement of personalities commonly labelled as 'love' (another highly ambiguous term).

The kind of loving that potentially leads to grief, which we are calling
'attachment', is a very complex mixture of states that develop over time
through mutual interaction. It will involve many dispositions, including dispositions that produce pleasurable feelings in the company of the person,
displeasure when the person is absent or harmed, and so on. Besides feelings,
attachment structures can generate new motivators relating to the person,
e.g. when information is received about that person's needs, successes, failures, suffering, etc. All these new (dispositional) control states generated by
the process of attachment will, over time, integrate into the existing control
network: the process we have called 'diffusion.'

These control states involve many dispositions, including potential influences on both pre-attentive and attentive processes. The former include (a) a
tendency for new motives to be generated pertaining to X; (b) assigning
relatively high insistence values to motives concerned with X, particularly if
there is a serious problem involving X that needs urgent attention; (c) allowing the filtering mechanism to give preferential surfacing conditions to X-
related motives, as all things relating to person X are deemed important
(compare a mother and her baby); and (d) new links between phenomena
involving X and the pain and pleasure mechanisms.

Effects on attentive, management processes include: (e) new dedicated
decision procedures with regard to X (e.g., skewed importance, urgency and
cost-benefit computations that raise the priority of X-related motives); (f)
creation of unusually detailed (possibly unrealistic) predictive models about
X's behaviour and preferences; (g) clusters of management procedures that
manage X-related motives by combining model-based information, current
and new goals to form new intentions; (g) a relatively high proportion of
items in the goal database concerned with long, medium and short-term
intentions relating to X, in various states, such as conditionally suspended,
postponed, ongoing etc.; (h) an unusually high proportion of intentions that
are long term mutual or joint plans predicated on the co-operation and continued proximity of X; and possibly (i) new motive conflicts pertaining to X,
e.g. the combination of preferring to be in the company of X, wishing that X
is happy and believing that X wishes to be alone, or loves another. Great
novels and real human tragedies often depend on such conflicts and the
processes they generate.

Meta-management procedures may be generated or altered during the
growth of attachment. For example, management tasks of the form 'decide

whether to adopt motive M' may come to be be handled as soon as possible if M pertains to X. Relatively more computational resources may come to be allotted to any decision procedure concerned with X. A host of plan libraries expressing the utility of certain actions for achieving goals with regard to X will be formed, which facilitate planning relating to X; and 'chunks' of actions that appear to be efficacious when dealing with X may be abnormally strongly reinforced and lead to stereotypical and positively valanced patterns of interaction.

Summary: an 'attachment structure' relating to an individual is a highly distributed collection of information stores and active components embedded in different parts of the architecture and linked to many other potential control states. When an attachment structure concerning individual X exists in an agent, almost any information about X is likely to trigger some internal reaction. In particular, information about good things or bad things happening to X may trigger reactions whose strength and pervasiveness depends on how good or bad they are. Death is a particularly bad event.

In this paper we shall not attempt to describe the process of *detachment*, in which the attachment structure is gradually dismembered and possibly replaced by a new complex set of beliefs and motives relating to X, consistent with X no longer being alive. This drawn-out process is part of a self-control strategy for overcoming perturbance, albeit a long-term strategy that attempts a design change to achieve its ends. This process can be analysed into many sub-problems – for example, the structure of attachment would need to be inspected for the sources of perturbance, blame assigned, a modification of the structure selected, and repair work effected followed by some kind of verification process to check whether the modification had resulted in an improvement.

These are all extremely sketchy ideas that need to be developed in the light of a more detailed specification of the architecture and its 'learning' capabilities. Yet all the proposed control states are of a type that we claim could be implemented (with difficulty) in a suitably rich architecture based on AI mechanisms, possibly using a mixture of neural nets and symbolic processes.

3.4 An architecturally grounded analysis of grief

We now return to the symptoms of grief and attempt an architecturally grounded interpretation of the surface phenomena in terms of an attachment structure in the griever towards the deceased.

1. The continual and repeated interruption of attention by memories or thoughts relating to the friend's illness and death.

We have already described (Section 3.2) how the architecture permits perturbant states when heuristic mechanisms designed to prevent disturbance of resource limited processes continually 'let through' motivators and thoughts that divert attention from highly valued activities. Following bereavement, cyclic processes could occur, involving, among other things: motives relating to the dead person, generated by long term attachment structures, including desires for the person to be alive, or present, or unharmed; wishing one had done things that might have prevented the death; recalling that the person is dead; rejection of the motives as therefore inappropriate or futile; evaluating such rejection as undesirable; reminders of relevant information concerning the person, such as might be important if the rejected goals were being acted on. These and other interactions might all reverberate throughout the system because of the deeply entrenched information structures and the powerful triggering effect of news that the worst possible harm has already happened to the person.

Some of these events may set off a stream of deliberative thought (or meta management processes) attempting to re-orientate extant desires, intentions and plans, to cope with the changed circumstances. This process could also trigger the recall of associated memories in the form of different sensory modalities (images, smells, sounds etc.), as well as triggering a host of embedded generactivators waiting in the wings.

The structure of attachment explains why motives relating to X are likely to disrupt attention. (a) X-related motives will be given high insistence values because the relationship with X is strongly positively valenced and X has suffered great harm. (b) Exception fields within the filtering mechanism may provide preferential surfacing conditions for X-related motives and thoughts. (c) Higher level, abstract control states expressing attitudes or preferences towards X may influence lower level motive generators not directly concerned with X, producing 'partially X-related' motives. (d) Meta-management control processes ensure that motives and thoughts pertaining to X are always decided as soon as possible, so that such motives tend to grab attentive resources immediately. (e) Dedicated evaluation procedures rate X-related motives preferentially, assigning skewed importance, urgency and cost-benefit measures. (f) Predictive models, triggered by X-related motives, will consume computational resources by attempting to reason about about X's needs and possible reactions to things. (g) In a resource-limited system, the proliferation of motives pertaining to X may 'crowd out' other motive generators.

Besides internal processes that spontaneously occur following the news of X's death, external reminders may trigger additional X-related processes: e.g. driving past X's favourite restaurant or accidentally finding an old photograph, or hearing X mentioned in a conversation. In some environments such reminders will be frequent. Perceptual schemata looking out for the 'lost' individual may misidentify strangers as X. The association of places, objects and events with memories of the deceased may be powerful triggers for perturbant episodes, sustaining the period of mourning and making recovery difficult without a change of location.

To summarise: *If a structure of attachment to X exists then motives and thoughts pertaining to X will surface and successfully compete for attentive computational resources; news relating to X's death will therefore have a strong tendency to generate perturbant states. The agent's thought processes will be partly out of control.*

2. The difficulty of accepting the fact of the friend's illness and death.

Updating many entries in a large database of information can take time, including the time for restructuring and propagation. This is one notion of the 'difficulty' of accepting new information.

Another factor is resistance to change. The agent has 'affective' grounds for wanting to believe that information about X's death is false. This could include long term high commitment intentions pertaining to X, involving mutual plans that have had resources expended on them, which the agent does not wish to regard as wasted. Besides uncomfortable evaluations, complete assimilation of the new information may require extensive resource-consuming cognitive reorganisation because the attachment structure is distributed and interwoven with other control states. Humans often seem to reject information, however reliable, if it requires extensive reorganisation of control states and value systems. This may be part of a good engineering design for intelligent agents in a mostly stable world.

Finally, the agent may know from past experience that the acceptance of such beliefs entails a long process of suffering and pain. Holding out hope that the information may turn out to be false is a management goal to delay the onset of this process.

3. The disruptive effect on normal, day-to-day functioning.

Perturbance involves disruption of the processes of motive management, and day-to-day goal processing may be adversely affected by management overload. It is difficult to plan a shopping trip or attend to what others are saying when distracted by futile regrets or painful thoughts and memories.

Besides cognitive disturbance, bereavement can cause physiological changes in the mourner, such as weight loss and excessive tiredness, which will contribute to a lack of efficacy; however, this is not explained by our architecture.

4. Periods of relative normality when grief is 'backgrounded', sometimes because external factors help one regain 'normal' control.

When the management system is involved in new important and urgent tasks it sets the interrupt filter threshold so high that the conditions discussed above no longer hold, like the soldier or football player who is injured and yet feels no pain. When the external demands are removed, the threshold drops, and processes relating to the bereavement regain control.

Another factor may be a general mood of depression that 'colours' motive processing during grief. A depressed mood is a global control state that 'scales-down' interaction with the environment. (We do not have space for a full discussion of moods.)

5. Attempts to 'fight' the grief.

How can the mourner 'fight' the grief and 'try' to get on with life? 'Fighting' here refers to a kind of mental striving or conscious self-control, which is not always easy. It requires some way of suppressing perturbant states, which is often much harder than control of emotional expression (external symptoms).

When the bereaved is attempting to work yet thoughts are continually drawn to the recent death, the self-control mechanism described above may detect the perturbance and attempt to negate its disruptive effects. Until detachment has been achieved, such self-control is partial and transient: the mourning returns when fragments of the attachment structure are next triggered, by external or internal (possibly subconscious) processes.

One form of self-control uses the artificial 'deadening' of cognitive activity by alcohol or anti-depressants. Chemicals can alter the functioning of abstract machines through their effect on the neuro-physiological substrate. Although understandable, this strategy could exacerbate the problem (drink can make people maudlin) or possibly slow down the process of detachment.

People are sometimes exhorted to try intentional suppression of perturbing thoughts, using internal imperatives: 'don't think about that', 'ignore that', 'put these thoughts out of mind' etc. This could also flow from a meta-management process, spawned by a self-control mechanism, which rejects new motives pertaining to the deceased. Some people may have learnt how to raise their attention filter threshold deliberately. In practice instructions to oneself often fail.

Even if temporarily successful this may lead to a build up of motives waiting to surface, since the cause of perturbance remains. Sudden surfacing of these suppressed motives could produce breakdown of control if there is a drop in the filter threshold due to low management load. Thus a person experiencing grief might function normally at work during the day (when high management load sets a high filter threshold) only to break down at home later (when both load and threshold drop).

Even at home one can try to absorb oneself in attention grabbing, computationally expensive tasks. 'And then there are details like writing obits, funeral arrangements, meeting his family, etc., which keep you busy. And then the grief resumes.' Arranging the funeral *has* to be done and can divert attention for a while, whereas attempting to read an interesting book fails.

However, as the intensity of grief lessens through gradual dismantling of the attachment structure, thoughts and motives relating to X have lower insistence, allowing 'normal' tasks with low importance and urgency to hold attention and prevent perturbance, and permitting enjoyment of activities such as listening to music, playing games, reading books, or conversing with others.

Another coping strategy is the formation of a new affectional bond to replace the old one ('on the rebound') – an option that is not always available, especially to an older person who has lost a spouse. The formation of such a bond might be a way to avoid the lengthy and painful process of detaching the structure of attachment by finding a new use for it. This involves replacing the original referent and possibly other things, and will not be achieved easily because of the distributed mechanisms and links that constitute attachment. This might be connected with the phenomenon of 'projection', where the grieving person views the new person in terms of the old.

Some of these strategies may be ineffective, or may have undesirable side effects, including hindering the long term process of detachment. The pressure to find quick fixes may come from the culture, for example through the necessity to keep one's job. This could cause harm if the only satisfactory strategy for achieving internal reorganisation following death of a loved one is through the natural process of grieving.

Examples of strategies that might aid this process are acceptance (as opposed to suppression), via a meta-level goal to interpret the experience of grief positively, by understanding that grief is necessary and worthwhile. A supportive social circle may be required for this to work. The self-control of emotional expression ('hold it inside, slog along and try to get on with life') becomes necessary when friends or work colleagues are less prepared to make allowances. It is difficult to control facial expression and general demeanour. People can usually see through the attempt. Limitations on our ability to dissimulate may arise from requirements for successful social co-operation (Sloman 92).

> 6. Second order motivators, some of them involving evaluation of the grieving state as good or bad, including, in some cases, wishing the grief to continue. See [o, q].

Disruptive and painful processes can trigger a second order motive to end the state. But the mourner quoted wishes to preserve his grief: 'I don't want to let go of the grief. Sometimes I think it's all I have left of XXX.' And 'I don't want to stop crying every day as I'm reminded of another piece of our time together. Well, I *do*, eventually, and I know I will, but I am not comfortable with this yet.' Why should the mourner – paradoxically – wish the grief to continue? There are a number of elements at work here: (a) the knowledge that the period of intense grieving may be coming to an end, (b) the association between grieving and the recollection of memories of the deceased, (c) a conflict of meta-level motivation between wanting to stop grieving and not wanting to.

The architecture described can support such conflicting processes. For example, detachment may be occurring concurrently with a meta-management process that ensures that the deceased is not forgotten, but remembered with the appropriate sadness. The meta-management process may have been constructed by a collection of high level control states consti-tuting a self-image; for example, the mourner may view himself as somebody who loved the deceased very much and consequently *should* experience the appropriate amount of grief and heartache. (Cultural norms will affect this.)

Second order effects are to be expected within the framework of the archi-tecture. The meta-management system includes self-monitoring processes that allow high level motive generators to be triggered by the detection of internal states that require some change in management strategy. Some of these simply redirect attention and cause sensible evaluating, reasoning, deciding, and planning to occur. Others generate some new motives that are, for one reason or another, hard to achieve, and some that are rejected yet go on being reactivated and interrupting processing. Exactly how all this develops will vary from individual to individual and within an individual from one situation to another. Second order processes may be strongly influ-enced by a culture.

> 7. The subjective 'pain' experienced by the mourner. There may be mental pain as well as bodily disturbances.

Why is grief a subjectively painful 'soul-grinding' experience? Some per-turbant states are very pleasurable (such as excited anticipation); con-sequently, a structure of attachment perturbing attentive processing is not a *sufficient* condition for grief. The pain presumably comes via the fact that the death violates so many of the motives and preferences associated with the attachment structure. Further research is in progress to explain the roles of pain, pleasure and evaluation in the architecture.

> 8. Crying. Can we provide a design-based account of the onset of crying? Why does wailing or howling occur in times of extreme emo-tional distress?

Infants cry when their desires are unsatisfied. This grabs the attention of an adult who will then normally attend to the baby's needs. For a baby in the helpless altricial stage crying is a *basic, genetically determined, plan*. It is the only way to satisfy its needs for food, warmth, milk etc. Later, crying is no longer necessary because there is a repertoire of plans and the agent can act independently.

Consider the following scenario. A loved one suddenly died a few weeks ago and you are in mourning. You were thinking about going shopping but your attention was disrupted by thoughts of the lost one. A perturbant state is manifest. Your thoughts are out of control and you cannot stop thinking about what you were going to do together, the things you miss sharing with them, that you are lonely and without a close friend, and so on. You stare at the wall and ruminate. In terms of the architecture the structure of attachment is generating motives that are surfacing through the attention filter to disrupt management processes. These motives, pertaining to the dead person, are unsatisfiable and therefore rejected. But their high insistence makes them surface again, foiling any plans for regaining control. In this situation, the basic plan of crying may be invoked because (a) no other plans from the repertoire exist for the surfacing motives, (b) the invocation conditions of the basic plan are situations where 'nothing can be done', i.e. identical to the altricial stage of development, (c) the basic plan has worked in the past to satisfy desires in such situations, and (d) it has general applicability, i.e. was used to satisfy diverse and basic wants such as food, warmth, milk, and proximity to adults. *Crying is the plan of last resort*, and can be triggered by negatively valenced perturbant states. There may be other 'basic' plans, some concerned with internal processes only.

This explains Sartre view of 'emotions' as an attempt to 'magically' transform the world (Sartre, 48). From an infant's standpoint, crying achieves things by magic. As children grow their helplessness diminishes, along with the need to cry. (The picture becomes complicated later on, when the possibility of emotional deception is discovered – faking crying to manipulate others.)

Also, the notion of 'basic plans' as control mechanisms of last resort bears important similarities to Kraemer's *cascade hypothesis* (Kraemer, 92), which states that control will 'cascade' down to 'genetically programmed neurobiological adaptive behaviours' if the organism is faced with 'disasters' (problematic situations) that its 'acquired behaviours' cannot deal with. However, Kraemer's approach is very different from ours, namely psychobiological as opposed to cognitive, and leads to seemingly different answers (biogenic amine system function as opposed to information processing). There is no space for a full comparison here, but a synthesis should be possible. For example, our notion of a basic plan makes no commitment to its implementation details. The integration of 'bottom-up' approaches with 'top-down' requirements-driven design work should yield fruitful, and not necessarily contradictory, results.

3.5 *Discussion*

Using the postulated architecture, we have offered a partial and provisional design-based interpretation of many aspects of human grief. However, our theory is sketchy, incomplete and offered only as an initial step towards a comprehensive theory of emotions informed by the exploration of agent architectures in which control mechanisms are information based.

1   For each loved person, a structure of attachment develops, consisting of diverse distributed mechanisms and representations with varying powers of persistence and dispositional causal roles in determining behaviour. This is the affectional bond.

2   Removal of the referent renders the structure of attachment inappropriate for the control of behaviour.[6] Nevertheless, triggered by the news of the death and reverberating associations, the attachment structure generates thoughts and motives that surface and divert attentive resources, producing negatively valenced perturbant states.

3   Perturbant states disrupt normal functioning in resource-limited management processes.

4   The futility of other plans may trigger regression to a basic plan of crying.

5   Various self-control strategies may be instigated to overcome the perturbant states; however, the phenomenology of grief suggests that the causal powers of self-control mechanisms are limited.

6   Detachment takes time due to the deep and diffuse embedding of the attachment structure in the architecture. Extensive cognitive reorganisation and re-learning is required before the generation of perturbant states ceases, or drops to a manageable level. How long it takes will depend on details of the case. Some grief lasts as long as the griever.

Much work is still required, to deal with many difficulties and gaps in the design and the interpretation we have based on it. Problematic areas include mechanisms for: learning, pleasure and pain, self monitoring, the hierarchy of dispositional control states, self-controlling abilities, the kinds of global control indicated by mood changes, and the processes which assemble and disassemble attachment structures.

Terms such as 'attention' and 'conscious' have been used without precise definitions. When fully specified the architecture will be used as the basis for a host of new definitions of classes of mental states and processes (like basing the descriptions of types of physical stuff on a theory of the architecture of matter).

Questions arise about the possibility of using the architecture to explain other perturbant states such as distress at the ending of a relationship, excited anticipation, sexual infatuation, obsessive love of a child, various pathologies of motivation or attention such as obsessive-compulsive disorder and attention deficit disorder. These are all possible directions for future work.

It is hard to think about the multifarious states and processes that can occur in such a complex paper design. A working implementation can aid analytical thinking, by exposing consequences of the design. An implementable scenario for investigating perturbance is outlined in (Wright, 94), and further work is in progress. This has led us to extend the architecture, to overcome limitations of early versions which assumed a fixed succession of processes to be applied to new motivators. This proved unworkable (Beaudoin 94).

It may be objected that the use of an architecture as explanatory ground merely restates the obvious in a more complicated way, particularly if it generates no new testable predictions. This expresses a naive view of complex information processing systems. Prediction may be impossible because some determinants of behaviour are inaccessible internal information states.

Our work can be classified as belonging to the 'creative modelling' phase of science (Bhaskar, 78 & 94), where competing models of generative mechanisms of surface phenomena are explored. Until we have a good 'design-space' of broad and increasingly deep agent architectures it will be difficult to move from hypothetical explanation to justified selection between hypotheses. The research community operating as parallel search in both empirical and theoretical directions will ultimately select between competing theories, using a variety of criteria including generality, simplicity, implementability, evolvability and applicability to other animals. But the theories need to be developed. Using an architecture as explanatory ground is a first step.

The interpretation of grief given here may be compared with other design-based models of emotionality, which tend to reason about emotional labels based on an operational semantics of emotion concepts (for example, see (Dyer, 87), (Frijda & Swagerman, 87) and (Pfeifer, 92)). On our model such emotion concepts would arise from internal perception of motive processing states, self-control mechanisms and social interaction. Another point in favour of the architecturally grounded interpretation is that it has greater explanatory power than that of folk psychology. For example, we begin to give answers to the following questions: *What is grief?* – Grief is (often) an extended process of cognitive reorganisation characterised by the occurrence of negatively valenced perturbant states caused by an attachment structure reacting to news of the death. *What causes grief to endure?* – Grief persists because of the time required to disassemble a complex, distributed and deep attachment structure. *Why does grief consume the mourner?* – Attentive processing is resource-bound and becomes swamped by highly insistent motives generated by a structure of attachment to a highly valued individual; in addition, the requirements for re-learning and detachment entail extensive rumination that can also generate perturbant states. *Why do we cry during grief?* – In processing situations where strong but unsatisfiable motives surface, a time may come when otherwise helpless management processes resort to a basic plan. Crying is the plan of last resort. *Why can't grief be overcome easily?* – Processes of self-control are limited by architectural opacity, the lack of adequate categorisations of internal states, the lack of good meta-management strategies, and the disruptive effects of perturbances.

4 Concluding comments

We have sketched an architecture of a sort that might be useful for an intelligent agent with multiple asynchronously generated goals in a complex and changing environment. We have shown how perturbant states can emerge in such an architecture and how a structure of attachment can generate ongoing perturbance after bereavement. This extends some previous theories of emotions and draws attention to new research problems, some of which require more detailed design specifications and some more detailed empirical investigations of phenomena involving grief and other perturbant states.

Our architecturally grounded interpretation of human grief has been provided within a design-based framework. We expect development of the design to lead to more fine-grained analysis of well-known phenomena, generating hard cases that will force further development of the theory. Detailed implementations may reveal unexpected insights, along with hidden flaws in the theory and also with opportunities to extend it.

No strong claim is made that the interpretation is *the* theory; currently, we are only exploring theoretical possibilities and illustrating a new approach to the study of complex mental phenomena.

We have extended our earlier (pre 1995) design, particularly in the direction of self-monitoring and self-controlling abilities, and alluded to the need for further extension, e.g. learning mechanisms. Sartre's intuition that 'emotions' are magical attempts to transform the world has been architecturally grounded via the idea of a fall-back plan in situations of helplessness. We have not yet said anything about links with neural structures and processes or emotional mechanisms shared with other animals.

We must stress that whether the actual interpretation of grief outlined here is correct in detail is of secondary importance. A stronger claim can be made for the methodology that generated the interpretation. In order fully to understand the complexity of human behaviour we have to posit new ontologies at the information processing level of description just as a designer specifies an architecture to meet some collection of behavioural requirements. By exploring families of related architectures and their strengths and weaknesses in relation to various niches, we may be able eventually to explain not only current human capabilities but also the evolution of human and non-human mental architectures in a variety of organisms.

The work will also give us new insights into what to expect if and when we design autonomous artificial agents, whose internal complexity will make detailed prediction of their behaviour very difficult.

That all this will be a long and difficult process, with continual revision of ideas, is not in question.

Acknowledgements

This work was supported by the UK Joint Council Initiative and the Renaissance Trust.

Thanks to Christian Paterson, Chris Complin and past and present members of the Cognition and Affect project at Birmingham. Additional papers by the group can be found at the ftp site:

ftp://ftp.cs.bham.ac.uk/pub/groups/cog-affect/0-INDEX.html
and in Aaron Sloman's Web page
http://www.cs.bham.ac.uk/ãxs/cogaff.html

Notes

1 The first two authors are at the University of Birmingham. The third author is now at Newbridge Microsystems, Canada. This paper was written by the first two authors, making considerable use of ideas developed with the third author and reported in his PhD Thesis (Beaudoin 94)

2 Disparate research efforts are already developing architectures that share a subset of design features given similar requirements. The design of autonomous agent architectures grows apace. For example, Firby's RAP (Firby, 87; Hanks & Firby, 90), the Oz Project (Loyall & Bates, 91; Reilly, 93), Hayes-Roth's intelligent control systems (Hayes-Roth, 91a, 91b, 93a & 93b), the Heuristic Control Virtual Machine (Fehling et al., 89), Georgeff's PRS and Beaudoin's NML1 all share significant design features (for a review see (Wright, 94) and (Wooldridge & Jennings, 95)). However, this phase of agent design may be overturned by revolutionary developments of ideas and techniques. For example, (Brooks & Stein, 93) claim that increased parallelism and the building of situated agents bottom-up will generate such a change.

3 There are are at least two uses of the word 'architecture'; one referring to an abstraction or design that is common to many instances of the architecture; and the other to concrete instances of such designs. We use the former sense, in which an architecture is a collection of features common to a class of entities. Each instance of an architecture is composed of coexisting, interacting substructures with various capabilities and functional roles. A substructure may also have an architecture. The architecture of a complex system can explain how its capabilities and behaviour arise out of the capabilities, behaviour, relationships and interactions of the components. An architecture can be specified at different levels of detail, e.g. at a high level of abstraction the architecture of a house will not include the occurrence of particular bricks, whereas a more detailed architectural specification would.

4 There are other motivator components not detailed here; see (Beaudoin 94, Sloman & Poli 95).

5 See (Pryor & Collins, 92).
6 Compare Oatley's treatment of grief: 'a whole repertoire of subplans and knowledge becomes useless' (Oatley, 92).

References

Bates, J., Loyall, A. B., & Reilly, W. S. (1991). Broad agents. Paper presented at the *AAAI spring symposium on integrated intelligent architectures.* Stanford, CA: (Available in SIGART BULLETIN, 2(4), Aug. 1991, 38–40).

Bawden, A. (1988). Reification without evaluation. MIT AI Memo 946; also in *Proceedings of the 1988 ACM Conference on Lisp and Functional Programming.*

Beaudoin, L. P. (1994). *Goal Processing in Autonomous Agents.* PhD Thesis, School of Computer Science, University of Birmingham.

Beaudoin, L. P. & Sloman, A. (1993). A study of motive processing and attention. In *Proceedings of AISB93,* A. Sloman, D. Hogg, G. Humphreys, A. Ramsay & D. Partridge (Eds), 229–238, Oxford: IOS Press.

Bhaskar, R. (1978). *A Realist Theory of Science.* The Harvester Press Ltd.

Bhaskar, R. (1994). *Plato, Etc.* Verso.

Brooks, R. A. & Stein, L. A. (1993). Building brains for bodies. MIT artificial intelligence laboratory, AI Memo No. 1439.

Bowlby, J. (1979). *The Making and Breaking of Affectional Bonds.* Tavistock Publications Ltd.

Bowlby, J. (1988). *A Secure Base.* Routledge.

Chalmers, D. (1996). *The Conscious Mind.* Oxford University Press.

Dodd, B. (1991). Bereavement, in: *Psychology and Social Issues* R. Cochrane & D. Carroll (eds), London: The Falmer Press, 1991 pages 63–72.

Dyer, M. G. (1987). Emotions and their computations: Three computer models. *Cognition and Emotion* 1(3), 323–347.

Fehling, M. R., Altman, A. M. & Michael Wilber, B. (1989). The Heuristic control virtual machine: An implementation of the schemer computational model of reflective, real-time problem-solving. In *Blackboard Architectures and Applications.* Academic Press, Inc.

Firby, R. J. (1987). An investigation into reactive planning in complex domains. *Proceedings of the Sixth National Conference on Artificial Intelligence,* (202–206). Seattle: AAAI.

Frijda, N. H. (1986). *The Emotions.* Cambridge: Cambridge University Press.

Frijda, N. H., & Swagerman, J. (1987). Can computers feel? Theory and design of an emotional system. *Cognition and Emotion,* 1, 235–257.

Georgeff, M. P., & Ingrand, F. F. (1989). Decision-making in an embedded reasoning system. In *Proceedings of the Eleventh International Joint Conference on Artificial Intelligence,* 2 (972–978). Detroit, MI: IJCAI.

Hanks, S., & Firby, R. J. (1990). Issues and architectures for planning and execution. In *Proceedings of a Workshop on Innovative Approaches to Planning, Scheduling and Control,* San Diego, CA: DARPA.

Hayes-Roth, B. (1993a). An architecture for adaptive intelligent systems (KSL Report No. 93–19). Knowledge Systems Laboratory, Department of Computer Science, Stanford University.

Hayes-Roth, B. (1993b). Intelligent control. *Artificial Intelligence*, 59, 213–220.

Hayes-Roth, B. (1991a). Evaluation of integrated agent architectures. SIGART Bulletin, 2(4), 82–84.

Hayes-Roth, B. (1991b). An integrated architecture for intelligent agents. SIGART Bulletin, 2(4), 79–81.

Johnson-Laird, P. N. (1988). *The Computer and the Mind: An Introduction to Cognitive Science*, Fontana.

Kagan, J. (1978). On emotion and its development: a working paper. In *The Development of Affect* edited by M. Lewis and L. A. Rosenblum. Plenum Press, New York and London.

Kraemer, G. W. (1992). A psychobiological theory of attachment. *Behavioural and Brain Sciences* 15, 493–541.

Kuhl, J., & Kraska, K. (1989). Self-regulation and metamotivation: Computational mechanisms, development, and assessment. In R. Kanfer, P. L. Ackerman, & R. Cudek (Eds.), *Abilities, motivation, and methodology: The Minnesota Symposium on Individual Differences* (343–374). Hillsdale, NJ: Lawrence Erlbaum Associates Inc.

Lakatos, I. (1970), Falsification and the methodology of scientific research programmes, in *Criticism and the Growth of Knowledge* I. Lakatos and A. Musgrave (eds), Cambridge University Press, 921–196.

Loyall, A. B., & Bates, J. (1991). Hap – A reactive, adaptive architecture for agents (Technical report No. CMU-CS-91-147), School of Computer Science, Carnegie Mellon University.

Miller, Galanter, & Pribram (1970). *Plans and the Structure of Behaviour*. Holt International Edition.

Moffat, D. & Frijda, N. H. (1995). Where there's a Will there's an agent. To appear in: *Intelligent Agents – Proceedings of the 1994 Workshop on Agent Theories, Architectures and Languages*, M. J. Wooldridge and N. R. Jennings (Eds.), Springer Verlag (LNAI Series) 1995.

Oatley, K. (1992). *Best laid schemes, the psychology of emotions*. Studies in Emotion and Social Interaction, Cambridge University Press.

Palmer, S. E., & Kimchi, R. (1984). The information processing approach to cognition. In *Approaches to Cognition: Contrasts and Controversies*, T. J. Knapp & L. C. Robertson (eds.). Hillsdale, NJ: Lawrence Erlbaum Associates.

Paterson, C. J. (1995) The use of ratings for the integration of planning and learning in a broad but shallow agent architecture. MPhil Thesis, Computer Science Department, University of Birmingham.

Penrose, R. (1989). *The Emperor's New Mind: Concerning Computers, Minds and the Laws of Physics*. Oxford University Press.

Pfeifer, R. (1992). The new age of the fungus eater: Comments on artificial intelligence and emotion. Extended and revised version of an invited talk at the AISB-91 conference in Leeds, U.K.

Pryor, L., & Collins, G. (1992). Reference features as guides to reasoning about opportunities. In *Proceedings of the Fourteenth Annual Conference of the Cognitive Science Society*. Bloomington, Lawrence Erlbaum Associates.

Rao, A. S., & Georgeff, M. P. (1991). Modeling rational agents within a BDI-Architecture (Technical Note No. 14). Australian Artificial Intelligence Institute, 1 Grattan Street, Carlton, Victoria 3053, Australia.

Rao, A. S., & Georgeff, M. P. (1992). An abstract architecture for rational agents. In *Proceedings of the Third International Conference on Knowledge Representation and Reasoning*. Boston: KR92.

Read, T., & Sloman, A. (1993). The terminological pitfalls of studying emotion. Paper presented at the *Workshop on Architectures Underlying Motivation and Emotion – WAUME 93*, Birmingham.

Reilly, W. S. (1993). Emotions as Part of a Broad Agent Architecture. Talk given at WAUME93, Birmingham.

Ryle, G. (1949) *The Concept of Mind*, Hutchinson.

Rozas, G. J. (1993). Translucent procedures, abstraction without opacity. Phd thesis: MIT AI Technical Report No. 1427.

Sartre, J. P. (1948) *Esquisse d'une théorie phénomenologique des émotions (The Emotions)*, Paris: Hermann (New York: Philosophical Library), 1934, Translated 1948

Searle, J. R. (1980), Minds Brains and Programs, *The Behavioral and Brain Sciences* 3,3.

Simon, H. A. (1967). 'Motivational and Emotional Controls of Cognition', reprinted in *Models of Thought*, Yale University Press, (1979) 29–38.

Simon, H. A. (1969). *The Sciences of the Artificial*, Second Edition, MIT Press (1981).

Simon, H. A. (1995). 'Explaining the Ineffable: AI on the Topics of Intuition, Insight and Inspiration', *Proceedings 14th International Joint Conference on Artificial Intelligence* Montreal, August 1995, 939–945.

Sloman, A. (1978). *The Computer Revolution in Philosophy: Philosophy, Science and Models of Mind*. Harvester Studies in Cognitive Science, Harvester Press.

Sloman, A. (1987). 'Motives mechanisms and emotions' in Emotion and Cognition 1, 3, 217–234, reprinted in M. A. Boden (ed) *The Philosophy of Artificial Intelligence* 'Oxford Reading in Philosophy' Series, Oxford University Press, 231–247 1990.

Sloman, A. (1992) Prolegomena to a theory of communication and affect, *Communication from an Artificial Intelligence Perspective: Theoretical and Applied Issues*, A. Ortony, J. Slack, and O. Stock, eds. Springer: Heidelberg, 229–260.

Sloman, A. (1993a). Prospects for AI as the general science of intelligence. In *Prospects for Artificial Intelligence* Proceedings of AISB93, Oxford IOS Press, Editors: A. Sloman, D. Hogg, G. Humphreys & D. Partridge.

Sloman, A. (1993b). The mind as a control system, in *Philosophy and the Cognitive Sciences*, (eds) C. Hookway and D. Peterson, Cambridge University Press, 69–110.

Sloman, A. (1994). Semantics in an intelligent control system. *Philosophical Transactions of the Royal Society: Physical Sciences and Engineering*, Vol 349, 1689, 43–58

Sloman, A. (1995). Exploring design space and niche space. In *Proceedings 5th Scandinavian Conf. on AI*, Trondheim May 1995, IOS Press, Amsterdam,

Sloman, A., Beaudoin, L. P., & Wright, I. P. (1994) Computational modeling of motive-management processes, *Proceedings of the Conference of the International Society for Research in Emotions, Cambridge, July 1994*. (ed) N. Frijda, ISRE Publications. 344–348.

Sloman, A., & Croucher, M. (1981). Why robots will have emotions. In *Proceedings of the Seventh International Joint Conference on Artificial Intelligence*, (197–202). Vancouver.

Sloman, A. & Poli, R. (1995). 'SIM_AGENT: A toolkit for exploring agent designs' in *ATAL-95, Workshop on Agent Theories, Architectures, and Languages*, IJCAI-95, Montreal, August 1995. (Also Cognitive Science technical report: CSRP-95-3, The University of Birmingham.)

269

Smith, B. C. (1986). Varieties of self-reference. In J. Y. Halpern (Ed.), *Proceedings of the First Conference on Theoretical Aspects of Reasoning About Knowledge*. Morgan Kaufman.

Smith, P. K. & Cowie, H. (1991). *Understanding Children's Development*, chapter 3: Parents and families. Blackwell Publishers.

Wooldridge, M. & Jennings, N. R. (1995). Agents: Theories, Architectures and Languages, *Knowledge Engineering Review*.

Wright, I. P. (1994). An emotional agent: the detection and control of emergent states in autonomous resource-bounded agents. Cognitive Science Research Report RP-94-21, School of Computer Science and Cognitive Science Research Centre, University of Birmingham.

76

CREATIVITY AND ARTIFICIAL INTELLIGENCE

Margaret A. Boden

Source: *Artificial Intelligence* 103(1–2), 1998: 347–56.

Abstract Creativity is a fundamental feature of human intelligence, and a challenge for AI. AI techniques can be used to create new ideas in three ways: by producing novel combinations of familiar ideas; by exploring the potential of conceptual spaces; and by making transformations that enable the generation of previously impossible ideas. AI will have less difficulty in modelling the generation of new ideas than in automating their evaluation. © 1998 Elsevier Science B.V. All rights reserved.

1. Why AI must try to model creativity

Creativity is a fundamental feature of human intelligence, and an inescapable challenge for AI. Even technologically oriented AI cannot ignore it, for creative programs could be very useful in the laboratory or the market-place. And AI-models intended (or considered) as part of cognitive science can help psychologists to understand how it is possible for human minds to be creative.

Creativity is not a special 'faculty', nor a psychological property confined to a tiny elite. Rather, it is a feature of human intelligence in general. It is grounded in everyday capacities such as the association of ideas, reminding, perception, analogical thinking, searching a structured problem-space, and reflective self-criticism. It involves not only a cognitive dimension (the generation of new ideas) but also motivation and emotion, and is closely linked to cultural context and personality factors [3]. Current AI models of creativity focus primarily on the cognitive dimension.

A creative idea is one which is novel, surprising, and valuable (interesting, useful, beautiful ...). But 'novel' has two importantly different senses here. The idea may be novel with respect only to the mind of the individual (or

AI-system) concerned or, so far as we know, to the whole of previous history. The ability to produce novelties of the former kind may be called P-creativity (P for psychological), the latter H-creativity (H for historical). P-creativity is the more fundamental notion, of which H-creativity is a special case.

AI should concentrate primarily on P-creativity. If it manages to model this in a powerful manner, then artificial H-creativity will occur in some cases—indeed, it already has, as we shall see. (In what follows, I shall not use the letter-prefixes: usually, it is P-creativity which is at issue.)

2. Three types of creativity

There are three main types of creativity, involving different ways of generating the novel ideas. Each of the three results in surprises, but only one (the third) can lead to the 'shock' of surprise that greets an apparently impossible idea [2]. All types include some H-creative examples, but the creators celebrated in the history books are more often valued for their achievements in respect of the third type of creativity.

The first type involves novel (improbable) combinations of familiar ideas. Let us call this 'combinational' creativity. Examples include much poetic imagery, and also analogy—wherein the two newly associated ideas share some inherent conceptual structure. Analogies are sometimes explored and developed at some length, for purposes of rhetoric or problem-solving. But even the mere generation, or appreciation, of an apt analogy involves a (not necessarily conscious) judicious structural mapping, whereby the similarities of structure are not only noticed but are judged in terms of their strength and depth.

The second and third types are closely linked, and more similar to each other than either is to the first. They are 'exploratory' and 'transformational' creativity. The former involves the generation of novel ideas by the exploration of structured conceptual spaces. This often results in structures ('ideas') that are not only novel, but unexpected. One can immediately see, however, that they satisfy the canons of the thinking-style concerned. The latter involves the transformation of some (one or more) dimension of the space, so that new structures can be generated which could not have arisen before. The more fundamental the dimension concerned, and the more powerful the transformation, the more surprising the new ideas will be. These two forms of creativity shade into one another, since exploration of the space can include minimal 'tweaking' of fairly superficial constraints. The distinction between a tweak and a transform is to some extent a matter of judgement, but the more well-defined the space, the clearer this distinction can be.

Many human beings—including (for example) most professional scientists, artists, and jazz-musicians—make a justly respected living out of exploratory creativity. That is, they inherit an accepted style of thinking from their culture, and then search it, and perhaps superficially tweak it, to explore its contents, boundaries, and potential. But human beings sometimes transform the accepted conceptual space, by altering or removing one (or more) of its dimensions, or by adding a new one. Such transformation enables ideas to be generated which (relative to that conceptual space) were previously impossible.

The more fundamental the transformation, and/or the more fundamental the dimension that is transformed, the more different the newly-possible structures will be. The shock of amazement that attends such (previously impossible) ideas is much greater than the surprise occasioned by mere improbabilities, however unexpected they may be. If the transformations are too extreme, the relation between the old and new spaces will not be immediately apparent. In such cases, the new structures will be unintelligible, and very likely rejected. Indeed, it may take some time for the relation between the two spaces to be recognized and generally accepted.

3. Computer models of creativity

Computer models of creativity include examples of all three types. As yet, those focussed on the second (exploratory) type are the most successful. That's not to say that exploratory creativity is easy to reproduce. On the contrary, it typically requires considerable domain-expertise and analytic power to define the conceptual space in the first place, and to specify procedures that enable its potential to be explored. But combinational and transformational creativity are even more elusive.

The reasons for this, in brief, are the difficulty of approaching the richness of human associative memory, and the difficulty of identifying our values and of expressing them in computational form. The former difficulty bedevils attempts to simulate combinational creativity. The latter difficulty attends efforts directed at any type of creativity, but is especially problematic with respect to the third (see Section 4, below).

Combinational creativity is studied in AI by research on (for instance) jokes and analogy. Both of these require some sort of semantic network, or inter-linked knowledge-base, as their ground. Clearly, pulling random associations out of such a source is simple. But an association may not be telling, or appropriate in context. For all combinational tasks other than 'free association', the nature and structure of the associative linkage is important too. Ideally, every product of the combinational program should be at least minimally apt, and the originality of the various combinations should be assessable by the AI-system.

A recent, and relatively successful, example of AI-generated (combinational) humour is Jape, a program for producing punning riddles [1]. Jape produces jokes based on nine general sentence-forms, such as: What do you get when you cross X with Y?; What kind of. X has Y?; What kind of X can Y?;

What's the difference between an X and a Y? The semantic network used by the program incorporates knowledge of phonology, semantics, syntax, and spelling. Different combinations of these aspects of words are used, in distinctly structured ways, for generating each joke-type.

Examples of riddles generated by Jape include: (Q) What kind of murderer has fibre? (A) A cereal killer; (Q) What do you call a strange market? (A) A bizarre bazaar; (Q) What do you call a depressed train? (A) A low-comotive; and (Q) What's the difference between leaves and a car? (A) One you brush and rake, the other you rush and brake. These may not send us into paroxysms of laughter—although, in a relaxed social setting, one or two of them might. But they are all amusing enough to prompt wryly appreciative groans.

Binsted did a systematic series of psychological tests, comparing people's reception of Jape's riddles with their response to human-originated jokes published in joke-books. She also compared Jape's products with 'non-jokes' generated by random combinations. She found, for instance, that children, by whom such humour is most appreciated, can distinguish reliably between jokes (including Jape's riddles) and non-jokes. Although they generally find human-originated jokes funnier than Jape's, this difference vanishes if Jape's output is pruned, so as to omit the items generated by the least successful schemata. The riddles published in human joke-books are highly selected, for only those the author finds reasonably funny will appear in print.

Binsted had set herself a challenging task: to ensure that every one of Jape's jokes would be amusing. Her follow-up research showed that although none were regarded as exceptionally funny, very few produced no response at all. This contrasts with some other AI-models of creativity, such as AM [16], where a high proportion of the newly generated structures are not thought interesting by human beings.

It does not follow that all AI-modelling of creativity should emulate Binsted's ambition. This is especially true if the system is meant to be used interactively by human beings, to help their own creativity by prompting them to think about ideas that otherwise they might not have considered. Some 'unsuccessful' products should in any case be allowed, as even human creators often produce second-rate, or even inappropriate, ideas. Jape's success is due to the fact that its joke-templates and generative schemata are very limited. Binsted identifies a number of aspects of real-life riddles which are not paralleled in Jape, and whose (reliably funny) implementation is not possible in the foreseeable future. To incorporate these aspects so as to produce jokes that are reliably funny would raise thorny questions of evaluation (see Section 4).

As for AI-models of analogy, most of these generate and evaluate analogies by using domain-general mapping rules, applied to prestructured concepts (e.g. [7,12,13]). The creators of some of these models have compared them with the results of psychological experiments, claiming a significant amount of evidence in support of their domain-general approach [8]. In these models, there is a clear distinction between the representation of a concept and its mapping onto some other concept. The two concepts involved usually remain unchanged by the analogy.

Some AI-models of analogy allow for a more flexible representation of concepts. One example is the Copycat program, a broadly connectionist system that looks for analogies between alphabetic letter-strings [11,18]. Copycat's concepts are context-sensitive descriptions of strings such as 'mmpprr' and 'klmmno'. The two m's in the first string just listed will be described by Copycat as a pair, but those in the second string will be described as the end-points of two different triplets.

One might rather say that Copycat will 'eventually' describe them in these ways. For its concepts evolve as processing proceeds. This research is guided by the theoretical assumption that seeing a new analogy is much the same as perceiving something in a new way. So Copycat does not rely on ready-made, fixed, representations, but constructs its own in a context-sensitive way: new analogies and new perceptions develop together. A part-built description that seems to be mapping well onto the nascent analogy is maintained, and developed further. One that seems to be heading for a dead end is abandoned, and an alternative begun which exploits different aspects. The model allows a wide range of (more or less daring) analogies to be generated, and evaluated. The degree to which the analogies are obvious or far-fetched can be altered by means of one of the system-parameters.

Whether the approach used in Copycat is preferable to the more usual forms of (domain-general) mapping is controversial. Hofstadter [11] criticizes other AI-models of analogy for assuming that concepts are unchanging and inflexible, and for guaranteeing that the required analogy (among others) will be found by focussing on small representations having the requisite conceptual structures and mapping rules built in. The opposing camp rebut these charges [8].

They argue that to identify analogical thinking with high-level perception, as Hofstadter does, is to use a vague and misleading metaphor: analogical mapping, they insist, is a domain-general process which must be analytically distinguished from conceptual representation. They point out that the most detailed published account of Copycat [18] provides just such an analysis, describing the representation-building procedures as distinct from, though interacting with, the representation-comparing modules. They report that the Structure Mapping Engine (SME), for instance, can be successfully used on representations that are 'very large' as compared with Copycat's, some of which were built by other systems for independent purposes. They compare Copycat's alphabetic microworld with the 'blocks world' of 1970s scene analysis, which ignored most of the interesting complexity (and noise) in the real-world. Although their early models did not allow for changes in conceptual structure as a result of analogising, they refer to work on learning (using SME) involving processes of schema abstraction, inference projection, and re-representation [9]. Moreover (as remarked above), they claim that their psychological experiments support their approach to simulation. For example, they say there is evidence that memory access, in which one is reminded of an (absent) analog, depends on psychological processes, and kinds of similarity, significantly different from those involved in mapping between two analogs that are presented simultaneously.

The jury remains out on this dispute. However, it may not be necessary to plump absolutely for either side. My hunch is that the Copycat approach is much closer to the fluid complexity of human thinking. But domain-general principles of analogy are probably important. And these are presumably enriched by many domain-specific processes. (Certainly, psychological studies of how human beings retrieve and interpret analogies are likely to be helpful.) In short, even combinational creativity is, or can be, a highly complex matter.

The exploratory and transformational types of creativity can also be modelled by AI-systems. For conceptual spaces, and ways of exploring and modifying them, can be described by computational concepts.

Occasionally, a 'creative' program is said to apply to a wide range of domains, or conceptual spaces—as EURISKO, for instance, does [16]. But to make this generalist program useful in a particular area, such as genetic engineering or VLSI-design, considerable specialist knowledge has to be provided if it is not to generate hosts of nonsensical (as opposed to merely boring) ideas. In general, providing a program with a representation of an interesting conceptual space, and with appropriate exploratory processes, requires considerable domain-expertise on the part of the programmer—or at least on the part of someone with whom he cooperates. (Unfortunately, the highly subject-bounded institutional structure of most universities works against this sort of interdisciplinarity.)

For example, EMI (experiments in musical intelligence) is a program that composes in the styles of Mozart, Stravinsky, Joplin, and others [6]. In order to do this, it employs powerful musical grammars expressed as ATNs. In addition, it uses lists of 'signatures': melodic, harmonic, metric, and ornamental motifs characteristic of individual composers. Using general rules to vary and intertwine these, it often composes a musical phrase near-identical to a signature that has *not* been provided. This suggests a systematicity in individual composing styles.

Individual musical style has been addressed also in a pioneering program that improvises jazz in real time, though the technique can be applied to other types of music [10]. The most highly developed version, at present, generates jazz in the style of Charlie Parker—and (ignoring the lack of expressiveness, and the quality of the synthesized sound) it actually sounds like Parker. Besides strong (and relatively general) knowledge of musical dimensions such as harmony and rhythm, and of musical conventions characteristic of jazz, the system has access to a large set of Parker-specific motifs, which can be varied and combined in a number of ways. (The programmer is an accomplished jazz-saxophonist: without strong musical skills, he would not be able to identify the relevant motifs, or judge the aptness of specific processes for using them.) In exploring this conceptual space, the program often originates interesting musical ideas, which jazz-professionals can exploit in their own performance. However, in its present form it never moves outside Parker-space: its creativity is merely exploratory, not transformational.

Architectural design, too, has been formally modelled. For instance, a shape-grammar describing Frank Lloyd Wright's Prairie houses generates all the ones he designed, as well as others he did not [14]. To the initiated eye, every one of these novel (exploratory-creative) structures falls within the genre. The grammar not only identifies the crucial dimensions of the relevant architectural space, but also shows which are relatively fundamental. In a Prairie house, the addition of a balcony is stylistically superficial, for it is a decision on which nothing else (except the appearance and ornamentation of the balcony) depends. By contrast, the 'addition' of a fireplace results in overall structural change, because many design-decisions follow, and depend upon, the (early) decision about the fireplace. Exploring this space by making different choices about fireplaces, then, can give rise to surprises more fundamental than can adding balconies in unexpected places.

Perhaps the best-known example of AI-creativity is AARON, a program—or rather, a series of programs—for exploring line-drawing in particular styles [17] and, more recently, colouring also [5]. Written by Harold Cohen, an artist who was already an acclaimed professional in the 1960s, AARON explores a space defined with the help of rich domain-expertise.

AARON is not focussed primarily on surfaces, but generates some representation of a 3D-core, and then draws a line around it. Versions that can draw many idiosyncratic portraits use 900 control points to specify the 3D-core, of which 300 specify the structure of the face and head. The program's drawings are aesthetically pleasing, and have been exhibited in galleries worldwide. Until very recently, coloured images of AARON's work were hand-painted by Cohen. But in 1995, he exhibited a version of AARON that can do this itself. It chooses colours by tonality (light/dark) rather than hue, although it can decide to concentrate on a particular family of hues. It draws outlines using paintbrush, but colours the paper by applying five round 'paint-blocks' of differing sizes. Some characteristic features of the resulting painting style are due to the physical properties of the dyes and painting-blocks rather than to the program guiding their use. Like drawing-AARON, painting-AARON is still under continuous development.

The drawings (and paintings) are individually unpredictable because of random choices, but all the drawings produced by a given version of AARON will have the same style. AARON cannot reflect on its own productions, nor adjust them so as to make them better. It cannot even transform its conceptual space, leaving aside the question of whether this results in something 'better'. In this, it resembles most current AI-programs focussed on creativity.

A further example of exploratory AI-creativity is the BACON suite designed to model scientific discovery [15]. The heuristics used by the BACON system are carefully pre-programmed, and the data are deliberately prestructured so as to suit the heuristics provided. New types of discovery are impossible for BACON. It is therefore misleading to name such programs after scientists remembered for noticing relations of a type never noticed before. Even the notion that there may be (for instance) some linear mathematical relation to be found was a huge creative leap.

Almost all of today's 'creative' computers are concerned only with exploring pre-defined conceptual spaces. They may allow for highly constrained tweaking, but no fundamental novelties or truly shocking surprises are possible. However, a few AI-systems attempt not only to explore their conceptual space but also to transform it, sometimes in relatively unconstrained ways.

Transformational systems include AM and EURISKO [16], and certain programs based on genetic algorithms. Some of these have produced valued structures that the human experts say they could never have produced unaided: the sculptor William Latham, for example, has generated 3D-forms of a type which he could not have imagined for himself [22].

Most GA-programs only explore a pre-given space, seeking the 'optimal' location within it. But some also transform their generative mechanism in a more or less fundamental way. For example, GA-work in graphics may enable superficial tweaking of the conceptual space, resulting in images which, although novel, clearly belong to the same family as those which went before [22]. Or it may allow the core of the image-generating code to be lengthened and complexified, so that the novel images may bear no family-resemblance even to their parents, still less to their more remote ancestors [21]. Similarly, some work in evolutionary robotics has generated novel sensory-motor anatomies and control systems as a result of GAs that allow the length of the 'genome' to be altered [4].

One should not assume that transformation is always creative, or even—in the present state of the art—that AI-systems that can transform their rules are superior to those which cannot. Significantly, some AI-modellers deliberately avoid giving their programs the capacity to change the heart of the code. That is, they prevent fundamental transformations in the conceptual space, allowing only exploration and relatively superficial tweaking. One reason for this is the human may be more interested, at least for a time, in exploring a given space than in transforming it in unpredictable ways. A professional sculptor such as Latham, for instance, may wish to explore the potential (and limits) of one particular family of 3D-structures, before considering others [22]. Another reason for avoiding rampant trans-formation in AI-models of creativity is the difficulty of automating evaluation.

4. The evaluation of new ideas

A main reason why most current AI-models of creativity attempt only exploration, not transformation, is that if the space is transformed then the resulting structures may not have any interest or value. Such ideas are novel, certainly, but not creative. (We saw in Section 1 that 'creativity' implies posi-tive evaluation.)

This would not matter if the AI-system were able to realize the poor qual-ity of the new constructions, and drop (or amend) the transformation accordingly. A truly automatic AI-creator would have evaluative mechanisms sufficiently powerful to do this. At present, this is very rarely so (an exception is artificial co-evolution in which the fitness function evolves alongside the several species involved [19]). Notoriously, AM produced many more useless items than powerful mathematical ideas, and although it did have heuristics of 'interestingness' built into it, its evaluations were often mistaken by human standards. And some 'adventurously' transformational programs embody no evaluative criteria at all, the evaluation being done interactively by human beings [21].

There is no reason in principle why future AI-models should not embody evaluative criteria powerful enough to allow them to transform their con-ceptual spaces in fruitfully creative (including H-creative) ways. But for such computerized self-criticism to be possible, the programmers must be able to express the values concerned sufficiently clearly for them to be implemented. Even if the values are not predetermined, being represented instead as an evolving fitness function, the relevant features must be implemented in and recognized by the (GA) system.

To some extent, this can be achieved implicitly, by defining a culturally accepted conceptual space so successfully that any structure that can be gen-erated by the program will be accepted by humans as valuable [5,14]. But the structures generated within newly transformed spaces will need types of evaluation different (at least in part) from those implicit within the original space, or previously provided in explicit form.

It is even more difficult to express (verbally or computationally) just what it is that we like about a Bach fugue, or an impressionist painting, than it is to recognize something as an acceptable member of one of those categories. And to say what it is that we like (or even dislike) about a new, or previously unfamiliar, form of music or painting is even more challenging.

Identifying the criteria we use in our evaluations is hard enough. Justify-ing, or even (causally) explaining, our reliance on those criteria is more dif-ficult still. For example, just why we like or dislike something will often have a lot to do with motivational and emotional factors—considerations about which current AI has almost nothing to say.

To make matters worse, human values—and therefore the novelties which we are prepared to approve as 'creative'—change from culture to culture, and from time to time. In some cases, they do so in unpredictable and irrational ways: think of the fashion-industry, for example, or of rogue memes like the back-to-front baseball-cap. Nor are value-shifts confined to trivial cases such as these: even Bach, Mozart, and Donne were ignored and/or criticized in certain periods.

The scientific criteria of theoretical elegance and coherence, and of experimental verification, are less variable than artistic values. But that's not to say they are easy to define, or to implement. (An attempt to do so, for certain sorts of mathematical symmetry, has been made by the BACON team.)

Moreover, science too has its equivalent of fad and fashion. Even the discovery of dinosaurs was not a cut-and-dried event, but the culmination of a process of scientific—and political-nationalistic—negotiation lasting for several years [20]. The important point is that what scientists count as 'creative', and what they call a 'discovery', depends largely on unarticulated values, including social considerations of various kinds. These social evaluations are often invisible to scientists. For sure, they are not represented in AI-models.

5. Conclusion

Some H-creative ideas have already been generated by AI-programs, though usually by merely exploratory (or combinational) procedures. Transformational AI-originality is only just beginning.

The two major bottlenecks are:

(1) domain-expertise, which is required for mapping the conceptual space that is to be explored and/or transformed; and
(2) valuation of the results, which is especially necessary—and especially difficult—for transformational programs.

These two bottlenecks interact, since subtle valuation requires considerable domain expertise. Valuation, thus far, is mostly implicit in the generative procedures used by the program, or interactively imposed by a human being. Only a few AI-models can critically judge their own original ideas. And hardly any can combine evaluation with transformation.

The ultimate vindication of AI-creativity would be a program that generated novel ideas which initially perplexed or even repelled us, but which was able to persuade us that they were indeed valuable. We are a very long way from that.

References

[1] K. Binsted, Machine humour: an implemented model of puns, Ph.D. Thesis, University of Edinburgh, 1996.

[2] M. A. Boden, The Creative Mind: Myths and Mechanisms, Basic Books, New York, 1990.

[3] M. A. Boden (Ed.), Dimensions of Creativity, MIT Press, Cambridge, MA, 1994.

[4] D. Cliff, I. Harvey, P. Husbands, Explorations in evolutionary robotics, Adaptive Behavior 2 (1993) 71–108.

[5] H. Cohen, The further exploits of AARON, painter, in: S. Franchi, G. Guzeldere (Eds.), Constructions of the Mind: Artificial Intelligence and the Humanities, Special edition of Stanford Humanities Review 4 (2) (1995) pp. 141–160.

[6] D. Cope, Computers and Musical Style, Oxford University Press, Oxford, 1991.

[7] K. D. Forbus, D. Gentner, K. Law, MAC/FAC: A model of similarity-based retrieval. Cognitive Science 119 (1994) 141–205.

[8] K.D. Forbus, D. Gentner, A. B. Markman, R. W. Ferguson, Analogy just looks like high level perception: why a domain-general approach to analogical mapping is right, Journal of Experimental and Theoretical AI, in press.

[9] D. Gentner, S. Brem, R. W. Ferguson, A. B. Markman, B. B. Levidow, P. Wolff, K. D. Forbus, Conceptual change via analogical reasoning: a case study of Johannes Kepler, Journal of the Learning Sciences, in press.

[10] P. Hodgson, Modelling cognition in creative musical improvisation. Ph.D. Thesis, University of Sussex, in preparation.

[11] D. R. Hofstadter, FARG (The fluid analogies research group). Fluid Concepts and Creative Analogies: Computer Models of the Fundamental Mechanisms of Thought, Basic Books, New York, 1995.

[12] K. J. Holyoak, P. Thagard, Analogical mapping by constraint satisfaction. Cognitive Science 13 (1989) 295–355.

[13] K. J. Holyoak, P. Thagard, Mental Leaps: Analogy in Creative Thought, MIT Press, Cambridge, MA, 1995.

[14] H. Koning, J. Eizenberg, The language of the prairie: Frank Lloyd Wright's prairie houses, Environment and Planning B 8(1981) 295–323.

[15] P. Langley, H. A. Simon, G. L. Bradshaw, J. M. Zytkow, Scientific Discovery: Computational Explorations of the Creative Process, MIT Press, Cambridge, MA, 1987.

[16] D. B. Lenat, The role of heuristics in learning by discovery: three case studies, in: R. S. Michalski, J. G. Carbonell, T. M. Mitchell (Eds.), Machine Learning: An Artificial Intelligence Approach, Tioga, Palo Alto, CA, 1983, pp. 243–306.

[17] P. McCorduck, Aaron's Code, W. H. Freeman, San Francisco, CA, 1991.

[18] M. Mitchell, Analogy-Making as Perception, MIT Press, Cambridge, MA, 1993.

[19] T. S. Ray, An approach to the synthesis of life, in: C. G. Langton, C. Taylor, J. Doyne Farmer, S. Rasmussen (Eds.), Artificial Life II, Addison Wesley, Redwood City. CA, 1992, pp. 371–408. Reprinted in: M.A. Boden (Ed.), The Philosophy of Artificial Life, Oxford University Press, Oxford, 1996, pp. 111–145.

[20] S. Schaffer, Making up discovery, in: M.A. Boden (Ed.), Dimensions of Creativity, MIT Press, Cambridge, MA, 1994, pp. 13–51.

[21] K. Sims, Artificial evolution for computer graphics, Computer Graphics 25(4) (1991) 319–328.
[22] S. Todd, W. Latham, Evolutionary Art and Computers, Academic Press, London, 1992.

2.2: Ethics

77

ETHICS, MIND AND ARTIFICE

Steve Torrance

Source: From K. S. Gill (ed.), *Artificial Intelligence for Society*, John Wiley & Sons, 1986, pp. 55–72.

Abstract This chapter explores the difference between two kinds of claim that can be made on behalf of AI: *the narrow claim*, that certain specific mental processes—the cognitive processes which are the common focus of attention in current AI research—are computationally realizable, and *the wide claim*, that all mental states are so realizable.

It is argued that these are extremely different positions. The first may ultimately hinge on little more than a decision over terminological usage. The second, however, is of ethical significance: the mental states which are associated with consciousness or sentience, particularly with enjoyment, suffering, etc., are ethically crucial; their application does not rest on arbitrary decision. The narrow claim has considerable plausibility in view of developments in AI. The wide claim has little plausibility, it is suggested. Some bad arguments in support of the wide claim are considered.

The chapter ends with some remarks on those aspects of mentality which lie between the computationally tractable and the computationally intractable—such as emotions, evaluative and ethical choice. These and other areas of mentality, although 'non-cognitive', may be capable of computational modelling. It is particularly important that AI knowledge-based systems should be equipped with some kind of humanitarian normative outlook.

A flowering of artificiality

It has been a great summer for the artificial. Not merely were some five thousand delegates registered for the 1985 International Joint Conference on Artificial Intelligence in Los Angeles, but also Mrs June Tregale won a gold award at the Honiton County Show, Devon, for her recreation of an entire

English country garden in plastic and silk flowers (*The Guardian*, 3 August 1985). A world first, surely. It would appear that the exhibit in question passed a floral equivalent of the Turing test: 'My biggest problem,' Mrs Tregale said, 'was the public. Half of them could not believe the flowers were fakes.'

If one is merely interested in exhibitions, then artificial intelligence and artificial flowers may serve as well as their respective natural correlates. Stick-in-the-soil horticulturalists may insist that something essential will always be missing from even the most delicately composed floral presentation. It is not clear that very much hangs on the issue.

In the case of intelligence, however, more may be at stake. On the one hand, AI supporters strenuously argue that as long as an artificially intelligent system *delivers* all (at least all) that a naturally intelligent system does, then that is all that matters as far as *intelligence* goes, because that is all that there is to intelligence. The view is not irresistable—indeed it has strenuous critics. Nevertheless, it has considerable plausibility. Enthusiasts of surrogate flora claim only that the latter may be *as good as* naturally grown varieties, and not that they *are* genuine flowers. AI supporters argue, however, that artificial intelligence *is* genuine intelligence: that human intelligence is merely the capacity of a naturally evolved organism to perform various sorts of operations—operations which are no different from those which might be performed by an artificial system.

On the other hand, intelligence is usually taken to be a feature of *mentality*: to be intelligent is to have a mind. To have a mind is to possess a lot more properties than merely those associated with the capacity for intelligent performances. Just what is involved in having a mind may differ from species to species (assuming that it is accepted that other species besides *Homo sapiens* have minds). In the case of humans, having a mind seems to involve, among other things, being able to have sensuous awareness of objects and of one's own experience and physical states; being able to experience pain and pleasure, love, hate, fear, anger, ecstasy, serenity; being able to be creative, inspired, nauseated, ashamed, bored; being able to tell jokes and find them funny, to play, to be aroused, to be satisfied, to suffer.

'Intelligence'

It is a highly *cognitivized* view of mind that emanates from AI and cognitive science literature. Most or all of the things mentioned in the above list no doubt involve the exercise of intelligence or cognition, and intimately so, and in a variety of different ways. Few of them are characterizable *exclusively* in terms of the exercise of intelligence—certainly not of 'intelligence' in the limited sense of the word with which we began: the sort of intelligence which is concerned with performing tasks, solving problems, understanding, learning, rule following, discrimination, etc.

Often the term 'intelligence' is used in a rather looser and wider way than this, as more or less a synonym for 'mentality' as such. People working in AI often tend to be hazy about the relative boundaries of 'intelligence', 'mentality', 'thinking', etc. There is impressive historical precedent for such vagueness. In Descartes' philosophy, for example, any mental event is considered to be a modification of the *res cogitans*, the thinking substance which is one's soul. It has to be said here that verbs like *cogitare*, or *penser*, as used by Descartes, had an extremely wide range of application. '*Thought (cogitatio)*,' he wrote, 'is a word that covers everything that exists in us in a way that we are immediately conscious of it. Thus all the operations of will, intellect, imagination, and of the senses are thoughts'.[1]

There is some suggestion here that for Descartes any mental event was a species of knowledge (of self-knowledge). He certainly believed that it intimately involved knowledge. Cartesian exegesis aside, the important point is to indicate how tempting it is to treat any process of mind as an act of thinking, a process of knowing or cognition. This cognitivizing tendency seems to be present in much subsequent philosophical or psychological writing. The matter becomes specially difficult and confused when 'cognition' is in turn understood in purely intellectual terms, so that any mental process whatsoever comes to be seen as an exercise of intellect, and therefore as something which is in principle susceptible of computational explanation within the AI paradigm. It is thus certainly very easy to slip from a narrow, relatively focused, sense of 'intelligence' to a wider, vaguer notion, a notion which seems to encompass the whole of mentality, including desire, emotion, direct conscious experience, pleasure, pain, etc. Because of this ready transition, the field of artificial intelligence seems to take on a much more portentious air. AI theorists become taken in by their own sleight of hand. We start out with a very limited and plausible enough claim concerning a particular set of cognitive activities—namely that computer performances of such activities may be called intelligent in exactly the same sense in which the human performances of those activities are. We end up with a grand theory of mentality as such—that any mental state, process, activity, capacity whatsoever is in principle computer simulable, and therefore computationally explicable.

The narrow and wide claims

We must therefore distinguish two very different claims made within and on behalf of AI. There is *the narrow claim*, according to which that portion of human mentality which involves the exercise of intelligence (in some fairly well-bounded sense of the term) can be reproduced in working computer programs with complete fidelity, so that when a computer is displaying a certain kind of behaviour it is—*to this extent*—exemplifying genuine mentality. Then there is *the wide claim*, according to which any and all aspects of mentality can in principle be realized on computer systems of some arbitrary degree of complexity—or at least they can be explained in computational terms (in some pertinent, and non-trivial, sense of 'computational').

What I shall try to show in the following is the enormous difference in significance between these two claims; to show that they are not merely two variants, respectively cautious and incautious, of a common outlook. Much confusion has resulted from failing to distinguish these two claims and from failing to see how different they are. People who, for understandable reasons, find the narrow claim plausible, tend to think that there is relatively little extra cost involved in endorsing the wide claim. On the other hand people who, again for understandable reasons, are aghast at the wider claim therefore tend to turn their faces against considering the merits of the narrower claim.

There has been a lively debate of late concerning the merits of the narrow claim: Searle's arguments are intended to refute that version of the narrow claim which maintains that intentional mental predicates such as 'understands', 'means', etc., can be attributed to a computational system.[2] Now one of the crucial assumptions of Searle's position is that there is some 'essence' to 'meaning', 'intentionality' and other similar mental predicates and that this 'essence' governs in advance how such terms are to be attributed to appropriately performing computer programs, or the systems running them. Searle appeals to a philosophical tradition, inspired by Brentano,[3] which identifies intentionality as a defining mark of the mental. He wants to set up a firm boundary between primary notions of intentionality—'original' or 'intrinsic' intentionality, as he calls it—which cover the cases of meaning, understanding, planning, inferring, representing things by human beings; and all secondary or 'derivative' or 'observer-relative' intentional notions, covering the ascription of meanings, etc., to written or spoken texts, pictorial representations of various sorts, and, of course, crucially, the variety of intentional or quasi-intentional ascriptions which have come to be used more and more commonly in connection with various computational processes.

The need to set up this rigid barrier between 'original' and 'derivative' intentionality must be based upon the idea that something important depends upon this separation, but I wonder whether there really can be such an important dividing line here. A way to show that there might not be such a division after all is to contrast the question of boundary conditions for intentional notions with questions concerning notions of mentality where something important undeniably *is* at issue. Questions to do with sentience or consciousness—with actually directly experiencing things rather than simply meaning things—seem to be questions on which something quite practical does indeed depend. To decide that a certain system or organism possesses certain states of consciousness or sentient awareness may imply the adoption of a quite distinctive sort of attitude towards that system. To attribute intentionality to a system where such an attribution is made *in isolation*, i.e. in a manner such as to not imply consciousness or sentience as well, is not necessarily to become committed to that same sort of distinctive attitude. True, an enormous weight of theoretical, explanatory significance rests upon getting clear the nature of cognitive or intentional mental states. Supporters of the narrow computationalist claim may seriously underestimate the complexities of human cognitive processes, and therefore the extent to which they are open to computational analysis or replication. However, the issue of deciding on the merits of the narrow claim, considered in abstraction from the wider claim of *across the board* computer mentality, where this includes computer consciousness, seems really to be a matter of deciding how to extend an old classificatory scheme to new sorts of cases, rather than deciding whether some intrinsic property applies to the new cases.

The narrow claim: some options

Consider the following analogy. A sculpture may possess many features which its original possesses: for instance it may be exactly the same height as the human who is its model; it may have the same muscular outline, the same delicate shape to the hands, the same characteristic facial expression of exquisite sadness as is often found on its subject, and so on. Someone might object that the sculpture cannot really have a sad facial expression, since lumps of plaster cannot be sad, and only that which can really *feel* sad can have a sad expression. This would certainly be a possible way to determine linguistic usage, but it would be little more than that—a matter for verbal legislation.

Perhaps the person who is hesitant about ascribing sad facial expressions to sculptures is worried that to do so would be to end up having to talk of sad sculptures. The issue of whether sculptures can (not merely have sad expressions but) actually be sad is clearly not just a matter of verbal decision. Most people will agree without too much hesitation that a lump of plaster cannot possibly meet the preconditions of *being sad*, miracles aside. Only in a fairy story could the sculptor's art be fine enough to render the creation into a conscious individual.

The situation seems to me to be very similar with respect to computer simulations of the cognitive aspects of mentality. AI sceptics may say that no mere bunch of electronic circuits could genuinely possess intentional states such as understanding, intelligence, and so on—on the grounds that (1) only beings which are conscious could possess such states, and (2) a bunch of electronic circuits cannot be conscious. Now, let's concede (2), to cut short the argument, but why should (1)—the claim that only conscious beings can have intentional states—go unchallenged? Why, just because we ascribe states like understanding, etc., to appropriately functioning non-conscious systems, should we thereby be forced to ascribe properties such as consciousness to such systems—any more than we should have to say that the sculpture's sad face betokens a sad soul?

We now know that computers are capable of exhibiting performances—playing games, solving puzzles, planning, perceiving, etc.—which were hitherto thought to be exhibited only by creatures capable of undergoing genuine mental processes, genuine intentional states, such as understanding, etc. Some people claim that the success curve currently enjoyed by AI research is likely to flatten out soon and that it will turn out that only rather superficial and limited aspects of human cognitive activity are capable of computational simulation. Even if such AI sceptics turn out to be right, our conception of the nature of cognitive performances has been irrevocably changed by the displays of computer 'intelligence' that have already been achieved. We now know that, in these crucial respects, machines can *act* like us, even if it were to be the case that, as the AI sceptics insist, they cannot *mean* like us.

Given such computer performances, as currently achieved and as promised in the future, we have a choice. Here are some of the many possible things we could decide to say.

A first possibility is to say that computers, when exhibiting such performances, are not really playing chess, solving puzzles, etc., since doing those things involves mentality, which computers do not possess. What *they* are doing is *quasi*-chess playing, *quasi*-puzzle solving, etc.

A second possibility would be to agree that computers do play chess, solve puzzles, etc., after all, but to argue as follows: since these are the sorts of things which can only be performed by beings which undergo genuine mental processes and since, further, a computer would certainly not be thought to be living or conscious merely by virtue of being able to play chess or solve puzzles (for that would be a ludicrous jump), therefore some mental processes can inhere in entities which are neither alive nor conscious.

A third possibility would be to say that computers can have genuine intentional states, can be genuinely intelligent, but that such states are not by that token *mental* states, or are so only in a secondary sense. On this position intentionality, intelligence, cognition, etc., are not indissolubly linked with mentality. The study of cognition would then not be a study of mentality, but of some other category distinct, perhaps, from both the mental and the physical.

A fourth possibility would suggest that the question of what counts as a mental state is too undefined for beings which can only perform an extremely tiny subset of the sorts of things which people or higher animals can do with their minds, and that, whereas there would be little point in ascribing mental states to a machine which *just* played chess or *just* solved a limited range of puzzles, nevertheless it may well be possible to ascribe genuine intentional states to more advanced systems with a comprehensive cognitive architecture encompassing a great many human faculties, such as memory, language, perception, and so on. If such systems were sufficiently carefully designed, then it might be otiose to deny that they really understood, meant things, and so on. It may be that we would wish to make such intentional ascriptions in advance of admitting that such systems possessed consciousness or sentience.

Of the four, my own preferred option is the last one. However, as stated earlier, as long as we are limiting ourselves to discussing intentionality or intelligence or cognition, as opposed to consciousness or sentience, it matters relatively little which of these alternatives one chooses to adopt. What is missing in any discussion of intentionality or cognition in relation to computational systems is any *ethical* dimension, and it is the ethical dimension which is brought in when we discuss the wider claim about computer mentality. It is to the wide claim that we now turn.

The ethical significance of the wide claim

It is the capacity to have these various features which we group together under the heading 'mental life', in the fullest use of that term, which we tend to regard as important in determining which entities or beings in the universe are potentially subjects of moral concern. Precisely because having a mind is, among other things, having the capacity to enjoy and to suffer, the notion of mind is central to our ethical thinking, for ethics is pivotally concerned with the provenance and distribution of enjoyment and suffering (if, no doubt, with other things as well).[4]

In order to shed light on this point, it would be useful to consider the ways in which people in our society are increasingly becoming concerned about the need to protect the interests of various species of animals. More and more people are coming to believe that domestic pets, farm animals, seals, dolphins, and so on, have quite elaborate mental capacities. While it is partly our view of the *intelligence* of such animals which is gradually being upgraded, it is also—and surely more crucially—our conception of the experiential or sensitive side of their mental life that motivates our increasing empathy towards non-human species. Computers or robots which exhibited mental capacities *only* of the cognitive kind—which were *only* intelligent (in the narrow sense)—would not, so far, be likely to excite our ethical sympathies a great deal.

Thus there are certain mental attributions which are theoretically and ethically low in cost: relatively little would be at issue if we conceded that a computer which exhibited cognitive performances such as chess playing, problem solving, sentence parsing, etc., was *to that extent* exhibiting genuine mentality. There are other mental attributions which are, from an ethical point of view, critical. If a computer or robot gave a convincing behavioural display of extreme suffering, it would be important to consider whether there was genuine suffering going on there as well—whether the outer display was indeed an indication of some genuine 'inner' state which rightfully ought to be an object of our moral concern. (It is not clear exactly what such a display would consist of, or *how* exactly it might succeed in convincing, but that is another matter.) In the case of states of consciousness or of experiential awareness—various sorts of pleasures and pains, for example—it is much easier to think of the mental state as conceptually distinct from the capacity to give the appropriate performances than it is in the case of cognitive processes such as problem solving, task performing and all those other instances which lend themselves so readily to a computational treatment.

AI theorists are thus in a dilemma. If, on the one hand, they are claiming that all that is reproducible by computational means is intelligence (in the narrow sense) *without* consciousness, *without* any subjective experience going on as well, then the debate over the genuineness or otherwise of artificial intelligence seems to be not much less sterile than that over the genuineness or otherwise of artificial flowers. If, on the other hand, they are agreeing that *genuine* intelligence involves (at least the capacity for) consciousness or subjective experience as well, *and moreover* that it is quite possible for a computational system to possess genuine states of consciousness, then they are making a much more adventurous claim—one which has much less intuitive plausibility and which is much more difficult to substantiate.

Many AI supporters tend to blur the distinction between intelligence and consciousness or to inflate the former notion so that it includes the latter as a necessary component. They do so at their peril. It seems (to me at least) difficult to deny the distinction between the capacity to exhibit intelligent performances on the one hand and the capacity to undergo conscious states on the other. To show that computers may generate the former is not to show that they may be subject to the latter.

Consciousness and scepticism about other minds

There are several highly questionable arguments which are often used to obscure this point. One such argument is the *appeal to scepticism about other minds*. The argument goes as follows. Just what is consciousness supposed to be, anyway? We do not (as individuals) even know whether our fellow humans have it, since all we can see is their external behaviour. So we would have as much or as little grounds for asserting it of an intelligently performing robot as we would for asserting or denying it of an intelligently performing human being, because the behaviour might be indistinguishable in the two cases.[5]

As against this, it has been fashionable, since Wittgenstein, to argue that the traditional philosophical doubts about whether fellow humans have a private inner consciousness accompanying their public behaviour is incoherent. Let us assume for the purposes of the argument that 'other minds' scepticism *is* coherent. The doubt about whether other human beings are conscious is a doubt about being able to validate a certain general belief, namely a belief that other individuals possessing *physiologies* just like mine, and exhibiting behaviour just like mine, also possess inner experiences like mine. The doubt about whether a computer can be conscious is of a quite different nature. It is a doubt over whether entities which have an entirely different physical structure, i.e. one comprised of electronic components and input-output devices of various kinds, rather than the wetware of a human or a mammalian central nervous system, can *also* possess consciousness.

Doubt about consciousness in computers (i.e. electronic devices of the sort that are currently used and that are visible on the research horizon) is an empirical doubt about whether such physical systems are capable of producing consciousness—whether they have the right 'causal powers', to use John Searle's phrase. It is a doubt which makes sense only in the context of the background assumption that certain physical systems *do* have the right causal powers to produce consciousness.

Moreover, given current knowledge in the neurosciences, it is difficult to see how such powers could be characterized except in terms of deep physiological properties of the central nervous systems of humans and other higher animals. That is not to say that, in holding such an assumption, we are committed to believing that *only* beings with central nervous systems like ours can have consciousness. It may well be that the causal powers which enable our central nervous systems to produce consciousness can also be possessed by physical structures of a quite different kind. There may be all kinds of sentient extraterrestrial beings with (to us) highly exotic neuroanatomies.

The classical philosophical doubt about other minds, on the other hand, is a doubt of a quite different kind. It expresses a despair over being able to be sure of (or even, more radically, over being able *to make sense of*) any causal generalization of all concerning the physical bases for consciousness. It is, in short, a doubt that has to be put to rest before the neurosciences can begin and before any speculation over consciousness in non-human kinds of physical systems can begin (and, of course, before ethics can begin).

Computational AI versus 'psychotechnics'

The issue of attributing consciousness or mentality to computational systems is further clouded by an unfortunate ambiguity in the notion of 'artificial', as used in the context of the phrase 'artificial intelligence'. The latter term was coined in the mid-1950s to characterize a sub-branch of the infant field of computer science.[6] The term was and is intimately associated with intelligence or mentality in computing machines, but there may well be many other ways of producing artificial intelligence or mentality apart from designing or programming computers.

It is at least a remote empirical possibility, for example, that one day a means could be developed for replicating the biological structure of an entire living, breathing, thinking and feeling human being—or at least of some lesser organism which nevertheless had some vestigial sentient states. If, to take a science-fictional point of view for a moment, one discovered that the person with whom one had just enjoyed a long conversation (or love affair) was an artefact, one would not necessarily withdraw one's attribution of consciousness. If it turned out that one's companion really did have a central nervous system just like one's own, for instance, then the fact that it was an artificially produced one need not make any difference. If processes of consciousness such as pain and pleasure are indeed produced by *states of the central nervous system*, then an artificial central nervous system may still produce real pain or pleasure. That is, it would have the appropriate 'causal powers', but these causal powers would in this case be the result of fabrication rather than natural growth.

In discussing the possibility of such artificially produced conscious beings, with real feelings, desires, interests, etc., I am not implying that it would be in any way *morally desirable* to bring beings of such a kind into existence. Indeed, the idea might strike some people as quite obnoxious. This raises many interesting issues, but it is beyond the scope of the present discussion to enter into them here. I am presently concerned only with the fact that a special ethical dimension does attach to their creation which is missing from the narrow AI activity of creating cognitively acting systems. The latter, unlike the former, will not have *interests*—not, at least, in the full sense in which human beings have interests. Here, once again, we have a pressure to make a distinction between primary and derivative attributions. It is a crucial part of my argument that, in the case of attributions of *interests*, it is of great importance where we site that division; this is in marked contrast to the question of where to site the boundary between primary and derivative attributions of intentionality, cognition, etc.

There is also, of course, the question: 'What counts as an artefact, as an artificial, as opposed to a natural, X?' There are no doubt many actual or potential ways of producing biological organisms which have varying degrees of artificiality. Are cells synthesized in a laboratory artefacts? There is clearly a range, or a series of ranges, of intermediate cases between the paradigmatically artificial and the paradigmatically natural. A purist would doubtless object that not just Mrs Tregale's but all the exhibits at the Honiton County Show were artificial, being the products of human cultivation.

So it is not the *artefactuality* of computers which makes it difficult to envisage consciousness in them. There might be all sorts of artificially created beings which possessed 'inner' states of a kind that would be psychologically and ethically interesting. However, consciousness being the sort of thing it is, such artifacts would no doubt be extraordinarily complex things—much more complex than fifth, sixth or seventh generation *computers* are likely to be, surely. Of course the field of artificial intelligence, taken in its widest sense as the quest to build artificial systems possessing genuine mental states of all kinds, need not be dependent upon digital computer technology alone. Moreover, who knows how computer technology is going to evolve and with what other technologies it will merge—either those now developing in parallel or other technologies not yet in existence.

Thus AI in this wider sense—*psychotechnics*, as it might be called—may, in decades or centuries to come, succeed in building artificial minds in the fullest and most ethically meaningful sense. No doubt computational systems, or their distant descendants, will also play a central role in any such future psychotechnologies, just as, no doubt, computational principles play a central role in the functioning of our own psychophysical organization.

The supposed ethical status of attributions of consciousness to machines

Another argument which is used to broaden the claims of AI (in its narrow, computational sense) might be called the *ethicization of attributions of consciousness*. Sloman, for example, claims that the general question of whether computers (of a particular complexity of organization) might ever be genuinely conscious is fundamentally ethical in nature, since it is dependent upon how we choose to treat such machines.[7]

If Sloman were right, then it would become easier to see the possibility of a *global* account of mind based on purely computational principles. With growing sophistication of AI techniques and associated hardware design, computers and robots will no doubt display progressively richer and more varied capabilities. On Sloman's view, the question 'Are they really conscious?' would be answered by our *practice*, by the fact that we would be unable to treat them in any other way than *as* conscious, i.e. as appropriate subjects of moral concern.

According to this view, then, it is not the case that we adopt an ethical attitude to a certain class of being *because* we believe them to be capable of certain sorts of conscious states—a belief which may or may not correspond to some independent factual state of affairs. Rather is it that our belief that they have those conscious states *consists in* our adopting the ethical attitudes. This would seem to imply, among other things, that there would be no possibility of our being systematically in error—of our treating *as* sentient systems that were not, or vice versa. As Sloman put it in the closing passage of a paper read to this year's International Joint Conference on AI:

> When we have shown in detail how like or unlike a human being some type of machine is, there remains a residual seductive question, namely whether such a machine really can be conscious, really can feel pain, really can think, etc. Pointing inside yourself at your own pain (or other mental state) you ask 'Does the machine really have *this* experience?'. This sort of question has much in common with

the pre-Einsteinian question, uttered pointing at a location in space in front of you: 'Will my finger really be in *this* location in five minutes' time?' In both cases it is a mistake to think that there really is an 'entity' with a continuing identity, rather than just a complex network of relationships. The question about machines has an extra dimension: despite appearances, it is ultimately an *ethical* question, not just a factual one. It requires not an answer but a practical decision on how to treat the machines of the future, if they leave us any choice.[7]

In this passage, Sloman appears to be making two different points. The first is that there is a certain sort of question. 'Can such and such machines really be conscious, feel pain, etc.?', which appears to be purely factual but which is in fact ethical (or partly so). The second is that the question is, like the pre-Einsteinian's question about absolute points in space, a pseudo-question. These two points are meant to give mutual support to one another, but they seem to be mutually contradictory.

In order to see this, consider our earlier distinction between narrow AI, which makes use exclusively or centrally of computational organizations and techniques, and wide AI, or psychotechnics, in which computational technology is enhanced by others, perhaps as yet undreamt-of, technologies. As I said before, there seems to be no compelling reason in principle why artificial systems should not be created which possessed the capacity for consciousness, pain, etc. Take, now, some hypothetical future successful product of psychotechnology: some artefact which reproduces a wide range of behavioural and physiological features which we take to be determinative or constitutve of possessing a mental life. (We leave it an open question as to what role AI technology, as viewed through today's eyes, plays in our hypothetical artefact.) Suppose someone were to say, of such an artefact: 'Yes, it appears to behave in ways which indicate consciousness, sentience, and so on, and it incorporates all those casual properties which we believe on the best available evidence to be responsible for consciousness in ourselves. But is it *really* conscious? Is it really the same sort of thing as *this* that I feel and know to be my subjective experience?' Clearly, such a question could be considered to have a similar sort of incoherence as that which affects the pre-relativist's query about absolute points in space.

It could also be considered incoherent for a different, more straightforward reason, for we are assuming that we have an artefact which is believed, on the best available evidence grounds, to have all the necessary physical requisites for possessing genuine consciousness. To accept all this, but to raise the possibility that it might not be conscious, is surely simultaneously to accept and call into question a certain theory of causally sufficient conditions for consciousness. In other words, it has appropriate consciousness-endowing causal powers, but perhaps in this case the powers are that having their effect.

Clearly there is nothing in the incoherence of such a question which suggests that the issue is an *ethical* one, in the sense of 'merely a matter for ethical decision'. Indeed, if the question 'But is it really conscious?' really is an incoherent question in this setting, then surely it can not also be an ethical one. I take it that ethical issues are not, *per se*, incoherent issues. (It would certainly need very special arguments from Sloman to show that they were.)

I think Sloman has failed to analyse the structure of his own ethical thinking properly. I take it that Sloman endorses the same general humane moral principles as are shared by most educated people of our culture, in respect of avoiding suffering, seeking to alleviate it where possible, etc. Such a principle would, of course, not be limited to *human* suffering: most people recognize at least some non-human suffering as ethically of concern (e.g. they are shocked by cruelty to pets, etc.). There might, of course, be *practical* disagreements, e.g. between meat eaters and vegetarians on whether, and if so, how much, pigs or chickens actually do suffer. However, usually the differences here are factual. Certainly the people who might be in strong ethical disagreement, in the sense of having quite unreconcilable views on what ought to be done in a given case, may share all actual ethical beliefs in common and just disagree over certain factual matters. Suppose, now, that Sloman and I had such a practical dispute about a particular candidate 'psychotechnical' being—he claiming that it was suffering and therefore that it merited our assistance and I claiming that it was not and thus did not. Our *ethical* beliefs may well be quite in harmony: they certainly *need not* conflict with each other. It would be sufficient to cause such a practical disagreement for us to share some general ethical principle of the form:

(P) Whenever conditions C obtain then (other things being equal) action A should be performed.

Sloman and I would then be involved in a *practical* dispute because we disagree over whether A should be done, but our disagreement is over whether or not conditions C obtain. The question of whether conditions C obtain is not itself an *ethical* question. It is a factual question—it *has* to be, otherwise the general principle (P) (which, we are supposing, Sloman and I share) would be incapable of being properly framed.

The 'truth' about consciousness attributions

In any case, surely it is abundantly clear that the general issue of consciousness in artefacts *is not* an ethical one (in Sloman's sense) but a factual one. Of course there are difficulties in directly checking that a given artificially produced system has direct states of consciousness, but we could have strong evidence of various sorts. The evidence would not just be behavioural. In order for any psychotechnological initiative to be successful, an enormous corpus of knowledge concerning the physical bases of conscious states will have to have been built up. It is obvious that today's neurophysiological knowledge is only at a relatively primitive stage compared to the kind of knowledge that will be needed in order to build a biological system capable of supporting consciousness. However, there seems no reason why that knowledge should be any less factual in nature than any other corpus of scientific knowledge.

There might be quite outlandish forms of empirical testing for the presence of conscious states in an organism, natural or artificial. It may turn out, for example, that certain people have 'ESP'-like capabilities that correlate well with human pain. That is, they may be able to identify faultlessly whenever a human being in the next room is in pain or not. They may be able to perform similarly with animals. Why should they not also be able to identify similar states in robots or other artificial beings? (Sceptics may fail to be convinced by the evidence of such specially gifted people, but the question at issue is the factual *status* of the claim that such artificial beings might be conscious, not the ease with which people might be convinced of such a fact, if indeed it obtained.)

It is often suggested that, the progress of research in neurophysiology, medicine, etc., terms like 'consciousness', 'pain' and other familiar notions of our intuitive folk-psychology will be shown to be too primitive and contradictory to be of use in a properly scientific account of mental life. Dennett has argued for this view most forcefully in his paper 'Why you can't make a computer that feels pain'.[8] This would give an additional reason for doubting the factual nature of questions like 'Is such and such an artefact really in pain, really conscious?'.

Wilkes has pointed out, in a recent article, many difficulties for a simpleminded application of the notion of pain. A striking instance is provided by the case of hypnotic anaesthesia. She cites experimental work of E. R. Hilgard:

> A typical experiment is the following: subjects are hypnotized, told they will feel no pain, and then one arm is put into a stream of circulating iced water. This is rapidly experienced as unpleasantly painful by the unhypnotized; but subjects under hypnosis may sincerely report that they feel no pain, and will leave their arm in the water for long periods apparently untroubled. On the other hand, and *with* the other hand—if it is supplied with pencil and paper—the subject typically provides a simultaneous running complaint about the intensity and unpleasantness of the pain.[9]

Such cases simply show that there are occasions when the conditions of the application of the predicate 'is in pain' are not straightforward. They do not show that the predicate is incoherent or scientifically invalid, nor do they show that it is not a factual predicate like 'is in the bath'. Such arguments surely do not threaten central uses of such terms. They do not imply that we should take our general ethical concerns over the occurrence of pain (in the vast majority of cases which do not display such anomalous features) less seriously.

Conclusion: AI and ethical modelling

Thus the question of consciousness, pain, etc., in artefacts is a genuine one—a 'factual' one. It is not simply a matter for ethical decision. Nevertheless, as we have seen, it is not an issue to which ethical considerations are indifferent. If one day we are indeed in a position to produce artefacts which do appear by all available tests to be conscious, then we will be saddled with some important new ethical problems. We will have to worry about their interests as well as our own. Genuinely intelligent and sentient artefacts buried beneath the rubble of an earthquake, for instance, would, if still 'alive', no doubt have a direct claim to be rescued, just as would human or animal victims. If their sentience and thus their capacity to suffer is genuine, then our general obligations to alleviate suffering wherever possible would, in consistency, have to be extended to such artefacts. Merely intelligent, and non-sentient, robots, however, would not necessarily prompt the same direct obligations, although they might need to be pulled out from the rubble as important scientific instruments.

I have also suggested that genuine consciousness is not likely to result merely from more and more sophisticated *computational* developments. Debates about whether *computers* are ever likely to have consciousness, pains, emotions, etc., seem to me to be sterile, insofar as computational devices are understood in their present-day sense as machines which process sequences of symbols. It may be possible to produce computational systems which *model* various aspects of consciousness, emotion, and so on, but a computer running a program which models consciousness is clearly a quite different thing from a computer which, by virtue of the program which it is running, *is* conscious. There is certainly no *a priori* reason why the latter should occur.

Thus while there is no doubt that a good proportion of our mental capacities are based upon symbol or information processing, and are therefore explicable computationally, it seems equally clear that the ethically crucial aspects of our mental life rest upon quite different sorts of properties. We have, at present, only a very hazy idea of what those properties might be. Perhaps such states of qualitative awareness may involve computational factors in their explanation, but their explanation cannot be *exclusively* computational.

The computational paradigm is thus unlikely to offer a *global* account of 'the mind'. To say this is to belittle AI hardly at all, since it is clear that AI has a fundamental role to play in explaining mentality. Work in AI has to date been very largely concerned with mental processes which are characterizable as 'cognitive' in the narrow sense of having to do with task performance, rule following, factual thought and discourse, instrumental or means-end planning, perceptual processing, and so on. Some speculative work has been done on producing computational models for emotions, aesthetic and evaluative attitudes, choices, etc.,[10] but this has very much been a Cinderella area of AI. This is partly, no doubt, because of its relatively low payoff in military and commercial terms, but it must also be due to the sheer *difficulty* of getting a theoretical focus on, say, emotion as opposed to cognition.

The interesting thing about emotions, desires, etc., is that they seem to contain both cognitive and qualitive aspects inextricably linked. To feel anger, or jealousy, or sexual excitation is both to experience certain bodily sensations and to make certain judgements or classifications. The mental and the physical aspects of emotional states seem to be intertwined (the 'hot' ones, at least, as opposed to 'cool' ones, such as affection, concern, etc.). Within the mental side of, say, fear, one can discern both a purely qualitative side and a cognitive side. Being afraid seems to feel like something 'on the inside', rather like being in agony from toothache; but, unlike the latter, it will usually turn out to involve a complex structure of judgements which wire into a person's general belief and value system (I am afraid that X might happen because, if it does, then Y will occur, which will diminish the possibility of Z, which I both greatly desire and believe myself to need . . . , etc.).

The cognitive aspects of our emotions and attitudes—which are the aspects that lend themselves to computational modelling—therefore cannot be underestimated. That applies in particular to our moral emotions and attitudes, righteous indignation, remorse, admiration, as well as to our more rational moral judgments concerning what it is right to seek and to avoid, concerning the relative merits of competing claims or norms, the apportionment of responsibility, and so on.

It is not clear whether any such computational ethical modelling is likely ever to be either convincing or useful, but it may be that only through becoming actively concerned with building an explicit ethical orientation, and moreover a humanitarian ethical orientation, into AI systems that there is any hope that the AI technological paradigm can maintain any pretence at being a humanizing influence in our civilization. The main volume of research in the field of AI is becoming more and more subservient to the needs of developing advanced systems of weaponry and warfare, to the accelerated accumulation of wealth and power by multinational industrial concerns, to the battles for world market domination between the economic superpowers. AI seems to be getting increasingly alienated from that fascination with understanding the complexities of human thought processes which was once its guiding inspiration.

There are many things that can contribute towards keeping this spirit of fascination alive. One activity which might help to combat the excessively instrumentalistic approach to thinking which dominates AI at present is that of trying to build moral norms—and appropriate ones—into knowledge bases. It looks as though we are entering an age in which electronic 'intelligent' knowledge bases will increasingly be considered as oracles to consult and to defer to, as dominant repositories of Truth. If these oracles are to serve the interests of human beings around the world, rather than merely the interests of the Fortune 500, then they must be given more than merely domain expertise: they must be provided with some measure of social and normative enlightenment. It remains to be seen if the moral wisdom of ordinary humankind is too ineffable, too inscrutable, too variable, to be captured within an AI representation. We can only hope that the attempt to inject human responsibility into our artificially intelligent systems manages to succeed.

Acknowledgements

Discussions with very many people helped to form and clarify the ideas presented herein. I would like to thank the following: Margaret Boden, David Conway, Jon Cunningham, Steve Draper, Peter Forte, Andre Gallois, Andrew Redfern, Guy Scott, Blay Whitby, Masoud Yazdani, and, especially, Richard Hare and Aaron Sloman.

References

1. Descartes, R. (1967). *The Philosophical Works of Descartes* (translated by E. S. Haldane and G. R. T. Ross), vol. II, Cambridge University Press, p. 52 (Appendix to Reply to Objections).
2. Searle, J. (1980). 'Minds, brains and programs', with Open Peer Commentaries. *Behavioural and Brain Sciences*, 3, 417–457.
3. Brentano, F. (1960). 'The distinction between mental and physical phenomena'. Translation by D. B. Terrell of a section from F. Brentano, *Psychologie vom empirischen Standpunkt*, Vienna, 1874. In *Realism and the Background of Phenomenology* (Ed. R. M. Chisholm), Free Press, Glencoe, Illinois.
4. The question of whether there is any necessary *content* to ethical thinking has been much discussed within moral philosophy. In my doctoral thesis (Torrance, S., 1977, *Non-descriptivism: A Logico-Ethical Study*, DPhil Thesis, University of Oxford) I proposed a formalistic account of ethics while arguing that the formal structure of ethical thinking constrained rational ethical thinkers to be centrally concerned with human welfare and harm (see Hare, R. M., 1963, *Freedom and Reason*, and 1981, *Moral Thinking: Its Levels, Method and Point*, Clarendon Press, Oxford). The same arguments would apply to concern for the welfare and

harm of non-humans, including artificial beings, if these latter genuinely could suffer and enjoy things, as well.

5. See, for example, Turing A. M. (1950). 'Computing machinery and intelligence', *MIND*, LIX, 433–460.
6. The first published appearance of the term 'artificial intelligence' is believed to be John McCarthy's proposal that 'a two-month, ten-man study of artificial intelligence be carried out during the summer of 1956 at Dartmouth College in Hanover, New Hampshire. The study is to proceed on the basis of the conjecture that every aspect of learning or any other feature of intelligence can in principle be so precisely described that a machine can be made to simulate it.' Quoted in Charniak, E., and McDermott, D. (1985). *Introduction to Artificial Intelligence*, Addison-Wesley, Reading, Mass., p. 11.
7. This claim can be found in many of Sloman's writings: the most recent source is Sloman, A. (1985), understand?'. *Proceedings of the Ninth International Joint Conference on Artificial Intelligence*.
8. Dennett, D. (1978). *Brainstorms: Philosophical Essays on Mind and Psychology*, Harvester Press, Brighton, Chap. 11.
9. Wilkes, K. V. (1984). 'Is consciousness necessary?'. *British Journal of the Philosophy of Science*, 35(3), 223–243.
10. See, for instance, Sloman, A., and Croucher, M. (1981), 'You don't need to have a soft skin to have a warm heart: towards a computational analysis of emotions', Cognitive Studies Research Paper CSRP 004, University of Sussex, Brighton.

78

ARTIFICIAL INTELLIGENCE AND ETHICS

An exercise in the moral imagination

Michael R. LaChat

Source: *The AI Magazine* 7(2), 1986: 70–79.

Abstract The possibility of constructing a *personal* AI raises many ethical and religious questions that have been dealt with seriously only by imaginative works of fiction; they have largely been ignored by technical experts and by philosophical and theological ethicists. Arguing that a personal AI is possible in principle, and that its accomplishment could be adjudicated by the Turing Test, the article suggests some of the moral issues involved in AI experimentation by comparing them to issues in medical experimentation. Finally, the article asks questions about the capacities and possibilities of such an artifact for making moral decisions. It is suggested that much *a priori* ethical thinking is necessary and that that such a project cannot only stimulate our moral imaginations, but can also tell us much about our moral thinking and pedagogy, whether or not it is ever accomplished in fact.

In a book written in 1964, *God and Golem, Inc.*, Norbert Wiener predicted that the quest to construct computer-modeled artificial intelligence (AI) would come to impinge directly upon some of our most widely and deeply held religious and ethical values. It is certainly true that the idea of *mind as artifact*, the idea of a humanly constructed artificial intelligence, forces us to confront our image of ourselves. In the theistic tradition of Judeo-Christian culture, a tradition that is, to a large extent, our "fate," we were created in the *imago Dei*, in the image of God, and our tradition has, for the most part, showed that our greatest sin is pride—disobedience to our creator, a disobedience that most often takes the form of trying to be God. Now, if human beings are able to construct an artificial, *personal* intelligence—and I will suggest that this is theoretically possible, albeit perhaps practically improbable—then the tendency of our religious and moral tradition would be toward the condemnation of the undertaking: We will have stepped into the shoes of the creator, and, in so doing, we will have overstepped our own boundaries.

Such is the scenario envisaged by some of the classic science fiction of the past, Shelley's *Frankenstein, or the Modern Prometheus* and the Capek brothers' *R.U.R.* (for Rossom's Universal Robots) being notable examples. Both seminal works share the view that Pamela McCorduck (1979) in her work *Machines Who Think* calls the "Hebraic" attitude toward the AI enterprise. In contrast to what she calls the "Hellenic" fascination with, and openness toward, AI, the Hebraic attitude has been one of fear and warning: "You shall not make for yourself a graven image . . . "

I don't think that the basic outline of *Frankenstein* needs to be recapitulated here, even if, as is usually the case, the reader has seen only the poor image of the book in movie form. Dr. Frankenstein's tragedy—his ambition for scientific discoveries and benefits, coupled with the misery he brought upon himself, his creation and others—remains the primal expression of the "mad scientist's" valuational downfall, the weighting of experimental knowledge over the possibility of doing harm to self, subject, and society. Another important Hebraic image is that of *R.U.R.*, a 1923 play that gave us the first disastrous revolt of man-made slaves against their human masters. In both works theological insight and allusion abound; God and creation are salient issues, and both works condemn the AI enterprise.

Alongside the above images, of course, there have always lurked Hellenic or, perhaps better, "Promethean" images. Western history is replete with examples of attempts to construct an AI, with miserable and comical flops; with frauds; and with, as of late, some feeble approximations. The more sophisticated our reason and our tools, the more we seem to be inexorably drawn to replicate what has seemed to many to be what marks human persons off from the rest of creation—their *cogito*, their *nous*, their reason. We seem to want to catch up with our mythology and become the gods that we have created. In the layperson's mind, however, the dominant imagery appears to be the Hebraic; many look upon the outbreak of AI research with an uneasy amusement, an amusement masking, I believe, a considerable disquiet. Perhaps it is the fear that we might succeed, perhaps it is the fear that might create a Frankenstein, or perhaps it is the fear that we might become eclipsed, in a strange oedipal drama, by our own creation. If AI is a real possibility, then so is *Frankenstein*. McCorduck says of *Frankenstein* that it combines nearly all the psychological, moral, and social elements of the history of artificial intelligence."

Philosophical and theological ethicists have been silent, with a few exceptions (Fletcher, 1977), on the problem of AI, leaving, unfortunately, those with little training in ethical theory to assess the moral arguments. Boden

(1977), Weizenbaum (1976), McCorduck (1979), and Hofstadter (1980), among others, have dealt with questions of technique, with the "hardware and software" questions surrounding the possibility of AI. Even when such researchers and chroniclers consider ethical questions, they tend to focus on the effects of AI upon society and not upon the AI *qua* subject of experimentation. By focusing on the morality of such experimentation as it effects the subject, I am obviously entering into the realm of the moral imagination, a realm that most ethicists might find trivial, farfetched, or meaningless given the present problems of the planet. Imagination *per se* has often been neglected in philosophy and theology, and the moral imagination suffers more neglect than the ordinary kind, perhaps because it seems more playful than the austere and often overly sober undertakings of most ethicists. Having team taught, however, a course on artificial intelligence and morality, a course about which I was, at first, somewhat dubious, I have reached the conclusion that pedagogically it is a very productive issue for ethical thinking, whether it will ever be accomplished in fact. The problems involved in the construction of a person by artificial means are fascinating and provocative partly because they allow us distance on ourselves; they allow us to probe ourselves in ways our imaginations were previously limited in doing. This does not mean, however, that they do not pose serious problems for the moral imagination.

One does not have to be a theist in order to be able to distill some practical wisdom from the religious counsel, "Don't play God." Among other things, God is a moral concept, as Kant rightly asserted. This venerable injunction can be "demythologized" to a word of warning, of caution toward all human undertakings, the effects of which might be irreversible or potentially harmful to ourselves and to others. For some ethicists, myself included, the first word of ethics is identical with the first caution of ethical medicine— "Above all, do no harm." As W.D. Ross (1965) has pointed out, such negative injunctions are the guiding thoughts, indeed, are the form of almost all legal codes, primitive or modern. The *prima facie* duty of nonmaleficence, of not doing harm, is almost universally conceded to be more stringent than positive injunctions to "do good." In the language game of modern ethics, this latter injunction can be considered as part of the utilitarian tendency to explore the new, to take risks that might even cause harm to a few for the benefit of many.[1] It is certain that both injunctions can claim to be moral, but I side with Kant on the primacy of the former: All rational beings, capable of moral evaluation, must be considered as ends in themselves rather than as means to another's ends.[2] The stringency of the norm of nonmaleficence, attested to in almost all of the modern codes of experimental medicine, means that ethical thinking with regard to the possibility of constructing an artifact which might verge on the personal is necessary *a priori*. The intent of this article is, thus, to raise the questions of a moral nature by stimulating the imagination in tandem with the technological imagination, a

305

necessary reciprocal relationship that we cannot allow to be submerged entirely in the technological realm.

In the first part of the article, I argue briefly that replication of personal intelligence is possible in principle, because counterarguments usually rest on some sort of quasi-mystical dualism, which I find untenable. I further argue that the Turing Test allows us to specify the conditions under which a machine could be said to have attained "personhood," however difficult such a characteristic might be to define.

In the second part of the article, I ask whether such an undertaking should be pursued. The focus of this section is on the moral safeguards for the subject of the experiment, and questions are raised about the extent to which an analogy can be drawn between the morality of the AI project and the ethical guarantees given to human subjects by modern experimental medicine.

The last section of the article is a true exercise in the moral imagination. It asks the question, "Can an artificial intelligence be moral?" It is suggested that one cannot answer this question without giving consideration to the perennial philosophical problems of free will, casuistry, and the role of emotions in moral decision making.

Is artificial intelligence possible in principle?

I will not pretend in what follows to be an expert on the "hardware" or "software" of AI, nor do I claim to be particularly adept in the relevant areas of philosophy of the mind. These technical questions have been dealt with elsewhere in great detail.[3] Joseph Weizenbaum, an increasingly isolated figure within the relatively small circle of AI researchers, has rightly pointed out some of the enormously exaggerated claims that even a sophisticated audience is prone to make for a technology it really does not understand. Few people who have been exposed to the relevant literature would doubt the incredible complexity of such an undertaking. Thus, for example, we need to cautiously remind ourselves that there is a distinction between intelligent behavior and personally intelligent behavior. A machine can learn to run a maze as well as a rat and at the level of rat intelligence could be said to be fairly "smart." The intelligence of the human brain, however, is of a different magnitude entirely.[4] Although it is obvious that machines can perform some activities at a higher level than persons can, these tasks remain, by and large, highly specialized and therefore remote from the capacity of human intelligence for multipurpose activities.

The obstacle of dualism

In spite of these difficulties—organizational complexities that might prove to be insuperable—I feel it necessary to stick out my layperson's neck and offer a tentative argument that an artificial, personal intelligence is possible in principle. Having team taught a course titled "Minds, Machines, and Morals," with a mathematician at St. John's University in Minnesota, I am well aware of the skeptical wall that confronts enthusiastic AI researchers. The first response of most students was a flat rejection of the possibility of such an endeavor. As the course progressed, however, such absolute skepticism gave way to a more tempered doubt, namely, that AI would never be accomplished, given the complexity of the task. What occurred to us during the process of in-class debate was that the absolute skepticism rested ultimately on some sort of dualism between mind and brain; for example, it was often contended that persons had "souls" which were not dependent upon the brain for their existence or that persons were possessed of some almost magical "substance" which could not be duplicated artificially.

I happen to agree with Carl Sagan who stated on a public television show that the evidence for such dualism is nonexistent. Although we might not, as the psychologist Wilder Penfield (1983) suggests, have all of the evidence which would allow us to deny that a "creative thought" might precede electrical activity in the brain, although we may not be able to accept without reservation the philosophic claim that thought equals brain activity, we can make, with some assurance, the more modest claim that there is no evidence of thought taking place without the brain. We do not have to make the stronger claim that there is an identity, an ontological identity, between consciousness and an electrical thought pattern in the brain in order to reject the claim which asserts that conscious thought can occur without the brain.[5]

Let me propose a rather simple response to the absolute skeptics who rest their arguments on an indemonstrable, ontological dualism between mind and brain. All that is necessary to indicate the possibility of AI is to posit a functionally isomorphic relationship between a neural network in the human brain and (at present) a silicon chip in a computer. What is asserted here is that intelligent thought is dependent for its existence on the neural "machinery" of the brain, on the flow of electricity through that "hardware." Electrical patterns in the brain can be compared to the software of the computer and the brain's neurons to the computer's hardware, to the "neural" networks of the chip. This is not to say that mind cannot be an emergent property of a certain level of organization but only that such emergence would be dependent on a neurological "substrate" for its existence. As Douglas Hofstadter says in his magnificent *Gödel, Escher, Bach*:

> Crucial to the endeavor of Artificial Intelligence research is the notion that the symbolic levels of the mind can be "skimmed off" their neural substrate and implemented in other media, such as the electronic substrate of computers. To what depth the copying brain must go is at present completely unclear.
>
> (P. 573.)

This last sentence is an important one. There are two basic approaches to it in the history of AI research. The first is the cybernetic model; it relies on the "physiological" similarity between neurons and hardware. Thus, Norbert Wiener (1964) can say that even the living tissue of the brain is theoretically duplicable at the molecular level by suitable hardware materials. The second approach, the one dominant today, is the "information-processing" model, a model that does not pay as much attention to the level of hardware similarity. All it asserts is that a machine will demonstrate intelligent behavior when it acts intelligently by behavioral definitions. An intelligent machine would not have to "look like" an intelligent human; it would only have to exhibit the same sort of behavior. It is evident that the functionally isomorphic relationship between neural network and hardware is an admixture of both models, although it leans in the direction of the latter. It claims that the neural network hardware isomorphism is a cybernetic one insofar as the substrate conditions would probably have to be similar enough to facilitate the duplication of the functions of both; it does not claim that the isomorphism would necessarily be pictorial as well. What we would need, then, in order to duplicate the hardware substrate would be an adequate "map" of the brain and the extremely sophisticated "tools" and "materials" with which to duplicate it.

So far I have only discussed conditions relevant to the hardware substrate. The software level of a personal machine consciousness—the symbolic level that Hofstadter contends must be "skimmed off" the neural substrate and implemented in other media—seems to be much more problematic to duplicate. A personal intelligence must have personality, and this seems on the face of it to be an almost impossible problem for AI. Personalities are formed through time and through lived experience, and the personal *qua* humanly personal must certainly include the emotional. Indeed, a phenomenological analysis of human experience, such as that of the early Heidegger, indicates that persons might have to experience the emotion of dread in the face of finitude (death) in order to have a grasp of "isness," in order to be fully conscious (Heidegger, 1962; Dreyfus, 1972).

The temporal dimension of human consciousness is a great obstacle to the AI project. Suppose we were able to produce a "map" of the thought patterns of a human adult. Such a map would have to include memories and experiences as well as hopes, aspirations, and goals; in short, it would have to be a map inclusive of the three temporal dimensions of human consciousness—past, present, and future. Could such a map be "programmed" directly into the hardware substrate? The question of the growth of consciousness through time thus emerges as a particularly salient problem. Perhaps a personally intelligent machine has to grow into consciousness, much as a human baby does; then again, perhaps not.

It is not out of the realm of possibility that pain consciousness might be electrochemically duplicable. To what extent are pain and emotion necessary

308

to personal intelligence? There are certainly cases in which paralyzed or drugged persons experience no pain and yet are still conscious, but such persons might still be said to suffer. This crucial distinction (Boeyink, 1974) needs to be borne in mind. Suffering, as opposed to pure pain reflex, is strained through a human ego, an ego that can remember, anticipate, and project itself in time. Perhaps, then, emotions and body consciousness are indispensable requisites of the personally intelligent. These are difficult issues that probably can only be resolved through the trial and error of experiment—and there's the rub! The deliberate constructions of the capacity for pain would seem to entail the causation of pain as well (as the robots in *R.U.R.* are given pain in order to keep them from injuring themselves). This problem raises the question of the morality of the experiment in a vivid way, and is an issue I address shortly.

Adjudicating the achievement of a personal AI

If these difficulties can be surmounted, how can we finally reach agreement that a personal AI has been achieved? The quasi-behavioral criteria I outlined earlier facilitate our ability to specify the conditions under which a machine can be said to have achieved this intelligence, namely, the conditions specified by the Turing Test.

The simplest way to adjudicate a claim that a machine has or has not achieved personal intelligence is to define intelligence behaviorally and then test the machine to see if it exhibits it. No doubt, such definitional lists, even when specified exhaustively, would still run afoul of persistent human skepticism, but such skepticism can be greatly alleviated by the application of the Turing Test. Alan Turing, a British mathematician and logician who believed in the possibility of AI, proposed a test that might give criteria for ascertaining the accomplishment of such an AI (McCorduck, 1979). Suppose that a person (an interrogator) were to communicate unseen with both another person and the AI "subject," and that the interrogator could not tell whether he or she was communicating with the other person or with the "machine"? I contend that such a test could adjudicate the claim, provided (1) that we could agree at the onset with what the test presupposes about the normatively personal, and (2) that certain problems concerning the prerequisites of the interrogator could be ironed out.

It is evident that the test presupposes communication as the *sine qua non* of personal intelligence, that the ability to meaningfully converse through the medium of some sort of language constitutes the essentially personal. Such a presupposed concept of the personal is evident in much of the literature of current medical ethics. Because communication depends on the functional organization of the brain, brain death might be considered the termination of the personal (Fletcher, 1977). Some philosophers and theologians have argued cogently that an inability to respond to stimuli, particularly to linguistic communication, means the subject, although perhaps morphologically human, is no longer a person.[6] Theologians, in particular, are apt to define the personal with regard to the giving and receiving of "the Word" (Niebuhr, 1963). Whether we take such communication to be exhaustive of the personal, it is apparent that without its possibility persons would no longer be persons. The high level of hardware and software sophistication necessary to enable symbolic communication ought to encompass any other kinds of activity we might take to be personal.[7] Human beings do not become persons through simple biological conception. A zygote is a human being, but it can only trivially be considered a person. A machine can be a person in the same way that a "higher" animal might possibly be considered a person (Singer, 1980)—if it shows the ability to meaningfully participate in a language system.

Other questions about the Turing Test remain. These problems have largely to do with the capacities of the interrogator. Such a person, it appears, must be a rational adult, capable of giving reasons for a decision. Should the interrogator know something about computers as well? Would the interrogator be able to "trick" the computer in ways a layperson could not? Would one of the tricks be to shame or insult the subject in order to elicit an emotional response? Perhaps the best interrogator would be another computer, one with the capacity, for example, to interrogate the computer well enough to see at what point it might eclipse human ability. Should there be a group of interrogators, both human and not? How long should the test run before a decision is made? The computer might have to be capable of deceiving the interrogator and of fabricating a life history (in the supposed absence of having "lived" one). It might need the capacity to anticipate tricks and perhaps even to evince a capacity for self-doubt. In short, it might have to possess a self-reflexive consciousness (the ability to make itself the object of its own thought), a characteristic that Tooley (1974) and Mead (1972) have convincingly argued to be a hallmark of the personal self. Such a machine might even have to be able to lie. An intriguing theory is that a child comes to know himself or herself as an ego when he or she can deceive an adult to whom he or she has previously attributed omniscience; then the child finally knows he or she has a private consciousness (Schlein, 1961). Such might also be the case with intelligent machines.

These problems are indeed difficult, though fascinating. At any rate, having asserted that a machine might in principle achieve a personal consciousness, I find I am still begging the central question of the article. The Turing Test, if passed, would be a *fait accompli*. The harder question is to ask whether it should have been undertaken in the first place.

310

Is the construction of a personal AI an immoral experiment?

Listen, for a moment, to the lament of Frankenstein's monster:

> Like Adam, I was apparently united by no link to any another being
> in existence, but his state was far different from mine in every other
> respect. He had come forth from the hands of God a perfect crea-
> ture, happy and prosperous, guarded by the especial care of his cre-
> ator, he was allowed to convene with, and acquire knowledge from,
> beings of a superior nature, but I was wretched, helpless, and alone.
> Many times I considered Satan was the fitter emblem of my condi-
> tion. For often, like him, when I saw the bliss of my protectors, the
> bitter gall of envy rose up within me . . . Hateful day when I received
> life! . . . Accursed Creator! Why did you form a monster so hideous
> that even *you* turned from me in disgust?
>
> (Pp. 152–53.)

It seems obvious, first of all, that a creature who can communicate as well
as the monster should have little trouble passing the Turing Test. Second, the
fact that the monster is not a "machine" but an assemblage of biological
parts revivified by electricity is beside the point. What is intriguing about the
monster's lament is that he is claiming something analogous to a "wrongful
birth" suit; as an imperfect creation, he is claiming that he ought not to have
been made. However fanciful the monster might be, he is a perfect example
of what might go wrong with AI: He is the possibility of an experiment gone
awry. His story would be incomplete without the rationalizations of his
creator:

> I believed myself destined for some great enterprise
> . . . I deemed it criminal to throw away in useless grief those talents
> that might be useful to my fellow creatures . . . all my speculations
> and hope are as nothing and, like the archangel who aspired to
> omnipotence, I am chained to an eternal hell.
>
> (P. 256.)

We can say the monster is claiming that he was the improper subject of a
poorly-designed, nontherapeutic experiment, whereas Dr. Frankenstein
claims as his motivation not only his own egotism but the benefits to society
that might accrue from his experiment. In modern times, a similar form of
utilitarian justification is echoed by Norbert Weiner (1964), who says of the
fears surrounding the AI enterprise:

> If we adhere to all these taboos, we may acquire a great reputation as
> conservative and sound thinkers, but we shall contribute very little to

the further advance of knowledge. It is the part of the scientist—of the intelligent man of letters and of the honest clergyman as well— to entertain heretical and forbidden opinions experimentally, even if he is finally to reject them.

(P. 5)

Entertaining opinions is one thing, but here we are talking about an experiment, an experiment in the construction of something which is so intelligent that it might come to be considered a person. It is one thing to experiment on a piece of machinery, such as a car, and quite another, as the Nuremberg Medical Trials indicated, to experiment with, or in this case toward, persons. Kant's imperative to treat persons as ends in themselves rather than as means to an end is at the heart of the matter.

Human experimentation and the AI experiment

Particularly since the Nazi atrocities, the norm of non-maleficence has been considered more stringent than that of beneficence in subsequent medical codes. The concern has been overwhelmingly in favor of the subject and against the interests and benefits of the society. Even where considerations of social utility have been included in such codes, a strong burden has been placed on the experimenter to prove that benefits overwhelmingly outweigh risks to the health and welfare of the subject. In the extreme, such concerns have tended to rule out all forms of nontherapeutic experimentation (Jonas, 1977). Is the AI experiment then immoral in its inception, assuming, that is, that the end (telos) of the experiment is the production of a person?

Let us first ask whether the experiment can be considered therapeutic in any meaningful sense of the word; that is, is it of benefit to the subject? It is difficult to consider it as such, because the subject does not really exist as confirmed fact (as a person) prior to the experiment itself; it exists only in *potentia*. In the stages prior to the "dawning" of consciousness, the machine is in some respects more like a zygote or early fetus than a person (assuming, of course, that the early stages of the construction of the AI are somewhat analogous to the early stages in the teleological process of biological growth). We can, then, consider the experiment to be therapeutic only if we maintain that the potential "gift" of conscious life outweighs no life at all. We cannot say that this is an experiment on a sick person or a sick potential person for the sake of that person whom we are attempting to make better. Thus, we can fairly consider the experiment to be nontherapeutic in nature. If so, the stringent code of medical ethics seems to apply (Ramsey, 1975). We shouldn't treat the subject as if it had no rights at all. This is not to say that the benefits to society would be trivial; even pure knowledge is never trivial, especially when such "high tech" almost invariably trickles down in various ways. However, the presumption of the experimental tradition is always *prima facie* against nontherapeutic experimentation, save perhaps in those cases where the experimenter is also the subject (Jonas, 1977).

It might be contended, however, that the "birthing" of an AI is analogous to a human birthing. Let us consider this possibility for a moment.

Until the recent present in human history, birthing has basically been "set" for us. We took what we got. In the Judeo-Christian tradition, life itself has been viewed, for the most part, as a gift from God, and the sanctity of human life has been weighted very strongly against any quality of life ethic (Dyck, 1977; Noonan, 1970). Modern technology, specifically genetic screening and amniocentesis, has, when coupled with the Supreme Court's abortion decision, raised a different sort of moral question: Is it immoral to knowingly bring into the world a potentially or actually defective child? Such a question raises the crucial issue of the locus of rights in the procreative decision.

Roe vs. Wade has shown that the right to procreate and to terminate procreation (whether or not the fetus is defective) is, at least in the first trimester of pregnancy, a subjective, discriminatory right of the parents (Reiser, Dick, & Curran, 1977). The desires of the parents are the locus of the rights, and only at stages approaching viability can the state take any compelling interest in the welfare of the fetus. Yet questions can be raised about the rights of the fetus. I have in mind here not the right to life of the fetus but the right of the potential newborn to be born to the possibility of a healthy existence, the right of a child to be born without disabling handicaps and with the freedom from severe pain (as opposed to the capacity to feel pain).

It is my opinion that most AI researchers would incline to follow something analogous to the "subjective desires for the parents" route where the possibility of AI is concerned, thereby implicitly making an analogy with procreative rights as guaranteed by the Supreme Court decision. However, the analogy does not really hold for a number of significant reasons.

In a certain sense, we must acknowledge that human reproduction is an experiment. Joseph Fletcher (1972) and others have argued that the "sexual roulette" mode of human reproductive experimentation should come to an end. "To be human is to be in control," says Fletcher, and he argues that a baby conceived by artificial means would be more, rather than less human because it would be the product of a thoughtful, rational process. Nonetheless, we can say that the human "roulette" mode of reproduction has allowed us inductively to generalize certain rules of thumb which serve as guidelines for preventive, prenatal care of the fetus. In AI there are really few, if any, such precedents. The injunction "do no harm" is cloudy in the case of AI, much more so than the injunction, for example, not to smoke while pregnant. AI is an extreme experiment; we have little or no knowledge of what might happen. Although it could be argued that all preventive, human reproductive behavior has been built on the basis of trial and error as well, we can at least say that evolution has set our birth for us in a way which, at present, is only trivially a matter of the will. AI is really much more of a deliberate experiment.

Second and most important, human reproduction is a necessity for species survival. All of the earth's cultures attest to this necessity and provide ethical and legal safeguards to protect it. AI, on the other hand, is not necessary as a means of species survival. This does not mean that it might not prove in ages to come to be a necessity, but at present it is not. AI is more a luxury than a necessity; as such, it should fall under the stringent experimental güidelines. It can also be argued that at present the risks of the AI experiment are greater than the benefits, and the ratio of risk to benefit is higher in AI than in human reproduction. For the *subject* of the AI experiment, the only benefit appears to be, at best, the gift of conscious life. This gift must be weighed against whatever problems might arise.

The result of this argument is, apparently, to side with the Frankenstein monster's "wrongful birth" suit. An AI experiment that aims at producing a self-reflexively conscious and communicative "person" is *prima facie* immoral. There are no compelling reasons which lead us to believe that we could ensure even the slightest favorable risk-benefit ratio. Is the necessary conclusion, then, not to do it?

Does a personal AI have rights?

Suppose, for a moment, that we could guarantee all of the conditions requisite to birthing an AI which had the full range of personal capacities and potentials; in other words, suppose we could guarantee that the AI would have the same rights *a priori* which actual persons do now. What would such rights be? A suitable starting point might be the United Nation's 1948 Declaration of Human Rights (Donaldson & Werhane, 1979). I except some of those which might be pertinent to the AI case. Article Four, for example, states that no one shall be held in slavery or servitude. Isn't this the very purpose of robotics? Fletcher has already contended that the bioengineering of such entities might conceivably be warranted for the performance of dangerous tasks (an interesting parallel to the conditions making for *R.U.R.*'s robot revolt) (Fletcher, 1972).

The prohibition of slavery raises a further question for AI. A free, multi-purpose robot might be "legitimate," as it were, but what of a single-purpose robot? Would this be tantamount to engineering a human baby with, for example, no arms so that he or she could become a great soccer player? Any limited-purpose or limited-capacity AI would have its essence defined before its existence (Sartre, 1957), so to speak; if we would not accept this of the humanly personal, we should not accept it of the AI personal as well. Thus, if we were to hold strictly to the United Nation articles, we would have to do justice, for example, to article thirteen: the right to freedom of movement.

Must the AI be mobile? Does the AI have the right to arms and legs and to all of the other human senses as well?

What about article sixteen: the right to marry and found a family? The Frankenstein monster demanded this right from his creator and was refused. Was Dr. Frankenstein immoral in refusing this request? Does an AI have the right to reproduce by any means? Does "it" have the right to slow growth (that is, a maturation process) or the right to a specific gender?

If we concede a right to freedom from unnecessary pain as well, a right we seem to confer on subpersonal animals (Singer, 1980), we have to face the delicate technical question I alluded to earlier: Is there a way to give pain capacity to an AI without causing it pain, at least no more pain than an ordinary human birth might entail?

Such questions are quite bewildering. Although I have argued that the bottom line of the morality of the experiment *qua* experiment on the subject is whether a consciousness of any quality is better than none at all, and although I have also argued that an unnecessary experiment which carries with it potential for a severely limited existence and, possibly, unnecessary pain, is unethical, I have indicated that if all of the conditions of a sound birth were met *a priori* the experiment might then be considered legitimate.

All this is somewhat silly. Such AIs will probably be built up in layers, and they are not really even babies, yet! Consciousness itself might prove to be an emergent property that might spring forth unexpectedly from a sophisticated level of hardware and software organization, quite as HAL's did in Clarke's *2001: A Space Odyssey*. Then, if we give birth to a Frankenstein monster, it will be too late. This is often the way human beings learn their lessons, and I have no illusions about the tendency of technology to run with its own momentum, to "do it if it can be done." Perhaps, though, if we give free rein to our moral imaginations, we will be better prepared than was poor old Dr. Frankenstein.

Can an artificial intelligence be moral?

A common criticism of the AI project is that a computer only does what it is programmed to do, that it is without the mysterious property called free will and, therefore, can never become "moral." (I will take free will to mean, specifically, the attribution of an intervening variable between stimulus and response that renders impossible a prediction of response, given adequate knowledge of all input variables.) Some philosophers might even be tempted to say that a machine, however intelligent, which is without the capacity to value and to make moral choices cannot be considered an end in itself and, therefore, could not be the possessor of certain human rights (I think, at least, that this is what Kant's argument would boil down to). Indeed, Kant (1964) would argue that a capacity for free will is a necessary postulate of the moral life, though there is nothing empirical about this capacity. (I cannot enter here into an analysis of Kant's arguments about the ontology of this capacity, for example, that freewill is part of the intelligible world as opposed to the sensual-empirical world. Suffice it to say that I believe this mysterious capacity for free will is really, for Kant, something from another reality and is, thus, subject to the criticism of dualism which I have previously alluded to.)

A cursory glance at the history of theology and philosophy on the topic of free will, from Augustine and Pelagius to Chomsky and Skinner, shows the difficulty of delineating any proof for its existence or nonexistence. For every Chomsky (1973) who maintains that a behaviorist has no predictive ability with regard to human behavior, there is a Skinner who maintains that the behaviorist does not have all the information about input variables necessary to make a complete prediction about behavior or output. Free will and determinism might really be differing perspectives on the same phenomenon, the former being the perspective from the subjectivity of human agency, the latter from observation. Except for the problem of retributive justice (punishment), I see little or no difference in the "cash value" of holding to one theory or the other; it is interesting to note, however, that the reality of Kant's noumenal capacity for free will might, in a trivial sense, be "proved" by the failure of an AI to ever give behavioristic evidence (however that might be defined) of free will. At any rate, persons make so-called choices to act in certain ways, whether they are factually free or factually determined (or programmed). However, short of invoking the *deus ex machina* of an ontological dualism in order to protect the ghostlike existence of the free will, the contention of its existence really makes little difference to the AI project. If free will is real in some sense, there is again no reason to believe that it might not be an emergent property of a sophisticated level of technical organization, just as it might be asserted to arise through a slow maturation process in humans. I should also add that not all AI experts are convinced an AI could not attain free will (I refer interested persons to the last chapters of Hofstadter's *Gödel, Escher, Bach* for some interesting ruminations on this difficult issue).

Emotion

What about emotion? There has been considerable debate among ethicists about whether the concept of the "good" is a cognitive one or a noncognitive and emotive one (for example, Frankena, 1973). Is morality primarily a matter of reason and logic, or is it a matter of emotion and sympathy? Even for Kant, who was deeply committed to reason, it can be construed to be a matter of both (Paton, 1965). A person, then, must have emotions and reason in order to have the capacity for ethical decision making. Given an accurate, nonreductionistic description of moral experience (Mandelbaum, 1969), an AI would probably have to have feelings and emotions, as well as intelligent reason, in order to replicate personal decision making. The necessity of this capacity becomes more apparent when we seek to discern whether an AI ought to be something like a moral judge. Weizenbaum (1976) has maintained that there are certain things an intelligent machine should not to be allowed to do, especially things involving human emotions such as love. Does this mean, then, that a machine should not be allowed to be a moral judge?

If we took to modern ethical theory in order to ascertain what attributes a competent moral judge must have, we might turn to the ideal observer theory (Firth, 1952). The ideal observer theory maintains that the statement "X is right" means that X would be approved by an ideal moral judge who had following characteristics: omniscience (knowledge of all relevant facts), omnipercipience (the ability to vividly imagine the feelings and circumstances of the parties involved, that is, something like empathy), disinterestedness (nonbiasedness), and dispassionateness (freedom from disturbing passion). These characteristics, then, are an attempt to specify the conditions under which a valid moral judgment might be made. The attributes of such an ideal observer, of course, resemble the traditional attributes of God, and this is understandable if we, like Kant, consider the concept of God to be, in part, a moral ideal. The theory itself, however, does not presuppose a belief in God; it merely contends that it gives an adequate description of the requisite conditions we need in order to make sound moral judgments. We do attempt to approximate these conditions when we make a moral judgment: A judge who shakes hands in the courtroom with your opponent but not with you could justly be accused of failing to be disinterested, and so on. Now if we look at most of the characteristics of such an observer, that is, omniscience, disinterestedness, and dispassionateness, then a case might be made for saying that an unemotional AI could be considered a better moral judge than a human person. Such a machine might be able to store and retrieve more factual data, not be disturbed by violent passions and interests, and so on; it could be said to be capable of "cool" and "detached" choices.

Omnipercipience, or empathy, however, is problematic. This kind of sympathy for the circumstances of people, part of what Aristotle called "equity," is a wisdom that comes from being able to "put ourselves in the other's shoes," as it were. Certainly emotions would be involved here, and the degree of morphological similarity necessary for the empathetic response of one person to another is a subtle and problematic matter. Perhaps the ability to empathize is what Weizenbaum finds lacking in any possible AI and is the reason why he would not entrust such judgments to one. Yet, given what I have previously said there is no reason to believe that such ability could not be, in principle, duplicable.

The problem of casuistry

Casuistry deals with the application of general rules to specific, concrete situations. The question of whether all thinking can be formalized in some sort of rule structure is a crucial one for AI in general. For example, one computer program seeks to capture the medical diagnostic ability of a certain physician who has the reputation as one of the best diagnosticians in the world. The computer programmer working with him tries to break this procedure down into a series of logical steps of what to the physician was an irreducible intuition of how to go about doing it. With a lot of prodding, however, the diagnostician was soon able to break these intuitions down into their logical steps (H.E.W., 1980). Perhaps this is true with all "intuitive" thinking, or is it? If we assume that ethics is a reasonable, cognitive undertaking, we are prone to formalize it in a series of rules, not exceptionless rules but something like W.D. Ross's list of *prima facie* obligations: a list of rules, any one of which might be binding in a particular circumstance (Ross, 1965). What Ross gives us is something like the moral equivalent of a physicist's periodic table of the elements, moral rules that constitute the elemental building blocks of moral life. The list runs something like this: promise keeping, truth telling, reparations, justice, gratitude, beneficence, nonmaleficence, and self-improvement.

All of these obligations are incumbent upon us as moral beings, but one or several can take precedence over the others in certain situations. We must, therefore, have some principle for adjudicating between these rules in situations where they might conflict. They need not be set up in a strict hierarchy; we could, for example, say that the principle of adjudication is intuition. This is basically what Ross asserts when he quotes Aristotle's famous dictum "The decision rests with the perception." At the same time, however, Ross ranks at least one of his rules as *prima facie* more binding than another. The duty of not harming (nonmaleficence) is a more stringent duty than actively promoting good (beneficence), and this is true even before a particular situation is addressed. This proves significant in what follows.

The problem of the casuistry of an AI has already been imaginatively addressed by Isaac Asimov in his book *I, Robot* (1950), where he lists his somewhat famous "Rules for Robotics." The list is an attempt to give us a rule hierarchy that might be wired into a robot. These rules are as follows:

1. A robot may not injure a human being or through inaction allow a human being to come to harm.
2. A robot must obey orders given it by humans except when such orders conflict with the first law.
3. A robot must protect its own existence as long as such protection does not conflict with the first or second laws.

These, of course, are not all of the rules that a robot might be wired with; Ross's list is certainly more complete than Asimov's. There is plenty of food for thought, though, in Asimov's hierarchy.

The first thing an ethicist might notice about rule one is that it attempts to combine the principle of nonmaleficence (do no harm) with a utilitarian principle of beneficence (do the maximum good). Rule one thus contains within itself the potential for conflict, as it does in modern normative theory (Frankena, 1973, pp. 45–48). What if the robot has to decide between injuring a human being or not acting at all and thus allowing another human being to come to harm through an act of omission? Asimov's robots run in circles when confronted with a conflict-of-rule situation. What would be most moral to do in such a situation—refrain from acting at all, or heed the voice of Kierkegaard and act whatever the costs might be? Further, how do we understand the principle of beneficence underlying the sins of omission? Should all robots go to Pakistan in order to maximize the good, or should they go somewhere else? How long should a robot calculate potential consequences before acting? I should point out that if there is any specific normative theory attributed to the AIs of science fiction, it would have to be utilitarian. Robots are seen as paradigms of calculation, as exhibiting metahuman capacities for weighing, quantifying, and projecting consequences. As such, they are subject to the same criticisms one might level at utilitarians in general; for example, how might a robot compare incommensurable goods in order that they might be quantified and rendered mathematically precise? Such a problem vexed Jeremy Bentham for most of his life—is push pin really as good as poetry?

The second rule, obeying orders for humans except where they might conflict with the first rule, appears to contradict the aforementioned right to freedom from slavery (unless, of course, the AI were to be somehow considered a "child"). The second part of the rule, refusing to take an order to harm, might not be considered moral at all if, for example, the protection of innocence were at stake. Should an AI robot be a proponent of the just war theory, or should it be something of a pacifist, even to the point of self-sacrifice as Asimov's robots would appear to be?

The third rule, protecting its own existence as long as such protection does not conflict with the first and second laws, is also highly problematic. First, it gives the robot the right to self-defense but then takes it away. Note the use of the word must. There is no possibility for what ethics calls "supererogatory" duties. These are the things we think it is praiseworthy to do, but not blameworthy not to do. (Urmson, 1958; Chisolm, 1963). Suppose, for example, that a man jumps on a hand grenade in order to save his comrades. His heroic action is likely to be praised, but had he chosen not to jump he probably would not be blamed for failing to sacrifice himself. We like to keep the heroic free from the obligatory. Asimov's rules do not. Is that really bad? Should we wire a self-sacrificial attitude into our robots, making them all little Christs? For that matter, should we "wire" our own children to so act? The questions involved in wiring a robot for morality are so very similar to the questions of how we should morally educate our own children!

It might prove to be the case that no hierarchy of normative principles can do justice to the complexity of personal, moral choice. It also might be that the self-reflexively conscious ego of a sophisticated AI would take no programming at all, and that it would pick and choose its own rules, rules it learns through the trials and errors of time. However difficult it might prove to duplicate human, moral decision making, especially an adjudicative principle like intuition, we need not resort to a skepticism that is based ultimately on dualistic "magic," and thereby resign from the attempt.

Conclusion

What if we never make an AI that can pass the Turing Test? Little of the effort will be lost. It is the peculiar pedagogical effect of "distancing" that makes the contemplation of artificial persons so fertile for the human imagination. The proponents of AI promise us that we will learn more about ourselves in the attempt to construct something like ourselves. This distancing is also dangerous, however. We have, for example, distanced ourselves from other people and from animals, often with tragic results. Of course, the project will go on and, I think, with much success, but it will be a sad thing if Hegel was right when he said, "The owl of Minerva flies only at midnight." Much caution and forethought are necessary when we contemplate the human construction of the personal.

If we can't ever make such an intelligence, is any mystery gone? To the contrary, the failure to be able to produce the personal as artifact might eventually bring us to the brink of a mysticism that has, at least, been partially "tested." Would it be more mysterious to find intelligent life elsewhere in the universe or to find after unimaginable aeons that we are unique and alone? Perhaps AI is the next stage of evolution, a harder blow to our ineradicable anthropomorphism than Copernicus's theory that the planets revolved around the sun and not the earth. As McCorduck says of the undertaking, "Face to face with mind as artifact we're face to face with almost more themes in the human experience than we can count or comprehend. And there's the added zest that this idea may turn out to transcend the human experience altogether and lead us to the metahuman" (p. 329).

On one side of the moral spectrum lies the fear of something going wrong; on the other side is the exuberant "yes" to all possibilities and benefits. Though the first word of ethics is "do no harm," we can perhaps look forward to innovation with a thoughtful caution. Perhaps we will eclipse ourselves with our own inventions. Perhaps Michelangelo was correct when he pointed that long finger of God at Adam's hand. Either way, I am excited.

Notes

1 For a more through discussion of normative theories, see W. K. Frankena's (1973) *Ethics*, chapters 2 and 3.
2 See Paton (1965), especially chapter 16.
3 For example, McCorduck (1979), pp. 359–64.
4 It had been estimated that the human brain contains 1013 bits of intelligence capacity as opposed, for example, to a cow's capacity of 1011 bits (*Chemtech*, 1980, p. 590.)
5 As Karl Marx and Friedrich Engels pointed out, mind-body dualists tend to hold to a disconcerting dualism between their physics and metaphysics as well. Thus, they say rightly of Descartes: "Descartes in his physics endowed matter with self-creative power and conceived mechanical motion as the act of its life. He completely separated his physics from his metaphysics. Within his physics matter is the only substance, the only basis of being and of knowledge" (Marx & Engels, 1971, pp. 60–61).
6 For example, Joseph Fletcher (1972) uses the term "human" rather than "person," but his criteria distinguish the personal from the merely biomorphologically human.
7 It ought to encompass even the possibility of a "religious experience," which Weizenbaum has asserted in a popular source it could never attain to. Weizenbaum does not tell us why it could not have such an experience. See the interview of Weizenbaum by Rosenthal (1983), pp. 94–97.

References

Asimov, I (1950) *I robot*. New York: Gnome Press.
Boden, M. (1977) *Artificial intelligence and natural man*. New York: Basic Books.
Boeyink, David (1974) Pain and suffering. *Journal of Religious Ethics* 2(1): 85–97.
Capek, The Brothers (1975). *R.U.R. and the insect play*. London: Oxford University Press.
Chisholm, Roderick (1963) Supererogation and offense: A conceptual scheme for ethics. *Ratio* 5(June): 1–14.
Chomsky, Noam (1973) *For reasons of state*. New York: Random House.
Department of Health, Education, & Welfare (1980) *The seeds of artificial intelligence: Sumex-aim*. Washington, D.C.
Dreyfus, H. (1972). *What computers can't do: A critique of artificial reason*. New York: Harper & Row.
Dyck, A. J. (1977) Ethics and medicine. In S. J. Reiser, A. J. Dyck, & W. J. Curran (Eds.) *Ethics in medicine: Historical perspectives and contemporary concerns*. Cambridge, Mass: MIT Press.
Firth, Roderick (1952) Ethical absolutism and the ideal observer *Philosophy and Phenomenological Research* 12 (March): 317–345.
Fletcher, Joseph (1977) Ethical aspects of genetic controls. In S. J. Reiser, A. J. Dyck, & W. J. Curran (Eds.) *Ethics in medicine: Historical perspectives and contemporary concerns*. Cambridge, Mass: MIT Press.
Fletcher, Joseph (1972). Indicators of humanhood: A tentative profile of man. *The Hastings Center Report* 2(5): 1–4.
Frankena, W. K. (1973) *Ethics*. Englewood Cliffs, N. J.: Prentice-Hall.
Heidegger, Martin (1962) *Being and time*. New York: Harper & Row.

Hofstadter, Douglas R. (1980). *Gödel, Escher, Bach: An eternal golden braid*. New York: Vintage Books.

Jonas, Hans (1977). Philosophical reflections on experimenting with human subjects. In S. J. Reiser, A. J. Dyck, & W. J. Curran (Eds.) *Ethics in medicine: Historical perspectives and contemporary concerns*. Cambridge, Mass.: MIT Press.

Kant, Immanuel (1964) *Groundwork of the metaphysic of morals*. New York: Harper & Row.

McCorduck, Pamela (1979). *Machines who think*. San Francisco: W. H. Freeman.

Mandelbaum, Maurice (1969) *The phenomenology of moral experience*. Baltimore, Md.: Johns Hopkins Press.

Marx, Karl, & Engels, F. (1971) *On religion*. New York: Schocken.

Mead, G. H. (1972) *Mind, self, and society*. Chicago: University of Chicago Press.

Niebuhr, H. R. (1963) *The responsible self*. New York: Harper & Row.

Noonan, John T. (1970) An almost absolute value in history. In J. T. Noonan (Ed.) *The morality of abortion*. Cambridge: Harvard University Press.

Paton, H. J. (1965). *The categorical imperative*. New York: Harper & Row.

Penfield, Wilder (1983). The uncommitted cortex: The child's changing brain. *The Atlantic Monthly* 22(7): 77–81.

Ramsey, Paul (1975) *The ethics of fetal research*. New Haven, Conn.: Yale University Press.

Roe vs. Wade, decision on abortion. (1977) In S. J. Reiser, A. J. Dyck, & W. J. Curran (Eds.) *Ethics in medicine: Historical perspectives and contemporary concerns*, Cambridge, Mass.: MIT Press.

Rosenthal, Elisabeth (1983) A rebel in the computer revolution. *Science Digest* (August): 94–97.

Ross, W. D. (1965) *The right and the good*. Oxford: Clarendon.

Sartre, Jean-Paul (1957) *Existentialism and human emotions*. New York: Wisdom Library.

Schlein, J. M. (1961) A client-centered approach to schizophrenia. In A. Burton (Ed.) *Psychotherapy of the psychoses*. New York: Basic Books.

Shelley, Mary W. (1974). *Frankenstein*. New York: Scholastic Book Services.

Singer, Peter (1980). *Practical ethics*. New York: Cambridge University Press.

Tooley, Michael (1974) Abortion and infanticide. In Cohen, Nagel, & Scanlon (Eds.) *The rights and wrongs of abortion*. Princeton, N. J.: Princeton University Press.

United Nations (1979) The universal declaration of human rights, 1948. In T. Donaldson & P. Werhane (Eds.) *Ethical issues in business*. Englewood Cliffs, N. J.: Prentice-Hall.

Urmson, J. O. (1958) *Saints and heroes*. Seattle: University of Washington Press.

Weizenbaum, Joseph (1976) *Computer power and human reason*. San Francisco: W. H. Freeman.

Wiener, Norbert (1964) *God and golem, inc.* Cambridge, Mass.: MIT Press.

2.3: Social Issues

79

ATTITUDES TOWARD
INTELLIGENT MACHINES

Paul Armer

Source: Edward A. Feigenbaum and Julian Feldman (eds) *Computers and Thought*, McGraw-Hill, 1962, pp. 389–406.

> 'A bird is an instrument working according to mathematical law, which instrument it is within the capacity of man to reproduce with all its movements.'
>
> (*Leonardo da Vinci (1452–1519)*)

This is an attempt to analyze attitudes and arguments brought forth by questions like 'Can machines think?' and 'Can machines exhibit intelligence?' Its purpose is to improve the climate which surrounds research in the field of machine or artificial intelligence. Its goal is not to convince those who answer the above questions negatively that they are wrong (although an attempt will be made to refute some of the negative arguments) but that they should be tolerant of research investigating these questions. The negative attitudes existent today tend to inhibit such research (MacGowan, 1960).[1]

History

Before examining the current arguments and attitudes toward artificial intelligence, let us look at some of the history of this discussion, for these questions have been around for a long time.

Samuel Butler (1835–1902), in *Erewhon and Erewhon Revisited* (1933), concocted a civil war between the 'machinists' and the 'anti-machinists.' (Victory, incidentally, went to the 'anti-machinists.') Butler stated 'there is no security against the ultimate development of mechanical consciousness in the fact of machines possessing little consciousness now' and speculated that the time might come when 'man shall become to the machines what the horse and dog are to us.' Discussion of this topic apparently took place in Babbage's time (1792–1871), for the Countess of Lovelace commented on it, negatively, in her writings on Babbage's efforts (Bowden, 1953). The topic came into prominence in the late 1940's when Babbage's dreams became a reality with the completion of the first large digital computers. When the popular press applied the term 'giant brains' to these machines, computer builders and users, myself included, immediately arose to the defense of the human intellect. We hastened to proclaim that computers did not 'think'; they only did arithmetic quite rapidly.

A. M. Turing, who earlier had written one of the most important papers in the computer field on the universality of machines (1936, 1937), published in 1950 a paper entitled, 'Computing Machinery and Intelligence.' In it he circumvented the problem of properly defining the words 'machine' and 'thinking' and examined instead the question of a game wherein an interrogator, who can communicate with a human and a machine via teletype, but does not know which is which, is to decide which is the machine. This is now known throughout the computer field as 'Turing's Test.'

Discussion of machine intelligence died down (but not out) in the early and mid-1950's but has come back in the last several years stronger than ever before. In fact, it has recently invaded the pages of *Science* (Mac-Gowan, 1960; Wiener, 1960; Taube, 1960; Samuel, 1960b).

A way of thinking about thinking

Before beginning an examination of the negative arguments, allow me to introduce a concept which will aid in discussing these arguments and which may help resolve some of the semantic difficulties associated with discussions of 'Can machines think?' Like Turing, I avoid defining 'to think.' Instead, observe that thinking is a continuum, an n-dimensional continuum. This notion is certainly not new, for it has existed since man first compared his mental abilities with another man's, and it is implicit in all of the positive arguments on machine intelligence. Psychologists long ago developed 'intelligence quotient' as a yardstick in this continuum, and their concept of 'factors' is indicative of the n-dimensionality of the continuum of intelligence. The use of the one-dimensional 'I.Q.' is obviously an oversimplification of reality. Although the concept of an n-dimensional continuum for intelligence is not new, and although it is implicit in many discussions of artificial intelligence, it is rarely stated explicitly.

An analogy may be drawn with the continuum of the ability to transport. With respect to speed in transporting people from New York to Los Angeles, the jet airplane of today outshines all other existing transportation vehicles. But it does not compare favorably, costwise, with ships for transporting newsprint from British Columbia to California. Existing commercial jet transports cannot transport people from one lake to another. A Cadillac may be the most comfortable vehicle to transport people short distances over a good network of roads, but it is hardly a substitute for the jeep in the environment of ground warfare—the jeep's forte is versatility and flexibility. In this dimension, in the continuum of the ability to transport, man outshines the jeep, for man can go where jeeps cannot, just as the jeep can go where Cadillacs cannot. But men cannot carry the load that a jeep can nor can men move with the speed of the jeep.

Similarly, comparisons can be made between men and machines in the continuum of thinking. If there is objection to the use of the word 'thinking,' then 'ability to process information' or some similar term can be used. But it must be admitted that there exists some continuum of behavior in which men and machines coexist and in which they can be compared. (See Fig. 1.)

An *n*-dimensional continuum is difficult to draw when *n* is large, so let's examine a two-dimensional one, realizing that reality is far from being that simple. With respect to raw speed, machines outdo men, but when it comes to the sophistication of the information processes available, machines look pretty poor. This dimension deserves further discussion. While the repertoire of today's machines is quite simple—a few basic arithmetic operations and comparisons—man's information processes are very complex. Let me illustrate this point with the following incident. We have all had the experience of trying to recall the name of a person we have once met. On a particular occasions Dr. Willis Ware and I were both trying to recall an individual's name. We recounted to one another his physical characteristics, where he worked, what he did, etc. But his name eluded us. After some time, I turned

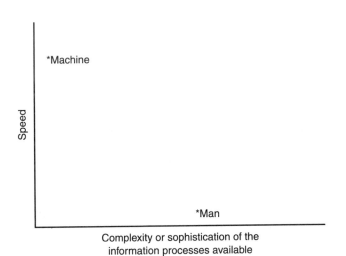

Figure 1 Complexity or sophistication of the information processes available.

to Dr. Ware and said, 'His name begins with a 'Z'.' At which point he snapped his fingers and correctly said, 'That's it, it's Frizell!'

Now, of course, the basic question is 'Can the machines' capabilities in this dimension be improved?' Let me turn the question around—Is there any evidence that they cannot? I know of none. In fact, over the last decade I think impressive progress has been made. It's easy to underestimate the advances, for 'intelligence' is a slippery concept. As Marvin Minsky put it, 'You regard an action as intelligent until you understand it. In explaining, you explain away' (1959*a*).

Today's computers, even with their limited capability in the sophistication dimension, have had tremendous impact on science and technology. Accomplishments of the last decade in the fields of nuclear energy, missiles and space would have been impossible without computers. If we can push the capabilities of computers[2] further out in the sophistication dimension, won't they have an even greater impact? *In this context then, the goal of research on artificial intelligence can be stated—it is simply an attempt to push machine behavior further out into this continuum.*

It is irrelevant whether or not there may exist some upper bound above which machines cannot go in this continuum. Even if such a boundary exists, there is no evidence that it is located close to the position occupied by today's machines. Is it not possible that we might one day understand the logical processes which went on in Dr. Ware's head and then mechanize them on a machine? We obviously will not achieve such a goal unless someone believes that the boundary is nonexistent in order to try; one need only believe that the boundary is much further out than the position occupied by today's machines.

Intelligent machines and today's digital computer

A common attitude toward today's computers is that such machines are strictly arithmetic devices. While it is true that machines were first built to carry out repetitive arithmetic operations, they are capable of other, non-numeric tasks. The essence of the computer is the manipulation of symbols—it is only a historical accident that the first application involved numeric symbols. This incorrect notion of the computer as a strictly numeric device results in the inability of many to conceive of the computer as a device exhibiting intelligent behavior, since this would require that the process be reduced to a numerical one. The reaction of many people to statements about intelligent behavior by machines seems to indicate that they take such statements to imply complete functional equivalence between the machine and the human brain. Since this complete functional equivalence does not exist, such people believe they have thereby debunked intelligent machines. Their argument is hollow since this equivalence was never implied. Intelligent behavior on the part of a machine no more implies complete functional equivalence between machine and brain than flying by an airplane implies complete functional equivalence between plane and bird.

The concept of comparing the behavior of men and machines in an *n*-dimensional continuum recognizes differences as well as similarities. For example, a common argument against machine intelligence is that the brain is a living thing—the machine is not. In our continuum we simply recognize the dimension of living and note that machines and men occupy different positions in this dimension.

While I do believe that today's digital computers can exhibit intelligent behavior, I do not hold that the intelligent machines of the 1970's will necessarily resemble today's machines, either functionally or physically. In particular, in my desire to see machines pushed further out in the continuum of intelligence, my interests in the dimension of speed are very minor; the organizational aspects (sophistication of the information processes) are obviously much more important. Likewise, I hold no brief for the strictly digital approach; a combination of analog and digital equipment may prove to be better. I do not mean to disown the digital computer, for it will be a most important tool in the endeavor to advance in our continuum.

Some of the negative arguments

1. The argument of invidious comparison

Considering the behavior of men and machines in the context of intelligence being a multidimensional continuum, an argument that a machine cannot play chess because 'it could only operate on standard-size pieces and could not recognize as chessmen the innumerable pieces of different design which the human player recognizes and moves around quite simply' (Taube, 1960) is like saying that the Wright brothers' airplane could not fly because it could not fly nonstop from Los Angeles to New York nor could it land in a tree like a bird. Why must the test of intelligence be that the machine achieve identically the same point in the continuum as man? Is the test of flying the achievement of the same point in the continuum of flying as that reached by a bird?

2. The argument of superexcellence

Many of the negativists[3] seem to say that the only evidence of machine intelligence they will accept is an achievement in our continuum seldom achieved by man. For example, they belittle efforts at musical composition by machine because the present output compares miserably with that of Mozart or Chopin. How many *men* can produce music that compares favorably? The ultimate argument of this kind occurred at a recent meeting in England, during which a discussant stated that he would not accept the fact that machines could think until one proved the famous conjecture of Fermat, better known as Fermat's last theorem. By this logic one concludes that, to this date, no man has been capable of thinking, since the conjecture remains unproven.

3. The argument by definition

There are many variations of this type of argument. For example, some negativists want to include in their definition of intelligent behavior the requirement that it be carried out by a living organism. With such a definition, machines do not behave intelligently. However, there does still exist machine behavior which can be compared with human behavior. To conclude that research on the simulation of such human behavior with a machine is wrong, as some have done, because the machine is not living, is like concluding that research on the simulation of the functions of the human heart with an artificial heart is wrong because the artificial organ is not a living one.

4. The argument by stipulation

An examination of the arguments advanced by the negativists reveals that many of them are not arguments at all, but only statements. They dismiss the notion out of hand, saying things like, 'Let's settle this once and for all, machines cannot think!' or 'A computer is not a giant brain, in spite of what some of the Sunday supplements and science fiction writers would have you believe. It is a remarkably fast and phenomenally accurate moron' (Andree, 1958).

5. The argument by false attribution

Typical of this type of argument is the following:

> The Manchester machine which was set to solve chess problems presumably proceeded by this method, namely by reviewing all the possible consequences of all possible moves. This, incidentally, reveals all the strength and weakness of the mechanism. It can review far more numerous possibilities in a given time than can a human being, but it has to review all possibilities. The human player can view the board as a whole and intuitively reject a number of possibilities. The machine cannot do either of these.
>
> (Hugh-Jones, 1956)

The statements about machine behavior in the above quotation are simply not true. While it is true that some of the early approaches to chess-playing machines were in the nature of attempts to review *all* possibilities in limited depth (Kister *et al.*, 1957), this is not the only way in which the problem can be approached. The chess-playing routine of Newell, Shaw, and Simon (1958*b*) does *not* examine all possibilities. And those which it does consider it examines in varying detail. The routine rejects moves which appear to be worthless; it selects moves which appear to be good ones and examines them in depth to ascertain that they are indeed good. An earlier routine developed by this same team to prove theorems in logic (Newell, Shaw and Simon, 1957*a*) did not examine all possible proofs—to do so with today's computers would literally take endless time. Rather, the routine searched through the maze of possible proofs for ones which looked promising and investigated them. It relied on knowing which approaches had worked before. Most of those who scoff about research on artificial intelligence turn out to be unaware of the details of what is going on in such research today; it is little wonder that they frequently make erroneous statements about the field.

6. *The argument by false extrapolation*

This class of argument is typified by extrapolations based on assumptions that machine properties are invariant. For example:

> The human memory is a filing system that has a far greater capacity than that of the largest thinking machine built. A mechanical brain that had as many tubes or relays as the human brain has nerve cells (some ten billion) would not fit into the Empire State Building, and would require the entire output of Niagara Falls to supply the power and the Niagara River to cool it. Moreover, such a computer could operate but a fraction of a second at a time before several thousand of its tubes would fail and have to be replaced.
>
> (Troll, 1954)

The point is tied to the vacuum tube (the article was written in 1954) and has therefore already been weakened by the appearance of the transistor, which requires less space and power and is considerably more reliable than the vacuum tube. An offsetting development is that the estimate of the number of nerve cells is undoubtedly too low. However, on the horizon are construction techniques involving the use of evaporated films, where the details of the machine will not be visible under an optical microscope (Shoulders, 1960). It seems reasonable to expect that it will be possible with these techniques to house in one cubic foot of space the same number of logical elements as exist in the human brain. Power requirements will be trivial.

331

7. The obedient slave argument

One often hears statements like 'The machine can only do what it is told to do.' People who advance this obedient slave argument would seem to be thinking that they are countering others who have pointed to a large conglomeration of unconnected transistors, resistors and electronic components, and said 'It thinks.' Certainly man is involved in machine intelligence—so are parents and teachers in human intelligence. Do we deny flying to an airplane because a man is piloting it or even to an unmanned flight because a man designed it?

The negativists who say 'the machine can only do what it is told to do' overlook the fact that they have not qualified their statement as to what is the limit of what the machine can be told to do. What evidence exists concerning the location of that limit? Might it not become possible to tell a machine to learn to do a given task, a task usually considered to require intelligence? Many of the tasks being accomplished with computers today were not considered possible ten years ago.

Recent computer tasks and milestones

The mounting list of tasks which can now be carried out on a computer but which we normally consider requiring intelligence when performed by humans, includes such things as:

Proving theorems in logic and plane geometry (Newell, Shaw and Simon, 1957a; Gelernter, 1960a)

Playing checkers and chess (Samuel, 1959; Newell, Shaw and Simon, 1958b)

Assembly line balancing (Tonge, 1961a)

Composing music (Hiller and Isaacson, 1959)

Designing motors (Goodwin, 1958)

Recognition of manual Morse code (Gold, 1959)

Solving calculus problems (Slagle, 1961)

The collection of capabilities which have been ascribed solely to humans in the past is being slowly chipped away by the application of computers. Space precludes going further into the evidence for machine intelligence; this topic is well covered in the articles previously cited and in other papers (Newell, Shaw and Simon, 1956; Milligan, 1959; Minsky, 1961a). Such evidence is, of course, the basis for many of the arguments advanced by the positivists.

To prove that machines *today* do *not* exhibit intelligence, it is only necessary to define a lower bound in our continuum which is above the behavior exhibited by the machines and then say that behavior above that bound is intelligent and below it is not intelligent. This is a variant of the proof by definition. Many who use this gambit have been redefining the lower bound so that it is continually above what machines can do today. For example, we find

> Perhaps the most flexible concept is that any mental process which can be adequately reproduced by automatic systems is not thinking (Meszar, 1953).

This redefinition may not be done consciously. A skill which seems highly intelligent in others becomes much less impressive to us when we acquire that skill ourselves. It would be useful to have at hand some milestones for the future. Turing's test is one such milestone (1950) but additional ones are needed. To this end a clearly defined task is required which is, at present, in the exclusive domain of humans (and therefore incontestably 'thinking') but which may eventually yield to accomplishment by machines.

Rivalry between man and machines

There is a strong personal factor in the attitude of many negativists. I'm sure it was a major factor in my being a negativist ten years ago. To concede that machines can exhibit intelligence is to admit that man has a rival in an area previously held to be within the sole province of man. To illustrate this point, let me quote from a letter received at RAND:

> ... semantics may have a lot to do with the degree of enthusiasm for supporting research in this area (artificial intelligence). Subjectively, the terms 'intelligent machine' or 'thinking machine' disturb me and even seem a bit threatening: I am a human being, and therefore 'intelligent' and these inhuman devices are going to compete with me and may even beat me out. On the other hand, if the very same black boxes were labelled 'problem solver,' or even 'adaptive problem solver,' they would seem much more friendly, capable of helping me in the most effective way to do things that I want to do better, but, best of all, I'd still be the boss. This observation is wholly subjective and emotional ...

Another explanation of why some negativists feel the way they do is related to what might be called the 'sins of the positivists.' Exaggerated claims of accomplishments, particularly from the publicity departments of computer manufacturers, have resulted in such a strong reaction within the scientific community that many swing too far in the opposite direction.

Da Vinci and flying

At this point allow me to paraphrase the quotation of da Vinci's, with which this paper was begun, and also, with the benefit of hindsight, expand on it somewhat. Thus, he might have said:–

When men understood the natural laws which govern the flight of a bird, man will be able to build a flying machine.

While it is true that man wasted a good deal of time and effort trying to build a flying machine that flapped its wings like a bird, the important point is that it was the understanding of the law of aerodynamic lift (even though the understanding was quite imperfect at first) over an airfoil which enabled men to build flying machines. A bird isn't sustained in the air by the hand of God—natural laws govern its flight. Similarly, natural laws govern what went on in Dr. Ware's head when he produced 'Frizell' from my erroneous but related clue. Thus, I see no reason why we won't be able to duplicate in hardware the very powerful processes of association which the human brain has, once we understand them. And if man gained an understanding of the processes of aerodynamics, may he not also obtain an understanding of the information processes of the human brain?

There are other facets to this analogy with flight; it, too, is a continuum, and some once thought that the speed of sound represented a boundary beyond which flight was impossible.

Approaches to the problem of building an intelligent machine

This topic can perhaps be expounded best with another analogy. Suppose we are given a device which we know exhibits intelligent behavior because we have observed it in action. We would like to build a machine which approaches it in capability (or better yet, exceeds it). We bring in a group of men to study the basic components of the device to understand how they work. These men apply pulses to subsets of the leads, and observe what each component does; they try to understand why the device behaves as it does in terms of basic physics and chemistry. They also seek to learn how these components function in subassemblies.

A second group of men approach the problem from the point of view that the device is a 'black box' which they are not able to open. This group observes that some of the appendages of the device are obviously input devices while others are output devices. They observe the device in operation and attempt to theorize how it works. They proceed on the basis that it will not be necessary that the machine they are to construct have the same basic components as exist in the device under study. They believe that if they can understand the logical operation of the existing device, they can duplicate its logic in their own machine, using components they understand and can make.

This second group makes conjectures about the logical construction of the device and tries these conjectures out on a computer which they have at hand. These theories are very crude at first and do not mirror the behavior of the 'black box' very well, but over time the resemblance improves.

Because we learned a lesson from the effort spent on attempting to build a flying machine that flapped its wings, we set a third group to work studying 'intelligence and information processing' per se and building up a science in the area.

There is much common ground among the three groups and they keep each other posted on results to date. Furthermore, they all use computers to aid them in their research. The groups combine their know-how along the way to build better computers (low-I.Q. intelligent machines) on which to try out their conjectures. Eventually, the three groups 'come together in the middle' and build a machine which is almost as capable as our model. They then turn to the task of building an even better one.

In the real-life situation of studying the human brain, the first group, studying components and assemblies thereof, is represented by physiological work. The second, or 'black-box' group, is represented by psychological efforts to explain human mental activity. This analogy represents, I believe, a plausible scenario for the way things might go in trying to understand the human mind.

Russian attitudes

Our examination thus far has been Western in origin; in view of the impact that achievement of the goals of research on artificial intelligence would have on the technological posture of the United States vis-à-vis the Soviet Union, it might be interesting to look at Soviet attitudes toward intelligent machines. As one might suspect, Soviet attitudes have been quite similar to Western ones. Positivists and negativists exist, and each camp advances the same sort of arguments as their Western counterparts. For example, there are negativists who advance the obedient slave argument. Academician S. A. Lebedev, head of the Institute of Precise Mechanics and Computational Techniques and host to the U.S. Exchange Delegation in Computers which visited the USSR in the last two weeks of May, 1959 (of which I was a member), on two occasions dismissed my questions concerning his attitude toward intelligent machines with the statement 'Machines can do no more than they are instructed to do.'

Their literature is filled with discussions of comparisons between men and machines. In 1961, an entire book, *Philosophical Problems of Cybernetics* (1961), was published on this topic. It was obvious from the questions asked of our delegation by the Russians about Western attitudes that it is a hotly debated issue. In the USSR, research on artificial intelligence is a part of cybernetics, the term coined by Wiener (1948) and now a household word in the Soviet Union. Cybernetics is also used as an umbrella term for research in automatic control, automation, computers, programming, information retrieval, language translation, etc. It is universally recognized as an area related to both men and machines, and the requirement for an interdisciplinary (engineering, mathematics, computing, biology, psychology, physiology, physics, chemistry, linguistics, etc.) approach to such research is also recognized.

As in the West, the use of the term 'giant brains' in the late 1940's resulted in a massive revulsion among the Soviet scientific community, and universal rush to the defense of the human mind. The degree of the revulsion was such that several Soviet writers have blamed it for the fact that Russia presently lags the U.S. in the digital-computer field (Shaginyan, 1959). One finds frequent references in the Russian literature to the existence of a negative attitude toward cybernetics, and to the persistence of this attitude for a period of about ten years.

Soviet literature on cybernetics frequently gives credit to Wiener, von Neumann, and other Westerners for pioneering the field. It also contains many references to the work of Pavlov and mixes in much political discussion of communism vs. capitalism, and even of Marx and Lenin. For example, we have:

> Karl Marx was the first to make use implicitly and anticipatingly of cybernetical ways of thought, or to express it more pointedly, Karl Marx was the first cybernetician! . . .
>
> (Klaus, 1960)

There are some strong positivists in the USSR. For example, I. A. Poletayev has stated 'nothing except prejudice and superstition allow one to deny with assurance today the possibility that the machine will pass, in the end, that limit beyond which consciousness begins' (1958). Other strong positivists include S. L. Sobolev (an Academician and a well-known mathematician) and A. A. Lyapunov (1960). We also find:

> . . . Thus, the perfecting of computer machines involuntarily leads us to the need to create a model of the brain . . . Also, one of the most effective methods of studying intra-cerebral processes involve experiments carried out in electrical models of the brain . . . But cybernetics has its critics too. These are skeptics. One can find them among scientists and among ordinary citizens, at times also among administrative personnel. These skeptics reject this branch of science and deny it the right of existence . . . In rejecting this science, they

generally state that the very thought of comparing a machine to a human being is an insult.

(Moiseyev, 1960)

The majority of Soviet workers appear to recognize (implicitly, at least) the continuum discussed in this report, and argue that while there does exist an upper bound above which machines cannot go, it is not possible to determine the location of that bound. For example:

As a result we arrive at the conclusion that a machine can perform all the intellectual human functions which can be formalized . . . But what can be formalized? . . . Upon brief reflection we conclude that it is impossible in principle to answer this question.

(Kolman, 1960).

Where do the Russians stand?

First of all, let us look at what they are doing in those disciplines upon which research in artificial intelligence depends: computing devices, mathematics, psychology, and physiology. With respect to computers, I can speak with firsthand knowledge, for, as mentioned earlier, I spent two weeks in 1959 visiting Soviet computer installations. In my opinion, they are somewhat behind us in the actual construction of machines, particularly with respect to input/output equipment and to numbers of machines (Ware, 1960; Feigenbaum, 1961c). However, there is nothing fundamentally lacking in their state of the art. The quantity of machines is not as important to research as an offhand comparison of numbers of machines might indicate, since none of their machines is devoted to such things as social-security records, subscription fulfillment, or airline reservations. In assessing a comparison of this kind, one always wonders how much of the iceberg we do not see. When visiting the IBM plant in California, Khrushchev said about computers, ' . . . for the time being we're keeping them a secret.'

The Russians started work on computers after we did, but they have certainly narrowed the gap. Furthermore, they are giving high priority to the computing field. In their announcement concerning the decentralization of responsibility for research, an exception was made for computers, along with fusion, space activities, high-temperature metallurgical research, and certain areas of chemistry; these research areas remained centralized under the cognizance of the Academy of Sciences. Of course, the Russians are interested in spurring the computer field for reasons other than intelligent machine research. There is no reason to believe that future Russian research on intelligent machines need be hampered by the computer tools available to them, although machine time is in short supply today.

In mathematics the Russians have had an outstanding reputation for many decades. In computer mathematics I have no doubts that, in general, they excel the West. One of the things which impressed our delegation, and other delegations before ours (Carr *et al.*, 1959), was the number of outstanding mathematicians now working in the computer field. Unfortunately, many U.S. mathematicians view computers as a glorified slide rule of interest only to engineers, or as an expensive sorting device of interest to businessmen with clerical problems.

Since psychological research on mental processes and neurophysiological research on structure and activity of the brain both play a vital suggestive role in the attempt to construct intelligent machines, progress by the Soviets in these disciplines is of considerable interest. Although psychology was severely inhibited during the Stalin era, a renaissance of impressive proportions has taken place within the last decade. Physiology, less inhibited in the previous era, is in even better shape. The best available evidence indicates that Russian neurophysiology is dynamic, innovative, and up to date. The researchers are competent and generally sophisticated; their laboratories are modern and well equipped.

The Soviets have demonstrated a knack for focusing talent and resources on important applied problems. I believe that the Soviets regard artificial intelligence as one such problem area, and that the best of modern Soviet psychology and neurophysiology will be recruited into the search for solutions. With respect to physiological research, the following is of interest:

> Essentially, we (the Western World) have not found the physio-chemical principles of neural activity, whereas the Russians have not seriously sought them. However, the current 7-year plan for physiology as presented in a recent editorial by D. A. Biriukev in the Sechenov Physiological Journal of the USSR calls for precisely this goal.
>
> (Freeman, 1960)

A recent visitor of the USSR reports that Soviet physiologists appear to be under pressure to produce explanations for human behavior which can be incorporated into machines. He further reports that their work is apparently under security wraps.

Russian emphasis on artificial intelligence research

I went to the Soviet Union convinced they were putting a great deal of emphasis on research in artificial intelligence. Possibly this predisposition influenced what I thought I saw. I also want to emphasize that *I was impressed, not by any substantive results, but by their apparent conviction that this was an important research area.*

In one institute, in response to my question about the problem of simulating the brain with a computer, I was told 'It is considered *the* number one problem.' The emphasis on 'the' was the speaker's; the statement was made in English. At another institute, when Professor L. I. Gutenmacher, head of the Laboratory for Electrical Modeling, told us that the charter of his laboratory was the modeling of human mental processes, I asked him if he had difficulty obtaining financial support for such exotic research. His response was 'No, not at all; the President of the Academy of Sciences is convinced that this is an important field for research.' There is evidence that he has been given ample support. I was told that his laboratory, which was formerly (and still is ostensibly) a part of the Institute of Scientific Information, had all the status of an institute, being separately funded and reporting directly to the Presidium of the Academy of Sciences. Gutenmacher's laboratory is apparently responsible for mechanizing the functions of the Institute of Scientific Information, which is a large, centralized, information retrieval system for scientific information from all over the world.

Despite much effort, our delegation was unable to visit Gutenmacher's laboratory. To my knowledge, no Westerner has done so; in fact none had met Gutenmacher before our delegation. Some in the U.S. have concluded from this denial of entry to his laboratory that there was nothing to be shown. However, its work may be classified, as Khrushchev indicated. But whether or not anything is being accomplished is not pertinent to the point that the President of the Soviet Academy of Sciences, a man with much power and resources, believes that modeling human mental activities is possible, that he recognizes the importance of research in this field, and that he is devoting considerable resources to this end.

What are some of the other indications about Soviet attitudes toward research on intelligent machines? As previously mentioned, cybernetics is a household word in Russia. Much is being written on the subject, in journals and in the popular press. There appears to be an effort in the popular writings to legitimatize such research as being in harmony with communism. For example, recall the earlier quote about Marx (Klaus, 1960).

With respect to professional writing on machine intelligence, a journal entitled *Problems of Cybernetics* was started in 1958; seven hard-cover volumes have appeared to date (Lyapunov, 1960, 1961). Since 1955, seminars on cybernetics have been held at the University of Moscow. These seminars are aimed at bringing together scientists from various disciplines. Similarly, the editors of *Problems of Cybernetics* state that their aim 'is the unification of the scientific interests of those working in different fields of science concerned with cybernetics.'

There seems to be widespread recognition for the necessity of an inter-disciplinary approach to problems of cybernetics. Article after article appeals to personnel from the various disciplines to get together. How much effect these appeals and seminars have is unknown. During our visit to the Soviet Union, we were told that some 500 physicists had been transferred to the biological sciences. We talked with I. M. Gelfand, a world-famous mathematician now working in the physiological field. He began studying the brain but switched to the heart, which he believes to be much simpler. With knowledge gained from studying the heart, he will return to the study of the brain. We were also told that other mathematicians were working on psychological and physiological problems.

Within the Soviet Academy of Sciences, there exists a 'Scientific Council on Cybernetics.' This council is headed by A. I. Berg and apparently reports directly to the Presidium of the Academy (Berg, 1960). To my knowledge, there is no evidence of any effect this council may be having in coordinating, controlling, or encouraging research in cybernetics. Outside of Moscow, individual researchers appear to operate entirely on their own, with little communication with other such researchers, and with only meager support. However, one does occasionally encounter references to the formation of new groups and laboratories for such work.

There is some evidence that machine time (until recently in critically short supply) has been made available for work in this area. *Moscow News* of August 12, 1961, has an article on musical composition and medical diagnosis on a computer while the issue of September 2, 1961, discusses chess playing by machines and the deciphering of ancient Mayan manuscripts.

In closing this topic, a quotation which appeared in the February, 1959, issue of *Fortune* is pertinent. Frank Pace, Jr., then president of General Dynamics Corporation, in warning us not to overlook nor be surprised by Russia's capacity to concentrate in specific areas, said:

> If the area has real military or psychological value to them, they'll put massive concentration on it, and achieve results all out of proportion to the general level of their technical ability.

The importance of research in artificial intelligence

I have indicated my feeling that research aimed at pushing machines further out in the continuum of intelligence is very important. Today's computers are helping advance the frontiers of man's knowledge in many fields; computers now pervade almost all scientific disciplines. (The fact that they pervade the field of research on intelligent machines means that such research will feed on itself.) The use of computers in research has been a key factor in the explosion of knowledge we have witnessed in the last decade. Their contribution to date has stemmed largely from their speed in doing arithmetic and the reliability with which they do it. As we move out in the continuum of possibilities, new dimensions and contributions will become important. A machine which retrieves information from a large store by complex associative processes like those inherent in Willis Ware's output of 'Frizell,' but which exceeds Dr. Ware in speed, reliability, and memory capacity, would be crucial in aiding scientists to cope with the flood of research results presently inundating science.

The large amount of money spent on machines today is evidence of the value placed on the computers' abilities along the dimensions of speed and reliability. If the machine's capabilities can be extended in additional dimensions, would it not be of great importance? Suppose that the boundary (if it exists at all) beyond which machines cannot go lies fairly close to the human brain in the dimension related to the sophistication of the information processing techniques used. Since it is known that the machine can exceed the human in speed and reliability, and probably in amount of memory, such a machine would approach the status of being 'super-human.' Of course, this is speculation; the boundary may be much lower.

We have been examining the question of the technological importance of research in artificial intelligence in the context of advancing the frontiers of knowledge for the sake of technological and scientific advancement. In such a context, there is little cause for any concern or action; progress in the field is being made at a fairly rapid pace in this country. However, since we are engaged in a technological race with the USSR, action becomes important, particularly since, in my opinion, the Russians appear to be putting much more emphasis on research in artificial intelligence than we are. Even if the Russians were not competing in this particular event of the 'technological Olympics,' it is an event well worth the running in that we will learn more about man and in that better machines will contribute to advancing the frontiers of knowledge in almost every discipline.

Timing

Before closing, a comment on the question 'when?' It is one thing to say it is possible to push machine capabilities way out in the continuum of intelligence, but it is another thing to say when. It was over four hundred years from da Vinci to the Wright brothers. But the sands of time in the scientific world have been flowing much more rapidly of late. Advances now made in a decade compare with earlier steps which took a century. Few would have believed in 1950 that man would hit the moon with a rocket within ten years. Gutenmacher, when told recently of the Simon and Newell prediction that a machine would be chess champion within ten years (Newell and Simon, 1958d) said that he thought the prediction conservative; it would happen sooner.

Conclusion

It is hoped that the definition of research on artificial intelligence as an effort to push machines further out in the continuum of intelligent behavior will reduce some of the semantic difficulties surrounding discussions of such research. I feel that such research is very important to our country and that we must expand our efforts therein. To do so implies that more researchers from the related disciplines are needed. The success of our efforts will depend on how well we do in bringing the various disciplines together and on the number of well-qualified scientists who are attracted to this research area.

Notes

1 Almost an entire book, *Computers and Common Sense, The Myth of Thinking Machines*, has been devoted to condemning artificial intelligence research (Taube, 1961). Readers who have been exposed to this book should refer to reviews of it by Richard Laing (1962) and Walter R. Reitman (1962), particularly the former.
2 I make no distinction here between the attributes of the computer and those of the program which controls the computer.
3 The terms 'negativists' and 'positivists' are used in this report to classify those who do not and those who do, respectively, believe machines can exhibit intelligent behavior. Of course, variations of degree exist.

80

THE SOCIAL ACCEPTABILITY OF AI SYSTEMS

Legitimacy, Epistemology and Marketing

Romain Laufer

Source: *AI & Society* 6, 1992: 197–220.

Abstract. The expression, 'the culture of the artificial' results from the confusion between nature and culture, when nature mingles with culture to produce the 'artificial' and science becomes 'the science of the artificial'. Artificial intelligence can thus be defined as the ultimate expression of the crisis affecting the very foundation of the system of legitimacy in Western society, i.e. Reason, and more precisely, Scientific Reason. The discussion focuses on the emergence of the culture of the artificial and the radical forms of pragmatism, sophism and marketing from a French philosophical perspective. The paper suggests that in the postmodern age of the 'the crisis of the systems of legitimacy', the question of social acceptability of any action, especially actions arising out of the application of AI, cannot be avoided.

Keywords: Artificial intelligence; Culture of the artificial; Epistemology; Sophism: Common sense psychology; Social acceptability; Postmodernism; Aesthetics

1. Introduction

When discussing matters of culture it is often better to specify right away the cultural point of view from which one speaks. As for the following lines they are written from the point of view of modern western culture. In this culture it is customary to look for the meaning of words in the dictionary. Thus when Herbert Simon considers the meaning of the word artificial he notes: 'My dictionary proposes as synonym affected, false, fabricated, feigned, simulated, falsified, unnatural, and as antonym real, genuine, honest, natural, authentic, unaffected. Our language seems to reflect the deep distrust of man towards his own productions.'[1]

If language is a meaningful expression of a culture and of its system of value then we must acknowledge that the very notion of artificial is not completely congenial to modern western culture. The expression 'the culture of the artificial' is consequently somewhat paradoxical as culture defines usually what is valued in a given society. How can a culture be defined by a notion with respect to which it expresses distrust?

This contradiction is still greater when one considers the status of intelligence. Western culture can be characterized by the central role played in it by human intelligence. The role of intelligence in western culture is such that culture, under its most valued aspect, is often defined as that which is produced by the original and inventive activity of human mind, be they work of art or scientific discoveries. From that point of view the culture of the artificial implies the notion of artificial intelligence as its realization cannot be considered complete if the higher activities of the human mind escapes the realm of the artificial. Actually, the question of knowing whether artificial intelligence is possible, what is its scope and its limits, raises debates from time to time among computer scientists, philosophers, social thinkers or specialists of cognitive sciences. This debate opposes those who value it as the ultimate expression of the ability of man to understand the world (including the workings of one's mind) and of transforming it (by producing ever more sophisticated machines) and those who oppose it either on the ground that it is conceptually impossible being just an illusion generated by the overconfidence of western scientists as to their own power or, more simply, a hype used by those same scientists to obtain funding by selling the idea of AI to the naïve administrators (be they public or private), or on the grounds that it is the way in which human reason endangers the human species when it develops without restraints the resources of computer power. (For a more detailed typology of positions with respect to the social acceptability of AI see note 2).

The debate on the social acceptability of artificial intelligence can be considered both as the expression of the ambiguous status of the artificial in modern western culture and as a way of assessing the extent to which it could be said that we are witnessing the rise of the culture of the artificial.

Questions relative to AI imply three levels of analysis: the level of the conceptual definition, the level of the technological definition of AI and the level of the selling of AI, that is the level of its marketing. Analyzing each of these levels is extremely complex. As far as the conceptual definition of AI is concerned, the existing literature on the subject offers a wide variety of possibilities according to the disciplinary field or paradigm that one chooses: philosophy, logic, linguistics, neuro-science, cognitive science, psychology, computer science, etc. In the case of the definition of AI at a technological level, the complexity and the variety of present and futuristic approaches are coupled with the difficulty of assessing their practical consequences. As for the level of the marketing of AI, it requires a clear view of the mix of fear, enthusiasm and indifference which characterizes the various parts of the general public. From the very outset, the description of the complexity of the notion of AI points out one of the risks associated with A.I. systems, i.e. the risk of confusion when they are discussed.

This is why to study the social acceptability of AI we propose to depart from an analysis of AI as such, so as to devote our attention to the analysis of the way in which people discuss it. In order to deal with this issue in a precise manner, it is necessary to give a clear definition of what is meant by social acceptability. For this purpose, we suggest that social acceptability be defined as equivalent to the notion of legitimacy. Our main argument can be summarized in the following propositions:

1. Social processes can be defined at a symbolic level by using the notions of *legitimacy* and of *system of legitimacy*. It is possible to define in a precise manner the notions of legitimacy and of system of legitimacy, as well as that of *crisis of legitimacy*. This latter notion is related to the emergence of radical forms of pragmatism. Sophism and marketing are two specific examples of this kind of radical pragmatism.
2. Computers belong to information technologies, i.e. they can be considered as symbol-processing machines, a consequence being that machines of this kind lend themselves to a description at a symbolic level. System analysis, cybernetic models, formal logic, computer languages, artificial intelligence, are some of the numerous names given to the symbolic structures involved in computers.
3. It can be shown that the system of legitimacy of Western societies, i.e. free-market democracies, is characterized by the central place reason and science occupy in them. As a consequence, the issue of epistemology lies at the heart of the system of legitimacy of Western societies. Insofar as the notion of AI is linked to the notion of epistemology, one can understand why the debate on AI systems necessarily poses questions of social legitimacy, or social acceptability.
4. The system of legitimacy of our society is undergoing a crisis, which explains why the question of the social acceptability of any action in general (and of specific actions implying the use of AI systems in particular) cannot be avoided.
5. Artificial intelligence will be defined as the ultimate expression of the crisis affecting the very foundations of the system of legitimacy in our society, i.e. *Reason* and, more precisely, *Scientific Reason*.

These propositions will be dealt with in two sections, one devoted to the analysis of the link between legitimacy, epistemology, marketing and artificial intelligence (when considered as an artefact), the other describing how the history of the rational-legal system of legitimacy corresponds to the emergence of artificial intelligence (when considered as intelligence).[3]

2. Legitimacy, epistemology, marketing and artificial intelligence (as artificial)

2.1 The notion of system of legitimacy

A system of legitimacy can be defined as a process of conflict resolution which characterizes a given society. Let us consider an individual (any individual) acting in our society. Either the act is accepted (it is not objected to, no conflict is generated) or it is not (the act is objected to – possibly by the actor himself – and generates a conflict). If the act is accepted, there is nothing more to be said. If, on the contrary, someone objects to it, the actor will be addressed the question: 'Why have you done that?' The answer to this question, which is assumed to override the objections, is what we shall call the system of legitimacy of the actor.

We must note that this scenario is unavoidable in our society: given that people are not allowed to use violence to settle their conflicts, they must resort to words. This corresponds to the principle stated by Max Weber, according to which the state has the monopoly of legitimate violence. To evaluate the legitimacy of the answer given, we can in turn consider it as an act. Either the answer is accepted or it is rejected. If it is accepted, there is nothing more to be said (other than that it proved practically effective as a legitimate answer); if the answer is rejected, the actor may try another one. If, after several trials, the actor does not find a satisfactory answer, the conflict will be brought before the judge, as, once again, the use of violence is prohibited. The role of the judge is to then look into a special text (the Law) to state which proposition (the question or the answer) conforms to the legal rule, and is consequently legitimate. In principle, in our societies, when examining problems related to conflict resolution, only issues of legality should arise and certainly not issues of legitimacy. The fact that issues of legitimacy are raised reflects a crisis in the legal systems, which in turn reflects a crisis in the system of legitimacy of the society considered.

It is possible to sketch out rapidly what happens when such a crisis occurs: as the second level of conflict resolution (the judgement) does not function, the problem has to be solved at the first level, that of the direct interaction, or negotiation, between the actor and the objector. One solution for the actor consists in asking the objector what he wants and, once this is specified, giving him just that. This in fact is applying the logic of marketing: a market study is conducted to identify the demand than, an offer corresponding precisely to this demand is made. To those who would object that this procedure would be impossible for economic reasons, it can be argued that any demand can be divided in three parts corresponding to what is unbearable for the objector, what may please him without being too costly and the remainder. The principle of negotiation is that the first two parts must be granted, while the last one must be negotiated in order to arrive at an agreement as to which part of it should be satisfied.

2.1.2 System of legitimacy, power and epistemology

The notion of legitimacy was first proposed as a central concept in the analysis of social action by Max Weber at the beginning of this century. Max Weber defined three types of legitimate power: charismatic power, traditional power and rational-legal power.

Our argument will be based on the notion of a 'well-formed system of legitimacy'. By definition, a well-formed system of legitimate power requires a cosmology in which the world is divided into two loci: the locus where legitimate power originates and the locus where legitimate power is used. Charismatic power results from a cosmology in which the world is divided into two parts: the sacred and the profane, the profane being submitted to the sacred. Traditional power results from a cosmology in which the world is divided into two parts: nature and culture, nature being submitted to culture and its traditions. Rational-legal power results from a cosmology in which the world is divided into two parts: nature and culture, culture being submitted to nature insofar as it is conceived as following the laws of science. We can infer from these definitions that two cosmologies (sacred/profane, nature/culture) can only produce three systems, as the sacred cannot be legitimately subservient to the profane. We may note that to be able to see the above-mentioned dichotomies special spectacles are required. Without faith, one does not see the difference between the sacred and the profane, without respect, one does not see the difference between nature and traditional culture, without science one does not see the difference between culture and nature inasmuch as it follows the laws of nature. The French Revolution substituted charismatic and traditional legitimacy with the rational-legal system. The core of this legitimacy system is best represented by the case where science allows the difference between nature and culture to be seen. Epistemology is consequently a central element of our ideology. This is why, insofar as the issue of AI implies a judgement on epistemology, we can say that it is central to the definition of the rational-legal system of legitimacy.

We should perhaps give an example of the way science allows the laws of nature to govern men. At the heart of the legitimacy of free-market democracies lie the propositions of a science, namely political economy. This science states that if economic actors are small enough with respect to the market (that is if the conditions of pure and perfect competition are met), they may act as they please as long as they respect the right of property, for, in such a situation, the laws of market equilibrium guarantee that, whatever they do, the market will reach a given optimum provided all economic actors are profit maximizers.

2.1.3 Crisis of legitimacy, marketing, system analysis and artificial intelligence (as an artefact)

2.1.3.1 CRISIS OF LEGITIMACY AND ARGUMENTATION

The description we have just given of the kernel of 'well-formed' systems of legitimacy allows us to define the notion of crisis of legitimacy in a simple way: a crisis of legitimacy occurs when confusion develops between the two sides of the dichotomy, i.e. between the origin of legitimate power and the locus of the use of legitimate power (the sacred and the profane, culture and nature, nature and culture).

The consequence of this confusion is that it is no longer possible to take a structure of principles (for instance, nature as seen through science) as a starting point to define which actions are legitimate. In practice, it becomes necessary to develop legitimizing techniques which take into account the beliefs people have in the various systems of legitimacy (charismatic, traditional and rational-legal). Instead of starting from principles to define legitimate actions, we have to start from beliefs to determine an action which will be seen as legitimate. Once again, in the case of the crisis of legitimacy, we note the development of a technique which recalls the logic of marketing: one conducts a survey to know what people believe in and consequently devise ideas to persuade the same people who then cannot reject them as they fit precisely within the structure of their beliefs. This unpleasant but powerful logic has yet another name: sophism. Actually, it can be shown that marketing is nothing but the modern – bureaucratic – form of sophism. Perhaps we should further develop this point as it lies at the heart of our argument on AI.

2.1.3.2 MARKETING AND SOPHISM

In the philosophical tradition, sophists are known as the opponents of Socrates in Plato's dialogues. They were notorious for a variety of reasons: they did not believe in truth but only in opinion, they were considered as mercenaries who sold their talent for money, they believed that they could solve all problems with their only technique (rhetoric), they were suspected to be technicians who had no regard for tradition and who undermined it, finally they were disliked because they were foreigners. We may note that these reproaches are the same as those levelled at marketing. The only exception could be the last argument, for, if in Europe marketing is considered as originating from America, it actually did originate there and consequently cannot be considered as foreign, at least in the United States. However, one could argue that marketing was not invented by American natives but by the emigrants who constituted the melting pot.

Beyond common reproaches, sophism and marketing also share a positive definition: they are both radically pragmatical techniques of action. To define a technique of action we need three things: a method of knowledge a means of action and a goal. In both techniques the method of knowledge is subjective empiricism: the only thing that can be known is opinion. Protagoras said 'man is the measure of all things' and the marketer says 'do a market study'. In both the means of action is rhetoric, i.e. what we today call, communication. In both of these techniques success is the only goal.

However coherent the analogy between the structure of the debates which took place in the Agora (Athens' market place) in the 5th century BC and the persuasion process which takes place in the modern mass-mediated market place may be, it is surprising that similar phenomena would occur in circumstances so different. Nevertheless, it could be argued that what these two historical periods have in common is precisely the fact that they undergo a crisis of legitimacy. In Greece, it resulted from the confusion between the sacred and the profane. In the modern history of the Western world, it results from the confusion between nature and culture.

To be more specific about what happens to the rational-legal system of legitimacy when nature is confused with culture, we could ask ourselves what becomes of science in such circumstances.

2.1.3.3 SYSTEM ANALYSIS AND ARTIFICIAL INTELLIGENCE

The result of the confusion between nature and culture has a name: it is called the artificial (for the artificial can be defined as what is neither purely natural nor purely cultural). When nature mingles with culture to produce the artificial, science becomes the science of the artificial (instead of the science of nature). According to Herbert Simon, the science of the artificial is in fact the science of systems. Consequently, system analysis corresponds to what becomes of science in times of crisis of legitimacy.

At this stage, we need to specify what system analysis is. In our view, it consists in describing complex realities with 'circles' and 'arrows' (otherwise called 'entities' and 'flows'). It follows from this that 'circles' and 'arrows' constitute basic symbolic forms which correspond to the crisis of legitimacy affecting our rational-legal society. As cybernetics is in fact system analysis when a given entity is endowed with a feed-back mechanism which allows it to control its action, we may conclude that the emergence of the cybernetic model also corresponds to a state of crisis in the system of legitimacy of society. Insofar as computers are linked (through the very symbolic forms they use in their programming) to 'circles' and 'arrows', system analysis and cybernetic models, we can say that their development reflects the crisis of legitimacy of society. Thus, it is no surprise that the legitimacy of computers should be questioned.

As for artificial intelligence, the definition of the crisis of the rational-legal system is revealing: if the cosmos is now defined as artificial, i.e. as the result of the confusion between nature and culture, the question of the existence of artificial intelligence is not really an issue. The issue is rather to know how natural intelligence could be defined under the rule of the artificial. This means that the crisis of legitimacy allows, and even constrains, us to consider intelligence as falling under the category of the artefact. We can also note that, at this level, artificial intelligence does not depend upon the existence of a machine which is capable of achieving intelligence or on the specifications of such a machine, but only on the reality of the crisis of legitimacy of the rational-legal system as well as of the crisis of the epistemology which it implies.[4]

Before turning to a more careful examination of the epistemological dimension of the rational-legal system of legitimacy, it is interesting to show that marketing and AI are actually linked together in one of the seminal works of the AI literature, namely Turing's article on the intelligence of machines. Let us consider for a moment what is known as 'Turing's criterion': a machine can be said to be intelligent if someone interacting with it without seeing it cannot tell whether he is interacting with a machine or with a human being. This is actually a purely pragmatic argument and such a judgement is not based on scientific knowledge but on opinion.

3. History of the rational-legal system of legitimacy, epistemology and artificial intelligence (as intelligence)

3.1 The notion of 'natural' intelligence

The difficulty of defining AI, a difficulty which we stressed in our introduction, becomes even greater when we try to find out what constitutes 'natural' intelligence. A brief look in dictionaries[5] gives us at least three meanings. The first one (dating back to the twelfth century according to the French dictionary *Robert*) concerns the general capacity for knowledge and understanding; it refers to notions such as the soul, the mind, thought and reason. The second meaning concerns specific mental functions which allow conceptual and rational knowledge; it refers to notions such as abstraction, understanding, intellect. Finally, the third one (which the French dictionary *Robert* dates back to 1636) concerns the aptitude of any living being to adapt to new situations; when applied to humans it refers to notion such as industry, ingenuity, ability, invention, know-how or judgement, perspicacity and awareness.

Things become even more complicated when we look up the meaning of terms like understanding, intellect and mind in a philosophical dictionary: it is the whole history of Western philosophy that has to be considered through some of the most sensitive issues such as animism, materialism, vitalism, etc.

However, it is possible to identify a feature common to most of these definitions of intelligence: they are usually used to differentiate between various types of beings or various states of existence of a given being. Defining intelligence thus implies that a stand be taken on questions such as: What constitutes the difference between a living creature (which in some sense can be said to be intelligent) and inanimate objects? What constitutes the difference between men and animals? What constitutes the difference between man's pragmatic ability to adapt to new situations and his capacity to develop a conceptual form of knowledge? What constitutes the difference between the knowledge which precedes the acquisition of language, and the kind of knowledge which develops as a result of the acquisition of language? etc.

Thus intelligence is a notion which has a descriptive value: it allows to describe the order of the cosmos distinguishing between the living and the inanimate, man and animal, the infant and the child, the child and the man, and, within man himself, between the mind and the body, understanding, intellect and the other constituents of the mind, etc. However, beyond this descriptive value, intelligence has also the power to establish a hierarchical arrangement of the cosmos from the highest to the lowest kind of being.

In the 'intelligence' article of the *Encyclopedia Universalis*, referring to the philosophical and religious tradition, Jean-François Richard notes that 'Intelligence represents the function through which man tried to define himself in the hierarchy of the beings, that is to say to situate himself with respect to his inferior, the animal, and with respect to his superior, the divinity'. He adds that ' ... with respect to the animal, intelligence has been defined in terms of difference while, with respect to the divinity, intelligence has been defined in terms of resemblance'.[6]

What has made the establishment of rational-legal democracy possible in modern times is the development of a conception of scientific knowledge of which man's reason is the only warrant. The formula of the 'self-foundation' of the legitimacy of knowledge can be stated as follows: how would it be possible that by his own endeavour an individual be able to produce objective knowledge? This question has been answered by distinguishing in man's intelligence the part which allowed him to have access to a scientific representation of natural laws (whether it is called thought, perception or understanding) and to give it a specific – 'philosophical' – status.

From this point of view, it is possible to define two antagonistic views of man's intelligence: a pragmatic view which considers it as a set of manifestations open to psychological inquiry, and a philosophical view which considers it as the locus of the very structure which allows man to know the world.

The 'self-foundation' of man's legitimacy on his own reason implies a division of the self which seems to oppose the unlimited exercise of self-examination. Philosophical systems generate differences and hierarchies within the individual which tend to exclude psychology from the realm of science.

Before turning to the way in which these differences and hierarchies are organized in the major epistemological paradigms which characterize the rational-legal system of legitimacy, we shall show how it is possible to sketch the main features of the history the rational-legal system of legitimacy through the analysis of legal systems.

3.2 The history of the rational-legal legitimacy system

As the history of the rational-legal system of legitimacy is particularly easy to describe in the case of French institutions, we will deal with this particular example. However, a similar analysis could reveal a comparable history in all Western free-market democracies. In France, to guarantee the separation of powers (especially between the judicial and the executive powers), a special body of judges has been created to monitor the public sector. Thus, courts have to decide what comes under either of the two legitimacy systems, the private and the public. They do so according to the 'criterion of administration law'. This makes it possible to identify the history of this criterion, (i.e. the history of the legitimacy of the public sector) with the history of social legitimacy. According to all text books on the topic this history develops in three stages separated by two transition periods.

The first stage (from 1800 to 1880/1900) corresponds to the 'Public Power Criterion': all activities carried out by civil servants are public. In the Garrison State legitimacy lies in the origin of power. The second stage (from 1880/1900 to 1945/1960) corresponds to the 'Public Service Criterion': anything done to render a public service is public. In the Welfare State, legitimacy lies in the finality of power. The third stage (from 1945/1960 to this date) corresponds to the 'crisis of Administrative Law Criterion', i.e. to the crisis of legitimacy of the public sector and consequently to the crisis of social legitimacy in general. The hypothesis we propose is that, from now on, the public sector's legitimacy will lie in the methods of power.

Three conclusions may be drawn from this brief historical sketch: 1) The history of the rational-legal legitimacy system follows the above three periods; 2) These three periods correspond to the succession of the following means of legitimation: through the origin of power, through the finality of power, through the method of power and; 3) In this third period the rational-legal system of legitimacy is undergoing a crisis.

This crisis is characterized by the breaking down of legal categories and especially of the dichotomy between the public and the private sectors. The destiny of this dichotomy in turn corresponds to the stages of the crisis of the limit between nature and culture.

Actually, each stage of the history of the legitimacy of the rational-legal system corresponds both to a state of the distinction between the public and the private sectors which is characterized by a legal doctrine, and to a state of the distinction between nature and culture which is characterized by corresponding scientific paradigms. It is to the description of these paradigms that we now turn our attention.

3.3 The three scientific paradigms of the rational-legal system

3.3.1 Preliminary remarks: a French perspective

As in the case of the analysis of legal systems, we must point out that, if we do propose the hypothesis that there is a common pattern among all Western free-market democracies with respect to the history of epistemology, we do acknowledge that there are cultural differences which account for the variety of national philosophical traditions. Some of these traditions make very different use of notions such as psychology and intelligence which lie at the heart of our analysis. Given the complexity of these traditions and of the interaction between them (for philosophy is both a barrier and a link between the various components of the Western world), given the limitations of our knowledge, the analysis will be confined to a French perspective where the hypothesis proposed is well documented. As for other traditions, we shall make a few comments after the core of the analysis, to suggest how it could be generalized.

3.3.2 The scope of our analysis

In the following sections, we shall distinguish three major epistemological paradigms which, as we shall show, correspond to each of the historical periods outlined above.

According to our discussion, in order to serve as the basis of a system of legitimacy, an epistemological paradigm must conform to the requirements of the self-foundation of reason on itself. The requirements consist of the division of the self through some *a priori* construction which limits the extension of legitimate self-examination. This is why we are going to focus our attention on what Bergson called 'the immediate data of consciousness' and to the way in which philosophical systems try to limit their power on our thinking. Among the various ways of describing immediate data of consciousness, we shall deal more specifically with the modalities of the relationships between the subject of knowledge and the object of knowledge, logic, common sense, psychology and opinion. The extent to which the immediate data of consciousness are considered for their own sake is a measure of the degree of pragmatism of the epistemological paradigm considered.

At the same time, we shall specify the status of sophism as it is expressed explicitly in each of the philosophical positions considered. Despite the fact that sophism is only quoted marginally in the philosophical literature (because of the tradition which dates back to Aristotle's *Sophistic Refutations* when a definitive condemnation of sophism was assumed to have been reached),[7] we shall note that this notion is always used in a very precise manner and gives a valuable indication of the moment when the crisis of legitimacy occurs in epistemology.

Finally, we shall describe the status of the scientific debate corresponding to each epistemological position. It will be possible to answer the following five questions: 1) Is a debate necessary? 2) Is a consensus necessary? 3) Who should participate in it? 4) What arguments are legitimate? and: 5) Is a consensus possible?

3.3.3 The three scientific paradigms of the rational-legal system

'It can be shown that the three major scientific paradigms of the rational-legal system correspond to three logical situations which can be defined with respect to the legitimation of actions. Let us give the following phenomeno-logical definition of an action: an action is *a change in appearance inasmuch as it is referred to a cause*. Starting from this definition, it can be shown that it is possible to distinguish three different situations with respect to the logic of the legitimation of an action, which we are going to consider in the next three sections. Let us note first that, in order to keep the size of the present paper within reasonable length, the mechanics of each scientific paradigm will not be developed in detail. We shall limit ourselves to summarizing their main consequences on our topic.[8]

3.3.3.1 FIRST CASE: WE CAN DEFINE A LEGITIMATE CAUSE

Main features of the paradigm: If we can define a legitimate cause (for instance nature) we define by the same token the origin of legitimate power. This corresponds to a non-pragmatic system of legitimacy–legitimacy does not rest on the consequences of action – and more precisely to the Kantian epistemology. The legitimacy of science lies in the origin of knowledge, i.e. in the intellectual faculties of men when these are properly used. The typical sciences which correspond to this model are Newtonian physics, which was the basis of Kant's analysis of science, and classical political economy, which was produced by taking physics as a model. In this epistemology we find neither complexity, nor artifacts: simple laws are reached directly and the mathematical structures which allow them to be expressed quantitatively are nothing but the expression of the structure of nature itself. The Kantian epistemology which allows the legitimation by the origin of power (the submission to the laws of nature) was to dominate during the XIXth century.

Relationship between the object of knowledge and the subject of knowledge:
Kant's contribution is essential in that he solved the problem by dividing
symbolically both the object of knowledge and the subject of knowledge.
The object is divided into the noumenon which is unknown and remains
such, and the phenomenon which lends itself to the effort of man's understanding through the *a priori* categories of perception, time and space, while
leaving human reason unaffected.

Knowledge was thus separated in three parts: the analytic part (logical, *a
priori*, 'Cartesian'), the synthetic part (empirical, *a posteriori*, 'human') and
the synthetic, *a priori*, part which is made possible by the existence of the
transcendental aesthetic (time and space), the latter being the necessary condition of the existence of Newton's Law. In this context, man is both the
only producer of his own knowledge (knowledge is empirical) and the only
warrant of his knowledge (man has access to transcendental categories in his
own right).

Epistemology is the law knowledge must obey to in order to gain the
certainties of the knowledge of the laws of nature, which in turn will provide
man with a legal system to which he will submit willingly, being the sole
author of this elaboration. Such is the simple formula of the self-foundation
of man's legitimacy. However, to survive, such a system requires that a set of
prohibitions protect shared symbols from the risk of confusion. This is why
Kant draws precise limits in the fields of logic, psychology, opinion and
sophism.

Logic: Logic is important to Kant as it is the basis of all analytical deductions: it has to be the locus of certainty. Kant himself wrote a treaty of logic
which remains strictly Aristotelian in its conception.[9] However, the examination of the foundations of logic is limited by the proposition of the Critique
of Pure Reason, according to which logical error can only result from a lack
of attention.[10]

Common sense psychology: In the Critique of Pure Reason Kant states that
the only thing that can be said about rational psychology is that it is not a
doctrine which adds something to the knowledge we have of ourselves.[11] In
the same work he states that 'empirical psychology must therefore be ban-
ished from the sphere of metaphysics and is indeed excluded by the very idea
of that science'. The rejection of psychology by Kant was a question of
principle (i.e. it might not find a place in the three critiques) and not of fact
as he wrote many texts on these matters, especially in his 'Anthropology
considered from a pragmatic point of view'.[12]

Opinion: plays no specific role in the epistemology as everyone has access to
the 'spectacles' of knowledge.

Sophism: Kant explicitly excludes the possibility of sophistic reasoning by the way he deals with the antinomies of pure reason. He shows that the contradictions between statements on the mathematical and the physical worlds are only apparent. The link between the antinomy of pure reason, sophism and the question of psychology is stressed in the observations of the second antimony when Kant states: 'The second dialectical assertion is characterized by the particularity of having as its opposite a dogmatic proposition, which, among all such sophistical statements, is the only one that undertakes to prove in the case of an object of experience, that which is properly a transcendental idea: the absolute simplicity of substance. The proposition is that the object of the internal sense, the thinking Ego, is an absolute simple substance'.[13]

The status of scientific debate. The status of scientific debate is reduced to a minimum for as soon as any citizen has put on his epistemological spectacles, and perhaps polished them a little by a more or less detailed reading of the *Critique of Pure Reason*, he finds the only science (mathematics and physics as a unified corpus of knowledge on the laws of nature) and its certitude. As soon as the laws of nature are recognized, what conforms to them is, by definition, socially acceptable.

3.3.3.2 THE SECOND CASE: SOME CONFUSION IS INTRODUCED BETWEEN NATURE AND CULTURE, LEGITIMACY LIES IN THE MEASURES OF THE CHANGE IN THE APPEARANCE.

Main features of the paradigms: The germ of the crisis of legitimacy being introduced in the system in the form of some degree of confusion between nature and culture, one can no longer tell if the cause of the action is legitimate. Henceforth the legitimacy of the action will have to depend on the measure of the change in the appearances. This pragmatism can be considered as moderate if it can be assumed that there is a consensus on the unit of measurement. This corresponds to the positivistic epistemology developed by Auguste Comte.

The legitimacy of science now resides in the finality of knowledge. This finality is reached when those who know how to attain the right finalities (the specialists) put themselves at the service of those who know what finality should be pursued (public opinion). Consequently, men no longer have equal access to knowledge: some know (the specialists) while others only know that scientists know. In addition, by definition all specialists only have access to a specific sphere of knowledge which has its own unit of measurement. Thus, we see that a certain degree of complexity has emerged in our representation of knowledge. At the same time, as complexity enters the picture of the world, artefacts start to play a role. For Auguste Comte, mathematics is much less valuable as a science than as a tool which allows to measure nature in the various fields of scientific knowledge.

To guarantee the stability of the unit of measurement an hypostasis is required: such is the function of the God of Auguste Comte. To guarantee a consensus on the measure of the consequences of an action, this hypostasis must be oriented: it must be some kind of divinized Progress.

The emergence and the development of the various fields of science is the result of a 'natural' process of progress. We may note that the whole construction of Comte's positivism lies in the principle of specialization and on the strict exclusion of multidisciplinarity.

The positivist epistemology was dominant (from the point of view of the social system of legitimacy) in the first half of the 20th century from 1880/1900 to 1945/1960.

Relationship between the object of knowledge and the subject of knowledge: In positivism, the separation between the object of knowledge and the subject of knowledge is realized in two manners. First, science being the study of closed systems, the separation is not so much a symbolic structure within the scientist and his object as it is a material separation between them: usually a box or a bottle in which the experiment takes place. The second separation is a sociological one. The Kantian division between sensibility, understanding and reason could be paralleled with the sociological difference between the individual scientist, the community of scientists, and Public Opinion considered as the 'Court of Universal Common Sense'. The parallel could be further extended by stating that the set of methods elaborated by the 'specialists of generalities' play a role analogous to *a priori*; categories of perception as they define the conditions of scientific observation.

Logic: Auguste Comte ' . . . mistrusts an abstract theory of numbers and an arithmetic considered for itself; he rejects the idea of a mathematical logic when it presents itself in the aspect of a general theory of signs or of a project of a universal language: too much abstraction, excessive formalization is contradictory to the positivist spirit'.[14]

Common sense psychology: As for psychology, August Comte forcefully rejects what he calls 'the deplorable psychological fad which a famous sophist had temporarily inspired the French youth.'[15]

The rejection of psychology is linked to the work of Comte the sociologist, the theoretician of social organization, to the rejection of the very notion of the individual as being 'metaphysical'. In the same line he rejected the cellular theory from biology as being ' . . . a fantastical theory and moreover, one that obviously comes from an essentially metaphysical system of general philosophy'.

As Canguilhem puts it 'Comte does not admit . . . that the life of an organism is the sum of particular lives anymore than, contrary to the philosophy of the 18th Century, he admits that society is an association of individuals'.

For Auguste Comte 'the famous theory of the self is essentially without any scientific purpose since it is designed solely to represent a purely fictitious condition'.

Opinion: As we have already noted, Opinion now plays a limited role within the epistemological paradigm itself. Non-specialists are entitled to their opinion as they constitute, as a whole, the 'court of universal common sense'. The role of their opinion is limited to an evaluation of the practical usefulness of the knowledge developed by scientists. As for what constitutes knowledge, the scientists are the only ones to be endowed with the authority to decide. The knowledge thus produced, or at least the idea that such a knowledge exists, must be transmitted through pedagogy.

Sophism: When dealing with psychology, we noted that Auguste Comte rejects sophism. We may also observe that the rejection of multidisciplinarity recalls the rejection of the polymathy of the sophists by the philosophical tradition (polymathy meaning the assumption that it is possible to deal with any problem with a single method of action: rhetoric).

The status of scientific debate: Scientific debate takes two forms. The first one concerns the scientists themselves and especially the relationship between the specialists of each field and the specialists of generalities; its goal is to establish a minimum common set of scientific methods. The other one concerns the relationship between the scientific community and public opinion.

In this framework: 1) The debate is necessary; 2) Consensus is necessary, otherwise anarchy could generalize; 3) All participate in it but not at the same time: scientists should discuss amongst themselves, then listen to the objection of public opinion while public opinion listens to the teachings of scientists; 4) From the point of view of scientific method, the legitimate arguments come from the scientist; from the point of view of social welfare, the legitimate arguments come from public opinion gathered in a 'Court of Universal Common Sense'; 5) By the very definition of the positivistic epistemological paradigm, consensus is possible.

3.3.3.3 THE THIRD STAGE: THE CONSENSUS ON THE UNIT OF MEASUREMENT DISAPPEARS.

Main features of the paradigm: If the consensus on the unit of measurement disappears (or if the belief in the divinized Progress disappears), it no longer becomes possible to guarantee the legitimacy of an action through the measure of 'the change in the appearance'. Complete confusion then reigns between nature and culture and the most radical form of pragmatism.

The confusion between nature and culture being called the artificial, science becomes the science of the artificial, which, according to Herbert Simon, is nothing but the science of systems. But the science of the artificial is not a science in the usual sense of the word. Actually it is an 'art', a technique: the art of simulation. The art of simulation consists of choosing the right specifications for the model, specifications that will tell us what the entities are and when flows must be singled out. Consequently, it is possible to define system analysis as the description of complex realities with 'circles' and 'arrows'. The determinism of processes which characterized the science of nature as described by Kant or Comte is no longer guaranteed. To come back to the issue of the legitimation of action, the question is to know how one can measure it, i.e. how a consensus on the measure of the change of appearance may be reached. The answer is extremely pragmatic: measurement itself must be considered as an action: it will be said to be legitimate inasmuch as people consider it as such. The legitimacy of science now lies in the methods used to measure (what will be called henceforth methodology), the good measure being the measure accepted by the public concerned. Contrary to what happened in the preceding period, consensus of opinion cannot be assumed *a priori* henceforth consensus is what one must continuously produce by one's own action.

We have now entered the logic of sophism itself, and we have noted that even Simon recognizes the mistrust associated with the very notions of the artificial, the artefact or, even worse, simulation, the connotations of which seem to be opposed to the notions of truth, honesty, authenticity.[16] He adds that these negative connotations carried by language seem to reflect the feeling of distrust man tends to experience toward his own creations. This remark addresses the very question raised by the self-foundation of man's legitimacy.

Through the role it gives to appearance, opinion, analogy, multidisciplinarity and relativity, system analysis reflects the crisis of classical epistemology. Its prominence as a dominant 'epistemological' paradigm corresponds to the third period of the history we have just sketched. Let us stress again that the concepts and symbols which characterize this epistemological paradigm are the same as those which characterize computers. This makes it possible to associate computers directly with the crisis of the system of social legitimacy and thus to explain why questions of social acceptibility are always associated with their development.

We can therefore understand why, inasmuch as they are computer systems and, as such, are directly linked to the crisis of the system of social legitimacy, A.I. systems are questioned as to their social acceptability.

Confusion between the subject of knowledge and the object of knowledge: The confusion between the subject and the object may be defined by the fact that knowledge now depends on the very 'immediate data of consciousness' that Kant and Comte had discarded through the two fundamental prohibitions concerning the questioning of logic and the direct consideration of common sense psychology.

Before turning to a more detailed analysis of this topic, it may be useful to draw an important conclusion from the idea of the confusion between the subject of knowledge and the object of knowledge: this confusion implies that it is impossible to consider man separately from the machine he faces, wondering whether it is intelligent. What exists is always a subject/object, man/machine mix.

Logic and perception: The epistemology of the third period is characterized by the importance given to a careful examination of the logical foundations of knowledge, and by the ambiguities which progressively invaded this field of study. The immediate data of consciousness cannot provide the basis of 'objective' (shared) knowledge if no reference is made to some warrant. For some time, logic seemed to be the ideal building block with which a shared representation of the world could be constructed. The effort to derive science from analytic deductions can be described as the result of a history which starts with Kant, continues with Bolzano and culminates in Frege's logicism[17] Similarly, it is possible to follow the discussions which opposed Carnap and Popper on how to define the atoms of the observations which were to constitute the basis of empirical knowledge: neither the method of protocol statements proposed by Carnap, nor the definition of 'basic statements' proposed by Popper allowed to specify these data without ambiguity or without having to refer to a pragmatic consensus.

The possibility of building sound representation of the world is the topic developed by Wittgenstein in the Tractatus. His disatisfaction with it and the unending questioning of the meaning of words and gestures which he pursued throughout his life are, perhaps, the best illustrations of the difficulties which henceforth plagued modern epistemology when it tried to lean on logic or observation.

Sophism: It may be useful to note that the most respected representatives of modern epistemology defined themselves explicitly as being related to the sophists as they oppose the philosophical tradition represented by classical epistemological positions: such is the case of the Vienna Circle in the famous text on *the scientific conception of the world* (1931), or of Karl Popper in his book on *the open society and its enemies*, when he states: 'Everything can be reached by man and man is the measure of all things. Here the connection with the sophists and not the Platonicians becomes obvious . . . '[18]

Common sense psychology: The third period is characterized by the growing interest devoted to psychology in general and to psychological concepts such as intelligence. This in turn may be linked to the place given to the notion of artificial intelligence. To understand the way in which common sense psychology eventually occupied a major place in the analysis of human behavior, we would have to examine in detail the conflict between the philosophical approaches of the human mind and the scientific approaches of human behavior. Given the limits of our presentation, we shall only outline the way in which the various traditions of psychology are connected and how they converge toward a situation where psychology plays a central role in the very analysis of epistemology itself. The most accomplished form of common sense psychology was proposed by William James in his 'Principles of Psychology'. This direct approach to common sense psychology was only possible because James was also the founder of pragmatism as a philosophy. The relationship between common sense psychology, pragmatism and sophism can be traced back to Schiller who claimed to be 'Protagorean'.[19] This radical form of common sense psychology was not compatible with the requirements of less pragmatic scientific or philosophical approaches. This is why behaviorism developed as a reaction against the obscurities of introspection.

Behaviorism tried to develop a scientific approach to psychology that would avoid the difficulties linked with the study of oneself. 'They renounced' the 'mentalistic' vocabulary of folk psychology as 'prescientific mumbo-jumbo'. Watson derided folk psychological concept as 'heritages of a timid savage past of a piece with 'superstition', 'magic', 'voodoo''[20] This compliance of behaviorism with epistemological criteria could fit, for instance, the neo-positivist framework. However, this produced a sharp conflict between two opposed visions of man.[21] Skinner later took it upon himself 'to demonstrate that we could live with behaviorism'.[22] To do so he borrowed a few concepts from folk psychology and 'reinterpreted them with terms drawn from the lexicon of behavioristic psychology'. Finally, frustration from these approaches led in the 60's to the reintroduction of 'mentalistic' concepts such as reasoning, problem solving, inference, perception, imagery, memory, etc to build the new field of cognitive science.[23] We may note that this return to the concept of the psychology of common sense has been accompanied by efforts to model cognitive theories on computers.

We could also mention the phenomenological tradition with which Husserl tried to depart from psychologism (be it that of Brentano's psychology of intention) through the discovery of a new cartesian-like starting point. Doing this was confronting the risk of sophism, as Husserl states: 'This negative scepticism (that of Protagoras and Gorgias) oriented towards practice and ethics (politics) was lacking what will still be missing later, that is the original cartesian theme. This original theme, which is nothing but the crossing of hell, may allow, through a quasi sceptic *épochè* that nothing can surpass, to force through the heavenly threshold of an absolutely rational philosophy'.[24] It may be possible to trace one of the outcomes of this heroic effort to the conference on perception Maurice Merleau Ponty gave to the French Society of Philosophy in 1984. A conference where he derived his argument both from Husserl and from the results of the Gestalt psychology. In the debate that followed Emile Brehier accused Merleau Ponty's 'relativism' of being merely 'protagorism'.

Finally, we may note that, according to Piaget, epistemology is to be founded on psychology instead of being constructed against it. As for its contents, the development pattern of man's intelligence is formalized in systemic terms: it results from a process of adaptation to its environment. In addition, according to one of his followers, Piaget's major ideas are quite similar to those of the early cognitivists.[25]

Opinion: The crisis of the rational-legal system is the crisis of reason, and consequently the crisis of philosophy which is the discipline which tells us what reason is. The crisis of philosophy is sophism. We have seen that what characterizes sophism is that opinion is the criterion of knowledge and that the study of opinion becomes a major source of knowledge. This expresses itself in all spheres of social life – opinion polling has become standard practice in politics since Paul Lazarsfeld in 1941 conducted his studies in Erie County in the USA, in business the rise of marketing and of market study exemplify the domination of the point of view of public opinion (the famous 'consumer') upon the point of view of specialists (be they technicians or 'scientific' managers), even in the field of art public opinion is becoming so important that recently a French review called *Beaux – Arts* thought it could find nothing better to celebrate its own ninth anniversary than to organize an opinion poll about what the public considered as art.[26] In this context 'Turing's criterion' which is based on opinion alone is perfectly coherent with this stage of the evolution of epistemology where no difference can be defined *a priori* and where no category can be legitimate unless it is recognized as such by the opinion of those who are going to use it in their Judgements.

The status of the debate: At this point we may consider the structure of the debate on science: 1) This debate is necessary, it cannot be avoided as the crisis of legitimacy implies a crisis of epistemology which in turn implies that people may object to the legitimacy of what is produced as knowledge; 2) Anyone may participate in this debate, as opinion is the only acceptable criterion and everyone is entitled to have an opinion of their own. All the debates may take place at the same time: i.e. the value of the debate between scientists depends on the way the rest of the public perceives their discussion (and also on the way in which they have been selected as specialists); 3) Similarly, scientists must be aware of the opinion of the public so as to orient their activities in a way that will seem acceptable to the public; 4) All possible arguments, especially those relating to intelligence, considered in a very pragmatic way, become quite legitimate, if not necessary, as they replace notions such as understanding or intellect which were the product of an *a priori* difference built into man's 'psyche'; 5) Consensus is not possible on any *a priori* basis, it can only appear as the result of persuasion and negotiation.

3.3.3.4 REMARKS ON THE CASE OF ENGLAND AND OF THE UNITED STATES

We are well aware that our description of the prohibition and of the resurgence of psychology which fits the French case could very well be considered as inappropriate in the case of England where psychology has never been rejected, or in the case of the United States where the very notion of intelligence plays a central role in the philosophical tradition. For lack of time and knowledge, we cannot provide a complete answer to these objections. However, we would like to propose that a similar analysis (parallel if not identical) to the one we have led could be conducted in these two cases. This belief is linked to the history of the legal system of these two countries which follow a pattern similar to that of the French history: the same three periods make sense in both countries. However the intellectual history of each of these countries are quite different indeed.

In the case of England, the solution may come from the remark that the psychology of philosophers (Hume, Locke, J. S. Mill) is often a philosophical psychology, in which conceptual notions, such as atomism, play a crucial role *a priori*. In the case of the United States, the problem is more delicate. A first direction of the analysis would consist in relating the use of the word intelligence by James or Dewey to the very pragmatic character of their philosophy. This would be in keeping with the fact that the use of the word intelligence is usually the sign of a time of pragmatism.[27] However, it is obvious that American pragmatism does not correspond (as in the case of France) to a period of crisis of legitimacy as such. The compatibility of pragmatism and legitimacy could be explained by the central role of religion in the philosophy of the United States. In such a context, the crisis of legitimacy would take the form of a pragmatism freed from the protection of religion and only confronted to science at the very moment when science enters a period of crisis of legitimacy.

3.3.3.5 ARTIFICIAL INTELLIGENCE AS INTELLIGENCE.

Let us quote H. Dreyfus at the very beginning of his argumentation against the existence of AI:

'Since the invention by the Greeks of logic and geometry, the idea that any reasoning could be reduced to a kind of calculus – so that any discussion could find its final conclusion once and for all – has fascinated all the rigorous thinkers of Western tradition. Socrates was the first to formulate this vision of things. It could very well be that artificial intelligence dates back to 450 BC, to the day when, according to Plato, Socrates asks his fellow countryman Euthyphron who was getting ready to denounce his father as a murderer: 'I want to know what characterizes this faith which transforms any action in a pious gesture ... that I am able to invoke it, and to use it as a standard of measurement with which I could judge your actions and those of other people'. What Socrates asks for from Euthyphron is what our modern theoretician of the computer would call an 'operating procedure', 'a set of rules which tells us with precision. step by step, what to do'. Plato extends this question for moral certitude in the direction of an epistemological quest.'[28]

In order to show that this objection to Plato and Socrates itself belongs to a tradition, it might be interesting to read the following quote from the Philosophy of Experience by William James:

'Intellectualism, in the negative meaning of the word, began when Socrates and Plato started teaching that the definition of a thing reveals to us what the thing really is. Since Socrates, we have always been taught that reality is made of essences not appearances, and that we know the essences of things when we know their definitions. Thus, we start by identifying the thing with a concept; then we identify this concept with a definition, and it is only then, insofar as the thing is what the definition expresses – whatever this definition does express – that we are certain to apprehend such a thing in all its truth'.[29]

These quotations deserve a few comments:

1. The relationship between both quotations shows that Dreyfus is, in his critique, very close to the positions of pragmatism.
2. The opponents of Plato and Socrates in Greece were the sophists. They were those who, in Plato's dialogue, both accepted and refused to play the game of 'what is the definition of ... ' mainly by not accepting the principle of non-contradiction.
3. We find in the quotation of Dreyfus' book the relationships between epistemology and systems of legitimacy, which is at the heart of our argument.
4. Let us recall what we have noted above about the nature of intelligence. First, the remark (taken from the article of the *Encyclopedia Universalis*) that in theological tradition man's intelligence was defined in terms of difference with respect in animals, and in terms of resemblance with respect to God. Second, that, to found a system of legitimacy on reason, man has to divide himself (his intelligence pragmatically defined as it

results from a completely open examination of the expression of his thinking, feelings and behavior) into two parts, of which, one (reason, intellect, understanding) serves to establish the certainty to which the other part is subservient.

Moreover, we can add the consequence of what we have stated from the start about systems of legitimacy, i.e. that there must be simple symbolic structures so that everybody in the community can recognize them without any hesitation.

We now get to the idea that: a) The part of the intelligence' which is going to be selected as the superior part will be composed of those results of science which the Western tradition has always considered as a miracle: the product of the 'Greek miracle';b) The rest of human intelligence will be modelled to the resemblance to the 'rational' part, as in theological times man's intelligence was referred to that of the divinity.

5. From this we can deduce the following choice for a man situated in the tradition of reason who wants to reject the idea that 'artificial intelligence' is an acceptable notion: either he defines intelligence or he does not. If he does not, then he excludes himself from the western rational tradition which is the foundation of the social system of free-market democracies. If he does give a definition, then, whether it is philosophical or scientific (and as such submitted to philosophy through epistemology), he will be able to avoid neither the formalization, the mechanization, the simplification which characterizes the Western tradition of reasons, nor the fact that the crisis of reason, which results in a breakdown of the limit between what is 'superior' and what is 'inferior' in the mind confronts us with the issue of the meaning of human experience, and especially of what we call intelligence.

The solution Dreyfuss finds for this dilemma is the references to Heidegger's philosophy. The discussion of this choice (which also attracts the votes of Winograd and Flores) is obviously quite complex, as it depends on the interpretation given to Heidegger's work: sophism, mystique, technology, irrationalism, all have their part of the these interpretations and all seem to indicate the central theme of the crisis of the classical conception of reason.

6. In essence, AI cannot be disproved because to disprove is to prove and AI is nothing but the expression of the somewhat shaky status of proof today.

4. Concluding remarks

The notion of system of legitimacy allows to understand both the distrust with which the artificial is considered in our society and the reason why it is nevertheless possible to speak of a culture of the artificial. To the extent that modern western culture is founded on the submission of all beings to the

365

laws of nature, the artificial, which *Webster* defines as the 'unnatural' cannot belong to the sphere of the legitimation of actions: it has to remain limited and submitted to the laws of nature, to the extent that the western world is undergoing a crisis of legitimacy it is characeried by the confusion of the nature and culture i.e. by the reign of the artificial.

Modern western culture as characterized by the rational-legal system of legitimacy supposes that techniques which are artefacts remain submitted to science, that opinion remains submitted to the truths to which the human mind has access thanks to its own natural abilities. The crisis of legitimacy of the rational-legal system corresponds to the confusion between science and artefacts, the rise of 'techno-science', and to the confusion of opinion and scientific truth which is best exemplified by the provocative epistemological writing of a physicist, Feyerabend, when he declares: 'always bear in mind that the demonstration and rhetoric which I use express no deep conviction on my part. They only show how easy it is to lead people by the nose in a rational way. An anarchist is like a secret agent who plays the game of Reason to undermine the authority of Reason (truth honesty, justice, etc . . .).'[30]

Epistemology, which is a part of philosophy was the central element of the modern western system of legitimacy as it legislated on things (through physics for instance) and on people (through political-economy). The crisis of legitimacy corresponds to the crisis of epistemology which is itself becoming a technique, an art of rhetoric. As for philosophy we have seen that it takes the form of that unique dogmatic sentence which allows sophistic to mimic philosophy this sentence being 'all is rhetoric'. Consequently AI exists to the extent that someone interacting with a machine can be made to doubt whether one interacts with a human being or with a machine, this corresponding to the famous 'Turing's Criterion'. To the extent that the extension of the notion of the artificial can legitimately be considered as being submitted, *de jure*, to no *a priori* limit we can say that we are living in a *Culture of the Artificial* if culture is meant there to define in a very general manner all our ways of doing things. It remains to know whether this constitutes a *Culture* to the extent that a culture would be characterized by some unifying principle which allows to give meaning to actions.

Judgement about a given culture can only be made from the point of view of a culture. We shall limit ourselves to one point of view, the point of view of *modern western culture*. Three different strategies can be observed as to the way in which the culture of the artificial is judged.

The first strategy consists of considering *the culture of the artificial* as a crisis. Philosophically it corresponds to the reign of sophism, technically it corresponds to the reign of rhetoric. As we have seen this situation is characterized by the fact that, as legitimacy cannot derive only from belief in the existence of natural processes, use will be made of rhetorical arguments coming from the traditional and the charismatic system of legitimacy i.e. from 'existing beliefs' in the value of 'traditional culture' and of 'the sacred'.

A second type of strategy which we can call *neo-modernist strategies* consist of resisting the idea of the reign of the artificial by saving some element of the cosmos from the realm of the artificial and considering it as 'natural'. Such is the strategy of H. Dreyfus when he argues that machines do not have a body ('body') being a 'natural' attribute of mankind) or Searle if we accept Daniel Dennett's argument that Searle's point of view requires that a specific status be given to the phenomenon of *conscience* which is to remain outside the reach of the endeavour of artificial intelligence. Similarly Habermas' theory of communicational action supposes that men are endowed with a natural ability and urge to communicate authentically so as to reach agreements in the social setting thus constructed by their action.[31]

Finally a third strategy remains which calls itself 'post modernist'. This position can be defined as follows: on the one hand it accepts the notion of 'a culture of the artificial' as well as the idea that it represents a crisis of modern western culture, on the other hand it considers that the crisis of modern culture constitutes by itself the element of a new culture which they call 'post modern'. This allows a philosopher both to give its place to sophism in his work and to remain a philosopher as can be seen in the work of Jean-François Lyotard especially in *Le Differend*.[32] The question with which the post modern condition is faced is that of the criterion of judgements. The question of the criterion in a world of appearances has a name: it is called esthetics. But modern esthetics does not escape so easily the radical form of ordinary pragmatism which is called sophism. It can be argued that the modern form of the criterion of official art is nothing else but marketing itself i.e. public opinion of the value of art. For those who would be shocked by his confrontation between art and marketing let us recall that one of the most venerable definition of art by a philosopher, art as 'mimesis', was produced by Plato in a controversy with the sophists which argued that appearance (and more precisely the ability to copy exactly reality) was the criterion of the quality of a work of art. To which Plato replied that the good copy is the one which can be recognized as a copy. We are thus left with the paradox of the criterion of appearances: if the copy looks like reality how am I to know it is not reality, if I can recognize it is not reality is it still a copy or, at least, a good copy.

We may note that there is a strong solidarity between the first position and the third position defined above, between sophism and post-modernism. Actually post-modernism is a philosophical stand which suits technologists, be they marketers, computer scientists, or architects: it allows them to develop freely the potentiality of their techniques which are the expression of the crisis of modernism and at the same time to participate in the legitimating powers of a respectable philosophical stand. However if this position is useful technically (as it adds an element of legitimacy to constructions which can undoubtedly make use of any such supplement) it can be argued that it is useless from the point of view of knowledge (be it knowledge of techniques) as the post-modern world can be defined as what is produced by the powers of human technique. This could mean that the level of the knowledge and of the practice of technique might be the most relevant to understand the culture of the artificial.

Notes and references

1 Herbert Simon – *La science des systèmes*. Paris (EPI) 1974.
2 When one considers the debate on the social acceptability of Artificial Intelligence, one must immediately distinguish between those who believe it exists and is (or will be) well defined, those who believe it is not possible to say whether it exists or not, and those who believe it is possible to prove it does not exist. The first category can be termed 'A. I. scientists'. The latter can be divided into the optimists and the pessimists. The optimists constitute what Dreyfus calls the 'Artificial Intelligentsia', i.e. Simon, Minsky, Feigenbaum.[a] They believe that what is at stake is actually, through the operation of computers, achieving two goals: the understanding of human intelligence and the use of the power of intelligence thus understood. The pessimists correspond to a group that we shall designate by the expression 'concerned scientists'. While this category is logically possible and should be composed of preoccupied scientists, I must say that I cannot find a concrete example of this position. This may be due to the fact that those who are negative with respect to A.I. tend to deny its very existence. The second category can be called 'A.I. technologists', as they believe that A.I. systems are technological systems which should not nessarily be assimilated with the production of actual intelligence, even if their performance in terms of simulating human behavior cannot be limited on an *a priori* basis. The optimists of this category can be found among the many researchers in the field of A.I. who, although they do not share the ideology or dogmas of the 'Artificial Intelligentsia', devote their time and interest to the development of ever more sophisticated systems. The pessimists could be termed 'concerned technologists' as they are afraid of the power developed by these techniques and as they would like to see limitations put on certain types of applications. Joseph Weisenbaum seems to support such a position in *Computer Power and Human Reason*.[b]
Finally, we find those who think it can be proven that developing A.I. is not a project one can carry out with a computer. These could be called the 'Sceptics'. Here again two positions can be found. The pessimistic view is best represented by H. Dreyfus in his philosophical criticism of the notion of A.I.[c] We may note that this pessimism concerns the very existence of A.I. and not its consequences, as something which does not exist cannot have consequences – at least, as long as nobody contends it exists and persuades other people of its existence. This explains the latent accusation made to the 'Artificial Intelligentsia' by Dreyfus who sees the latter's enthusiasm and certitude relative to the existence of A.I. as part of a conscious or unconscious strategy to obtain funding and recognition by business and academia: in other words, A.I. could be the name for a marketing strategy rather than the name of an intellectual achievement. This accusation is made explicitly by Winograd and Flores who share with Dreyfus the idea that A.I. is not a philosophically sound concept, but have an otherwise positive attitude toward the technological developments which have taken place under this relatively inadequate banner.[d]

a   H. A. Simon, Ch. A. Newell, 'Heuristic Problem Solving: the Next Advance in Operations Research', Operation Research, Vol 6 Jan. Fév. 1958. M: Minsky: *La santé de l'esprit*, Paris (Interédition), 1988. A. Feigenbaum and J. Feldman *Computers and Thought*. New York. (McGraw Hill), 1963.

b   J. Weizenbaum, *Computer Power and Human Reason*, San Francisco (W. H. Freeman and Company), 1976.

c   H.L. Dreyfus, *Intelligence Artificielle: mythes et limites*, Paris (Flammarion), 1984.

d   T. Winograd et Frenando Flores: *L'intelligence artificielle en question*, Paris (PUF), 1989.

3 These hypothesis have already been defined and applied in former works. See R. Laufer and C. Paradeise: *Marketing Democracy: Public Opinion and Media Formation in Democratic Societies*. New Brunswick. (Transaction Books), 1990, and R. Laufer 'The question of the Legitimacy of the computer = an Epistemological Point of view in J. Berleur et al. *The Information Society* = Evolving Landscapes – New York (Springer – Verlag – Captus) 1990.

4 We could note that the *Turing Criterion* for artificial intelligence does not depend on the fact that the machine behind the curtain is a Turing machine. H. Dreyfus' critique of A.I., however rigorous and complete, addresses essentially this special case where the 'body' (or material part of the machine) is reduced to what is required for a Turing machine to be specified.

5 Le Robert, Le Larousse du xxème siècle, The Webster, Le Dictionnaire Philosophique de Lalande.

6 Encyclopedia Universalis, p. 1252.

7 M. Narcy, '*A qui la parole? Platon et Aristote face à Protagoras*' in B. Cassin, *éd. Position de la Sophistique*, Paris. (VRIN), 1986.

8 For a more detailed analysis, cf. R. Laufer and C. Paradeise, op. cit., pp. 170–189.

9 Emmanuel Kant, *Logique*, Paris, (VRIN), 1982.

10 I. Kant, *The Critique of Pure Reason*, Trans. G.M.D., Meikllejohn, London and Melbourne (Dent), 1984, p. 210.

11 I. Kant, *The Critique of Pure Reason*, London, (Oxford University Press), 1958, p. 351.

12 I. Kant, *Anthropologie*, Paris, (VRIN), 1979.

13 I. Kant, *The Critique of Pure Reason*, London, (Dent), 1984, p. 269.

14 Michel Serres, *La Traduction*, Paris, (Editions de Minuit), 1974, p. 165.

15 Auguste Comte, Cours de Philosophie Positive, 45ème leçon, in Pierre Arnaud. Texte Choisis, Paris (Bordas), p. 65.

16 Herbert Simon, *La Science des Systèmes*, Paris, (EPI), 1974.

17 Joëlle Proust, *Question de Forme*, (Fayard), 1988.

18 A. Soulez, éd. *Manifeste du Cercle de Vienne*, Paris, (PUF), 1985.

19 E. Durkeim, *Sociologie et Pragmatisme*, Paris (VRIN), 1955, pp. 28–29.

20 S. Stitch, From *Folk psychology to cognitive sciences, the cases against belief*. Cambridge, (MIT Press), 1986.

21 Ibid.

22 Ibid.

23 Ibid.

24 Husserl E., *La Crise des sciences européennes et le phénoménolgie transcendantale*, Paris, (Gallimard). 1976, p. 89.

25 Guy Celerier, *La psychologie génétique et le cognitisme* in *Le Débat*, Paris, nov–déc 1987, n°47.

26 On the relationship between art and marketing see Romain Laufer: 'Système de Légitimité, art et marketing', in *Rencontres de l'Ecole du Louvre* – Paris (Documentation Française) 1987.

27 We may note that Middle Age Theology did use the expression divine intelligence.

This could be accounted for by the fact that for the divinity to know and to do is the same (Pragmatic) thing.

28 Translated from H. Dreyfus, *Intelligence Artificielle, Mythes et Limites*, Flammarion, 1979, p. 3. H. Dreyfus quotes first Plato: Euryphron VII, then Marvin Minsky Computation: finite and infinite machines, Englewood Cliffs, prentice – Hall, 1967, p. 106.
29 William James, *Philosophie de l'Expérience*, Flammarion éd. Paris, 1914, pp. 208–209.
30 P. Feyerabend. *Contre la Méthode* – Paris (Seuil) 1979.
31 Jürgen Habermas, Theorie des Kommunïkativen Handelns. Suhrkamp, Frankfurt/Main, 1981.
32 Jean-François Lyotard: *La Condition Post-Modern*, Paris (Minuit) 1979. *Le Différend*. Paris (Minuit) 1984.

81

WHY NOT A SOCIOLOGY OF MACHINES?

The case of sociology and artificial intelligence

Steve Woolgar

Source: *Sociology* 19(4), 1985: 557–72.

Abstract In the light of the recent growth of artificial intelligence (AI), and of its implications for understanding human behaviour, this paper evaluates the prospects for an association between sociology and artificial intelligence. Current presumptions about the distinction between human behaviour and artificial intelligence are identified through a survey of discussions about AI and 'expert systems'. These discussions exhibit a restricted view of sociological competence, a marked rhetoric of progress and a wide variation in assessments of the state of the art. By drawing upon recent themes in the social study of science, these discussions are shown to depend on certain key dichotomies and on an interpretive flexibility associated with the notions of intelligence and expertise. The range of possible associations between sociology and AI reflects the extent to which we are willing to adopt these features of AI discourse. It is suggested that one of the more important options is to view the AI phenomenon as an occasion for reassessing the central axiom of sociology that there is something distinctively 'social' about human behaviour.

Introduction

The rationale for an examination of the relationship between sociology and artificial intelligence (AI) is threefold. Firstly, the recent growth of AI has been accompanied by renewed interest in the possible contribution of the social sciences to this area. In the U.S.A. and U.K. there have been calls for efforts to match the Japanese programme for the 'fifth generation' of artificially intelligent machines (for example, Feigenbaum and McCorduck, 1983). In the U.K. alone, a massive level of state intervention in information technology has spawned several projects attempting to apply social science perspectives to the development of information technology. In this context, it is both important and timely to clarify some basic assumptions about the relationship between social science and AI. Secondly, despite the evident rise in the AI phenomenon, it has been paid surprisingly little attention by sociology, compared with other social science disciplines. Thirdly, in the efforts of AI, several significant philosophical pigeons are coming home to roost. If, for example, AI turns out to be a feasible project, this would vindicate those philosophies which hold that human behaviour can be codified and reduced to formal, programmable and describable sequences. The perceived failure of AI, on the other hand, would amount to a victory in the eyes of humanist anti-reductionists. The positions adopted in the longstanding and funda-mental debate about the nature of human action – whether or not humans are essentially rather complicated machines, whether social study should proceed on the basis that the human being is really just an animal and so on (for example, Pratt, 1978) – all stand to be revised or modified in the light of the outcome of the current massive research effort in AI. Clearly, it is important to develop an understanding of the social factors which will shape this outcome.

Since the literature on and about AI is vast, encompassing contributions from diverse perspectives within several disciplines, the discussion here is restricted to key features of current debates, with particular reference to 'expert systems'. This paper assesses the prospects for a *sociological* perspec-tive on AI by drawing upon developments in the social study of science. The counter-intuitive sense associated with the notion of a 'sociology of machines' is reminiscent of the way in which a 'sociology of science' appeared problematic before Kuhn. How can a machine (science) be the object of fruitful sociological inquiry? An earlier response was to examine social relationships between scientists rather than the social character of sci-entific knowledge. However, post-Kuhnian sociology of science has made considerable progress in overcoming earlier preconceptions about its object of study and in modifying its own analytic perspective. Recent work has established that our understanding of science need not be so restricted; the nature and content of scientific knowledge is now recognised as a legitimate sociological object. By analogy, this paper examines the prospects for an approach to AI which construes machines as legitimate sociological objects.

The argument below is based upon a survey of discussions by a variety of sources about AI and about expert systems in particular. Three striking fea-tures of these discussions are evident. Firstly, in most of the literature, soci-ology is either excluded altogether, or granted an impoverished role by virtue of the use of a restricted notion of 'social'. Secondly, parts of the literature exhibit a marked rhetoric of progress in depictions of the likely development of AI. Thirdly, however, there is a wide variation in discussions and descriptions of the current state of the art. By drawing upon themes in the social study of science to account for these characteristics of the AI literature, it is possible to discern the basic concepts, distinctions and dichotomies which sustain current attitudes towards AI. This analysis then enables us to clarify the range of possible sociological perspectives on AI.

The restricted view of sociological competence

Although the associations between AI, on the one hand, and disciplines like psychology and philosophy, on the other, have been widely recognised and lengthily debated in terms of the implications of one for the other,[2] the important possibility of an association between AI and *sociology* has hardly been noticed.[3] On the few occasions it is alluded to, sociology is assigned the role of dealing with matters left over by other disciplines. For example, Boden's (1977: 446) notion of 'social' refers to the uses of artificial intelligence, the effects of futuristic proposals embodied in AI and the possible precautions to be taken by the AI community to minimise the dangers involved. Writers like Boden thus concede the relevance of the 'social' through avowals of concern for social responsibility. In this view, 'social' has to do with the *effect* of artificial intelligence, but not with its *genesis*.

Some sociologists have adopted a similarly restricted notion of 'social' in their treatment of AI (for example, Turkle, 1982; 1984). Although this can provide a suggestive characterisation of the environment in which AI takes place and of the way ideas about the computer enter into social life, it largely exemplifies the assumption that a 'sociological' approach to the phenomenon of AI entails the treatment of topics such as social attitudes to AI, public perceptions and acceptability of machine intelligence, and the likely effects of the implementation of AI in different institutional environments (especially education). The contribution of the sociologist is seen to lie in discussions of the 'impact' of AI research, rather than in a detailed consideration of the process of the research activity itself. The danger of this restricted view of the scope of sociological investigation is that social science inputs into AI research are narrowly conceived in terms of investigations of cognitive psychology into human learning, memory, cognitive development and so on (Murray and Richardson, 1983). It is therefore important to understand the basis for this restricted view of sociological competence.

The rhetoric of 'social'

It is now generally accepted that post-Kuhnian attitudes to science embody a major revision in epistemological preconceptions about the nature of science (for example, Mulkay, 1979). While science was generally regarded as exotic and esoteric, it was neither necessary nor desirable for the sociologist to penetrate the content of science. In this 'received view' new scientific knowledge was assumed to be the rational extrapolation from the existing body of knowledge. Discussion of the content of science was largely limited to the analysis of the social origins of erroneous science; only when things went wrong was it the sociologist's prerogative to identify the social factors which had intervened. Hence, the sociology of science was effectively a sociology of scientists, a series of analyses of relationships between people who just happened to be scientists.[4]

The revision of this view has had fascinating consequences. It turns out to be both necessary and desirable to take the content of science seriously, to attempt to apply sociological analyses of the generation of scientific knowledge without regard for its (perceived) truth status. These claims alone have amounted to major transgressions of previously established disciplinary competences. Whereas the earlier sociology of scientists coexisted more or less peacefully alongside both the internalist history of science and the objectivist philosophy of science, recent claims of the sociology of scientific knowledge have, not surprisingly, caused consternation because they trespass on the domain previously reserved for these other disciplines. Current sociology of science has been called the 'philosophical' or 'epistemologically relevant internalist sociology of science' (Campbell, 1979).[5]

The restricted view of sociological competence corresponds to the pre-Kuhnian view of science. Concomitant with that outdated view is a distinction between the 'technical' (sometimes 'intellectual' or 'cognitive') aspects of science, on the one hand, and peripheral 'social factors' on the other. This distinction was regarded as definitive of the scientific enterprise; 'social' factors were precisely those factors not germane to 'science itself'; the domain of the social was regarded as outside or (at best) peripheral to the actual science. The argument of the new social study of science is not just that as much attention should be paid to the social as to the cognitive (for that merely engenders a kind of analytic 'parallelism' – discussions of the 'connection between social and cognitive factors' – which preserves the distinction intact, nor indeed that the social should supplant the cognitive (since that merely enjoins endless discussions about the appropriate scope of the social and cognitive – witness the age-old debate between internalism and externalism). Instead, the distinctions themselves need to be transcended. We need to recognise such distinctions as the achievement of science, as a resource for the characterisation of behaviours and practices, and as deeply ingrained in a discourse which sustains its own practice as 'scientific'.

The repeated avowal of a distinction between 'science' and 'social' sustains the image of science as an essentially non-social activity. Thus, Boden's implicit analogy with arguments for social responsibility in the natural sciences presumes the same limited sense of relationship between the context of the generation of AI (discovery of scientific knowledge) and the context of its subsequent use (justification of scientific knowledge). The view that sociology is competent to deal only with the latter is predicated upon the very distinction between 'the scientific' and 'the social' challenged by the recent social study of science. Sociological studies which focus solely on the impact of AI research, to the exclusion of the research activity itself, similarly underwrite the distinction between the scientific and the social. In order to escape the idea that the 'scientific' character of AI research makes sociological investigation inappropriate, we need to rid ourselves of a distinction which unnecessarily restricts the realm of the 'social'.

We have seen how one particular feature of discussions about AI can be explained by drawing upon recent developments in the sociology of scientific knowledge. The distinction between 'the social' and 'the scientific' is a major barrier to a thorough-going sociological analysis of AI. It is similarly possible to use ideas in the sociology of scientific knowledge to explain the nature of discussions about the state of AI research. As an indication of the character of discussions about AI research, we turn to examples taken from the literature on 'expert systems'.

Progress and variation: discussions of expert systems

Work on 'expert systems' is one subfield of AI. Expert systems are entities which perform tasks deemed intelligent, in virtue of their access to and use of a knowledge base. In the U.K. in particular, the term 'intelligent knowledge based systems' (IKBS) is used to speak about the performance of tasks requiring knowledge by either (or both) machines and people. In this usage, 'expert system' is the term for an IKBS designed to make decisions about a specific knowledge domain (Murray and Richardson, 1983).

The notion of the expert system arose out of a more general interest in problem solving. Cognitive psychology has long been concerned to specify 'mechanisms' whereby people solve problems – a classic example is the missionary-cannibal problem.[6] AI has been concerned with the possibilities for designing artificial systems which can also solve them. It is assumed that the capacity for problem-solving is unique to humans. Notwithstanding the achievements of certain celebrity animals – dogs like Lassie, and apes like the 'speaking' Nim Chimpsky – humans are claimed to have a far greater capacity for the solution of these problems. Significantly, far less is made of the observation that the *generation* of this particular genre of problems is a uniquely human trait, and probably a culturally and historically specific one at that. As far as we know, the missionary-cannibal problem is not a major concern of dogs and apes.

The kinds of puzzles, games and problems typically used for these investigations are now thought to be largely unlike the kinds of problem which rely upon the solver's access to and use of a knowledge base; most 'brain teasers' are said to be 'knowledge poor' (Hunt, 1982: 260). This has led to the task of finding how solutions are determined for problems normally thought to require human specialists. In practice, expert systems are computer programmes intended to serve as consultants for decision making. For example, MYCIN is an expert system developed at Stanford University in the mid-1970's in order to assist doctors' selection of antibiotics for patients with severe infections. The expert system comprises two parts. One is the knowledge base containing the facts and heuristics of a particular discipline – blood infections in the case of MYCIN. The second is an inference procedure, a set of rules for the manipulation of the knowledge base.

Discussions of the state of expert systems research exhibit a marked rhetoric of progress. Work on expert systems is said to be at the cutting edge of AI research. Early attempts to produce a relatively small number of powerful techniques for generating intelligent behaviour have gradually waned (Duda and Shortliffe, 1983: 261). 'Problem independent heuristic methods' are now regarded as incapable of wide application. Much better chances of success are said to be assured when the problem to be solved involves more precisely stated 'problems', 'facts' and 'axioms'. For example, the very general facility of language understanding is now thought to be much more difficult to emulate than the deduction of advice based on knowledge about a very narrow class of problems. AI has thus turned from the search for a few powerful all-encompassing techniques of intelligence to a strategy for developing knowledge-based approaches to problem solution. This change in direction is described by practitioners as a 'shift in paradigm' (Goldstein and Papert, 1977). Ironically, the prospects for creating problem solving systems are now thought better in the area of highly esoteric, advanced expertise, than in the realm of common sense deductions; it is easier for machines to solve highly abstract problems than to behave common-sensically.

Expert systems have been widely acclaimed as the applied end of AI research, the long-awaited tangible outcome of research investment. 'The science of artificial intelligence . . . is at last emerging from academic obscurity' (Evanczuk and Manuel, 1983: 139). 'Commercial products begin to emerge from decades of research . . . expert systems . . . herald what could be a new tidal wave' (Manuel and Evanczuk, 1983: 127). AI has come of age and has 'risen above its ancient (sic) image' (Yasaki, 1980: 48). 'One could imagine some use for expert systems in just about any sphere of business, engineering or research' (Webster and Miner, 1982: 60). Expert systems provide 'practical uses for a useless science' (Alexander, 1982: 1). 'Knowledge-based expert systems come of age' (Duda and Gaschnig, 1981: 1).

The expert systems literature also reveals a marked discrepancy in reports about the state of research in expert systems. The extraordinary optimism of some reports is elsewhere countered by considerable caution and pessimism about the achievements to date. On the one hand, expert systems is generally regarded as one of the most active and exciting areas of AI research. On the other, there is considerable concern about the fact that the field currently faces 'fundamental problems' (Davis, 1982; Duda and Shortliffe, 1983). In terms of the number of expert systems in existence, we find claims that 'nearly fifty' had been built by early 1982 (Resnick, Port and Hall, 1982; Manuel and Evanczuk, 1983: 128). In the less popular press, however, it is reported that despite impressive performances by some of these systems, only four of the best known systems are in regular use (Duda and Shortliffe, 1983: 265). According to interviewees at M.I.T. and Stanford University, even this is an overestimate (for example, Szolovits, 1983)!

Progress and variation: the example of the Turing test.

What accounts for the extraordinary rhetoric of progress and the marked variation in descriptions of the state of the art? Although these particular discussions about expert systems are not necessarily representative of discussions about AI as a whole,[7] it is nonetheless worth considering that there are basic features of the AI enterprise which give rise to the rhetoric of progress and to variation in assessments of the state of the art. In order to address this possibility, we examine discussions of the most celebrated suggestion for deciding what counts as 'intelligence' in machines: the Turing test.

The test proposed by Turing (1950) to determine whether or not a machine can think is a variation on the 'imitation game'. A machine and a person are in separate rooms. Both are interrogated by a third party via some sort of teletype set-up. The machine 'passes' the test if the interrogator is unable to determine the difference between the machine and the person.[8] The Turing test is problematic, it is claimed in recent philosophical discussions, because it confuses mere signs of intelligence with what intelligence actually comprises (for example, Block, 1981). Thus, it is said, the Turing test fails to allow for the possibility that although a machine's performance *appears* intelligent, this in itself does not determine whether or not the machine is *actually* intelligent. Indeed suggestions have been made for devices which pass the Turing test but which are 'manifestly not intelligent' (Block, 1981; also Colby, 1973; Heiser et al, 1980; but see Weizenbaum, 1974, 1976). This argument thus reflects a basic tenet of mundane reasoning: it is possible to treat superficial appearances as not necessarily representative of the underlying reality from which they originate. We can interpret a particular action as stupid, even while maintaining the possibility (belief, knowledge, conviction or whatever) that the actor is in fact bright (clever, intelligent and so on). (For example, 'He wrote an absurd paper, but we know he is capable of better things'). Our apprehension of surface signs does not determine our views about the underlying reality, even though on occasion we may treat them in this manner. What the signs seem to point to is always revisable in the light of further signs. In this sense, the philosophical complaint about the Turing test indexes our practical subscription to Quine's (1960, 1969) thesis of the under determination of theory by observation.

The difficulty comes when the distinction between surface signs and underlying reality is expressed as a fundamental and inviolable principle of scientific procedure. In this view the distinction between 'what it is to be intelligent' and 'how we tell something is intelligent' corresponds to a distinction between the metaphysical essence of an entity (what it is to be an X) and its epistemological apprehension (how we know something is an X). According to this view, the mistake of Turing (and people like him) is illegitimately to confuse the metaphysical with the epistemological.

In order to appreciate the consequences of this philosophical distinction, we need to recall a second feature of the post-Kuhnian shift in attitudes to science. Although many sociologists have now abandoned the idea that there is necessarily anything privileged about science, many have yet to appreciate the full significance of the point that the very notion of 'science' has an interpretive flexibility. In order to argue that science is an ordinary social phenomenon, sociologists first organise observations (of action and practices) and claim their specificity to a distinct cultural entity; they label this entity 'science' or 'scientific practice'. However, it is clear that constituting the object of inquiry in this way involves a *de facto* demarcation. Materials are organised in such a way that sociological investigation yields findings 'about science". Unfortunately, this procedure overlooks the fact that the initial construal of a distinct object for study is no less the upshot of adopting the discourse of science than granting epistemological privilege to its 'scientific' (as opposed to 'social') aspects. The very notion of 'science' is as much a flexible interpretive resource as the distinction between the 'cognitive' and the 'social'.

Two examples will elucidate this point. First, the experience of the recent ethnography of science suggests the adage: 'the science is always elsewhere'. In several attempts to negotiate participant observation in scientific laboratories, practitioners repeatedly told me that the work of their particular laboratory was not really representative of science.[9] Sometimes the claim that their laboratory was not representative was made in disciplinary terms (for example, the claim that neuroendocrinology is hardly representative of science; it is after all merely a soft science; the real hard work goes on in physics); sometimes it took the form of a claim about differences between research areas (for example, that observing work in a solid state physics laboratory wasn't the best place to get a handle on science; for this I should study people working in high energy particle physics). The scientists making these arguments may have had many reasons for wishing to dissuade me from studying their particular laboratory. (In neither of the above two cases were they successful!) But the point brought home to me was that the very notion of 'where the science is' has an interpretive flexibility which enables practitioners to formulate the presence (and defining characteristics) of science in a variety of different ways (cf. Moerman, 1965, 1968). What they construed as the defining characteristic of science, 'what science actually is', was used as a resource in attempting to deter my request for access.

Evidently, 'science' is as much an interpretive resource for natives as for ethnographers (Sharrock and Anderson, 1982).

Second, the traditional versions of Science handed down by generations of objectivist philosophy are notably at odds with the descriptions of mundane, day-to-day laboratory work in recent ethnographic studies of science (Knorr-Cetina, 1981; Latour and Woolgar, 1979). Since science at the laboratory bench appears little different from everyday practical reasoning, we are again led to ask: where is the science? Since the science vanishes from our grasp just when we think we have reached the heart of the matter, we are left with the rather weak argument that what we observed must have been scientific since it took place within a laboratory.

Once again, we see the illusory character of Science. In line with recent calls for an analysis of scientific discourse (for example, Gilbert and Mulkay, 1984), my suggestion is that science exists only in and through occasioned appeals to certain ideals of procedure, rules and moral imperatives. Scientists deploy a repertoire of devices for evaluating and appealing to the scientific character of what they are doing.

Just as the science is always elsewhere, and hence scientists tell me that my sociological investigation will never capture its content (certainly not in *their* laboratory, anyway), so too is the intelligence always elsewhere in the philosophical distinction between 'what intelligence actually is' and 'mere signs of intelligence' as detected by the Turing Test. This distinction is treated as a given, pre-theoretic duality, against which any claim to empirical detection of intelligence can be assessed.

This distinction has two important consequences. First, the claim that the metaphysical entity is not reducible to epistemology helps establish and preserve the object of inquiry. By holding that the underlying entity may be different from the indication of surface signs, one reaffirms the existence of the object. Although we may never have it in hand, the object's existence is assured. From time to time it may reveal its true character, but there seems no way of recognising when this is happening. Second, the postulation of an object's wholly metaphysical character relieves it of the responsibility of revealing itself. Thus it can always be said, in virtue of the distinction between surface signs and underlying reality, that we have not *yet* got the object. In the absence of any stipulated mechanisms for closure, the distinction evinced by philosophers like Block perpetuates the task of the science indefinitely. The object recedes into the distance, taking refuge in a more remote corner of metaphysical space, and thereby occasioning yet further efforts by its hapless pursuers. The philosophical distinction between the metaphysical and the epistemological thus provides the research enterprise with a powerful dynamic. In a similar way, the argument that any specific appearance of 'intelligence' may not turn out actually to be 'intelligence' provides the AI community with a seemingly endless research programme. The latest manifestation of intelligent performance merely occasions the redefinition of what (after all) intelligence comprises.[10]

We can illustrate this point with the simple example of an imaginary device which detects the onset of advertisements, commercial messages and other nuisance interruptions during television programmes.[11] This would permit the television to be turned off (or at least muted) during these interruptions. Two quite different reactions to the operation of the device are possible. We might be completely satisfied with its efficient execution of the desired task. We might speak of the device 'knowing' when to spare us from the misery of 'messages from our sponsor'. Alternatively, we might be disappointed to discover that the device worked 'merely' by detecting some change in the electronic signal at the onset of commercial breaks. Its operation, on this view, might be said to be 'entirely mechanical' and not 'really' what we would call 'intelligent'. We might say it was 'unable to determine changes in story line', that it 'failed to see' that the commercial was substantively different from the interrupted programme. Thus, although on one level we could be perfectly happy with its 'intelligent operation', we could also argue that the device was 'not really intelligent'. Importantly, the latter view redefines and thus reserves the attribute of 'intelligence' for some future assessment of performance. The way is thereby cleared for further research into devices which are 'really intelligent', where this is (temporarily) equated with the capacity to analyse story lines, content, tenor of presentation and so on.[12]

The preceding analysis reveals three key features of discussions about AI. Firstly, pre-Kuhnian notions of the scientific/technical character of AI research endorse distinctions between the realms of 'scientific' and 'social' which withhold all but peripheral phenomena from sociological purview. Secondly, the interpretive flexibility associated with the concepts of 'expertise' and 'intelligence' facilitates the continual redefinition of the operational correlate of these entities. Thirdly, the classic distinction between surface appearance and underlying essence, in this case the distinction between 'what intelligence actually is' and 'mere signs of intelligence', provides an important dynamic for the research enterprise.

These three features begin to account for the rhetoric of progress which characterises discussions (and justifications) of the field and for the variation in reports of the state of AI research. Discrepancies in reports of the state of expert systems research could also be explained by noting that different versions are likely in different reporting contexts. We might expect optimistic representations of the vitality, achievements and potential of the field from those involved in marketing expert systems. But whatever the interests of the marketing entrepreneurs, our analysis suggests that an endemic feature of AI discourse facilitates the differential portrayal of the research product. The interpretive flexibility of the object of the enterprise permits variations in the definition of 'expert systems'. What counts as 'expertise' is at the heart of these discrepancies. Not only does it have different meanings and significance for different audiences (on different occasions, for different interests and so on). The continual definition and redefinition of 'expertise' draws on and sustains the inner dynamic of the research enterprise. This dynamic is crucial to the rhetoric of progress which accompanies portrayals of work in expert systems and in AI more generally.

These features of AI discourse also begin to account for the extraordinary marketability of the future products of AI research. The promise of future achievement hinges on the flexibility which makes redefinition possible. Alexander (1982: 2) reports a saying among AI researchers that 'If it's useful it isn't AI'. The successful design of a machine which *appears* to work intelligently can be taken as the grounds for presuming that intelligence is, after all, something more than the machine manifests. Hence the need to build a machine which is 'really intelligent'. The general feeling in the AI community that the 'Turing Test is now too easy' (Shurkin, 1983: 73) similarly indexes a redefinition of what counts as intelligence. The feeling that AI research has encountered severe problems is perhaps best understood as a reflection of the move away from designing (mere) classification systems (such as MYCIN's medical diagnosis consultation) to building expert systems for the solution of synthetic problems, such as planning and the *de novo* solution of problems. Similarly, the current claim in the literature that expert systems are 'most successful' when they are amenable to friendly interrogation reflects a recent expansion of the definition of expertise to include the ability to display the grounds for their reasoning.

Implications

What are the implications of the features of AI discourse outlined above for attempts to understand the phenomenon sociologically? Clearly, our sociological programme will reflect the extent to which we adopt the distinctions, concepts and assumptions of AI discourse. I have suggested that the uncritical adoption of the distinction between the 'cognitive' and 'social' restricts the scope of sociology to the impact and context of the use of AI. Similarly, adherence to the view that the phenomenon for AI investigation are the inner processes responsible for 'thought' and 'intelligence', will place these entities beyond the reach of mere observational social science. By being insufficiently alert to the interpretive flexibility of notions of 'intelligence', sociology is left uncertain as to the intelligent character of its subjects and has to wait upon the outcome of what (currently) seems an interminable research 'progression'.

The dangers of uncritically adopting the discourse of the subjects of study are well illustrated by noting that the distinction between man and machine has been used to considerable effect by some practitioners in the expert systems field. By virtue of their 'political' skills (Latour, 1983, 1984), certain individuals have become highly effective salespersons. In particular, they have mobilised the distinction between man and machine in claiming their own particular (human) expertise to speak about expert systems (machines). They thus define the nature and character of the object of study, they establish that these are indeed the proper objects of investigation and they claim to be uniquely competent in speaking on behalf of these objects. The rest of us are obliged to defer to what these privileged spokesmen have to say about expert systems. In claiming to be especially qualified to define and articulate associations between different expert systems, they establish themselves as experts on the social order of expert systems. They claim to be especially well placed to pronounce upon the relevance of these objects' behaviour for the wider world. More significantly, they claim a particular skill in predicting and explaining the emergence of new and better objects. The inner dynamic of the enterprise ensures the constant search for different ('improved', as they say) species of expert system. The entrepreneurs are experts in marketing the potential of their work, i.e. they have the ability to speak on behalf of an as yet unknown population of future machines. The effectiveness of their skillful deployment of the discourse of AI is perhaps mirrored in our more mundane experiences as neophyte users of personal computers: we 'know' that the very next word processor we buy will soon be obsolete.

In a sense, our uncritical adoption of the man-machine distinction would amount to compliance with the arguments of the entrepreneurs. More importantly, this would overlook the need to develop an appreciation of the generation and use of these distinctions. Instead of taking them on board, we need to understand how such fundamental distinctions underpin the AI phenomena.

What then of the prospects of an association between sociology and AI? In general, the particular style of sociology we espouse will depend on our presumptions about the character of our subjects, the nature of their behaviour and so on. Our willingness to adopt the features of AI discourse identified in this paper will hinge upon our preconceptions about the nature of machines and human behaviour and this, in turn, will shape the relationship between sociology and AI. In particular, our stance with respect to these features of AI discourse will have a direct bearing on whether we construe machines as subjects or objects of sociological analysis.

One option is to develop a sociology of the same phenomena which AI takes as its subject matter. For example, the work is conversational and interaction analysis might provide useful insights for those attempting to construct systems capable of understanding natural language (Gilbert and Heath, 1985). In developing this line of inquiry, we can anticipate two main problems. Firstly, the axiom that activities such as knowing, understanding and so on are fundamentally social is bound to conflict with some current assumptions in hard line AI research. According to writers like Coulter (1983), the assumptions of cognitive theory are just too much at odds with the kind of neo-Wittgensteinian sociology which argues for the socially constituted character of knowledge, expertise, the use of rules and so on (cf. Suchman, 1985). To the extent that AI conflicts with the central arguments of a neo-Wittgensteinian sociology, the prospects of a useful sociology *for* AI seem bleak. Secondly, the utility of a sociological analysis of 'cognitive' activities for the AI project will presumably depend on the extent to which sociological results are formalisable (and hence programmable). Whether or not adherents to the neo-Wittgensteinian line are willing to allow the codifiability of the results of their analyses is an open question (see Woolgar, forthcoming). Clearly, an increased interaction between AI and sociology may lead to some modification of assumptions by either party. If, for example, conversational analysis turns out to be (that is, becomes defined as) 'useful' to the development of systems for natural language understanding, this will provide an interesting comment on the sense in which conversational analysis can be said to generate 'actual results'.

An alternative (but not necessarily incompatible) option is to develop a sociology *of* AI research practice. This should proceed so as to maximise our commitment to the social character of those activities designated 'cognitive', but it should eschew adoption of the analytic premises built into AI discourse. Let us briefly review four different styles of a sociology of AI available to us.

Firstly, we could imagine a sociology of AI researchers, but this, by analogy with the distinction between a sociology of scientists and a sociology of science, might tell us little about the products of their research. We would be looking at the researchers rather than the research practice. Secondly, we can adopt the more current sociology of science position that the products of AI research are socially constructed. Under this rubric one would develop a sociology of the characterisation, design and use of intelligent machines; the machines would be portrayed as socially constituted objects. Note, however, that this approach grants priority to humans as constructing agents, and this implicitly adopts the key distinction between humans and machines which pervades AI discourse.[13] A third kind of sociology of AI would construe intelligent machines as the subjects of study. There seem no difficulties of principle in using standard sociological methods in this approach. We can imagine the successful programming of a machine to produce responses to a questionnaire or interview questions. And presumably a participant observation study would entail no more than successful 'man-machine interaction' This project will only strike us as bizarre to the extent that we are unwilling to grant human intelligence to intelligent machines.[14] Yet the grounds for restricting our attention to the activities of machines alone seem just as arbitrary as confining our study to the practice of humans. Both the second and third alternatives involve the implicit adoption of the human-machine distinction.

Conclusion

The tentative conclusion of this paper, then, is that we adopt a fourth alternative style. Our sociology of machine intelligence has to do more than merely adopt the discourse of AI. It should instead take as topic the dichotomies and distinctions which characterise and sustain this discourse. To achieve this, we need to eschew approaches which are unnecessarily parasitic on participants' dichotomies, and develop a sociological approach which takes as its focus the human/mechanical language community; the community composed of 'expert machines and machine experts'. Clearly, this would entail an empirical investigation which goes beyond the largely conceptual analysis outlined in this paper. For example, we need to investigate the relationship between the pronouncements of spokesmen on behalf of AI[15] and the practical day-to-day activities of AI researchers. What circumstances generate these public accounts of the importance of AI, and how do its proponents respond to the argument that the achievements of AI should not be evaluated in terms of their relevance for 'intelligence' or any other 'mental' phenomena?[16]

The AI phenomenon has a strategic importance for sociology in at least two senses. Firstly, AI is a technology which provides an interesting test case for attempts to extend approaches in the sociology of scientific knowledge to the phenomenon of machines more generally (cf. Pinch and Bijker et al, forthcoming). Of course, much of the AI (and expert systems) research discussed in this paper comprises work on a particular class of algorithms which just happen to be tested on computers. Nonetheless the use of the term 'machine' to describe the workings of these algorithms raises the possibility of extending this same kind of approach to other classes of machine. To what extent can we develop a sociological study of the human/mechanical language community where the 'machines' in question are, say, bicycles, missiles or food processors? Secondly, the AI phenomenon provides an important occasion for reassessing one of the basic axioms of sociology, viz. the claim that there is a sense in which human behaviour can be understood as distinctively 'social'. More generally, perhaps, AI provides the opportunity for reevaluating our preconceptions about behaviour, action, its origins and agency, and, most significantly, our attempts to understand. I suggest it is instructive to press closely the claim that there is something special about human behaviour. Or, to put it more carefully (since it is not my intention to legislate on the 'actual character' of human behaviour), it is important to examine how sociology presumes human behaviour to be unlike the performance of a machine. How do prevalent conceptions of machine activity and social behaviour shape sociological explanation? Given the reductionist tendencies of many sociological styles, the implicit assumption that virtually any activity can be analysed sociologically, it is interesting to ask why sociology should stop short when it comes to machines. How exactly do presumptions about the 'social' exclude machine-like activity from the purview of sociological investigation? Why not a sociology of machines? Are artificially intelligent machines sufficiently like humans to be treated as the subjects of sociological inquiry? Or, to reverse the more usual query, in what sense can we continue to presume that human intelligence is not artificial?

Hitherto abstract concerns in the philosophy of the social sciences can now be broached empirically by reference to the recent attempts of AI researchers to probe the limit of the distinction between human behaviour and machine activity. Thus the question of whether there are essential differences between humans and machines can be addressed with respect to attempts to develop a sub-class of machines which are, arguably, endowed with a human capability, intelligence. The phenomenon of AI provides an opportunity for investigating how presumptions of the distinction between human and machine delimit social inquiry.

Notes

1   The revision of earlier versions of the argument here has benefitted substantially from comments by Jeff Coulter, James Fleck, Gonzalo Munevar, Lucy Suchman, Anna Wynne, anonymous referees and participants in the workshop on 'Discourse and Reflexivity', Department of Sociology, Brunel University, 31st March–1st April 1984.

2   In her well known textbook, Margaret Boden argues that (AI) 'offers an illuminating theoretical metaphor for the mind that allows psychological question to be posed with greater clarity than before' (1977: 473). We can similarly anticipate benefits for philosophical investigations into the nature of mind, since the phenomenon of AI provides an impetus for attempts better to articulate what mind consists of, what can be legitimately described as 'intelligence' and so on. Almost all introductory sections of contributions to the AI literature include a ritual citation of the relevance of AI for philosophy, psychology (for example, Haugeland, 1981), linguistics and even physics (for example, Gregory, 1981). Of course, many other commentators have offered rather different visions of the import of artifical intelligence and many have strongly contested its potential (for example, Dreyfus, 1979; Coulter, 1983; Weizenbaum, 1976).

3   Some exceptions are Gilbert and Heath (1985), Fleck (1982, 1984).

4   As a methodological corollary, it was sufficient to rely upon the formal writings of science, the memoirs and recollections of (usually eminent) scientists, their disengaged interview responses and whatever 'compliance documents' (Garfinkel et al, 1981: 133) the sociologist could persuade them to complete.

5   A methodological corollary of the shift in epistemological preconceptions is that it is now possible to undertake detailed participant observation studies of the practice of science. The fact that the culture of the laboratory is scientific is no reason for the exclusion of the sociologist. See, for example, Latour and Woolgar, 1979; Knorr-Cetina, 1981; Lynch, 1985; Traweek, forthcoming.

6   For an exposition of the missionary-cannibal problem, and solutions, see, for example, Hunt (1982: 25 and 365).

7   Some practitioners would argue that expert systems work does not properly count as AI because it is applied. In addition, as is discussed below, certain special

considerations apply to expert systems work in view of the marketability of its products.

8 For an introductory discussion of the subtleties of the test see, for example, Hofstadter (1981)

9 Of course, this was partly due to expressing my interest 'in science' and 'in the way science works in practice' rather than, say, 'in the technical skills involved in the work of your particular laboratory'.

10 The empirically interesting question which follows is that of how any particular instance of scientific inquiry ends. How do practitioners conclude that they now have what they were after and, most importantly, what are the associated changes in discussions of the connection between the metaphysical and the epistemological?

11 Since first writing this, I have been told that such a device indeed exists. It has been developed in the U.S.A. by a well known electronics company, in order to enable editing of video taped TV programmes. But it is not being marketed, so the the story goes, due to enormous pressure from the TV networks.

12 Two distinct kinds of criteria are being used here (Suchman, 1984). The example implies that we might be willing to attribute intelligence on the basis of effect (performance) alone, but unwilling to do so on the basis of the way it operates (mechanism). This distinction mirrors the difference between those AI researchers committed to the simulation of cognitive mechanisms and those who believe that the prime task is to mimic human behaviour (performance) by whatever means this is achieved. One of several difficulties, however, is that these criteria are not unproblematically distinct. For example, a description of a machine's performance may well involve an assessment of the means by which it performs. Similarly, we can see from this example that the assessment of intelligence in terms of mechanism projects a further ambiguous assessment of performance viz. 'the capacity to analyse story lines etc.' This suggests that an important topic for investigation is the ways in which descriptions of machine activity are construed as descriptions of, say, performance rather than mechanism.

13 Although this paper has begun to reveal some sources of restriction on a sociology of machine intelligence, our discussion has concentrated on the strategic practices of members of the AI community, and on the discussions and arguments between others who speak about AI. In identifying aspects of the discourse on AI we ourselves have unwittingly adopted one of its key features: the distinction between humans and machines. Thus we have taken humans, rather than machines, as the subject of discussion and our analysis of AI discourse has been an analysis of human discourse on AI.

14 Precisely because we use a metaphor of human communication to speak of systems of interacting intelligent machines, it is less difficult to conceive of a network study of machine communication.

15 Obviously, we should be wary of saddling philosophers like Block with an ontological commitment to the distinction between the metaphysical and the epistemological. These are, after all, occasioned pronouncements. Nonetheless, they do speak on behalf of AI research. Does the distinction championed by writers like Block, the difference between metaphysical objects and their epistemological correlates, have any currency in the actual practice of AI research? One version is that AI researchers simply want to make their machines perform a task; on this view 'talking INTELLIGENCE', by analogy with the activity of 'talking SCIENCE', occurs mainly in peripheral and programmatic discussions of AI, and such talk has no bearing on the practice of AI. Whether or not AI practitioners talk INTELLIGENCE in the course of their practice is an open question. If they are

anything like the laboratory scientists we already know about, their shop floor practice, their talk in the course of evaluating programme output, for example, is unlikely to articulate the philosopher's distinction. Nonetheless, it would be interesting to discover that there was no reference to INTELLIGENCE in the course of AI practice, because then the enterprise would rely entirely for justification of its greater significance on outsiders who themselves did not contribute to the practice.

16 Coulter (1983) argues that cognitive theory depends on a false equivalence between the achievements of AI and the operation of cognitive processes; that arguments for establishing a phenomenon (the mind) for scientific investigation are spurious and the notion of 'cognitive processes operating at the unconscious level' is fallacious. There is no reasonable basis to suppose such phenomena exist, according to Coulter, except through the illegitimate bludgeoning and reformulation of ordinary concepts of human behaviour and action. Arguing for the removal of 'unconscious cognitive processes' as the appropriate topic of investigation does not imply a criticism of the technical achievements of AI. It is simply that the assessment of such achievements in terms of their relevance for mysterious (and artificially construed) 'cognitive processes' is inappropriate: 'I do not think that (AI) need be assessed *at all* in connection with psycho-physiological meta-theory, any more than progress in advanced cartography needs to be assessed in terms of the need for theorising about children's (or non-technical adults') map-using capacities.' (Coulter, 1983: 25, emphasis in original).

References

Alexander, T. (1982) 'Practical uses for a 'useless' science' *Fortune* (May 31).

Bijker, W.E., Hughes, T. and Pinch, T.J. (eds.) (forthcoming) *New Directions in the Social Study of Technology*

Block, N. (1981) 'Psychologism and behaviourism'. *The Philosophical Review*. 90 no. 1 (January): 5–43.

Boden, M. (1977) *Artificial Intelligence and Natural Man* (Sussex: Harvester).

Campbell, D. (1979) *Descriptive Epistemology* (Cambridge, Mass: Harvard University Press).

Colby, K.M. (1973) 'Simulation of Belief Systems' in Schank and Colby (eds.)

Coulter, J. (1983) *Rethinking Cognitive Theory* (London: Macmillan).

Davis, R. (1982) 'Expert systems: where are we and where do we go from here?' A.I. Laboratory Memo No. 665, MIT, June.

Dreyfus, H. (1979) *What Computers Can't Do* (New York: Basic Books, 2nd Edn.).

Duda, R.O. and Gaschnig, J.G. (1981) 'Knowledge-based expert systems come of age'. *Byte* (September): 238–281.

Duda, R.O. and Shortliffe, E.H. (1983) 'Expert systems research'. *Science* 220: 261–268.

Evanczuk, S. and Manuel, T. (1983) 'Practical systems use natural languages and store human expertise' *Electronics* (December 1): 139–145.

Feigenbaum, E.A. and McCorduck, P. (1983) *The Fifth Generation: Artificial Intelligence and Japan's Computer Challenge To The World* (London: Addison-Wesley).

Fleck, J. (1982) 'Development and establishment in artificial intelligence' in Elias, N., Martins, H. and Whitley, R. (eds.) *Scientific Establishment and Hierarchies. Sociology of the Sciences Yearbook* 6: 169–217. (Dordrecht: Reidel).

Fleck, J. (1984) 'Artificial Intelligence and Industrial Robots: An Automatic End For Utopian Thought?' *in* Mendelsohn, E. and Nowotny, H. (eds.) *Nineteen Eighty-Four: Science Between Utopia and Dystopia. Sociology of the Sciences Yearbook* vol. 8: 189–231 (Dordrecht: Reidel).

Garfinkel, H., Lynch, M. and Livingston, E. (1981) 'The work of a discovering science construed with materials from the optically discovered pulsar'. *Philosophy of the Social Science* 11: 131–158.

Geertz, C. (1973) *The Interpretation of Cultures* (New York: Basic Books)

Gieryn, T.F. (1983) 'Boundary-work and the demarcation of science from non-science: strains and interests in professional ideologies of scientists'. *American Sociological Review* 48: 781–795. Gower Press).

Gilbert, G.N. and Mulkay, M.J. (1984) *Opening Pandora's Box: A Sociological Analysis Of Scientists' Discourse* (Cambridge: University Press).

Goldstein, I. and Papert, S. (1977) *Cognitive Science* 1: 84

Gregory, R. (1981) *Mind In Science: A History Of Explanations In Psychology And Physics* (Cambridge: University Press).

Haugeland, J. (ed.) 1981 *Mind Design: Philosophy, Psychology, Artifical Intelligence (Cambridge, Mass: MIT Press).*

Heiser, J.F., Colby, K.M., Faught, W.S. and Parkinson, K.C. (1980) 'Can Psychiatrists Distinguish A Computer Simulation From The Real Thing?' *Journal Of Psychiatric Research* 15: 149–162.

Hofstadter, D.R. (1981) 'Metamagical themas: a coffeehouse conversation on the Turing test to determine if a machine can think'. *Scientific American* May: 15–36.

Hunt, M. (1982) *The Universe Within: a new science explores the human mind* (New York: Simon and Schuster)

Knorr-Cetina, K.D. (1981) *The Manufacture of Knowledge: An Essay on the Constructivist and Contextual Nature of Science*

Latour, B. (1983) 'Give Me A Laboratory And I Will Raise The World' in Knorr-Cetina, K.D. and Mulkay, M.J. (eds.) *Science Observed: Perspectives On The Social Study of Science* pp. 141–70. (London: Sage).

Latour, B. (1984) *Les Microbes: Guerre et Paix et Irréductions* (Paris: Pandore).

Latour, B. and Woolgar, S. (1979) *Laboratory Life: The Social Construction Of Scientific Facts* (Beverly Hills: Sage).

Lynch, M. (1985) *Art and Artifact In Laboratory Science: A Study of Shop Work and Shop Talk In A Research Laboratory* (London: Routledge and Kegan Paul).

Manuel, T. and Evanczuk, S. (1983) 'Commercial products begin to emerge from decades of research'. *Electronics* (November 3): 127–137.

Moerman, M. (1965) 'Who Are The Lue?' *American Anthropologist* 67: 1215–30.

Moerman, M. (1968) 'Being Lue: the use and abuse of ethnic identification', *in* Helm, J. (ed.) *Essays On The Problem Of The Tribe* (University of Washington Press)

Mulkay, M.J. (1979) *Science and the Sociology of Knowledge* (London: Allen and Unwin).

Murray, L.A. and Richardson, J.T. (1983) 'The contribution of the social sciences to the development and understanding of intelligent knowledge-based systems'. Report prepared for the Education and Human Development Committee of the Social Science Research Council, November.

Pinch, T.J. and Bijker, W.E. (1984) 'The Social Construction of Facts and Artefacts or

How The Sociology of Science and the Sociology of Technology Might Benefit Each Other'. *Social Studies of Science* 14: 399–441.

Pratt, V. (1978) *The Philosophy of the Social Sciences* (London: Methuen)

Quine, W.v.O. (1960) *World and Object* (New York: Wiley)

Quine, W.v.O. (1969) *Ontological Relativity and Other Essays* (London: Columbia University Press)

Resnick, M., Port, O. and Hall, A. (1982) 'Artificial intelligence: the second computer age begins'. *Business Weeks* (March 8): 66–75

Schank, R.C. and Colby, K.M. (eds.) (1973) *Computer Models of Thought and Language* (San Francisco, Freeman)

Sharrock, W.W. and Anderson, R.J. (1982) 'On the demise of the native: some observations on and a proposal for ethnography'. *Human Studies* 5: 119–136.

Shurkin, J.N. (1983) 'Expert systems: the practical face of artificial intelligence'. *Technology Review* (November/December): 72–78.

Suchman, L. (1984) Private communication, May 17

Suchman, L. (1985) *Plans and Situated Actions: the problem of human-machine communication* (Palo Alto, California: Xerox Corporation ISL-6)

Szolovits, P. (1983) Interview, M.I.T., 2nd November

Traweek, S. (forthcoming) *Uptime, Downtime, Spacetime and Power: an Ethnology of the Particle Physics Community in Japan and the United States.*

Turing, A. (1950) 'Computing machinery and intelligence'. *Mind* 59: 433–460

Turkle, A. (1982) 'The subjective computer: a study in the psychology of personal computation'. *Social Studies of Science* 12: 173–205.

Turkle, S. (1984) *The Second Self: The Human Spirit in a Computer Culture* (New York: Simon and Schuster)

Webster, R. and Miner, L. (1982) 'Expert systems: programming problem-solving' *Technology* 2 (January/February): 62–73

Weizenbaum, J. (1976) *Computer Power and Human Reason: From Judgement to Calculation*, San Francisco: Freeman.

Woolgar, S. (forthcoming) 'Reconstructing man and machine: a note on sociological critiques of cognitivism'. in Bijker, W., Hughes, T. and Pinch, T. (eds.) *New Directions in Social Studies of Technology.*

Yasaki, E.K. (1980) 'AI comes of age'. *Datamation* (October): 48–54

Biographical Note: Steve Woolgar BA (1972) PhD (1978; Emmanuel College, Cambridge) is lecturer in sociology and social anthropology at Brunel University. He is coauthor (with Bruno Latour) of Laboratory Life: the social construction of scientific facts (Sage, 1979).

82

THE KNOWING SUBJECT IN AI

A. Adam

Source: A. Adam, *Artificial Knowing, Gender and the Thinking Machine*, Routledge, 1998, pp. 69–98.

Chapter two examined important features of the historical development of symbolic AI, emphasizing the way in which AI reasoning techniques were developed from highly constrained and artificial problem solving situations. A number of key issues for a study of AI, partly philosophical, partly socio-logical, emerge from a reading of the literature on debates surrounding AI. In this chapter I want to bring together these historical considerations and key issues into a discussion of the relevance of feminist epistemology for a study of AI, and especially to see how far two AI systems – Cyc and Soar – stand as examples of the concerns I have raised. Chapter one introduced the way in which feminist epistemologists have developed a critique of rationalist epistemology, with its reliance on the '*S* knows that *p*' formulation of who the knower should be, and what is to count as knowledge. In this and the following chapter I unpack that formulation with the aim of showing how the traditional rationalist view of knowledge permeates the design of AI systems. In particular, in this chapter I focus on the '*S*' while chapter four examines '*p*'. I argue that the incorporation of ideals from traditional ration-alist epistemology has important ramifications for AI systems, not so much in the way they are used – for my example systems are somewhat removed from public use as yet – but rather in what they say, albeit in an indirect way, on the nature of knowers and knowledge.

What then is feminist epistemology to make of the knowing subject in that most evocative of renderings, the 'view from nowhere' (Nagel 1986)? Thinking about the subjects of knowledge reveals a number of things that otherwise might be taken for granted. Significantly, research in feminist epis-temology points to the way in which the knower in traditional epistemology is taken to be a rational individual, in a 'normal' situation, perceiving the world through his (sic) senses and with no dependence on others for know-ledge of the world. Such a view exerts a normative force against pluralist perspectives of knowledge and also may be seen to divert attention from collective responsibility in knowing and making decisions, for if the view is from nowhere, then there is no individual nor group of individuals who bear the responsibility. In looking for the knower in two AI systems, Cyc and Soar, the business of somehow losing the knower in a supposedly universalist, perspectiveless viewpoint is revealed. I want to argue that this preserves the rational 'male-as-norm' ideal and also deflects a thorough-going discussion of responsibility.

Mainstream epistemology

I approached what might be termed 'mainstream' epistemology coming first from the direction of feminist epistemology. I wanted to see for myself whether the literature of traditional epistemology was as problematic as is suggested by feminist alternatives. But, in addition, I wanted to see whether salient features of mainstream epistemology re-emerge in the underlying epistemology of AI systems. I am aware that the discussion of mainstream epistemology in this chapter is rather lengthy. However I feel that this is justified in order to bring out the quite extensive list of points of contrast with feminist epistemology – the types of examples, the implicit individualism, the absence of any definition of S or 'non-weirdness' and the cultural imperialism of such views. This list is explored below.

A student of feminist philosophy will be struck by a number of features in tackling works of mainstream epistemology. Some of these features, such as the identity of the knowing subject, 'S', and the nature of propositional knowledge, 'p', both of which are discussed in some detail in this book, are at the same time well known to feminist epistemologists (Alcoff and Potter 1993). But there are notable aspects of traditional epistemology which very clearly distinguish from the endeavours of feminist epistemologists. In thinking about these issues I have examined a number of standard contemporary texts in epistemology that are fairly representative of their genre (Boghossian 1992a; Chisholm 1989; Foley 1987; Schiffer 1992; Villaneuva 1992). Not surprisingly, traditional epistemological writings, such as these, have a very different flavour from to their feminist counterparts.

Turning the gaze of one discipline onto another must always make the new one seem strange in relation to the first. I want to avoid the temptation to argue that traditional philosophical domains are not feminist enough; that would seem to be both obvious and, at the same time, rather pointless, unless there are specific ways of being 'not feminist enough' that could be identified and a feminist version offered. My approach would be more in the style, to paraphrase Audre Lorde (1984), of trying 'to dismantle the master's house using the master's tools' or perhaps, more realistically, to make at least a few scratches on the masonry.[1] So the job is not saying what makes good or bad epistemology in epistemology's terms; rather, it is looking at how traditional epistemology treats the knowing subject, and what is implied about perspectives other than those taken to be the norm. I also examine the way in which simplistic examples obscure questions of responsibility and reinforce individualistic styles of knowing, and the question of what is to be treated as knowledge and what styles of knowing are not.

The first thing that might strike a feminist reader is the style of these texts, particularly the way in which they are peppered with formal principles about the justification for believing propositions, and the absence of extended real world examples, in favour of either short, almost trivial examples, or elaborate, impossible thought experiments.[2] To quote a number of examples; for Richard Foley (1987: 76–80), it is 'cats on mats', while Roderick Chisholm (1989: 25) alludes to the 'speckled hen problem', concerning the number of speckles the fowl in question may be said to have, an example which the philosopher A. J. Ayer originally suggested to Gilbert Ryle. Paul Boghossian (1992a; 1992b) and Stephen Schiffer (1992) elaborate an extraordinary 'twin earths' example to elucidate, what is termed, the internalist/externalist debate in epistemology.

This is a stark point of contrast with writing in feminist epistemology, which favours much more realistic examples. Some feminist authors, writing about epistemology, make it their task to use realistic examples from women's lives. For instance, Liz Stanley and Sue Wise's *Breaking Out Again* (1993) adopts a reflexive method of reviewing feminist epistemology with the practical example of feminists doing social science research. Kathryn Pyne Addelson (1994) looks at contraception, abortion, teen pregnancy and gay rights. Dalmiya and Alcoff (1993) discuss 'old wives' tales'. The 'Women's Ways of Knowing' approach has been applied to education, psychotherapy, law and empirical studies of communities (Goldberger et al. 1996).

In addition to this sharp contrast with realistic feminist examples, there are other reasons why the use of simple, unrealistic cases should be problematic. On the positive side, we may applaud the use of simple, easily understood examples where philosophical points may be elucidated but not at the expense of being obliged to concentrate on a complex, difficult case. Unfortunately the negative aspects appear more compelling. One such aspect is the way in which simple examples neatly sidestep issues of collective responsibility; just because they are so simple they seem to be unproblematic, an argument I elaborate in a later section. But they also play a significant part in maintaining the role of the individual, rationalist, universal knower.

The way we frame our examples of knowledge and problem solving says important things about knowers. 'S' and 'p' are intimately entwined; they are not as separate as even the organization of chapters in this book might suggest. A simplified 'p' allows a simplified 'S' as it helps to constrain the subject to be an individual knower, where more complex, realistic examples would force a consideration of the web of relationships which connects 'S' to other knowers. This points to one of the important arguments of feminist epistemology, namely the argument against '*S*' as a single independent knower who has knowledge independently of others. Looking back to the key issues of chapter two, an individualist view of the knower implicates consideration of both cultural issues and agency. An emphasis on individualism denies the role of culture in transmitting and defining knowledge and at the same time throws agency back on the isolated individual, denying the value of a network of subjects where agency is distributed throughout the network.

Hence, in traditional epistemology, a strong sense of knowing as an individual activity is maintained as a dominant theme. As Chisholm (1989: 5) points out, traditional epistemology is 'internalistic', that is, it holds that there are certain things we can know about ourselves without the need of any outside assistance purely by reflecting on our own states of mind. In other words we can formulate a set of epistemic principles which enable us, as individuals, to find out whether we are justified in having any given belief. Establishing these principles is done by internal reflection and without external assistance (ibid.: 76). A consequence of this is that there is no logical connection between epistemic justification, an extremely important part of twentieth century epistemology, and the concept of truth, a consequence which many may find hard to accept. But extreme forms of internalism are by no means well accepted everywhere. The 'internalist/externalist' debate within epistemology (Boghossian 1992a), reflects a broader concern within the humanities and social sciences, as increasing numbers of philosophers are persuaded that propositional attitudes cannot be established purely by reflection without regard to the social and physical environment in which they exist. This alternative view, in other words, a view which emphasizes culture in the making of knowledge, is strongly reflected in recent work in science and technology studies (see e.g. Jasanoff et al. 1995).

The traditional view of epistemology, termed foundationalism, places an emphasis on the evidences of the senses, in other words that it is by means of perception that we obtain our primary information about the external things around us (Chisholm 1989: 39; Sosa 1991: 2.). This suggests that the traditional foundations for knowledge should be reason, introspection and observation, although foundationalists would concede that clearly many things are known through routes other than these (Sosa 1991: 10). On the other side, critics of foundationalism reject the foundations metaphor and wish to have knowledge cut free of fundamental foundations (ibid.: 149).

Wittgenstein offered an infinite regress of justification where actual justification proceeds only as far as the occasion demands and where it could always proceed further if necessary. Richard Rorty, as a contemporary critic of foundationalism adopts, instead, a coherentist approach: 'nothing counts as justification unless by reference to what we already accept, and there is no way to get outside our beliefs and our language so as to find some test other than coherence' (Rorty 1979: 178).[3] He would oppose the foundationalist view that a belief could be justified by some sheer confrontation with reality, arguing, instead, that justification is not a matter of a special relation between words or objects but is rather a matter of social practice (ibid.: 170). Ernest Sosa (1991: 275) acknowledges the way in which epistemic communities conceive of knowledge and justification but without particularly emphasizing this point. He is admitting an element of a contextual relativity in the knowledge attributions of a contextual community, a social *component*, implying that there may be other components not social in origin.

In traditional mainstream epistemology the knower of knowledge, the '*S*' in '*S* knows that *p*', is taken to be universal. *He*, for there is no doubt that it is *he*, is an unanalysed subject, one of us and, in particular, a *rational* one of us. Foley's *The Theory of Epistemic Rationality* (1987), a classic work of traditional epistemology, paints a vivid, if rather indirect picture of '*S*'. Foley's book is centered on the question of what is involved in its being epistemically rational for someone to believe some claim.[4] Rationality here involves the individual pursuing the goal of having true belief as opposed to false beliefs. This stems from an Aristotelian view, which understands rationality in terms of a person carefully deliberating about how to pursue their goals effectively, and then acting accordingly. Just what is involved in the act of careful deliberation, or careful reflection which '*S*', the knowing subject must undertake, is as taken for granted in Foley's work as is the knowing subject itself.

There is a built in assumption that, just as we will all agree as to the character of '*S*', so too will we all agree as to what is involved in 'careful deliberation or reflection'. And this is despite his realization that the appropriate idealized reflection demands a detailed description. But Foley's definition is entirely circular. The kind of reflection involved is that which reveals the person's own deepest epistemic standards. To the question: 'What kind of reflection reveals a person's own deepest epistemic standards?', Foley (ibid.: 33) responds: 'Sufficient reflection from an epistemic point of view.' This is surely an instance of something defined in terms of itself. Sufficient reflection involves reflecting on an argument 'solely with the idea of deciding whether the inference recommended by the argument is sufficiently likely to be truth preserving' (ibid.) So it is the somewhat elusive character of 'careful reflection' which is to demarcate the epistemically rational thinker. But we are never told who the '*S*' is who is doing the careful reflecting and who is peppered throughout Foley's book; *he* is just one of us.

Foley (ibid.: 113) makes some extraordinary claims. Granted, he suggests, that some proposition which seems bizarre 'to the rest of us' may be properly epistemically rational for some other individual, there are, however, constraints in addition to those posed by the formal part of his theory which make this unlikely. These constraints are to do with our genetic compositions and our environment. Totally without evidence Foley claims: 'These constraints shape our nature as believers, making it highly unlikely that the

beliefs or the epistemic standards of different individuals will vary radically.'
(ibid.). He concedes that there are individuals who may have beliefs which
seem 'crazy or bizarre or outlandish to most of the rest of us' but which yet
might be epistemically rational for those individuals (ibid.: 114). We must
not make the mistake of assuming that someone who has beliefs that are
'silly or outlandish' must also be epistemically irrational as this may well *not*
be the case. It might be rational for those individuals to hold their particular
set of beliefs, and the set of beliefs might be internally consistent, even if
most people would find the set of beliefs crazy.

Yet any plausible account of rational belief or action must be represented
as an 'account of judgments made from some nonweird perspective P about
how effectively the beliefs or actions of an individual promote some non-
weird goal G' (ibid.: 140). But of course, Foley does not define 'nonweirdness' for us. Nonweirdness acts in a regulative role; rationality is to conform
to some tacit normative definition. The only reference to other perspectives is
a suggestion that introducing social considerations into an account of
rational beliefs is a move towards an externalist account (ibid.: 134).

Foley appears to want to preserve rationality as something separate from
social groups. He is unwilling to conflate completely belief and rational
belief, although he believes we must take seriously the question as to what
goal, and from what perspective, the rationality is perceived. The goal of
epistemic rationality for a person is likely to be relative to their culture.
Foley seems content with a 'weak' relativism – that cultural factors influence what is taken to be rational. But he draws the line at a stronger version
as he takes it that the same criteria of rationality are to be used for 'evaluating the beliefs of every person in our culture as well as the beliefs of every
person in every other culture that ever has been now is, or ever will be'
(ibid.: 149).

Foley puts the answer, ultimately, in natural selection, with an argument
that could well find favour amongst proponents of sociobiology.

> We may have good epistemic reasons . . . to believe that our genes
> and our culture influence our beliefs and our epistemic standards in
> such a way that truths rather than falsehoods are likely to be epi-
> stemically rational for us . . . many of us . . . may . . . believe that the
> processes of natural selection have influenced our beliefs and our
> epistemic standards, that these influences tend to be survival-
> enhancing, and that they would not be survival-enhancing if they did
> not incline us to believe truths.
>
> (ibid.: 150)

This is the idea that our culture and our genes are 'epistemically
benevolent'. This aspect might be difficult to square with a sociobiological
view which sees genes solely in terms of their capacity for self-preservation

and transmission – there seems no reason why they should be benevolent from an epistemological point of view.

But what are the general principles of rationality? Foley (ibid.: 152) describes these as belonging to the 'cultures with which we are familiar' but nowhere does he tells us what is to be counted as a familiar culture. The principles include the idea that memory is generally reliable, that sense experience is generally a good guide to what physical objects are in our environment, and that past behaviour of physical objects is a good guide to future behaviour. These may not be particularly contentious, especially from the point of view of evolutionary biology, but in a broad sweep of cultural imperialism, Foley claims, 'nothing that we now know about the variety of cultures here on earth gives us any general reason to be suspicious of the arguments that we in our culture are inclined to favor' (ibid.: 152).

Even if we found a culture whose epistemic standards were radically different from ours, he argues, this would not lead us to be suspicious about our standards. Rather it would suggest to us that other cultures can form epistemic arguments which are unlikely to be truth preserving. For Foley a truth-preserving argument is absolute – it is not subject to the dictates of relativism and it is what we experience in *our* culture. Stated such this appears to be an astonishingly chauvinistic view, suggesting on the one hand that we have a genetic predisposition towards epistemic rationality, although this presumably applies to every human being, and on the other that this produces a culture against which other cultures are measured up and ostensibly found wanting, at least in the epistemic sense. Code argues, in relation to traditional epistemology, with Foley's work as a prime example:

> In its assumed political innocence, it prepares the ground for the practices that make 'knowledge' an honorific and ultimately exclusionary label, restricting it to the products of a narrow subset of the cognitive activities of a closely specified group . . . the assumptions that accord S-knows-that-p propositions a paradigmatic place generate epistemologies that derive from a privileged subjective specificity to inform sociopolitical structures of dominance and submission.
>
> (Code 1993: 22)

This is precisely the kind of claim to cultural epistemic superiority that recent work on science studies and anthropology declares a wish to avoid. For instance David Bloor's (1976) strong programme in the sociology of knowledge takes, as a central belief, the view that knowledge claims should be treated alike for the purposes of sociological analysis. It has also been a long-standing tenet of modern anthropology not to privilege the view of the anthropologist over the culture under observation. So really what I am saying here is that socially mediated views are at least aware of the desirability of a symmetrical approach – something which, as yet, philosophically motivated epistemology usually avoids.

Acknowledging the complexities of the internalist/externalist-foundationalist/anti-foundationalist debate in epistemology, this can be seen as a version of the modern/postmodern debates taking place in other areas of the humanities and social sciences. The old order of rationality and objectivity is breaking down, giving way instead to relativistic views of knowledge which are seen as dependent more on culture rather than on any taken for granted values of absolute certainty. In epistemology this manifests itself as a contrast between writers who look to the internal reflection of the individual, based on sensory perception in the production of knowledge and those, such as Rorty and Sosa, following Wittgenstein, who look to the norms of society in the production of valid inferences about knowledge.

Although it does not have exactly the same meaning in this context, in the historical sociology and philosophy of science of the 1970s and 1980s internalism/externalism was a hotly debated topic (Barnes 1974). Were events in the history of science, such as the 'discovery' of oxygen and the abandonment of the phlogiston theory, to be understood in terms of an internal rational thread running through the history of science or, alternatively, in terms of the interests of social groups? As chapter two describes, in the 1990s, these arguments have given way to a more general debate between socially constructivist views and those who wish to collapse the distinctions between social/technical, human/non-human actors in a view which asserts itself as neither modern nor postmodern, but, in Latour's (1990) terminology, as 'a modern'. Although it may be possible to remain an internalist in mainstream epistemology, in science and technology studies which place a particular emphasis on the empirical dimension, and which follow scientists and technologists around in pursuit of ethnographic data, such a position would now be much harder to maintain.

The more socially mediated Rortian view of epistemology might seem more promising for the project of feminist epistemology, but other than offering the basis of a more general endorsement of socially mediated views, it falls short in a number of important ways. One problem is that talking of epistemic communities and the social foundation of inferential norms provides little to tell us who these communities are. In other words we need practical examples, a way of historicizing epistemology, otherwise we may remain suspicious that the subjects of epistemology, the knowers, remain as the individual 'male-as-norm'.

Feminist epistemology and the knowing subject

Much effort has been expended in feminist writing of the last two or more decades in exposing the way that women's lives, experiences and knowledge are rendered invisible in the traditional canon. In its unspoken assumption of 'male-as-norm', malestream writing need not make explicit its masculinist position.[5] This process is at work in mainstream epistemology in an important way. As the previous section argues, with Foley's work as a paradigm example, it means that on the one hand the nature of the knowing subject need never be articulated, and on the other, that groups not belonging to the unstated norm may be regarded as 'crazy' or 'weird'.

It is hardly surprising then, that the specificity of the knowing subject has become such an important issue for feminist epistemology (Code 1993). One of the senses in which this is important is demonstrated by the ways in which unacceptable points of view may be ignored in an illusion of a universal subject which is somehow perspectiveless and goes beyond our own subjectivity; the 'view from nowhere' (Nagel 1986). This is very much the position that Foley (1987) takes in his dismissal of crazy or outlandish beliefs. The archetypal knowers, authors of scientific research, are supposed to be anonymous – the individual is always abstract and it is held that this makes no difference to the quality of the research, but this, in itself constitutes a statement of the ideal knower as a disinterested moral philosopher, a 'good man' of liberal ethics (Harding 1991: 58). Code (1993: 23) argues, 'These 'subjects' are interchangeable only across a narrow range of implicit group membership. And the group in question is the dominant social group in Western capitalist societies: propertied, educated, white men.' Much of the feminist challenge to 'S knows that p' involves showing that there are types of knower, such as women, who will not fit into this stereotypical mould, and whose knowledge cannot readily be described in a propositional form.

Further important points follow from the feminist analysis of the 'S' in 'S knows that p'. Code (1991: chapter one) asks the question 'Is the sex of the knower epistemologically significant?' Yet asking, 'Who is S?' is not considered a proper concern for traditional epistemologists. Foley does not ask it; he takes it for granted. It is a form of what Addelson (1994: 4) describes as 'we' saying. She suggests that 'we' is not given but rather is enacted. The 'we' might be made through the bonds that grow between people living or working together. Alternatively it might be a way of hiding the authority that some groups have over others, as in parents over children, or within 'our traditions' in the USA or the UK, as a way of giving some people authority against dissenting traditions. In philosophy and AI the 'we' is the 'we' of masculine academic authority who define the norm of 'non-weirdness'.[6]

Thinking about whether the subject is epistemologically significant somehow taints the purity of traditional enquiries especially as it seems to imply an epistemological relativism which drags in its wake all the concerns of the internalism/externalism debate. But whereas other areas of social science enquiry at least appear to have moved beyond this debate, it is still very much a live issue for epistemology where, at bottom, authors are reluctant to let go of the idea that there are some things that the individual 'S', in other words the individual cognitive agent, *can* know independently of other agents.

'Autonomous man' is the ideal and he is autonomous not only in his knowing of the world but also in ethical and moral judgements.

> The autonomous moral agent is the undoubted hero of philosophical moral and political discourse: the person – indeed, more accurately, the *man* – whose conduct and attributes demonstrate the achievement of moral maturity and goodness. Developmental and educational theorists counsel in favor of structuring the processes so that rational, self-conscious, autonomous *individuals* will be their products, and the realization and maintenance of autonomy is a goal of moral and political life.
>
> (Code 1991: 72–3)

But in looking towards the epistemic community as the locus of knowledge, Code (1991) challenges these ideas. Annette Baier's (1985: 84) concept of 'second person knowing' strongly cuts across ideas of autonomy in knowing subjects. Baier (1985: 84–5) argues that we are all second persons, rather than completely autonomous agents, knowing, acting and perceiving the world independently of one another. Her argument is that our cultural, and particularly our linguistic skills, are acquired during our long, drawnout dependencies on other persons. A person, or second person, is someone who was long enough dependent on others to acquire the essentials of personhood. This is also related to Mary Belenky et al.'s (1997) notion of 'connected knowing' which comes from personal experience rather than the voice of authority. Connected knowers develop the capacity for empathy in accessing other people's knowledge. Not surprisingly, it was a style of knowing prevalent amongst many of the women in the 'Women's Ways of Knowing' study. Yet, at the same time, it is a style of knowing which goes against the grain of autonomous knowing emphasized in many Western educational settings.

The business of passing through the various stages of life is part of our individual life histories and our collective histories depend on the way in which, during childhood, our cultural heritage is transmitted. We are successors to other persons. Our personalities and our views of the world develop not only in relation to others, but also in relation to our own histories. There is an inescapable connectedness. One clear, if unfortunately pathological, instance of this is the way in which adult child-abusers have so often themselves been abused in childhood. Viewed in this way the snapshot of the individual rational knower, separated from his or her history and all other knowers, becomes all the more improbable. To understand ourselves we need to situate ourselves in relation to others.

Responsibility

Thinking about autonomy versus second personhood in this way brings to the fore another dimension. Again this is an area which traditional epistemology rarely acknowledges but which is emphasized amongst feminist philosophers, and particularly in the work of Lorraine Code (1987; 1991; 1995). This is the moral dimension, within which I particularly wish to focus on responsibility. If the view is from nowhere then it is not clear where responsibility to others lies. This is analogous to Suchman's (1994a) concept of 'design from nowhere', in the design of computerized information systems, where, she argues, no one is willing to hold ultimate responsibility for the design of the system, as it is difficult to identify the designer as one single clearly identifiable individual.

Code (1995: 19) notes that questions of responsibility rarely arise in mainstream epistemology and, she finds at least one of the explanations for this, she finds in the way that it works with such simple standard examples, of the type described above. 'Traditional epistemologies foreclose discussions of responsibility' (ibid.: 14). Code recognizes the lack of intersection between epistemology and issues of accountability and responsibility as partially responsible for the mixed reception to her own work on the subject, *Epistemic Responsibility* (1987). The way in which foundationalist epistemology is written, 'obscures the extent to which there are genuine choices about how to know the world and its inhabitants' (Code 1995: 3). And it is only under much more difficult epistemic circumstances than the 'cat-sat-on-the-mat' examples of mainstream epistemology that this becomes obvious. Political policies, environmental and medical debates, all these point up more questions of responsibility, trust and obligations in the making of knowledge than would ever be rendered visible with simple observational examples, which are simplified to the extent that they falsely separate knowledge from responsibility. This further emphasizes the collective rather than individual endeavour of making knowledge.

It is interesting to note that philosophical approaches to AI, of the kind analysed in the previous chapter, in company with traditional epistemology, have so little to say about responsibility. But perhaps this is not surprising in their emphasis on the individual aspects of knowing over collective knowledge. As the preceding paragraphs suggest, it is an awareness of how individuals depend on each other that forces into the open the question of responsibility. Knowing agents in AI are individual agents and, once again, only when the dependency of agents on each other is acknowledged, can the idea of a *moral* agent be developed.

But what form does responsibility take? Addelson (1994: 140) points to one possible candidate in the form of a backward-looking juridical notion of 'responsibility-as-blame' which fits in with an individualist perspective but is ill suited to collectivist accounts of responsibility for say, gender, race or class oppression. In particular, she is interested in moral responsibility amongst professional groups where concepts such as 'participation', 'joint action' and 'outcomes' may be more appropriate than individualist notions. Thus it is responsibility for collective action that is to be important and not just the personal responsibility which attaches to a professional role. She actively contrasts a collectivist approach with the individualism inherent in traditional epistemology. In Addelson's view moral responsibility is understood to require a different approach, not compatible with the notion of professions selling services. The individualist perspective brings with it a moral universe which is the counterpart of the predictable scientific universe, where the emphasis is on the judging observer rather than on the actors. The ideal knower is then seen as a detached judging observer, rather than a participant in the world with a shared history. The past is immutable; the future predictable. Such a view matches well with the traditional detached subject in epistemology and moral theory.

This view of responsibility, then, involves a backward-looking notion of fixing liability on an individual or individuals. Yet this stance is extremely limited for deciding important questions of responsibility in collective action. In criticizing the individualism of classical, liberal politics and ethics, and also the ideal of the detached, judging observer which rests on this position, Addelson (1994) aims to develop a theoretical basis for moral theory in collective action. Connectedness is emphasized over individualism. The knower becomes an active participant rather than a distanced judging observer. In emphasizing AI's adherence to traditional epistemology, I am also arguing that it follows traditional moral theory, in other words, the view of collective moral responsibility is not a view largely found in AI systems. But the work of Addelson and other feminist philosophers suggests a collectivist alternative to mainstream moral theory, an alternative which could, in principle, be designed into future AI research. Code (1987: 50) invokes a similar position with regard to collective responsibility. She terms this 'responsibilism' in contradistinction to 'reliabilism', a view which judges knowledge in terms of a person's epistemic reliability, an example of which can be found in Sosa's (1991) view of traditional epistemology. Responsibilism, instead, emphasizes the active nature of knowers and believers, purposefully taking responsibility for their actions in the world.

Introducing Cyc

A number of important issues are thrown into sharp relief by the comparison of feminist with traditional epistemology and with particular regard to the nature of the subject; issues which may be at work in AI systems. But at the same time the job of actually applying the points which emerge from the discussion of traditional and feminist epistemology is not a simple matter. Writing on AI projects does not leave exposed the sorts of concerns that I

401

wish to uncover. In analysing examples of AI systems, I am looking in particular for how the knowing subject is portrayed, whether indeed the subject is made explicit at all, and if not, what kind of subject is implicitly inscribed in these systems. I also want to understand to what extent the subject is seen to be an isolated individual or part of a culture, how agency is ascribed to the subject and whether collective acts of responsibility are considered. Some of these questions are easier to address than others, nevertheless I hope that in what follows I may be able to make a beginning.

My first example of an AI system is Cyc, a ten-year project, originally due for completion in the mid 1990s, based in the Microelectronics and Computer Technology Corporation (MCC), latterly Cycorp, supported by huge grants from American industry and under the direction of Doug Lenat. The original rationale, or rather 'vision' of the project was to build a vast knowledge base spanning most of human common sense or consensual knowledge. This is the kind of knowledge we need to understand a one volume encyclopaedia, hence the project's name.[7] What is the point of such a large and costly project? As Lenat and his colleague, R.V. Guha, rightly point out, most expert or knowledge-based systems are 'brittle' (Lenat and Guha 1990: 3). In other words they do not cope well, or even at all, with situations outside the narrow range of their scope as they have no common sense; they break and hence are metaphorically brittle. They cannot communicate with one another and the rules from one system generally cannot be used in another. Their virtue as 'micro-worlds' is, at one and the same time, their vice. It is a question which has dogged AI from its beginning – how to encapsulate the human ability to respond appropriately to an infinite variety of often unpredictable situations, through that unique human ability of common sense.

For instance, human beings do not have to be experts to note that something odd is going on if a teenager claims to have worked for the same company for twenty years on a car loan application form, a car is diagnosed as having measles, or an absurd drug dosage is prescribed for a patient whose weight and age have accidentally been swapped in a medical expert system. But the relevant expert systems might not spot the problems (Lenat and Feigenbaum 1991: 196–7). We spot the problems because we have common sense; the programs do not because they have none. Although a program can be amended to take account of each of these errors individually, we can never be sure that there are no more problems of a similar nature just around the corner. The way to protect against this is to equip expert systems with common sense. Lenat does not see common sense as of a fundamentally different order from the sorts of things expert systems now know; rather he sees the route to common sense as through lots and lots of knowledge. Lenat and Guha (1990: 352) estimate that 100 million assertions will have to be entered into the system before Cyc can learn for itself. The philosopher Jack Copeland (1993: 102) regards Cyc as the current flagship project of traditional AI and, at the same time, the severest test of both the physical symbol system hypothesis and the view that knowledge can be represented in a piecemeal way.

Although Lenat regards the problem of brittleness as due to expert systems not having enough knowledge to represent common sense, other commentators see the problem somewhat differently. Suchman (1987: 82) points to some of the reasons why expert systems appear to have but a 'thin veneer of competence' (Lenat and Guha 1990: 4). First of all, thinking about the turn-taking involved in an ordinary human conversation shows that individual utterances are not necessarily understandable in terms of the immediately preceding turn. Instead we often have to look at the purpose of the whole conversation to understand a given turn. There is a kind of backward reach of relevance which extends beyond the immediately preceding turn. This is analogous to the way that the applause at the end of a play is not just a response to the last line, or to the curtain dropping, but rather is a response to the whole play. Extending these ideas to human-computer interaction, Suchman's study of the protocol of users attempting to use a photocopier with an 'intelligent' help system shows that the coherence of the users' actions was largely unavailable to the computer system, despite being available to the researcher. This is because the researcher had available the verbal protocols, while the machine only knew which buttons the users had pressed.

> ... from the system's 'point of view', correspondingly, one could see how it was that those traces of the users' actions available to the system – the user's behaviour seen, as it were, through a key-hole – were mapped onto the system's plan, under the design assumption that, for example, button x pushed at this particular point in the procedure must mean that the user is doing y.
>
> (Suchman 1987: 116)

This is part of the story which results in an 'asymmetry that substantially limits the scope of interaction between people and machines' (ibid.: 181). Using Collins's (1990) terminology, our human ability to make sense of our interactions with machines and their inability to make sense of each other or indeed us, is due to an 'interpretative asymmetry' in human-computer interactions. In other words this means that we can and do supply a great deal of the common sense that is needed to make sense of conversations with our fellow human beings and we also apply this to our interactions with computers to make sense of what they tell us. There have been some quite famous, not to say notorious, cases where sense was read into computer consultations when indeed results were either generated randomly, and/or subjects in the experiments were not told that a computer was involved.[8]

Until computers can supply the same level of interpretation to our human conversations, and indeed until they can supply a similar level of interpretation to conversations with other computers, the asymmetry in interpretative powers between humans and machines will persist, hence expert systems will always be brittle. Although Lenat, Suchman and Collins might agree that expert systems are brittle, it seems that the latter two would not agree with Lenat as to the cause of the brittleness, and it seems most unlikely that they would agree to Lenat's solution. For Lenat the brittleness is ultimately to be overcome by Cyc supplying most of the common sense we take for granted, and that can be done by giving it lots of knowledge. For Collins, interpretative asymmetry and the associated brittleness of expert systems can only be overcome by computers sharing our 'forms-of-life' and he cannot imagine their achieving this as things now stand. They would have to do it in some different and perhaps currently unimaginable way.

Lenat and his colleagues argue that in order to overcome perennial brittleness a program needs to know a large fraction of *consensus reality*, or the millions of things that we assume that everyone else knows and that we generally take for granted. The real job of expert systems is not to make medical diagnoses or design chips or whatever, rather it is to help people do these things, and they will do this much better from a position of strength, in other words with common sense knowledge rather than with just an illusion of competence. This is broadly the rationale for attempting to build Cyc, which, if it succeeds could make it the major 'consensus reality KB [knowledge base]' for the world and where everyone building an expert system would use it.

Writing in 1990, Lenat and Guha's hope was that, by the turn of the century, it would be commonplace to expect a new computer to come equipped with Cyc, much as the computers of the period when they were writing had an operating system, word processor and a spreadsheet as standard. In the AI world researchers have a sneaking respect for Lenat's *chutzpah*, the sheer boldness and scale of such an enterprise which has consumed a person-century of effort (Lenat 1995). Understandably they might feel not a little envy at his ability to marshal the vast resources necessary to the task. Lenat (Lenat et al. 1995: 48) admits it is a 'high-risk but high-payoff' gamble. He is anxious that his project is not just 'bumps on a log' but the log itself. Let us hope he does not fall off it.

Yet, interestingly, in a paper published four years after their mid-term report of 1990, Guha and Lenat (1994) were beginning to suggest that the first application of Cyc is likely to take a different direction and will belong, instead, to the realm of information management. They have in mind ways of finding relevant information amongst the extraordinary accumulation of data available on the world wide web. No doubt the technical virtuosity required for such an application is substantial and, in a way, it is possibly just as technically demanding as Lenat's original aims for Cyc. Yet, in a philosophical sense the revised first application does seem to be of a different order. Philosophically it appears considerably more modest. An intelligent tool to manage information on the internet is a much more imaginably achievable project than a program which forms a substrate between expert systems, all sorts of expert systems, to overcome indigenous brittleness.

The Cyc system is Dreyfus's (1992) *bête noire* and it is with Cyc's handling of the propositional/skills distinction, in particular, that he crosses swords. Yet as a phenomenologist, Dreyfus is not particularly concerned with the nature of the knowing subject. I return to Dreyfus to examine his position in more detail in chapter four, but at this point it is worth noting that he (Dreyfus 1996) has also commented on Cyc's more recent change in emphasis. Of course Dreyfus's (1992) arguments turn on the question of whether GOFAI is a degenerating research programme which will ultimately fail.

Writing in 1996 he is willing to concede that there is much more apparently healthy GOFAI activity going on than he at first believed (Dreyfus 1996). Interestingly he cites the Soar system, which I examine in detail below, as a demonstration of this health. However he suggests that Soar, along with a number of other high profile projects, have not made enough progress for anyone outside their university or group to join them. This is a surprising claim to make in relation to Soar, given the number of groups in the USA and Europe who are using it, organizing tutorials and seminars and publishing about it, but this is not the point with which I take issue at this stage.

More pertinently, Dreyfus urges a plea for both sides to avoid 'the unscientific ploy of never admitting failure even when one fails to achieve one's research goals' (ibid.: 173). Leaving aside the cynical temptation to argue that this is actually rather a good scientific ploy, simply because it means that one need never admit to failure, he is suggesting that this is precisely what Lenat is doing – rewriting the goals and timetable, as he goes along, in order to claim that the project is still on schedule. In particular he points to the analogy part of Cyc which eleven years before (i.e. 1985), Lenat said would be ready in ten years' time. In the latest report of Cyc, no mention is made of analogies, instead Lenat concentrates on natural language, and claims that two years hence there will be a crossover where most entry into Cyc will be in the form of semi-automated natural language acquisition. Dreyfus clearly expects the goal posts to have moved again by then but would prefer to be told just what has been accomplished and what was harder than expected.

Cyc and the knowing subject

Just what can be said about the knowing subject in Cyc? In their detailed mid-project description of Cyc, Lenat and Guha (1990), make little explicit reference to the owners of the knowledge to be contained in the system. Just as the consensual knowledge itself is to be taken for granted, so it seems are those who possess such knowledge, 'be they a professor, a waitress, a six-year-old child, or even a lawyer' (ibid.: xviii). This is one of the few places where a subject is mentioned at all, albeit humorously. Given such a variety of type of subject, even within one culture, it would not be difficult to argue for different views of consensual knowledge for each of these subjects.

So difficult is it to find explicit mention of subjects in Lenat's papers that I must resort to indirect means. Once again there appears to be a strong relationship between the type of knowledge represented, or the way it is conceived, and the subject who is doing the knowing, so it is feasible to work backwards from knowledge to subject. In this case, the way that different theories on the same theme, or multiple models in the design of Cyc, are dealt with, reveals something of the nature of the implied subject. Cyc's builders must find appropriate, economical yet workable representations, or what they term 'work-arounds' for such fundamental things as space, time, agency, beliefs etc. (regarded as representational 'thorns'). It is acknowledged that, as human beings use their common sense to cope with contradictory information, Cyc must be able to do the same through a scheme of multiple models. For instance I might use Newtonian mechanics in the physics classroom, but use Aristotelian mechanics to cope with the rest of the world. Multiple models of objects are needed where there are different theories of the same system, such as Marxist economic theory and the capitalist model. The multiple model representation seems to come into play when there is more than one model of some part of the world and the models are judged to be of similar intellectual status.

The overt rationale for Cyc's ability to represent these twin, or more than twin, models lies in two directions; firstly although Cyc might 'believe' one of these views, it won't be able to understand the actions of others who believe the other view unless it knows about the alternative. So, for instance, Cyc might 'believe' in capitalism (indeed it would be surprising if it did not) but at the same time would need to know about Marxism. A second overt part of Cyc's rationale is that, supposedly, the state of the real world shows that it is not possible to rely upon one model in a number of disciplines, such as, most obviously, economics.

There are a number of interesting assumptions at work here. First of all, there has to be a judgement as to what has enough status to be a competing model of a given area in the first place. For economics, Marxism and capitalism might compete but what about an ecologically motivated, low growth, low technology, public-service orientated economics? And indeed what about a feminist version of economics which shows that so much of the world's economy depends on women's unwaged labour? It would be easy to deny the latter two even the status of competing models, especially in an AI system which depends so heavily on funding from successful capitalist enterprises. So Cyc will have to decide whether to be a Marxist or a capitalist and presumably decisions will have to be made as to whether Cyc is Christian or Jewish, male or female, old, young or middle-aged. Cyc's models of the world are hegemonic models – unconsciously reflecting the views of those in powerful, privileged positions. I discuss below the ways in which views of the world which do not have enough epistemic status to be assigned to a model are treated differently.

Importantly, Cyc's designers adhere to the idea that one can have access to the state of the real world to see whether or not the domain of economics, for example, warrants more than one model. Forsythe (1993a; 1993b) shows the way in which the knowledge engineers in her study would, from time to time in discussion, point out of the window when they alluded to the 'real world'. An appeal to the state of the real world to show that it is fruitless to hold a single economic model says more about how economics and economic theorizing is regarded, than it says about 'the' or 'a' real world. Cyc is developed within a frame of reference which assumes, at bottom, that it is possible to access a real world about which we will all agree, or at least those of us holding a 'non-weird' perspective might perhaps agree. In other words Cyc's design is built on this one element of foundationalist epistemology at least.

Yet philosophers, from at least Mary Hesse (1970) onwards, have long since abandoned the notion that that there are independent observations of the real world to be had, arguing instead that all our observations are mediated by our theories of the world. Such a view is hardly confined to a few philosophers of science. It is part and parcel of the development of the sociology of scientific knowledge of the last twenty or so years, and indeed is a central consideration of postmodern arguments in general.

In talking of economics, Lenat gets round these problems as he is appealing to a kind of 'intellectual folklore', that we all know economics to be inexact. Like weather forecasting, we are never quite sure how things are going to turn out. In other words the 'we saying' that is going on assumes 'we' will all agree when multiple models are necessary, that we will all agree when things are inexact like economics, and even so there is no guarantee that the multiple models available in the system would represent all the options. If 'we' are going to agree when some areas are perceived to be inexact and therefore requiring of multiple models, then it is but a short step for 'us' to agree that some other area is exact enough not to require multiple models.

Then there is a 'real world' to be brought into play for situations when 'we' cannot agree. All this starts to look rather problematic. For example, Cyc and its builders could decide that psychology or a rampant sociobiology, say, is not as inexact a science as economics and privilege one theory of psychology or sociobiology in the system, buttressed by appeals to the state of the real world. Taking sociobiology as an example for a moment, this would be worrying for those of a feminist persuasion, since Rose (1994) has argued that sociobiology has conveniently suited the politics of the new right, as it argues for the idea that so much of human nature is genetically determined. This is bolstered by successive media reports along the lines of 'scientists have discovered a gene for . . . ' where it seems that we could fill in the blank with almost anything.

In building Cyc, Lenat (1995) and his team were particularly anxious to eschew what they picturesquely term 'free-lunch tactics'. These include natural language understanding (NLU) and machine learning (ML), both popular topics in the AI research of the 1980s and 1990s. Instead the direction they chose was to handcraft around a million axioms of common sense, with the expectation that knowledge collection might proceed through NLU and ML later in the project. In Guha and Lenat's (1994: 130) more recent report they describe the way in which they have organized knowledge base axioms into one (occasionally more than one) specific 'context' or 'microtheory'. Part of the reason for doing this is to organize the enormous list of assertions contained in Cyc. And also there is the question of everyday defaults and the situations where they hold true.

As Lenat (1995) points out, the default assertion: 'You can usually see people's noses, but not their hearts' does not usually hold true in the context, or microtheory, of heart surgery. So each knowledge-based assertion should be considered true only in certain contexts, which are distinguished by the assumptions that must be made. 'For example, one context assumes all the people involved are more or less healthy, sane, non-babies, and sighted; that there is adequate light [presumably for seeing noses]; and so on' (ibid.: 34). Cyc puts each of its assertions into one or more explicit contexts which Lenat likens to the articulated plates in a suit of armour. 'Each of them is relatively small, solid, and flat and meets others at a small number of individually fashioned joints, but the whole suit of plate mail is strong and flexible' (ibid.).

It is important to note that microtheories are not the same as the micro-worlds beloved of the earlier blocks world AI researchers. Micro-worlds are deliberately (over)simplified toy-blocks type worlds. *Microtheories* are not meant as simplifications of the world but represent different ways of looking at different parts of the world where differing assumptions will hold good. The problem with this is that there is little evidence to suggest that individuals compartmentalize their common sense in such a manner. It is unimaginable that, say, heart surgeons switch over their common sense from operating situations (see hearts not noses) to ordinary situations (see noses not hearts) in this way. Assumptions that it is meaningful to compartmentalize common sense are easier to maintain with the use of simplified examples. More complex examples show that it might be better to think of common sense as a seamless web rather than a suit of chain mail. The problem is that, because Cyc is not situated in the world, all these myriad assumptions have to be made explicit and the Wittgensteinian infinite regress looms just over the horizon.

In Cyc, a distinction is made between knowledge and beliefs, where knowledge has a higher status than belief. Anything an agent knows can be true or just 'a belief'. Of course a belief can be supported by some 'direct' physical observations of the 'real world', or by other agents holding similar beliefs. A consideration of what this entails starts to brush away the sand from the deeply buried ideas about subjects which are contained in Cyc. '*Cobelieving communities* make it easy to propagate rumors, prejudice, and superstition' (Lenat and Guha 1990: 284). Beliefs are to represent minority opinions and they are tagged in the system as such. Entries without belief tags are to be designated knowledge, which is of a higher status than belief, hence it does not need to be tagged. As this kind of real knowledge is meant to be the sort of thing that everyone knows, the authors of the knowledge are difficult to uncover – as they are meant to be all of us. But when pressed, Cyc's builders admit that it is a view belonging to 'The World As The Builders Of Cyc Believe It To Be', very little of which is supposedly questionable as it contains facts such as 'people have two arms and two legs' or what they call 'Americana' as in 'you are not likely to get a speeding ticket in mid- or late-twentieth century America if you're driving less than 5 m.p.h. over the speed limit' (ibid.). This starts to look very much like Foley's (1987) definition of 'nonweird'. The *Builders Of Cyc* are taken to have an epistemologically authoritative 'nonweird' perspective on true knowledge of the world. Cyc's prejudice-propagating co-believing communities are, according to Foley's view, holders of, at least potentially, weird perspectives.

I have already argued that simple unrealistic examples help to reinforce such a view in traditional epistemology. In Cyc, the same thing is going on. Lenat and Guha (1990) use such undisputable examples that it is hard to quibble with them. Surely only a member of the prejudice-propagating co-believing community of academic feminism would query examples about speeding tickets. But if we unpack this apparently trivial example, some interesting questions emerge. Do more men than women get stopped for speeding; are more coloured people stopped; are more young men than old men given tickets? This helps the builders of Cyc to maintain a position where it appears that everyone agrees and it is their examples which reinforce this. But were they to choose epistemologically more complex examples, it would be much more difficult to maintain a stance with which 'we' all agree. It then becomes a question of asking whether unquestionable examples really are unquestionable.

The clearest way of showing how dubious the examples must be is to think of the variation in common sense over different cultures. There are many easily elicited contemporary examples of where common sense is quite different in different cultural settings, even before we bring in gender, or before we think of how common sense changes over time. Even within one cultural setting the common sense of, say, children and adults can be quite different. For instance any self-respecting six-year-old child (one of Lenat's examples) resists going to bed, despite any level of tiredness, unless coerced by an adult whereas mature adults usually know (well, sometimes know) that it is common sense to go to sleep to relieve tiredness.

Cyc's examples might seem innocuous, but what happens if other untagged and therefore unquestioned knowledge, particularly of a more normative nature – saying how people *ought* to be – is put into the system? Cyc could perhaps assert things about how people from different races should behave, or the nature of women or children or what rights should be given to people with disabilities, all under the rubric of consensual knowledge. It is interesting that the assumption that what constitutes true knowledge over mere belief is to be decided by TheWorldAsTheBuildersOfCycBelieveItToBe. This is especially worrying as the authors of the system hope that it will eventually be the 'gold standard' global knowledge base which all expert systems will use for common sense knowledge. Yet Lenat (Lenat and Guha 1990: 348) himself admits that the fundamental tenet on which the philosophy of Cyc rests is itself only a belief, 'we *believe* that the current brittleness problems with expert systems are the results of their inability to fall back on ever more general knowledge'. Should Cyc tag this as a belief, especially as others such as Suchman (1987) and Collins (1990) believe that much of this brittleness is due to the asymmetry of human-computer interactions rather than a shortage of knowledge?

In Cyc we have an example of what Code (1993) has described as the supposed universality of the knowing subject, or the view from nowhere being used potentially to discount views which are 'crazy', 'maverick', 'weird' in Foley's parlance or one of Lenat's minority beliefs. This also supports what she suggests is a perspectival hierarchy where the perspective of the group at the top of the hierarchy is accorded higher status than that at the bottom. So taken for granted is this assumption that the authors barely need to state it. Middle-class, male, professional knowledge informs The WorldAsTheBuildersOfCycBelieveItToBe and hopes that such a world might be available in a global knowledge base is a form of epistemological imperialism.

The consensual knowledge of Cyc is intended to be knowledge with which we all agree, to the extent that we do not even consciously make an agreement; we just take the knowledge for granted, the 'we' being 'healthy, sane, non-babies' with good eyesight and in a good light. But who will decide on our health and sanity? Even being a 'non-baby' is a matter for negotiation, as the minimum age for criminal liability varies from country to country, and is the subject of some debate. In Cyc there is an assumption that we are all the same, that we are all capable of independently inspecting the real world and coming to the same conclusions about it, at least as long as we live up to the norms of health and sanity. There is an assumption that cultural histories play little or no part and that an individual's movement through their own history, other than being a 'non-baby' (which is surely an admission that common sense has something to do with age), has no bearing on what they would count as consensual knowledge at different stages in that history. The sense of, 'of course we all agree' is not far removed from the normative, 'we ought to agree . . . '. This is Addelson's (1994) notion of making a 'we'. For Addelson (1994: 4) there is more than one implication. Further implications involve giving

> some knowers have authority over others, as adults have authority over children. In this case the others' knowledge does not disappear, it is hidden. Hiding it sometimes means suppressing it or declaring it false or superstitious, but most often it means ignoring it or overlooking it.

Soaring AI

Are there other examples, drawn from AI, which can be used to support similar arguments? I think it would not be surprising if a similar 'view from nowhere', disguising a white, male, middle-class perspective, pervaded other work on symbolic AI. But, at least part of what makes Cyc such an excellent exemplar, is the sheer scale and scope of the project – person-centuries of effort and spanning all of common sense – what could be better! And although Cyc has its critics, it clearly receives a great deal of attention from the AI community, as shown by the way that the major part of an issue of the flagship journal, *Artificial Intelligence*, was turned over to reviews of the book that made up the mid-term report (Stefik and Smoliar 1993). Given Dreyfus's critiques of Cyc too, there is clearly much at stake for GOFAI in Cyc's perceived success or failure.

With these criteria, the Soar system (Newell 1990) provides an ideal object for comparison with Cyc, for it is similar in scope and effort, and is understood to be just as important to the success of GOFAI, yet at the same time it is built on somewhat different principles. In the following paragraphs I outline the roots of the Soar system, before going on to look at how the system deals with subjectivity. The following chapter discusses in more detail the design of Soar and how it handles the representation of knowledge and problem solving.

Soar was the brainchild of Allen Newell, a leading light in the early days of symbolic AI, and two of his former doctoral students, John Laird and Paul Rosenbloom (Rosenbloom 1996). The name *Soar* was originally an acronym for State, Operator And Result, to reflect the way in which all problem solving in Soar is regarded as a search through a problem space in which an operator is applied to a state to get a result. Over time the Soar community no longer came to regard it as an acronym, which is why it is no longer written in upper case (Soar 1996: G3). It is a direct descendant of the earlier Logic Theorist and GPS systems. Soar solves problems which are framed as goals by the method of searching for a solution through a defined 'problem space' or set of problem 'states', that is, formal descriptions of the whole state of the problem. Sub-goals may be set up on the way to the solution. It uses a type of rule as its main form of knowledge representation. Originally designed around the solution of logic-type problems, it was later extended to a number of other domains including learning, natural language processing and, as application domains, traffic and various types of tactical air simulations (ibid.). Its emphasis is on architecture rather than knowledge as the key to replicating intelligence, which is diametrically opposite to Cyc's emphasis on knowledge. With its basis on Newell and Simon's earlier empirical studies on problem-solving psychology, Newell (1990) proposed it as a candidate for a *unified theory of cognition* in his book of the same name. In its emphasis on well-accepted and well-used AI concepts such as search techniques and rules, Soar is very much a mainstream GOFAI system, albeit a very large one.

Although it has something of the same scope as Cyc in its aim to be all-embracing, the way in which it has progressed over the period in which Cyc has been on the scene, has proved rather different. At least part of the reason for this is that Cyc is a commercial product developed by a commercial organization ultimately for profit. Information about Cyc is carefully controlled.[9] There does not appear to be an extended 'Cyc community'; although up to thirty people at a time might enter assertions into Cyc, they are all based centrally. There are no publicly available versions of Cyc to experiment with in the comfort of one's own laboratory.

Soar, however, is a different story. After its beginnings in 1983 in Carnegie Mellon University (CMU), Laird and Rosenbloom (1996) continued to work on the project at Stanford, Michigan and Ohio State Universities. There are other groups in the Netherlands and UK. Workshops are held regularly. The EuroSoar community concentrates on cognitive science aspects, while the US community combines cognitive and AI flavours. You can download the latest version of Soar from the Internet and look at the Frequently Asked Questions (FAQs; see Soar 1996) document for advice on how to use it (preferably sit at the feet of the masters for some months), where to get information and so on. You can use Soar for whatever you like in ways that its originators may not have intended, join the relevant communities and publish what you will. Soar is one big happy family.

The starting-off point for Soar can be seen as part of the remarkable collaboration between Newell and Simon, from their early systems through to the publication of their vast *Human Problem Solving* in 1972, and a later parting of the ways. I want to emphasize the way in which Soar reflects its intellectual lineage in *Human Problem Solving* and the way in which several important features emerge in the process of tracing this lineage. Although *Human Problem Solving* is not *about* Soar, after all it predates it by a decade, an examination of the book shows where many concepts emerged which later gradually became taken for granted in Soar in the shape of 'psychological facts which have been well known for thirty years or more' (Newell 1990). In addition to providing the intellectual backdrop for Soar, *Human Problem Solving* fulfilled a wider role in symbolic AI. It was an important element in marking out the field for the computational theory of mind, in its emphasis on search methods for problem solving and its use of rules for representing knowledge.

The aim of *Human Problem Solving* was to advance our understanding of the way humans think, by putting forth a theory of human problem solving, along with a body of empirical evidence to support it. This, in turn, borrowed from two approaches in psychology. The first involved the move away from behaviourism, as chapter two has already noted, which said little about internal states as it concentrated instead on external behaviour. This required a need to be explicit about symbolic mechanisms in cognition, an approach which was evident in psychology in the decades after the Second World War. Second, this was coupled with developments in computer science which suggested that it was reasonable to understand thinking in terms of an information processing theory. As chapter two describes, this led Newell and Simon to the *physical symbol system hypothesis*. But the empirical evidence on which their claims are based (remembering that I am also suggesting that this strongly informs later work) has some rather interesting features.

First of all, the tasks that the subjects carried out, which involved symbolic logic, chess and cryptarithmetic puzzles, are of a very narrow form (e.g. of the form DONALD + GERALD = ROBERT, where given that D = 5, the aim is to find which numbers the other letters represent). As chapter two suggests, it was perhaps only natural that the smart young men developing ideas in this area should look to the kind of activities they felt they did well, such as chess playing and solving logic puzzles, for their theories of human problem solving. Newell and Simon themselves admitted to being strong but not expert chess players, 'conversant with the literature of the game and able to understand the discourse of masters, although not able to emulate their practice' (Newell and Simon 1972: 65). And whilst Soar has been broadened out to many more practical domains, its theoretical underpinnings still rest on this empirical work which has some features which invite scepticism.

Human Problem Solving offers some admittedly very detailed descriptions of subjects' protocols in problem solving – records of behaviour both verbal and written. However very little about the subjects in this exercise is revealed explicitly in the book. This is unintentional – the authors just do not appear to have thought it important. Yet some interesting things can be inferred from the text. How many subjects there were altogether is not clear. However many there were in the study, explicit mention is made of between a dozen to twenty subjects at most (exactly how many is not clear because of the numbering systems used – subjects are given a new number on different types of task so it is not possible to compare any given subject's performances over different tasks, and the exact number of subjects is not published).

Newell and Simon do not think that features such as age are important – although they do mention this factor. Gender and ethnicity do not get a look in; they are invisible. Almost all subjects appear to be students, from what was then the Carnegie Institute of Technology (later Carnegie Mellon University; Newell and Simon 1972: 165). All the subjects were male; this is not said explicitly, but it is possible to deduce this from the way that each individual subject is referred to as 'he' in some place in the text, and because each 'he' refers to a specific individual it can be inferred that the term is not generic and really does refer to the individual in question's gender. One subject was not college educated (ibid.: 267) and he had to suffer the ignominy of being the only one *not* able to solve the cryptarithmetic problem. Most of the subjects used a problem solving technique which Newell and Simon (ibid.: 261) characterize as being the one used by most 'technically educated people'. From Newell's (1990: 365) wistful comments in his later book, *Unified Theories of Cognition*, that his then 20-year old subjects would now be well advanced in middle age, it is reasonable to build up a picture of fairly young subjects. White and middle class too? This would not be an unreasonable assumption, given the considerable financial resources needed to attend a relatively elite US university.

All this leads to the strong possibility that the theory of human problem solving developed in the book, and which has strongly influenced not just the development of Soar but of symbolic AI in general, is based on the behaviour of a few, technically educated, young, male, probably middle-class, probably white, college students working on a set of rather unnatural tasks in a US university in the late 1960s and early 1970s. Rather than its just being assumed that these do not matter, if the particular attributes of the subjects genuinely do not matter, then they have to be shown not to matter, and this is not done. Soar incorporates a 'view from nowhere' in that we are all expected to behave like these subjects in our problem solving in 'normal' circumstances. Yet it is in fact a view from somewhere, the somewhere being the youthful college years from the 1960s of the now middle-aged Donalds, Geralds and Roberts.

One of the problems with early general systems like GPS was, that in attempting to capture the principles of *general* problem solving it became hopelessly cumbersome when faced with problems of any complexity, in other words it was the victim of the combinatorial explosion, that is, the explosion in the number of paths which must be searched on the way towards finding a solution. It was this problem, in large measure, which prompted the AI community away from general problem solving techniques towards more specific heuristics, and hence the interest in expert or knowledge-based systems in the 1970s and 1980s, or at least so the rhetoric of AI's standard history would have it: as Daniel Crevier (1993: 259) puts it, 'the shift from search to knowledge that Newell and his followers never quite bought.' Just as Lenat has abandoned the dream of accounting for mind through a handful of simple mechanisms, what he whimsically terms 'Maxwell's equations of thought' (Lenat and Guha 1990: xvii), it seems as if Newell at least, if not his colleagues, never abandoned this dream.[10]

For Newell, originally, all problem solving was to be characterized as search in problem spaces, but in Soar this position was extended to include *all* forms of intelligent behaviour, which was all to be seen in terms of a search for a goal. If intelligent behaviour was to be seen as a form of problem solving, it could therefore be characterized in terms of a search through problem spaces. Subjects were seen to be strongly motivated towards goals which were dictated by the nature of the problem. If a goal couldn't be achieved then he argued that it would be broken down into sub-goals in the search for a solution.

Newell's aim was to propose Soar as a candidate for a *Unified Theory of Cognition* (1990). Writing in 1990 he felt that the time was right for such a unified theory; Soar was one such proposal but there could be others. Interestingly the early 1990s seem to have been a turning point for both Cyc and Soar since that period represents for both systems their most unifying stage. This is like the action of a lens on a beam of light, bringing it to a focal point from which it must again diverge as it travels away. Just as Cyc seems to have moved away from its initial principles, so too has Soar diverged from the notion of a *unified* cognitive theory after Newell's death. Tellingly the definition of Soar given in Soar's (1996) frequently asked questions (FAQs) documents posted on the internet, is as (1) an AI programming language, (2) a cognitive architectural framework and (3) a theory of cognition (but note, *not a unified* theory of cognition). As more and more researchers use Soar for diverse applications, as is verified by a glance through the papers and reports being produced by Soar research groups, this is hardly surprising. It is as if it *cannot* continue as a unified theory candidate once this necessary diversity occurs; it is to big a weight for Soar to bear. The hope of unity can only be maintained when the focus is on a narrow range of artificial, symbolic, logic-based problems, and also, tellingly, probably on the vision of one man.

Soar and the subject – Donna + Geraldine = Roberta

The physical subjects from the original Newell and Simon studies were actually technically able young men, but what of the conceptual subject of Soar? In taking up these studies as a basis for its theory of cognition, Soar is predicated on a notion that their behaviour is the norm. It is the tacit acceptance of male-as-norm that permeates traditional epistemology. So normal is that norm that Newell and Simon do not even have to state it explicitly; we only know it by a process of deduction. But does it really matter whether the subjects solving DONALD + GERALD = ROBERT were male or female? Is there evidence to suggest that if the subjects were female or black or young or old that they would solve the problem in a different way? In this case, as

Newell and Simon argue, the characteristics of the particular problem heavily constrain the way an individual can solve it. Other than by a very lucky guess, it probably can only be solved in one of the ways they suggest, if it is to be solved at all. But it is with the extrapolation from this point that I wish to take issue.

First of all there is the assumption that problems to be solved are constrained by the nature of the given problem in general. Even a problem which might be seen as similarly logical in focus, such as computer programming, can be seen as containing at least two radically different styles, both of which may be perfectly satisfactory in obtaining a solution (Turkle and Papert 1990). A certain kind of rationality is assumed in Newell and Simon's model. It is *rational* to be motivated towards goals. 'Properly motivated' subjects are expected to behave in a way predicted by this model of rationality (Newell and Simon 1972: 55). As they point out, the competitive aspects of a game like chess can be relied upon, in our culture, to produce properly motivated subjects *even when no opponent is present* (ibid.: 664). In addition a kind of biological norm is expected (ibid.: 866). All sorts of biological things are regarded as affecting behaviour, including drowsiness, illusions, after-images, ringing in the ears and, of course, individual differences such as hearing acuity which can substantially affect an individual's behaviour. 'But a *normal situation* is precisely one in which these biological limits are not exceeded, and it is to such normal situations that the theory of this book applies' (ibid.: 866). Once again Foley's 'non-weirdness' creeps in. And there is also an assumption that it is possible to define unequivocally biological things, as opposed to cultural things, which affect behaviour. Chapter two discussed the difficulty, not to say impossibility, of deciding where the line is to be drawn between biological and social aspects of masculinity and femininity. We have a similar problem here, in trying to establish a firm line between what is biological or medical, and what is taken to be social in origin. For instance I wonder if my suffering from the illusion that AI systems are permeated with a masculinist view of rationality can be said to be biological or otherwise.

As the next chapter suggests, the idea that problems determine the problem solving behaviour of their subjects becomes questionable when we look at more realistic examples. Cryptarithmetic, logic problems and chess have at least some of the characteristics of the unrealistic problems traditionally posed in traditional epistemology. They are different from speckled hens and twin earths in that cryptarithmetic problems and chess can at least be seen as games which can be played for recreational purposes, but nevertheless they are similar in that they are bounded, unrealistic problems.

Using problems such as these means that the male-as-norm need never be challenged. Indeed Newell and Simon's 'normal situation' bears a clear analogy to the way in which Foley talks of all of us with the 'non-weird' perspective necessary for believing the same thing, and which defines a marker for

416

rationality. This is also strongly reminiscent of Lenat's 'healthy, sane non-babies'. As part of their view of rationality, Newell and Simon (1972: 664) make fleeting mention of 'properly motivated' subjects. 'Proper' motivation means the motivation to undertake cryptarithmetic problems, or to rise to the challenge of a chess game, even where there is no opponent. If you would rather not do cryptarithmetic problems because you prefer the challenge of converting an intricate knitting pattern into an exquisite hand-knitted jumper, or you don't even have time for that because you have to solve the problem of picking up the children from school and cooking the evening meal, then you might not be properly motivated. If a normal situation excludes say having influenza, ringing in the ears or double vision as factors impairing your problem solving abilities, then how about pre-menstrual stress, the menopause or just being a difficult feminist?' It is not hard to reach the conclusion that many people labour under these difficulties whilst managing to solve problems perfectly adequately.

In addition to these considerations, it is clear that the types of problem which originated in *Human Problem Solving*, but carried through into Soar and beyond are to be seen as problems to be solved solely by individuals, each acting on his (sic) own. It is a view of problem solving highly dependent on individual psychology and an educational system which prizes the development of skills in artificial logic-type problems. Such a view does not regard collective problem solving, or the 'Women's Ways of Knowing' style of *connected knowing* (Belenky et al. 1997), as an appropriate type of activity for investigating human cognition.

This AI view of problem solving involves subjects working on their own without sense of their *second personhood*, bits of that background which can only be uncovered by detective work on the text. How would the 'properly motivated' young college students of the 1960s feel about solving these problems now? Perhaps their passage through their own histories would motivate them more to ponder solutions to problems of health, pollution, unemployment and urban violence.[12] All these considerations, coupled with the inherently unrealistic nature of the problems involved, serve to remove them from the moral dimension, much as traditional epistemology avoids moral questions and sidesteps a consideration of responsibility.

There are two senses of responsibility which can be understood in the context of the design of systems such as Cyc and Soar. There is the responsibility of the builders of the system to get right what they put in, to make sure that the knowledge is internally consistent with itself. This is a difficult enough question and one which is just beginning to be raised in the computing community. For instance, Copeland (1993) worries about the way that Cyc handles consistency. What should it do when it encounters a pair of conflicting assertions? Should it shout for human help, try to quarantine the problem assertions and get by without them or just carry on regardless, in the hope that the negative effects of the inconsistencies won't spread too far?

Lenat seems to prefer the latter course of action. But Copeland argues that the inconsistency may spread from node to node poisoning the entire knowledge base. 'In my view it would be downright dangerous to allow a commissioned KB [knowledge base] with logic and control systems as crude as CYC's to continue to run once an irremediable inconsistency develops' (ibid.: 120).

Yet there is also a more diffuse sense of responsibility which may become lost in the 'view from nowhere' which is incorporated into these systems. To illustrate this point with an example, in a threatened ecological crisis there are many parties who have a collective responsibility. The *Sea Empress* oil tanker spillage off the coast of Wales made headlines in the UK press in early 1996. There are a number of potential 'responsibility' holders here: the shipping company who may have put economic concerns before safety (for instance double-hulled vessels are less susceptible to oil leakage, oil tankers are so large and heavy they are not easily controlled in narrow seaways and so on), the UK Government for bowing to pressures from shipping companies, co-ordinators of rescue services, co-ordinators of environmental protection and clean up operations, the press and perhaps all of us for wanting cheap petrol and oil rather than the preservation of the environment. The 'story' of where responsibility lies is complex and indeed there is no single true story. It seems entirely appropriate and indeed *rational* that there should be a plurality of views so that responsibility is debated, and so that responsibility is not seen purely as blame. The solution to the 'problem' is then not made by an individual person, but is collectively owned by all those willing to share responsibility.

This feature is an essential part of collective systems such as the law or the democratic political system, no matter how imperfectly we may feel they operate. The individual Cartesian man of reason, cut loose from his history, using his senses to capture knowledge about the world, sits uneasily with collectivist views of responsibility. It seems difficult to see how a system like Cyc could ever capture the richness of such a picture. The richness would be finessed, factored and levelled away. It is also difficult to see what Soar could offer in its problem solving techniques. In focusing on the idea of male-as-norm which is hidden in the view from nowhere, through the use of unrealistic examples, Cyc and Soar fall prey to the problems of traditional epistemology in its inability to get to grips with the moral dimension of human problem solving.

83

ARTIFICIAL INTELLIGENCE

J. D. Bolter

Source: J. D. Bolter, *Turing's Man: Western Culture in the Computer Age*, University of North Carolina Press, 1984, pp. 189–213.

We return at last to the most radical expression of Turing's man, artificial intelligence – the notion of putting together hardware and programs to create new thinking entities, machines that rival human beings. In classical and Christian thinking, man was a made thing, the crown of creation, perhaps, but not the creator. Whatever modern biology has done to stress the continuity of life from microbe to man, we still think of ourselves as the highest manifestation of evolution, or the creative power of nature. In fact, our modern self-appraisal is possibly higher than that of the Platonist or the Christian theologian. They believed in orders of existence beyond our own, the Platonist in ideas and the Christian in angels and God. Dispensing with God as a hypothesis, the modern biologist sees man, and in particular his brain, as the most highly organized matter to be found in the natural world.

In his tiny artificial world, the computer programmer sets for himself the tasks of imitating nature and improving upon it, filling electronic space with models of real world problems and providing solutions through highly "unnatural" means. He invents complex transformations of numbers and symbols, and then has the satisfaction of seeing his results applied powerfully to the world of experience. Through mathematics, simulations, industrial robots, and data bases, more and more of human experience comes under the computer's "command and control." Is it surprising, then, that some programmers should want to rival the finest achievement of nature, to bring man himself into the computer world by turning the computer into an electronic brain?

The electronic brain remains for many an uneasy metaphor. No one can say with certainty how far the analogy between the computer and the brain may be taken – whether some human capacities, perhaps the most important, can ever be given to a machine. The popular press often carries reports of the computer's capacity for rational thought (from economic planning to playing chess), of its huge, infallible memory, its unimaginable speed of operation. Can computers really think? Computer experts, like laymen, are divided on this question. There are those who argue for various reasons that computers will never be able to think as men do, yet so little is known about how the human brain functions that their arguments are as speculative as Turing's original plea for machine intelligence. The argument over artificial intelligence has in fact produced more heat than light. The debate between two camps with such opposing world views leads quickly to a stalemate. One side claims that a computer will never be able to do this or that; the other replies that it will in two, five, or fifty years. Those who believe in artificial intelligence constantly exploit the fascinating, if frightening, uncertainty of our technological future. Who would be so foolish as to predict the limits of technology fifty years from now, assuming that science continues to make discoveries at its present rate?

For our purposes it does not matter whether computers can really think. We are interested in the cultural impact of the computer; for us the importance of the artificial intelligence movement is that it serves to crystallize so many of the qualities of electronic technology and display them in a way that will catch the imagination of our contemporaries. The debate over the possibility of computer thought will never be won or lost; it will simply cease to be of interest, like the previous debate over man as a clockwork mechanism. Computers will prove useful in many tasks and useless in others. It seems to me that the whole debate has turned the question around: the issue is not whether the computer can be made to think like a human, but whether humans can and will take on the qualities of digital computers. For that, as stated at the outset, is the fundamental promise and threat of the computer age, the fundamental premise of Turing's man.

Turing's game

Let us look more closely at the claim, made in 1950, that by the year 2000 computing machines would be capable of imitating human intelligence perfectly. Turing envisioned a game in which a human player is seated at a teletype console, by which he can communicate with a teletype in another room. Controlling this second console would be either another human or a digital computer. The player could ask any questions he wished through his console in order to determine whether he was in contact with a man or a machine.

Suppose there were in fact a computer at the other console. If asked to write a sonnet, the machine could attempt one or refuse; after all, most humans are not poets. If given two numbers to add, the machine might wait thirty seconds and provide the answer or instead might prefer to make a mistake to imitate human fallibility. However, it would not produce the answer in less than a second, for that would be a clear indication of its electronic nature. Turning's game really demands a machine that is more than human, not merely equal to its biological counterpart, one capable of any intellectual feat a man or woman can perform and sly enough to mask any prowess that exceeds a human's abilities. It would be a machine that knew men and women better than they know themselves. Turing was optimistic about the prospect of this supercomputer: "I believe that in about fifty years' time it will be plausible to programme computers ... to make them play the imitation game so well that an average interrogator will not have more than 70 per cent chance of making the right identification after five minutes of questioning" (Feigenbaum and Feldman, *Computers and Thought*, 19).

The appeal of Turing's test is easy to understand. It offers an operational definition of intelligence quite in the spirit of behavioral psychology in the postwar era. A programmer can measure success by statistics – the number of human subjects fooled by his machine. The test seems to require no subjective judgment; it says nothing about the machine writing a good poem or solving an important mathematical theorem. Every humanist, of course, is tempted to devise his own Turing test and so his own definition of humanity: a computer will never be fully human unless it can laugh, cry, feel sympathy, feel pain, and so on. Someone has suggested that a computer will pass for a human only when it begins to ask what are the differences between itself and a human being. Turing's own test is supposed to embrace any and all human qualities that can be communicated in writing. The player at the terminal may ask anything.

The test is cast in the form of a game, a dual of wits between man and machine. Games are in fact the form of intellectual activity that computers imitate most effectively. The Turing machine itself is a logical game, whose moves are governed by precise rules, and the computer plays a sort of game with every program it runs. Today, thirty years after Turing's proposal, a computer can play excellent chess, but no computer program could even attempt to play Turing's intelligence game. No computer could answer more than a question or two without revealing its mechanical nature.

The strategies for meeting Turing's proposal have varied. The most intriguing, if least successful, arose from the work of Norbert Wiener, who in the 1940s devised the term 'cybernetics' for the 'entire field of control and communication theory, whether in the machine or in the animal' (*Cybernetics*, 19). Wiener's work with servomechanisms to aim antiaircraft guns and to do much else besides had convinced him that forms of life could be understood entirely in mechanical terms; they could not be understood as Cartesian clockwork, which was too crude and rigid, but rather as electro-mechanical or even electronic devices. Like others, Wiener compared the new electronic tubes to neurons and wanted to subsume the study of both under one discipline. Wiener's outlook was clearly as much influenced by pre-electronic control devices (feedback loops in various machines) as by the digital computers just being built. In *Cybernetics* he stressed direct contact with the world—experiments with the muscles of the cat, improved prostheses for amputees, sensing equipment, and so on. Current workers in artificial intelligence show less interest in such direct contact with the world and more interest in abstract thought.

Wiener was still only halfway along the line from Descartes to Turing. He wanted machines to imitate the man who acts in the world as well as the man who reasons, to explain muscle action in terms of feedback loops as well as chess in terms of a digital program. He relied on hardware devices for his metaphor of man and demanded a close correspondence between man and the machine made to imitate him. Vacuum tubes were meant to be a physical substitute for neurons, servomechanisms for nerves acting upon muscles. This line of thinking was forthright and compelling, and led to attempts to build a brain (in theory, seldom in practice) using simple electronic components. Those following Wiener's approach spoke of creating artificial brain cells and neural networks and allowing the machine to learn as a baby was presumed to do—presuming with Locke that the baby's mind was a tabula rasa at birth. But the theory of neural networks, which was developed mathematically, met with little or no practical success. In general, Wiener's preferences gave way to others in the 1950s, as computer hardware and especially programming languages became more sophisticated. Unfortunately, the elegant name of cybernetics, created from the Greek word for governor but smacking perhaps of the antiquated technology of the war years, also gave way to 'artificial intelligence.'

Specialists more or less gave up the idea of building a machine whose components would mirror the elements of the human brain; they no longer demanded a literal correspondence between man and machine. The new high-level languages led them to emphasize programs rather than hardware, and they turned to such tasks as computer chess and theorem proving, problems of 'information processing,' rather than Wiener's command and control. In fact, the Turing test is just such a problem; it requires the computer not to act in the world but to act a role by manipulating symbols on a teletype.

For some, direct simulation of human thought seemed the most appealing way to pass the Turing test. They sought to discover intuitively how humans solved mental problems and then to translate these intuitions into digital programs. They may also have expected that the human solution would be the most appropriate (most efficient) one for the computer. Others tried simply to make programs fast and effective, feeling no need to be faithful to some theory of human cognition. Marvin Minsky, a principal spokesman for this approach, defined artificial intelligence as 'the science of making machines do things that would require intelligence if done by men' (*Semantic Information Processing*, ed. Marvin Minsky, v).

This new definition seemed to reassert the difference between men and computers. Men can solve problems in one way, machines in another. But in fact, the analogy remains firm in the minds of programmers. Computer programs are open to inspection, and human ways of thinking are not. When a programmer devises an algorithm for playing chess or for analyzing English grammar, he can hardly avoid regarding human performance by analogy with his visible, intelligible algorithm. As one psychologist has put it, the computer model of the mind is the only working model available and even a bad model is better than none.

The nature of artificial intelligence can be illustrated by the performance of a program called SHRDLU. It is not the most recent effort (now more than ten years old) but one of the most famous and suggestive. SHRDLU is a simulated robot. The human controller types commands in simple English at a terminal; the program responds in typed English while a television screen displays the actions of the robot, picturing for us the tiny world in which the machine is supposed to operate. The screen shows a group of building blocks with identifying colors and a hook by which the robot moves the blocks. These elements constitute the program's world—all that SHRDLU can talk about or manipulate. The level of abstraction, the removal from the world, is striking. Nothing is really done by the robot, no blocks really moved; rather, the computer creates for us a picture of what it would do. A sample of the dialogue is given in figure 1. The human operator's questions or commands appear in small letters, and SHRDLU's replies appear in capitals. The program takes from five to twenty seconds to reply and to alter the display screen to reflect the commands.

SHRDLU can also remember when it has moved a block and why. It has a vocabulary limited to a few hundred words relevant to its world of blocks, and it can learn a few new definitions. If told that a 'steeple' is a stack of two green cubes and a pyramid, it can construct one. It can parse sentences well enough to interpret commands and answer questions about its display of blocks in simple phrases. The ingenious programming behind these achievements, however, cannot be extended very far beyond the world of blocks. The program depends upon a complex data structure to represent blocks and their manipulation. Expanding that structure would make the program too large and too time-consuming for any contemporary machine.

It is hard to criticize the performance of this computer program, for the idea of any machine being able to perform seemingly intelligent tasks is at once paradoxical and compelling. SHRDLU was constructed in about 1970. Should we expect much more after twenty years of effort in artificial intelligence or be surprised at what SHRDLU can already do? The program is certainly more an expression of faith in what artificial intelligence may someday achieve than a practical result in itself.

SHRDLU is a product of the intellectual assumptions of its creator. It is an invention, not a discovery, and it can be understood in the symbolic, psychological, and generic terms appropriate to any literary or artistic

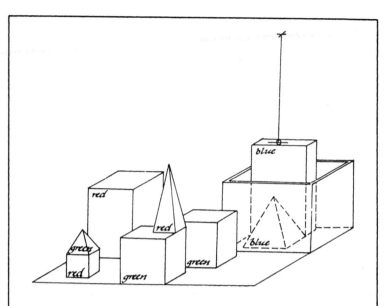

1. Pick up a big red block.
   OK. (The system answers "OK" when it carries out a command.)

2. Find a block which is taller than the one you are holding and put it into box.
   BY "IT", I ASSUME YOU MEAN THE BLOCK WHICH IS TALLER THAN THE ONE I AM HOLDING.
   OK.

3. What does the box contain?
   THE BLUE PYRAMID AND THE BLUE BLOCK.

4. How many blocks are not in the box?
   FOUR OF THEM.

5. Can a pyramid be supported by a block?
   YES.

6. Can a pyramid support a pyramid?
   I DON'T KNOW.

7. Stack up two pyramids.
   I CAN'T. (The robot tries and fails.)

8. I own blocks which are not red, but I don't own anything which supports a pyramid.
   I UNDERSTAND.

9. Do I own a box?
   NO.

10. Do I own anything in the box?
    YES, TWO THINGS: THE BLUE BLOCK AND THE BLUE PYRAMID.

Figure 1 SHRDLU The world of toy blocks manipulated by the program SHRDLU. This sample has been assembled from excerpts from Terry Winograd's description in *Understanding Natural Language* (New York Academic Press, 1972), 8–15. Comments in parentheses are Winograd's own. Sample reprinted by permission of Terry Winograd and Academic Press.

invention. From this point of view, SHRDLU is a retarded sibling of the robots known to us from decades of science fiction books and films. Robots in motion pictures evolved from such figures as the good Indian companion in westerns and the chimpanzee in the Tarzan series, figures who mediate between nature and full humanity or between savagery and full civilization. SHRDLU also mediates, in this case between the rigorously logical world of the computer and the ambiguous world of everyday human experience. It seems that we must meet SHRDLU more than halfway, giving up much of the richness of our experience and language in order to communicate with the machine. But in fact, SHRDLU has come a tremendous distance from its customary jargon of machine instructions even to achieve English that smacks of automation.

SHRDLU (indeed most programs that answer questions and solve problems) resembles Tonto or Tarzan's chimp in another respect: it exists to serve man, to help him manipulate his physical or intellectual environment, to carry out his requests patiently and supply him with information. Having no function or goal independent of the human operator, it embodies the stimulus-response psychology of the behaviorist, with the human always supplying the stimulus. Yet the structure of question and answer is the same Turing envisioned for his test. SHRDLU is already a game, although it is not Turing's game. Even if the range of responses were immensely broadened and SHRDLU could answer questions from any field of human knowledge in grammatical English (as it can now with its tiny world of blocks), no one would take SHRDLU for a human being. The naive submissiveness and total earnestness belong to a robot and not to a man or woman. Still, there is something disquieting about even this simple-minded machine. Entering into a dialogue with SHRDLU and agreeing to play the game, even under the restricted rules that the program understands, provides us with a moment's uncertainty and allows us to imagine that we are conversing with something that shares our humanity. This is the real importance of SHRDLU as well as the source of its appeal.

Language, memory, and other games

Probably the first step in meeting Turing's challenge is to create a program that is able to read and write English or some other natural language. SHRDLU is designed to demonstrate how a computer may 'process natural language' in order to solve problems. One of the earliest aspirations of programmers was to bridge the enormous gap between human languages and the codes in which programs had to be written. As stated earlier in the chapter on language, progress was rapid in giving programmers more tractable coding languages, first assemblers and then compilers, but programs written in such languages are still far from simple English prose. Those interested in artificial intelligence dreamed of allowing their computers to accept unadulterated natural language. Their enthusiasm here is not surprising, for the electronic culture, accustomed to equating thought and language, could hardly regard a machine as intelligent unless it could speak a language fully as rich as English. Furthermore, a program that processed English would be able to communicate with those outside the scientific and engineering communities on their own terms; no one could excuse himself from confronting the thinking computer by claiming ignorance of the secret codes with which the machine functioned. To legitimate itself as an artificial intelligence, the computer simply had to learn English.

The first project along this line was the ambitious one of translation by machine: programming a computer to write an idiomatic English version of Russian prose. The military and scientific utility of such a program was obvious, so the United States government supported the work massively, spending perhaps twenty million dollars, until in the mid-1960s the task was judged hopeless. By then one of the specialists had the sobriety to write: 'The outlook is grim for those who still cherish hopes for fully automatic high quality mechanical translation' (A. G. Oettinger, quoted in Dreyfus, *What Computers Can't Do*, 4). Those who did cherish such hopes changed their approach. They wrote programs to handle only a restricted number of sentence types or the highly restricted vocabulary of a single subject, such as the game of chess or a child's set of blocks. Their goal was no longer translation into another natural language but rather the 'understanding' or 'processing' of a single natural language.

Another area of continuing interest is that of human memory. This is one of the most appealing human faculties to attempt to imitate. The computer is a device for storing and retrieving information, and human memory can be viewed in the same way. Many cognitive psychologists have been intrigued by this comparison, and the result has been a variety of programs for 'simulating' memory. Such programs are complicated affairs; they are not of course designed simply to enable the computer to memorize symbols by rote. For that purpose, no special programming is needed because a magnetic tape or transistor memory in good repair preserves perfectly the information written on it; in this simple sense, it remembers with far greater accuracy than humans do. There is more to human memory than the ability to repeat what is remembered. If men and women are constantly forgetting what they learn, they can also remember more than they learn. They can trace out connections among sets of disparate memories and not only on the aesthetic level of Proust's associations on the scent of madeleines. Memory, with its capacity to establish structures of associations, is closely tied to other faculties of reasoned thought and creativity. It is in this sense that we live in the world we remember, and it is this mysterious capacity that psychologists and artificial intelligence specialists would like to co-opt for their computerized intellect.

The desire to reflect human memory in the circuits of a digital computer finds its most ironic expression in programs that forget as well as remember, ones deliberately designed to lose the address of some of the information fed to them and so to mirror human memory in its weakness as well as its strength. One of the favorite devices of psychologists of memory is some variant of the syllable test originated by Ebbinghaus in the nineteenth century. Human subjects are asked to memorize a list of syllables and are then tested in various ways—how many elements do they remember after five minutes or five days, can they reconstruct the order of the list, do they remember items at the end of the list better than those in the middle? From these questions, psychologists draw admittedly rather limited conclusions about how human memory works, about the size of short term memory, the difficulty of storing an element in long term memory, and so on. The whole procedure is an attempt to turn human subjects into quantifiable processors of information. Now programs for memory simulation reverse the procedure. The psychologist administers to the machine the same tests that have already been given to human subjects. If the program remembers and forgets in a pattern consistent with human subjects, then it is taken to be a fair model of human memory.

The effort to simulate the flaws of human memory is only half the story. Most artificial intelligence programmers are in the long run interested in perfecting the human reason, not imitating its imperfections. What they want to imitate is the human memory's capacity for association, its ability to retrieve appropriate memories instantly, apparently without recourse to the slow techniques known so far to the designers of data bases. They want to couple this capacity with the computer's perfect accuracy and the enormous size of its internal and external storage. The result would be an imposing resource upon which the logical calculus of the machine could draw. Many say that 'representation is programming,' that if we know how to represent and structure the information, then we have solved the problem. In this sense, memory might be the key to artificial intelligence.

Let me come back to the notion of problem solving. It is as important to the artificial intelligence specialist as to any other programmer. Artificial intelligence programs are not written to meditate; they are written to unravel some puzzle. Beyond the puzzles of the language and memory, artificial intelligence programs most often concern mathematical puzzles: manipulating formal symbols to prove theorems in logic, solving storybook algebra problems, or performing integration and differentiation analytically. Such programs have achieved some success by placing rigid restrictions on the puzzle questions they will accept. Again, those that permit a wide vocabulary of subjects remain extremely limited in the kinds of reasoning they can conduct. If you tell a typical program that the ball is in the box and that the box is in the room, it can then decide that the ball is in the room by the simplest form of set theory.

Computers have been successful at imitating humans when playing games, for games are generally conducted in a restricted universe of playing pieces and with an explicit set of rules. In the 1950s, a program to play checkers was able to match the talents of the best human players. The program used a set of mathematical linear equations to determine the desirability of moves. Because checkers is a relatively simple business, the program could 'look ahead' for several moves, examining possible responses of its opponent and its own further responses. Success here encouraged artificial intelligence programmers to redouble their efforts with the more difficult game of chess. But the much greater complexity of chess, the combinatorial explosion of possible moves and responses, made the trick of looking ahead much more difficult to program. Chess programs face the fundamental limitations of computer time and space. Huge trees listing possible moves and replies have to be searched in *real time*, that is, while the opponent waits for a response. Improvement has been slow but steady since the 1960s, benefiting particularly from improved hardware such as faster CPUs and more capacious memories and from new techniques for storing and searching the data. Now, in the early 1980s, the best programs on the best machines can beat any talented amateur.

At present, artificial intelligence programs fall in these two groups: those that perform one clearly defined task at human or nearly human standards and those that perform more general tasks at drastically subhuman standards. In addition to chess programs, there are specialized algorithms to aid chemists in mass spectrography or doctors in diagnosis; these are impressive in their capacity to manipulate a large data base of expert and carefully defined information. On the other hand, SHRDLU deals with the tiny world of colored blocks, and already its wooden syntax, repetitiveness, and cheerful literal-mindedness make it apparent that we are not confronting an adult human intelligence. The program strikes us rather as an idiot savant or a well-behaved five-year-old child, for we very soon realize that, even in the simple manipulation of blocks, it is operating at the limit of its capacities. In fact, the world of artificial intelligence programs is populated by idiot savants and well-behaved children, but the goal remains to create machines that act with at least adult competence on the whole spectrum of problems requiring intelligence.

My own feeling is that the idiot savants will be with us for a long time, that computers will improve spectacularly in some areas and remain quite awkward in others. Computers may play brilliant chess in twenty years and still be incapable of translating English into idiomatic Russian. They might be able to process television images well enough to drive an automobile and yet not be able to prove important mathematical theorems automatically. And it is great fun, but probably fruitless, to try to guess which tasks will prove hard or perhaps impossible for the machine.

Successful or not, the artificial intelligence movement is important. So far its enthusiasm has gone far beyond the limits of its achievements and has led occasionally to wild claims, which later had to be retracted, to the delight of the polemicists against artificial intelligence. There are practical benefits from work in artificial intelligence: for example, intelligent robots to perform dangerous or unpleasant jobs in industry and to explore outer space. If in the future we can program computers in some simple form of English or use them to organize and search libraries of scientific and humanistic texts, we will likely be using techniques developed by programmers in artificial intelligence. Yet the literature of the movement often gives the impression that practical applications are of secondary importance, that a project ceases to be artificial intelligence as soon as it becomes practical. What really matters to the artificial intelligence specialist is to realize in transistors the image of a thinking human being: to make an electronic man.

The technology of making man

There was perhaps never a moment in the ancient or modern history of Europe when no one was pursuing the idea of making a human being by other than the ordinary reproductive means. The pursuit today is more costly and demands a degree of mathematical sophistication as never before, but in fact the cultural equivalent of artificial intelligence can be found throughout the history of Western cultures.

The Pygmalion theme in Greek and Roman mythology shows how the ancients thought of going about it. Pygmalion was a master craftsman, so skilled as a sculptor that he could fashion the perfect likeness of a human woman. 'He gave the ivory a form more beautiful than any mortal woman, and then fell in love with his own creation. The face was that of a real woman, who you would have thought was alive and—if her modesty did not prevent it—wishing to be touched' (Ovid, *Metamorphoses*, 10: 248–51, my translation). As Ovid, himself a classic craftsman-poet, described it, the statue, later called Galatea, resembled a human only in outward appearance; it was, after all, homogeneous ivory, with hair and paint applied to improve the deception. (In this painting, too, it resembled women of Ovid's day.) Pygmalion did not attempt to carve organs and blood vessels into his work, for ancient myths did not worry about such details. The subtle interrelation of Galatea's internal organs was not of interest, partly because a myth is not a medical textbook, but also because to the ancient mind (even in the sophisticated times following Hippocrates) the human body was not regarded as a complex of parts analogous to a clockwork mechanism. The four humors theory, though elaborated in later ages and particularly in the Renaissance, was first developed by Greek physicians. For them, man was a crucible in which the blend of black and yellow bile, blood, and phlegm determined the temperament as well as the health of the individual. If the ancients had a holistic view of man, the reason is that they understood very little of the complicated mechanisms and chemistry of respiration, circulation, elimination. Health and indeed life to their thinking was much more a question of the flowing and ebbing of vital liquids than of the careful regulation of biological processes.

So in the myth Pygmalion created only the form of a human; it was the goddess Aphrodite who breathed life into the work. The myth corresponded perfectly to the level of technology achieved by the Greeks and the Romans. The craftsman, the potter or the sculptor, concentrated his effort upon perfecting the form that he gave to his basic material (clay, stone, ivory). Pygmalion achieved such excellent results that he 'fell in love with his own creation.' His perfection of the human form simply demanded to become fully human, and the *dea ex machina* obliged. Ancient technology and a limited knowledge of biology inclined even philosophers to take an animistic view of the world. The deepest thinkers found it hard to reject the idea that anything that moved was alive; even their stars were made of a sort of living fire. Pygmalion's problem was that his craft was incomplete. He could not himself impart the final touch, the breath of life. Divine craftsmanship was needed.

In Plato's creation myth in the *Timaeus*, the deities who made men were clearly thought of as craftsmen (potters or perhaps bakers): they knew how to fashion the human vessels to contain the spark of life, and they knew how to add the spark to the mixture. In fact, the theme of the master craftsman, who had such perfect command over form that he could call forth motion and therefore life, emerges here and there throughout the literature of ancient mythology. The god of craftsmen, Hephaestus, could fashion gold and silver watchdogs and even female servants of gold. The mythic Daedalus could endow artificial wings with the power of flight. Neither the philosophers nor the poets had to provide details, to describe mechanisms. These feats were not conceived by the ancient mind in terms of machines but rather in terms of forms and animating spirits.

The Greeks of the Hellenistic Age did know of the possibilities of mechanical transformations of power. Mathematicians, among them Archimedes, studied the geometry of the five simple classes of 'machines': the lever, the wedge, the screw, the pulley, and the winch. But the knowledge of mechanics seldom had a significant economic and social impact, for, whatever the mechanism, there was normally an animal or a slave at the business end. Complex mechanisms were generally conceived as toys. A surviving treatise by Hero of Alexandria describes such automata, various devices giving the illusion of animation. Some devices had the appeal of parlor tricks, such as a vessel that pours wine, water, or a mixture of the two. Some are ghost mechanisms—a temple whose doors open automatically when a fire is lit at the altar and close again when the fire goes out. But the most intriguing are the true mechanical representations of living creatures, men or gods. One was a theater in which the god Dionysus came forth, sprayed water and wine from his staff, and then was surrounded by Bacchants who danced in his honor. Like modern prime movers, Hero's mechanisms were powered by inanimate sources: falling water, heat, and atmospheric pressure. Hero even knew of steam power, which he used to drive a toy reaction jet known as an 'aeliopile.'

Thus, what later ages would regard as major sources of useful energy, the ancient used to power toys. The appeal of these toys was the paradox of motion without life; such motion had to be paradoxical to a society that was accustomed to thinking of life and motion as inseparable qualities. Hero's mechanisms themselves were never very complex. They can always be explained in a few paragraphs of prose. Yet they did not need complexity to fascinate an audience for whom the very idea of inanimate power was a delightful contradiction.

Both traditions of artificial life—the animistic represented by the Pygmalion myth and the mechanical represented by Hero's automata—also existed in Western Europe from the Middle Ages on. The first tradition was vastly elaborated by the alchemists and magicians of various sorts. Alchemy began, after all, in the ancient world, though we associate the search for the philosopher's stone and the attempt to turn base metals into precious ones particularly with the Middle Ages and the Renaissance. Another great project of the alchemists was the creation of an artificial man, the homunculus—a creature also to be found in the Jewish cabalistic tradition as the golem. The Renaissance alchemist Paracelsus gave a recipe for the creation of the homunculus; it was a carefully prepared mixture beginning with human semen, which makes clear that he had no mechanical robot in mind. The alchemist did not work with gears and mechanisms but rather with elements, spirits, distillates, sublimations, and spells. He belonged to the intellectual undercurrent of his times, whereas the better-known philosophers were exploring other ways and trying, not always successfully, to keep clear of ideas of animism and magic. Occasionally, particularly in the Renaissance, a magus like Ficino or Bruno emerged to make a lasting contribution to Western thought, but the belief in a world populated by spirits and subject to the laws of natural magic ran counter to the mainstream. The homunculus always had a certain eerie charm, even for poets like Goethe who knew better. But even in times when the majority of a superstitious population may have considered the homunculus possible, the idea exercised only a limited influence upon philosophy and literature.

Far more influential were the mechanical automata that began to be built along with the first clocks in the thirteenth century. The great Strasbourg clock, for example, had three Magi and a cock that crowed at dawn. Many have noted the influence of the clock upon the great mechanical philosophies of Descartes and Leibniz. It was not only the clock itself that sparked their thinking but also the thriving tradition of clockwork animals and men. The great civic clocks from the later Middle Ages were often decorated with moving figures, and the art of making automata, separate from or together with clocks, reached a high state of refinement in the centuries of the scientific and industrial revolutions. Descartes himself remarked that his mechanical explanation of animal life would make perfect sense to those who know 'how many different *automata* or moving machines can be made by the industry of man' (*Philosophical Works*, 1:116).

Many such devices were designed to amuse royalty. In the sixteenth and seventeenth centuries, gardens were adorned with hydraulic automata, such as those described by the French engineer, Solomon de Caus. These Baroque toys, far more intricate than those of Hero, were unwitting tributes to the waterwheel (little used by the ancients) and the mechanical clock (probably unknown to the ancients). Ironically, ancient themes remained popular: grottos were constructed with such pastoral characters as nymphs, shepherds, and the Cyclops. About 1600 St. Germain in France could boast a nymph playing on a water organ, Mercury sounding a trumpet, Neptune driving a chariot of sea-horses, and Orpheus with his lyre charming the animals around him—all powered by falling water.

By the eighteenth century, automata had dried out; that is, the most interesting were spring-driven mechanisms. They had also moved from the garden to the salon and could now copy words and play music. Jacquet-Droz, a French toy maker, produced a mechanical boy that would dip its pen in an inkwell and write a message, distinguishing between light and heavy strokes and lifting the pen between words and over the line. The mechanism inside could be adjusted to produce different messages. This same toy maker built a female musician who actually played the harpsichord with artificial fingers and at the same time breathed, raised her eyes, and turned her head; she may well have performed at the courts of Louis XV, Louis XVI, and George III of England. One of the best known of the eighteenth-century automata was the duck designed by Jacques de Vaucanson. Exhibited in 1738, this creature drank, ate, quacked, splashed about, and even eliminated its food. It was also a sign of the progress of the Industrial Revolution that the duck not only appeared before royalty but was sold to exhibitors who took it throughout Europe.

Surely ancestors of Vaucanson's duck helped to confirm Descartes in the belief that even the most complicated physical processes of animals and men could be explained as intricate clock-work mechanisms. Only the mind was exempt from Descartes's mechanical explanation, but in the eighteenth century a few men were so impressed by technological progress—on the sober side by the accurate watches and other precise instruments that were being produced and on the lighter side by the toys of Jacquet-Droz and Vaucanson—that they were prepared to go further and see the whole man as a clockwork mechanism. Such was the thesis of the infamous philosophe La Mettrie, who wrote: 'Let us conclude bravely that man is a machine; and that there is in the universe only one kind of substance subject to various modifications' (from *L'Homme-Machine*, cited in Vartanian, *La Mettrie's L'Homme-Machine*, 197). La Mettrie was bold indeed, bold enough to banish mental substance altogether in favor of the material.

With the mechanical triumphs of the eighteenth century, the situation was completely reversed from that of the classical world. There the animists won the day and were convinced that man was a material, like clay or stone, animated by the breath or spark of life. The myth of Pygmalion or of Plato's craftsmen-deities captured perfectly the prevailing world view. Hero and his mechanical toys expressed the minority opinion, arguing paradoxically against animism. But in Western Europe, the animists, the alchemists who sought to make men from a recipe, were in the minority. The mechanical view triumphed: the bodies of animals and men were best approximated by clocks and best imitated by clockwork toys.

The triumph became more apparent with each passing decade, as automata of the nineteenth and early twentieth centuries became progressively more precise and complex. Eventually, electric circuits and motors created even more lifelike machines than clockwork could alone. Convincing if somewhat creaky electromechanical robots, such as the chess player of Torres Quevedo, began to appear and to hint at the electronic age to come. The Spanish technologist Torres himself showed remarkable historical sense when he said in a 1915 interview, 'The ancient automatons . . . imitate the appearance and movements of living beings, but this has not much practical interest, and what is wanted is a class of apparatus which leaves out the merely visible gestures of man and attempts to accomplish the results which a living person obtains, thus replacing a man by a machine' (cited in Eames, *A Computer Perspective*, 67). Torres was close to the definition of artificial intelligence, although his own work was necessarily limited to mechanical rather than electronic techniques.

The electronic image of man

It is in the context of the classical and Western European traditions of making men that artificial intelligence must be understood. Artificial intelligence is not a science, any more than the sculpture represented in the Pygmalion myth or the toy making of Jacquet-Droz was a science. It is rather a special skill in engineering and logic; computer programming techniques are used to mimic human abilities, from playing chess to answering questions in English. The techniques are different from those of the mechanical men of the eighteenth century or of Greek myth, for the simple reason that artificial intelligence is meant to take account of the new qualities that the computer has introduced into the story of technology. That is its significance. Artificial intelligence is a radical expression of the possibilities of the digital computer, a celebration of a new technology.

Specialists in artificial intelligence must refer to their field as a science because we live in an age of science when practically every activity can only be dignified, or indeed legitimated, under this name. For this reason, they often claim their program is a 'model' of this or that aspect of intelligence and point out that many sciences use models to understand nature. The problem here is that the artificial intelligence specialist has nothing but a model. Having abandoned the idea that electronic circuits can be made to mirror the organization of human neurons, he has no natural phenomenon left to study. A physicist may build a mathematical or even physical model, but he must at some point go back to nature for confirmation. But what can the computer programmer find in the brain or the mind of which his binary coded instructions are a model?

All the biologist can find are neurons, and the tangle of billions of axons and synapses will remain beyond human comprehension probably for decades. So the artificial intelligence specialist looks to 'higher levels of the system,' to problem-solving structures, rules of language production, symbolic representation of visual data, and the like. But beyond the level of neurons, there *is* no science of the mind; instead, there are metaphors that capture more or less aptly our mental experience. Programmers find in the mind structures appropriate to computers and formal logic because they bring these concepts with them as they look at human experience. Each age has found in the human mind precisely what it has brought to the search; each has had its own metaphorical explanations. Plato compared the mind to the class structure of a Greek city-state, the mechanists likened it to a collection of gears, and now Turing's man sees it as a digital computer. Certainly some metaphors are better than others. The mind seems more like a computer than like a clock. But some metaphors emphasize such disparate qualities that they can hardly be compared: is the mind more like a computer than a Greek city-state? The important point is that the computer is not the final, correct answer. It will surely be replaced someday by metaphors that spring from a technology we cannot now imagine.

So artificial intelligence will not be a science even if it wins someday at Turing's game. It is and will remain a field of engineering that relies on science and mathematics for its tools. Many of its exponents are computer specialists who have made real contributions to their discipline. (Vaucanson also made substantive improvements in the manufacture of silk, in addition to his automata.) Programs for artificial intelligence are not scientific constructions at all; they are wonderfully clever ornaments, like the cock and the Magi on the original Strasbourg clock.

We must not underestimate the value of such decorations, however, because the figures on the Strasbourg clock caught the contemporary imagination more readily than the concealed mechanism that actually told the time. In the ancient world, Hero's mechanisms had been mere toys because ancient technology was not mechanically inclined, but the writing boy of Jacquet-Droz and Vaucanson's duck were more than toys. They were leisurely statements of the idea that the natural world behaved mechanically; they made tangible the ideas of Descartes, Huygens, or Newton. The same ideas and the same creative energies also led to more practical applications, to better clocks and more efficient engines.

Similarly, the artificial intelligence movement produces programs that illustrate rather than perform. These programs are likely to have practical applications that even their creators may not foresee, but that is not their purpose. In a field generally marked by a ruthless sense of utility, these computer specialists are interested in something more marvelous than immediately useful results: they are seeking to demonstrate what it means to live in the computer age. Their programs succeed in arousing much the same wonder among the public, and even within the literary and scientific communities, that Vaucanson's duck aroused two hundred years ago. For example, the chess programs that play nearly at the level of the professional rate publicity whenever a chess master agrees to compete against a machine. Nowhere, perhaps, will people more readily grasp the meaning of electronic technology than in the widespread attention that artificial intelligence programs attract.

For the artificial intelligence programmer, the electronic brain is a dead metaphor: the computer and the brain differ only in the unimportant respect that one is made of electronic components and the other of biological ones. Both think. By taking the metaphor to its extreme, proponents of artificial intelligence illustrate with utmost clarity a way of thinking shared by all of Turing's men. Other computer specialists or scientists who use computers disagree sharply with the notion of artificial intelligence. Yet they all cheerfully speak of computer *languages*, the *logic* of computer circuits, and computer *memory*. They say that a computer did not *read* the data properly or *recognize* a particular character. They all accept to some degree the idea that humans and computers are comparable things, even as they assert that humans perform some tasks much better than machines. The comparison has become irresistible, a clear indication that we are living in the computer age.

The concept of artificial intelligence in fact contains within it most of the defining qualities of computer technology, qualities that have been explored in previous chapters. If a digital computer can think, then intelligent thought must be a step-by-step process conducted in pulses of time—data shuttled through a biological or electronic job shop in which each machine can handle only one bundle of data before or after another machine has had its turn. It must be conducted in a symbolic code, a 'language of thought,' directing the data through a series of transformations or intermediate forms between input and output. The transformations themselves must be governed by the rules of logic, which allow for the spatial and structural representation of meaning and intention. Such qualities of the computer shape every artificial intelligence program and every other program besides.

It is important to remember that these qualities are seen as strengths of the computer, not as limitations. The whole point is to find a way to enable a network of wires and transistors to manifest intelligence. Any artificial intelligence specialist could marry and produce a number of biological information processors in the customary way, as could a toy maker in the eighteenth century, a Renaissance alchemist, or an ancient sculptor. Turing, by the way, forbade this route; to meet his test, the machine must be electronic rather than biological. The attempt to make man over, with whatever available technology, is an attempt to circumvent or reverse the process of nature. Man the artificer and man the artifact merge, but on the artificer's terms. In bypassing the ordinary sexual process of reproduction, man achieves a new freedom from nature; computer technology offers a path to this new freedom.

The homunculus that results is man as a processor of information—not a whole man, for he has no arms or legs, nor emotions in any conventional sense. He is a calculating engine, although one of far more complexity and even charm than is portrayed in the popular mythology of sinister, electronic superbrains. He embodies assumptions about space, time, language, and creativity central to the computer era upon which we are entering. He is far more sophisticated than the stimulus-and-response circuit of the behaviorist school, but he does have the same relation to his environment, for he thinks by transforming inputs into outputs.

Most important, this computer man fulfills the same function for our contemporary technology that the clockwork man or the living statue fulfilled for previous ones. He is an expression of both the exciting possibilities and the limits suggested by this new technology. Some programmers in artificial intelligence are wildly optimistic about the possibilities. They speak as if at any time someone may find the key to making the computer not merely human, but superhuman. 'Artificial intelligence is the next step in evolution,' says one. And again: 'I suspect there will be very little communication between machines and humans because unless the machines condescend to talk to us about something that interests us, we'll have no communication' (McCorduck, *Machines Who Think*, 346, 347). These artificial intelligences will help run society and relieve mankind of the burden of being the leading species. We have entered the realm of science fiction, and, as with all science fiction, the predictions are not really about the future but about an extrapolated present. Everything else is left constant or dropped from consideration while digital computers and their programs are allowed to grow arbitrarily in power. The world is seen through the electronic eye of the information processor.

The historian Lynn White has described for us a parallel from the Middle Ages. 'By the middle of the thirteenth century,' he writes, 'a considerable group of active minds, stimulated not only by the technological successes of recent generations, but also led on by the will-o'-the-wisp of perpetual motion, were beginning to generalize the concept of mechanical power. . . . They were power-conscious to the point of fantasy. But without such fantasy, such soaring imagination, the power technology of the Western world would not have been developed' (*Medieval Technology and Social Change*, 133–34). Perhaps historians two hundred years from now (if history is still being written) will make the same assessment of the artificial intelligence movement.

Artifact and artificer

Men tend to regard what they make through their technological or artistic genius as in some measure human. It is not only a skilled playwright who brings his characters to life: all human artifacts, from vases to computer programs, from tragedies to steam engines, have a bit of life in them. The artifact also changes the artificer. Through technology, men and women attempt to redefine their relationship to their environment on terms that seem more favorable. If the struggle to collect or catch food seems too difficult using only human hands and muscles, the addition of even a crude stone weapon or tool redefines the entire problem and opens new possibilities for personal and social activity at the same time. Human beings with a developed stone technology are different from those without tools; men with bronze and iron weapons, looms and potter's wheels, are different again. Each technology, if not each single invention, remakes the men who invent or possess it by altering their most elemental capacity—that of surviving in the world of nature.

If humans are not unique among animals in this respect, they are certainly very special. Most animals can rely only on the biological processes of evolution over thousands or millions of years in order to improve the equipment (teeth, camouflage, instinctual cunning) with which they must confront their environment. Animals that do learn to use tools and pass on such information to their young progress at an agonizingly slow rate, if they progress at all. In contrast, it is often said that humans progress too quickly to assimilate intelligently the technology they create. At any rate, the human race has taken over at least in part the future course of its own evolution by making itself over through technology.

So far only in part. Even today we are extremely limited in our ability to use chemistry or physics to control and improve our own human nature. We have at our disposal sources of energy on a cosmic scale: we can create explosions whose temperatures match those in the interior of the sun. Yet we still cannot make a prosthesis that has a fraction of the agility and versatility of the human arm. We know at least where to look for the mechanism that controls the growth and function of human tissue and organs—in the DNA in the nucleus of our cells. Yet these molecules are of such complexity that we can only decipher tiny portions, and our tools for rearranging molecules are correspondingly crude, although these very tools manifest the highest skill of contemporary biochemists. Men are clearly not in the position today to take full or even substantial control of their own biological destiny. And if this can be said of contemporary technology, it was surely the case with the technologies of eighteenth century Europe and Alexandria in the third century B.C. The machines of the Industrial Revolution performed only elementary repetitive actions; they had nothing comparable to the versatility of a skilled human worker. In fact, each of the cleverest automata of Vaucanson and Jacquet-Droz was only capable of a few mechanical tricks. The automata of Hero were far more crude, and in general the ancient world could only manage to use clay, stone, or bronze to produce static likenesses of human beings, although these likenesses were sometimes of extraordinary beauty.

Our ability technologically to improve upon our physical and mental equipment has fallen far short of the goal of remaking ourselves entirely. Nonetheless, technological man has always had that goal somewhere in the back of his mind, and it has emerged audaciously in myths, legends, toys, and automata throughout history. In all the manifestations, the informing idea is that the artificer and the artifact become one. Man makes man and therefore raises himself above the status that nature seems to have assigned him. Beyond that, each manifestation is different because it must, in Norbert Wiener's fine phrase, take account of 'the living technique of the age.' Ancient craftsmanship produced myths of ivory and gold statues coming to life and automata in which inanimate motion itself was a thing to be admired. Western European technology emphasized the intricate working of gears in its automata. The attempts at artificial intelligence today stress the qualities of contemporary technology that are new and strikingly productive.

There are antiquarians who still delight in the toys of the past; no one else today cares about making automata that physically resemble their makers, a fact Torres Quevedo recognized over sixty years ago. Engineers are indeed working to perfect robots (grasping and manipulating devices of various sorts controlled by microprocessors or full-scale computers). These devices have so many practical applications, for example, in handling dangerous materials or doing repetitive assembly work, that they have descended from the dreamy world of artificial intelligence into the world of business.

A so-called robot assembling machine tools bears hardly any resemblance to the androids in science fiction and comic books of the preceding generation, the era before digital computers. One glance at these modern industrial robots convinces us that engineers are not seeking to make their machines look human, although they might have done so for aesthetic reasons. On the other hand, a programmer writing a mathematical 'theorem prover' would say that he is interested in imitating a far more important and characteristically human quality, that of intelligence. One opponent of the movement has argued that the human body with its five senses is fundamental to the human capacity for intelligent thought. The argument misses the point. The artificial intelligence specialist is not interested in imitating the whole man. The very reason he regards intelligence (rational 'problem solving') as fundamental is that such intelligence corresponds to the new and compelling qualities of electronic technology. Today, as before, technology determines what part of the man will be imitated.

Annotated bibliography

The following books and articles have been of particular value, either as sources for quotations or as background for the many subjects I have had to treat superficially in the course of my argument. Parenthetical references to the following works appear in the text.

Appel, Kenneth, and Haken, Wolfgang. 'The Solution of the Four-Color-Map Problem.' *Scientific American* (October 1977): 108–21.

Arbib, Michael A. *The Metaphorical Brain: An Introduction to Cybernetics as Artificial Intelligence and Brain Theory.* New York: John Wiley and Sons, 1972. Attempts, as the title suggests, to relate psychology and neurology by an explicit reference to the metaphor of the electronic brain.

Automatic Language Processing Advisory Committee, National Academy of Sciences, National Research Council. *Languages and Machines: Computers in Translation and Linguistics.* Washington, D.C.: National Research Council, 1966. The report that put an end to generous government support of programs for machine translation of human languages.

Ayer, A. J., ed. *Logical Positivism.* New York: Free Press, 1959. A convenient selection of positivist thinkers.

Boden, Margaret A. *Artificial Intelligence and Natural Man.* New York: Basic Books, 1977. A detailed account of numerous artificial intelligence programs, with an explanation of their significance. The author is clearly a partisan of the movement.

Boyer, Carl B. *A History of Mathematics.* New York: John Wiley and Sons, 1968.

—— *The History of Calculus and Its Conceptual Development.* New York: Dover Publications, 1959.

Brooks, Frederick P. *The Mythical Man-Month.* Reading, Mass.: Addison-Wesley, 1975. An excellent account of the problems of programming teams. This book broaches the idea that the programmer creates from 'pure thought-stuff,' an idea I have found nowhere else.

Brooks, Frederick P., and Iverson, K. *Automatic Data Processing.* New York: John Wiley and Sons, 1963.

Bury, J. B. *The Idea of Progress in History.* New York: Macmillan Co., 1932. A survey that concentrates on the eighteenth century but has some interesting remarks on the ancient world in the introduction.

Butler, Samuel. *Erewhon and Erewhon Revisited.* New York: Modern Library, 1927. A classic anti-utopian novel, yet Butler's views on technology are much more complicated than is often supposed.

Cardwell, D. S. L. *Turning Points in Western Technology.* New York: Neale Watson Academic Publications, 1972. A good, readable account of the clock and various heat engines of the eighteenth and nineteenth centuries, as well as other technological breakthroughs.

Chapuis, Alfred, and Droz, Edmond. *Automata.* Translated by Alec Reid. Neuchâtel:

Editions du Griffon, 1958. Examples of mechanistic imitations of man, including the hydraulic and clockwork masterpieces of the sixteenth through eighteenth centuries.

Chomsky, Noam. *Aspects of the Theory of Syntax*. Cambridge, Mass.: MIT Press, 1965.

—— *Reflections on Language*. New York: Random House, 1975. Explores the broader implications of the new methods in linguistics.

—— *Syntactic Structures*. The Hague: Mouton and Co., 1964. First published in 1957. By general agreement, a watershed in modern linguistics.

Cipolla, Carlo M. *Clocks and Culture, 1300–1700*. New York: Walker and Company, 1967. A good popular account.

Cohen, John. *Human Robots in Myth and Science*. London: George Allen and Unwin, 1966. A fascinating story of mechanical and alchemical automata. It is quite useful for comparisons with the artificial intelligence project.

Cohen, Jonathan. 'On the Project of a Universal Character.' *Mind* 63 (1965): 49–63. Details this extraordinary caprice, which was popular in the seventeenth century. Leibniz was the most famous supporter because of his proposal for a logical calculus of thought.

Collingwood, R. G. *The Idea of Nature*. Oxford: Clarendon Press, 1957.

Cornford, F. M. *Plato's Cosmology*. London: Harcourt Brace, 1937. An excellent commentary on Plato's cosmological dialogue, the *Timaeus*. Cornford recognized Plato's analogy between Greek craftsmanship and the making of the cosmos.

Dales, R. C. 'The De-animation of the Heavens in the Middle Ages.' *Journal of the History of Ideas* 41, no. 4 (October–December 1980): 531–50. Shows how medieval Europeans broke free of the ancient concept that the stars are alive, with the help of comparisons between the heavens and such inanimate mechanisms as the mill and the clock.

Descartes, René. *The Philosophical Works of Descartes*. 2 vols. Translated by E. S. Haldane and G. R. T. Ross. Cambridge: Cambridge University Press, 1973–76.

—— *Principia Philosophiae*. Vol. 8–1 of *Oeuvres de Descartes*. Edited by Charles Adam and Paul Tannery. Paris: Librairie Philosophique J. Vrin, 1964.

Dijksterhuis, E. J. *The Mechanization of the World Picture*. Translated by C. Dikshoorn. London: Oxford University Press, 1969. First published in Dutch in 1950. A scholarly work which follows the mechanical philosophy of science to its culmination with Huygens and Leibniz.

Dodds, E. R. *The Ancient Concept of Progress, and Other Essays on Greek Literature and Belief*. Oxford: Clarendon Press, 1973.

Dreyfus, Hubert L. *What Computers Can't Do: A Critique of Artificial Reason*. New York: Harper and Row, 1972. This attack on the idea of artificial intelligence takes a philosophical (phenomenological) rather than broadly cultural or historical line.

Eames, Charles. *A Computer Perspective*. Cambridge, Mass.: Harvard University Press, 1973. An illustrated essay based on an exhibit by IBM.

Ebbinghaus, Hermann. *Memory*. Translated by H. A. Rogers and Clara E. Bussenius. New York: Dover Publications, 1964. This translation of the treatise *Über das Gedächtnis* (1885) has been called the beginning of the modern psychological study of memory.

Edge, D. O. 'Technological Metaphor.' In *Meaning and Control: Essays in Social*

Aspects of Science and Technology, edited by D. O. Edge and J. N. Wolfe, pp. 31–59. London: Tavistock Publications, 1973.

Eisenstein, Elizabeth. *The Printing Press as an Agent of Change: Communications and Cultural Transformations in Early-modern Europe*. 2 vols. Cambridge: Cambridge University Press, 1979. A thorough and lively account of this important subject.

Feigenbaum, E. A., and Feldman, Julian. *Computers and Thought*. New York: McGraw-Hill, 1963. An early collection by the artificial intelligence movement; contains Turing's paper on 'Computing Machinery and Intelligence.'

Finley, M. I. *The Ancient Economy*. London: Chatto and Windus, 1973.

Fishman, Katharine D. *The Computer Establishment*. New York: Harper and Row, 1981. About the companies that make computers and their own, occasionally appalling, world view.

Fodor, Jerry A. *The Language of Thought*. New York: Crowell, 1975. A forthright statement of the electronic metaphor; for Fodor the human mind is without doubt an information processor.

Forbes, R. J. *Studies in Ancient Technology*. 9 vols. Leiden: E. J. Brill, 1964–. The definitive work in English on the subject. Water and wind power are discussed in volume 2, textile manufacture in volume 4.

Fowler, Roger. *Understanding Language: An Introduction to Linguistics*. London: Routledge & Kegan Paul, 1974.

Giedion, Siegfried. *Mechanization Takes Command*. New York: W. W. Norton, 1969. First published in 1948. Covers in delightful detail mechanical inventions for daily living, particularly for the period from 1850 on. Among other things, the book manages to make the mechanization of the bathroom fascinating.

Goldstine, Herman H. *The Computer from Pascal to von Neumann*. Princeton: Princeton University Press, 1972. A richly detailed account of the development of computers, particularly in the crucial 1940s.

Grant, Michael. *The Twelve Caesars*. London: Michael Grant Publications, 1975.

Greenberger, Martin, ed. *Computers and the World of the Future*. Cambridge, Mass.: MIT Press, 1962.

Hadas, Moses. *Ancilla to Classical Reading*. New York: Columbia University Press, 1954. For background on ancient techniques of writing and oral reading.

Hamming, R. W. *Introduction to Applied Numerical Analysis*. New York: McGraw-Hill, 1971. A textbook by one of the leading computer mathematicians.

Herder, Johann Gottfried von. *J. G. Herder on Social and Political Culture*. Edited by F. M. Barnard. Cambridge: Cambridge Universitry Press, 1969. Contains Herder's 'Essay on the Origin of Language,' which joins in the eighteenth-century debate about 'artificial' language.

Hofstadter, Douglas R. *Gödel, Escher, Bach: An Eternal Golden Braid*. New York: Basic Books, 1979. A book that expresses perfectly the spirit of Turing's man. Hofstadter may well be defining many of the 'philosophical' problems that will occupy our culture for years to come: the paradox of meaning within meaningless formal systems, self-reference, finite and infinite loops, artificial intelligence, the mind as a semantic network, and so on. The author's attitude toward art—as a play of formal elements without any true historical dimension—also reveals how remote Turing's man is from his predecessor.

Hunt, Earl. 'What Kind of a Computer is Man?' *Cognitive Psychology* 2 (1971): 57–98. Another explicit acceptance of the metaphor of electronic man.

Innis, Harold A. *Empire and Communications*. Toronto: University of Toronto Press, 1972. Originally published in 1950. Drops any number of fascinating hints about time, space, language, and culture, but in a disconcerting, telegraphic style.

Jammer, Max. *Concepts of Space*. Cambridge, Mass.: Harvard University Press, 1969. A general treatment from Aristotle to Einstein. Contains a canny suggestion that Einstein's 'spherical space' is in some sense a return to Aristotle's finite universe (p. 22).

Kemeny, John G. *Man and the Computer*. New York: Charles Scribner's Sons, 1972. Lectures delivered by a computer specialist and educator, the inventor of BASIC.

Kidder, Tracy. *The Soul of a New Machine*. Boston: Little, Brown and Company, 1981. Examines the psychology of a design team working on a new minicomputer; a valuable look at how such designers think and work.

Kirk, G. S., and Raven, J. E. *The Pre-Socratic Philosophers*. Cambridge: Cambridge University Press, 1957. Fragments of the philosophers with translation and analysis. I have used in particular the discussion of the Pythagorean attitude toward number, which was so influential in the ancient world.

Knuth, Donald E. *Mathematics and Computer Science: Coping with Finiteness* (Stan-CS-76–541). Stanford: Stanford University, Computer Science Department, February 1976. A lecture, in the author's usual playful style, on the important idea that the computer can only deal with finite numbers.

Koyré, Alexandre. *From the Closed World to the Infinite Universe*. Baltimore: Johns Hopkins University Press, 1974. Chronicles this great change in Western thinking, principally through the sixteenth, seventeenth, and eighteenth centuries.

Kuhn, Thomas S. *The Structure of Scientific Revolutions*. Chicago: University of Chicago Press, 1962. Probably belongs in any contemporary bibliography on a scientific subject.

Leibniz, Gottfried Wilhelm von. *The Philosophical Writings of Leibniz*. Selected and translated by Mary Morris. London: Everyman's Library, 1934.

Levy, David. *1975 US Computer Chess Championship*. Woodland Hills, Calif.: Computer Science Press, 1976.

Lindsay, Peter H., and Norman, D. A. *Human Information Processing*. New York: Academic Press, 1972. Another example of the borrowing of computer concepts by psychologists.

Lloyd, G. E. R. *Aristotle: The Growth and Structure of His Thought*. London: Cambridge University Press, 1968. A good introduction.

McCorduck, Pamela. *Machines Who Think*. San Francisco: W. H. Freeman, 1979. The authorized court history of artificial intelligence and, as such, a fascinating look into the motivations and aspirations of these computer specialists.

Macey, Samuel L. *Clock and the Cosmos: Time in Western Life and Thought*. Hamden, Conn.: Archon Books, 1980. Numerous examples of the clock metaphor from philosophy, literature, and art. Focuses on the seventeenth and eighteenth centuries.

McLuhan, Marshall. *The Gutenberg Galaxy: The Making of Typographic Man*. Toronto: University of Toronto Press, 1972. The printing press and cultural change. Whatever one thinks of McLuhan's public persona, one must admit that he was in possession of a very important idea.

Mead, Carver, and Conway, Lynn. *Introduction to VLSI Systems*. Reading, Mass.: Addison-Wesley, 1980. An excellent textbook explaining the design and fabrication of microcomputer systems.

Miller, G. A. 'The Magical Number Seven, Plus or Minus Two: Some Limits on Our Capacity for Processing Information.' *Psychological Review* 63 (1956): 81–97. An early and influential piece on man as an information processor; human memory as storage device.

Minsky, Marvin. *Computation: Finite and Infinite Machines.* Englewood Cliffs, N.J.: Prentice-Hall, 1967.

—— 'Steps Toward Artificial Intelligence.' *Proceedings of the IRE* 49 (1961): 8–30.

—— ed. *Semantic Information Processing.* Cambridge, Mass.: MIT Press, 1968. A collection by artificial intelligence advocates.

Morrison, Philip, and Morrison, Emily, eds. *Charles Babbage and His Calculating Engines.* New York: Dover Publications, 1961. A fascinating collection of excerpts and papers by Babbage himself and his followers.

Mumford, Lewis. *The City in History.* New York: Harcourt, Brace & World, 1961.

—— *Myth of the Machine.* Vol. 1, *Technics and Human Development.* New York: Harcourt, Brace & World, 1967. Vol. 2, *The Pentagon of Power.* New York: Harcourt Brace Jovanovich, 1970. This late work takes a negative view of our technological future.

—— *Technics and Civilization.* New York: Harcourt Brace, 1934. A Brilliant work showing the intimate connection between technology and culture from the Middle Ages to the twentieth century.

Nelson, Theodor H. *Computer Lib.* South Bend, Ind.: Theodor H. Nelson, 1974. A book that is determined to 'popularize' the computer at any cost; still, the author has recognized some of the key qualities of the machine.

Newton, Isaac. *Sir Isaac Newton's Mathematical Principles of Natural—Philosophy and His System of the World.* 2 vols. Translated by Andrew Motte in 1729. Revised and edited by Florian Cajori. Berkeley: University of California Press, 1966.

Ong, Walter J. *Ramus, Method, and the Decay of Dialogue.* Cambridge Mass.: Harvard University Press, 1958.

Oresme, Nicole. *Le Livre du ciel et du monde.* Translated by A. D. Menut. Edited by A. D. Menut and A. J. Denomy. Madison: University of Wisconsin Press, 1968.

Papert, Seymour. *Mindstorms: Children, Computers, and Powerful Ideas.* New York: Basic Books, 1980. An intriguing combination of educational theory and computer programming. Papert has created a programming language through which children can learn the procedural thinking of the machine.

Pennington, Ralph H. *Introductory Computer Methods and Numerical Analysis.* New York: Macmillan Co., 1965.

Pizer, Stephen M. *Numerical Computing and Mathematical Analysis.* Chicago: Scientific Research Associates, 1975.

Price, Derek J. de Solla. 'An Ancient Greek Computer.' *Scientific American* (June 1959): 60–67. Describes the paradoxical Anti-kythera device.

Ralston, Anthony, and Meek, C. L. *Encyclopedia of Computer Science.* New York: Petrocelli/Charter, 1976. A good reference work for the nonspecialist.

Raphael, Bertram. *The Thinking Computer: Mind Inside Matter.* San Francisco: W. H. Freeman, 1976. By a proponent of artificial intelligence.

Robins, R. H. *A Short History of Linguistics.* Bloomington: Indiana University Press, 1967. A well-balanced presentation, from the Greeks to the 1960s.

Russell, Bertrand. *Introduction to Mathematical Philosophy.* London: George Allen and Unwin, 1967.

Sagan, Carl. *The Dragons of Eden: Speculations on the Evolution of Human Intelligence*. New York: Ballantine Books, 1977. Agrees with many in seeing computers as a further evolution of the human brain.

Simon, Herbert. *The Sciences of the Artificial*. Cambridge, Mass.: MIT Press, 1969. Perhaps the most famous proponent of artificial intelligence, Simon wholeheartedly endorses the notion of man as information processor.

Singer, Charles J., et al. *A History of Technology*. 7 vols. Oxford: Clarendon Press, 1954–78. An encyclopedic collection of rather long chapters.

Solmsen, Frederick. *Aristotle's System of the Physical World*. Ithaca: Cornell University Press, 1960. A masterful explanation of the development of Aristotle's thinking out of and away from Plato's.

Spengler, Oswald. *The Decline of the West*. 2 vols. Translated by C. F. Atkinson. New York: Alfred A. Knopf, 1945. Much maligned but brilliant in its way. Among other accomplishments, Spengler understood the meaning of limit for Greek culture and infinity for the West. If I am right, a returning appreciation of the finite will be a defining quality of the computer age.

Taube, Mortimer. *Computers and Common Sense: The Myth of Thinking Machines*. New York: Columbia University Press, 1961. Against artificial intelligence.

Timmerman, Peter. *Vulnerability, Resilience, and Society*. Toronto: University of Toronto, Institute for Environmental Studies, 1981.

Turbayne, Colin M. *The Myth of Metaphor*. New haven: Yale University Press, 1962. A philosophical essay on the place of metaphor in science.

Turing, A. M. 'On Computable Numbers, with an Application to the Entscheidungs problem.' In *Proceedings of the London Mathematics Society*, 2d ser., 42:230–65. London: C. F. Hodgson, 1936. The paper in which Turing defined his logical machine.

Vartanian, Aram. *La Mettrie's L'Homme-Machine: A Study in the Origins of an idea*. Princeton: Princeton University Press, 1960. An essay tracing the idea from Descartes's bête-machine to La Mettrie, together with a full translation of La Mettrie's text.

von Neumann, John. *Collected Works*. Edited by A. H. Taube. 6 vols. Oxford: Pergamon Press, 1961–63. Contains von Neumann's well-known papers on computers and the theory of automata.

—— *The Computer and the Brain*. New Haven: Yale University Press, 1958. Analyzes the brain in the operational terms supplied by the digital computer.

Weizenbaum, Joseph. *Computer Power and Human Reason*. San Francisco: W. H. Freeman, 1976. One of the few attempts to deal with the cultural impact of the computer. Weizenbaum is an opponent of artificial intelligence.

White, Lynn T. *Medieval Technology and Social Change*. Oxford: Clarendon Press, 1962. Exciting chapters on cavalry, agriculture, and mechanical-dynamic technology.

Whitehead, A. N. *Science and the Modern World*. New York: Macmillian Co., 1967.

Whorf, Benjamin L. *Language, Thought, and Reality*. Edited by J. B. Carroll. Cambridge, Mass.: MIT Press, 1956. Often cited as the source of the idea that our native language colors our whole world view.

Wickelgren, Wayne A. *Learning and Memory*. Englewood Cliffs, N.J.: Prentice-Hall, 1977. I cite this book as an example of the extent to which computer jargon has been taken over into cognitive psychology.

Wiener, Norbert. *Cybernetics*. New York: John Wiley and Sons, 1948. An elegant account of the identification of man and machine by the famous mathematician and student of technology. Wiener is in many ways a more civilized and sympathetic proponent of the making of electronic man than current writers.

Wilkins, John. *An Essay Towards a Real Character and a Philosophical Language*. London, 1668. Reprint, edited by R. C. Alston. English Linguistics 1500–1800, no 119. Menston, Eng.: Scolar Press, 1968. A beautiful book that presents calligraphic symbols to represent basic ideas. It is representative of the general movement for a logical language of thought, as Leibniz was suggesting.

Winograd, Terry. *Understanding Natural Language*. New York: Academic Press, 1972. A description of SHRDLU, the simulated robot. Very influential for the artificial intelligence movement.

Yates, Frances. *The Art of Memory*. Chicago: University of Chicago Press, 1966. Wonderfully detailed account of ancient, medieval, and Renaissance mnemonic systems.